Where to watch birds in

# Australasia and Oceania

## THE *WHERE TO WATCH BIRDS* SERIES

*Where to watch birds in Africa*
Nigel Wheatley

*Where to watch birds in Asia*
Nigel Wheatley

*Where to watch birds in Australasia and Oceania*
Nigel Wheatley

*Where to watch birds in South America*
Nigel Wheatley

Where to watch birds in

# Australasia and Oceania

Nigel Wheatley

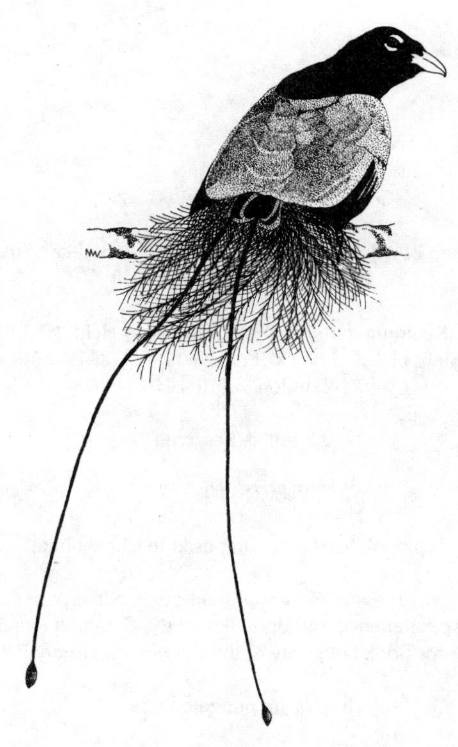

Princeton University Press

Princeton, New Jersey

Published by Princeton University Press, 41 William Street,
Princeton, New Jersey 08540

In the United Kingdom, published by Christopher Helm (Publishers) Ltd,
a subsidiary of A & C Black (Publishers) Ltd, 35 Bedford Row,
London WC1R 4JH



ISBN 0-691-00231-2

This book has been composed in Cheltenham

Princeton University Press books are printed on acid-free paper and meet the
guidelines for permanence and durability of the Committee on Production
Guidelines for Book Longevity of the Council on Library Resources

http://pup.princeton.edu

Printed in Great Britain by Hillman Printers (Frome) Ltd, Frome, Somerset

1 3 5 7 9 10 8 6 4 2

# CONTENTS

# ACKNOWLEDGEMENTS

It would have been impossible to produce this book without the help of many birders who have not just travelled to Australasia and Oceania in search of birds, but who have also been unselfish enough to record their experiences for the benefit of others. Most of these people have made their information generally available and, to me, are some of the pillars of the birding world.

I would like to express my heartfelt thanks to the following friends, birders and organisations who have generously allowed me to use the information contained within their reports, papers, books and letters, and/or covered some country accounts in honest red ink: BirdLife International, Birdquest, Tim Blackburn, Ian Burfield, Cygnus Wildlife Holidays, Detlef Davies, John Day, Anne-Grete Ditlevsen, John Edge, Nick Gardner, David Gibbs, Mark Hardwick, Kerry Harrison, Hugh Harrop, Alun Hatfield, Sam Hicks, Jon Hornbuckle, Mike Hunter, Erling Jirle, Geoff Morgan, Tony Palliser, Bent Otto Poulsen, Jan Reinemo, Gerry Richards, David Rosair, Richard Rowland, Roger and Lesley Safford, Peter Sandford, Dave Sargeant, Spotter (John Mason), Steve Smith, Barry Stidolph, Sunbird, Jan Vermeulen, Duncan and Paul Walbridge, Nick Wall, Michael Warren and Richard Webb.

Naturally, many thanks also go to the many birders who accompanied these people in the field, helped to find the birds, and no doubt contributed their own information. I have spoken to numerous other people on the telephone, in the field and in the pub about minor, but important, matters, who I have unwittingly omitted from the above list. I sincerely hope these people will accept my profuse apologies if I have failed to acknowledge their help in this edition, and hope they will let me know before the next edition.

There is one name missing from the above list. Mike Entwistle, who was so tragically killed in Peru, would no doubt have shared his detailed knowledge of the area with infectious enthusiasm because he was such a good egg. His report on birding in Australia, *600+: A Birder's Guide to Australia*, which was based on his extensive travels throughout the country in 1986, is still one of the best around.

Unfortunately, it has to be said at this juncture that there are some birders, including a few with a wealth of experience in Australasia and Oceania, who have never written any trip reports! Or, if they have done so, they have not made their information generally available. Fortunately, such people are few and far between, and sharing information comes naturally to the vast majority of birders. Writing a trip report can be a very enjoyable undertaking because it enables the author to relive the experience, absorb as many birds as possible and cement the memories, hence I can only say to those who don't bother, have a go next time.

Once I had come up with the idea for the book I had to convince a publisher it would be popular. Fortunately, Robert Kirk, the editor at Helm, saw the potential and deserves thanks for taking on the original idea and developing it. When I started compiling the basic information for the book it seemed as though every bird had at least three different names. This major headache was cured by James Clements, to whom I am very grateful for giving me permission to use his *Check List* as the baseline for this book.

I would also like to thank Mike Carter, Neil Cheshire, John Cox, Steve Holliday, Phil Maher, Dave Percival, Gerry Richards, Rob Roberts, Trevor Quested and Barry Stidolph, with whom I have shared many successful and enjoyable days in the field. John Cox and his wife were also good enough to let Barry Stidolph, Rob Roberts and myself crash on their floor for a couple of nights, after many amusing and enlightening hours chatting about birds over a few beers. Finally, my old friend Rob Roberts and his wife Sarah deserve special thanks for being more than happy to let two dishevelled birders use their cosy house in Sydney as a base for a couple of weeks, despite having a newly born child to attend to. Sarah also put up with Barry and I tempting Rob into the odd birding excursion with a smile, even though these included a 1600 km round trip to Deniliquin!

# INTRODUCTION

Shortly after shambling out of Darwin Airport at four o'clock in the morning, 30 hours after leaving London, I was knee-deep in mud. Dave Percival was leading Barry Stidolph and myself through the mangroves at Sadgroves Creek in search of big red chooks, alias Chestnut Rails, which are big and red(ish), and look like chickens to the local fishermen. Dave warned us not to stray too close to the deep channel alongside us because a saltwater crocodile lived in it. Suddenly, the sandflies and stepping barefoot on spear-tipped mangrove shoots didn't seem so painful, but I began to wonder if, after a serious lack of slumber, plodging through muddy mangroves in the hope of seeing a 'big red chicken' was the best way to begin an antipodean adventure. My first Red-headed Myzomelas were stunning, but they were no compensation for the lack of Chestnut Rails, and when we returned, with some relief, to *terra firme* I was a little disappointed with my introduction to birding in Australia.

After then walking the length of the 2 mile long East Point beach in a warm wind and searing heat, and not seeing any Beach Thick-knees, I began to think that my first carefully researched and meticulously planned birding trip to Australasia and Oceania was going to be a complete failure. A wonderful flock of Rainbow Bee-eaters and a huge manta ray flying out of the sea kept my lifeless legs going, but it was not until I sought shade in the mangroves at the top of the beach, and a sparkling new gem of a bird appeared, that I really began to enjoy birding in this part of the world. The pristine black, white and golden yellow Black-tailed Whistler was the first of a run of brilliant birds which turned my first day down under into one of my best birding days ever. Suddenly, everything came together, as it always does eventually, and two bizarre Bush Thick-knees, a couple of confiding Rainbow Pittas, some perfect Pied Herons and a fence full of five fantastic Forest Kingfishers took the day total of new birds to beyond fifty, despite the conspicuous absence on the list of Chestnut Rail and Beach Thick-knee! Hence, once the tent was up, it was with some satisfaction that Barry and I walked up to the nearby bar at beer o'clock. "Two beers please, the best you've got," I said to the two barmen, one of whom brusquely replied, "Give 'em anything, they're poms!". Ah, it was good to be birding abroad again, out all day in the field, without a care in the world, surrounded by new birds in new landscapes, and absorbing it all over a welcome cold beer at the end of a long, hot day .... with the friendly natives!

One of the main aims of that trip to Australia was to see the continent's ten endemic shorebirds, and the itinerary was geared heavily towards achieving that goal. When I was researching the trip, with this target always in mind, it became apparent that to virtually guarantee seeing Banded Stilt, one of the best-looking endemic shorebirds as far as I was concerned, it would be wise to visit the St Kilda Saltworks near Adelaide, and that to do so it would be necessary to contact a local birder who could arrange access to this private site. So I wrote to John Cox, who very kindly offered to take me and whoever else turned up, to the Saltworks for a day's birding. It took some time to fix up mutually convenient dates, but taking time to plan such excursions before embarking on a birding trip is crucial to the trip's success, and so it proved! Thanks to John Cox, I saw my first seven endemic Australian shorebirds in as many hours, including 25,000 Banded Stilts.

John Cox also told Barry, my old friend Rob Roberts, who had joined us in Adelaide, and I where to look for the best Australian shorebird of all. I shall never forget lying on my stomach, on the white sand of wild Waitpinga Beach, watching two exquisite Hooded Plovers at eye-level, with waves like waterfalls crashing on to the shore in the background. It was one of those precious times that enhance the lives of birders, a few minutes of magic when I actually felt like I was part of nature, one of those all too rare moments in the company of a wonderful bird in a wild place. Such mortal moments don't come along very often, even for birders, but a few weeks later I was fortunate enough to find myself in the same position, only with a different bird. This time I was lying on my stomach on the hard grassy plains which surround Deniliquin, in a universe so full of stars it was difficult to see the sky, and a female Plains-wanderer, complete with white-spangled black ruff and rufous gorget, walked right up to my nose!

Other particularly vivid memories of birding in Australasia and Oceania include my first Inland Dotterels, straw-striped specialities of the outback, vanishing into the tawny grass of the Great Stony Desert alongside the Strzelecki Track; dazzling Cezanne-blue birds with what looks like snow on their backs, known in the books as White-winged Fairywrens; watching an Albert's Lyrebird bend its shimmering mass of silvery tail plumes over its head to form a veil as it prepared to sing and dance; my first Regent Bowerbird, a velvet black and golden yellow shock of a bird complete with fiery forehead; *pterodromas* whizzing and wheeling above the waves; and, last but by no means least, the sight of a colossal Wandering Albatross slicing through the wind as it tore towards the boat, where it banked and zoomed off without so much as a flick of its wings, all in one beautiful flowing movement. It would have been worth travelling half way around the world just to have experienced one of these moments, but, fortunately, in Australasia and Oceania there are plenty of such delights. The region is one hell of a flight away for most visiting birders, but those endless hours in the air are well worth enduring because the vast majority of the region's birds inhabit some of the best birding terrain on the planet, and many of the colourful and intricately marked species actually look as neat, clean and bright as they are portrayed in the field guides.

These personal memories and the hope of many more have inspired me to research and compile the information contained within this book, and in sharing this information I hope I might encourage fellow birders to travel to the region's wild places in search of the birds they dream of. It is possible, even easy, to achieve such dreams, but to ensure success it is essential to prepare thoroughly, hence I have aimed to include the information that will help birders to plan their own successful and enjoyable birding trips to Australasia and Oceania for years to come.

Birders who are thinking of organising a trip to Australasia and Oceania will probably want to know, first and foremost, where to look for certain species and which species to concentrate on. In this case, they may be thinking about such birds as Emu, the three cassowaries, the three kiwis, penguins, Wandering* and other albatrosses, plenty of *pterodroma* petrels and shearwaters, tropicbirds, strange waterfowl such as Musk and Pink-eared Ducks, Pied Heron, rare raptors like Letter-winged Kite and New Guinea Eagle*, some scrubfowl, seven button-quails, Chestnut Rail, Kagu*, Brolga, Comb-crested Jacana, Tuamotu Sandpiper*, Plains-wanderer*, Bush and Beach Thick-knees, Black* and Banded Stilts, Red-necked Avocet, Hooded* and Shore* Plovers, Red-kneed Dotterel, Wrybill*, Inland Dotterel, Grey-backed Tern, Common White-Tern, Spinifex, Wonga and Pheasant Pigeons, some fabulous fruit-doves, Orange, Golden and Velvet* Doves, the three crowned-pigeons, what is arguably the most varied selection of parrots on earth, three frogmouths, owlet-nightjars, Moustached Treeswift, the world's five kookaburras, Blue-black*, Forest, New Britain, Beach and Moustached* Kingfishers, the world's eight paradise-kingfishers, Rainbow Bee-eater, Rifleman, South Island Wren*, Black-headed*, Rainbow, Noisy and Black-faced* Pittas, the seven Australasian treecreepers, the two lyrebirds, the two scrub-birds, catbirds, Golden*, Flame, Regent and Satin Bowerbirds, fifteen fantastic fairywrens, three emuwrens, eight grasswrens, four pardalotes, three bristlebirds, three whitefaces, honeyeaters galore, Crimson, Orange and Yellow* Chats, Kokako*, Saddleback*, some stunning red-black-and-white robins, two sittellas, Crested Shrike-tit, some lovely whistlers, six pitohuis, Wattled Ploughbill, Logrunner, three whipbirds, five quail-thrushes, three jewel-babblers, Blue-capped Ifrita, many monarch flycatchers, Yellow-breasted and Black-breasted Boatbills, forty-four of the world's forty-six birds-of-paradise, nine woodswallows, six butcherbirds, Magpie-lark, White-backed Swallow, six firetails, seven parrotfinches, Gouldian Finch*, Crested Berrypecker and the Hawaiian honeycreepers.

Once birders have decided on what they would like to see, further questions may spring to mind. Which country supports the best selection? When is the best time to visit that country? Where are the best sites within that country? How easy is it to get from site to site? How much time will be needed to bird each site thoroughly? What other species are there at these sites? Which birds should I concentrate on? Are there any endemics? How many species am I likely to see? The list goes on.

Such questions need careful consideration if the proposed birding trip is going to be an enjoyable success, and without months of painstaking preparation a trip may not be anywhere as near as exciting as it could be. Hence this book's major aim is to answer those questions birders may ask themselves before venturing to Australasia and Oceania for the first or fortieth time. It is not meant to direct you to every site and bird in the minutest detail, but to be a first point of reference, an aid to your own research and planning, a *guiding light*. It is no substitute for up-to-date reports and I urge readers to seek these reports out (see p. 424) once they have decided on their destination, and to write their own reports on their return.

Birders are notoriously hard to please, so writing this book has been all-consuming. I began by compiling a list of sites and the species recorded at them, from every imaginable source. Reports written by independent birders were the major goldmine and without the generous permission of the writers the book you are now reading would not exist (see Acknowledgements). While compiling the site lists it became apparent that many species were known by more than one name, hence I needed a baseline list to cure what was fast becoming a bad headache. So I began looking for the world list of species which I thought was the most logical, easy to use and popular, in terms of individual species names and taxonomic order, and it did not take long to settle on *Birds of the World: A Check List*, by James Clements (Fourth Edition, *Ibis*, 1991, together with the supplements), and I am most grateful to James for being kind enough to allow me to use it. Some of the names he uses are significantly different from those used in other books covering the region, and in some birders' trip reports, hence I have compiled a table to compare these (p. 428).

Although the 'English' names of New World birds should be spelt in the American way (e.g. 'colored' instead of 'coloured', and 'gray' instead of 'grey'), I have written all bird names in English, simply because my busy fingers refused *not* to press the 'u' in 'coloured' or *to* press the 'a' in 'grey' instead of the 'e', while whizzing (no, stumbling) across the keyboard.

Using birders' reports and a wide variety of other sources as my database, most, if not all, of the best birding sites, spectacular and endemic species, as well as those birds hard to see beyond the region's boundaries, have been included, albeit in varying amounts of detail. Absolute coverage and precision would have resulted in the staggered publication of several thick volumes.

The result is over 200 major sites, listed in the Contents and Site Index, over 100 maps, lists of endemic and near-endemic species at the end of each country account, and a Species Index. Hence birders interested in a particular species can look it up in the Species Index, see the page number(s) and turn straight to the site(s) where it occurs. Birders with an interest in a site or sites they have heard about can refer to the Contents or Site Index, see the page number(s) and turn directly to the required site(s).

After much consideration the book has taken the following shape. Countries and island groups have, on the whole, been split according to political boundaries, although having taken into account the distribution of the birds of Oceania it has seemed reasonable to me to lump together some individual countries, overseas territories, republics and self-governing states into larger regions. For example, Fiji, Samoa and Tonga are dealt with in one section; the Federated States of Micronesia, as well as Guam, the Marshall Islands, the Northern Mariana Islands and Palau are dealt with in one section entitled Micronesia; and the Cook Islands, French Polynesia, Kiribati, Nauru and the Pitcairn Islands are dealt with in one section entitled Polynesia. Although Hawaii is a state of the USA, its avifauna most closely resembles that of the nearest islands in Polynesia, hence it has been included in this book under Oceania. These countries and regions are treated alphabetically (except for Antarctica, which is discussed at the end) and details for each country are dealt with as follows.

The **Country Introduction** includes:

A brief **summary** of the features discussed below.

The **size** of the country in relation to England and Texas.

The basics of **getting around** the country.

The range of **accommodation and food**.

Details relating to **health and safety** where, although general advice is given, it is still important to find out the latest information on immunisation requirements (immunisation against yellow fever may be compulsory, not 'just' recommended) and personal safety levels, especially if you are planning to visit Irian Jaya or Papua New Guinea.

A section on **climate and timing**, where the best times to visit are given (these are summarised in the Calendar, p. 422).

An outline of the **habitats** within the country.

Any pertinent **conservation** issues.

The total number of **bird species** recorded in the country (where known), followed by a short list of non-endemic specialities and spectacular species which is intended to give a brief taste of what to expect (rarely seen species are not usually included in this brief list).

The total number of **endemic species** and near-endemic species (where appropriate), followed by a short list of the most spectacular birds in this category.

**Expectations**, where an idea of how many species to expect is given.

Some of these sections may be missing for the less well-known countries, and the details given are intended to be as brief as possible. There seems little point here in repeating the vast amount of information now available in travel guides, and it makes much more sense to save room for more information on the birds and birding in this book.

---

**FIGURE 1: A LIST OF THE 100 BIRD FAMILIES WHICH REGULARLY OCCUR IN AUSTRALASIA AND OCEANIA**

The 20 families listed below in **BOLD CAPITAL** type are endemic to Australasia and Oceania.

| | |
|---|---|
| **EMU** | **Endemic to Australia** |
| **CASSOWARIES** | **Endemic to Australia and New Guinea** (One of the three species belonging to this family, Southern Cassowary*, occurs outside the region on Seram, but it is thought to have been introduced there.) |
| **KIWIS** | **Endemic to New Zealand** |
| Grebes | |
| Penguins | |
| Albatrosses | |
| Petrels and shearwaters | |
| Storm-petrels | |
| Diving-petrels | |
| Tropicbirds | |
| Frigatebirds | |
| Gannets and boobies | |
| Cormorants and shags | |
| Anhingas | Represented by Australian Darter |
| Pelicans | |
| Waterfowl | |
| Herons | |
| Ibises and spoonbills | |
| Storks | Represented by Black-necked Stork |
| Osprey | |
| Kites, hawks and eagles | |
| Falcons | |

| | |
|---|---|
| Scrubfowl | |
| Quails | |
| Buttonquails | |
| Rails | |
| **KAGU*** | **Endemic to New Caledonia** |
| Cranes | |
| Bustards | Represented by Australian Bustard |
| Jacanas | Represented by Comb-crested Jacana |
| Painted-snipes | Represented by Greater Painted-snipe |
| Snipes and sandpipers | |
| **PLAINS-WANDERER*** | **Endemic to Australia** |
| Thick-knees | |
| Oystercatchers | |
| Stilts and avocets | |
| Pratincoles | |
| Plovers | |
| Gulls and terns | |
| Skuas | |
| Pigeons | |
| Parrots | |
| Cockatoos | |
| Lories and lorikeets | |
| Cuckoos | |
| Coucals | |
| Barn-owls | |
| Owls | |
| Frogmouths | |
| Owlet-nightjars | |
| Eared-nightjars | |
| Nightjars | |
| Treeswifts | Represented by Moustached Treeswift |
| Swifts | |
| Kingfishers | |
| Bee-eaters | |
| Rollers | Represented by Dollarbird |
| Hornbills | Represented by Blyth's Hornbill |
| **NEW ZEALAND WRENS** | **Endemic to New Zealand** |
| Pittas | |
| **AUSTRALASIAN TREECREEPERS** | **Endemic to Australia and New Guinea** |
| **LYREBIRDS** | **Endemic to Australia** |
| **SCRUB-BIRDS** | **Endemic to Australia** |
| **BOWERBIRDS** | **Endemic to Australia and New Guinea** |
| **FAIRYWRENS** | **Endemic to Australia and New Guinea** |
| Australo-Papuan warblers | Includes pardalotes, bristlebirds, mouse-warblers, scrubwrens, thornbills, gerygones and whitefaces, and, of which, only three species out of 68 occur |

| | |
|---|---|
| | outside the region |
| Honeyeaters | |
| **NEW ZEALAND WATTLEBIRDS** | **Endemic to New Zealand** |
| Australasian robins | Includes 44 species, of which only one species occurs outside the region |
| Whistlers | Includes sittellas, shrike-thrushes and pitohuis |
| **LOGRUNNERS** | **Endemic to Australia and New Guinea** |
| **PSEUDO-BABBLERS** | **Endemic to Australia and New Guinea** |
| Whipbirds and quail-thrushes | Includes wedgebills and jewel-babblers, and of which, only one species, Malaysian Rail-babbler, occurs outside the region |
| **WHITE-WINGED CHOUGH and APOSTLEBIRD** | **Endemic to Australia** |
| Monarch flycatchers | Includes fantails, shrikebills and boatbills |
| Drongos | |
| Crows | |
| Birds-of-paradise | Includes 44 of the 46 known species |
| Woodswallows | |
| **BUTCHERBIRDS** | **Endemic to Australia and New Guinea** |
| **MAGPIE-LARK and TORRENT-LARK** | **Endemic to Australia and New Guinea** |
| Orioles | |
| Cuckoo-shrikes | |
| Shrikes | Represented by Long-tailed Shrike |
| Thrushes | |
| Starlings | |
| Old world flycatchers | |
| Swallows | |
| White-eyes | |
| Cisticolas | |
| Warblers | Includes grassbirds, songlarks and thicketbirds |
| Larks | Represented by Australasian Bushlark |
| Old world sparrows | |
| Waxbills | Includes firetails, finches, parrotfinches and munias |
| Wagtails and pipits | |
| Flowerpeckers | |
| Sunbirds | |
| **BERRYPECKERS** | **Endemic to New Guinea** |
| **TIT and CRESTED BERRYPECKERS** | **Endemic to New Guinea** |
| **HAWAIIAN HONEYCREEPERS** | **Endemic to Hawaii** |

On some country or region maps the **sites** are numbered, roughly, along a more or less logical route through the country, or in 'bunches', and discussed in that order under each country account. Naturally, different birders will prefer their own routes, but I felt this was a better method than dealing with the sites alphabetically because those birders intending to visit just one area of a country or region will find all the sites dealt with in the same section of the book.

**Sites** are dealt with as follows:

The **site name** usually refers to the actual site. However, if it is nameless, or it involves a number of birding spots which are in close proximity, the best city, town, village, lodge or road name, however remote, from which to explore the site, is used.

The **site introduction** gives its general location within the relevant country (where appropriate) before describing its size, main physical characteristics, habitat make-up and avifauna, including the number of species recorded, where such information is known, and particular reference is made to the endemic and speciality species best looked for at that site. It is *important* to remember here that specialities of the given site are mentioned in the introduction and do not include all the birds listed under the section headed **Non-endemic specialities** in the list for that site (see full explanation, below).

The site's altitude (where known) is also given in metres and feet. Both measurements are given as some birders prefer metres and some prefer feet, whereas only kilometre readings are given for distances (except in the case of Hawaii where miles are used) because most birders now have a grasp of kilometres. For those that don't, remember that one mile equals 1.6093, or roughly 1.6, km.

Restrictions on access, if any, are also given in the site introduction. Such a negative start is designed to eliminate the extreme disappointment of discovering that the site is inaccessible to all but the most well-prepared and adventurous *after* reading about the wealth of avian riches present at the site. Where personal safety is an issue it is *imperative* to check the current situation within some countries, or parts of countries, with the relevant authorities before even considering a visit. Birds are beautiful, but so is life.

The **species lists** for the site follow the introduction and include:

**Endemics:** species only found in the country the site is in (not species endemic to the site). Some birds listed here may only occur at one or two sites within the country so it is important to make a special effort to see them. Such species are mentioned in the site introduction. Others are more widespread, but still endemic to the relevant country.

**Non-endemic specialities:** species which have i) restricted ranges which cross country boundaries, or ii) wider distributions throughout Australasia and Oceania, but are generally scarce, rare, or threatened, or iii) rarely been mentioned in the literature consulted in preparing this book.

It is important to remember here that the species listed under **Non-endemic Specialities** are *not* specialities of the site (such species are mentioned in the site introduction). Some species which are listed under **Non-endemic Specialities** may be very rare at the given site. Nevertheless they *still* fit the criteria given above and merit the 'status' of speciality as far as this book is concerned.

**Others:** species that are widely distributed, but uncommon, spectacular or especially sought after for a variety of reasons.

Some species are **Non-endemic Specialities** in one country, but not in others, hence they may appear under **Non-endemic Specialities** for one country and **Others** for another.

At the end of the bird lists there is also a list of **Other Wildlife** which includes species of mammal, reptile, amphibian, fish, insects, etc., which are listed in alphabetical order.

The lists, particularly the **Others** section, are not comprehensive and many more species may have been recorded at the given site. Such species are common and likely to be seen at many sites in that region of the country, or throughout the country, or across a large part of Australasia and Oceania. By restricting the numbers of species listed under **Others** I have hoped to avoid repetition. These abundant, widespread, but no less spectacular species which are not normally listed include Emu, Australasian Grebe, Australian Gannet, Brown Booby, Little Pied, Pied and Little Black Cormorants, Australian Pelican, Black Swan, Grey Teal, Pacific Black Duck, White-faced Heron, Striated Heron, Australian and Straw-necked Ibises, Whistling Kite, Brown Goshawk, Brown Falcon, Purple Swamphen, Dusky Moorhen, Pied Oystercatcher, Masked Lapwing, Silver Gull, Crested Pigeon, Peaceful Dove, Red-cheeked Parrot, Galah, Sulphur-crested Cockatoo, Brush and Fan-tailed Cuckoos, Glossy, White-rumped and Uniform Swiftlets, Laughing Kookaburra, Collared and Sacred Kingfishers, Dollarbird, Brown Treecreeper, New Holland Honeyeater, Noisy and Yellow-throated Miners, Red Wattlebird, White-fronted Chat, Jacky-winter, Yellow Robin, Varied Sittella, Golden and Rufous Whistlers, Grey Shrike-Thrush, Willie-wagtail, Northern, Grey and Rufous Fantails, Broad-billed and Restless Flycatchers, Spangled Drongo, White-breasted Wood-swallow, Grey and Pied Butcherbirds, Australasian Magpie, Pied and Grey Currawongs, Black-faced and White-bellied Cuckoo-shrikes, Common Cicadabird, Pacific and Welcome Swallows, Tree and Fairy Martins, Silver-eye, Zitting and Golden-headed Cisticolas, Tawny Grassbird, Australasian Bushlark, Mistletoebird and Olive-backed Sunbird.

No one, not even the most experienced observer, is likely to see all the species listed under each site in a single visit, or over a period of a few days, or, in some cases, during a prolonged stay of weeks or more! This is because a number of Australasian species, especially the forest species, apart from being hyper-skulkers, are very thin on the ground, and because a lot of the species which occur in the interior of Australia are nomadic.

Although you may not wish to take this book into the field once you have decided on your destination and itinerary, it, or a photocopy of the relevant section, may prove useful if you are prepared to scrawl all over it. For, by crossing out those species you have seen on a previous trip, or at a previously visited site, or already at the site you are at, you will be able to see what species you still need to look for. It is all too easy, in the haze of excitement generated by birding in a new country or at a new site, to see a lot of good birds and be satisfied with your visit, only to discover later that you have missed a bird at that site which does not occur at any other, or that you have just left a site offering you the last chance to see a certain species (on your chosen route) and are unable to change your itinerary.

Within these lists those species which have been marked with an **asterisk** (*) have been listed as threatened, conservation-dependent, data-deficient, or near-threatened by BirdLife International/IUCN in *Birds to Watch 2: The World List of Threatened Birds*, Collar N *et al.*, 1994. It is important to report any records of these species, and those described as rare in the text, to BirdLife International, Wellbrook Court, Girton Road, Cambridge, CB3 0NA, UK. The excellent BirdLife book deals in detail with Australasia and Oceania's rarest and often most spectacular species, hence all birders planning a trip to the region should seriously consider using it for their pre-trip research.

After the bird lists, directions to the site from the nearest large city, town or village, or previous site, are given. Then the best trails, birding 'spots' and birds are dealt with. Distances are usually given to the nearest kilometre (miles in Hawaii) because speedometers and tyres vary so much, and directions are usually described as points of the compass rather than left or right so as not to cause confusion if travelling from a different direction to that dealt with. These directions are for the most part aimed at birders with cars, as this is the most effective mode of transport in most places, especially in Australia, Hawaii and New Zealand. However, it is important to note that, in some countries, planes, buses, taxis and trails connect most islands and settlements, hence a vehicle would be superfluous. This is particularly true of Irian Jaya and Papua New Guinea. I have decided not to repeat the vast amount of information available about public transport in birders' trip reports or compete with the mindboggling detail presented in the various guidebooks. These can be used by those birders requiring them, thus allowing more room in this book to talk birds.

Where access to a site is limited or permission is required to visit it, this is stated and a contact address given, sometimes in the **Additional Information** section at the end of each country account. If the site details seem scant, this is usually because most birds are easily seen or one or more severely endangered species is present at that site.

Under **Accommodation** I have included the names of hotels, lodges and so on recommended by birders for their safety, economy, comfort, position and, especially, opportunities for birding in their grounds. I have not listed all the types of accommodation available at every site, as it would be foolish to waste so much space on repeating all the information which exists in the general guidebooks.

Prices of accommodation are marked as follows (prices refer to per person per night): (A) = over £10/US$15 (usually a long way over!); (B) = £5 to £10/US$7.5 to US$15; and (C) = under £5/US$7.5. In a few cases these price codes have been used to indicate other costs, such as boat hire and guide fees.

Under some major sites other nearby spots worth birding are mentioned. These usually offer another chance of seeing those species already listed under the major sites, but, in some cases, include sites, especially new ones, where information is scant and a deal of pioneer spirit is required. Veterans of Australasia and Oceania may wish to find out more about such sites (and send me the details for inclusion in the next edition).

Near the end of each country account there is an **Additional Information** section which includes lists of **Books and Papers**, for further research and field use, and **Addresses**, to contact for more information, permits, booking accommodation in advance and so on.

Each country account ends with a list of **Endemic Species** and the sites where they are most likely to be seen. Many birders will consider these species to be the most important and may wish to plan their itinerary based solely on this list, and that of **Near-endemics** which follows, especially if some of the near-endemics are difficult to get to, or see, in the neighbouring countries or regions which they also occur in. A few of the species listed under these headings, mainly those which are **Endemic Species**, are so rare or little known that there are no sites where they are 'likely to be seen'. This is the time to leave this book behind, put your exploring boots on, and set out to find these rarely reported birds that may still survive somewhere off the beaten track. If successful, please send the details to me for inclusion in the next edition (see **Request**, p. 421).

Finally, it is important to remember that this book is not an up-to-the-minute trip report. Some sites will have changed when you get there, some may not even be there and some new ones may have been discovered. Still, a little uncertainty is what makes birding so fascinating. It would be a poor pastime if every bird was lined up and guaranteed at an 'x' on the map, and whilst some birds are lined up (none are guaranteed) in this book, I hope there are not too many. I have aimed to leave enough room, in the major part of the book, for you to 'find' your own birds and, perhaps even more importantly, to provide just the right amount of guidance to help birders to plan a successful and enjoyable birding trip to Australasia and Oceania.

# INTRODUCTION TO BIRDING IN AUSTRALASIA AND OCEANIA

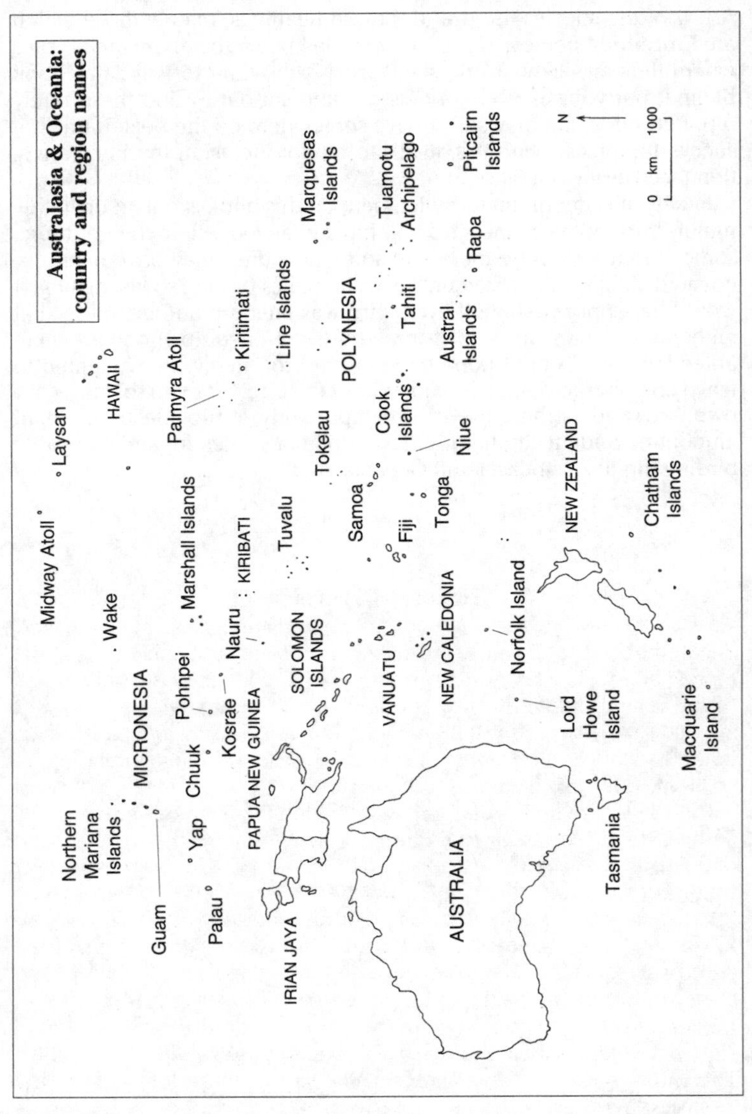


Only 16% of the world's bird species occur in Australasia and Oceania, which for the purposes of this book includes New Guinea, Australia, New Zealand, New Caledonia, Vanuatu, the Solomon Islands, Fiji, Samoa, Tonga, Micronesia, Polynesia and Hawaii. The total number of species which regularly occur in this region is 1,563, over 1,500 less than in South America and over 1,100 less than in Asia, but only 750 less than in Africa. The vast majority of species occur in New Guinea and Australia, with diversity decreasing through Micronesia, the Solomon Islands, Hawaii, Fiji and New Zealand to New Caledonia, Vanuatu and Polynesia.

**FIGURE 2: SPECIES LISTS OF FOUR OF THE WORLD'S MAJOR ZOOGEOGRAPHICAL ZONES**

The figures below relate to regularly occuring species. They are approximate and are based on *Birds of the World: a Check List* (Fourth Edition), Clements J, 1991, together with the supplements, which list approximately 9,700 species.

| Region | List | % of world total | % of Australasia and Oceania total |
|---|---|---|---|
| SOUTH AMERICA | 3,083 | 32 | 197 |
| ASIA | 2,689 | 28 | 172 |
| AFRICA | 2,313 | 24 | 148 |
| AUSTRALASIA and OCEANIA | 1,563 | 16 | – |

## Habitat Diversity

Australasia and Oceania stretches from New Guinea, Australia and New Zealand across the Pacific to Hawaii, and covers a massive area of the planet, although away from the continental landmass of Australia much of the region is taken up by the Pacific, the earth's largest ocean. It accounts for nearly 40% of the world's total area of sea, reaching a maximum breadth of 16,000 km from west to east, and a maximum length of 11,000 km from north to south.

Irian Jaya, the Indonesian province which takes up the western half of the island of New Guinea, is one of the wildest parts of the world, and one of the few where vast expanses of land remain inaccessible by road. Together with parts of Papua New Guinea, the country which takes up the eastern half of the island, it supports the largest tract of rainforest away from Amazonia and the Congo Basin. All but four of the world's 46 species of birds-of-paradise inhabit these moist lowland and mossy montane forests, including those on offshore islands, as well as numerous other endemic species (two birds-of-paradise are endemic to Halmahera to the west and two are endemic to Australia to the south). The snow-capped mountains which rise above these forests form the central spine of New Guinea and rise to 5029 m (16,499 ft) at Gunung Jaya in Irian Jaya and 4508 m (14,790 ft) at Mount Wilhelm in Papua New Guinea. Both of these peaks are higher than Mount Kinabalu in north Borneo, which rises to 4107 m (13,455 ft), and Gunung Jaya is the highest mountain between the Himalayas, which rise to 8848 m (29,029 ft) at Mount Everest, and the Andes, which rise to 6960 m (22,835 ft) at Aconcagua.

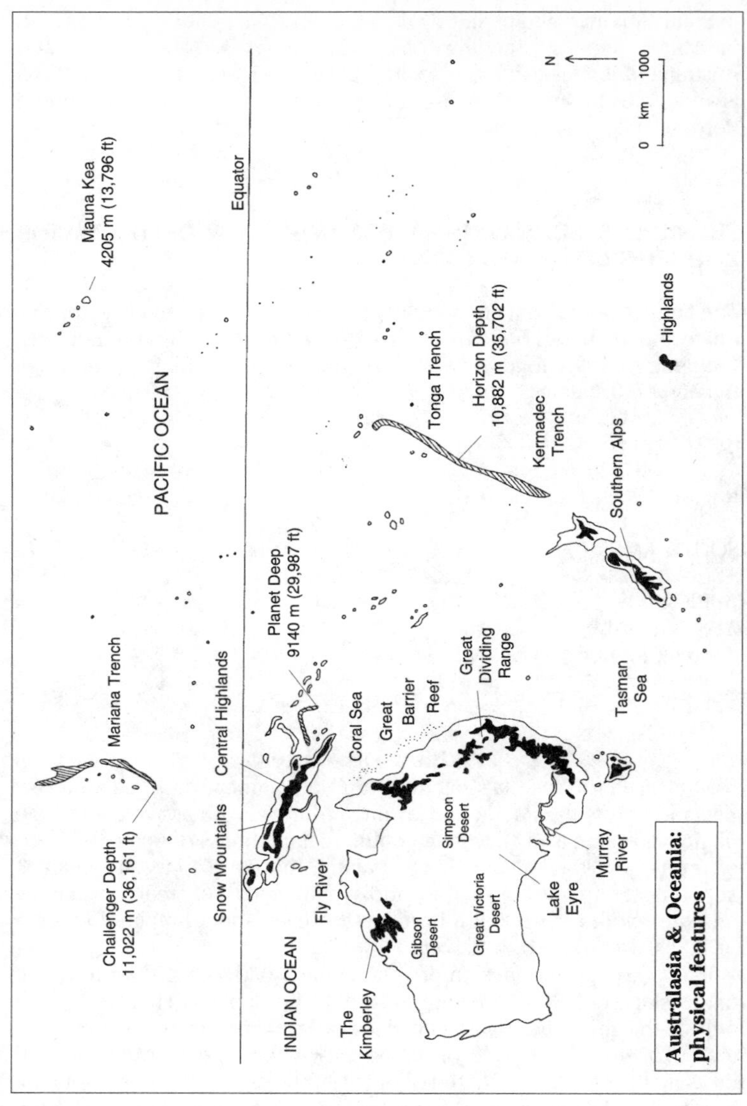


**Australasia & Oceania: physical features**

These precipitous mountains are lofty enough to support alpine grasslands, alpine lakes and elfin moss forests, as well as the luxuriant montane forests. Numerous streams tumble down the steep slopes into the lowlands where they form wide, meandering muddy rivers. Those to the north of the central highlands, including the Mamberamo in Irian Jaya and the Sepik in Papua New Guinea, flow through lowland forests across a relatively narrow coastal plain, while those to the south, such as the Digul in Irian Jaya and the Fly in Papua New Guinea, flow through vast swathes of seasonally flooded savanna in the region known as the Trans-Fly. Masses of waterbirds and some lowland landbird specialities occur here, the vast majority of which also occur in the wetlands of northern Australia, a short distance away to the south across the Arafura and Coral Seas.

Much of Australia, in stark contrast with New Guinea, is low-lying, flat and arid, with the vast majority of the continent comprising grassy plains and stony and sandy deserts with ephemeral saline wetlands and low shrublands, hence the terrestrial avifauna is very different. Numerous creeks, lined with eucalypts such as red river gums, criss-cross the outback, but they are usually dry, and there is only one major river system on this huge continent. The Murray–Darling flows for 3750 km, 29 km less than the Mississippi, across the southeast, draining the only real highlands to the east. These mountains, known as the Great Dividing Range, lie a little way inland from the east coast, run parallel to it for some 2000 km, and rise to 2230 m (7316 ft) at Mount Kosciusko, between Sydney and Melbourne. They support temperate, subtropical and tropical rainforests full of birds, with diversity reaching a peak in the north near Cairns. Elsewhere in Australia there are open, park-like eucalyptus woodlands, dry and wet sclerophyll forests, wet heathlands, remnant patches of dense, dwarf eucalypts known as *mallee*, and, in semi-arid areas, degraded shrublands known as *mulga*, each of which support highly distinctive avifaunas.

Cliffs, lagoons, beaches, mangroves and mudflats line the coasts of New Guinea and Australia, where numerous shorebirds, many of which breed in Siberia, spend the winter, especially around Australia. Offshore there are reefs, cays and islands, most notably in the 2000 km long strip of ocean off northeast Australia where the Great Barrier Reef is situated.

New Zealand is more like New Guinea than Australia, in that it too is a high, scenically spectacular, verdant island with snow-capped peaks, albeit with a rather cooler climate. Its ancient ferny forests may lack birds-of-paradise and a great diversity of terrestrial species, but they do support representatives of three endemic bird families. Unfortunately, most of these are now restricted to translocated populations on offshore islands free from introduced predators. The mountains reach 3754 m (12,316 ft) at Mount Cook in the Southern Alps on South Island and give rise to some unique braided rivers where endemic species such as Black Stilt* breed. These mountains are high enough and sufficiently far south to support glaciers and the wild coast to the west of the Southern Alps is full of fantastic fiords inhabited by penguins. Numerous other seabirds roam the rich coastal waters and breed on offshore islands, while the pillars of rock which form the Subantarctic Islands between New Zealand and Antarctica support some of the world's largest colonies of penguins and albatrosses.

East of New Guinea, Australia and New Zealand the Pacific Ocean is dotted with the archipelagos of the Bismarcks, the Solomon Islands, Vanuatu, New Caledonia and Fiji, Samoa and Tonga. Humid, tropical lowland and mossy montane rainforests on the rugged volcanic islands in these archipelagos, which reach their highest point at 2447 m (8028 ft) at Mount Makarakomburu in the Solomon Islands, support their own endemic avifaunas, but only New Caledonia can boast an endemic family, represented by Kagu*. Most of the unique birds of these islands are restricted to montane forests, which occur mostly on the wet windward slopes, because a lot of lowland forest has been cleared to make way for subsistence farming and coconut plantations. Offshore from the palm-fringed beaches which surround the majority of these islands there are reefs which support a good selection of seabirds.

Further north and east, within Micronesia and Polynesia, there are numerous low-lying chains of coral islands known as atolls, which rarely reach 10 m (33 ft) and support a few specialised endemics such as Tuamotu Sandpiper*, and some high, rugged volcanic islands, rising to 2241 m (7352 ft) in Polynesia, with remnant wet montane, mostly fig, forests which support endemic pigeons, monarch flycatchers and white-eyes.

The remotest archipelago on earth, the Hawaiian Islands, lies at the northeastern edge of Australasia and Oceania, in the middle of the northern Pacific. Here, the natural forests, allied to the eucalptus and acacia clans, are virtually confined to the high, steep slopes above 1219 m (4000 ft) on the precipitous volcanic peaks, which reach 4205 m (13,796 ft) at Mauna Kea on Big Island. These permanently damp 'cloud' forests support a sadly depleted endemic avifauna. The lowlands are virtually devoid of endemic plants and birds, but the deep waters surrounding these islands provide food for numerous seabirds which breed on the rocky headlands and offshore islets throughout the archipelago.

## Country Lists

The top country lists for Australasia and Oceania fall well short of the top eight in South America, the top five in Asia and the top ten in Africa. Australia's list of a little over 800 is under half that for Brazil despite being nearly the same size, over 400 less than China's, despite being only slightly smaller, and nearly 300 lower than Kenya's, despite being thirteen times larger. In fact, Australia's list, which is the largest in this region, is bolstered by rarities and only around 650 are usually regarded as regular visitors, a total similar to Irian Jaya and Papua New Guinea. These two largely forested regions which lie near the equator compare favourably with similarly situated forested countries in South America, Asia and Africa. Venezuela, which is roughly twice the size of Irian Jaya and Papua New Guinea, supports about twice as many species; Thailand, which is 1.4 times larger than Irian Jaya and a little larger than Papua New Guinea, supports 1.4 times as many birds (nearly 300 more species); and Cameroon, which is 1.3 times larger than Irian Jaya and about the same size as Papua New Guinea, supports 1.4 times as many birds (over 200 more species).

The other countries and island groups in Australasia and Oceania have far smaller lists. New Zealand's total of over 320 is higher than Madagascar's 250 or so, despite being less than half the size of that Afrotropical island and much further south of the equator, but Japan, which is roughly the same distance north of the equator as New Zealand is south of the equator, and only 1.4 times larger, has a list of over 580, over 250 higher than that for New Zealand.

Both Hawaii and Micronesia have lists in excess of 200, but the rest of the island groups in this region have rather impoverised avifaunas and fail to make the 200 mark, a milestone easily reached by much smaller archipelagos in the world's other continents, including Trindad and Tobago (430), the Canary Islands (315+) and the Seychelles (220+). Hence birders hoping to see the widest possible diversity of species on a short trip to Australasia and Oceania should read the accounts for Irian Jaya, Papua New Guinea and Australia first, and those visiting the other countries and island groups should not expect to see over 100 species in most places.

**FIGURE 3: COUNTRY AND REGION SPECIES LISTS (approximate figures) (see Figure 4)**

| | Country | Species |
|---|---|---|
| 1 | AUSTRALIA | 800+ |
| 2 | IRIAN JAYA | 650+ |
| 3 | PAPUA NEW GUINEA | 646+ |
| 4 | NEW ZEALAND | 320+ |
| 5 | MICRONESIA | 225+ |
| 6 | HAWAII | 200+ |
| 7 | SOLOMON ISLANDS | 190+ |
| 8 | FIJI, SAMOA and TONGA | 130+ |
| 9 | VANUATU | 120+ |
| 10 | POLYNESIA | 100+ |
| 11 | NEW CALEDONIA | 90+ |

**FIGURE 4: COUNTRY AND REGION SPECIES LISTS**

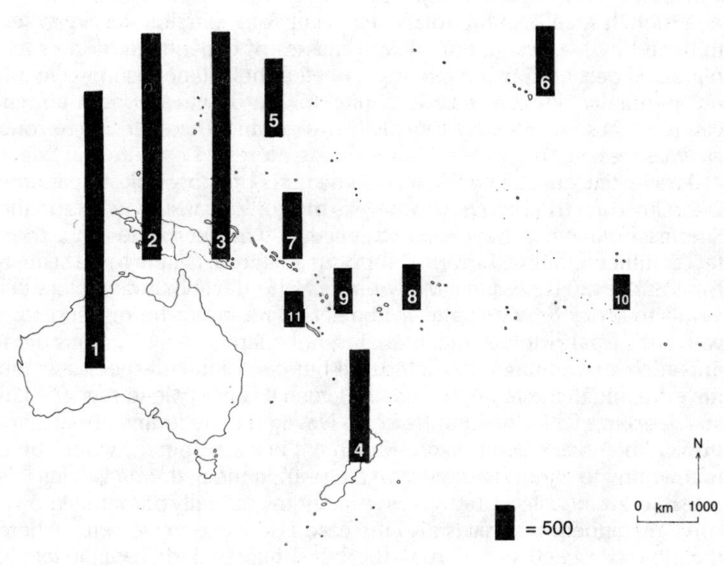


## Trip Lists

In Australasia and Oceania the best way to see the most species on a trip lasting three or four weeks is to fly between the major cities in the eastern half of Australia and bird the sites nearby. If such a trip was undertaken between October and March a trip total of 420 or more would be possible. Between April and September it would be very difficult to reach 400. Some birders take a year out to cover the country more thoroughly, in which case 600 species are possible, while others concentrate on taking shorter trips to different parts of the continent, in which case it would be possible to see between 270 (in the west) and 300 (in the north and east) in three weeks.

Australia is able to compete with Asia when it comes to lengthy trip lists, but not Africa and South America. In Asia the best totals possible on trips lasting three to four weeks range from 440 (northeast India) down to 350–400 (north India, Malaysia and Thailand) and 330 (Nepal and Vietnam), but in Africa it is possible to see 730 species on Sunbird's three-week thrashes to Kenya, and a 25-day tour to Kenya led by Brian Finch in November 1991 amassed an amazing 797 species. In South America Birdquest have recorded 707 species in three weeks in Ecuador, but the unofficial 'World Bird Tour Record' belongs to the Danish Ornithological Society, who recorded a mindblowing 844 species on a 27-day trip to Ecuador in 1992! The birders who took part in these trips therefore had to cope with more species than the total number which regularly occur in the whole of Australia or New Guinea.

On the island of New Guinea it is possible to see 300 species during a month's trip to mainland Papua New Guinea, including up to 20 of the 25 mainland endemics (80%) and up to 26 of the world's 46 birds-of-paradise (57%). In Irian Jaya it is possible to see over 250 species in a month, including about 35 of the 44 endemics (80%) and up to 24 of the world's 46 birds-of-paradise (52%).

Although such high trip totals are usually only possible on organised tours led by leaders equipped with masses of experience of the sites, birds and best birding techniques, as well as hefty tape-recorders to lull out the many skulkers, thorough preparation by independent birders can result in similar totals for small 'teams' of fanatics, especially beyond New Guinea.

Away from Australia and New Guinea it is only possible to pass the 100 mark for a trip lasting a few weeks in New Zealand, Hawaii and the Solomon Islands. In New Zealand seeing 100 native species on a short trip is difficult, but with over 20 introduced species likely to be seen, a trip total of 120 is possible. Many birders who travel halfway across the world to scour New Zealand for birds will no doubt be disappointed with such a paltry total, but it is quality, not quantity, which counts here, and such a total may well include all but one of the 43 species which are endemic to the main islands. In Hawaii it is possible to see 100–120 species during a fortnight in October–November, including about 20 of the 35 known surviving endemics (57%), but 100 species would be a noteworthy total during the rest of the year. In the Solomon Islands it is possible to see at least 100 species, including virtually all of the known surviving endemics. This is also the case elsewhere in Oceania, where the trip totals will be well below 100, but should include most, if not all, of the endemics, especially in Micronesia, New Caledonia and Vanuatu.

## Site and Day Lists

The top site and day lists in Australasia and Oceania fall well short of those for South America, Africa and Asia. The top ten site lists in South America all exceed 430 and reach 1,000, the top ten site lists in Africa all exceed 400 and reach 535 and the top five site lists in Asia all exceed 350 and reach 480, whereas the best this region can muster in a relatively small area is around 275 at Kakadu National Park in northern

Australia. About 250 species have also been recorded in the environs of nearby Darwin, as well as Sydney, Melbourne, Perth, Broome, Cairns and Brisbane in Australia, and Port Moresby and Wau in Papua New Guinea.

The total of 275 species for the rivers, seasonally flooded grasslands and woodlands of Kakadu is over 200 fewer than that of the 480 recorded in the similar habitats present at Chitwan National Park in Nepal, which is less than a tenth the size of Kakadu, and 260 less than that of the 535 recorded in Ruwenzori National Park in Uganda, which is less than half the size of Kakadu.

There are plenty of sites in Australia with lists in excess of 200, including Wilson's Promontory National Park, which is situated on the south coast a long way south of the equator, but such totals are rare elsewhere in the region, even in New Guinea where the habitat is primarily forest. These forests may be inhabited by birds-of-paradise, but they support a relatively low diversity of species overall, especially when compared with forested sites near the equator in the other major continents. In South America even small but largely forested sites boast lists in excess of 500; in Africa the admittedly huge Ituri Forest in the Congo Basin has a list of over 400; and in Asia over 350 species have been recorded at the top forested site of Taman Negara in Malaysia.

There are few places in Australasia and Oceania where it is possible to see over 100 species in a day, but they include the environs of Sydney, Deniliquin, Melbourne, Adelaide (where over 130 is possible), Perth, Darwin, Cairns and Brisbane in Australia, and Port Moresby in Papua New Guinea. Such totals are easily achieved in the other major continents. In Asia it is possible to record over 180 species in a day at Bharatpur (India) and over 150 at Chitwan National Park (Nepal), Kosi (Nepal) and Hong Kong (in spring). In South America such totals are possible at plenty of sites and on one day in 1986 a total of 331 species was recorded in Manu National Park, Peru, the best day total for any one site on earth. However, Africa is probably the best continent for notching up incredible day totals, and on a November day also in 1986, the world day list record of 342 was set in Kenya with the aid of a light aircraft.

## Family Diversity

Australasia and Oceania supports 100 different bird families, 52% of the world's total (see Figures 1 and 5, p. 15 and 30). Asia, the most diverse continent on earth in terms of bird families, has 16 more and Africa eight more, but South America has eight less.

Australasia and Oceania may be poor in terms of numbers of species, but their avifauna is highly endemic. They support 20 endemic bird families (see Figure 1), 14 more than Asia, 11 more than South America (but five less than South and Central America combined) and five more than Africa (including the five which are confined to Malagasy). The 20 families unique to Australasia and Oceania include five which are only found in Australia [Emu, Plains-wanderer*, lyrebirds (two species), scrub-birds (two species) and the *Corcoracidae* (White-winged Chough and Apostlebird)], eight families which are restricted to Australia and New Guinea [cassowaries, Australasian creepers, bowerbirds, fairywrens, logrunners, pseudo-babblers, butcherbirds and the *Grallinidae* (Magpie-lark and Torrent-lark)], two families which are endemic to New Guinea [Berrypeckers and the *Paramythiidae* (Tit and Crested Berrypeckers)], three families which only occur in New Zealand [kiwis, New Zealand wrens and wattlebirds (Kokako and Saddleback)], one family which is endemic to New Caledonia and is represented by the Kagu*, and one family which is endemic to Hawaii (the Hawaiian honeycreepers). Australia is the best place to see the widest range of these families, with 13 out of the 20 being possible, while Irian Jaya and Papua New Guinea both offer the opportunity to see ten.

Apart from the strictly endemic families, Australasia and Oceania also support a few families which are virtually restricted to the region, including megapodes, cockatoos, owlet-nightjars, australo-papuan warblers (scrubwrens, thornbills and gerygones), honeyeaters, Australasian robins, whistlers, whipbirds and quail-thrushes, birds-of-paradise (all but two of the world's 46 species) and woodswallows. Representatives of these ten families can be encountered in Australia and New Guinea, but far fewer are likely to be encountered elsewhere.

Unique genuses include the three crowned-pigeons of New Guinea, the five kookaburras of Australia and New Guinea, the four pardalotes of Australia, the three bristlebirds of Australia, the three mouse-warblers of New Guinea, the two sittellas of Australia and New Guinea, the five shrike-thrushes of Australia and New Guinea, the six pitohuis of New Guinea, the three jewel-babblers of New Guinea, and the two boatbills of Australia and New Guinea.

The region is particularly rich in albatrosses, petrels and shearwaters, cormorants and shags, buttonquails, oystercatchers, plovers, pigeons, parrots, kingfishers and monarch flycatchers, but there are no flamingos, trogons, barbets, woodpeckers, nuthatches, bulbuls nor babblers.

## FIGURE 5: FAMILY LISTS OF THE WORLD'S MAJOR ZOOGEOGRAPHICAL ZONES

The figures below are based on *Birds of the World: A Check List* (Fourth Edition). Clements J, 1991, together with the supplements, which list 194 families.

| Region | List | % of World total | % of Australasia and Oceania total |
|---|---|---|---|
| ASIA | 116 | 60 | 116 |
| AFRICA | 108 | 56 | 108 |
| AUSTRALASIA and OCEANIA | 100 | 52 | – |
| SOUTH AMERICA | 92 | 47 | 92 |
| CENTRAL AMERICA and the CARIBBEAN | 89 | 46 | 89 |
| NORTH AMERICA | 68 | 35 | 68 |
| EUROPE | 66 | 34 | 66 |

## Endemic Species

Regions of the world with concentrations of restricted-range birds have been identified as Endemic Bird Areas (EBAs) in BirdLife International's *Putting Biodiversity on the Map*, 1992. Of the world total of 221 EBAs, Australasia and Oceania have 46 (21%), 11 less than Asia with 57, nine less than South America with 55, and nine more than Africa with 37.

Half of the EBAs in Australasia and Oceania are situated in New Guinea and Australia, where there are 14 and nine respectively. In New Guinea the five which cover the forests of the central highlands and the wetlands of the Trans-Fly region are shared between Irian Jaya and Papua New Guinea, while Irian Jaya has three of its own, and Papua New Guinea has six of its own, although five of these encompass the off-shore islands and only one is on the mainland. All of the New Guinea EBAs apart from that covering the Trans-Fly region are in forested regions. Although the interior outback of Australia supports the most endemics, these species are widely distributed and do not qualify as restricted-range species, hence the six mainland Australian EBAs are liberally sprinkled around the periphery of the continent, near Sydney, Melbourne, Perth, Darwin and Cairns, and on the Cape York Peninsula.

The remaining 23 EBAs in Australasia and Oceania are distributed between Polynesia (five), Micronesia (four), New Zealand (four, including North and South Islands), Hawaii (three), the Solomon Islands (three), Fiji, Samoa and Tonga (two), New Caledonia (one) and Vanuatu (one).

---

**FIGURE 6: AUSTRALASIA and OCEANIA ENDEMIC BIRD AREAS (46)**

| Name of Endemic Bird Area | Country or Region |
|---|---|
| WEST PAPUAN ISLANDS and VOGELKOP LOWLANDS | Irian Jaya |
| VOGELKOP MOUNTAINS | Irian Jaya |
| GEELVINK BAY ISLANDS (Biak, etc.) | Irian Jaya |
| NORTH NEW GUINEA MOUNTAINS | Irian Jaya and Papua New Guinea |
| NORTH NEW GUINEA LOWLANDS | Irian Jaya and Papua New Guinea |
| CENTRAL NEW GUINEAN HIGH MOUNTAINS | Irian Jaya and Papua New Guinea |
| CENTRAL NEW GUINEAN MID MOUNTAINS | Irian Jaya and Papua New Guinea |
| TRANS-FLY and UPPER-FLY | Irian Jaya and Papua New Guinea |
| ADELBERT and HUON MOUNTAINS | Papua New Guinea |
| ADMIRALTY ISLANDS | Papua New Guinea |
| ST MATTHIAS ISLANDS | Papua New Guinea |
| NEW BRITAIN and NEW IRELAND | Papua New Guinea |
| D'ENTRECASTEAUX and SOLOMON SEA ISLANDS | Papua New Guinea |
| LOUISIADE ARCHIPELAGO | Papua New Guinea |
| KIMBERLEY and the TOP END (Darwin) | Australia |

| | |
|---|---|
| CAPE YORK | Australia |
| ATHERTON REGION (near Cairns) | Australia |
| SOUTHWEST AUSTRALIA | Australia |
| MURRAY-DARLING REGION and ADJOINING COAST | Australia |
| SOUTHEAST AUSTRALIA | Australia |
| TASMANIA | Australia |
| NORFOLK ISLAND | Australia |
| LORD HOWE ISLAND | Australia |
| FIJIAN ISLANDS | Fiji |
| SAMOAN ISLANDS | Samoa |
| NORTHWESTERN HAWAIIAN ISLANDS | Hawaii |
| HAWAIIAN ISLANDS (Kauai, Oahu, Molokai, Maui) | Hawaii |
| HAWAII (Big Island) | Hawaii |
| MARIANA ISLANDS | Micronesia |
| PALAU | Micronesia |
| YAP | Micronesia |
| MICRONESIAN ISLANDS (Pohnpei, Chuuk, Kosrae) | Micronesia |
| NEW CALEDONIA and the LOYALTY ISLANDS | New Caledonia |
| CENTRAL NORTH ISLAND | New Zealand |
| SOUTH ISLAND | New Zealand |
| CHATHAM ISLANDS | New Zealand |
| AUCKLAND ISLANDS | New Zealand |
| LOWER COOK ISLANDS | Polynesia |
| PITCAIRN ISLANDS | Polynesia |
| SOCIETY ISLANDS (Tahiti, etc.) | Polynesia |
| TUAMOTU ARCHIPELAGO | Polynesia |
| MARQUESAS ISLANDS | Polynesia |
| SOLOMON ISLANDS (not San Cristobal nor Rennell) | Solomon Islands |
| SAN CRISTOBAL | Solomon Islands |
| RENNELL | Solomon Islands |
| VANUATU and the SANTA CRUZ ISLANDS | Vanuatu |

Australia and New Guinea may support relatively low numbers of species compared with countries in South America, Asia and Africa, but this relatively low diversity is more than compensated for by the high degree of species endemism, with both mainland Australia (313) and mainland New Guinea (324) supporting over 300 unique species. These two totals are second only to Indonesia (338), where the total is boosted by the presence of so many islands, in the world league table, and way ahead of the rest of the pack, which is led by the Philippines (185), Brazil (180+) and Madagascar (102).

If New Guinea was a single country it would be able to boast the highest number of endemics in the world. The grand total of 399 endemics, including those confined to the offshore islands, is over 60 more than the total for the whole of Indonesia and all the more remarkable considering that Borneo, an island of similar size and situated a similar distance from a large continental landmass, only has 37 endemics, and nearby Sumatra only 18. Even Madagascar, which has a highly endemic avifauna, can only muster 102 endemics, just 26% of New Guinea's total. As it is, the island is divided into two, and 269 of the New Guinea endemics occur in both Irian Jaya and Papua New Guinea. The majority (86) of the remaining 130 endemics are confined to Papua New Guinea, although only 25 of these occur on the mainland. The other 61 are restricted to the islands east of Papua New Guinea and 50 of these occur only in the islands of the Bismarck Archipelago, mainly (35) on New Ireland and New Britain. The 44 Irian Jaya endemics are shared between the mainland (30) and the offshore islands (14) where nine are confined to islands such as Biak in Geelvink Bay, and five occur only on West Papuan Islands such as Batanta.

Australia's long list of endemics is almost as impressive as that of New Guinea. A total of 332 birds occurs only in this country, including 13 which are restricted to Tasmania, four which only occur on Norfolk Island and two which are confined to Lord Howe Island. This leaves a total for the mainland of 313, only 11 short of the total for the much more luxuriant mainland of New Guinea, and a figure far more impressive than that for other large countries in the world such as Brazil (180+) and China (59), although they do not have the advantage of being an island continent. The species unique to mainland Australia are concentrated in the east, but 66 are more or less confined to the arid interior and 20 are restricted to the southwest.

New Zealand also has a high number of endemics. Of the total of 61, ten only occur in the Subantarctic Islands and seven are confined to the Chatham Islands, leaving 43 species which are endemic to the main islands, a far higher total than for Japan (12), which is a similar distance from the equator.

There are also plenty of endemics in Oceania, with over 30 in most of the large island groups. The avifauna of the Solomon Islands is particularly rich in endemics, with 45 species being unique to the islands within the political boundaries, and 70 within the zoogeographical limits, as 25 species are shared only with the islands of Bougainville and Buka, which lie at the northern end of the archipelago, but are politically part of Papua New Guinea. Forty-one species only occur on the islands of Fiji, Samoa and Tonga, of which 25 are endemic to Fiji. Micronesia (40) and Polynesia (42) support an almost equal number of endemics, with the most concentrated on the Caroline Islands (15) and Palau (10) in Micronesia, and on the Marquesas Islands (10) in Polynesia. Hawaii, the world's most isolated archipelago, also supports an impressive number of endemics, although there used to be a lot more than 35 and of these ten or so are on the brink of extinction. Although New Caledonia has the distinction of supporting an endemic family, represented by Kagu*, it only supports 22 endemics in total, the same as Halmahera and its satellites in Indonesia. The islands of Vanuatu support just nine endemics, which is the same as Samoa, but less than the two Indonesian islands of Timor (11) and Buru (10).

In Irian Jaya and Papua New Guinea most of the species seen in the forests on the central mountains will be endemic to the island of New Guinea, but seeing a high percentage of the species endemic to each half of the island is more difficult. In Irian Jaya it is possible to see about 35 of the 44 endemics (80%), including all five endemic birds-of-paradise, on a trip lasting about a month. In Papua New Guinea it is possi-

**FIGURE 7: COUNTRY and REGION ENDEMIC LISTS and ENDEMIC BIRD AREA TOTALS (see Figure 9)**

| COUNTRY | Number of Endemic species | Number of Endemic bird areas |
|---|---|---|
| AUSTRALIA | 332 | 9 |
| PAPUA NEW GUINEA* | 86 | 11 |
| NEW ZEALAND | 61 | 4 |
| SOLOMON ISLANDS | 45 | 3 |
| IRIAN JAYA* | 44 | 8 |
| POLYNESIA | 42 | 5 |
| FIJI, SAMOA and TONGA | 41 | 2 |
| MICRONESIA | 40 | 4 |
| HAWAII | 35 | 3 |
| NEW CALEDONIA | 22 | 1 |
| VANUATU | 9 | 1 |

* The total number of species endemic to New Guinea is 399.

**FIGURE 8: SELECTED ENDEMIC LISTS**

| Country or Region | Total |
|---|---|
| NEW GUINEA MAINLAND | 324 |
| AUSTRALIAN MAINLAND | 313 |
| SOLOMON ISLANDS, BOUGAINVILLE and BUKA | 70 |
| ISLANDS OFF PAPUA NEW GUINEA | 61 |
| IRIAN JAYA | 44 |
| NEW ZEALAND MAINLAND | 43 |
| HAWAII | 35 |
| FIJI | 25 |
| PAPUA NEW GUINEA MAINLAND | 25 |
| NEW CALEDONIA | 22 |
| NORTHEAST AUSTRALIA | 21 |
| SOUTHWEST AUSTRALIA | 20 |
| CAROLINE ISLANDS (Micronesia) | 15 |
| TASMANIA (Australia) | 13 |
| KIMBERLEY and DARWIN AREAS (Australia) | 11 |
| MARQUESAS ISLANDS (Polynesia) | 10 |
| PALAU (Micronesia) | 10 |
| SUBANTARCTIC ISLANDS (New Zealand) | 10 |
| SAMOA | 9 |
| VANUATU | 9 |
| GUAM and NORTH MARIANA ISLANDS (Micronesia) | 8 |
| CHATHAM ISLANDS (New Zealand) | 7 |
| COOK ISLANDS (Polynesia) | 6 |
| TUAMOTU ARCHIPELAGO (Polynesia) | 6 |
| PITCAIRN ISLANDS (Polynesia) | 5 |
| TAHITI (Polynesia) | 5 |

ble to see up to 20 of the 25 mainland endemics (80%), including six to nine of the ten birds-of-paradise which are endemic to the mainland. A further few weeks travelling through the Bismarck Archipelago to the east should be enough to see the vast majority of the 50 species endemic to these islands. The 11 remaining endemics, including two birds-of-paradise, inhabit the East Papuan Islands, which are off the beaten track but actually fairly easy to get to and around.

One of the joys of a first time visit to Australia is that most of the species encountered will be new, because they are endemic, but seeing a large percentage of these birds will take a lot more time than that available on a three or four week trip. The 313 mainland endemics are scattered throughout this huge continent, from the southwest (20) and the Kimberley and Darwin region (11) to the southeast and northeast, and through the interior where many species are nomadic and take time to pin down. Hence to see a high percentage of Australia's endemics it will be necessary to make several trips, or perhaps a single trip lasting anything from a few months to a year.

A two or three week trip to New Zealand should be enough to see all but one of the mainland endemics (42 of 43 species), but catching up with the 18 species which occur on the Chatham (7) and Subantarctic (10) Islands (one species is possible in both) will require considerable good fortune, in the case of the former, and considerably large amounts of money, in the case of the latter. It is now easy to get to the main island in the Chatham Islands, but very difficult to arrange a visit to the island of Rangatira where four of the endemics, including Shore Plover*, are only likely to be seen. The only realistic way of seeing the Subantarctic endemics is to join one of the expensive and irregular cruise-ship tours.

Most of the 45 Solomon Islands endemics, plus the 25 species shared only with Bougainville and Buka which lie within the political boundaries of Papua New Guinea, can be seen on an island-hopping trip which lasts a few weeks, but seeing the 42 Polynesian and 39 Micronesian endemics will involve a lot more time and travel. Although most of the Polynesian endemics are fairly easy to see once the individual islands and archipelagos have been reached, some of these are virtually impossible to get to without joining a number of separate expensive and irregular cruise-ship tours. In Polynesia it will be necessary to visit the Cook Islands (six), the Austral Islands (three), the Pitcairn Islands (five), Tahiti (five), the Tuamotu Archipelago (six), the Marquesas Islands (ten), the Line Islands (one) and Nauru (one) to look for all of the endemics, some of which are very rare. In Micronesia it will be necessary to visit the Northern Mariana Islands (eight) and Palau (ten), as well as Yap (three), Chuuk (three) and Pohnpei (five) in the Caroline Islands, to look for all of the endemics. Most of these islands are readily accessible, given plenty of time, and most of the birds are fairly easy to see once on site.

There are also over 40 endemics to look for in Fiji, Samoa and Tonga, the majority of which are fairly easy to see, especially on Fiji. Some of the 35 Hawaiian endemics are on the edge of extinction, hence it is impossible to see a large percentage of the endemics there, and a realistic target for a two week trip would be about 20 (57%). In New Caledonia (22) and Vanuatu (nine) the situation is very different, for on both archipelagos it is possible to see virtually all of the known surviving endemics in a few days.

**FIGURE 9: COUNTRY and REGION ENDEMIC LISTS (See Figure 7)**

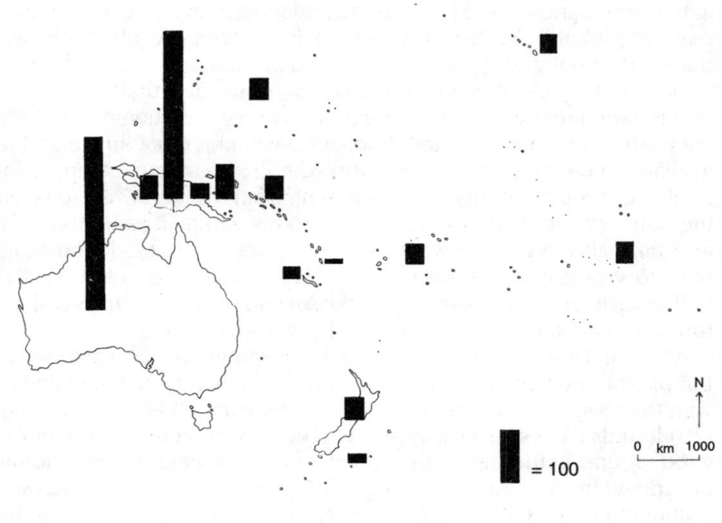


## Exploration

John McKean, who died in early 1996, was the pioneer of listing in Australasia and during his extensive travels he set a target which is going to be hard to beat, having amassed a total of 1,279 species in Australia and New Guinea alone. Although several birders have passed the 1,000 mark, and 20 or so are over 800, his nearest competitor is Phoebe Snetsinger who, by the end of 1995, had reached 1,164, still over 100 behind. In Australia around 30 birders have seen more than 600 species, a total which Mike Entwistle, a British birder now also sadly departed from the birding world, managed to achieve during a 12-month tour of the continent. Mike Carter, an Australian resident, leads the field, having amassed an awesome 756 by October 1996. John McKean was on 743 when he died. The leader's nearest competitors are Tony Palliser (731), Fred Smith (729), Alan McBride (713) and Glen Holmes (710), with a further seven birders on 700 or more and 19 with lists in excess of 600.

Those birders keen to add the little known and rarely seen species to their burgeoning lists, or those birders in search of something new and exciting, will be busy planning possible trips to the region's remote nooks and crannies, having carried out extensive and painstaking research into previous ornithological explorations, in order to identify those areas which have been least studied or perhaps completely neglected, and the habitat preferences (and their present distributions) of those species which are rarely reported these days.

Australia and New Zealand have been thoroughly grilled, although new birds are still being added to the their lists on an almost regular basis. This is especially true in Australia, where pioneering seabird fanatics continue to spring surprises. There have been numerous pelagic trips off Wollongong near Sydney for years, and yet in October 1996 a probable Murphy's Petrel was seen. If accepted, this Polynesian *pterodroma* will be a new bird for Australia. Also in October 1996 the hardcore Australian seabirders ventured out of Broome and discovered Matsudaira's Storm-Petrels and probable Jouanin's Petrels in Australian waters.

The chances of finding a species new to science in Australia and New Zealand are extremely slim, although a potential new species of grasswren, allied to Dusky Grasswren, was photographed in The Kimberley in 1991 and rumours of a new species of fruit-dove, which supposedly occurs on a single mountain in the Atherton Tablelands of northeast Australia, persist. There may be a faint chance of rediscovering one or two species, however. Could a couple of Paradise Parrots, presumed to have been extinct since around 1927, be surviving somewhere in the remote outback of Australia? They are still reported occasionally. Could those rarely visited rugged and remote parts of New Zealand, especially on South Island, still support a few Laughing Owls, last recorded in 1914, or Bush Wrens, seen as recently as 1972? Only time will tell. One endemic Australian bird that does still exist, but which has eluded most of the country's birders, is the nocturnal Night Parrot*. This mysterious bird was reported 15 times between 1984 and 1994, but all attempts to pin it down have so far failed.

Remote and rarely visited forested regions exist in New Caledonia, where the endemic rail and owlet-nightjar have not been recorded for many years, and in the Solomon Islands, where Choiseul Pigeon* has not been recorded since 1904 and San Cristobal Moorhen* was last reported in the 1950s—the last time anyone from outside the region who knew anything about birds bothered to look for it. Little Vanuatu, where Mountain Starlings* were seen for the first time for 30 years in 1991, could even conjure up a new species. Such an achievement would be unlikely in Fiji, although some birders may wish to try and pin down Long-legged Warbler*, which has only been reported four times this century, or even rediscover Bar-winged Rail, which has only been reported once this century and is presumed to be extinct.

In Micronesia and Polynesia there are a number of rarely reported species, but this is probably partly due to problems of access to remote atolls and islands, rather than the rarity of most species. The trickiest large forested areas to reach are probably those on the Marquesas Islands, where in the far-flung corners there may reside a new species of ground-dove or monarch flycatcher. There is little chance of finding a new species in Hawaii, but every chance for those who can get off the beaten track of finding one of the many species which may or may not be extinct. Some of the most spectacular Hawaiian endemics became extinct long ago and have been looked for in earnest since, so there is virtually no chance of them surviving, but if someone did manage to track down the stunning Ula-ai-hawane, last recorded in 1890, or the brilliant Hawaii Mamo, last seen in 1898, birders of the world would rejoice.

Leaving the realms of fantasy behind, it is fair to say that some parts of Papua New Guinea will definitely be worth exploring if and when they are accessible and safe to visit, as they may offer the chance to track down the forest-dwelling rails and owlet-nightjars which are rarely heard of these days. However, Papua New Guinea has been relatively well covered compared with its neighbour Irian Jaya. This wild province of Indonesia is without doubt the hot-spot as far as the opening up of new areas goes, and pioneering birders have already been in, where it has been possible, and discovered new delights. In the Fakfak Mountains, for example, a short trip in 1991 revealed that the rarely visited forests on their slopes probably support a new bowerbird, two new honeyeaters and a new bird-of-paradise. These birds may only be versions of very similar species, but who knows what the even remoter forests in places such as the Foya Mountains and the Mamberamo River basin support? Irian Jaya probably offers birders the best chance of rediscovering rarely reported New Guinea endemics and is arguably the most likely place on earth where new species may still be discovered. The probable new species of bird-of-paradise in the Fakfak Mountains is only a paradigalla with a different sized tail to the others, but, if a new bird-of-paradise is waiting to be discovered elsewhere in the country—it might just be more spectacular than any of the others.

# CONSERVATION

Despite the fact that most of Australasia and Oceania is relatively sparsely populated, much of the natural habitat has been destroyed or degraded as a result of human interference. Habitat loss and degradation are by far the biggest problems facing the birds of the region, although hunting, foolish introductions of non-native birds, mammals, reptiles and disease-carrying mosquitoes, and the international trade in some species, especially parrots, also need to be addressed.

The endemic avifaunas of Oceania, often represented by very small, single-island bird populations, are particularly vulnerable to the direct and indirect impact of humans. In Hawaii at least 16 species, including some beautiful and unique birds, have become extinct since 1800, mainly because virtually all of the lowland forest has been cleared and, it is believed, because of the introduction of disease-carrying mosquitoes. The similarly stupid introduction of the Brown Tree Snake, a voracious predator of eggs and nestlings, to the island of Guam in Micronesia has led to the extinction of the endemic flycatcher, the extinction in the wild of the endemic rail, and the extinction of a number of more widespread Micronesian endemics on the island.

In New Zealand, forest destruction, hunting and the introduction of non-native mammalian predators such as cats and rats has led to the total extinction of ten species since 1870 and the extinction on the main two islands of many more endemic species, so that most now survive only on predator-free offshore islands to which they have been translocated. These islands act as zoos fenced in by the surrounding seas. In Australia it has been the introduction of rabbits, sheep and cattle to the semi-arid grasslands and shrublands which has led to severe habitat loss and degradation. This, coupled with the fact that more land has been cleared for agriculture in the past 50 years than in the preceding 150, has resulted in the serious decline of almost half of the country's passerines.

Where substantial areas of natural habitat do survive in Australasia and Oceania, notably the large tracts of forest which remain on New Guinea, the Solomon Islands and Vanuatu, they are invariably under threat from international organisations, especially mining and logging companies. Fortunately, much of the land they have their evil eyes on is owned by large, extended families, making it very difficult for these otherwise all-conquering companies to purchase land. However, some governments are trying to enforce individual ownership. If such government officials, who are supposed to represent their country's people, get their way, it will almost certainly lead to a sudden massive loss of habitat, as individuals are much more likely to sell their land when they see the colour of the conglomerate's money.

However, even if the indigenous people of the region do manage to keep the international axes at bay, the natural habitats, especially the forests, in which they survive, will only remain intact if their populations remain stable. In Australasia and Oceania the human population is increasing particularly fast in Micronesia, Papua New Guinea (with a population already at four million), the Solomon Islands and Vanuatu, all of which have an annual population increase of over 2.3%. The annual population increase in the UK is only 0.3%, in the USA 0.9% and even China (1.3%) and India (2.1%) have lower annual increases than these regions. Subsistence farmers need somewhere to build their 'nests', some land to grow food on and some fresh water. These are the basic requirements for survival of the human race and they result in habitat loss and degradation, which the environment can only take so much of before other species start to suffer.

Eventually we suffer too, for there comes a point where our quality of life declines. Those of us who think the quality of our lives has improved with time should stop and think. Is living in a centrally heated concrete box surrounded by tarmac or chemically sterilised, lifeless farmland better than living in a so-called primitive 'hut in the woods' surrounded by butterflies and birdsong? Most people would, given the choice, probably plump for a combination of both, but most don't have a choice—because there are so many of us!

Ironically, it therefore seems logical to think about ourselves first, and then perhaps we will realise how vital it is to conserve natural habitats and the wildlife which inhabits them. We must restore, maintain and improve the quality of our lives by ensuring we continue to live alongside life on earth. In the long term there is little point in trying to persuade governments to protect areas, even those where the current land use by local people benefits birds, when they advocate increasing human populations as a necessary prerequisite of economic growth and stability. Some governments will boast about how much land they have protected, in the form of National Parks for example, but while these areas may be worthy of protection, they are little more than lines on a map, and, in many cases, far from being wildernesses. People live and farm in many of them and so they should, and they are not always sacrosanct as far as development goes, which is a good job, because when the human population has increased enough to fill up all of the gaps between these so-called protected areas, the next generations will be able to hop over the fence and settle there.

So, unless the quality of our lives is to sink to even greater depths, with people living in smaller and smaller boxes, stacked higher and higher, all that will be left of the natural world will be contained within the odd oasis amongst one vast desert of concrete. Then the day will come when everyone, not just the few of us who are already awake, will decide that they want to 'get away from it all', only to discover when they try to drive out of the city that they can't, because one city merges into the next and that there is, and never will be ever again, absolutely no where away from it all.

Hence, the logical way to ensure that there will be enough room for us and the birds in the future is to stabilise human population growth. Better still, we should aim to decrease it. However, since stemming population growth seems impossible, and indeed, undesirable to some governments, it may be worth considering some smaller initiatives to help preserve bits of what we have left, ready for the time when these governments see the folly of their ways. For example, integrating local needs with sustainable use of the natural habitat, through such schemes as ecotourism, could be implemented. Some governments have catered for ecotourists interested in wild places for many years, but providing specifically for birders is still in its infancy. Bird tourism, be it on an organised or casual basis, has the potential to boost the economy of many local communities in Australasia and Oceania and this is a strong argument for conserving natural resources at a given site. So, when visiting any of the sites described in this book, please make sure every person in the area, especially local business people, knows why you are there, and why more will follow if the birds and their habitats are protected.

I hope this book, in its own small way, will help to convince local people and governments, via encouraging bird tourism to their countries, that protecting their natural habitats is the only way to restore, maintain and improve the quality of their lives in the long term.

# GENERAL TIPS

The following words of advice are by no means comprehensive. They are little more than a mishmash of miscellaneous points resulting from personal experience and birding tales shared between friends. However, they may help to maximise the enjoyment of a birding trip to Australasia and Oceania.

The best birding trips usually result from extensive research and months of planning. Take time to find out where you are most likely to locate the species you wish to see before embarking on any trip and work out an itinerary very carefully (the best itineraries are normally the result of several drafts). Allow plenty of time in the itinerary to track down forest species, especially in Hawaii, Irian Jaya and Papua New Guinea. The distances between some sites in Australia are huge, so make the appropriate allowances in the itinerary for this, especially if travelling by road during the day when there may be plenty of roadside species worth stopping for.

When in the field, walk quietly and slowly, especially in forests, and make use of vegetation for patient stalking. These basic field skills are well known to most birders, but they are all too easily forgotten in the frenzy of new and exciting birds. Early morning is usually the best time for birding anywhere in the world and Australasia and Oceania is no exception. The middle of the day is a good time to move from one site to another, or, if this is not appropriate, to take a siesta before a late afternoon bash, the evening owl and nightjar search, and the appropriate celebration of another great day in the field. Some fanatical birders will argue that it is still possible to see plenty of birds around midday, especially where there is some shade or water, and the hours of darkness after the owls and nightjars have been seen are the best time to move from site to site! Travelling by road between sites at night could be dangerous in some countries, especially where the roads are bad, but overnight drives do help to keep accommodation costs down, and may produce a few otherwise unexpected birds and mammals. However, while a couple of night drives may save some money and be good fun, too many may result in overtiredness which could impair your enjoyment of the whole trip. Its not much fun returning home after a successful and enjoyable trip full of glorious moments only to discover that you can't remember much because you were too tired.

Forest birding in Australasia and Oceania, especially in Irian Jaya and Papua New Guinea, can be very frustrating, and hours may pass without seeing a single bird (despite the fact that many seem to be singing and calling throughout the forest), but when a wave (feeding flock) appears, or an avian jewel in the form a pitta or a jewel-babbler pops out on to the trail, all those hours of pre-trip planning and patient stalking will suddenly seem worthwhile. Bird waves are a feature of forests and woodlands in Australasia and Oceania. They often seem to appear from nowhere and move all too quickly, but try sticking with the birds as long as possible, even after it seems like they have all moved on, because the stragglers often turn out to be the real goodies. For example, the last honeyeater in a wave at Glen Davis, near Sydney, Australia, could be the Regent. If the forest or woodland canopy seems devoid of avian life, remember that many of the rarest and most spectacular forest and woodland birds are ground dwellers such as cassowaries, crowned-pigeons, pittas and jewel-babblers, and that walking silently and slowly with your eyes riveted to the ground on and either side of the trail may turn out to be the most worthwhile birding technique.

Tracking down every unknown call, especially whistles (pittas), is essential, but more often than not requires the patience of a saint. It is easy to get the tape recorder out in such a situation, but this devious birding method is *not* appropriate for use with threatened or near-threatened species (not knowing the call means it could be such a species), if any species at all. It distracts birds from feeding and causes them undue excitement. Trying to pin down a bird which you can hear but not see is extremely frustrating, but surely there is more joy to be gained from seeing the bird after a long and hard hunt, than by standing next to a tape recorder waiting for the unfortunate creature to come and peck at it!

Pigeons, parrots, bowerbirds, honeyeaters, some birds-of-paradise, flowerpeckers, berrypeckers and Hawaiian honeycreepers are good examples of birds which are attracted to flowering and fruiting trees. On first impressions such trees may seem to be lacking in avian life, as the birds quietly set about feeding, but on waiting a while under such a tree and watching out for movements near the flowers and fruits, they can slowly come alive. In some cases there may be so many birds in an individual tree that watching it for a couple of hours or so will probably prove to be more productive than frantic wandering.

A little knowledge is dangerous, but it is worth brushing up on a bit of botany before birding in Australasia and Oceania, because knowing the habitats and some individual flowering plants may help in locating a number of localised specialities, especially in Australia and Hawaii. If a species is not present in its preferred habitat at one known site, make a note of that habitat and look out for it elsewhere. In the Australian outback such habitats may only appear after recent rainfall, hence a number of bird species are nomads, wandering around the interior of the continent, following the random and unpredictable rains from one fresh flush of flowering shrubs to the next. A good example is Pied Honeyeater, a species which is usually faithful to its favoured food-plant, *Eremophola*. This shrub, also known as emu-bush, takes about six weeks to produce its long, tubular red flowers after rainfall. Birders travelling through the outback should therefore be on the alert for areas where rain has fallen during the previous few weeks, because once such an area has been located, shrubs such as *Eremophola* may be on the brink of flowering and, in turn, attracting their avian followers.

Some birding sites in Australasia and Oceania, especially in Irian Jaya, Papua New Guinea and on high islands throughout the Pacific, are in high-altitude montane forests where rain and wet mist are more or less permanent features of the climate. This damp, humid, often downright wet and rotten, weather rarely seems to affect bird activity, however, hence it is necessary to carry on birding in such conditions if you wish to see certain birds. In which case, wet weather gear, a small, easy-to-handle umbrella, and, most importantly, air- and water-tight binoculars are essential items of equipment.

Although there is plenty of montane forest in Australasia and Oceania, altitude sickness is a potentially serious problem in only a few places. In Hawaii, Irian Jaya and Papua New Guinea it is worth remembering the following: most people can travel up to 3000 m (9843 ft) in a short time and manage 4500 m (14,764 ft) after a night at 3000 m (9843 ft), but going straight to 4500 m (14,764 ft) can be dangerous and one in three people who attempt it usually end up with a severe headache, or, even worse, feel dizzy and begin to vomit. If that person then turns blue or coughs up pink mucus they should descend immediately to below 3000 m (9843 ft), where a quick recovery is normal. Otherwise, high-altitude health problems can be alleviated by eating lightly, taking it easy, using maximum sun block and keeping warm when the sun goes down.

It is worth taking an altimeter and a compass if you are unsure of the terrain you are visiting, or if the only information you have on a certain species is the altitude at which it has been recorded. Vehicles may be a problem at high altitudes. If you have difficulty starting your engine in the early mornings, try pouring petrol directly into the carburetter.

Apart from a few parts of Irian Jaya and Papua New Guinea which are best avoided due to the possibility of kidnapping or violent crime, the most dangerous area to go birding in Australasia and Oceania is probably the Australian outback. Although this is a modern country with the infrastructure and all the facilities one would expect in a westernised society, there are still a few very wild and remote areas in the interior where it is possible to die if you don't drink enough water or your vehicle breaks down, you run out of emergency supplies and no one else comes along. However, some of the best birds in the region occur only here, so prepare properly for a mini-expedition and enjoy the birds which complete what is great birding country.

# GLOSSARY

**2WD:** Two-wheel-drive vehicle.
**4WD:** Four-wheel-drive vehicle.
**Atoll:** A group of very small, very low, sparsely vegetated coral islands, which usually occur in a circular or horseshoe-shaped chain, surrounding a saltwater lagoon. Each island in the chain rarely reaches more than 10 m (33 ft) in height.
**FR:** Forest Reserve.
**Gallery forest/woodland:** Waterside (riparian) forest and woodland, usually where forested areas merge into more open areas such as savanna.
**NP:** National Park.
**NR:** Nature Reserve.
**NWR:** National Wildlife Refuge.
**Secondary:** This term usually refers to forested areas which have been cleared, but since regenerated, albeit usually in fragments alongside the newly established land use.
**SF:** State Forest.
**SP:** State Park.
**SW:** Sewage Works.

# MAPS

Birders, understandably, are more interested in finding and watching birds than noting down distances and directions when in the field, so although every effort has been made to make the maps in this book as precise as possible, they may not be entirely accurate, at least in terms of exact scale and compass points. The main purpose of the maps is to facilitate birding at the sites, so more often than not 'direction pointers' such as rivers and buildings and on-site detail such as trails have been exaggerated and are not drawn to scale. Each country account begins with a map of the country with the main sites numbered and there are also some maps of regions within countries to show how 'bunches' of sites are distributed. These are intended to aid birders in their production of trip routes and itineraries during the planning stage.

It is important to remember that site details change, hence old signs may have fallen down or been taken down, new signs may have been put up, trails may have become tracks, tracks may have become roads, buildings may have been knocked down, buildings may have been put up, marshes, lakes and rivers may have dried up or been drained, rivers may have changed course, habitats may have been totally destroyed and some sites may no longer exist by the time you come to use these maps. If you do arrive at a site which no longer exists or which looks totally different to what you have perceived as a result of reading this book, don't blame the birders who have been before you and don't blame me: blame the ever increasing human population on the planet. And, remember, this book is a guiding light, not a substitute for up-to-the-minute information.

The **map symbols** used are as follows:

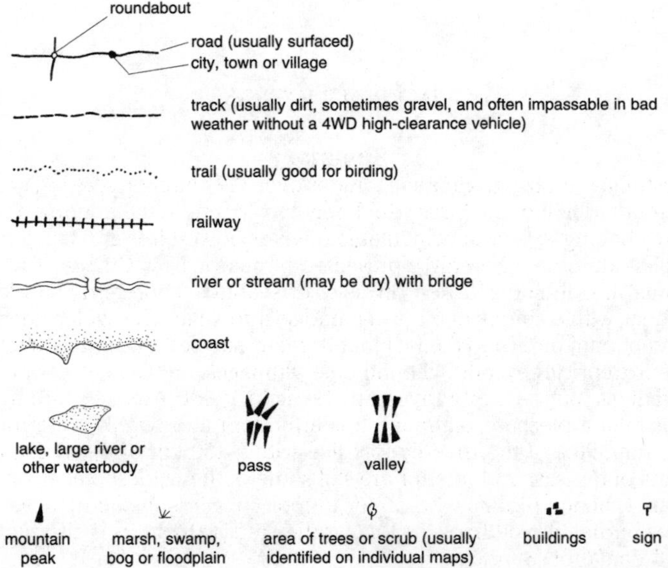

# AUSTRALIA

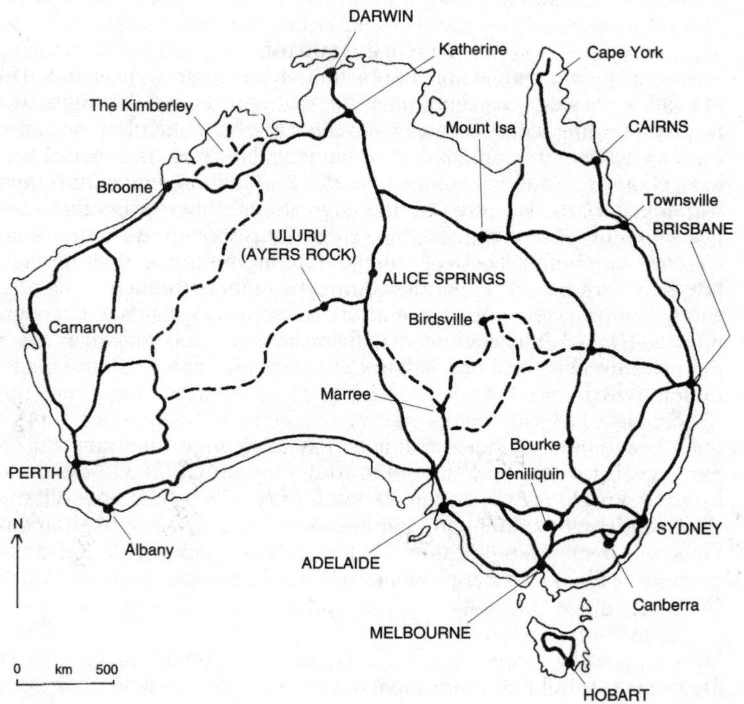


## INTRODUCTION

### Summary

Australia's amazing avifauna includes over 330 endemic species, which amount to half of the birds which regularly occur in the country. These birds belong to such spectacular families as bowerbirds and fairywrens, which are otherwise only represented in nearby New Guinea. The avifauna also includes a rich diversity of seabirds, shorebirds and kingfishers, with a couple of birds-of-paradise thrown in. This wide variety of exceptional birds and the fact that so many species, even those such as the Regent Honeyeater with intricate plumages, are as neat, clean and bright as they are portrayed in the field guides, makes birding in Australia a pleasure. Although it is a modern, thoroughly westernised country, 90% of the friendly folk live within 150 km of the coast, and parts of the vast arid interior are still some of the wildest places on the planet, hence birders who prefer to look for birds in such places will love birding the outback, so long as they realise that this is also remote and dangerous territory.

## Size

At 7,682,300 sq km, this huge country is a little smaller than Europe and the USA. It is 4000 km from west to east, 3200 km from north to south and the coastline is about 37,000 km long. The largest state is Western Australia (2,525,500 sq km), followed by Queensland (1,727,000), which is 13 times larger than England and 2.5 times larger than Texas.

## Getting Around

Seeing a wide cross-section of Australian birds on a short trip will involve a considerable amount of air and road travel. All but a few remote sites are accessible in 2WD vehicles, even most of those in the outback where there are many 'roadhouses', complete with petrol stations, shops, pubs and some form of accommodation, hence travelling by car is the best way to go birding in Australia. However, road distances are vast (see below), so if time is short it is wise to use the internal air network to travel between the major birding areas, even though interstate airfares are expensive. Airpasses help to reduce costs and some airlines often throw in a few free domestic flights for foreign tourists. The only real alternative to flying between major bases is to use the extensive bus network, as the rail network is slow, expensive and rather limited.

Some examples of road distances (km): Sydney–Canberra (287), Sydney–Melbourne (868), Melbourne–Adelaide (728), Adelaide–Lyndhurst (610), Adelaide–Alice Springs (1542), Adelaide–Albany (2684), Albany–Perth (409), Perth–Broome (2248), Broome–Darwin (1865), Darwin–Alice Springs (1511), Darwin–Cairns (2727), Cairns–Brisbane (1717), Brisbane–Sydney (996), Alice Springs–Ayers Rock (450).

Birders planning to spend more than a month or so birding throughout the country should consider buying a second-hand vehicle on arrival, then selling it on departure, for there is little depreciation in the price of such vehicles. The best place to buy and sell second-hand vehicles is the Kings Cross area of Sydney. Make sure the vehicle is a reliable, popular model with high ground clearance, such as a Ford Falcon or Holden Kingswood. When on the road beware of trucks with two or three huge wagons in tow, known as road-trains, and, especially at night, watch out for kangaroos, because most 2WDs are not equipped with 'roo-bars' and hitting a 'roo at full speed could seriously damage your vehicle and you! Only travel in the remotest parts of the outback with a 4WD, backed up with spares, a flying doctor radio set and full camping and survival equipment.

## Accommodation and Food

The cheapest and often most enjoyable way to go birding in Australia is to make full use of the ubiquitous, cheap, conveniently situated and very well equipped campsites. Many of these have water, fireplaces and/or built-in barbecue grills, firewood, hot showers and even ovens, microwaves and washing machines! Where there are no campsites it is normally no problem to 'go bush' and camp anywhere, but beware of flash floods in cosy looking dried-up watercourses. The only other alternative to the expensive motels and hotels are caravan parks and the 130 or so Youth Hostels.

'On the road' food is nothing to shout about and unless you take your own be prepared to live on 'junk food' or local delicacies such as a floater: a meat pie floating in pea soup. Beer is arguably the national drink and there are numerous varieties on offer, from the light Four X to the strong Toohey's Red. In pubs, which are often called hotels, beer is available in schooners (large glasses) or stubbies (small bottles). Australian wines are, on the whole, excellent, but avoid the cheap varieties.

## Health and Safety

Immunisation against yellow fever is essential if arriving from an infected country. Great care needs to be taken when birding in the remote outback, one of the harshest places on earth. As recently as the early 1990s a visiting birder from Britain died of hyperthermia on the Birdsville Track, despite having an adequate supply of water. Preparation is one thing, survival is another. If you have water, drink it whether you feel thirsty or not. Most people who die in the outback do so because their vehicle breaks down and no one else comes along in time, so check the latest information on all tracks in the nearest town or roadhouse, take plenty of water, fuel, spares, tools and, if on a serious excursion, a high-frequency radio unit which is set up for the Royal Flying Doctor Service. Such units are extremely expensive to buy, but they can be hired in major cities at a fair price. Remember that it can be bitterly cold in the desert at night, especially during the austral winter (May–Oct) and throughout the year it is wise to use high-factor sunscreen. In the wet eastern forests some people have almost been killed by leeches, which can be a serious problem during the wet season at such sites as Lamington National Park. There are 130 species of snake in Australia and 20 of them are venomous. The fierce snake, which occurs in southwest Queensland and northeast South Australia, is the most poisonous snake on the planet and a clean bite from one of these, or the taipan, will probably stop you from adding any more species to your life-list. Even spiders can kill you in Australia, so beware of the stocky black Sydney funnel-web and the redback.

In Australia there are a number of places where it is possible to go on pelagic birding trips. On such trips it is possible to see many rare and exciting seabirds, but seasickness can affect even the most hardy seafarers and spoil what would otherwise be a wonderful birding experience, so it is wise to take some sort of precaution against this. Travacalm and Kwells are the most popular forms of prevention, but they can cause drowsiness. Other people prefer anything from patches to pressure bracelets, but some of the best ways to prevent a day in hell is to get a good night's sleep beforehand, eat a wholesome breakfast, stand up as much as possible when on board, concentrate on the horizon and keep busy by constantly scanning for goodies. Also be sure to step aboard with a packed lunch, warm and windproof clothing, sunglasses and sunscreen.

## Climate and Timing

Timing is very important in the world's driest inhabited continent. The best general time to visit is during the austral spring, in October and November, when many resident species are most active, northern migrants are arriving and subantarctic seabirds are moving into coastal waters. The austral summer, December to February, is almost as good, but it is very wet, hot and humid around Darwin and The Kimberley, wet in northern Queensland and dangerously hot in the outback at this time. The best time to be in the outback is August and September, which usually coincides with the end of the rains, if there have been any. This is also the peak time to visit western Australia as many plants are in bloom at this time. During the austral winter, from June to August, it can be downright wet and cold from Adelaide to Sydney, but this is a good time to visit the Darwin area.

## Habitats

Australia is, for the most part, rather low-lying and flat. There are no really high mountains and few permanent large rivers. However, the winter snowfields are larger than those in alpine Switzerland on the Great Dividing Range, which runs parallel to the east coast for over 2000 km and rises to 2230 m (7316 ft) at Mount Kosciusko. There is a narrow, fertile coastal plain to the east of these mountains, but to the west there lies a vast expanse of flat, arid sandy and stony deserts and grassy plains dotted with ephemeral salt lakes and the odd mountain range or monolith. After thousands of kilometres the land rises to the Western Plateau and The Kimberley range.

Spiny *spinifex*, also known as porcupine grass, which covers about 30% of Australia's land surface, dominates desert areas and is the preferred habitat of a number of grasswrens and emuwrens. Where the surface of sparsely vegetated desert is covered with small shiny stones this is known as **Gibber**, a habitat also characterised by open, low shrubland dominated by bluebush and saltbush, and vegetated creeks which remain dry for long periods, even years. Other desert plants include canegrass, which is a pale yellow thin-stemmed tangled low shrub and looks nothing like a grass, and lignum, which is a tall tangled spindly bush which can reach 5 m. *Eremophola* or emu-bush is another outback speciality. It is a relatively large grey bush with narrow leaves and long red tubular flowers which attract many nomadic honeyeaters. Semi-arid areas and rocky hillsides were originally dominated by acacia shrubland known as **Mulga**, but much of this habitat has been severely degraded because vast areas are leased for cattle grazing. In the low rainfall belt to the south of the deserts the vegetation used to be dominated by dense dwarf *Eucalyptus* trees, which form a habitat known as **mallee**, but much of this habitat has been cleared since the 1960s when successive years of above-average rainfall encouraged farmers to try growing wheat. Both mulga and mallee support distinct avifaunas, particularly the latter. Semi-arid zones in the southwest and east also support open **woodlands** dominated by acacia and *casuarina* (wispy medium-sized conifers) species. Tall, open forests dominated by *Eucalyptus* species which grow in wet areas are known as **wet sclerophyll forests**. These forests, characterised by trees with peeling bark, are confined to the southeast, including Tasmania, and the southwest where the high seasonal rainfall sustains the lofty 'karri' forests where the trees may exceed 70 m (230 ft). Tall, open forests dominated by *Eucalyptus* species which grow in dry areas are known as **dry sclerophyll forests**. These are confined to the north and east and the tree species include the ironbarks, which often have rust-coloured bark and are a magnet for honeyeaters when in flower. The lowlands and mountain slopes of the extreme east support luxuriant **tropical**, **subtropical** and **temperate rain forests**, and in some regions of the south and east which receive high rainfall, particularly those near the coast, there are

**heathlands**, a diverse habitat which supports a rich and distinct avifauna. The coastline of Australia is a wonderful mixture of cliffs, beaches, dunes, mangroves, estuaries, saltmarshes and lagoons, and offshore there are a number of islands and cays, most of which lie along the **Great Barrier Reef**, the largest reef on earth, which runs parallel to the Queensland coast for around 2000 km.

## Conservation

A census conducted by the Royal Australasian Ornithologists Union since 1989 has revealed that nearly 50% of the country's passerines have declined dramatically in recent years, especially south of the Tropic of Capricorn where much of the land has been cleared for agriculture. In fact, as much native bush has been cleared in the past 50 years as in the preceding 150, with five million hectares being destroyed between 1983 and 1993 alone, and the spread of agriculture seems set to proceed north. Hence the future looks bleak for many of the 89 threatened and near-threatened species which occur in Australia, despite the presence of over 2,000 National Parks, Nature Reserves and Wildlife Sanctuaries.

## Bird Families

Five bird families are endemic to Australia: Emu, Plains-wanderer*, lyrebirds, scrub-birds and the *Corcoracidae* (White-winged Chough and Apostlebird). A further eight families are shared only with New Guinea: cassowaries, Australian creepers, bowerbirds, fairywrens, logrunners, pseudo-babblers, butcherbirds and the *Grallinidae* (represented in Australia by the Magpie-lark). Hence 13 of the 20 families endemic to Australasia and Oceania are present.

## Bird Species

Over 800 species have been recorded in and around Australia, of which about 650 are regarded as being regular visitors and about 575 as regular breeding species. Over 130 species of seabird have been recorded, the highest total for any country in the world. Non-endemic specialities and spectacular species include Southern Cassowary*, Little Penguin, Wandering* and Royal* Albatrosses, Providence* and White-headed Petrels, Buller's Shearwater*, White-faced Storm-Petrel, Red-tailed Tropicbird, Great-billed* and Pied Herons, Black and Australasian* Bitterns, Black-necked Stork, Red-necked and White-browed Crakes, Chestnut Rail, Brolga, Australian Bustard, Comb-crested Jacana, Latham's Snipe*, Little Curlew, Grey-tailed and Wandering Tattlers, Great Knot, Bush and Beach Thick-knees, Australian Pratincole, Double-banded and Oriental Plovers, Black-fronted Dotterel, White-fronted, Sooty and Fairy* Terns, Brown and Black Noddies, Papuan and Marbled Frogmouths, Australian Owlet-Nightjar, Azure and Little Kingfishers, Blue-winged Kookaburra, Forest Kingfisher, Buff-breasted Paradise-Kingfisher, Rainbow Bee-eater, Noisy Pitta, Varied Sittella, Logrunner, Yellow-breasted Boatbill, Magpie-lark and Blue-faced Parrotfinch.

## Endemics

Australia supports 332 endemics, 50% of the regularly occurring species. These species occur throughout the country, although most are confined to the arid outback (66), the Melbourne and Sydney areas of the southeast (47), the eastern forests (43), the north and northwest

(39) and the southeast and southwest (38). Other areas where there is a concentration of endemics include the Cairns region (21), the Perth region (20) and Tasmania (13). Only 37 could reasonably be described as widespread. The grand total includes seven raptors, five button-quails, nine shorebirds (including the unique Plains-wanderer*), 15 pigeons, 45 parrots, cockatoos and lories, four owls, two kingfishers, a pitta, six 'treecreepers', two lyrebirds, two scrub-birds, eight bower-birds, 20 fairywrens, emuwrens and grasswrens, 59 honeyeaters, 12 robins, eight whistlers, four quail-thrushes, two birds-of-paradise, four woodswallows and 14 'finches'.

Australia also supports nearly 150 near-endemic species, many of which are shared with southern New Guinea, and the vast majority of these can be seen in the Darwin and Cairns regions.

### Expectations

It is possible to see over 420 species on a 25-day trip between October and March that takes in the Darwin, Cairns, Brisbane, Sydney, Adelaide and Melbourne regions, including 40 shorebirds and 46 honeyeaters. On a 35-day trip to the same areas 470 species are possible. On a similar trip between April and September to Darwin, Adelaide, the outback, Melbourne, Brisbane and Sydney it is possible to see around 380–400 species. Species totals possible on three week trips include; the southwest (270), the Kimberley and Darwin regions (240), the Darwin, Alice and Cairns regions (300), and the southeast (Lamington to Tasmania) (300+). In six to twelve months it is possible to see over 600 species across the continent.

The sites are dealt with in a more or less circular route around Australia, beginning in Sydney and ending in Brisbane, via Melbourne, Adelaide, Perth, The Kimberley, Darwin and Cairns, before moving inland to the outback sites and finishing up with Tasmania and the other offshore islands. A year or so spent on this amazing birding trail should enable birders to see virtually every Australian endemic and many more species besides.

## *NEW SOUTH WALES*

## SYDNEY

There are plenty of excellent places to go birding in and around this sprawling, mainly low-rise, pleasant coastal city where it is possible to see such delights as Double-banded Plover, White-fronted Tern, Powerful Owl*, Tawny Frogmouth and Crested Shrike-tit, as well as some excellent seabirds in suitable weather conditions.

### Localised Australian Endemics

Powerful Owl*.

### Other Australian Endemics

Maned Duck, Chestnut Teal, Sooty Oystercatcher, Crested Pigeon, Australian King-Parrot, Eastern Rosella, Red-rumped Parrot, Galah, Scaly-breasted and Musk Lorikeets, Tawny Frogmouth, Laughing

## SYDNEY AREA

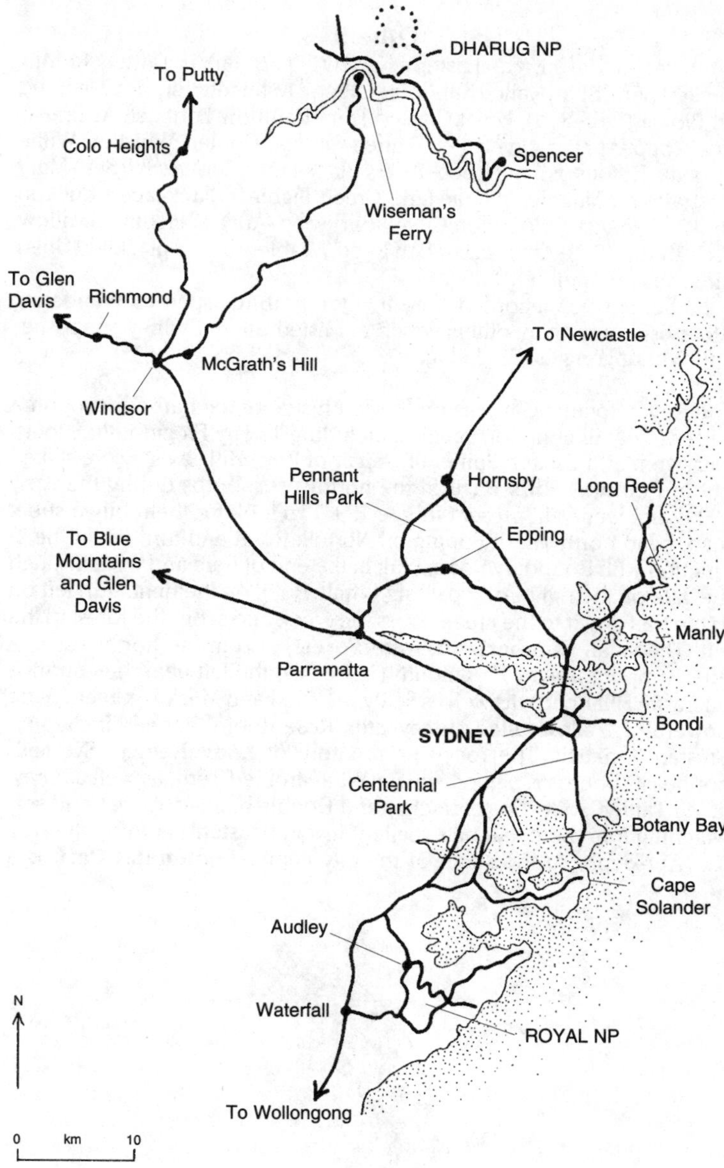


Kookaburra, White-throated Treecreeper, Satin Bowerbird, Superb Fairywren, Spotted Pardalote, Yellow-rumped and Yellow Thornbills, Brown Gerygone, Lewin's, Yellow-faced, Yellow-tufted, White-plumed, New Holland and White-cheeked Honeyeaters, Eastern Spinebill, Bell and Noisy Miners, Red Wattlebird, Rose and Yellow Robins, Crested Shrike-tit, Australian Raven, Pied Currawong, Red-browed Firetail.

## Non-endemic Specialities

White-fronted Tern (Apr–Sep).

## Others

White-faced Heron, Far Eastern Curlew*, Grey-tailed Tattler, Rufous-necked Stint, Sharp-tailed Sandpiper, Pied Oystercatcher, Double-banded Plover (Feb–Sep), Great Crested-Tern, Rainbow Lorikeet, Australian Koel (Sep–Apr), Jacky-winter, Varied Sittella, Golden Whistler, Willie-wagtail, Rufous Fantail (Sep–Apr), Black-faced Monarch (Sep–Mar), Australasian Magpie, Magpie-lark, Green Figbird, Black-faced Cuckoo-shrike (Sep–Apr), Common Cicadabird (Sep–Apr), Welcome Swallow, Tree Martin (Sep–Apr), Australian Reed-Warbler (Sep–Apr), Little Grass-bird, Australasian Pipit.

(Other species recorded here include seabirds such as Wandering Albatross* and many others which are listed under Sydney (opposite) and Wollongong (p. 57) Pelagics).

The Royal Botanic Gardens on the south side of the harbour support a wide variety of common species, including Tawny Frogmouth, Superb Fairywren and Eastern Spinebill. A pair of Powerful Owls* were staked out in **Pennant Hills Park** in the northwest suburbs during the early 1990s and were still present in late 1996. To look for them buy a street map, head north out of Epping on Norfolk Road and turn left at the T-junction with Boundary Road. Park at the end of here and walk through the gate on the right. After passing Whale Rock on the right, turn left on to the trail down to the creek, cross the creek and scour the forest to the left. The small **Cumberland State Forest**, also in the northwest suburbs, supports Tawny Frogmouth (in trees to the left near the entrance on Castle Hill Road), as well as Scaly-breasted and Musk Lorikeets, Satin Bowerbird, Yellow-tufted Honeyeater, Rose Robin, Varied Sittella and Crested Shrike-tit. The rocky promontory of **Long Reef** in Sydney's northeast suburbs is a good site for White-fronted Tern, as well as Grey-tailed Tattler, Sooty Oystercatcher and Double-banded Plover, and sea-watching from here can be excellent in southeasterlies during the winter (Apr–Sep). To the south of the city centre **Centennial Park** is a

*The Tawny Frogmouth is a widespread Australian endemic which even occurs in the suburban parks of Sydney. However, its excellent camouflage makes this strange bird difficult to detect*

good place for waterbirds, while **Botany Bay** supports shorebirds including Far Eastern Curlew*, and Red-capped and Double-banded Plovers. The bay can be approached via Foreshore Road, east of the airport, at the northern end, and from Captain Cook Drive at the southern end, where Woolooware and Quibray Bays are the best areas. This road leads to **Cape Solander**, another excellent seawatching site in suitable conditions.

**Sydney Pelagics** usually take place aboard the *Halicat,* a strong 50 ft catamaran which leaves Rose Bay Public Ferry Wharf (15 minutes by road from the city centre) near the floating restaurant along New South Head Road at 0700 and returns at about 1500 on the second Saturday of every month. To book in advance or to find out about all Australian pelagics, contact Tony Palliser, Unit 11, 520 Mowbray Road, Lane Cove, Sydney, NSW 2066, Australia (tel: 02 9900 1678 or 02 427 7563; fax: 02 9900 1669; e-mail: tpallise@au.oracle.com or palliser@zip.com.au, Web Site: http://www.zip.com.au./~palliser). Species recorded are almost exactly the same as those listed for Wollongong (p. 57) but the *Halicat* is a fast boat hence it is possible to reach the continental shelf, 30 nautical miles out, in just one and a half hours, and therefore spend more time in deeper waters.

## ROYAL NATIONAL PARK

Over 200 species have been recorded in this 150 sq km reserve just 40 km south of Sydney. The combination of coastal heathland, with its selection of specialities including Southern Emuwren, wet sclerophyll and subtropical rainforests and open eucalypt woodland supports a superb assortment of species and it is one of the easiest places in Australia to see Superb Lyrebird. In early 1994 much of the park was burnt to a cinder in serious bush fires, but it has recovered well.

### Localised Australian Endemics

Green Catbird.

### Other Australian Endemics

Maned Duck, Crested, Wonga and Topknot Pigeons, Australian King-Parrot, Crimson and Eastern Rosellas, Yellow-tailed Black-Cockatoo, Laughing Kookaburra, White-throated and Red-browed Treecreepers, Superb Lyrebird, Satin Bowerbird, Superb and Variegated Fairywrens, Southern Emuwren, Yellow-throated, White-browed and Large-billed Scrubwrens, Chestnut-rumped Hylacola, Brown, Yellow-rumped, Yellow and Striated Thornbills, Brown Gerygone, Scarlet Myzomela, Lewin's, Yellow-faced, White-eared, White-plumed, White-naped, New Holland, Tawny-crowned and Striped Honeyeaters, Eastern Spinebill, Noisy Miner, Spiny-cheeked Honeyeater, Brush and Red Wattlebirds, Flame, Rose and Yellow Robins, Crested Shrike-tit, Eastern Whipbird, Australian Raven, Grey Butcherbird, Pied Currawong, Red-browed Firetail.

### Others

Australasian Grebe, Grey and Brown Goshawks, Dusky Moorhen, Brush (Sep–Apr) and Fan-tailed Cuckoos, Shining (Aug–Apr) and Horsfield's

## ROYAL NATIONAL PARK

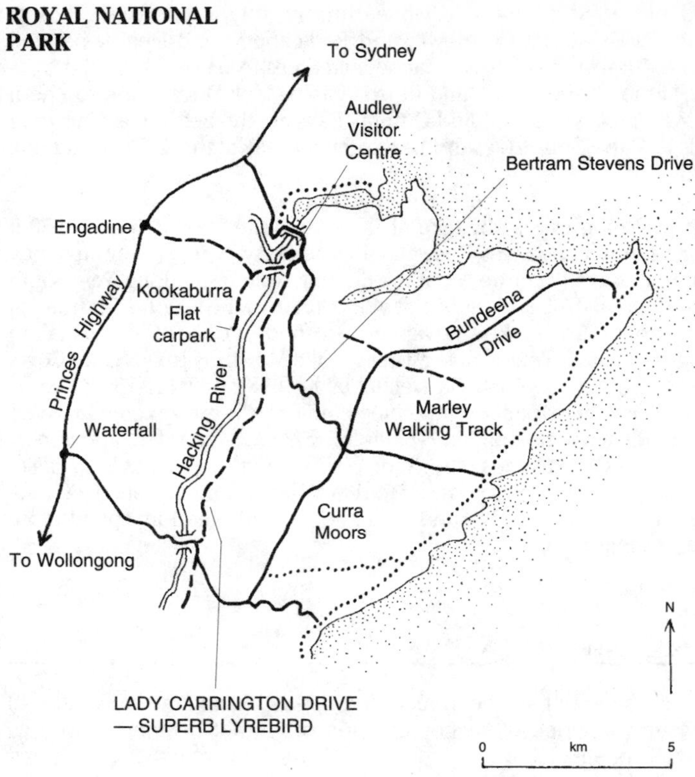


Bronze-Cuckoos, White-throated Needletail (Oct–Apr), Azure and Sacred Kingfishers, Rainbow Bee-eater (Sep–Apr), Dollarbird (Sep–Apr), Varied Sittella, Golden and Rufous Whistlers, Grey Shrike-Thrush, Grey and Rufous (Sep–Apr) Fantails, Black-faced Monarch (Sep–Mar), Leaden Flycatcher (Sep–Apr), Magpie-lark, Olive-backed Oriole, Black-faced (Sep–Apr) and White-bellied Cuckoo-shrikes, Olive-tailed Thrush, Welcome Swallow.

(Other species recorded here include Greater Sooty-Owl, Powerful Owl*, Rock Warbler* and Beautiful Firetail.)

The park is signposted from the Princes Highway, 36 km south of Sydney. Turn east on to Farnell Avenue to reach the visitor centre at Audley (02 542 0666), where the best walking track, **Lady Carrington Drive**, starts and continues through wet sclerophyll (in sheltered gullies) and subtropical rainforests alongside the Hacking River. In midweek or at dawn on weekends, this gently rising 9.5 km long track is a good place to look for Superb Lyrebirds which sing and display right next to the track at times. The last 2 km at the south end of this track are worth walking at night in search of Greater Sooty-Owl and Powerful Owl* (which has also been recorded at roost in the lush area of forest about 100 m along the river from Kookaburra Flat car park). With two cars, one parked at the Waterfall (south) end and one at the Audley (north) end of this track, it is possible to spend a very pleasant morning or day on the gentle descent from the bridge near Waterfall to Audley. Heathland specialities such as Southern Emuwren, Chestnut-rumped Hylacola and Tawny-crowned Honeyeater occur on the Curra Moors, reached by heading south from Audley, and alongside Bundeena Drive and its side tracks, especially the Marley Walking Track, but don't expect the hat-trick in a single visit.

*The Eastern Spinebill, a member of the huge honeyeater family, occurs at most sites in east Australia, but few birders will tire of seeing this beautiful cross between a hummingbird and a bee-eater*

## WOLLONGONG PELAGIC

The monthly boat trip from Wollongong, 80 km south of Sydney, out to the edge of the continental shelf 30 nautical miles offshore, where upwelling nutrients attract numerous seabirds, is a seawatcher's dream. There are few distant fly-past dots to dwell on after going on one of these trips—some of the birds, including albatrosses, come within touching distance! Over 90 seabird species, a third of the world total, have been recorded and they include the colossal Wandering Albatross*, plenty of wonderful *pterodromas* and lots of rarities.

The trips take place on the tiny and very fragile-looking *Sandra K*, which usually leaves Bellmore Basin at 0700 and returns around 1600 on the fourth Sunday of every month, and places must be booked in advance through Tony Palliser (see Sydney Pelagics, p. 55).

### Non-endemic Specialities

Wandering Albatross* (Mar–Nov), Providence Petrel*, White-fronted Tern.

### Others

Little Penguin, Black-browed (Mar–Nov), Shy (Apr–Nov) and Yellow-nosed (Apr–Nov) Albatrosses, Antarctic (May–Nov) and Hall's* (May–Sep) Giant Petrels, Cape (May–Nov), Great-winged and White-headed (Mar–Nov) Petrels, Fairy Prion (Apr–Oct), Wedge-tailed (Sep–Apr), Flesh-footed (Sep–Apr), Sooty, Short-tailed (Sep–Jun), Fluttering and Hutton's* Shearwaters, Wilson's and White-faced Storm-Petrels, Australian Gannet, Australian Pelican, Kelp and Silver Gulls, Great

Crested-Tern, Brown Skua, Pomarine (Sep–May), Parasitic (Sep–May) and Long-tailed (Sep–Apr) Jaegers.

## Other Wildlife

Australian fur seal, common dolphin, humpback and sperm whales, sunfish.

(Other species recorded include 'Northern' Royal* (May–Nov), Grey-headed* (May–Sep), Buller's* (May–Nov), Sooty* (May) and Light-mantled (Sep–Oct) Albatrosses, Southern Fulmar (Sep), Kerguelen (Jul–Nov), Tahiti (Nov–Mar), Black-winged (Oct–Apr), White-necked (Jan–Mar, Sep), Mottled (Oct), Gould's (Jan–Apr), Cook's* (Sep–Apr), Herald (Apr, Aug), Kermadec (Mar–Apr, Oct), Juan Fernandez (Aug), Murphy's (the potential first for Australia was recorded in October 1996) and Soft-plumaged (Aug–Oct) Petrels, Antarctic (May–Sep) and Slender-billed (May–Sep) Prions, White-chinned (Sep–Nov), Parkinson's* (Oct–Jan) and Westland* (Oct) Petrels, Streaked (Nov–Mar), Buller's* (Sep–Mar), Pink-footed* (Mar), Manx (Oct), Audubon's (Mar, Aug–Oct) and Little (May–Nov) Shearwaters, Grey-backed (Sep), Black-bellied (Sep–Nov) and White-bellied (May–Sep) Storm-Petrels, Common Diving-Petrel (Apr–Jun), Red-tailed (Apr) and White-tailed (Oct–Apr) Tropicbirds, Brown Booby (Mar, Nov), Wandering Tattler (harbour), Pacific* (May–Jun) and Sabine's (Oct–Mar, Jun) Gulls, Sooty Tern (Apr, Sep), Common White-Tern (Mar–Apr), Blue-grey Noddy (Mar) and South Polar Skua (Jun–Oct).)

The smaller albatrosses, shearwaters and storm-petrels soon start to follow the boat once 'chumming' (throwing food overboard) commences, and birds often approach to within a few feet of the boat. The larger albatrosses and pterodromas don't tend to follow so closely but the commotion caused by the other birds at the stern entices them close enough for stunning views.

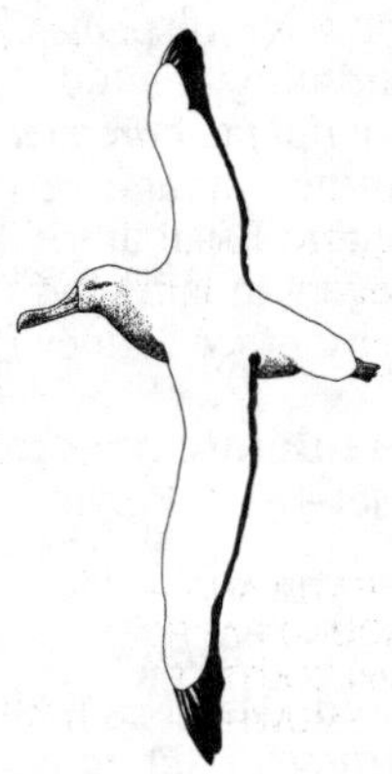

*When the first Wandering Albatross* banks by the boat during the Wollongong Pelagic, try to remember you are on a tiny boat, because the sight of this gigantic glider zooming over the ocean tends to make most birders forget that they have to hang on for dear life aboard the Sandra K!*

## BARREN GROUNDS NATURE RESERVE

This small reserve (20 sq km) protects heathland, reminiscent of the New Forest in England, where Dartford Warblers are replaced by the equally delightful Southern Emuwrens, scrub where skulkers such as Eastern Bristlebird* hide and woodland which supports Pilotbird.

### Localised Australian Endemics

Ground Parrot*, Eastern Bristlebird*, Beautiful Firetail.

### Other Australian Endemics

Brush Bronzewing, Wonga and Topknot Pigeons, Crimson Rosella, Yellow-tailed Black-Cockatoo, Gang-gang Cockatoo, White-throated and Red-browed Treecreepers, Superb Lyrebird, Satin Bowerbird, Southern Emuwren, Pilotbird, Chestnut-rumped Hylacola, White-eared, White-naped, Crescent and Tawny-crowned (scarce) Honeyeaters, Eastern Spinebill, Flame, Rose and Yellow Robins.

### Other Wildlife

Long-nosed potoroo, pygmy possum.

This reserve is accessible from the Robertson–Jamberoo Road, about 110 km south of Sydney and 30 km southwest of Wollongong. From

**BARREN GROUNDS NR**

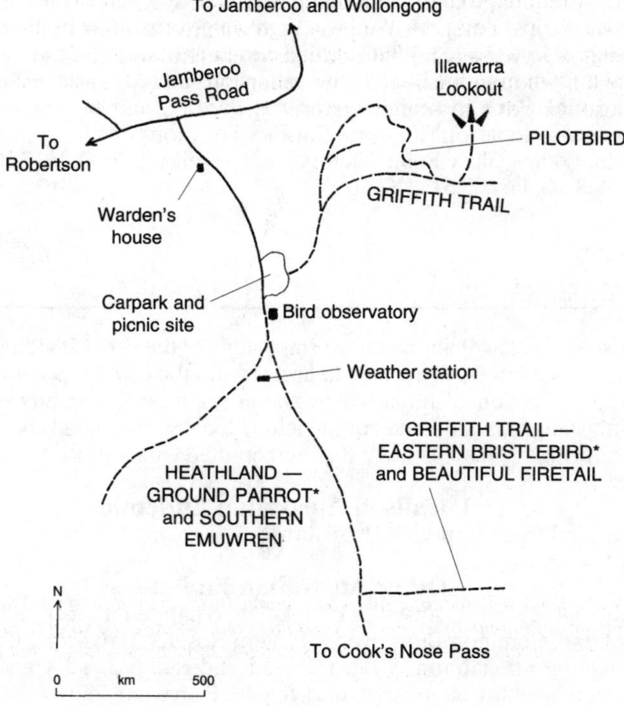

Jamberoo take the narrow Jamberoo Pass Road towards Robertson and the track to the bird observatory and car park is on the left-hand side of the road after 7 km, about 14 km from Robertson. Ground Parrot* (most likely at dusk) and Southern Emuwren frequent the heathland above the car park. Take the trail to the left and look for Beautiful Firetail at its junction with the Griffith Trail further on, and walk down the Griffith Trail for Eastern Bristlebird*. The forest alongside the track which descends the escarpment from the Griffith Trail and loops back to it further on is the best for Pilotbird, although this bird also occurs in the wet sclerophyll forest alongside the road up from Jamberoo, along with Red-browed Treecreeper and Superb Lyrebird, although the latter is most likely to be seen in the Minnamurra Rainforest Reserve, a few km east of Jamberro.

*Accommodation*: can be arranged through The Wardens, Barren Grounds Bird Observatory, PO Box 3, Jamberoo, NSW 2533 (tel: 042 360 195, fax: 042 360 537), or there is a campsite 1 km further up the road, or hotels in Jamberoo.

Other sites worth visiting in southeast New South Wales include **Jervis Bay Nature Reserve**, 32 km southeast of Nowra, where Eastern Bristlebird* occurs around the car park at the ruined Cape St George lighthouse. Regular whale-watching trips run out of **Eden** in October and November in search of humpback whale, and on such trips it is possible to see seabirds such as Wandering Albatross* and White-faced Storm-Petrel. Just across the border in southeast Victoria is **Gipsy Point Lodge**, an expensive guesthouse which caters specifically for birders at the eastern edge of Croajingolong National Park. One of the highlights of boat trips along the Wallagaraugh River organised by the lodge is being able to watch White-bellied Sea-Eagles swoop down to snatch fish thrown from the boat. Other excursions include visits to **Ben Boyd National Park** in search of Ground Parrot*, and the area north of **Genoa** to look for Turquoise Parrot*. For more details contact Gipsy Point Lodge, Gipsy Point, Victoria 3891 (Freecall: 1800 063 556, tel: 03 5158 8205, fax: 03 5158 8225).

## CANBERRA

Australia's capital lies on the western slope of the Great Dividing Range, 287 km southwest of Sydney. In and around the city it is possible to see a fine selection of birds which should include the locally common Gang-gang Cockatoo and could include locally distributed species such as Freckled Duck*, Lewin's Rail and Spotted Quail-thrush.

### Localised Australian Endemics

Freckled Duck*, Spotted Quail-thrush.

### Other Australian Endemics

Blue-billed Duck, Australian Crake, Red-capped Plover, Red-kneed Dotterel, Common Bronzewing, Eastern Rosella, Gang-gang Cockatoo, Laughing Kookaburra, White-throated and Red-browed Treecreepers, Superb Lyrebird, Satin Bowerbird, Superb Fairywren, Pilotbird, Speckled

Warbler, White-eared (Apr–Sep), Fuscous (Apr–Oct), Brown-headed and Crescent (Apr–Sep) Honeyeaters, Eastern Spinebill, Flame (Apr–Sep) and Rose (Oct–Mar) Robins, White-winged Chough.

### Others

Australian Shoveler, Lewin's Rail, Baillon's and Spotless Crakes, Latham's Snipe* (Oct–Mar), Black-fronted Dotterel, Satin Flycatcher (Nov–Mar).

Gang-gang Cockatoos may be seen around the university and botanic gardens with some ease, especially between April and September when wintering birds from the surrounding hills join the resident population. The dry sclerophyll forest and other stands of trees in the Botanic Gardens also support Speckled Warbler, White-eared, Fuscous and Crescent Honeyeaters, and Flame Robin. The wet sclerophyll forest in the 55 sq km **Tidbinbilla Nature Reserve** (open 0900–1800), 40 km to the southwest, supports Red-browed Treecreeper (Fishing Gap Firetrail), Superb Lyrebird (Lyrebird Trail), Pilotbird, Brown-headed Honeyeater, Rose and Flame (Fishing Gap Firetrail) Robins, and Spotted Quail-thrush (Camelback Firetrail). During the summer (Nov–Mar) it is worth visiting the **Jerrabomberra Wetlands** where Lewin's Rail, crakes, Latham's Snipe*, Red-capped Plover and Red-kneed and Black-fronted Dotterels occur. These wetlands lie at the east end of Lake Burley Griffin around which the city lies and can be viewed from the two hides overlooking Kelly's Swamp, along Dairy Flat Road about 5 km southeast of the city centre. The sewage farm opposite is also worth checking (ask permission to enter or view from outside). Up to 600 Freckled Ducks* have been recorded on **Lake George**, about 35 km northeast of Canberra, and smaller numbers of this rare nomad are often present year round on this lake, mostly in the southwest corner which is viewable from Lake Road, which leads off the road to Bungendore from the Federal Highway. For more information on birding around Canberra, contact the Canberra Ornithologists Group, PO Box 301, Civic Square, ACT 2608, Australia.

## DHARUG NATIONAL PARK

This reserve is one of the best birding sites north of Sydney, having recovered well from the devastating bush fires of early 1994. The subtropical rainforest, eucalypt woodland and stands of *casuarinas* combine to support a fine selection of birds, including a number of localised species.

### Localised Australian Endemics

Glossy Black-Cockatoo*, Green Catbird, Rock Warbler*, Spotted Quail-thrush.

### Other Australian Endemics

Brown Cuckoo-Dove, Wonga Pigeon, Gang-gang Cockatoo, Superb Lyrebird, Satin Bowerbird, Large-billed Scrubwren, Scarlet Myzomela, White-naped, Crescent and White-cheeked Honeyeaters, Rose Robin, Eastern Whipbird.

**DHARUG NP**

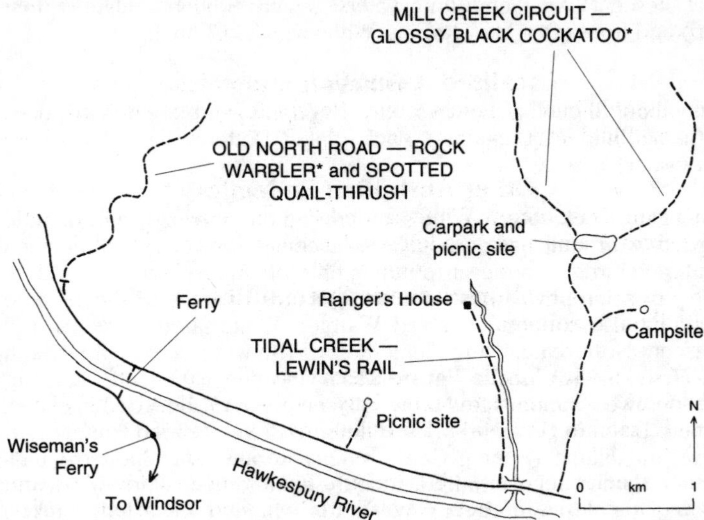


## Others

Lewin's Rail, Olive-backed Oriole.

To reach the park, cross the Hawkesbury River at Wiseman's Ferry about 80 km north of Sydney, then head east for about 4 km and turn north on to a track which leads to a car park and picnic site. Glossy Black-Cockatoo* occurs along the 11 km long Mill Creek Circuit which begins here. Lewin's Rail occurs along the tidal creek which runs alongside the track to the ranger's house, but is not seen very often. The Old North Road, west of where the ferry docks, is the best place to look for Rock Warbler* (on scree 1 km up the road) and Spotted Quail-thrush.

To the west of Dharug National Park the Putty Road between Windsor and Putty, particularly the exposed rocky ridges near **Colo Heights**, is a good place to look for Spotted Quail-thrush, and the area also supports Gang-gang Cockatoo, Red-browed Treecreeper, Pilotbird and Rock Warbler*. To the south of here, around **Windsor**, there are some good wetlands worth exploring. Latham's Snipe* (Oct–Mar) occurs at the sewage works 1 km southeast of McGraths Hill (visible from Musgrave Road), the large lagoon close to RAAF Richmond at McGraths Hill and at Longneck Lagoon, where there is a field studies centre, along with Red-kneed and Black-fronted Dotterels, Tawny Frogmouth, Speckled Warbler and Fuscous Honeyeater.

## NORTH NEW SOUTH WALES

This part of Australia supports two very localised species: the very rare Rufous Scrub-bird*, which is only likely to be seen here and at

Lamington National Park near Brisbane (p. 153), and Relict Raven, as well as a number of northern species at the southern edge of their ranges.

## Localised Australian Endemics

Rufous Scrub-bird*, Green Catbird, Regent Bowerbird, Relict Raven, Paradise Riflebird*.

## Other Australian Endemics

Australian Brush-turkey, White-headed Pigeon, Superb Lyrebird, Satin Bowerbird, Flame and Rose Robins, Australian Raven.

## Non-endemic Specialities

Noisy Pitta, Logrunner.

## Others

Wedge-tailed Shearwater, Pacific Baza (Nov–Dec), Beach Thick-knee, Satin Flycatcher (Oct–Nov), Torresian Crow, Olive-tailed Thrush.

(Other species recorded here include Black-winged (Nov–Mar) and Gould's (Nov–Mar) Petrels, Red-tailed (Nov) and White-tailed (Feb–Apr) Tropicbirds, Blue-grey Noddy (Mar) and Common White-Tern (Mar).)

One of the few known sites for the rare Rufous Scrub-bird* is near **Gloucester**, which is 267 km north of Sydney via Newcastle, at the eastern edge of Barrington Tops National Park, a montane forest World Heritage Area. To look for the scrub-bird, turn west towards Faulkland 9 km south of Gloucester and follow signs to Invergordon and Gloucester Tops. Stay left where the Kerripit Road forks right and bird alongside the rest of the track. From Gloucester head north 207 km to **Armidale** in the heart of the New England Tablelands to look for the localised Relict Raven which occurs in the wet sclerophyll forests and adjacent farmland around here. The subtropical forest in **Dorrigo National Park**, about 140 km east of Armidale, supports a number of species which are relatively common further north in Queensland, including White-headed Pigeon, Noisy Pitta, Regent Bowerbird, Logrunner and Paradise Riflebird*. To the east of Dorrigo National Park Relict Raven also occurs, along with Torresian Crow and Australian Raven, around **Coffs Harbour**, where Black-winged Petrel has been recorded regularly at the Wedge-tailed Shearwater colony on Muttonbird Island (walk out along the northern harbour wall to reach the island) and Pacific Baza breeds in the botanic gardens. Gould's Petrel, an endemic breeding species, breeds on the Cabbage Tree Islands offshore, where the Australian Nature Conservation Agency run ringing studies. Thirty-seven kilometres north of Coffs Harbour, turn off the Pacific Highway to reach Red Rock Beach (6 km away), where Beach Thick-knee is regularly recorded. Seawatching from the lighthouse at **East Ballina** has produced Red-tailed and White-tailed Tropicbirds, Blue-grey Noddy and Common White-Tern. The best conditions for seawatching are southeasterlies during March, northeasterlies during October, and, especially, cyclones.

## BLUE MOUNTAINS

The forested gullies of the cool Blue Mountains, which lie in the Great Dividing Range west of Sydney, support Pilotbird and Rock Warbler*, as well as Gang-gang Cockatoo and the delightful Crescent Honeyeater.

### Localised Australian Endemics

Rock Warbler*.

### Other Australian Endemics

Australian King-Parrot, Crimson Rosella, Yellow-tailed Black-Cockatoo, Gang-gang Cockatoo, Galah, White-throated and Red-browed Treecreepers, Satin Bowerbird, Pilotbird, White-browed Scrubwren, Brown Gerygone, Lewin's, Yellow-faced, Crescent and New Holland Honeyeaters, Eastern Spinebill.

The cockatoos occur around the 275 m (902 ft) Wentworth Falls, about 100 km west of Sydney on the Great Western Highway, and at **Katoomba**, the Blue Mountains tourist hub which is situated at 1017 m (3337 ft) 104 km west of Sydney. Bird Echo Point, 3 km south of Katoomba, where Gang-gang Cockatoo visits the feeders outside the window of the Information Centre, Red-browed Treecreeper, Pilotbird and Rock Warbler* all occur along the path which starts by the Information Centre, and Crescent Honeyeater occurs in the forest alongside the steep Scenic Railway Trail. Pilotbird and Rock Warbler* also occur at **Pierce's Pass**, which can be reached by turning off the road between Richmond and Lithgow to the picnic area, alongside which there is a small, well-vegetated gulley which the two little skulkers frequent. Prepare to wrap up warm in these mountains during the winter (May–Oct).

## GLEN DAVIS

Beyond the Blue Mountains at the west side of the Great Dividing Range 200 km west of Sydney a number of inland birds, here at the eastern edge of their ranges, mix with a star cast of localised little beauties which include Regent Honeyeater* and Diamond Firetail. Hence this is one of the best birding sites in southeast Australia and one of the few where it is possible to see over 100 species in a day.

### Localised Australian Endemics

Turquoise Parrot*, Regent Honeyeater*, Plum-headed Finch.

### Other Australian Endemics

Maned Duck, Common Bronzewing, Red-rumped Parrot, Yellow-tailed Black-Cockatoo, Galah, Little Lorikeet, White-throated and Brown Treecreepers, Superb Fairywren, Speckled Warbler, Chestnut-rumped Hylacola, Weebill, Western Gerygone, Yellow-tufted, Fuscous, White-plumed, Black-chinned and Brown-headed Honeyeaters, Red-capped, Flame, Hooded and Yellow Robins, Crested Shrike-tit, White-browed Babbler, White-winged Chough, Dusky Woodswallow, Rufous Songlark (Sep–Apr), Diamond and Red-browed Firetails, Double-barred Finch.

## Others

Wedge-tailed Eagle, Brown Falcon, Brown Quail, Painted Buttonquail, Shining (Aug–Apr) and Horsfield's Bronze-Cuckoos, Black-eared Cuckoo (Sep–Apr), White-throated Gerygone (Sep–Apr), Jacky-winter, Scarlet Robin, Grey-crowned Babbler, Common Cicadabird (Sep–Apr), Zebra Finch.

## Other Wildlife

Eastern grey kangaroo, wallaroo, wombat.

(Other species recorded here include Red-chested Buttonquail, Swift Parrot*, Glossy Black-Cockatoo*, Gang-gang Cockatoo, Red-browed Treecreeper, Rock Warbler* and Spotted Quail-thrush.)

Take the Western Freeway beyond Katoomba towards Mudgee and turn northeast at Capertree, 35 km west of Lithgow. Bird the 35 km road that runs down the valley from here, especially at KM 10 and between KM 14 and KM 17 for Regent Honeyeater*, and the reedy creek at KM 20 for Plum-headed Finch. The rare honeyeater has also been recorded in the grounds of Rockview Lodge, off Crown Station Road, along with Red-chested Buttonquail and Speckled Warbler.

*One of the highlights of birding in Australia is the pristine plumage of intricately marked birds, so that all spots, stripes, bars and crescents are usually present and correct, as is the case with the rare Regent Honeyeater**

If *en route* to Deniliquin via Wagga Wagga it is worth looking out for Superb Parrots* (Nov–Feb) near **Yass**, especially along the road to Temora which leads off the Hume Highway 14 km west of Yass. Near Narrandera it is worth stopping at **Leeton Swamp**, 11 km north of the Sturt Highway, especially between November and March. Head north out of town and turn right at the second supermarket to reach the swamp on the left side of this road. Possible goodies include Plumed Whistling-Duck, Freckled Duck*, Black-backed Bittern, Greater Painted-snipe, Long-toed Stint (Oct–Mar) and Red-kneed Dotterel. **Back Yamma State Forest**, 17 km northwest of Eugowra on the Parkes Road, supports Turquoise Parrot*, Speckled Warbler, Red-capped and Rose Robins, Apostlebird and Diamond Firetail.

## ROUND HILL NATURE RESERVE

This area of pristine mallee is the best site in Australia to look for the very rare Red-lored Whistler*. There are a number of other mallee specialists here, including Chestnut Quail-thrush, while the nearby areas of mulga support such localised goodies as Spotted Bowerbird and Pink Cockatoo*.

### Localised Australian Endemics

Spotted Bowerbird, Red-lored Whistler* (Sep–Oct).

### Other Australian Endemics

Mallee Ringneck, Mulga Parrot, Pink Cockatoo*, Splendid Fairywren, Shy Hylacola, Yellow-plumed, White-fronted, Striped and Spiny-cheeked Honeyeaters, Red-capped Robin, Southern Scrub-Robin, Gilbert's Whistler, White-browed Babbler, Chestnut Quail-thrush.

### Others

Black-eared Cuckoo (Sep–Apr), Spotted Nightjar, Grey-crowned Babbler.

(Other species recorded here include Malleefowl*, Red-chested and Little Buttonquails, Black, Pied and Grey-fronted Honeyeaters, Crimson Chat and White-browed Woodswallow.)

The reserve is 75 km northeast of Hillston. 41 km northwest of Euabalong towards Mount Hope turn south towards Lake Cargelligo. A little way along here turn west to the reserve where the whistler occurs along the track leading northwest from the corner of the old field. They have also been seen along the road to Lake Cargelligo. The mulga areas alongside the road back to Euabalong support Pink Cockatoo*, Spotted Bowerbird and Striped Honeyeater.

Malleefowl*, Painted Buttonquail, Spotted Nightjar and Chestnut Quail-thrush occur in the oasis of mallee at **Pulletop Nature Reserve**, reached by turning west along Heaths Road about 30 km north of Griffith. Turn right at the T-junction with Pulletop Road to reach the reserve after 6 km. Other species recorded here include Bluebonnet and Yellow-plumed Honeyeater. **Griffith Sewage Works** on the western edge of town near the cattle market may be worth a look, since Freckled Duck* has been recorded here in the past. The grasslands between Coleambally, 66 km south of Griffith, and Deniliquin, support Spotted Harrier, Black Falcon, Banded Lapwing and Apostlebird.

## DENILIQUIN

This small, pleasant town stands on the Steam Plains either side of the Murray River, 795 km southwest of Sydney and 285 km north of Melbourne. It is possible to see over 100 species in a day in the surrounding grasslands, wetlands, woodlands and riverside red river gums, including Plains-wanderer*, a unique species in a family all of its own which is most closely related to the seedsnipes of South America. The Plains-wanderer* pilgrimage has been completed by many birders and

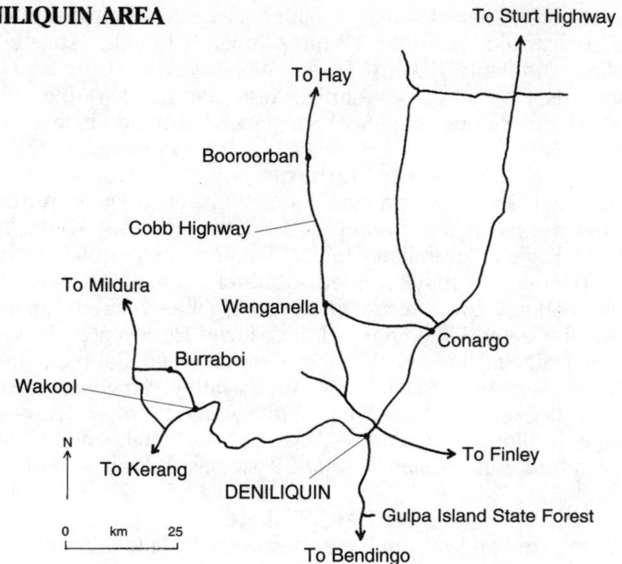


few return home without fond memories of watching this nocturnal shorebird under so many stars it is difficult to see the sky. The pilgrims also usually come away with a bagful of other goodies which might include Black Falcon, Superb Parrot*, Painted Honeyeater*, Stubble Quail, up to three buttonquails and Australian Owlet-Nightjar. Hence this is one of those sites every birder intending to visit Australia should include in their itineraries from day one.

Phil Maher is the man who knows where to look for the wanderer and all of the other goodies. He is a professional guide who runs bird tours throughout Australia, hence it is crucial to contact him well in advance about dates, prices and so on, at Inland Bird Tours, PO Box 382 (172 Whitehorse Road), Balwyn, Victoria 3103 (tel/fax: 03 9817 6555, mobile: 041 931 0200).

## Localised Australian Endemics

Plains-wanderer*, Banded Lapwing, Superb Parrot*, Painted Honeyeater* (Sep–Apr).

## Other Australian Endemics

Emu, Plumed Whistling-Duck, Musk and Pink-eared Ducks, Pacific Heron, Yellow-billed Spoonbill, Australian Kite, Black Falcon, Stubble Quail, Little Buttonquail, Black-tailed Native-hen, Red-kneed Dotterel, Common Bronzewing, Diamond Dove, Mallee Ringneck, Crimson Rosella (yellow *flaveolus* race), Bluebonnet, Red-rumped Parrot, Galah, Long-billed Corella, Southern Boobook, Tawny Frogmouth, Laughing Kookaburra, Red-backed Kingfisher, White-throated and Brown Treecreepers, White-winged and Superb Fairywrens, Striated Pardalote, Buff-rumped, Yellow-rumped, Chestnut-rumped and Yellow Thornbills, Weebill, Western Gerygone, Southern Whiteface, Singing, White-plumed, Black-chinned, Brown-headed and Striped Honeyeaters, Noisy Miner, Spiny-cheeked Honeyeater, White-fronted Chat, Red-capped and

Hooded Robins, Crested Shrike-tit, Gilbert's Whistler, White-browed and Chestnut-crowned Babblers, White-winged Chough, Apostlebird, Australian and Little Ravens, Dusky Woodswallow, Grey and Pied Butcherbirds, Ground Cuckoo-shrike, Australian Reed-Warbler, Brown (Aug–Apr) and Rufous (Aug–Apr) Songlarks, Diamond Firetail.

## Others

Hoary-headed Grebe, Australian Darter, White-eyed Duck, Australian and Straw-necked Ibises, Swamp and Spotted Harriers, Wedge-tailed and Little Eagles, Australian Hobby, Painted Buttonquail, Latham's Snipe* (Oct–Mar), Black-fronted Dotterel, Peaceful Dove, Pallid Cuckoo, Barking Owl, Australian Owlet-Nightjar, Sacred Kingfisher, Rainbow Bee-eater, Little Friarbird, Blue-faced Honeyeater, Jacky-winter, Varied Sittella, Rufous Whistler, Grey-crowned Babbler, Restless Flycatcher (Sep–Apr), Black-faced Woodswallow, Magpie-lark, Black-faced Cuckoo-shrike (Sep–Apr), White-winged Triller (Aug–Mar), Welcome Swallow, Fairy Martin (Aug–Feb), Golden-headed Cisticola, Little Grassbird, Australasian Bushlark, Australasian Pipit, Mistletoebird.

## Other Wildlife

Eastern grey, red and western grey kangaroos, fat-tailed dunnart.

(Other species recorded here include Freckled Duck*, Black-backed and Australasian* Bitterns, Letter-winged Kite (at least 25 birds were present in August 1994 when there was a mouse plague), Red-chested Buttonquail, Baillon's, Australian and Spotless Crakes, Greater Painted-snipe, Bush Thick-knee, Australian Pratincole (Sep–Apr), Inland Dotterel (Sep–Apr), Budgerigar, Cockatiel, Black Honeyeater, Orange Chat (Sep–Apr), Masked and White-browed Woodswallows, White-backed Swallow.)

The area includes **Gulpa Island State Forest**, 18 km south of Deniliquin near the Cobb Highway, where Superb Parrot*, Painted Honeyeater* and Diamond Firetail occur.

**GULPA ISLAND STATE FOREST**

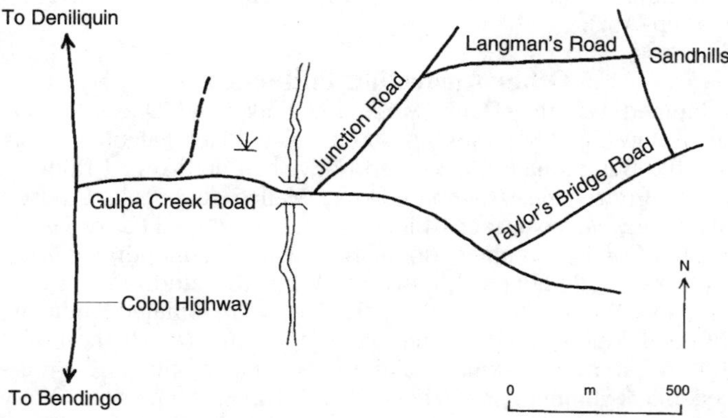

Phil Maher also has access to the evaporation pools at Tullakool, 12 km south of Burraboi about 100 km west of Deniliquin, where species recorded include Musk and Freckled* Ducks, Australian Shoveler, Pink-eared and White-eyed Ducks, Banded Stilt, Red-necked Avocet, Red-capped Plover and Red-kneed Dotterel. The Kerang Lakes near Kerang to the south support similar species, as well as a large colony of cormorants and ibises, Blue-billed Duck, Australian Shelduck, Australian Crake and Black-tailed Native-hen.

*Deniliquin should be included in every Australian birding itinerary because the unique Plains-wanderer* may well end up being bird of the trip*

## *VICTORIA*

**Chiltern State Forest** in northeast Victoria between Albury and Wangaratta is a good site for Painted Buttonquail (on ridges east of Cyanide Road) and White-throated Nightjar (hawking insects over Cyanide Dam between November and March), as well as Turquoise* and Swift* (Apr–Sep) Parrots, Gang-gang Cockatoo, Musk and Little Lorikeets, Chestnut-rumped Hylacola, Fuscous, Black-chinned and Regent* (rare) Honeyeaters, Crested Shrike-tit, Rufous Songlark (Aug–Apr) and Diamond Fire-

**CHILTERN STATE FOREST**

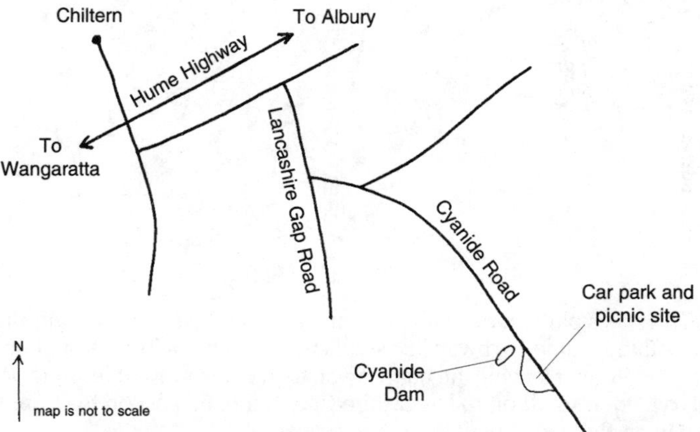

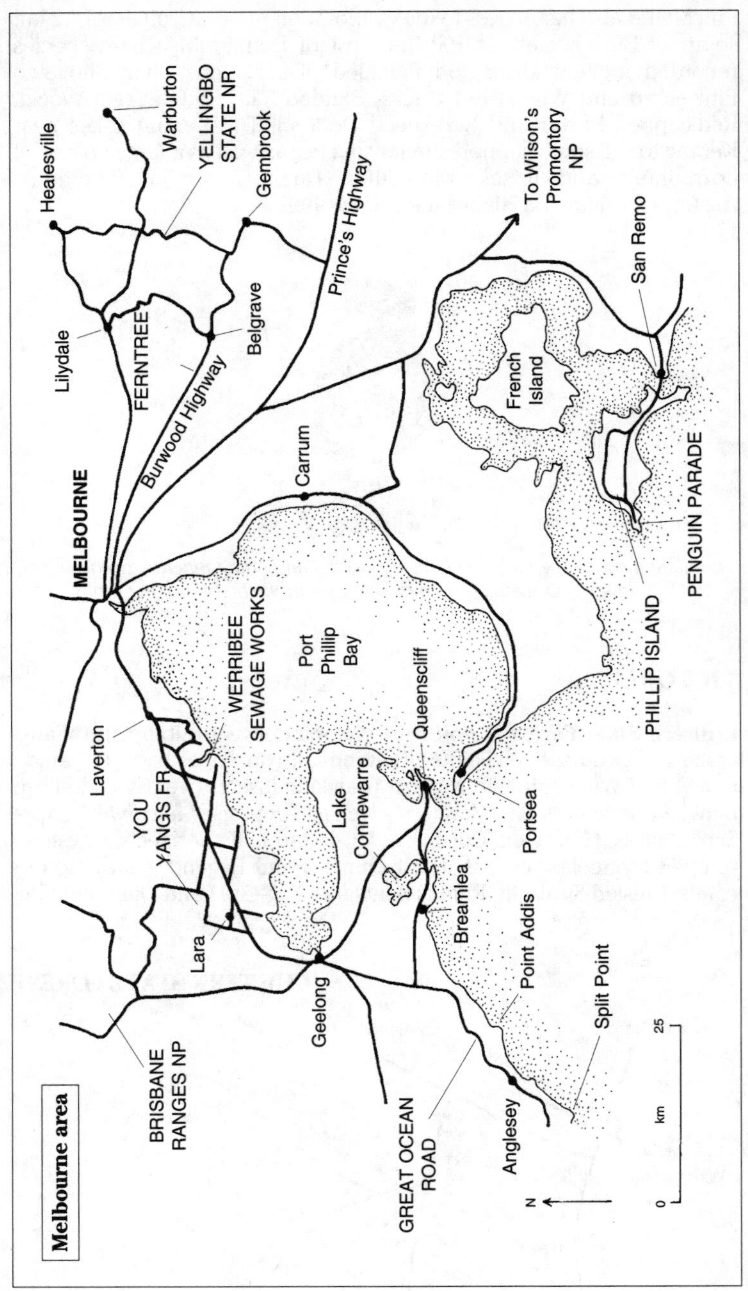


tail. This site is particularly good in spring and can be reached by turning south off the Hume Highway just southeast of Chiltern. Turn east almost immediately after leaving the highway on to the narrow road running parallel to it, then south on to Lancashire Gap Road and east on to Cyanide Road up to the dam where there is a car park.

## DANDENONG RANGE

These mountains, which rise to 633 m (2077 ft) just to the east of Melbourne, support tall ferny forests, where the lofty mountain ash trees reach over 50 m (164 ft), and which are inhabited by such good birds as Powerful Owl*, Superb Lyrebird and Olive Whistler.

### Localised Australian Endemics

Powerful Owl*, Olive Whistler.

### Other Australian Endemics

Australian Kite, Brush Bronzewing, Australian King-Parrot (Apr–Sep), Crimson and Eastern Rosellas, Yellow-tailed Black-Cockatoo, Gang-gang Cockatoo (Mar–Sep), Purple-crowned Lorikeet, Laughing Kookaburra, White-throated and Red-browed (scarce) Treecreepers, Superb Lyrebird, Pilotbird, Large-billed Scrubwren, Brown Thornbill, Yellow-faced, White-eared, Yellow-tufted (including *cassidex* race), White-naped and Crescent Honeyeaters, Eastern Spinebill, Bell Miner, Red Wattlebird, Rose (Nov–Mar) and Pink Robins, Crested Shrike-tit, Eastern Whipbird, Dusky Woodswallow, Red-browed Firetail.

### Others

Brown Goshawk, Wedge-tailed Eagle, Greater Sooty-Owl, Scarlet Robin, Rufous Fantail (Sep–Apr), Satin Flycatcher (Sep–Mar), Olive-tailed Thrush.

Dandenong Ranges National Park comprises Sherbrooke Forest Park and Ferntree Gully National Park. **Sherbrooke Forest Park**, 40 km east of Melbourne via Belgrave and Kallista, is a good site for Superb

**FERNTREE GULLY NP**

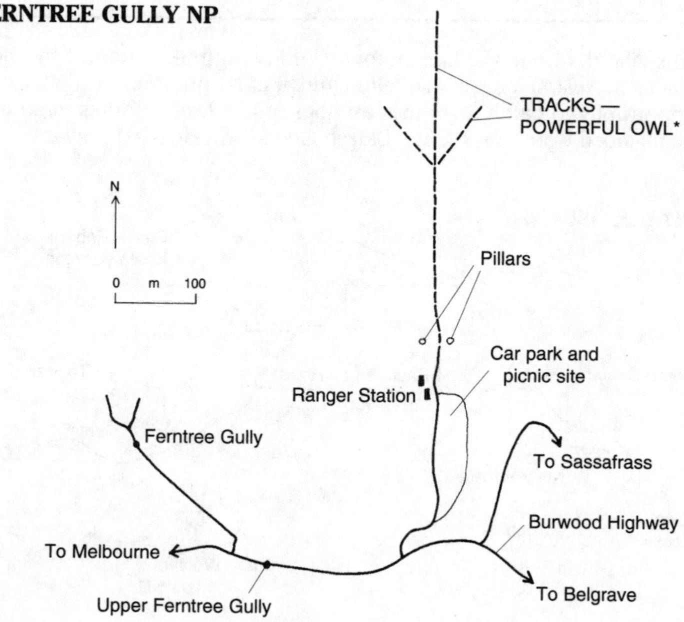

Lyrebird and Pilotbird (along Ridge Track at dawn), as well as Red-browed Treecreeper and Olive Whistler. The lyrebird and pilotbird, as well as Powerful Owl*, also occur in **Ferntree Gully National Park**, 36 km east of Melbourne via the Burwood Highway. After passing through Upper Ferntree Gully, take the road north to the ranger station (leave vehicle outside park after 1700 hours), walk north through the pillars and explore the three-pronged fork in the track for Powerful Owl*, which is normally most vocal at dusk. The rare *cassidex* race of Yellow-tufted Honeyeater, known as 'Helmeted Honeyeater', is restricted to **Yellingbo State Nature Reserve**, about 50 km east of Melbourne. To reach here from Ferntree Gully head east towards Gembrook, turn north towards Woori Yallock and the reserve is on the left after 6 km. The honeyeater, which occasionally associates with Bell Miners, occurs in creek-side eucalypts. **Toolangi State Forest** is another good site for Superb Lyrebird, as well as Crescent Honeyeater and Pink Robin.

Flowering eucalypts in the domestic terminal car park at Tullamarine International Airport, **Melbourne**, are some of the most reliable in Australia for the elusive Purple-crowned Lorikeet, as well as Musk Lorikeet, while the city's botanical gardens are a good site for the localised Rufous Night-Heron, which roosts by the main pond, and grey-headed flying-fox. *En route* to sites southeast of Melbourne it may be worth stopping at **Carrum Sewage Works** (ask permission to enter at the office), where Blue-billed Duck, Chestnut Teal, Australian Shoveler, Pink-eared Duck, Red-necked Avocet, Red-capped Plover, and Red-kneed and Black-fronted Dotterels occur, and where Freckled Duck* is a rare visitor.

## PHILLIP ISLAND

This island, about 150 km southeast of Melbourne, is one of the best places in Australia to see Little Penguin at close quarters, and offers the opportunity to catch up with a number of localised goodies including Black-faced Cormorant, Cape Barren Goose and Hooded Plover*.

**PHILLIP ISLAND**

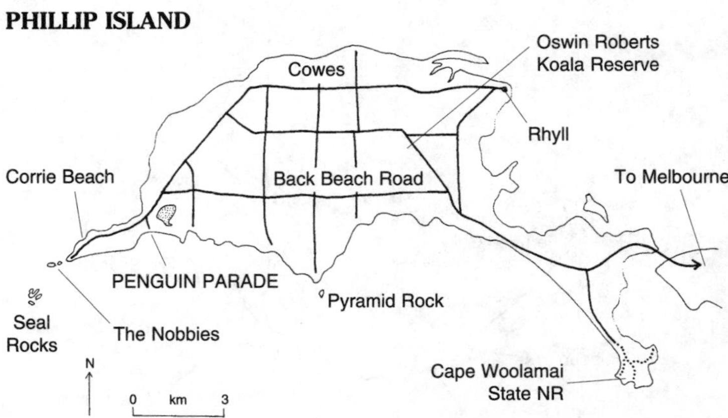

### Localised Australian Endemics

Black-faced Cormorant, Cape Barren Goose, Hooded Plover*.

### Other Australian Endemics

Australian Shelduck, Chestnut Teal, Sooty Oystercatcher, Pacific Gull*, Common and Brush Bronzewings, Superb Fairywren, Brown Thornbill, White-plumed and New Holland Honeyeaters, White-fronted Chat, Flame Robin (Apr–Sep), Dusky Woodswallow.

### Others

Little Penguin, Black-browed (Mar–Nov) and Shy (Apr–Nov) Albatrosses, Short-tailed Shearwater (Oct–Mar), Australian Gannet, Australian Pelican, Straw-necked Ibis, Royal Spoonbill, Swamp Harrier, Australian Hobby, Brolga, Pied Oystercatcher, Black-fronted Dotterel.

### Other Wildlife

Australian fur seal, koala.

Once on the island take the Back Beach Road along the south side and check roadside paddocks for Cape Barren Goose. Just after the end of this road continue west to Penguin Parade where Little Penguins can be seen returning to their burrows at dusk from a grandstand overlooking the floodlit Summerland Beach, along with Short-tailed Shearwaters. The penguins are present all year but peak numbers are usually recorded between October and January. West of here check the beaches such as Berry's and Cowrie for Hooded Plover*. If there is no sign of them here it may be worth checking Cape Woolamai State Nature Reserve at the eastern end of the island before returning to the mainland.

*The Hooded Plover* inhabits wild white sandy beaches, a wonderful habitat in which to see what is one of the world's most beautiful shorebirds*

## WILSON'S PROMONTORY NATIONAL PARK

This headland, which rises to 754 m (2474 ft) at Mount La Trobe, forms the southernmost point of Australia, jutting out into the Bass Strait 250 km southeast of Melbourne. The tidal mudflats, mangroves, grasslands, heathlands, wetlands and small areas of rainforest within this large park (490 sq km) support a diverse avifauna (over 250 species have been recorded) which includes Cape Barren Goose, Hooded Plover*, Ground Parrot*, Forest Raven and heathland specialities such as Beautiful Firetail.

## WILSON'S PROMONTORY NP

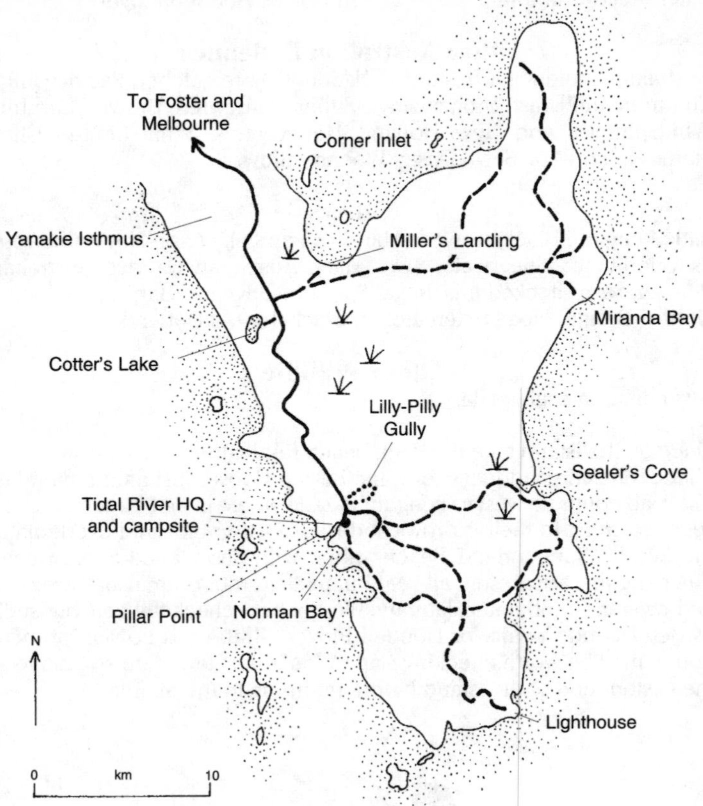


### Localised Australian Endemics

Black-faced Cormorant, Cape Barren Goose, Hooded Plover*, Blue-winged (Apr–Oct) and Ground* Parrots, Olive Whistler, Forest Raven, Beautiful Firetail.

### Other Australian Endemics

Emu, Musk Duck, Black Swan, Chestnut Teal, Sooty Oystercatcher, Pacific Gull*, Brush Bronzewing, Crimson Rosella, Yellow-tailed Black-Cockatoo, Gang-gang Cockatoo, Southern Emuwren, Striated Field-wren, Chestnut-rumped Hylacola, Striated Thornbill, Crescent, New Holland and Tawny-crowned Honeyeaters, Eastern Spinebill, Brush Wattlebird, Flame, Rose (Nov–Mar) and Yellow Robins, Crested Shrike-tit, Grey Currawong.

### Others

Far Eastern Curlew*, Great Knot, Rufous-necked Stint, Sharp-tailed Sandpiper, Pied Oystercatcher, Double-banded Plover (Feb–Sep), Scarlet Robin, Golden Whistler, Rufous Fantail (Sep–Apr), Satin Flycatcher (Sep–Mar).

## Other Wildlife

Australian fur seal, eastern grey kangaroo, koala, swamp wallaby, wombat.

The park entrance is south of Foster. Crescent Honeyeater occurs around the Tidal River Campsite, along with wombat. There are two excellent trails: the 5 km long Lilly-Pilly Gully Nature Walk which starts near this campsite (Gang-gang Cockatoo, robins, Olive Whistler) and the 2.5 km long Miller's Landing Nature Walk to the north (Black-faced Cormorant, Sooty Oystercatcher and Ground Parrot*). The area around Cotter's Lake is the best for heathland specialists such as Blue-winged and Ground* Parrots, Southern Emuwren and Striated Fieldwren, and Hooded Plover* has been recorded at the west end of the lake. Pacific Gull* occurs in Norman Bay and it is possible to see Australian fur seals on the islands visible from Pillar Point.

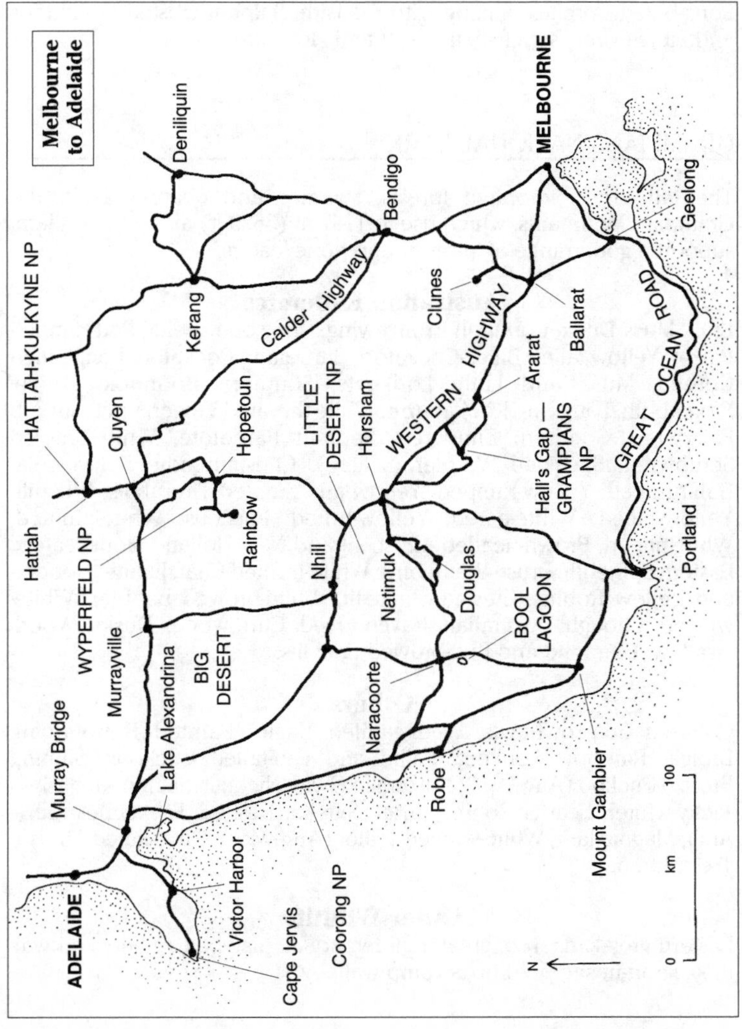

*Accommodation:* Tidal River Campsite.

There are two possible birding routes between Melbourne and Adelaide: inland on the **Western Highway** via large areas of protected mallee, where such specialities as Malleefowl* occur, or along the coast on the Great Ocean Road and **Prince's Highway**, via wetlands and coastal scrub which support Orange-bellied Parrot* and Rufous Bristlebird*.

Along the **Western Highway** the first site worth stopping at is **Clunes State Forest**, one of the most reliable sites in spring (Oct–Nov) for the beautiful Painted Honeyeater*. From Clunes, 34 km north of Ballarat, head northeast towards Campbelltown, then turn left towards the forest. Turn left at the junction 1.5 km along here and stop by the gate after 200 m. Check the large tree infested with mistletoe 50 m beyond the gate. The honeyeater also occurs in the dry **Muckleford Forest** near Maldon, 32 km north of Campbelltown. Back on the highway look for Long-billed Corellas, mixing with roadside Sulphur-crested Cockatoos and Little Corellas, between Ararat and Horsham.

## GRAMPIANS NATIONAL PARK

The tall, dry sclerophyll forests, swamps and heathlands in the Grampian Mountains, which rise to 1167 m (3829 ft) at Mount William, support a good range of 'parrots' and honeyeaters.

### Australian Endemics

Emu, Musk Duck, Common Bronzewing, Crimson Rosella, Red-rumped Parrot, Yellow-tailed Black-Cockatoo, Gang-gang Cockatoo, Long-billed Corella, Musk and Little Lorikeets, Southern Boobook, Tawny Frogmouth, Laughing Kookaburra, White-throated Treecreeper, Superb Fairywren, Southern Emuwren, Spotted Pardalote, White-browed Scrubwren, Speckled Warbler (scarce), Chestnut-rumped Hylacola, Buff-rumped, Yellow-rumped, Yellow and Striated Thornbills, Weebill, Yellow-faced, White-eared, Yellow-tufted, Fuscous, White-plumed, White-naped, Brown-headed, Crescent and New Holland Honeyeaters, Eastern Spinebill, Brush Wattlebird, White-fronted Chat, Flame, Hooded and Yellow Robins, Crested Shrike-tit, White-browed Babbler, White-winged Chough, Australian Raven, Pied Currawong, Dusky Wood-swallow, Diamond and Red-browed Firetails.

### Others

Collared Sparrowhawk, Wedge-tailed Eagle, Painted Buttonquail, Brolga, Rainbow Lorikeet, Pallid and Fan-tailed Cuckoos, Shining Bronze-Cuckoo (Aug–Apr), Australian Owlet-Nightjar, Sacred Kingfisher, Jacky-winter, Scarlet Robin, Varied Sittella, Restless Flycatcher (Sep–Apr), Magpie-lark, White-winged Triller (Aug–Mar), Olive-tailed Thrush, Tree Martin.

### Other Wildlife

Eastern grey kangaroo, greater glider, koala, platypus, red-necked wallaby, short-nosed potoroo, swamp wallaby.

(Other species recorded here include Powerful Owl* and Spotted Quail-thrush.)

Leave the Western Highway at Ararat and head west to Hall's Gap, 260 km northwest of Melbourne. Gang-gang Cockatoo and Long-billed Corella occur around Hall's Gap on the numerous walking tracks. Painted Buttonquail occurs in the open woodland alongside the road to Wartook, west of Zumsteins, which is 22 km northwest of Hall's Gap. The Victoria Valley Road, which is actually a track, southwest of Hall's Gap, passes through heathland where Southern Emuwren occurs. Heathlands, a small expensive guesthouse in the middle of a 40 ha bird sanctuary, is run by Graham Pizzey, author of *A Field Guide to the Birds of Australia*. It lies near Dunkeld at the south end of the park, and details of the accommodation and Graham's birding excursions can be obtained from Heathlands, PO Box 41, Dunkeld, Victoria 3294 (tel: 055 77 2501).

At Stawell, back on the Western Highway, it is worth considering a detour to **Donald**, 92 km to the north, where the nearby lakes have attracted Freckled Duck* and support a good variety of other waterfowl. The 30 or so shallow saline lakes between **Natimuk** and **Douglas**, west of Horsham, support large numbers of breeding Banded Stilts and Red-necked Avocets when conditions are suitable. The lakes normally fill in winter and early spring, attracting, in the best years, over 50,000 Banded Stilts (mainly between September and November) and over 5,000 Red-necked Avocets (mainly between July and October) before they dry up in late summer. In 1996 most of these birds were on Oliver's, Mitre, Centre, Heard and Bow Lakes, all waters which also support a fine variety of other waterbirds.

The mallee in **Little Desert National Park** (353 sq km), northwest of Natimuk, supports Shy Hylacola, White-eared and Purple-gaped Honeyeaters, Southern Scrub-Robin, Gilbert's Whistler and Diamond Firetail, as well as short-beaked echidna. North of Little Desert is **Big Desert Wilderness**, traversed by the 146 km long rough track between Nhill and Murrayville. The rare and elusive Red-lored Whistler*, along with Regent Parrot, Shy Hylacola, Purple-gaped and White-fronted Honeyeaters, and Southern Scrub-Robin, has been recorded around Big Billy Bore, recognisable by a windmill and a dam on a sweeping left-hand bend 33 km south of Murrayville, and the area 15 km further south has also been productive in the past. Malleefowl* and Mallee Emuwren* are known from the rest of Big Desert.

## WYPERFELD NATIONAL PARK

Most of the mallee in northwest Victoria has been replaced with farmland, but there are a few big reserves which protect what is left of the natural vegetation and this is arguably the best. As well as about 1000 sq km of mallee, there are also riverine woodlands and heathlands, hence over 220 species have been recorded, including most mallee specialities. This is also one of only seven known sites where the very rare Black-eared Miner* occurs.

## WYPERFELD NP

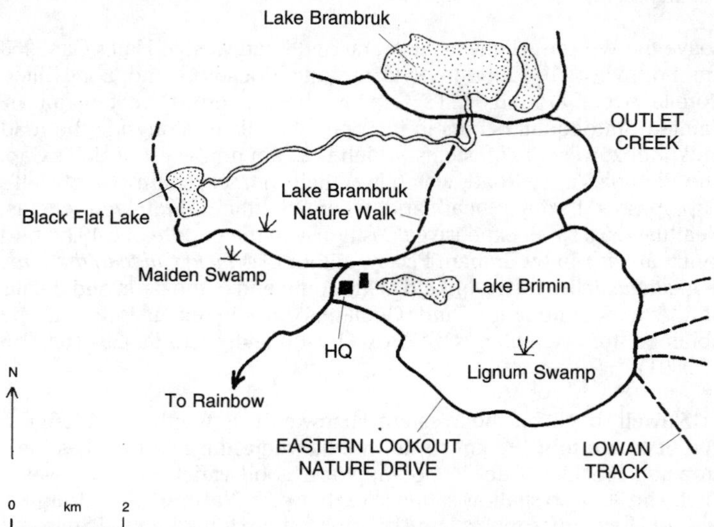


### Localised Australian Endemics

Malleefowl*, Regent Parrot, White-browed Treecreeper, Purple-gaped Honeyeater, Black-eared Miner*, Chestnut Quail-thrush.

### Other Australian Endemics

Emu, Common Bronzewing, Mallee Ringneck, Bluebonnet, Red-rumped and Mulga Parrots, Budgerigar, Pink Cockatoo*, Galah, Southern Boobook, Tawny Frogmouth, Brown Treecreeper, Splendid and Variegated Fairywrens, Spotted and Striated Pardalotes, Redthroat, Shy Hylacola, Inland, Yellow-rumped, Chestnut-rumped and Yellow Thornbills, Weebill, Southern Whiteface, White-eared, Yellow-plumed, Brown-headed, White-fronted, Tawny-crowned and Striped Honeyeaters, Yellow-throated Miner, Spiny-cheeked Honeyeater, White-fronted Chat, Red-capped and Hooded Robins, Southern Scrub-Robin, Crested Bellbird, Gilbert's Whistler, White-browed Babbler, White-winged Chough, Australian Raven, Masked (nomadic) and Dusky Woodswallows, Grey Currawong, White-backed Swallow.

### Others

Collared Sparrowhawk, Wedge-tailed and Little Eagles, Brown Falcon, Little Corella, Pallid Cuckoo, Horsfield's Bronze-Cuckoo, Australian Owlet-Nightjar, Spotted Nightjar, Rainbow Bee-eater (Sep–Apr), Jacky-winter, Restless Flycatcher, White-winged Triller (Aug–Mar), Tree Martin.

### Other Wildlife

Sand goanna, stumpy-tailed lizard, western grey kangaroo.

(Other species recorded here include Mallee Emuwren*, Striated Grass-wren and White-browed Woodswallow.)

This reserve is 450 km northwest of Melbourne and 500 km east of Adelaide. On arrival, ask at the HQ if there are any active Malleefowl* mounds. Viewing screens are usually erected by those that are active, with the most recent being along a track leading off the Eastern Lookout Nature Drive near post 12. The best time of year to see Malleefowl* is October, when they lay around 20 eggs in their large mounds. Otherwise cruise around the 15 km long Eastern Lookout Nature Drive and walk the Lowan Track, which is usually the best for the scarce and shy Chestnut Quail-thrush, as well as other mallee specialities and the very rare Black-eared Miner*, one or two individuals of which may still exist in this area, alongside the commoner Yellow-throated Miner and assorted hybrids. White-browed Treecreeper is restricted to the north end of the park, accessible via Patchewollock, and occurs alongside the track between the entrance gate and the campsite. This is also the best area for Budgerigar, Southern Whiteface and White-browed Woodswallow.

*Stands of old trees in the mallee country of northwest Victoria are one of the best places to look for the widespread Australian Owlet-Nightjar*

## HATTAH-KULKYNE NATIONAL PARK

Sandy, semi-arid mallee with *spinifex* covers most of this 480 sq km park, but there are also red river gums, open eucalypt woodlands, sandhills and ephemeral billabongs and lakes on the floodplain of the Murray River, hence over 200 species have been recorded, including Mallee Emuwren* and Striated Grasswren.

### Localised Australian Endemics

Malleefowl*, Regent Parrot, Mallee Emuwren*, Striated Grasswren, Chestnut-crowned Babbler, Chestnut Quail-thrush.

### Other Australian Endemics

Little Buttonquail, Black-tailed Native-hen, Mallee Ringneck, Crimson Rosella (yellow *flaveolus* race), Mulga Parrot, Pink Cockatoo*, Tawny Frogmouth, Splendid and Variegated Fairywrens, Spotted Pardalote, Shy Hylacola, Inland, Chestnut-rumped and Yellow Thornbills, Yellow-plumed, Brown-headed, White-fronted and Striped Honeyeaters, Hooded Robin, Southern Scrub-Robin, Crested Bellbird, Gilbert's Whistler, White-browed Babbler, White-winged Chough, Apostlebird, Masked (nomadic) and Dusky Woodswallows, Grey Currawong.

**HATTAH-KULKYNE NP**

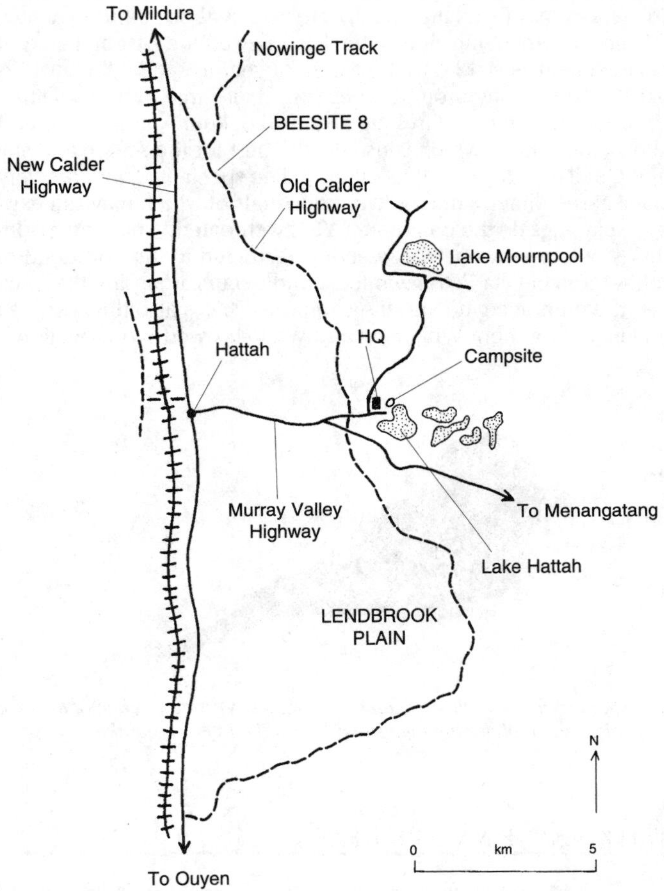


## Others

Black-eared Cuckoo (Sep–Apr), Australian Owlet-Nightjar.

## Other Wildlife

Red and western grey kangaroos.

To reach this park turn off the Murray Valley Highway 4 km east of Hattah. Mallee Emuwren* and Striated Grasswren occur in the *spinifex* between the Old Calder Highway (now a track) and the New Calder Highway, north of the Murray Valley Highway, as well as west of the railway line a few kilometres northwest of Hattah, and on the Lendbrook Plain. Mallee Emuwren* also occurs, along with White-fronted Honeyeater, at Beesite 8, which is 8 km north of the park entrance track along the Old Calder Highway, and Malleefowl*, Striated Grasswren and Chestnut Quail-thrush occur along the Nowinge Track, a little further north.

The first site worth birding along the **Prince's Highway** between Melbourne and Adelaide is **Laverton Saltworks**, about 25 km south-west of Melbourne city centre. This is a good site for shorebirds, which often include Banded Stilt. Just west of Laverton, turn south off the highway on to Aviation Road towards Point Cook. Ask permission at the entrance, 3 km along here, to enter the works and explore the salt-pans which are divided by drivable tracks.

## WERRIBEE SEWAGE WORKS

The mudflats, marshes, lagoons and samphire flats about 35 km west of Melbourne on the Port Phillip Bay shoreline support a superb selection of waterbirds as well as the very rare Orange-bellied Parrot*. Access is restricted, especially at weekends, but, ironically, this is probably the best time to go because this is Melbourne's mecca as far as birders are concerned and there will probably be someone around to advise visiting birders on where to go and what to look out for in this complex area.

### Localised Australian Endemics

Black-faced Cormorant, Blue-winged (Apr–Sep) and Orange-bellied* (Mar–Jul) Parrots.

### Other Australian Endemics

Blue-billed and Musk Ducks, Black Swan, Australian Shelduck, Chestnut Teal, Pink-eared Duck, Yellow-billed Spoonbill, Australian Kite, Stubble Quail, Australian Crake, Black-tailed Native-hen, Banded Stilt, Red-necked Avocet, Red-capped Plover, Pacific Gull*, White-browed Scrubwren, Striated Fieldwren, White-fronted Chat.

### Others

Hoary-headed Grebe, Little Pied, Pied and Little Black Cormorants, Australian Shoveler, Australian and Straw-necked Ibises, Royal Spoonbill, Whistling Kite, Swamp and Spotted Harriers, Wedge-tailed and Little Eagles, Brown Falcon, Australian Kestrel, Buff-banded and Lewin's Rails, Baillon's and Spotless Crakes, Latham's Snipe* (Oct–Mar), Far Eastern Curlew*, Grey-tailed Tattler, Great Knot, Rufous-necked Stint, Sharp-tailed Sandpiper, Pied Oystercatcher, Double-banded Plover (Feb–Sep), Fairy Tern*, Fairy Martin (Aug–Feb), Golden-headed Cisticola, Little Grassbird.

(Other species recorded here include Freckled Duck* (over 200 on at least one occasion) and Black-fronted Dotterel. Rarities have included Letter-winged Kite and a number of shorebirds including Asian Dowitcher*, Long-toed Stint, Pectoral Sandpiper and the hybrid Pectoral/Curlew Sandpiper, formerly known as 'Cox's Sandpiper'.)

Turn south off the Prince's Highway onto 29 Mile Road and, access permitting, bird the whole area. There is a large pool along the track with the most inappropriate name of Paradise Road, which is sometimes used by shorebirds as a roost site. This track leads to a bridge over Little River. Scour the river channel south of the bridge, on the east side, for Lewin's Rail. Back on the west side of the bridge turn south onto anoth-

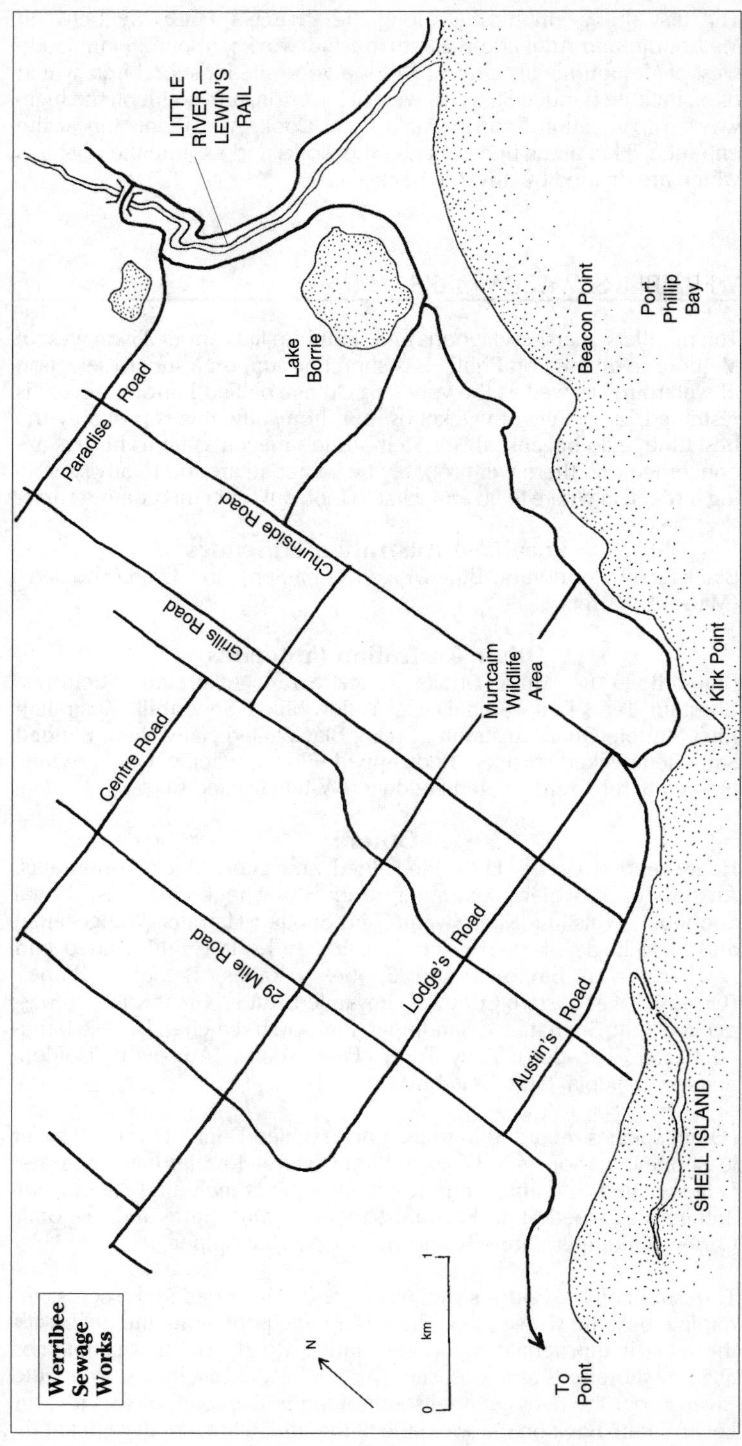
Werribee Sewage Works
LITTLE RIVER — LEWIN'S RAIL
Lake Borrie
Beacon Point
Port Phillip Bay
Paradise Road
Churnside Road
Grills Road
Centre Road
Murtcaim Wildlife Area
Kirk Point
Lodge's Road
29 Mile Road
Austin's Road
SHELL ISLAND
To Point
N
0
km
1

er track which leads to the huge Lake Borrie where Freckled Duck* has been recorded. Before this track rejoins 29 Mile Road west of Lake Borrie it is possible to walk out to a spit and across to Shell Island (wading across channels may be necessary) where Orange-belllied Parrots* feed on the samphire flats and the surrounding coastal lagoons are full of shorebirds including Banded Stilt, Red-necked Avocet and Double-banded Plover. Back at 29 Mile Road continue south and west to Point Wilson, another good shorebird spot. For details of the latest access arrangements contact the RAOU.

*The large Pacific Gull* has a huge puffin-like bill.*

**Avalon**, a beach community on the northwest edge of Port Phillip Bay, south of Lara, lies near a large area of salt-pans which attract Banded Stilt, Red-necked Avocet, Red-capped Plover and Black-fronted Dotterel, while the surrounding scrub supports Striated Fieldwren and Little Grassbird. The dry, open eucalyptus woodland in **You Yangs Forest Reserve**, a few kilometres north of the Prince's Highway between Werribee and Geelong, is a good site for Swift Parrot* (Apr–Sep) and Speckled Warbler (around Big Rock picnic area), and other species recorded here include Musk, Little and Purple-crowned Lorikeets, Brown-headed Honeyeater, Flame Robin (Apr–Sep), Crested Shrike-tit, White-winged Chough, Satin (Sep–Mar) and Restless Flycatchers, White-browed Woodswallow, Fairy Martin (Aug–Feb), Brown Songlark (Aug–Apr) and Diamond Firetail. In **Brisbane Ranges National Park**, about 30 km north of Geelong, it is possible to see Powerful Owl*, Speckled Warbler and Spotted Quail-thrush, as well as koala. Head northwest out of Geelong on Anakie Road, fork left at Anakie Junction towards Ballan, then turn right after about 2 km to the Stony Creek picnic area which is reached after a steep descent. Take the path north from here towards Lower Stony Creek Reservoir and turn left almost immediately on to Outlook Walk which runs through a gully where Powerful Owl* occurs, especially at dusk between May and July. Head south from the Stony Creek picnic area to look for koalas. A good site for Orange-bellied Parrot* (Mar–Jul) is **Swan Island**, only accessible via a causeway from Queenscliff and with prior permission from the army (tel: 052 520 011). Once on the island head for the golf course and ask for permission to walk around its perimeter to the saltmarsh at the far side where the parrots feed, along with Buff-banded and Lewin's Rails. The island is also a good place to see Black-faced Cormorant.

## GREAT OCEAN ROAD

West of Geelong take the Great Ocean Road to reach a number of excellent birding sites and the best area in Australia for Rufous Bristlebird*.

### Localised Australian Endemics

Hooded Plover*, Blue-winged Parrot (Apr–Sep), Rufous Bristlebird*.

### Other Australian Endemics

Brush Bronzewing, Crimson Rosella, Superb Fairywren, Southern Emuwren, White-browed Scrubwren, Yellow-rumped Thornbill, White-naped and New Holland Honeyeaters, Grey Currawong.

(A number of seabirds are possible offshore during the austral summer (Mar–Nov) including Royal* (rare), Black-browed, Shy and Yellow-nosed Albatrosses.)

The protected beach at **Breamlea**, 18 km south of Geelong, supports Hooded Plover*. The bristlebird occurs at a number of sites from **Point Addis** west and have become rather easy to see at a number of tourist spots in recent years, particularly **The Arch**, 5 km west of Port Campbell, and **Split Point**, near Airey's Inlet just west of Anglesey (105 km south-west of Melbourne), where this normally highly secretive species can be seen feeding on the lawns of the houses alongside the road just before the lighthouse, with Eurasian Blackbirds. Keep a look out across all remnant roadside heathlands for Blue-winged Parrot (especially at Point Addis) and Southern Emuwren.

There are a few good birding sites along the **Warrnambool–Port Fairy** stretch of the Prince's Highway, 264–291 km west of Melbourne. Tower Hill Lake, between Warrnambool and Port Fairy, is good for waterbirds, Long-billed Corella and Australian Reed-Warbler, as well as koala, while the Port Fairy area supports Hooded Plover* (on coastal pools), plus Pacific Gull*, Striated Fieldwren and Singing Honeyeater, as well as swamp wallaby. Offshore, look out for Hall's Giant Petrel* and White-chinned Petrel, as well as southern right whales which visit the coastal waters between May and October and are most likely to be seen from the viewpoints on the cliffs at Logan's Beach.

**Portland Pelagics** depend on the availability of trawlers and the unpredictable weather. It may be possible to arrange a pelagic trip out of Portland with local fishermen, and regular trips are organised by local birders who can be contacted via the RAOU, 21 Gladstone Street, Moonee Ponds, Victoria 3039 (tel: 03 370 1422). The best time to set sail (from the harbour where Forest Raven is possible) is during the austral winter (Apr–Sep), when Subantarctic species not usually seen off Sydney or Wollongong are possible. Previous trips have turned up as many as nine species of albatross (July 1992) and such great rarities as Sooty* and Light-mantled Albatrosses, Southern Fulmar, and Kerguelen, Blue and Grey Petrels, alongside common birds such as Royal*, Grey-headed and Buller's* Albatrosses, White-headed and Soft-plumaged Petrels, Antarctic and Slender-billed Prions, and Grey-backed Storm-Petrel.

## *SOUTH AUSTRALIA*

### BOOL LAGOON

This lagoon is one of the largest and most important freshwater wetlands in Australia and it supports one of the richest assemblages of waterbirds in the country, including Black-backed and Australasian* Bitterns, Lewin's Rail and Brolga.

**Localised Australian Endemics**
Black-backed Bittern.

**Other Australian Endemics**
Blue-billed and Musk Ducks, Black Swan, Australian Shelduck, Maned Duck, Chestnut Teal, Pink-eared Duck, Australian Kite, Stubble Quail, Australian Crake, Red-capped Plover, Long-billed Corella.

**Non-endemic Specialities**
Australasian Bittern*.

**Others**
Hoary-headed Grebe, Australian Shoveler, White-eyed Duck, Rufous Night-Heron, Royal Spoonbill, Swamp Harrier, Buff-banded (scarce) and Lewin's Rails, Baillon's and Spotless Crakes, Purple Swamphen, Brolga (Mar–Sep), Latham's Snipe* (Oct–Mar), Rufous-necked Stint, Sharp-tailed Sandpiper, Double-banded Plover (Apr–Sep), Little Grassbird.

(Other species recorded here, mainly in drought years, include Plumed Whistling-Duck, Freckled Duck* and Greater Painted-snipe, while reintroduced species include Magpie Goose and introduced species include Cape Barren Goose.)

To reach this lagoon, which is a reserve, turn west at Struan, 17 km south of Naracoorte. The best birding areas within the reserve vary according to water levels, so the best bet on arrival is to have a chat with the rangers. Otherwise bird the boardwalk, the observation platform and Gunawar Walk, which is usually best for Australasian Bittern* and rails. The breeding season for waterbirds is September to January. Beware of tiger snakes.

*Accommodation:* there is an excellent campsite at Naracoorte Caves Conservation Park, 8 km northeast of Bool. Purple-crowned Lorikeet, Chestnut-rumped Hylacola and Black-chinned Honeyeater have been recorded along the forest trail here, as well as around Mosquito Creek, south of Victoria Fossil Cave, which is reputed to be one of the top three fossil sites in the world.

Sooty Albatross* and Blue Petrel have been recorded on the occasional **Robe Pelagics**. For more details of these trips, which usually take place aboard the *MV Cheynne*, contact Tony Palliser (see p. 55). The rare Rufous Bristlebird* occurs in **Coorong National Park**, a narrow series of coastal lagoons separated from the sea by the 130 km long Younghusband Peninsula, 185 km south of Adelaide. The bristlebird occurs alongside the old Melbourne Road south of Pipeclay Lake at Salt

Creek, along with Southern Scrub-Robin and Beautiful Firetail. The park is also good for Buff-banded Rail, and Baillon's, Australian and Spotless Crakes, and is one of the prime shorebird sites in Australia. Large numbers are usually present, especially during the summer (Dec–Mar), including Banded Stilts, and the best area is between Magrath Flat and Policeman's Point.

## FLEURIEU PENINSULA

This large windswept peninsula south of Adelaide is a good place to see Black-faced Cormorant, Cape Barren Goose and Hooded Plover*. In suitable weather conditions seawatching can be exceptional, with even species such as Light-mantled Albatross amongst the possibilities.

### Localised Australian Endemics

Black-faced Cormorant, Cape Barren Goose, Hooded Plover*.

### Other Australian Endemics

Pacific Gull*, Purple-crowned Lorikeet.

### Others

White-bellied Sea-Eagle, Wedge-tailed Eagle.

### Other Wildlife

Great white shark, southern right whale (Jun–Sep).

(In suitable conditions, usually during winter (May–Oct) westsouthwesterlies, possible seabirds include Black-browed, Shy and Yellow-nosed Albatrosses, Antarctic and Hall's* Giant Petrels, Southern Fulmar, Cape, Great-winged and White-headed Petrels, Fluttering Shearwater, and even rarities such as Royal*, Grey-headed* and Light-mantled Albatrosses.)

Cape Barren Goose occurs around **Lake Alexandrina**, alongside the track to Narrung from Meningie at the south end (especially around Poltallock), and alongside the Wellington–Milang Road at the north end (especially where the road runs close to the shore). Black-faced Cormorant and Pacific Gull* occur at **Port Elliot**, about 10 km east of Victor Harbor, and Hooded Plovers* inhabit wild **Waitpinga Beach**, 15 km southwest of Victor Harbor. Great white sharks are occasionally recorded offshore here, along with southern right whales. **Newland Head**, at the eastern end of Waitpinga Beach, is the top seawatching spot for birders based in the Adelaide area.

The rare Western Whipbird* has been recorded in dense mallee-heath at Cape du Couedic and West Bay in Flinders Chase National Park, at the western end of **Kangaroo Island**, which is accessible by air or ferry (from Port Adelaide and Cape Jervis, at the western tip of the Fleurieu Peninsula). The island also supports Bush Thick-knee, Rock Parrot, Southern Emuwren and Shy Hylacola. (Cape Barren Goose has been introduced.)

## ADELAIDE

The extensive St Kilda Saltworks and the surrounding saltbush and mangroves north of Adelaide support one of the greatest concentrations of waterbirds in Australia. It is possible to see about 130 species in a day here, including over 25 species of shorebird, Fairy Tern* and some superb landbirds, including Elegant Parrot and White-winged Fairywren. Thirty-four species of shorebird have been seen in a day, and 51 in total. Many of them are often present in amazing numbers, and up to 150,000 Banded and White-headed Stilts have been recorded in February and March, which is usually the peak time for these species. Rufous-necked Stints and Sharp-tailed Sandpipers winter in tens of thousands, and there are usually small numbers of these and many other species present through the summer. A day here and a day touring the other local wetlands should be enough to see most of the species listed below.

The Saltworks are only accessible with a key and permit holder, but access can usually be arranged through the South Australian Ornithological Association, c/o South Australian Museum, North Terrace, Adelaide, SA 5000, Australia.

### Localised Australian Endemics

Banded Lapwing, Elegant Parrot (Apr–Sep), Slender-billed Thornbill*.

### Other Australian Endemics

Blue-billed and Musk Ducks, Black Swan, Australian Shelduck, Chestnut Teal, Pink-eared Duck, Yellow-billed Spoonbill, Australian Crake, Black-tailed Native-hen, Sooty Oystercatcher, Banded Stilt, Red-necked Avocet, Red-capped Plover, Red-kneed Dotterel, Crested Pigeon, Red-rumped Parrot, White-winged and Superb Fairywrens, White-browed Scrubwren, Singing Honeyeater, Red Wattlebird, White-fronted Chat, Australian Reed-Warbler.

### Others

Hoary-headed Grebe, Little Pied, Pied and Little Black Cormorants, Australian Darter, Australian Shoveler, White-eyed Duck, Australian Ibis, Royal Spoonbill, Swamp Harrier, Little Eagle, Baillon's and Spotless Crakes, Purple Swamphen, Far Eastern Curlew*, Marsh and Terek Sandpipers, Great Knot, Rufous-necked Stint, Sharp-tailed Sandpiper, Pied Oystercatcher, White-headed Stilt, Black-fronted Dotterel, Great Crested-Tern, Caspian and Fairy* Terns, Fan-tailed Cuckoo, Sacred Kingfisher, Little Grassbird.

(Other species recorded here include Blue-winged Parrot and White-browed Woodswallow (Oct–Nov), as well as a long list of shorebirds including Long-toed Stint, Baird's and Pectoral Sandpipers, Red-necked Phalarope and a few hybrid Pectoral/Curlew Sandpipers. This hybrid was originally thought to be a new species by some experts and was named 'Cox's Sandpiper', even though the finder, John Cox, thought it was a hybrid and had to put up with the birds being given his name against his wishes. The welcome outcome of all this is that the next edition of *Shorebirds* will be even better than the first, because this hybrid will be replaced with Plains-wanderer*.)

## ADELAIDE AREA

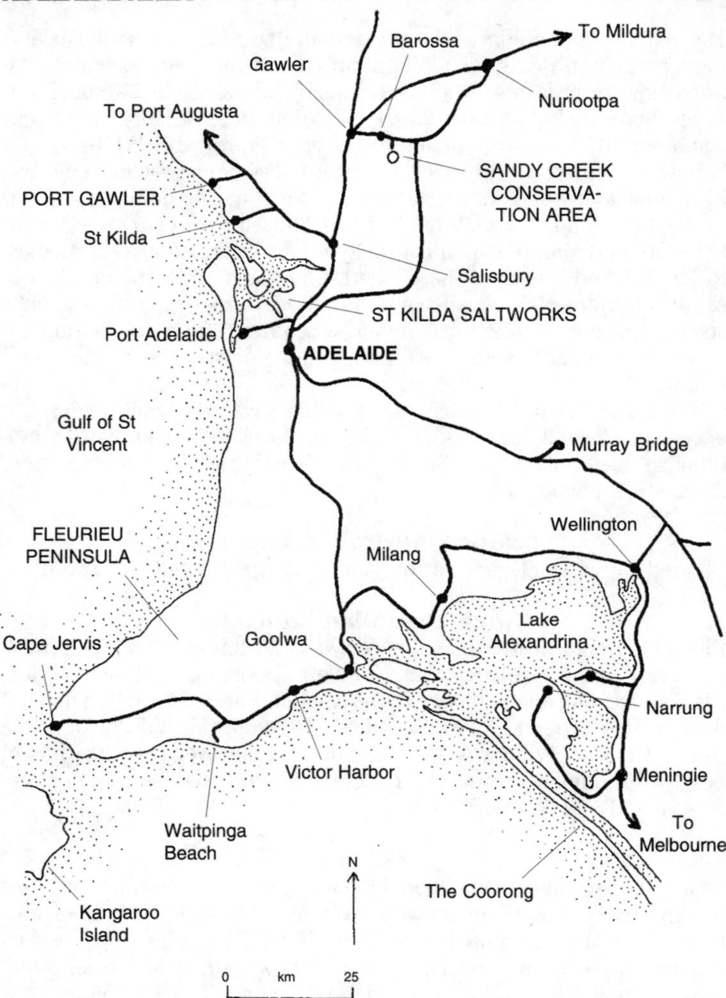


Some of the lagoons within the saltworks, 19 km northwest of the city, can be viewed from the surrounding roads, such as St Kilda, Plain and Thompson (off Port Wakefield Road) Roads, but this is a poor substitute for a long day inside the fence, preferably with a local birder who knows every nook and cranny. At low tide some of the shorebirds which feed in the saltworks fly out to the adjacent Gulf of St Vincent, joining Sooty Oystercatcher and many other waterbirds. Other sites in the Adelaide area worth visiting include Greenfields Nature Reserve, where Black-fronted Dotterel occurs. Banded Lapwing has been recorded alongside Waterloo Road, where a new reserve was being created in 1993.

Elegant (mainly Nov–Mar) and Rock Parrots, and Slender-billed Thornbill* (in the samphire flats) occur around **Port Gawler** and **Port Prime**, both of which can be covered in half a day from Adelaide. To reach Port Gawler, head north from Adelaide on the Prince's Highway towards Port Wakefield and turn west 5 km north of Virginia. Bird the samphire flats alongside this road and at the coast. To bird Port Prime, continue north along the Prince's Highway, turn left between Lower Light and Dublin and repeat the performance. The mixed forest in the small **Sandy Creek Conservation Area**, which is situated in the Barossa Valley 50 km northeast of Adelaide and is accessible via the Gawler–Nuriootpa Road, supports Elegant Parrot, Pallid Cuckoo, Rainbow Bee-eater (Sep–Apr), Weebill, Black-chinned and Brown-headed Honeyeaters, Red-capped Robin, Crested Shrike-tit, White-winged Chough, Dusky Woodswallow, White-winged Triller (Aug–Mar), White-backed Swallow and Diamond Firetail.

*Any birder with even the slightest interest in shorebirds should visit the St Kilda Saltworks near Adelaide, if only to see the huge mixed flocks of elegant Red-necked Avocets and Banded Stilts*

## BROKEN HILL

Although much of the extreme west of New South Wales is flat and arid, this is excellent birding country where birders with enough time have a fair chance of finding a number of outback nomads within 150 km of Broken Hill, including Black and Pied Honeyeaters, and Crimson and Orange Chats.

### Localised Australian Endemics

Grey Falcon*, Bourke's Parrot, Black and Pied Honeyeaters, Crimson and Orange Chats, Hall's and Chestnut-crowned Babblers, Chirruping Wedgebill.

### Other Australian Endemics

Emu, Australian Shelduck, Pink-eared Duck, Black Falcon, Little Button-quail, Black-tailed Native-hen, Bluebonnet, Mulga Parrot, Budgerigar, Pink Cockatoo*, Cockatiel, Red-backed Kingfisher, Variegated Fairy-wren, Southern Whiteface, Singing, White-fronted, Striped and Spiny-cheeked Honeyeaters, White-fronted Chat, Red-capped Robin, Crested Bellbird, Apostlebird, Little Raven, Masked and White-browed Wood-swallows, Ground Cuckoo-shrike, White-backed Swallow, Brown (Aug–Apr) and Rufous (Aug–Apr) Songlarks.

### Others

Hoary-headed Grebe, Wedge-tailed and Little Eagles, Australian Pratincole, Little Corella, Pallid Cuckoo, Australian Owlet-Nightjar, Spotted

Nightjar, Rainbow Bee-eater (Sep–Apr), Black-faced Woodswallow, White-winged Triller (Aug–Mar), Fairy Martin (Aug–Feb).

## Other Wildlife

Yellow-footed rock-wallaby.

Broken Hill is 517 km northeast of Adelaide. The large lakes, sandy savanna and open eucalypt woodlands in **Kinchega National Park** (440 sq km), on the west bank of the Darling River 111 km southeast of Broken Hill, support Black Falcon, Little Buttonquail, Spotted Nightjar, Crested Bellbird, Chirruping Wedgebill and White-backed Swallow. The park entrance is 2 km west of Menindee and the HQ 16 km further on. The dry sandstone ranges with wooded gullies, gibber and mulga in **Mootwingee National Park** (689 sq km), which is 135 km northeast of Broken Hill via the Silver City Highway Track, support Bourke's Parrot, Pink Cockatoo* and White-fronted Honeyeater, as well as the localised yellow-footed rock-wallaby. Homestead Creek is a particularly good area and Grey Falcon*, Black Honeyeater and Hall's Babbler have been recorded here. Black and Pied Honeyeaters, and Crimson and Orange Chats, are all, at the very least, occasional visitors to these two parks. Other sites worth birding in this region include the nationally important wetlands in **Currawinga National Park** and the woodland in **Pilliga State Forest**.

*Accommodation*: campsites.

The boundary of the huge (3106 sq km) **Sturt National Park** lies a little way north of Tibooburra, in the outback 337 km north of Broken Hill. At the HQ in Tibooburra check if it is OK to continue in a 2WD as it is not usually possible to do so after rain, and ask about any recent sightings of Grey Grasswrens* if you intend to look for these great rarities. At the park boundary just outside Tibooburra, Cinnamon Quail-thrush, as well as Rainbow Bee-eater (Sep–Apr) and White-winged Fairywren, occur along the Granites Nature Trail. Beyond here it may be worth stopping for a while where the Silver City Highway crosses Twelve Mile Creek, for if there has been enough rain there is often a marsh here which attracts Cockatiel, as well as Masked, White-browed and Black-faced Woodswallows. These beautiful birds also occur along the Jump Up Loop Trail, which leads from the park campsite at Olive Downs, but even they may be overshadowed here by the presence, in suitable conditions, of Pied Honeyeater and Crimson Chat. These are hard birds to see anywhere in Australia, but not as hard as Grey Grasswren*, which occurs in lignum clumps in the ephemeral maze of swamps that make up the **Bulloo Overflow** between Tibooburra and Thargomindah (see p. 157). To look for this great rarity, head back down the Silver City Highway and take the Wompah Gate Road towards Onepah and the border between New South Wales and Queensland. Six kilometres beyond the border, which is marked by a dog-fence, ask permission from the people at the old Pyampa property station to take a 15-minute walk to the windmill and bore, visible from the metal sheds alongside the track, followed by another 15-minute walk northeast to a stand of trees, cane grass and lignum where the elusive little tinker resides, along with Budgerigar, Redthroat, Crimson and Orange Chats, Chirruping Wedgebill, and Masked and Black-faced Woodswallows. Otherwise try heading for Tuerika Station, ask permission to camp, and drive towards Adelaide Gate. About 15 km south of Adelaide Gate try the lignum clumps at the creek crossing at dawn and dusk. The best time of year to visit this region is between May and September. Other species recorded in the vast expanse of hot, arid gibber in Sturt National Park include Letter-winged and Black-breasted Kites, Grey* and Black Falcons, Australian Bustard, Australian Pratincole, Inland Dotterel, Red-browed Pardalote and Desert Chat.

The wide beaches, sheltered bays, cliffs, saline lakes, and extensive heathlands and mallee in the spectacular **Innes National Park** at the tip of the Yorke Peninsula, west of Adelaide, support Rock Parrot and Western Whipbird*, as well as Malleefowl* (rangers may know where there is an active mound), Brush Bronzewing, Sooty Oystercatcher, Pacific Gull*, Rufous Fieldwren (around Cape Spencer lighthouse), Purple-gaped Honeyeater and Gilbert's Whistler. To look for Western Whipbird* take the track to West Cape for 300 m, climb up the dunes on the left and scour the vegetation on the dunes and in the bushy hollow below, or try 2.5 km south of Brown Lake or by the Loop camping area.

## EYRE PENINSULA

The remnant mallee on this large peninsula west of Port Augusta supports three species which are otherwise more or less confined to southwest Australia: Blue-breasted Fairywren, Grey-breasted Robin and Western Whipbird*, and the peninsula wetlands and beaches support a fine variety of waterbirds, including Cape Barren Goose and Hooded Plover*.

### Localised Australian Endemics

Cape Barren Goose, Hooded Plover*, Blue-breasted Fairywren, Purple-gaped Honeyeater, Grey-breasted Robin, Western Whipbird*, Chestnut Quail-thrush.

### Other Australian Endemics

Red-necked Avocet, Rock Parrot, White-browed Scrubwren (spotted *maculatus* form), Grey Currawong (brown *intermedia* form), Diamond Firetail.

(Other species recorded here include Freckled Duck*.)

The fairywren and robin occur at Lake Gilles Conservation Park, an area of mallee reached by turning north about 17 km east of Kimba. At the south end of the peninsula the fairywren, robin and whipbird occur in Lincoln National Park, southeast of Port Lincoln via Tulka, along with the *maculatus* form of White-browed Scrubwren, Chestnut Quail-thrush, the *intermedia* form of Grey Currawong and Diamond Firetail. About 21 km northwest of Port Lincoln the road to Elliston crosses Big Swamp, where Cape Barren Goose and Red-necked Avocet occur, and where Freckled Duck* has been recorded. Hooded Plover*, Rock Parrot and Blue-breasted Fairywren occur in Coffin Bay National Park, which can be reached by turning west 32 km northwest of Port Lincoln. The parrots and plovers feed around Point Avoid and the parrots roost on Golden Island, which is just offshore.

'Nullarbor Quail-thrush', the bright, black-breasted *alisteri* race of Cinnamon Quail-thrush, considered by some taxonomists to be a full species, occurs on the **Nullarbor Plain** and it can be found near Nullarbor Roadhouse on the Eyre Highway, 1088 km west of Adelaide. About 1 km east of the roadhouse turn north on to a rough track, continue parallel to a fence on the right for 6–7 km and explore the saltbush. Other species recorded here and elsewhere on the plain include Stubble Quail, Australian Bustard, Inland Dotterel, Banded Lapwing, the isolated *narethae* race of Bluebonnet, Pink Cockatoo* (Madura Roadhouse), Black-eared Cuckoo, White-winged Fairywren, Redthroat, Rufous Fieldwren, Shy Hylacola, Southern Scrub-Robin, Crested Bellbird and Brown Songlark (Aug–Apr).

The only place where the endemic Scarlet-chested Parrot* may be seen in Australia is in the **Great Victoria Desert**, and to look for this bird you will need (i) permission to pass through aboriginal land, obtainable from Maralinga Tjarutja Incorporated, Ceduna, SA (tel: 086 252 946), (ii) permission to enter the Unnamed Conservation Park, obtainable from National Parks and Wildlife Office, Ceduna, SA, (iii) a 4WD vehicle (in a convoy if possible) and (iv) the full set of equipment needed for traversing one of the wildest places on earth, including some form of communication with the outside world. Birders have broken down here in the past and been lucky to survive, because few people venture this far into the outback, and it may be weeks before another vehicle passes by. Let someone reliable in Cook know your planned return date. To reach the best area, turn north off the Eyre Highway 42 km west of Nullarbor Roadhouse and head to Cook. North of here the track deteriorates rapidly and it takes up to ten hours hard driving (255 km) to reach Vokes Hill Corner, which is also accessible from Perth to the west and Coober Pedy to the east. This is where the parrots are most likely to be seen, especially alongside the track up to 10 km to the south, and up to 52 km along the Beadle Highway to the west. Other species to look out for include Ground Cuckoo-shrike, White-browed Treecreeper, Slaty-backed Thornbill and Crimson Chat.

## *WESTERN AUSTRALIA*

Malleefowl*, Blue-breasted Fairywren, Grey-breasted Robin and Chestnut Quail-thrush, as well as the isolated *narethae* race of Bluebonnet, Mulga Parrot and Pink Cockatoo* occur around **Eyre Bird Observatory**, which is situated about 50 km southeast of Cocklebiddy and well signposted from the Eyre Highway about 16 km east of there (about 450 km west of Nullarbor Roadhouse). Parts of the rough entrance track may only be passable in a 4WD, so contact the warden before tackling it. Accommodation (A) can be booked in advance by contacting The Wardens, Eyre Bird Observatory, Cocklebiddy, via Norseman, WA 6443 (tel: 090 39 3450, fax: 090 39 3440). Near Esperance, 641 km west of Cocklebiddy, over 10,000 Banded Stilts and up to 240 Hooded Plovers* have been recorded at **Lake Warden Nature Reserve** (just north of Esperance), and many Banded Stilts and up to 390 Hooded Plovers* have been recorded on **Lake Gore**, the highest number ever recorded at one site. To reach Lake Gore, turn

## SOUTHWEST AUSTRALIA

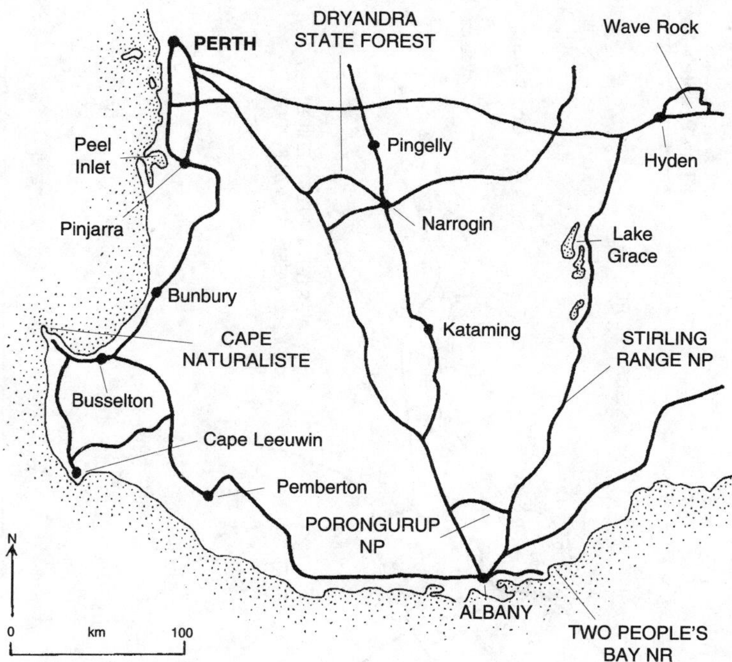


south off the South Coast Highway about 35 km west of Esperance on to McCall's Road, then follow this to the end and explore.

The rare Western Bristlebird* and Western Whipbird* occur in **Fitzgerald River National Park**, along with Southern Emuwren and mallee specialists such as the Shy Hylacola, Purple-gaped Honeyeater and Southern Scrub-Robin. Ask at the park HQ, along Hamersley Drive about 10 km west of Hopetown, for details of the latest sightings and best places to see these birds.

## TWO PEOPLE'S BAY NATURE RESERVE

The coastal heathland in this important 46 sq km reserve, 40 km east of Albany, supports three very rare and elusive birds: Noisy Scrub-bird*, Western Bristlebird* and Western Whipbird*, as well as other heathland specialities such as Southern Emuwren.

### Localised Australian Endemics

Red-capped Parrot, Western Rosella, Slender-billed Black-Cockatoo*, Noisy Scrub-bird*, Red-winged Fairywren, Western Bristlebird*, Western Spinebill, Little Wattlebird, White-breasted Robin, Western Whipbird*, Red-eared Firetail*.

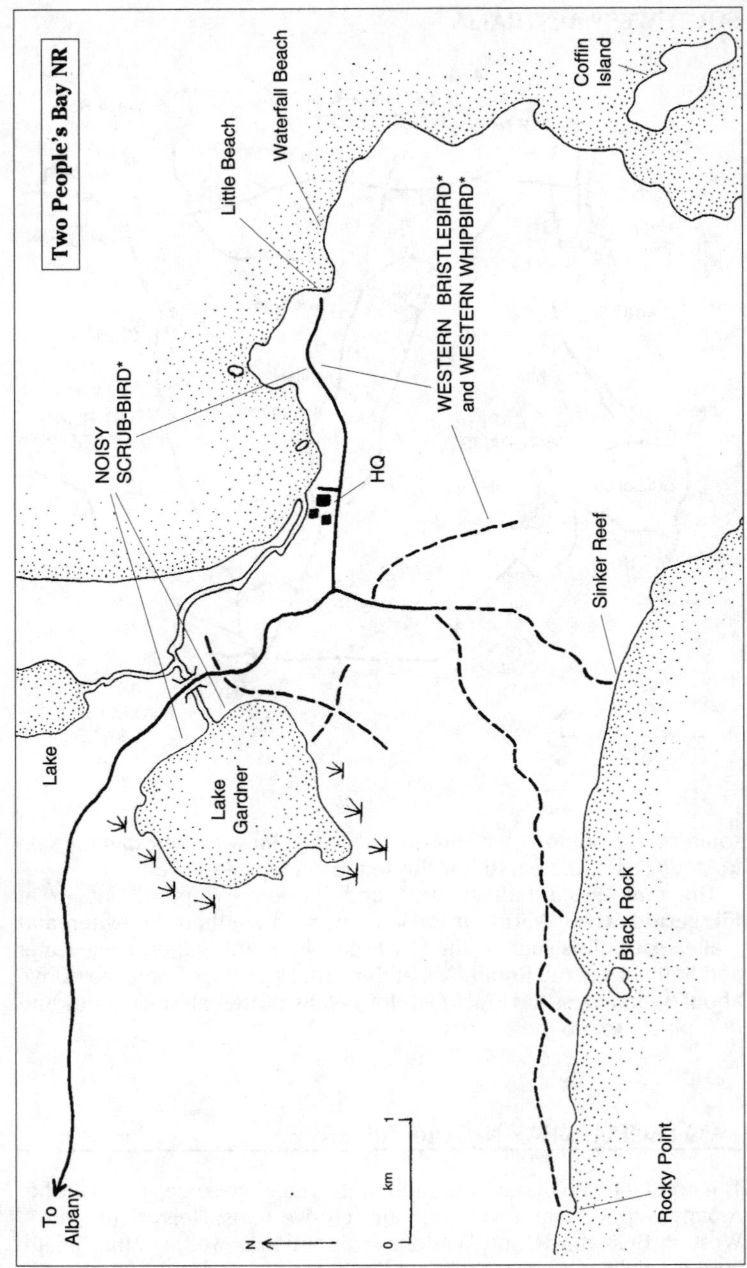


## Other Australian Endemics

Sooty Oystercatcher, Red-necked Avocet, Red-capped Plover, Pacific Gull*, Common and Brush Bronzewings, Crested Pigeon, Rock Parrot, Tawny Frogmouth, Splendid Fairywren, Southern Emuwren, Spotted Pardalote, Rufous Fieldwren, Shy Hylacola, Yellow-rumped Thornbill,

White-naped, New Holland, White-cheeked and Tawny-crowned Honeyeaters, Red Wattlebird, Australian Raven, Grey Butcherbird, Grey Currawong.

## Others

Australian Gannet, White-bellied Sea-Eagle, Brown Falcon, Australian Kestrel, Brown Quail, Grey-tailed Tattler, Pied Oystercatcher, Silver Gull, Great Crested-Tern, Caspian Tern, Spotted Nightjar, Golden Whistler, Willie-wagtail, Australasian Magpie, Magpie-lark, Black-faced Cuckoo-shrike, Welcome Swallow.

## Other Wildlife

Carpet python, short-nosed bandicoot, western grey kangaroo.

(Other species recorded here include Australasian Bittern* and Square-tailed Kite*. Possible seabirds include Yellow-nosed Albatross, and Southern and South Polar Skuas, while the offshore islands support breeding Little Penguin, Great-winged Petrel, Flesh-footed and Little Shearwaters, and White-faced Storm-Petrel. Introduced species include Laughing Kookaburra.)

To reach the reserve turn south off the South Coast Highway just west of King River. Noisy Scrub-bird*, Western Bristlebird* and Western Whip-bird* are all extremely difficult species to see. Their position can be located fairly easily during the breeding season (Apr–Sep) when they are singing, especially the aptly-named Noisy Scrub-bird*, but to stand a chance of glimpsing one of these super skulkers it is best to ask the rangers where the best sites are and make sure you are in position at dawn. Expect a frustrating time and under no circumstances attempt to tape any of them out! The rangers may say something along the following lines; the scrub-bird occurs between the entrance road and Lake Gardner, and, along with the bristlebird and whipbird, in the heath and scrub above Little Beach car park, which is probably the best area to concentrate your efforts on. Drive into this car park at dawn, park so that the vehicle is facing back up the slope and look out for bristlebirds running across the road to the traffic island where they have been known to show relatively well in the small bushes. The bristlebirds also occur alongside the track to and in the vicinity of the toilets at the beach. Seawatching off Little Beach in onshore winds may produce a variety of seabirds. Another area worth trying for the whipbird is alongside the track to Sinker's Reef. They occur near the beach along with Red-capped and Rock Parrots. If all else fails the rangers may suggest visiting Waychinicup, an hour or so by road east of Albany and a good site for all three rarities.

*Accommodation:* Albany—Havana Chalets, Emu Beach (Rock Parrot).

Between Two People's Bay and Albany it is worth checking the **Kalgan River Estuary** for Banded Stilts. In Albany Rock Parrots are possible, Southern Skuas can usually be found wintering (Apr–Sep) in the docks and the natural harbour also supports Great Knot and Pied and Sooty Oystercatchers. 'The Gap' and, to a lesser extent, 'The Blowholes', two popular tourist spots in **Torndirrup National Park**, 16 km south of Albany, are two of the best seawatching sites in southwest Australia, especially in strong southwesterlies when pelagic possibilities include

Royal*, Grey-headed* and Yellow-nosed Albatrosses, Soft-plumaged Petrel, Flesh-footed and Hutton's* Shearwaters, Pacific Gull*, Great Crested-Tern, and Southern and South Polar Skuas.

## THE COAST BETWEEN ALBANY AND PERTH

Any birders who can conjure up the time to drive leisurely between Perth and Albany via the scenic coastal route may be rewarded with a wonderful variety of birds along the way. The rich diversity of habitats here in the extreme southwest corner of Australia, including ocean, beaches, heathlands, forests, lakes, swamps and estuaries, supports all sorts of stunning birds, from Red-tailed Tropicbird to Regent Parrot.

### Localised Australian Endemics

Hooded Plover*, Banded Lapwing, Regent Parrot, Red-eared Firetail*.

### Other Australian Endemics

Australian Shelduck, Maned Duck, Chestnut Teal, Pacific Heron, Yellow-billed Spoonbill, Australian Crake, Sooty Oystercatcher, Banded Stilt, Red-necked Avocet, Red-capped Plover, Red-kneed Dotterel, Pacific Gull*, Common and Brush Bronzewings, Crested Pigeon, Rock Parrot, Splendid Fairywren, Southern Emuwren, Spotted Pardalote, Rufous Fieldwren, White-fronted Chat.

### Non-endemic Specialities

Red-tailed Tropicbird.

### Others

Little Penguin, Hoary-headed Grebe, Australian Shoveler, White-eyed Duck, Straw-necked Ibis, Swamp Harrier, Collared Sparrowhawk, Buff-banded Rail, Baillon's and Spotless Crakes, Purple Swamphen, Black-fronted Dotterel, Bridled and Fairy* Terns, Black-faced Woodswallow.

### Other Wildlife

Australian sealion, tiger snake.

(Other species recorded here include Royal Albatross*, Freckled Duck*, and Black-backed and Australasian* Bitterns.)

Ten kilometres west of Albany, alongside the road to Elleker, there is a nature reserve at **Grasmere Lake** which supports a wide variety of waterbirds, as well as Splendid Fairywren, Southern Emuwren and Rufous Fieldwren. When the water levels are low, this is a cracking place for crakes. Along the coast Hooded Plover* occurs on **Ocean Beach**, 8 km south of Denmark (which is 55 km west of Albany), with Pacific Gull*, while seawatching from here has produced Royal Albatross*. Between Cape Leeuwin and Cape Naturaliste, Rock Parrot and Southern Emuwren occur at **Hamelin Bay**, by the trail along the cliffs left of the car park which also looks over a Bridled Tern colony on Hamelin Island. A few kilometres south of **Cape Naturaliste**, 40 km northwest of Busselton, there is a small Red-tailed Tropicbird colony on Sugarloaf Rock, which lies about 50 m offshore. These lovely birds are probably present all year round, but their numbers appear to peak between December and February. Look for them around the rock or on the water further out to sea, and, in winter, remember there may be other seabirds around. The **Vasse** and **Wannerup Estuaries** along Layman's Road 10 km east of Busselton support numerous waterbirds. Freckled Duck* and both bitterns have bred at **Benger Swamp**, at the end of Swamp Road, off Route 20 in Benger near Bunbury (beware of tiger snakes). Between Bunbury and Perth it is worth stopping at **Peel Inlet**, one of the most important wetlands in southwest Australia, and nearby **Preston Lake**, south of Mandurah, where the masses of waterbirds usually include Banded Stilt, Red-necked Avocet, Red-kneed Dotterel and Banded Lapwing, and rarities such as Freckled Duck* are possible. The north, east and south shores of this estuary, accessible via Coodanup, Yunderup and Pinjarra, respectively, are usually the best. From the old coast road which enables access to the west shore, head north towards Perth and turn west onto Safety Road East just north of Lake Walyungap to look for Regent Parrots, which are possible on the farm to the north just west of the old coast road. Continue west, over the new Mandurah–Perth Highway, for several kilometres to **Rockingham** where, at the southwest end of Arcadia Drive, it is possible to join organised boat trips to Penguin Island. Little Penguins breed here (mainly Sep–Nov), in the boulders along the southeast coast, and other species present include Buff-banded Rail, and Bridled and Fairy* Terns, as well as Australian sea-lions.

## PORONGURUP AND STIRLING RANGES

Although the inland road route between Albany and Perth does not offer the opportunity to see such a wealth of birds as the coastal route, the towering 'Karri' forests and heathlands of the Porongurup and Stirling ranges do support such localised southwestern endemics as Rufous Treecreeper and Western Thornbill.

### Localised Australian Endemics

Western Rosella, Elegant Parrot, White-tailed* and Slender-billed* Black-Cockatoos, Rufous Treecreeper, Blue-breasted Fairywren, Western Thornbill, Purple-gaped Honeyeater, Western Spinebill, Grey-breasted and White-breasted Robins, Red-eared Firetail*.

### Other Australian Endemics

Purple-crowned Lorikeet, Southern Emuwren, White-naped, White-cheeked and Tawny-crowned Honeyeaters, Southern Scrub-Robin.

### Others

Australian Owlet-Nightjar, Spotted Nightjar.

The towering 'karri' trees in the wet sclerophyll forests of **Porongurup National Park**, 45 km north of Albany via Chester Pass Road and Napier, support Rufous Treecreepers. If they fail to appear on the trees, try the tables at the Tree in the Rock picnic site. This is situated at the end of Bolganup Road which is about 7 km northwest of Napier *en route* to Mount Barker. This park also supports Western Rosella, Blue-breasted Fairywren, Western Thornbill, White-breasted Robin and Red-eared Firetail*. The granite outcrops of the Porongurup Range rise to 670 m (2198 ft), but the **Stirling Range**, all of which also lies within a National Park about 40 km north of Napier, rises to 1073 m (3520 ft) at Bluff Knoll. Western Thornbill occurs north of the creek on the east side of the road at Gold Holes, about 5 km south of the Visitor Centre (tel: 098 279230) which is on Chester Pass Road. Spotted Nightjar has been recorded along the road north of here. The ranger's house is further north at the junction of Chester Pass Road and Bluff Knoll Road. Purple-crowned Lorikeet and Australian Owlet-Nightjar occur around the house and along the trail through the heath which begins behind the house it is possible to see Blue-breasted Fairywren, as well as Elegant Parrot and Southern Emuwren. The fairywren may also be found south of Bluff Knoll Road, between 500 m and 1 km east of the junction where the ranger's house is.

The road north from the Stirling Range to **Lake Grace** passes a number of saline lakes where Banded Stilt, Red-necked Avocet and Banded Lapwing occur. **Wave Rock**, an overhanging 13 m (42 ft) high cliff of smooth granite near Hyden, 200 km northeast of Narrogin and 310 km east of Perth, is a popular tourist attraction and in the general area it is also possible to see Western Rosella, Elegant Parrot, Blue-breasted Fairywren, White-eared and Spiny-cheeked Honeyeaters, Crested Bellbird, White-browed Babbler and White-backed Swallow. The areas known as The Humps and King Rocks, north of Wave Rock, are the best for birding. This site is on the edge of the mulga country fringing the out-back and by driving east on the track towards **Norseman** species such as Australian Bustard, Mulga Parrot, Shy Hylacola, White-fronted Honeyeater, Gilbert's Whistler, Chestnut Quail-thrush, Black-faced Woodswallow and Brown Songlark become possibilities.

## DRYANDRA STATE FOREST

Over 100 species have been recorded in the open wandoo woodlands of this important reserve, 165 km southeast of Perth, including Malleefowl*, Rufous Treecreeper and the western race of Crested Shrike-tit, as well as the rare numbat, a tiny marsupial anteater.

### Localised Australian Endemics

Malleefowl*, Regent and Red-capped Parrots, Western Rosella, Elegant Parrot, Rufous Treecreeper, Blue-breasted Fairywren, Western Thornbill, Western Spinebill.

### Other Australian Endemics

Maned Duck, Common and Brush Bronzewings, Port Lincoln Parrot, Galah, Purple-crowned Lorikeet, Southern Boobook, Tawny Frogmouth, Splendid Fairywren, Striated Pardalote, White-browed Scrubwren, Chestnut-rumped Thornbill, Weebill, Western Gerygone, Singing, Yellow-plumed, White-naped, Brown-headed, New Holland and White-cheeked Honeyeaters, Red-capped and Hooded Robins, Crested Shrike-tit (western *leucogaster* race), White-browed Babbler, Dusky Wood-swallow, Grey Currawong, Rufous Songlark (Aug–Apr).

### Others

Collared Sparrowhawk, Wedge-tailed Eagle, Brown Falcon, Australian Kestrel, Painted Buttonquail, Bush Thick-knee, Pallid Cuckoo, Rainbow Bee-eater (Sep–Apr), Brown Honeyeater, Scarlet Robin, Varied Sittella, Golden Whistler, Grey Shrike-Thrush, Grey Fantail, Restless Flycatcher, Tree Martin.

### Other Wildlife

Brush-tailed bettong, common ringtail possum, numbat (rare), red-tailed phascogale, tammar (rare) and western brush wallabies, western grey kangaroo.

(Other species recorded here include Square-tailed Kite*, Little Buttonquail and Black Honeyeater.)

This reserve is 32 km northwest of Narrogin, about 25 km south of the Wandering–Pingelly Road. Head along Kawana Road to the forest village which lies at the centre of a web of tracks, most of which are worth birding. The best one for numbat is the Ochre Trail.

## PERTH

It is possible to see well over 100 species in a day in and around this large city on the Swan River, including over ten of the species which are restricted to southwest Australia and a wide variety of waterbirds.

### Localised Australian Endemics

Banded Lapwing, Red-capped Parrot, Western Rosella, Elegant Parrot, White-tailed* and Slender-billed* Black-Cockatoos, Western Corella*, Red-winged Fairywren, Western Spinebill, Little Wattlebird, White-breasted Robin, Red-eared Firetail*.

### Other Australian Endemics

Blue-billed and Musk Ducks, Black Swan, Australian Shelduck, Maned and Pink-eared Ducks, Australian Kite, Australian Crake, Black-tailed Native-hen, Banded Stilt, Red-necked Avocet, Red-capped Plover, Red-kneed Dotterel, Common Bronzewing, Port Lincoln and Rock Parrots, Galah, White-winged and Splendid Fairywrens, Striated Pardalote, White-browed Scrubwren, Yellow-rumped Thornbill, Weebill, Western Gerygone, Singing, New Holland and White-cheeked Honeyeaters, Red Wattlebird, White-fronted Chat, Red-capped Robin, Australian Raven, Grey Butcherbird.

### Others

Australasian and Hoary-headed Grebes, Australian Gannet, Little Pied and Little Black Cormorants, Australian Darter, Australian Pelican, Australian Shoveler, White-eyed Duck, White-faced Heron, Rufous Night-Heron, Australian Ibis, Swamp Harrier, Australian Hobby, Buff-banded Rail, Baillon's and Spotless Crakes, Dusky Moorhen, Purple Swamphen, Far Eastern Curlew*, Grey-tailed Tattler, Great Knot, Rufous-necked and Long-toed Stints, Sharp-tailed Sandpiper, Pacific Golden-Plover, Greater Sandplover, Black-fronted Dotterel, Silver Gull, Caspian Tern, Great

**PERTH**

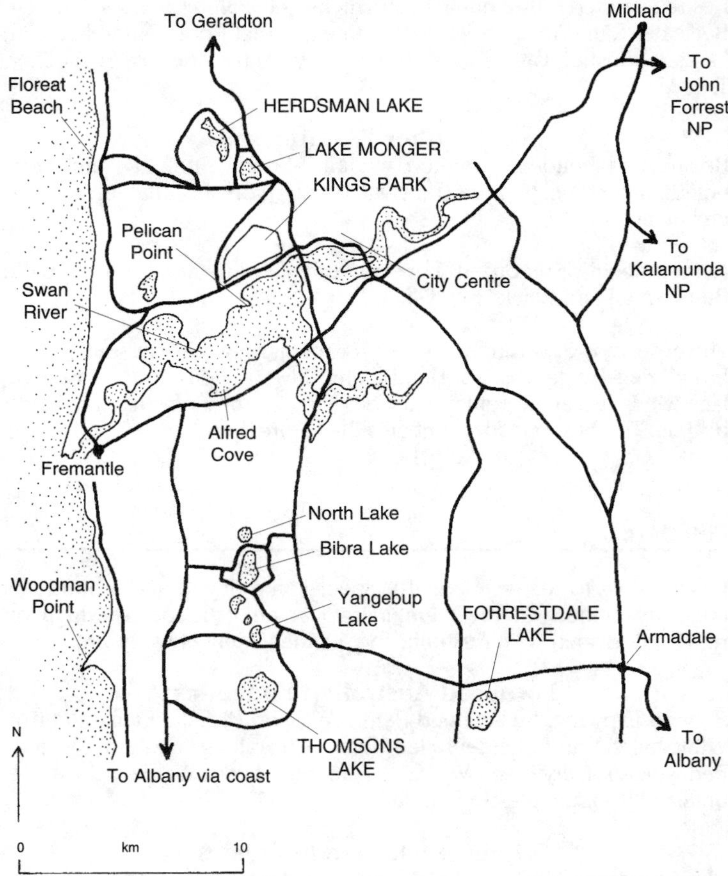


Crested-Tern, Bridled (Nov–Mar) and Fairy* Terns, Southern Skua, Rainbow Lorikeet, Pallid Cuckoo, Sacred Kingfisher (Sep–Apr), Rainbow Bee-eater (Sep–Apr), Brown Honeyeater, Scarlet Robin, Varied Sittella, Golden and Rufous Whistlers, Willie-wagtail, Grey Fantail, Australasian Magpie, Magpie-lark, Black-faced Cuckoo-shrike (Sep–Apr), Welcome Swallow, Tree Martin (Sep–Apr), Australian Reed-Warbler, Little Grassbird.

## Other Wildlife

Black-gloved wallaby, quokka, tiger snake.

(Other species recorded here include Freckled Duck*, and Black-backed and Australasian* Bitterns. Seawatching, mainly between May and September, has produced Wandering*, Black-browed, Shy and Yellow-nosed Albatrosses, Antarctic Giant Petrel, Cape Petrel, Wedge-tailed Shearwater, Wilson's Storm-Petrel and Red-tailed Tropicbird (Rottnest Island). Introduced species include Laughing Kookaburra.)

The semi-natural **King's Park**, 2 km west of the city centre on the north side of the Swan River, supports a fine selection of birds, including Western Rosella, White-tailed Black-Cockatoo*, Rainbow Bee-eater, Western Thornbill, Little Wattlebird and Western Spinebill. Concentrate on the area around the botanic gardens. **Pelican Point** to the south of King's Park is a good spot for shorebirds and terns, but **Alfred Cove**, on the opposite shore of the Swan River, is better, especially at Point Waylen, accessible via Burke Drive. To the south of here there are a number of lakes worth birding, including **Thomsons Lake**, which lies within a nature reserve 34 km southwest of the city centre on Russell Road in Success. Red-capped Parrot occurs in the woodland here, along with tiger snakes. **Forrestdale Lake**, another nature reserve, off Moore Street in Forrestdale, is also worth a look. Fairy Tern* occurs off **Woodman Point**, also in the southern suburbs. The 11 km long **Rottnest Island**, a popular tourist destination 19 km offshore and accessible by ferry from Fremantle, supports Banded Stilt, Red-necked Avocet (both on saline lakes), Banded Lapwing, Bridled Tern, Rock Parrot, a subspecies of Singing Honeyeater and Red-capped Robin, which is rare on mainland southwest Australia, as well as a small wallaby known as quokka. In winter it is worth looking for seabirds from the ferry and Cape Vlaming at the western end of the island. Private vehicles are not allowed on Rottnest and the best way to get around is by bicycle, although there is also a bus service. The island is surrounded by limestone reefs which make excellent snorkelling or scuba-diving sites. North of Perth city centre and the Swan River there are two other lakes well worth visiting. **Lake Monger** is a good site for Blue-billed Duck and Western Corella* (at southern end), and nearby **Herdsman Lake**, where there is an excellent visitor centre, supports a fine range of waterbirds which, in suitable conditions, have included both bitterns, plenty of crakes and shorebirds such as Banded Stilt, Red-necked Avocet and Red-kneed Dotterel. The White-winged Fairywren is localised in southwest Australia, but it does occur in the scrub to the south of Dog Beach car park at **Floreat Beach**, west of Herdsman Lake. The forested Darling Range, east of the city, supports White-tailed Black-Cockatoo* and

**ROTTNEST ISLAND**

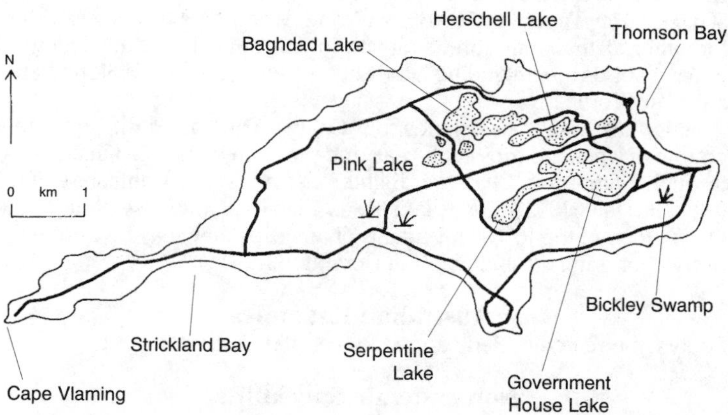

black-gloved wallaby, both of which occur around **Mundaring Weir** in Kalamunda National Park. In August 1996 the first **Perth Pelagic** took place, producing Kerguelen and Soft-plumaged Petrels. Local birders hope to run regular trips from Hillarys Boat Harbour using Mill's Charters. For more information contact Tony Palliser (see Sydney Pelagics, p. 55).

The small **Yanchep National Park**, about 50 km north of Perth, is a good site for White-winged Fairywren which occurs in the coastal heath and scrub north of Leeman's Landing at Two Rocks Beach, accessible via Yanchep Beach and Two Rocks Roads. Other species recorded here include Red-capped Plover, Bridled Tern (Nov–Mar), Inland Thornbill, Tawny-crowned Honeyeater, Black-faced and Dusky Woodswallows, and White-backed Swallow.

*The lazy but buoyant flight of the White-tailed Black-Cockatoo* is typical of all the large black-cockatoos of Australia*

## HOUTMAN ABROLHOS ISLANDS

This small archipelago of low-lying islands, 64 km west of Geraldton on Australia's west coast, supports masses of breeding seabirds, including 500,000 Sooty Terns, 260,000 Brown Noddies and 70,000 Lesser Noddies, the latter at their only breeding site in Australia. There are plenty of other seabirds too, including Little Shearwater, White-faced Storm-Petrel and Fairy Tern*.

Few boats visit these islands, but Coate's Tours in Perth organise a couple of weekend trips each year, and they can be booked in advance through Naturetrek, Chautara, Bighton, Nr Alresford, Hampshire SO24 9RB, UK (tel: 01962 733051, fax: 01962 733368). Otherwise write to the Perth office of the RAOU for details of any trips they may be arranging, or try chartering a fishing boat in Geraldton.

### Australian Endemics

Sooty Oystercatcher, Red-capped Plover, Pacific Gull*

### Non-endemic Specialities

Lesser Noddy (Sep–Mar).

### Others

Wedge-tailed (Sep–Mar) and Little (Aug–Dec) Shearwaters, White-faced Storm-Petrel (Aug–Feb), White-bellied Sea-Eagle, Buff-banded Rail, Spotless Crake, Far Eastern Curlew*, Grey-tailed Tattler, Great Knot, Rufous-necked and Long-toed Stints, Sharp-tailed Sandpiper, Pied Oystercatcher, Greater Sandplover, Silver Gull, Caspian Tern, Great Crested-Tern, Roseate, Bridled, Sooty and Fairy* Terns, Brown Noddy.

### Other Wildlife

Australian sea-lion, bottle-nosed dolphin.

The islands are accessible from Geraldton (contact Greenough Tourist Bureau on freecall 008 014 700), which is 485 km north of Perth. The sea crossing, which can be very rough, usually takes three hours, and the islands are often windy and cool. **Pelsaert Island**, the most southerly of the group, supports the greatest variety and largest numbers of seabirds, including White-faced Storm-Petrel, Bridled, Sooty and Fairy* Terns, and Brown and Lesser Noddies. The latter breeds in mangroves at the north end of the island and also on Wooded and Morley Islands.

The mulga either side of **Route 123** east of Geraldton, between Mullewa and Mount Magnet, and south of Mount Magnet alongside the Great Northern Highway to Paynes Find and Dalwallinu, supports Bourke's Parrot, Redthroat, Slaty-backed Thornbill, Pied and Grey Honeyeaters, Crested Bellbird, the western *marginatum* form of Chestnut-breasted Quail-thrush (also around Mount Magnet golf course) and Ground Cuckoo-shrike. The wide, usually dry, creek on the north side of Route 123, 99 km west of Mount Magnet, is one of the few sites where Grey Honeyeater has been recorded.

## KALBARRI NATIONAL PARK

The heathland in this large coastal park 130 km north of Geraldton supports one of the richest floras in Australia. The peak time to observe the profusion of plants, their fancy flowers and the birds which are attracted to them, is from August to November, and at this time nomadic nectar-lovers such as Black and Pied Honeyeaters are often present.

### Localised Australian Endemics

Blue-breasted Fairywren, Black (nomadic) and Pied (nomadic) Honeyeaters.

### Other Australian Endemics

Sooty Oystercatcher, Red-tailed Black-Cockatoo, White-cheeked, White-fronted, Tawny-crowned and Spiny-cheeked Honeyeaters, Crimson Chat (nomadic), Red-capped and Hooded Robins, Crested Bellbird, Masked Woodswallow (nomadic).

### Others

Bridled Tern, Rainbow Bee-eater (Sep–Apr).

Bird alongside the Ajana–Kalbarri Road which runs through the park and its side tracks, especially those to Hawks Head and Ross Graham Lookout, both of which overlook the 80 km-long Murchison River Gorge.

**Shark Bay**, south of Carnarvon, is a World Heritage Area rich in cetaceans such as bottle-nosed dolphin, dugong, humpback whale (Jun–Oct) and whale shark (Apr–Jun), as well as manta ray, terrestrial mammals such as banded hare-wallaby, burrowing bettong and western barred bandicoot, and the most ancient form of life on earth—colonies of blue-green algae known as stromatolites. The western *textilis* race of Thick-billed Grasswren* occurs on the **Peron Peninsula**, which penetrates the middle of Shark Bay, along with Pied (nomadic) and White-fronted Honeyeaters, Chiming Wedgebill and Mangrove Fantail. The grasswren occurs around the '26th Parallel' signpost 10 km south of Denham, which is 135 km west of the North West Coastal Highway from the Overlander Roadhouse on the road to Monkey Mia. It also occurs just to the east of Denham. Turn left to a lagoon here and park by the first bend in the track, then walk along the track to the right which leads back to the Monkey Mia road. This secretive species is most likely to be seen at both sites at dawn or dusk. At **Monkey Mia**, 26 km east of Denham, it is possible to swim with bottle-nosed dolphins as Fairy Terns* fly overhead. To the west of the Peron Peninsula lies **Dirk Hartog Island** where the black-and-white *leucopterus* race of White-winged Fairywren occurs.

Slender-billed Thornbill*, as well as Dusky Gerygone and Orange Chat, have been recorded at the samphire flats and mangroves to the south of New Beach, reached by turning left off the North West Coastal Highway about 40 km south of **Carnarvon**. The beach, mudflats and mangroves at the harbour 2 km southwest of Carnarvon town centre support Grey-tailed Tattler, Great Knot, Fairy Tern* and Dusky Gerygone. The nomadic Crimson Chat, as well as White-winged Fairywren and Chiming Wedgebill, have been recorded along the road to Rocky Pool, reached by turning east off the main highway 7 km north of Carnarvon, then left after about 38 km. Further north, *en route* to Cape Range National Park, Roseate, Bridled and Fairy* Terns can be seen off **Coral Bay** which lies close to the Ningaloo Reef, an excellent offshore snorkelling spot.

## CAPE RANGE NATIONAL PARK

The rugged gorges in this coastal reserve supports a number of outback specialities whose ranges stretch to the west coast of Australia, including Western Bowerbird and Rufous-crowned Emuwren.

### Localised Australian Endemics

Western Bowerbird, Rufous-crowned Emuwren, Pied Honeyeater (nomadic), Chiming Wedgebill, Spinifex-bird, Painted Firetail.

### Other Australian Endemics

Spinifex Pigeon, Red-backed Kingfisher, Red-browed Pardalote, Grey-headed Honeyeater, Masked and Little Woodswallows.

### Others

Black-eared Cuckoo, Australian Owlet-Nightjar.

### Other Wildlife

Black-footed rock wallaby, humpback whale, leatherback (Feb–Mar) and loggerhead (Feb–Mar) turtles.

Bird the Shothole Canyon Road approach near Exmouth, 371 km north of Carnarvon. Rufous-crowned Emuwren occurs around the second creek along here, beyond the first car park. Western Bowerbird frequents the area 100 m behind the information board at the park entrance and the camping area at Yardie Creek where the nearby gorge is a good site for black-footed rock wallaby. Pied Honeyeater has been recorded on Vlaming Head and humpback whale off it.

Black-breasted Kite, Spinifex Pigeon, Blue-winged Kookaburra, Red-backed Kingfisher, Black-tailed Treecreeper, Painted Firetail and Star Finch* have been recorded at the **Ashburton River Crossing** on the North West Coastal Highway, and Black Bittern, Painted Firetail and Star Finch* at **Maitland River and Mairee Pool**, a camping area which is well signposted off the North West Coastal Highway about 60 km west of Roebourne. From nearby Dampier it may be possible to visit **Barrow Island**, where the black-and-white *leucopterus* race of White-winged Fairywren occurs. White-breasted Whistler, as well as Dusky Gerygone, Mangrove Robin, Black-tailed Whistler, Mangrove Fantail, Shining Flycatcher, Australian Yellow White-eye, Painted Firetail and Star Finch*, have been recorded in the mangroves by the bridge over the wide creek about 2 km south of **Point Samson**, 19 km north of Roebourne. The south side of the creek on the east side of the road is the best area for the birds *and* millions of mosquitoes.

## BROOME

The small town of Broome is about as far away from the other major centres in Australia as it is possible to get: 2248 km north of Perth and 1865 km west of Darwin, to be exact. It lies at the north end of Roebuck Bay and Eighty Mile Beach, where up to 850,000 shorebirds may be present at peak times, the fifth highest concentration on earth. These birds are supported by extensive areas of mud exposed at low tide, thanks to the rare combination of a gently sloping shoreline and a huge tidal range, which averages around 8 m (26 ft). The majority of birds are Bar-tailed Godwits, Great and Red Knots, Rufous-necked Stints and Curlew Sandpipers, but this selection of Siberian shorebirds also includes added attractions such as Asian Dowitcher*, Oriental Plover and Common Redshank, which is so rare elsewhere in the country that many Australian listers have had to make a pilgrimage to Broome where they are almost annual.

### Localised Australian Endemics

Dusky Gerygone, White-breasted Whistler.

### Other Australian Endemics

Little Buttonquail, White-gaped and Grey-headed Honeyeaters, Black-tailed Whistler, Australian Yellow White-eye, Brown and Rufous Song-larks.

## Non-endemic Specialities

Asian Dowitcher*, Yellow-tinted Honeyeater.

## Others

Lesser Frigatebird, Brown Quail, Brolga, Bar-tailed Godwit, Little and Far Eastern* Curlews, Common Redshank (scarce), Great and Red Knots, Sanderling, Rufous-necked Stint, Sharp-tailed, Curlew and Broad-billed Sandpipers, Australian Pratincole, Oriental Plover, Mangrove Gerygone, Red-headed Myzomela, Lemon-bellied Flycatcher (*tormenti* race), Mangrove Fantail.

(Other species recorded here include Letter-winged and Square-tailed* Kites, Grey Falcon*, Red-backed and Red-chested Buttonquails, Swinhoe's Snipe (Oct–Apr), Black, Pied and White-fronted Honeyeaters, Barn Swallow, Yellow Wagtail, Painted Firetail, Pictorella Munia*.)

Eighty Mile Beach is accessible from the Great Northern Highway between Port Hedland and Broome, but one of the best places to see shorebirds is by **Broome Bird Observatory**, which can be reached by turning south 9 km east of Broome. The **Anna and Roebuck Plains**, inland from Eighty Mile Beach and Broome, support wintering Little Curlew and Oriental Plover, as well as Brolga, Australian Pratincole, and Brown and Rufous Songlarks. The dunes at Broome Port support Grey-headed Honeyeaters and attract local migrants such as Black, Pied and White-fronted Honeyeaters, Painted Firetail and Pictorella Munia*. To reach here take the road past the silos and fishing club to a car park, just before reaching the town wharf. Walk in to the dunes from here. The area by the car park is also a good spot for Sanderling. Ask at the observatory where the best places to see mangrove specialities such as White-breasted Whistler are (e.g. Crab Creek, 2–3 km away), and try seawatching from **Gantheaume Point** south of town if weather conditions seem suitable.

*Accommodation*: chalets and camping, bookable in advance via The Wardens, Broome Bird Observatory, PO Box 1313, Broome, WA 6725 (tel: 091 93 5600, fax: 091 92 2294).

*Between Broome and Darwin it is worth checking any areas of pristine mangrove for specialities such as White-breasted Whistler*

In October 1996 a bold bunch of pioneering seabird fanatics boarded the *Jodi Anne II* and headed northwest out of Broome to the deep waters between the **Scott and Ashmore Reefs**. A week later they returned with triumphant tales of Bulwer's Petrels, Matsudaira's Storm-Petrels and probable Jouanin's Petrels. An amazing hat-trick, ably supported by Tahiti Petrel, Streaked and Hutton's* Shearwaters, Leach's and probable Swinhoe's Storm-Petrels, Red-tailed Tropicbird, Masked and Red-footed Boobies, Roseate, Black-naped, Bridled and Sooty Terns, and Brown and Black Noddies, as well as bottle-nosed, rough-toothed and spinner dolphins, Bryde's, humpback and melon-headed whales, and flatback turtle. The waters in this area of the Indian Ocean appear to be so rich that a return trip may even turn up Mascarene Black Petrel* and Band-rumped Storm-Petrel.

Between Broome and Derby check short grass areas for Oriental Plover and open eucalypt woodland for Black-tailed Treecreeper. **Fitzroy River Crossing**, 157 km east of Broome, is a good place to stop for a while. Blue-winged Kookaburra occurs here. **Derby Sewage Works** are also worth a look, especially between November and March when Garganey, Little Curlew, Long-toed Stint, Australian Pratincole, Oriental Plover, and Yellow Chat* have been recorded. The mangroves at Derby support the white-breasted *tormenti* race of Lemon-bellied Flycatcher, as well as Dusky and Mangrove Gerygones, Mangrove Robin and White-breasted Whistler. Head southwest out of town along the causeway and take the last left before the jetty. Check the mangroves here and opposite the boat ramp further on.

## THE KIMBERLEY

The Land of Wait a While, alias The Kimberley, is a massive rugged sandstone plateau split by a maze of magnificent gorges. It covers an area the size of Britain, but it is inhabited by less than 25,000 people and there are only a few roads and tracks. Many of the rivers tumble off the *spinifex*-covered plateau as waterfalls, forming pools before flowing through the tree-lined gorges, open savanna woodlands and grassy plains dotted with baobabs, termite hills and cattle. The wild terrain is traversed by a rough track known as the Gibb River Road, which enables access via its 4WD-only side tracks to such rare, localised and delightful birds as Black Grasswren*, which is endemic to The Kimberley, and Purple-crowned Fairywren*. This is also one of the few places in Australia where Red Goshawk* is reported with any regularity.

The best way to bird The Kimberley is to hire a 4WD and spend at least a few days in the area during the dry season (Jul–Sep), although it is possible to see Black Grasswren*, the region's only endemic, by driving to Mount Elizabeth Station in a 2WD and organising transport from there. Before tackling the Gibb River Road it is crucial to check its current condition at the Derby Tourist Bureau, 2 Clarendon Street, PO Box 48 (tel: 091 911 426), or the Kununurra Visitor Centre, 75 Coolibah Drive (tel: 091 681 177).

### Localised Australian Endemics

Chestnut-backed Buttonquail*, Partridge Pigeon*, White-quilled Rock-

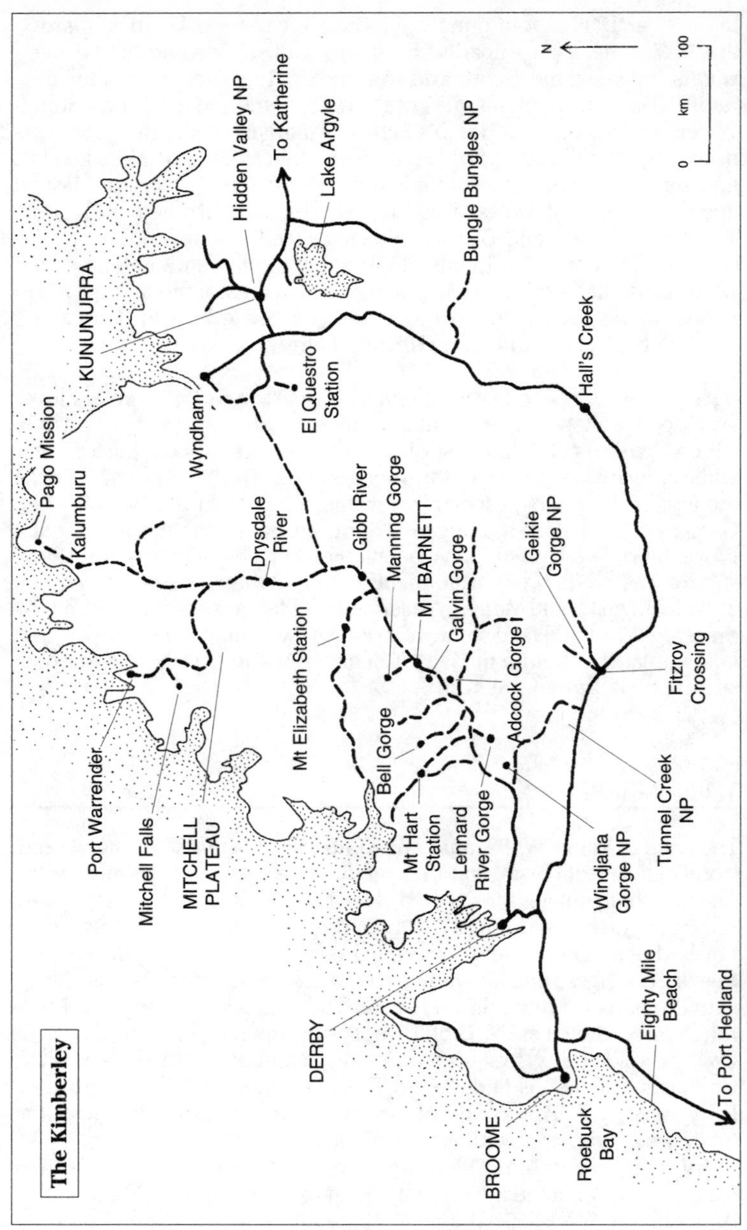


Pigeon, Northern Rosella, Varied Lorikeet, Purple-crowned Fairywren*, Black Grasswren*, White-lined Honeyeater.

## Other Australian Endemics

Square-tailed* and Black-breasted Kites, Black Falcon, Little Button-quail, Spinifex Pigeon, Diamond Dove, Budgerigar, Red-tailed Black-Cockatoo, Galah, Cockatiel, Tawny Frogmouth, Red-backed Kingfisher,

Black-tailed Treecreeper, Great Bowerbird, Red-backed and Variegated Fairywrens, Red-browed Pardalote, Banded, White-gaped, Grey-fronted and Golden-backed Honeyeaters, Silver-crowned Friarbird, Bar-breasted and Rufous-throated Honeyeaters, Sandstone Shrike-Thrush, Masked and Little Woodswallows, Grey Butcherbird, Double-barred, Masked and Long-tailed Finches.

## Others

Intermediate Egret, Rufous Night-Heron, Black Bittern, Black-necked Stork, Pacific Baza, Spotted Harrier, Grey and Brown Goshawks, Wedge-tailed and Little Eagles, Australian Kestrel, Australian Hobby, Brown Quail, Buff-banded Rail, Brolga, Australian Bustard, Bush Thick-knee, Oriental Plover (Oct–Apr), Peaceful Dove, Red-winged Parrot, Little Corella, Rainbow Lorikeet (red-collared *rubrotorquis* race), Black-eared and Channel-billed (Sep–Apr) Cuckoos, Pheasant Coucal, Barking Owl, Australian Owlet-Nightjar, Spotted Nightjar, Azure Kingfisher, Blue-winged Kookaburra, Rainbow Bee-eater, Dollarbird (Sep–Apr), Green-backed and White-throated Gerygones, Brown, Yellow-tinted and White-throated Honeyeaters, Little Friarbird, Blue-faced Honeyeater, Lemon-bellied Flycatcher (white-breasted *tormenti* race), Varied Sittella, Grey-crowned Babbler, Northern Fantail, Leaden, Broad-billed and Restless Flycatchers, Torresian Crow, Green Figbird, White-winged and Varied Trillers, Crimson and Zebra Finches, Chestnut-breasted Munia.

## Other Wildlife

Freshwater crocodile, wallaroo.

(Other species recorded here include Red Goshawk*, Grey Falcon*, Red-backed Buttonquail, Flock Bronzewing*, Rainbow Pitta, Yellow Chat*, Crested Shrike-tit (northern *whitei* race), Star* and Gouldian* Finches, Yellow-rumped* and Pictorella* Munias and a potential new species of grasswren, allied to Dusky Grasswren, photographed at Pinnacle Creek in 1991.)

**BACHSTEN GORGE**

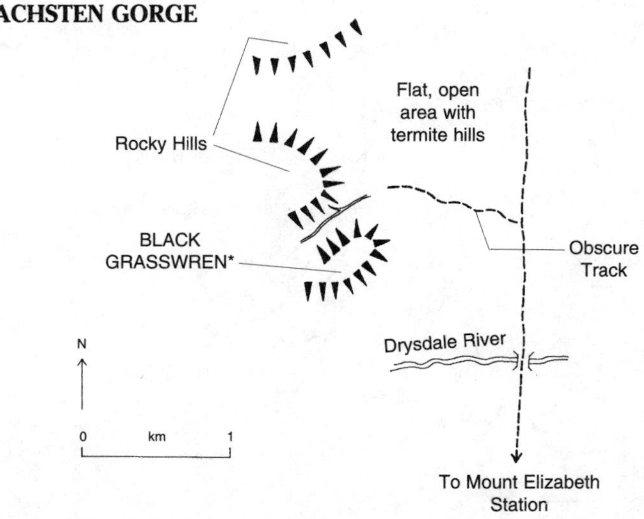

The following distances are from Derby (KM 0) and the distances given in parentheses are those from the Gibb River Road to the particular site. The turn-off to **Windjana Gorge** (21 km) and **Tunnel Creek** (55 km), both of which are National Parks, is at KM 118. Black Bittern, Great Bowerbird, Green-backed Gerygone, White-gaped Honeyeater and Sandstone Shrike-Thrush may be seen on a walk up Windjana Gorge. At KM 315 the Gibb River Road reaches Mount Barnett road station (tel: 091 917 007, to check the fuel for your vehicle is available) and the turn-off to **Manning Gorge** (7 km), which is accessible via a trail which starts opposite the camping area, or by walking along the river. Black Bittern, Red Goshawk*, White-quilled Rock-Pigeon and Sandstone Shrike-Thrush occur here. The turn-off to **Mount Elizabeth Station** (30 km), where it is possible to stay and to organise transport (A+) to **Bachsten Gorge** on the Mitchell Plateau where Black Grasswren* occurs, is at KM 347. To arrange accommodation and/or transport in advance, telephone 091 914 644. The **Hann River** at KM 363 is lined with paperbark eucalypts which, when in flower, attract most of the honeyeaters listed above. Further downstream there is a swamp where Red Goshawk* has been recorded.

The stronghold of the Black Grasswren* is the **Mitchell Plateau** (243 km). Turn north off the Gibb River Road at KM 419 (293 km from Kununurra) to reach here, on what is definitely a 4WD-only track. After 60 km this track crosses **Drysdale River**, a good site for Purple-crowned Fairywren*, which inhabits dense pandanus stands along the river. It is possible to re-fuel and camp at the nearby Drysdale River road station (tel: 091 614 326). About 98 km north of here, turn west on to the Mitchell Plateau Track. Along this track it is worth birding at the King Edward River after 6.5 km and Camp Creek after 66.5 km, but more avian excitement lies further ahead. After 70 km turn off to **Merten's Creek**, where there is a car park and campsite, 15 km from the Mitchell Plateau Track. At dawn look for Black Grasswren* on the rocky outcrop

**MITCHELL PLATEAU**

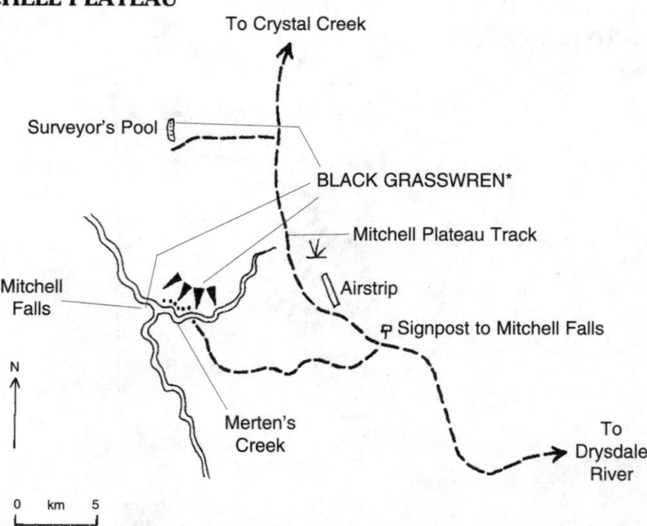

on the opposite side of Merten's Creek (straight on from where the obscure trail leads left to Mitchell Falls), or continue for a few hundred metres along the trail to Mitchell Falls and search the area nearer the head of the Merten Falls. Once the sun gets up these birds become very difficult to find because they tend to seek shade amongst the rock crevices. Other species which may be seen along the trail from Mertens Creek to Mitchell Falls include Black Bittern, Chestnut-backed Button-quail*, Partridge Pigeon*, White-quilled Rock-Pigeon, Green-backed Gerygone and White-lined Honeyeater. The final chance of seeing Black Grasswren* comes at **Surveyor's Pool**, reached by returning to the Mitchell Plateau Track and continuing north for 20 km or so to the turn-off to the pool, which is 7 km down a rough track. The grasswrens occur around the pool. After 115 km the Mitchell Plateau Track reaches Crystal Creek and an adjacent mangrove-lined bay.

The eastern section of the Gibb River Road, beyond the turning to Drysdale River and Merten's Creek, is much rougher than the western, especially the 200 m wide tidal Pentecost River crossing, and there are few notable birding sites. At KM 667 the Gibb River Road joins the Victoria Highway between Wyndham (48 km northwest) and Kununurra (53 km east).

*Accommodation*: Mount Barnett/Manning Gorge Camping Ground (C). Mount Elizabeth Station (A–C, including camping). Drysdale River Camping Ground (C).

*The Black Grasswren* is endemic to The Kimberley*

Gouldian Finch* regularly visits Three Mile (Wyndham) Caravan Park in the coastal town of **Wyndham** to drink during the dry season (May–Oct). Check wet areas near sprinklers and any pools in the usually dry creek alongside the park. Spinifex Pigeon, Black-eared Cuckoo, Yellow-tinted and Rufous-throated Honeyeaters, and Star*, Masked and Long-tailed Finches also occur here. It is possible to take boat trips on the Ord River near Wyndham in search of Great-billed Heron*, Black Bittern and many other waterbirds. The sandstone gorge known as The Grotto supports Spinifex Pigeon (birds visit the permanent waterhole), White-quilled Rock-Pigeon, Sandstone Shrike-Thrush and Little Wood-swallow, as well as the localised short-eared rock-wallaby. The swamps and lily-covered lagoons in the Marlgu Bird Sanctuary support Wandering Whistling-Duck, Radjah Shelduck, Green Pygmy-goose, and Oriental (Oct–Apr) and Australian Pratincoles.

## KUNUNURRA

The irrigated fields and wetlands surrounding this small town support lots of waterbirds and seedeaters, including the rare endemic Yellow-rumped Munia*, which is more likely to be seen here than anywhere else in Australia, while nearby Lake Argyle is one of only a few sites where the endemic Yellow Chat* is seen regularly.

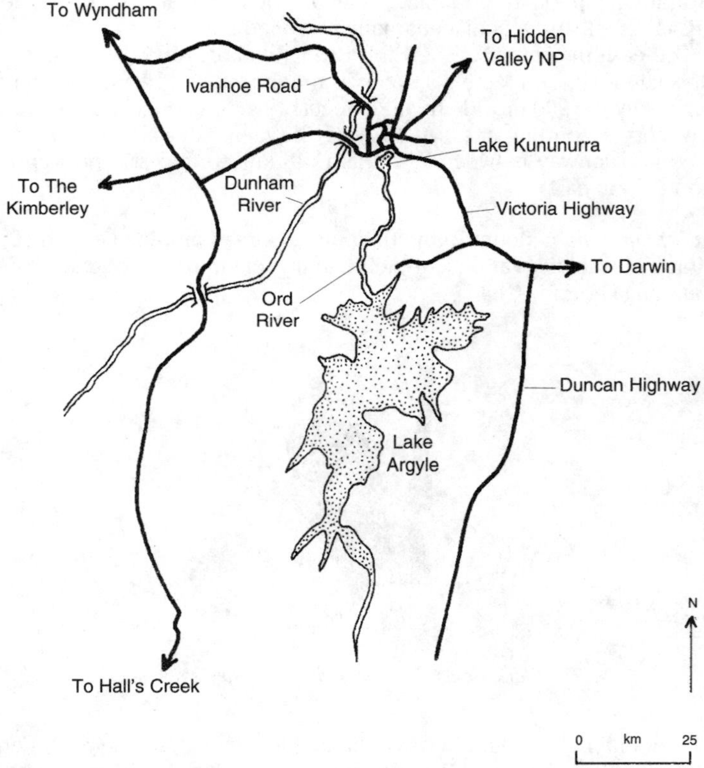


### Localised Australian Endemics

Red-chested Buttonquail, White-quilled Rock-Pigeon, Yellow Chat*, Gouldian Finch*, Yellow-rumped* and Pictorella* Munias.

### Other Australian Endemics

Black-tailed Treecreeper, White-browed Robin (*cerviniventris* race).

### Others

Wandering Whistling-Duck, Green Pygmy-goose, Intermediate Egret, Pied Heron, Black Bittern, Black-necked Stork, White-browed Crake, Brolga, Comb-crested Jacana.

At the west side of the town, turn north off the Victoria Highway on to Ivanhoe Road, park by the third irrigation ditch and walk west along the north side of this to search the reedbeds for Yellow-rumped Munia*. Beware of Yellow-rumped/Chestnut-breasted Munia hybrids. Pure Yellow-rumped Munias* also occur at Lake Kununurra, formed by the construction of Diversion Dam on the Ord River, just south of town where the highway crosses the river. Take the track on the east side of the lake to reach a small marsh along the river bank. Both of these sites also support a fine selection of waterbirds, including Pied Heron, White-browed Crake and Comb-crested Jacana. The buff-flanked *cerviniventris* race of White-browed Robin, as well as Black Bittern, occur in the forest along the west bank of Dunham River, south of the Victoria Highway, about 8 km west of Kununurra. It is possible to take boat trips on the Ord River or a six-hour cruise on **Lake Argyle**, about 70 km south of Kununurra, during which it is possible to see up to 100 species. The best area of shoreline around the lake can be reached by road by turning south off the Victoria Highway 40 km east of Kununurra on to Golden Gate Drive, a rough 19 km track. Bird along here (Red-chested Buttonquail, Black-tailed Treecreeper and Pictorella Munia*) and at the shore (waterbirds and Yellow Chat*). White-quilled Rock-Pigeon occurs in **Hidden Valley (Mirima) National Park**, which is on the northeastern edge of Kununurra, and in **Keep River National Park** (along the track from the camping area to the sandstone escarpment), along with Red-chested Buttonquail, Gouldian Finch* and Pictorella Munia*. A permanent pool in **Dingo Creek**, 56 km east of Kununurra, is used as a drinking hole by Gouldian Finches* during the dry season. Walk south for 300 m at dawn.

The only reliable place in Australia to see the rare Alexandra's Parrot* is along the 1700 km **Canning Stock Route**, which runs between Halls Creek, 371 km south of Kununurra, and Wiluna, 958 km northeast of Perth. This track, the longest and roughest on the continent, crosses endless sand dunes as it traverses the Great Sandy and Gibson Deserts, and can only be completed safely in July in 4WD convoys with pre-arranged fuel drops and full survival gear. However, the parrots are usually recorded between 400 and 500 km south of Hall's Creek, near Lake Tobin, and it is possible to make this return journey alone in a 4WD, so long as you have plenty of fuel, food and, especially, water, and some way of contacting the outside world in case of breakdown.

**Victoria River Roadhouse**, 310 km east of Kununurra and 200 km southwest of Katherine, is an excellent place for an overnight stop because the delightful Purple-crowned Fairywren* occurs in the long grass south of the bridge over the Victoria River and opposite the car park in nearby Gregory National Park. This park is signposted 2 km west of the roadhouse and the trail from the car park leads to an escarpment where White-quilled Rock-Pigeon and Sandstone Shrike-Thrush occur. Other possibilities in this area include Grey Falcon*, Barking Owl (on petrol pumps at the roadhouse at night), Blue-winged Kookaburra, Great Bowerbird, White-browed Robin, and plenty of honeyeaters and 'finches'.

## *NORTHERN TERRITORY*

### KATHERINE

During the northern dry season a number of wide-ranging rarely seen arid country specialists, including two of the rarest: Hooded Parrot* and Gouldian Finch*, use regular drinking holes, and some of the most popular over the years have been those in Chinaman Creek, 16 km southwest of Katherine.

#### Localised Australian Endemics

Hooded Parrot* (Apr–Sep), Gouldian Finch* (Apr–Sep).

#### Other Australian Endemics

Black-tailed Treecreeper, Great Bowerbird, Banded, Grey-fronted, Golden-backed and Rufous-throated Honeyeaters, Masked and Long-tailed Finches.

#### Others

Brown Quail, Yellow-tinted and Blue-faced Honeyeaters.

#### Other Wildlife

Freshwater crocodile.

(Other species recorded here include Grey Falcon*.)

About 150 m east of where the Victoria Highway crosses Chinaman Creek, turn north on to a track which leads to the old highway (which runs parallel with the new one). At the old highway turn west and park by the bridge over the creek. Walk north along the usually dry creek to the first pool and settle down at a reasonable distance to wait for the birds to fly in for a drink. The best time to be in position is dawn.

Great Bowerbird occurs in and around the car park and campsite in **Katherine Gorge (Nitmiluk) National Park**, about 25 km northeast of Katherine. The rarely reported Chestnut-backed Buttonquail* occurs near the **Edith River**, about 45 km north of Katherine along the Stuart Highway. A couple of kilometres north of the river, turn east on to a track which passes over an old railway line. After 5 km check the bare ridge alongside the track for the buttonquail. Hooded Parrot* (this is a good wet season site for this species) and Gouldian Finch* have also been recorded further along this track and at the permanent pools in the **Fergusson River**, 60 km north of Katherine. Walk east at dawn.

Over 200 species have been recorded in the pockets of monsoon forest, woodland and watercourses on and around the sandstone plateau in **Litchfield Park**, including Red Goshawk* (rare), Partridge Pigeon*, Northern Rosella, Rainbow Pitta and Brown Whistler, as well as Rose-crowned Fruit-Dove, Red-tailed Black-Cockatoo, Rufous Owl, Little and Red-backed Kingfishers, and Bar-breasted and Rufous-throated Honeyeaters. The park is 100–140 km southwest of Darwin via Batchelor or the Cox Peninsula Road, and also supports Antilopine Wallaroo.

## DARWIN

The big beaches, large areas of mangroves, pockets of monsoon forest, marshes, lagoons and savanna that surround the small town of Darwin at Australia's 'Top End' support a profusion of high quality birds, ranging from Beach Thick-knee through many mangrove specialists, including Chestnut Rail, to forest skulkers such as Rainbow Pitta and savanna dazzlers such as Rainbow Bee-eater. With so many waterbirds around as well it is easy to see over 100 species in a day.

### Localised Australian Endemics

Partridge Pigeon*, Northern Rosella, Varied Lorikeet, Rainbow Pitta, Brown and White-breasted Whistlers.

### Other Australian Endemics

Pink-eared Duck, Pacific Heron, Black-breasted Kite, Red-capped Plover, Red-kneed Dotterel, Red-tailed Black-Cockatoo, Galah, Red-backed Kingfisher, Great Bowerbird, Red-backed Fairywren, Banded and White-gaped Honeyeaters, Silver-crowned Friarbird, Yellow-throated Miner, White-browed Robin (*cerviniventris* race), Grey and Pied Butcherbirds, Australian Yellow White-eye, Rufous Songlark, Double-barred and Long-tailed Finches.

### Non-endemic Specialities

Great-billed Heron*, Red-backed Buttonquail, Chestnut Rail, Swinhoe's Snipe (Oct–Apr), Beach Thick-knee.

### Others

Australasian Grebe, Little Pied and Pied Cormorants, Australian Darter, Magpie Goose, Wandering Whistling-Duck, Radjah Shelduck, Green Pygmy-goose, White-eyed Duck, Intermediate Egret, Pied Heron, Black Bittern, Glossy, Australian and Straw-necked Ibises, Royal Spoonbill, Black-necked Stork, Whistling and Brahminy Kites, White-bellied Sea-Eagle, Swamp Harrier, Brown Goshawk, Australian Kestrel, Australian Hobby, Orange-footed Scrubfowl, Brown and Blue-breasted Quails, Buff-banded Rail, Brolga, Comb-crested Jacana, Little (Oct–Apr) and Far Eastern* Curlews, Grey-tailed Tattler, Great Knot, Rufous-necked and Long-toed Stints, Sharp-tailed Sandpiper, Bush Thick-knee, Pied Oystercatcher, Oriental (Oct–Nov) and Australian Pratincoles, Mongolian Plover, Greater Sandplover, Oriental Plover (Oct–Apr), Silver Gull, Caspian Tern, Great and Lesser Crested-Terns, Emerald, Peaceful and Bar-shouldered Doves, Rose-crowned Fruit-Dove, Torresian Imperial-Pigeon (Aug–Apr), Red-winged Parrot, Little Corella, Rainbow Lorikeet (*rubritorquis* race), Oriental (Sep–Apr) and Brush Cuckoos, Little and Horsfield's Bronze-Cuckoos, Australian Koel (Sep–Apr), Pheasant Coucal, Rufous Owl, Azure and Little Kingfishers, Blue-winged Kookaburra, Forest, Collared and Sacred Kingfishers, Rainbow Bee-eater, Dollarbird (Sep–Apr), Green-backed, Large-billed and Mangrove Gerygones, Brown Honeyeater, Dusky and Red-headed Myzomelas, White-throated Honeyeater, Little and Helmeted Friarbirds, Rufous-banded and Blue-faced Honeyeaters, Lemon-bellied Flycatcher, Mangrove Robin, Black-tailed Whistler, Rufous Shrike-Thrush, Willie-wagtail, Northern and Mangrove Fantails, Leaden, Broad-billed and Shining Flycatchers, Torresian Crow, Black Butcherbird, Magpie-lark, Olive-

**DARWIN**

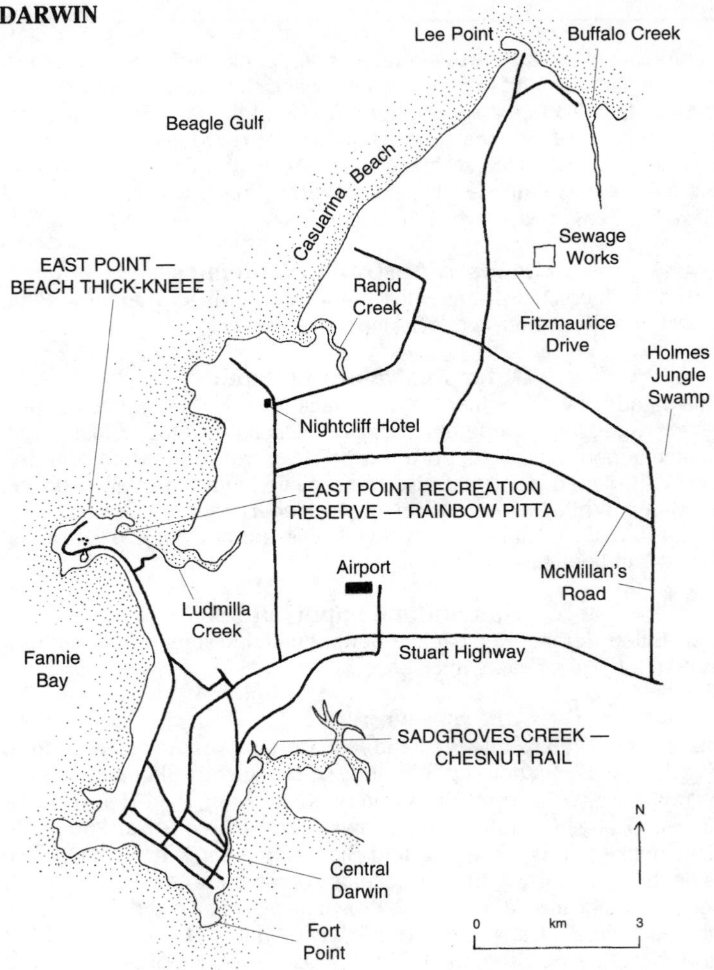


backed and Green Orioles, Green Figbird, Black-faced and White-bellied Cuckoo-shrikes, White-winged and Varied Trillers, Tree Martin, Golden-headed Cisticola, Tawny Grassbird, Australasian Bushlark, Crimson Finch, Chestnut-breasted Munia, Australasian Pipit.

## Other Wildlife

Agile wallaby, black flying-fox, humpback and Irrawaddy dolphins, humpback whale (Oct), manta ray, northern brushtail possum, salt-water crocodile.

(Other species recorded here include Streaked Shearwater (Oct–Mar), Garganey (Oct–Apr), Pintail Snipe (Oct–Apr), Nordmann's Greenshank* (Sep–Apr), Asian Dowitcher* (Sep–Apr), Yellow Wagtail (Sep–Apr) and Star Finch*.)

One of the best places to start birding on arrival in Darwin (apart from the airfield where Australian Pratincole is possible) is **East Point Recreation Reserve**, 5 km north of the town centre. Orange-footed Scrubfowl, Rose-crowned Fruit-Dove, Rainbow Pitta (in the monsoon forest opposite the car park *en route* to the point) and Black-tailed Whistler (in mangroves east of the point) occur here, and the huge beach supports plenty of shorebirds, including Beach Thick-knee (check the beach to the east of the point at low tide and the point at high tide). Humpback dolphin, humpback whale and manta ray (leaping out of the sea) are all possible offshore. The small patch of mangroves in Ludmilla Creek within the reserve supports a number of mangrove specialities such as Mangrove Gerygone, as do the mangroves a little further north at Nightcliff. One of the few known and accessible sites in the world for Chestnut Rail is not far from the centre of Darwin, in the mangroves at **Sadgroves Creek**, accessible from Frances Bay Drive at the eastern edge of town near its junction with Tiger Brennan Drive. There are a couple of tracks from which it is possible to scan some of the mangroves, and part of the area was being destroyed by development in late 1996, opening up what mangroves remain for further scrutiny, but the best way to see one of these rails is to plodge in! However, this is a dangerous technique because a few saltwater crocodiles cruise the creeks and there are sandflies galore. Fortunately, it is also possible to see what the locals call 'Red Chooks' at Middle Arm (p. 119).

**Darwin Sewage Works**, at the end of Fitzmaurice Drive, off Lee Point Road north of the airport, is an excellent place for waterbirds, including Pied Heron and Red-kneed Dotterel, and Star Finch* has been recorded here with Crimson Finches. The grassy surrounds of the military area (beware of trespassing) along **Lee Point Road** are good for Little Curlew and Oriental Plover, especially on passage, as well as

**LAGOON ROAD PONDS**

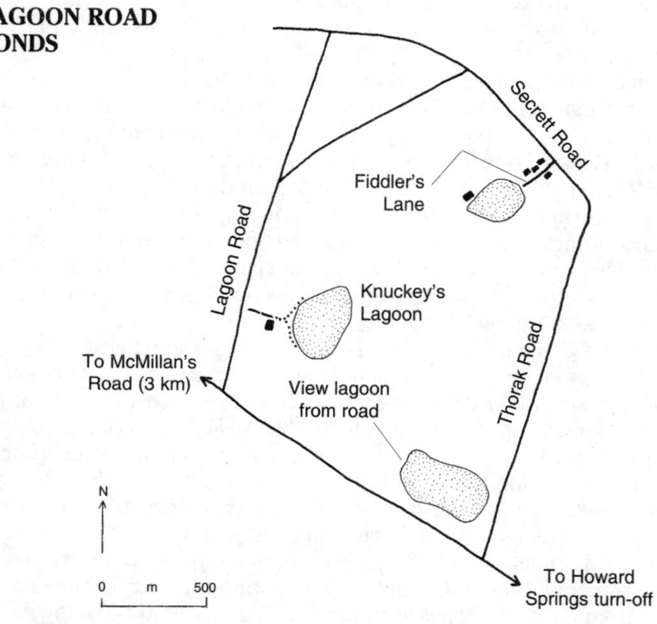

## HOWARD SPRINGS

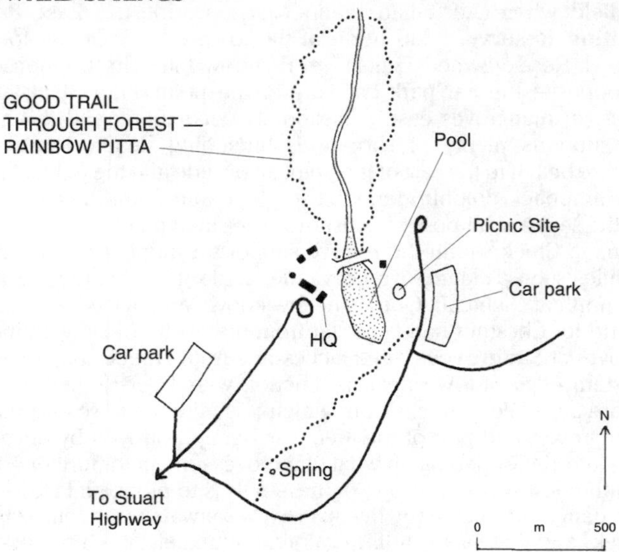


Rufous Songlark. **Lee Point Beach**, at the end of Lee Point Road 20 km northeast of the town centre, is excellent for shorebirds, including Red-capped Plover. Mangrove specialities including White-breasted Whistler and Australian Yellow White-eye occur at **Buffalo Creek** and Great-billed Heron*, Chestnut Rail, Little Kingfisher and Brown Whistler have also been recorded here. Turn east off Lee Point Road about 1 km south of the point and check the mangroves around the boat-ramp at the end of this road. **Holmes Jungle Swamp**, a tiny reserve which protects an isolated patch of monsoon forest, wetlands and grasslands off Vanderlin Drive, is open from 0700 to 1900. It supports Brown and Blue-breasted Quails, as well as Red-backed Buttonquail (in tall grass around the sharp right-hand bend a couple of kilometres along the main track into the reserve). The three lagoons enclosed by **Lagoon**, **Secrett** and **Thorak Roads**, 3 km southeast of the junction of McMillan's Road and the Stuart Highway, just out of Darwin, support a great selection of waterbirds including Green Pygmy-goose, Comb-crested Jacana, Swinhoe's Snipe, Little Curlew, Long-toed Stint, Oriental and Australian Pratincoles, and Red-kneed Dotterel, as well as Tawny Grassbird. This area is also one of the best in Australia for scarce visitors such as Garganey and Yellow Wagtail.

**Howard Springs**, an isolated patch of monsoon forest and open eucalypt woodland surrounding a semi-natural swimming pool (complete with several large barramundi), 27 km southeast of town at the end of Howard Springs Road off the Stuart Highway (keep straight, ignoring signs to village), is well worth a prolonged look. Species occurring here include Black Bittern, Azure Kingfisher, Blue-winged Kookaburra, Rainbow Pitta (on lawns in wet season) and Brown Whistler, as well as black flying-fox. In October and November most of the world population of Little Curlews passes through the Darwin area and these confiding birds can be seen on virtually every piece of short grass, from football pitches to traffic islands in the middle of town.

*Accommodation*: Howard Springs Caravan Park and Campsite (complete with Great Bowerbird bower in hedge at south end).

The safest site to look for Chestnut Rail is **Middle Arm**, 60 km south of Darwin. Turn west off the Stuart Highway 45 km south of Darwin on to the Cox Peninsula Road towards Berry Springs, and after 1.7 km turn north on to Middle Arm Road, a track which reaches a boat-ramp after 14 km. Partridge Pigeon* occurs on this track, usually near dawn. Once at the boat-ramp scan, preferably with a 'scope, the muddy margins of the mangrove-lined creek, or, better still, ask the local fishermen to take you out in search of the 'Red Chook'. Other species recorded here include Great-billed Heron*, Little Kingfisher, Red-headed Myzomela and Mangrove Robin, as well as Irrawaddy dolphin.

*Rainbow Pitta* is one of the easiest members of its family to see, but like any pitta it still stirs a birder's blood when one is seen bouncing along the forest floor*

## FOGG DAM

Between Darwin and Kakadu National Park it is worth spending a morning or afternoon birding the shallow lagoons, left over from a failed rice-growing project, and monsoon forest at this site. Now a worthy reserve, it is signposted 60 km southeast of Darwin off the Arnhem Highway and supports some cracking waterbirds such as White-browed Crake, as well as forest-dwelling beauties such as Rainbow Pitta and Rose-crowned Fruit-Dove.

### Localised Australian Endemics

Varied Lorikeet, Rainbow Pitta, Brown Whistler.

### Other Australian Endemics

Plumed Whistling-Duck, Pacific Heron, Black-breasted Kite, Red-kneed Dotterel, Double-barred, Masked and Long-tailed Finches.

### Non-endemic Specialities

White-browed Crake.

### Others

Australian Darter, Magpie Goose, Wandering Whistling-Duck, Radjah Shelduck, Green Pygmy-goose, Intermediate Egret, Pied Heron, Rufous

Night-Heron, Royal Spoonbill, Black-necked Stork, Swamp Harrier, Baillon's Crake, Brolga, Comb-crested Jacana, Little Curlew (Oct–Apr), Australian Pratincole, Rose-crowned Fruit-Dove, Torresian Imperial-Pigeon (Aug–Apr), Little Corella, Rainbow Lorikeet (*rubritorquis* race), Little Bronze-Cuckoo, Pheasant Coucal, Blue-winged Kookaburra, Forest Kingfisher, Dusky Myzomela, White-throated and Rufous-banded Honeyeaters, Rufous Fantail, Leaden, Broad-billed and Restless Flycatchers, Black-faced Woodswallow, Magpie-lark, Varied Triller, Tawny Grassbird, Crimson Finch.

(Other species recorded here include Garganey (Oct–Apr), Letter-winged Kite, and Pintail (Oct–Apr) and Swinhoe's (Oct–Apr) Snipes.)

To reach the car park, turn north off the Arnhem Highway 60 km south-east of Darwin. On the way out to the shallow lagoons from the car park, look for Rainbow Pitta behind the sign which says 'Look for Rainbow Pitta'! There is also a trail through the forest from the car park, along which it is possible to see Rose-crowned Fruit-Dove. The roadside marshes at **Humpty Doo Dam**, 2 km east of the turn-off to Fogg Dam, are also worth a long look, with Black-necked Stork and Brolga being just two possibilities.

*Gorgeous Pied Herons feed alongside unique Magpie-larks in the wetlands of northern Australia*

## KAKADU NATIONAL PARK

This huge park (13,000 sq km) in *Crocodile Dundee* country is a World Heritage Site, and no wonder! The beautiful landscape of rivers, seasonally flooded grasslands, eucalypt woodlands and monsoon forests is alive with birds. Around 275 species have been recorded, including a wonderful variety of waterbirds, the rare Chestnut-backed Buttonquail* and the localised White-lined Honeyeater. In addition, the park lies at the western edge of the deeply incised sandstone massif known as Arnhem Land, and it is the only site in Australia where it is possible to see all three Arnhem Land endemics: Chestnut-quilled Rock-Pigeon, Black-banded Fruit-Dove* and the splendid White-throated Grasswren*.

### Localised Australian Endemics

Chestnut-backed Buttonquail*, Partridge Pigeon*, Chestnut-quilled

Rock-Pigeon, Black-banded Fruit-Dove*, Northern Rosella, Varied Lorikeet, Rainbow Pitta, White-throated Grasswren*, White-lined Honeyeater.

### Other Australian Endemics

Emu, Plumed Whistling-Duck, Pacific Heron, Yellow-billed Spoonbill, Square-tailed* and Black-breasted Kites, Red-kneed Dotterel, Red-tailed Black-Cockatoo, Galah, Tawny Frogmouth, Black-tailed Treecreeper, Great Bowerbird, Red-backed and Variegated Fairywrens, Weebill, Banded and White-gaped Honeyeaters, Silver-crowned Friarbird, Bar-breasted and Rufous-throated Honeyeaters, White-browed Robin, Sandstone Shrike-Thrush, Masked and Little Woodswallows, Pied Butcherbird, Double-barred, Masked and Long-tailed Finches.

### Non-endemic Specialities

Great-billed Heron*, White-browed Crake.

### Others

Australasian Grebe, Little Pied and Little Black Cormorants, Australian Darter, Magpie Goose, Wandering Whistling-Duck, Radjah Shelduck, Green Pygmy-goose, Pacific Black Duck, Intermediate Egret, Pied Heron, Rufous Night-Heron, Glossy, Australian and Straw-necked Ibises, Royal Spoonbill, Black-necked Stork, White-bellied Sea-Eagle, Spotted Harrier, Wedge-tailed and Little Eagles, Grey Goshawk, Collared Sparrowhawk, Brown Falcon, Orange-footed Scrubfowl, Brown Quail, Brolga, Comb-crested Jacana, Little Curlew (Oct–Apr), Bush Thick-knee, Australian Pratincole, Oriental Plover (Oct–Apr), Black-fronted Dotterel, Peaceful and Bar-shouldered Doves, Torresian Imperial-Pigeon (Aug–Apr), Red-winged Parrot, Little Corella, Rainbow Lorikeet (*rubritorquis* race), Oriental (Sep–Apr) and Pallid Cuckoos, Little Bronze-Cuckoo, Black-eared Cuckoo, Pheasant Coucal, Rufous and Barking Owls, Australian Owlet-Nightjar, Spotted Nightjar, Azure and Little Kingfishers, Blue-winged Kookaburra, Forest Kingfisher, Rainbow Bee-eater, Dollarbird (Sep–Apr), Green-backed Gerygone, Brown Honeyeater, Dusky Myzomela, White-throated Honeyeater, Helmeted Friarbird, Rufous-banded and Blue-faced Honeyeaters, Lemon-bellied Flycatcher, Rufous Whistler, Grey Shrike-Thrush, Grey-crowned Babbler, Willie-wagtail, Northern Fantail, Leaden, Broad-billed, Restless and Shining Flycatchers, Torresian Crow, Black-faced Woodswallow, Olive-backed and Green Orioles, Green Figbird, Black-faced and White-bellied Cuckoo-shrikes, White-winged and Varied Trillers, Golden-headed Cisticola, Tawny Grassbird, Crimson Finch, Mistletoebird.

### Other Wildlife

Agile wallaby, antilopine kangaroo, barramundi, black and little red flying-foxes, black wallaroo (rare), dingo, freshwater and saltwater crocodiles.

(Other species recorded here include Red Goshawk* (most sightings have been from the Arnhem Highway), Black Falcon and Yellow Chat* (Nov–Mar)).

The HQ is situated 247 km east of Darwin (180 km east of Fogg Dam) next to the Kakadu Highway, 2.5 km south of the junction with the Arnhem Highway. Between Darwin and here it is worth stopping for a look from the hide at **Mamukala**, 25 km west of the HQ. This overlooks seasonally flooded grassland which attracts Little Curlew, Australian Pratincole and Oriental Plover. Look out for Partridge Pigeons* alongside the road from here to the HQ and in the HQ grounds. The campsite at **Merl**, 45 km northeast of the HQ, lies in an excellent birding area. Partridge Pigeon* occurs in and around the campsite and the rare Chestnut-backed Buttonquail* may be found with patience and persistence in the eucalypt woodland between there and the East Alligator River, which forms the border between Kakadu and Arnhem Land. To look for the buttonquails try and locate the 20 cm diameter circular cleared areas, known as platelets, which they leave in the leaf litter as they search for food. Birds are usually present near fresh platelets where they can be heard amongst the leaf litter and seen with careful stalking. Rainbow Pitta occurs in the monsoon forest alongside the river from the boat-ramp and picnic area 3 km southeast of the campsite, and both species of flying-fox roost alongside Mangarre Walk. **Obiri (Ubirr) Rock**, 3 km north of the campsite, is adorned with some of the best aboriginal art in Australia and is well worth visiting.

**KAKADU NP**

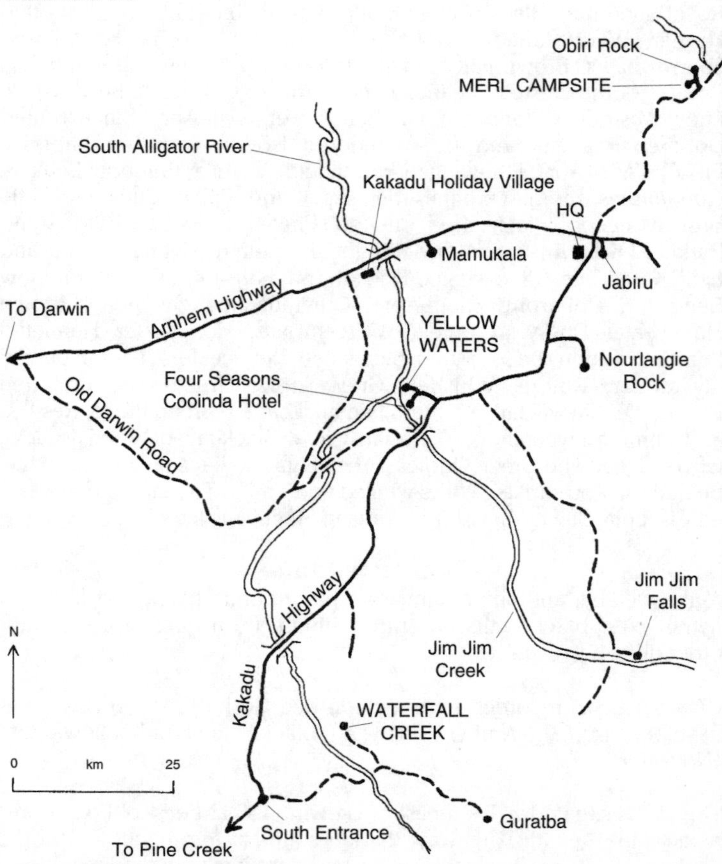

## MERL AREA

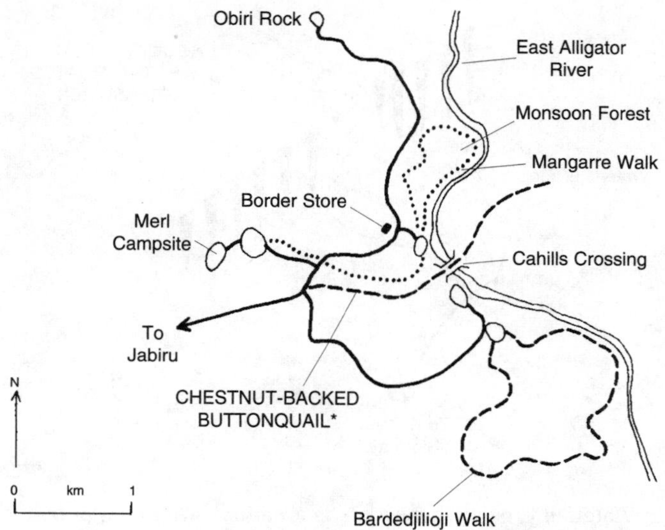


**Nourlangie Rock**, about 35 km southwest of the HQ, is another high-quality aboriginal art gallery, around which Chestnut-quilled Rock-Pigeon, Black-banded Fruit-Dove*, White-lined Honeyeater and Sandstone Shrike-Thrush have all been recorded, although only the honeyeater is seen regularly. About 55 km southwest of the HQ the road reaches a billabong known as **Yellow Waters**. There are regular two-hour boat trips along this billabong, during which it is possible to see 70 or so species, including Plumed Whistling-Duck, Great-billed Heron*, White-browed Crake, Tawny Frogmouth and Little Kingfisher, as well as saltwater crocodiles. On these trips photographers may think they are in paradise, so long as they forget about the mosquitoes. To guarantee a place on the boat, book in advance at the nearby Four Seasons Cooinda Hotel. Chestnut-backed Buttonquail* and Black-tailed Tree-creeper occur in the woodland on the north side of the **Old Darwin Road**, up to 300 m west of its junction with the Kakadu Highway, 8.5 km south of Yellow Waters Junction.

The best place to see the three Arnhem Land endemics is **Waterfall Creek** (also known as UDP Falls or Gunlom Falls), a nature park which is situated about 180 km southwest of the HQ, technically just outside Kakadu National Park. During the wet season it is usually easier to reach Waterfall Creek from Pine Creek, which is situated on the Stuart Highway 110 km to the southwest (tel: 089 792101, for details of road and track conditions). To see the Arnhem Land endemics walk up the steep 91 m (300 ft) escarpment from the campsite, looking for Black-banded Fruit-Dove* as you ascend, and once at the top scour the boulder country, especially where there is lots of *spinifex*, for the grasswren. They are elusive birds which seem to spend an inordinate amount of time in deep, shady crevices, especially once the sun is high in the sky, hence dawn is the best time to look for them. The pigeons can usually be found while looking for the grasswrens. At the base of the escarp-

## WATERFALL CREEK

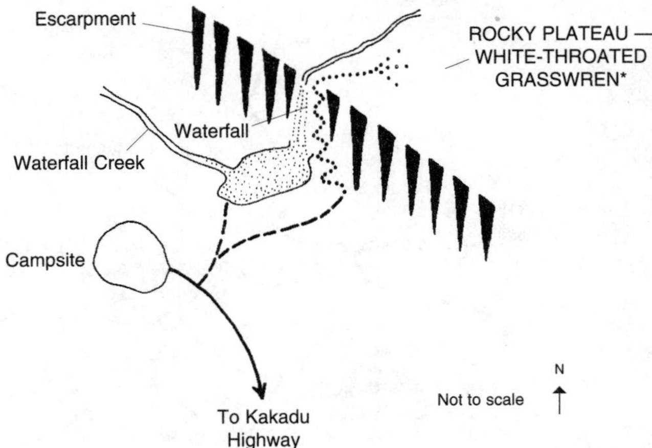


ment at Waterfall Creek, where there is a natural swimming pool and some monsoon forest, there are plenty of other birds worth looking out for, including Bush Thick-knee, Northern Rosella, Rufous Owl (along the creek towards South Alligator River), Azure Kingfisher, Rainbow Pitta, Banded Honeyeater, Sandstone Shrike-Thrush and Little Wood-swallow, as well as mammals such as black wallaroo. The endemic fruit-dove and White-lined Honeyeater, along with Rainbow Pitta and White-browed Robin, also occur along **Stag Creek**, which lies alongside the track 7.8 km back towards the Kakadu Highway from Waterfall Creek. Follow the creek eastwards. Rufous Owl also occurs on the north side of Pine Creek Road, 3 km west of the Kakadu Highway. Throughout the Kakadu area do not stray on to land owned by uranium mining companies for they may well hit you with a hefty fine.

*Accommodation:* Gagudju Lodge Cooinda (A). Campsites at Kakadu Frontier Lodge, East Alligator River (Merl), Waterfall Creek, etc.

*The lovely Black-banded Fruit-Dove* is one of the three Arnhem Land endemics which can be seen only in Kakadu National Park*

## CARANBIRINI SPRINGS

The sandstone escarpment near Caranbirini Springs is one of only two reasonably accessible sites in Australia where it is possible to see the rare Carpentarian Grasswren*. Although this species also occurs near Mount Isa, which is at least reasonably close to the beaten track, the form present there may be a separate species to the form present here, hence birders in search of every potential Australian endemic face a long, long crawl to Caranbirini, because it is around 1000 km from Darwin and Alice Springs, the nearest major birding bases, and about 2000 km from Cairns!

**CARANBIRINI SPRINGS**

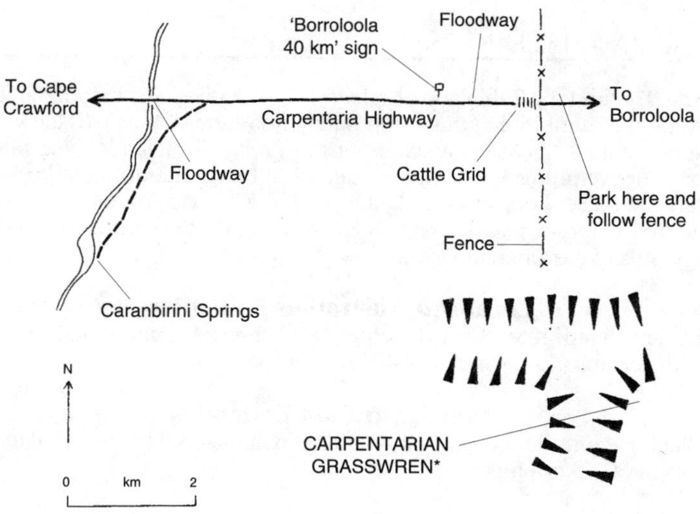


### Localised Australian Endemics

Northern Rosella, Carpentarian Grasswren*, Gouldian Finch* (Apr–Sep), Pictorella Munia* (Apr–Sep).

### Other Australian Endemics

Spinifex Pigeon, Banded, White-gaped, Grey-headed and Golden-backed Honeyeaters, Sandstone Shrike-Thrush, Little Woodswallow, Long-tailed Finch (Apr–Sep).

### Others

Spotted Nightjar, Yellow-tinted Honeyeater, Crimson Finch.

(Other species recorded here include Purple-crowned Fairywren*.)

Carpentarian Grasswren* occurs 40 km south of Borroloola alongside the Carpentaria Highway. Park east of the 'Borroloola 40 km' signpost and walk south directly towards the rough sandstone escarpment. Traverse this escarpment and continue to the second, where the grasswrens frequent the *spinifex* amongst the big slabs of rock. Don't expect to see these birds without a great deal of effort because they hide in shady fissures, especially when the sun is high in the sky, and, if the area has been recently burned, end up in the dense *spinifex* in the deepest gullies. Take a compass when leaving the road because it is easy to get lost here. Purple-crowned Fairywren* has been recorded at Caranbirini Springs, 5 km west of the grasswren site, and at the height of the dry season birds such as Gouldian Finch* use this as a drinking hole.

*Accommodation:* Borroloola Inn (A—tel: 089 75 8766). Borroloola Holiday Village (A—tel: 089 75 8742). McArthur River Caravan Park (C—tel: 089 75 8734).

## BARKLY TABLELANDS

The 374 km long Tablelands Highway between Cape Crawford, 66 km south of Caranbirini Springs, and Barkly Roadhouse, traverses the vast, sun-scorched treeless grasslands of the Barkly Tablelands. Few birds can survive in this harsh environment, but those that do include such rare outback specialities as Letter-winged Kite and Yellow Chat*. In addition, these sparse grasslands are one of the major wintering grounds of the Oriental Plover.

### Localised Australian Endemics

Letter-winged Kite, Grey Falcon*, Red-chested Buttonquail, Flock Bronzewing*, Crimson and Yellow* Chats.

### Other Australian Endemics

Black Falcon, Budgerigar, Masked and White-browed Woodswallows, Ground Cuckoo-shrike.

### Others

Australian Bustard, Australian Pratincole, Oriental Plover (Oct–Apr).

It is hellishly hot here during the summer (Oct–Apr) and with a good air-conditioned vehicle it is wise to spend the middle part of the day covering as many km as possible. Dawn and dusk is the time to bird, especially around waterholes, which are usually hidden from the road by raised bushy banks. These attract birds such as Flock Bronzewings*, and those with plenty of emergent vegetation may also support Yellow Chats*.

*Accommodation:* Barkly Roadhouse—where there is a cool pub, restaurant and camping area with showers.

## *QUEENSLAND*

The deep sandstone gorges in **Lawn Hill National Park**, which is about 320 km north of Camooweal, support Grey Falcon*, Great Bowerbird, Purple-crowned Fairywren* (around the campsite and along Lawn Hill Creek), White-browed Robin, Sandstone Shrike-Thrush, and Masked and Long-tailed Finches, as well as rock ringtail possum and solitary wallaroo.

### MOUNT ISA

The *spinifex*-covered hills around the large mining town of Mount Isa, 1111 km southwest of Cairns, support Dusky and Carpentarian* Grasswrens, both of which also occur elsewhere, but in different forms which may be separate species.

#### Localised Australian Endemics

Dusky (*ballarae* race) and Carpentarian* Grasswrens, Spinifex-bird, Painted Firetail.

#### Other Australian Endemics

Spinifex Pigeon, Mallee Ringneck (*macgillvray* race), Grey-headed and Golden-backed Honeyeaters.

#### Others

Latham's Snipe* (Oct–Apr).

The rare Carpentarian Grasswren* has been recorded along the road to **Lady Loretta Mine**, 90 km northwest of Mount Isa. Its habitat here is very different to that at Caranbirini Springs, indicating perhaps that the birds here are a different species altogether! Turn off the Barkly Highway 66 km north of Mount Isa in response to the 'Lady Loretta Project' signpost and search the tall *spinifex* on the east side of this track between 7.8 and 8.2 km, looking out for the isolated *macgillvray* race of Malle Ringneck, known as Cloncurry Ringneck, and Golden-backed Honeyeater as well. The striking *ballarae* race of Dusky Grasswren occurs on the rocky hills just before **Mica Creek**, along with Grey-headed Honeyeater and Painted Firetail, 13 km south of Mount Isa on the Diamantina Developmental Road, around **Sybella Creek**, and about 20 km west of there along the road to **May Downs**. Latham's Snipe* and other waterbirds occur at Lake Moondarra, an artificial reservoir 20 km north of Mount Isa. Turn east 5 km north of town and head for the picnic area 15 km further on, checking the roadside *spinifex* for Spinifex Pigeon and Spinifex-bird.

Australia's most mysterious bird, the virtually unknown Night Parrot*, is very rarely reported, but one area where they may be present is near **Cloncurry**, 117 km east of Mount Isa. In 1993 two birds were reported around KM 37 alongside the road to Duchess, reached by turning south off the Barkly Highway 9 km west of Cloncurry.

Waterholes around **Burke and Wills Roadhouse**, 180 km north of

Cloncurry, attract Plumed Whistling-Duck, Black Bittern and Flock Bronzewing*, while other birds of the surrounding area include Spinifex Pigeon, Crimson Chat and Brown Songlark. About 195 km further north is **Normanton**, where birding along the Norman River may produce Magpie Goose, Plumed and Wandering Whistling-Ducks, Radjah Shelduck and Comb-crested Jacana. Look out for Pied Heron, Black-necked Stork, Sarus Crane* and Australian Bustard between Normanton and Karumba. At **Karumba**, a small shrimp-fishing town on the Gulf of Carpentaria 70 km to the northwest, White-breasted Whistler, as well as Mangrove Gerygone, Red-headed Myzomela, Mangrove Robin, Black-tailed Whistler, Mangrove Fantail and Australian Yellow White-eye, occur in the mangroves to the northeast of town. Beware of saltwater crocodiles here.

## GEORGETOWN

The arid woodlands and shrubby desert dotted with numerous termite hills around Georgetown support a number of arid outback specialists, including Squatter Pigeon and Gouldian Finch*.

### Localised Australian Endemics

Squatter Pigeon, Plum-headed, Black-throated and Gouldian* (Feb–Apr) Finches, Pictorella Munia* (Feb–Apr).

### Other Australian Endemics

Plumed Whistling-Duck, Black-breasted Kite, Diamond Dove, Pale-headed Rosella, Budgerigar, Cockatiel, Red-backed Kingfisher, Brown Treecreeper, Great Bowerbird, Red-browed Pardalote, Weebill, Banded, Grey-fronted, Golden-backed and Rufous-throated Honeyeaters, Yellow-throated Miner, Ground Cuckoo-shrike, Double-barred and Masked Finches.

### Others

Brolga, Australian Bustard, Latham's Snipe* (Oct–Apr), Australian Pratincole, Yellow-tinted and Blue-faced Honeyeaters, Grey-crowned Babbler.

(Other species recorded here include Spinifex Pigeon and Zebra Finch.)

Bird alongside the Gulf Developmental Road between Normanton and Georgetown, especially around **Cumberland Dam**, 20 km west of Georgetown on the south side of the road.

## ATHERTON TABLELANDS

Over 90% of the original montane rainforest cover on this highly fertile 800 m (2625 ft) high volcanic plateau, 80 km southwest of Cairns, has been replaced with tobacco, rice, maize and peanut farms. The remaining dark, cool, epiphyte-laden ferny forests lie within a World Heritage Site known as the Wet Tropics, and together with remnant savanna and wetlands they make the Atherton Tablelands one of the richest areas for birds in Australia. Many of northeast Queensland's endemics occur here, including Golden Bowerbird*, Pied Monarch and Victoria's Riflebird, as well as a whole host of other goodies shared only with New Guinea, including Buff-breasted Paradise-Kingfisher and Yellow-breasted Boatbill.

Many of the species which occur here can also be seen at Julatten and Mount Lewis (p. 133).

## Localised Australian Endemics

Squatter Pigeon, Lesser Sooty-Owl*, Australian Swiftlet, Tooth-billed Catbird*, Golden Bowerbird*, Lovely Fairywren, Fernwren*, Atherton Scrubwren*, Mountain Thornbill*, Yellow-spotted, Bridled*, Yellow and Macleay Honeyeaters, Grey-headed Robin*, Bower's Shrike-Thrush*, Chowchilla, Pied Monarch, Victoria's Riflebird, Black-throated Finch.

## Other Australian Endemics

Plumed Whistling-Duck, Maned Duck, Pacific Heron, Australian Kite, Australian Brush-turkey, White-headed Pigeon, Brown Cuckoo-Dove, Topknot Pigeon, Australian King-Parrot, Crimson and Pale-headed Rosellas, Scaly-breasted Lorikeet, Southern Boobook (*lurida* race), Laughing Kookaburra, White-throated Treecreeper (*minor* race), Great Bowerbird, Red-backed Fairywren, Striated Pardalote, Yellow-throated and Large-billed Scrubwrens, Brown Gerygone, Scarlet Myzomela, Lewin's and Yellow-faced Honeyeaters, Silver-crowned Friarbird, Eastern Spinebill, Pale-yellow and White-browed Robins, Eastern Whipbird, Pied Butcherbird, Ground Cuckoo-shrike, Australian Reed-Warbler.

## Non-endemic Specialities

Sarus Crane*, Double-eyed Fig-Parrot, Australian Masked-Owl, Australasian Grass-Owl, Buff-breasted Paradise-kingfisher (Oct–Mar), Spotted Catbird, Graceful and Brown-backed Honeyeaters, Yellow-breasted Boatbill.

## Others

Australasian Grebe, Little Pied and Little Black Cormorants, Australian Darter, Magpie Goose, Wandering Whistling-Duck, Radjah Shelduck, Green and Cotton Pygmy-geese, White-eyed Duck, Intermediate Egret, Pied Heron, Rufous Night-Heron, Black Bittern, Australian and Straw-necked Ibises, Royal Spoonbill, Pacific Baza, Whistling Kite, Spotted Harrier, Brown Falcon, Orange-footed Scrubfowl, Brown Quail, Buff-banded Rail, Rufous-tailed Bush-hen, Baillon's and Spotless Crakes, Purple Swamphen, Dusky Moorhen, Brolga, Australian Bustard, Comb-crested Jacana, Latham's Snipe* (Oct–Apr), Bush Thick-knee, Emerald and Peaceful Doves, Wompoo, Superb and Rose-crowned Fruit-Doves, Torresian Imperial-Pigeon (Aug–Apr), Red-winged Parrot, Rainbow Lorikeet, Brush Cuckoo, Little (Sep–Mar), Gould's and Shining (Aug–Apr) Bronze-Cuckoos, Australian Koel (Sep–Apr), Channel-billed Cuckoo (Sep–Apr), Pheasant Coucal, Rufous and Barking Owls, Australian Owlet-Nightjar, Spotted and Large-tailed Nightjars, White-throated Needletail (Oct–Apr), Fork-tailed Swift (Oct–Apr), Azure Kingfisher, Blue-winged Kookaburra, Forest Kingfisher, Rainbow Bee-eater, Dollarbird (Sep–Apr), Fairy, White-throated and Large-billed Gerygones, Dusky Myzomela, White-throated Honeyeater, Little, Helmeted and Noisy Friarbirds, Blue-faced Honeyeater, Rufous Shrike-Thrush, Grey-crowned Babbler, Willie-wagtail, Rufous Fantail, Black-faced (Sep–Mar) and Spectacled Monarchs, Leaden, Satin (Sep–Mar), Restless and Shining Flycatchers, Torresian Crow, Australasian Magpie, Magpie-lark, Olive-backed Oriole, Green Figbird, Black-faced and Yellow-eyed Cuckoo-shrikes, Common Cicadabird (Sep–Apr), Olive-tailed Thrush (*cuneata* race), Golden-headed Cisticola, Tawny Grassbird, Crimson Finch, Chestnut-breasted Munia, Australasian Pipit, Mistletoebird, Olive-backed Sunbird.

## Other Wildlife

Carpet python, common and mountain brushtail possums, dingo, greater glider, green, Herbert river and lemuroid ringtail possums, long-nosed bandicoot, Lumholtz's tree-kangaroo, musky rat-kangaroo, platypus, red-legged pademelon, spectacled flying-fox, striped possum, white-tailed rat and birdwing butterflies, including Cape York birdwing.

There are many sites worth birding on the Atherton Tablelands, but the one to concentrate on is arguably **Crater National Park**, which is about 20 km south of Atherton via the Kennedy Highway. This park lies on Mount Hypipamee, which rises to nearly 1000 m (3281 ft), hence it supports most of the high-altitude forest specialities, including the small *minor* race of White-throated Treecreeper, Tooth-billed Catbird*, Golden Bowerbird*, Fernwren*, Atherton Scrubwren*, Mountain Thornbill*, Bridled Honeyeater and Chowchilla (which are often found in groups accompanied by musky rat-kangaroos, one of Australia's few diurnal mammals). Bird the forest alongside the entrance road to the car park (Golden Bowerbird* in fruiting trees), around the car park (Lesser Sooty-Owl*, Southern Boobook) and the trail down to the crater from the car park (Atherton Scrubwren* occurs in the gulley to the left of this track after the second bridge). To look for Golden Bowerbird*, which attend their bowers mostly between October and January, park in the gravel lay-by 2.2 km south of the turning to the crater and take the track west. After 270 m or so there is an obscure trail north to a bower which is attended by a bird used to visitors. The whole area is also good for spotlighting mammals such as long-nosed bandicoot and Lumholtz's tree-kangaroo.

**CRATER NP**

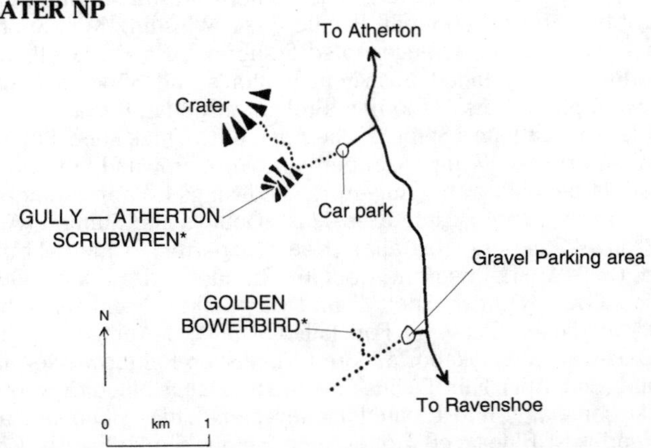

If Crater National Park is closed, try the **Wongabel Botanical Walk** south of Atherton for Tooth-billed Catbird* and Victoria's Riflebird. In suitable conditions **Hasties Swamp**, 3 km south of Atherton, supports Plumed Whistling-Duck, crakes and rails (including Rufous-tailed Bush-hen), Sarus Crane* (which fly in to roost at dusk), Comb-crested Jacana, Latham's Snipe* and Tawny Grassbird. Turn west off the Kennedy Highway on to Hasties Road, then south on to Koci Road to reach the swamp. East of Atherton platypus occurs in the river 3–4 km west of Yungaburra (look south from the bridge in the late afternoon). The forests surrounding **Lake Eacham**, about 4 km east of Yungaburra, and **Lake Barrine** (Wandering Whistling-Duck), about 10 km east of Yungaburra, both of which are accessible via 6 km long circular walking tracks, support a similar selection of birds to Crater National Park. There are plenty of leeches here and at all forest sites on the Atherton Tablelands. North of Atherton bird **Nardellos Lagoon**, west of the Kennedy Highway 1 km north of Walkamin, where Latham's Snipe*, as well as Green and Cotton Pygmy-geese occur; **Tinaroo Creek Road**, a few kilometres east of Mareeba, where Black Bittern (along stream which crosses the track to the right at the first crossroads), Squatter Pigeon (most likely at dawn), Channel-billed Cuckoo, Blue-winged Kookaburra, Silver-crowned Friarbird and Black-throated Finch occur; and the rice fields alongside **Pickford Road**, west off the Kennedy Highway a couple of kilometres south of Biboohra, where Black Bittern, Sarus Crane* and Black-throated Finch occur.

*Victoria's Riflebird is one of Australia's two endemic birds-of-paradise. Males are few and far between, and difficult to see well, so one in full display would be a real prize*

The rarely reported Buff-breasted Buttonquail*, along with Painted Buttonquail, has been recorded in the short, sparse grassy areas east of the Mareeba–Mount Molloy Road about 1.5 km south of **Big Mitchell Creek**, which is about 20 km north of Mareeba. White-browed Robin occurs along the creek (walk west from the road towards the dam), as well as Red-winged Parrot, Great Bowerbird (which also occurs in Mount Molloy cemetery), Red-browed Pardalote, Banded Honeyeater, Silver-crowned Friarbird, Lemon-bellied Flycatcher and Black-throated Finch. The rare buttonquail, along with Painted Buttonquail, has also been recorded along **Baker's Road** which leads west from the Mareeba–Mount Molloy Road, south of Mount Molloy. Look for this elusive bird on the small hill between the two tracks leading north after the

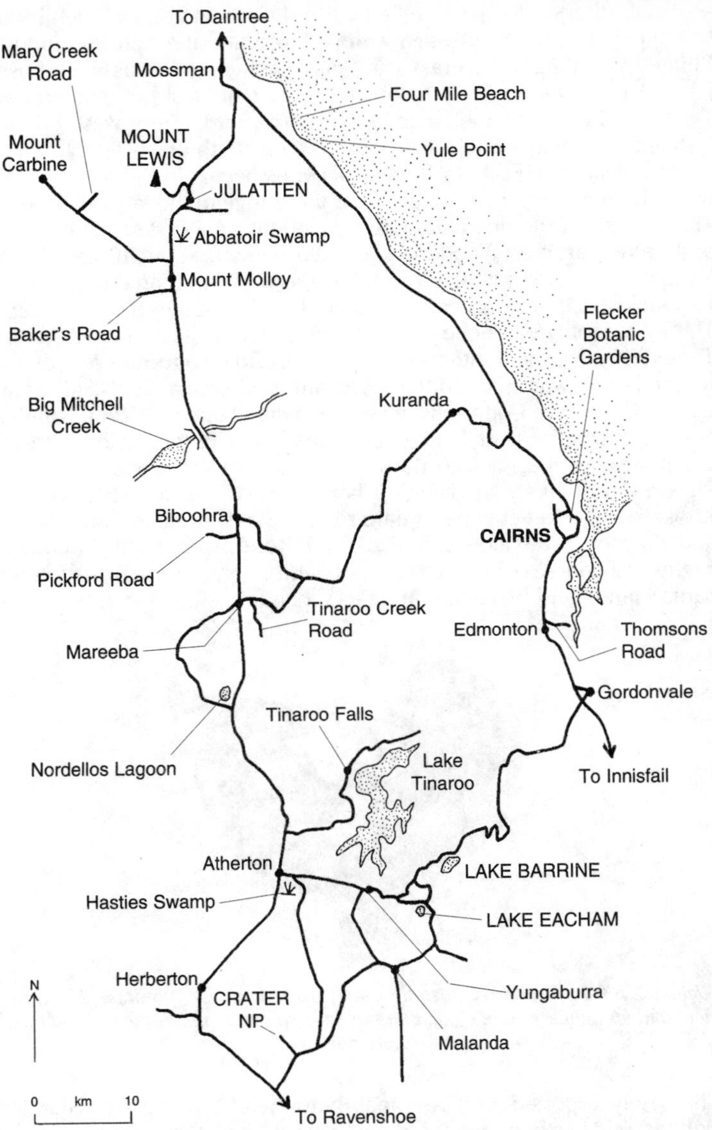


fourth cattle grid along this road. Near Mount Molloy turn northwest to bird the **Mount Molloy–Mount Carbine Road**, where Australian Bustard occurs in roadside fields full of termite hills 4 km north of Station Creek, and along Mary Creek Road, which leads east a little further north, especially around the orchid farms after a few kilometres. Check the clumps of trees to the east of the main road a little further north of the Mary Creek Road turn-off for Red-tailed Black-Cockatoo and the power lines alongside the stretch of road north of here for Red-backed Kingfishers. After the wolfram quarry at Mount Carbine comes into view look out for telegraph pole number CAR 196 on the east side of the road and take the obscure track opposite to reach a small dam after 500 m, which is a good site for Squatter Pigeon. Other species recorded along the Mount Molloy–Mount Carbine Road include Pale-headed Rosella, Blue-winged Kookaburra, Great Bowerbird, Grey-crowned Babbler and Black-throated Finch. In suitable conditions the wetland known as **Abbatoir Swamp** near Hunter's Creek, situated a couple of kilometres along McDougall's Road which leads east off the Mount Molloy–Julatten Road, supports a good assortment of waterbirds including Green Pygmy-goose and White-browed Crake.

## JULATTEN AND MOUNT LEWIS

The rainforests at the northern end of the Atherton Tablelands around the small settlement of Julatten and on nearby Mount Lewis, about 100 km northwest of Cairns, support most of the northeast Queensland endemics, including Golden Bowerbird* and Victoria's Riflebird, as well as a number of other specialities shared only with New Guinea, including Buff-breasted Paradise-Kingfisher and Yellow-breasted Boatbill, and the widespread but localised Red-necked Crake and Blue-faced Parrotfinch.

Many of the species which occur here can also be seen at the southern end of the Atherton Tablelands (see p. 129).

### Localised Australian Endemics

Lesser Sooty-Owl*, Australian Swiftlet, Tooth-billed Catbird*, Golden Bowerbird*, Lovely Fairywren, Fernwren*, Atherton Scrubwren*, Mountain Thornbill*, Yellow-spotted, Bridled*, Yellow and Macleay Honeyeaters, Grey-headed Robin*, Bower's Shrike-Thrush*, Chowchilla, White-eared and Pied Monarchs, Victoria's Riflebird.

### Other Australian Endemics

Pacific Heron, Australian Brush-turkey, Brown Cuckoo-Dove, Topknot Pigeon, Scaly-breasted Lorikeet, Southern Boobook (*lurida* race), Tawny Frogmouth, Laughing Kookaburra, Satin and Great Bowerbirds, Red-backed Fairywren, Yellow-throated and Large-billed Scrubwrens, Brown Gerygone, Scarlet Myzomela, Lewin's Honeyeater, Pale-yellow Robin, Eastern Whipbird, Red-browed Firetail.

### Non-endemic Specialities

Red-necked Crake, Papuan Frogmouth, Buff-breasted Paradise-kingfisher (Oct–Mar), Noisy Pitta, Spotted Catbird, Graceful and Brown-backed Honeyeaters, Yellow-breasted Boatbill, Blue-faced Parrotfinch.

### Others

Pacific Baza, Grey Goshawk (white phase), Collared Sparrowhawk, Australian Hobby, Orange-footed Scrubfowl, Buff-banded Rail, Bush Thick-knee, Wompoo and Superb Fruit-Doves, Torresian Imperial-Pigeon (Aug–Apr), Little (Sep–Mar) and Gould's Bronze-Cuckoos, Channel-billed (Sep–Apr) Cuckoo, Rufous and Barking Owls, Australian Owlet-Nightjar, Large-tailed Nightjar, Azure and Forest Kingfishers,

Dollarbird (Sep–Apr), Fairy Gerygone, Dusky Myzomela, White-throated Honeyeater, Grey Whistler, Rufous Fantail, Black-faced (Sep–Mar) and Spectacled Monarchs, Black Butcherbird, Olive-backed and Green Orioles, Green Figbird, Yellow-eyed Cuckoo-shrike, White-winged and Varied Trillers, Metallic Starling (Jul–Apr), Chestnut-breasted Munia, Olive-backed Sunbird.

## Other Wildlife

Agile wallaby, amethystine python, coppery brushtail possum, greater glider, green, Herbert river and lemuroid ringtail possums, long-nosed and northern brown bandicoots, Lumholtz tree-kangaroo, platypus, red-necked pademelon, short-beaked echidna, spectacled flying-fox, striped possum.

(Other species recorded here include Chestnut-breasted Cuckoo (Sep–Apr/Mount Lewis), Australian Masked-Owl and Australasian Grass-Owl).

Julatten is arguably the best base for birding in the Cairns area of north-east Queensland, and **Kingfisher Caravan Park**, which is run by friendly birders, is probably the best place for independent birders to stay. It is situated just north of the small village of Julatten, which is about 10 km north of Mount Molloy, off the road to Mossman, and should not be confused with Julatten Caravan Park. Birding begins in earnest in the grounds, where Red-necked Crakes are regularly seen near dusk by the pool at the back of orchard, Buff-breasted Paradise-kingfishers sometimes breed and Noisy Pittas can be quite tame. To boot, platypuses paddle along Bushy Creek just behind the park. Many of the other species listed above also occur in the park, but the montane forest specialities and Blue-faced Parrotfinch are restricted to nearby **Mount Lewis**. This state forest reserve is accessible via Mount Lewis Road which leads left a few kilometres north of the caravan park, off the road to Mossman. The parrotfinch can be very elusive, but occurs most regularly about 3 km up the road, in a lush gulley on a sharp left-hand bend 300 m below the 'State Forest' sign, and in the clearing 12 km up the road. There is a trail leading from this clearing along which montane specialities such as Tooth-billed Catbird*, Lovely Fairywren, Atherton Scrubwren*, Mountain Thornbill* and Bridled Honeyeater occur. A couple of kilometres along this trail, take the left fork to a small dam, backtrack about 70 m and enter the forest to the right on an obscure trail, which after 50 m reaches a bower which belongs to a Golden Bowerbird*. The best time to look for this forest gem is between October and January when the bower receives the most attention. Lesser Sooty-Owl* and Southern Boobook also occur on Mount Lewis. The birders who run Kingfisher Caravan Park will probably know the whereabouts of any species which are proving dificult to find, especially owls, if they are around, and what the latest arrangements are for visiting Mount Lewis, as a permit is sometimes required.

*Accommodation:* Kingfisher Park Birdwatchers Lodge, PO Box 3, Julatten 4871, Queensland (tel: 070 94 1263; fax: 070 94 1466)—cabins (A/including free birding information and guided walks), campsite (B).

At Kingfisher Caravan Park, Red Mill House B&B (tel: 070 98 6169) or the Daintree General Store (tel: 070 98 6146) it is possible to book a place on the daily two-hour **Daintree River Cruise**, a very pleasant way to almost certainly see Great-billed Heron*, Black Bittern, Little Kingfisher and Papuan Frogmouth, as well as saltwater crocodile. Beach Thick-knee occurs on the beaches alongside the large area of mangroves at **Yule Point** near Port Douglas, 55 km north of Cairns. Head for Pebbly Beach, which is well signposted from the Captain Cook Highway, and walk north, also looking out for Varied Honeyeaters in the mangroves. Beach Thick-knee also occurs at **Cape Tribulation**, a national park and very popular tourist destination where the rainforest begins at the beach. Other birds recorded here include Chestnut-breasted Cuckoo (Sep–Apr), Lovely Fairywren and Metallic Starling (Jul–Apr), all of which have been recorded in the Noah's Beach area.

## CAPE YORK

The low-lying Cape York peninsula which forms the northeast tip of Australia is a land of eucalypt woodlands, grasslands, swamps and, most importantly, large tracts of tropical coastal rain forest, which together support 20 species which are found nowhere else in Australia. Most of these are widespread outside the country, particularly in New Guinea, but they also include two endemics: Golden-shouldered Parrot*, which occurs in the arid southern half of the peninsula, and White-streaked Honeyeater.

The northern end of this far-flung corner of the continent is only accessible by road (4WD only) during the dry season (May–Nov) when some specialities are absent, and the peak time to visit is during the wet season (Dec–Apr) when the only way in is by air.

### Localised Australian Endemics

Buff-breasted Buttonquail* (May–Nov), Squatter Pigeon, Golden-shouldered Parrot*, Lovely Fairywren, White-streaked Honeyeater, White-eared Monarch.

### Cape York Non-endemic Specialities

Red-cheeked and Eclectus Parrots, Palm Cockatoo*, Chestnut-breasted Cuckoo (Sep–Apr), Yellow-billed Kingfisher, Red-bellied Pitta (Dec–Apr), Fawn-breasted Bowerbird, Beccari's Scrubwren, Green-backed and Tawny-breasted Honeyeaters, Yellow-legged Flycatcher, White-faced Robin, Northern Scrub-Robin, Black-winged (Oct–Mar) and Frilled Monarchs, Trumpet Manucode, Magnificent Riflebird, Black-backed Butcherbird.

### Other Australian Endemics

Black-breasted Kite, Southern Boobook (*lurida* race), Great Bowerbird, Banded Honeyeater, White-browed Robin, Pied Butcherbird, Masked Finch.

### Other Non-endemic Specialities

Red-necked Crake, Beach Thick-knee, Double-eyed Fig-Parrot (*marshalli* race), Marbled Frogmouth, Buff-breasted Paradise-kingfisher (Oct–Mar), Noisy Pitta, Spotted Catbird, Graceful Honeyeater, New Guinea Friarbird, Yellow-breasted Boatbill.

## Others

Great and Lesser Frigatebirds, Emerald Dove, Wompoo, Superb and Rose-crowned Fruit-Doves, Torresian Imperial-Pigeon (Aug–Apr), Oriental Cuckoo (Oct–Apr), Gould's Bronze-Cuckoo, Rufous Owl, Little Kingfisher, Blue-winged Kookaburra, Dollarbird (Oct–Apr), Fairy Gerygone (*personata* race), White-throated Honeyeater, Grey Whistler, Lemon-bellied Flycatcher, Northern Fantail, Broad-billed, Satin (Sep–Mar) and Shining Flycatchers, Metallic Starling (Jul–Apr).

## Other Wildlife

Green python, grey cuscus, native cat, spiny-haired bandicoot, spotted cuscus.

(Other species recorded here include Southern Cassowary*, Red Goshawk*, Papuan Frogmouth and Blue-faced Parrotfinch.)

Golden-shouldered Parrot* occurs sparingly in the grassy roadside woodlands dotted with termite hills near **Musgrave**, around 310 km north of Mount Molloy on the rough Peninsula Developmental Road, especially around Windmill and Fifteen Mile Creeks, along with Black-backed Butcherbird (which occurs alongside the road from Laura northwards). The best time to look for the parrot is between September and November, at the end of the dry season, when they are most likely to be seen visiting the few remaining areas of water. Dawn at the dam on the east side of the Peninsula Developmental Road, south of Windmill Creek (16 km south of Musgrave), is a good starting point. Otherwise try the roadside between there and Fifteen Mile Creek, 7 km further south. All of the other Cape York specialities occur in **Iron Range National Park**, 90 minutes by air north of Cairns, which encompasses the largest remaining tract of lowland tropical rainforest in Australia and is the premier birding site on the peninsula. There are no facilities where the best birding is, so it is necessary to camp with all supplies (there is usually some freshwater fit for drinking in the creeks) to get the best out of this site. The best birding area is about 10 km north of Lockhart River Airport, around the Coen Road turn-off along the road to Portland Roads. It is possible to arrange a lift to the turn-off, but most birders end up walking. Concentrate on the patches of forest around here, although it will also be necessary to visit drier areas further

**IRON RANGE NP**

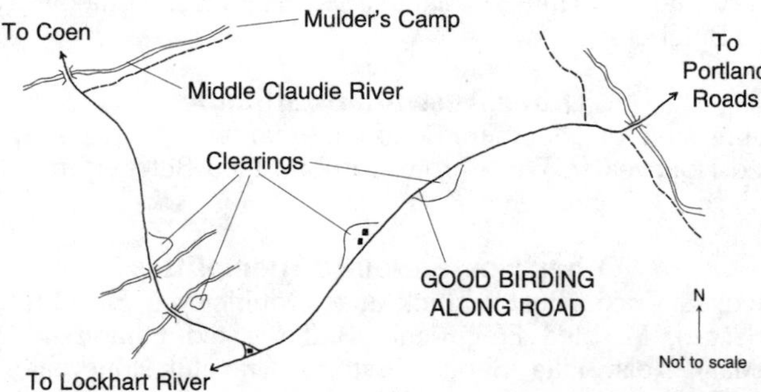

towards Portland Roads for Fawn-breasted Bowerbird and White-streaked Honeyeater. Both frigatebirds can be seen at the coast off Portland Roads. Around 230 species have been recorded around **Pajinka Wilderness Lodge**, which lies just 400 m from the northern tip of the peninsula, including White-streaked Honeyeater and all of the peninsula's non-endemic specialities, as well as Great Frigatebird, Beach Thick-knee and Noisy Pitta. The lodge is accessible by air and road, and there are 4WD vehicles available for exploration of the surrounding area.

*Accommodation:* Iron Range National Park—Lockhart River Aboriginal Community Guesthouse (A—tel: 070 60 7139). Chili Beach Camping Ground (a few kilometres south of Portland Roads), camping (take all supplies). Pajinka Wilderness Lodge—rooms (A+), camping (C), bookable in advance via PO Box 7757, Cairns 4870 (tel: 070 313 988, fax: 070 313 966) or at Cape York 4876 (tel: 070 692 100, fax: 070 692 110).

**Saibai Island**, at the northern end of the Torres Strait between Cape York and New Guinea, forms part of Australian territory and attracts a few species normally only associated with New Guinea, including Grey-headed Goshawk, Singing Starling and Red-capped Flowerpecker.

## CAIRNS

This tropical town in northeast Australia is the gateway to some exceptional birding, but the town itself should not be ignored because the Esplanade is famous the world over for providing close-up views of shorebirds at high tide, and the lowland tropical rainforest nearby supports a superb selection of 'town park' birds, including Red-necked Crake, Papuan Frogmouth, Little Kingfisher, Buff-breasted Paradise-Kingfisher, Noisy Pitta and Pied Monarch.

### Localised Australian Endemics

Australian Swiftlet, Lovely Fairywren, Yellow-spotted, Yellow and Macleay Honeyeaters, Pied Monarch.

### Other Australian Endemics

Yellow-billed Spoonbill, Red-capped Plover, White-headed Pigeon, Scaly-breasted Lorikeet, Laughing Kookaburra, Lewin's and Bar-breasted Honeyeaters.

### Non-endemic Specialities

Red-necked Crake, Double-eyed Fig-Parrot (*macleayana* race), Papuan Frogmouth, Buff-breasted Paradise-kingfisher (Oct–Mar), Noisy Pitta, Spotted Catbird, Graceful, Varied and Brown-backed Honeyeaters, New Guinea Friarbird.

### Others

Little Pied Cormorant, Australian Pelican, Australian Darter, Magpie Goose, Wandering Whistling-Duck, Green Pygmy-goose, Intermediate Egret, Rufous Night-Heron, Australian and Straw-necked Ibises, Royal Spoonbill, Black-necked Stork, Pacific Baza, Whistling and Brahminy Kites, White-bellied Sea-Eagle, Grey Goshawk, Australian Hobby, Orange-footed Scrubfowl, Buff-banded Rail, Purple Swamphen, Comb-crested Jacana, Latham's Snipe*, Little (Dec–Apr) and Far Eastern* Curlews, Marsh and Terek Sandpipers, Grey-tailed Tattler, Great Knot, Rufous-necked Stint, Sharp-tailed and Broad-billed (scarce) Sandpipers, Bush Thick-knee, Pied Oystercatcher, Pacific Golden-Plover, Mongolian Plover, Greater Sandplover, Silver Gull, Gull-billed and Caspian Terns, Lesser Crested-Tern, Peaceful Dove, Wompoo, Superb and Rose-crowned Fruit-Doves, Torresian Imperial-Pigeon (Aug–Apr), Rainbow Lorikeet, Fan-tailed Cuckoo, Gould's Bronze-Cuckoo, Pheasant Coucal, Rufous Owl, Little, Forest, Collared and Sacred Kingfishers, Rainbow Bee-eater, Dollarbird (Sep–Apr), Fairy and White-throated Gerygones, Brown Honeyeater, Dusky Myzomela, Noisy Friarbird, Mangrove Robin, Willie-wagtail, Rufous Fantail, Black-faced (Sep–Mar) and Spectacled Monarchs, Black Butcherbird, Magpie-lark, Olive-backed and Green Orioles, Green Figbird, Yellow-eyed and White-bellied Cuckoo-shrikes, Common Cicadabird (Sep–Apr), Varied Triller, Metallic Starling (Jul–Apr), Welcome Swallow, Chestnut-breasted Munia, Mistletoebird, Olive-backed Sunbird.

## Other Wildlife

Spectacled flying-fox.

(Other species recorded here include Southern Cassowary*, White-browed Crake, Wandering Tattler, Pectoral Sandpiper, Beach Thick-knee, Sooty Oystercatcher, Double-banded Plover (Feb–Aug), Masked Woodswallow and Pacific Swallow. Introduced species include Common Myna and Scaly-breasted Munia.)

Over 26 species of shorebird have been recorded along **The Esplanade** which overlooks extensive tidal mudflats. At low tide most birds are just specks in the distance, but at high tide, especially during the late afternoon and evening when the light is from behind, the views can be out of this world. Check the esplanade fig trees and adjacent gardens for Double-eyed Fig-Parrot, as well as Rufous Night-Heron, Varied Honeyeater and New Guinea Friarbird. Centenary Park, between Collins Avenue and Greenslopes Street, and Flecker Botanic Gardens, on the lower slopes of Mount Whitfield north of Collins Avenue, at the northern end of town, support a superb selection of birds, with possibilities including Rufous Owl and Papuan Frogmouth, as well as Red-necked (near dusk in forest patch traversed by Centenary Boardwalk) and White-browed Crakes, Latham's Snipe*, Bush Thick-knee (also occurs in Cairns Cemetery), Double-eyed Fig-Parrot, Little Kingfisher (at the saline one of the two Centenary Lakes), Graceful, Yellow and Brown-backed Honeyeaters, Mangrove Robin (in mangroves along the central channel) and Metallic Starling. The adjacent **Mount Whitfield Environmental Park** supports Buff-breasted Paradise-kingfisher, Noisy Pitta, Lovely Fairywren and Pied Monarch. There is also a boardwalk through the mangroves next to **Cairns Airport** where Little Kingfisher and Varied Honeyeater occur, and Little Curlew is possible on the airfield.

Southern Cassowary* and Red-necked Crake are just two birds on John and Rita Squire's garden list. They live at Cassowary House, Black Mountain Road, Kuranda, Queensland 4872, Australia (tel/fax: 070 937 318), which is situated in a forest clearing at 305 m (1000 ft) east of **Kuranda**, 27 km north of Cairns, and serves as an excellent, if expensive, guesthouse (A+). Other birds which visit the feeding station in the garden include Graceful, Yellow-spotted and Macleay Honeyeaters, and Victoria's Riflebird, while the adjacent forest supports Australian Brush-turkey, Wompoo Fruit-Dove, Lesser Sooty-Owl*, Buff-breasted Paradise-Kingfisher (Oct–Mar), Black-faced (Sep–Mar), Spectacled and Pied Monarchs, Yellow-breasted Boatbill and Spotted Catbird. The Squires cater especially for birders and a week's all-inclusive visit may produce up to 180 species within a 100 km radius of the house.

Little Kingfisher and Mangrove Robin occur in the mangrove-lined creek at the end of **Thomsons Road** in Edmonton, about 15 km south of Cairns. Park at the speedway track and walk north to the creek. South of the Thomsons Road turning off the Bruce Highway there are two **Turf Farms** where the short grass attracts a variety of shorebirds between December and April, including Little Curlew and Oriental Plover, as well as Oriental and Australian Pratincoles, and, occasionally Yellow Wagtail. Edmonton Turf Farm is well signposted and Yarrabunda Turf Farm is a little way along the road to Yarrabunda.

## GREAT BARRIER REEF

The Great Barrier Reef, which stretches for about 2000 km along the northeast coast of Australia, is one of the world's natural wonders, where everyone should go, at least for a day, especially birders in search of seabirds such as Black Noddy and the chance to relax a little with a bit of snorkelling. Fortunately, it is easy to visit Michaelmas Cay, where there is a sprinkling of Black Noddies amongst the Brown Noddies and several thousand Sooty Terns, on a day trip from Cairns.

It is best to book a few days in advance at the Tourist Information Centre (tel: 070 31 1751), which is at the south end of the Esplanade in Cairns.

### Non-endemic Specialities

Black Noddy.

### Others

Great and Lesser Frigatebirds, Brown Booby, Pacific Reef-Egret, White-bellied Sea-Eagle, Terek Sandpiper, Grey-tailed Tattler, Great and Lesser Crested-Terns, Roseate, Black-naped, Bridled and Sooty Terns, Brown Noddy, Emerald Dove, Rose-crowned Fruit-Dove, Torresian Imperial-Pigeon (Aug–Apr).

### Other Wildlife

Snorkelling and scuba-diving may reveal giant clam, green turtle and a kaleidoscope of tropical fishes.

(Other species recorded here include Masked and Red-footed Boobies, and Wandering Tattler. Some birders believe the white-eyes on Green Island include Ashy-bellied White-eye which, in Australia, is confined to islands off the northeast Queensland coast.)

Several companies in Cairns operate regular boat trips to the Barrier Reef. A day-trip to Michaelmas Cay (make sure you will be allowed to

land—usually for a couple of hours) and Hastings Reef (superb snorkelling and scuba-diving) on the *Seastar II* (A+), which leaves daily from Pier B, Marlin Marina, Cairns, is recommended. Tea, coffee and snorkelling gear is provided, but you must take your own food (don't eat just before snorkelling or scuba-diving). Thousands of seabirds breed on the small, sandy island (100 x 200 m) of **Michaelmas Cay**, mainly Sooty Terns and Brown Noddies, along with a few pairs of Black-naped Terns and Black Noddies. **Hastings Reef**, 54 km offshore, will be as exciting as Michaelmas Cay if you go snorkelling or scuba-diving, for this reef is alive with an astonishing variety of multi-coloured and multi-shaped fish, including such wonders as banana fish, harlequin parrot-fish, humphead wrasse, sweetlips and Valentin's pufferfish, as well as white-tipped reef-shark. It used to be possible to visit the low-lying forested coral cay known as **Green Island** (13 ha), 27 km east of Cairns, on the same trip as that to Michaelmas Cay, but the island now appears to be satisfied with being an exclusive resort. Black-naped Tern, Emerald Dove and Rose-crowned Fruit-Dove occur here, along with Grey-tailed Tattler, and there is an underwater observatory where numerous marine creatures including green turtle can be seen.

*Sooty Tern should be one of the highlights of a trip to Michaelmas Cay on the Great Barrier Reef.*

## MISSION BEACH

The dense lowland rainforest around this small coastal resort 130 km south of Cairns is the best site in Australia for Southern Cassowary*.

### Localised Australian Endemics

Yellow-spotted and Macleay Honeyeaters, Pied Monarch, Victoria's Riflebird.

### Non-endemic Specialities

Southern Cassowary*, Double-eyed Fig-Parrot, Buff-breasted Paradise-Kingfisher (Oct–Mar), Noisy Pitta, Graceful Honeyeater, Yellow-breasted Boatbill.

### Others

Black Bittern, Pacific Baza, Grey Goshawk, Orange-footed Scrubfowl, Rufous-tailed Bush-hen, Superb Fruit-Dove, Torresian Imperial-Pigeon (Aug–Apr), Fan-tailed Cuckoo, Azure Kingfisher, Fairy Gerygone, Spectacled Monarch, Black Butcherbird, Yellow-eyed Cuckoo-shrike, Metallic Starling (Aug–Apr).

(Other species recorded here include White-eared Monarch.)

**MISSION BEACH**

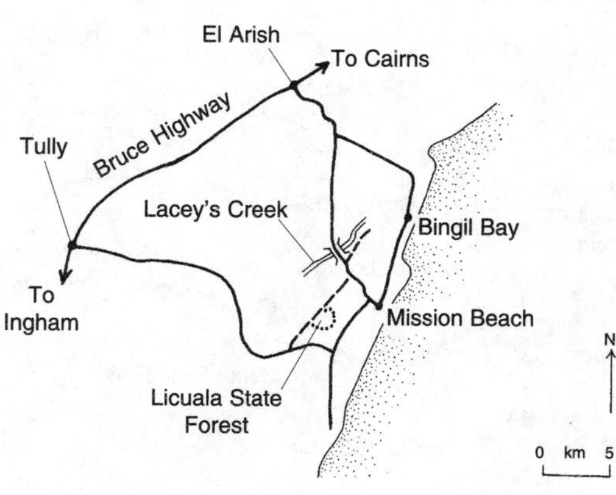

To reach the forest inland from this 14 km long string of beach settlements, turn east off the Bruce Highway at El Arish 35 km south of Innisfail. Southern Cassowaries* used to come to food at the Lacey's Creek car parks, but they became so tame and unwary that over 15% of the local population were killed by cars in 1990, and feeding was stopped. The best place to look for them now is along the trail through Licuala State Forest at dawn. Otherwise, it is probably best to ask the locals about recent sightings, or try the other roads and tracks at Lacey's Creek and near Hull River boat-ramp at South Mission Beach, accessible via Jackey Jackey Street off Kennedy Esplanade. Although they are big birds which can weigh over 50 kg and become dangerous if cornered, most cassowaries keep to the thickest parts of the forest where they are extremely difficult to see. The best time to look for them is probably in October and November when the adults should have young in tow.

Beach Thick-knees occur on the beach at **Cardwell**, between Tully and Ingham on the Bruce Highway, and these birds can be seen from the pier. Australian Masked-Owl (alongside entrance road to Broadwater Forest Park near Trebonne) and Australasian Grass-Owl have been recorded around freshly cut cane fields in the **Ingham** area. Southern Cassowary* (along the track to the falls and around the campsite), Lesser Sooty-Owl* (around the campsite), Noisy Pitta, Spotted Catbird, Chowchilla and Russet-tailed Thrush, as well as Platypus, have been recorded around the 280 m (917 ft) **Wallaman Falls**, 48 km west of Ingham via Trebonne.

## PALUMA AND MOUNT SPEC NATIONAL PARK

Mount Spec National Park, which straddles the Paluma Range 65 km southwest of Ingham, supports many of the northeast Queensland endemics, including Golden Bowerbird*, and the tea garden in Paluma offers the opportunity to see birds such as Victoria's Riflebird at very close range.

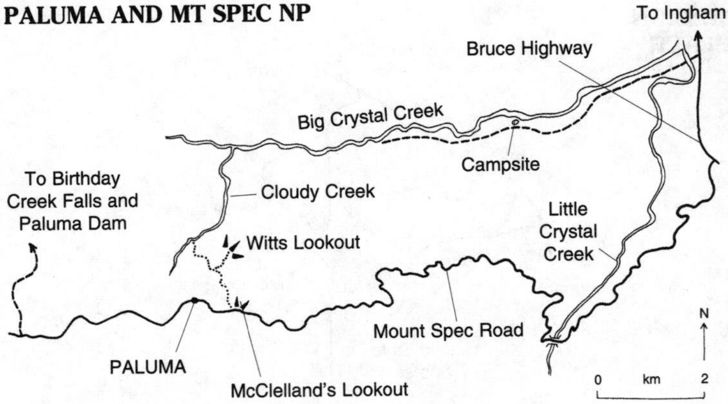

## Localised Australian Endemics

Lesser Sooty-Owl*, Tooth-billed Catbird*, Golden Bowerbird*, Fernwren*, Mountain Thornbill*, Yellow-spotted, Bridled* and Macleay Honeyeaters, Grey-headed Robin*, Chowchilla, Bower's Shrike-Thrush*, Pied Monarch, Victoria's Riflebird.

## Other Australian Endemics

Australian Brush-turkey, White-headed and Topknot Pigeons, Scaly-breasted and Little Lorikeets, White-throated Treecreeper (*minor* race), Yellow-throated and Large-billed Scrubwrens, Brown Gerygone, Scarlet Myzomela, Lewin's and White-cheeked Honeyeaters, Eastern Spinebill, Pale-yellow Robin, Eastern Whipbird, Red-browed Firetail.

## Non-endemic Specialities

Papuan Frogmouth, Buff-breasted Paradise-Kingfisher (Oct–Mar), Noisy Pitta, Spotted Catbird, Graceful Honeyeater.

## Others

Grey Goshawk, Emerald Dove, Fan-tailed Cuckoo, Shining (Aug–Apr) and Horsfield's Bronze-Cuckoos, Channel-billed Cuckoo (Sep–Apr), White-throated Needletail (Oct–Apr), Fairy Gerygone, Dusky Myzomela, Rufous Shrike-Thrush, Grey and Rufous Fantails, Spectacled Monarch, White-winged and Varied Trillers, Olive-tailed Thrush (*cuneata* race).

## Other Wildlife

Striped possum.

To reach the hamlet of **Paluma**, which is situated in montane rainforest at 800 m (2625 ft), turn west off the Bruce Highway 47 km south of Ingham (66 km northwest of Townsville). It is worth birding alongside the steep, narrow and twisting 18 km long road up to Paluma from here, and once there be sure to visit the Ivy Cottages Tea Garden (closed on Mondays) where the rewards for indulging in the extravagance of a cream tea go far beyond the taste buds, for here it is possible to see some otherwise elusive montane forest birds at close quarters. Don't forget a camera and plenty of film for the likes of Spotted Catbird, Yellow-spotted, Lewin's, Bridled, Macleay and White-cheeked Honeyeaters, Grey-headed Robin* and, best of all, Victoria's Riflebird. A walk along the forest trail at the bottom of the garden may reveal Chowchilla. At **Mount Spec National Park**, which lies to the north and east of Paluma, the best places to bird are McClellands Lookout (Lesser Sooty-Owl*), the trails to Witt's Lookout and Cloudy Creek (Papuan Frogmouth, White-throated Treecreeper, Fernwren* and Chowchilla, as well as striped possum at night), and the Birthday Creek Falls area, west of Paluma, where Golden Bowerbird* occurs. Ask at the craft shop in Paluma for precise locations of bowers or try the following: turn north 4 km west of Paluma on to the road to Paluma Dam (a rough track well worth birding anyway) and park in the car park after the right-hand bend at 6.8 km. Take the path opposite the car park up to a ridge, turn right and proceed to two fallen logs across the path. Walk directly downhill (left) from here for about 70 m to where there is a bower. The birds spend most of their time near the bower between October and January.

## TOWNSVILLE

Over 240 species have been recorded in the 33 sq km Townsville Common Environmental Park, and in suitable conditions it attracts an impressive variety of waterbirds, including Little Kingfisher, and grassland specialists such as Red-backed Buttonquail.

### Localised Australian Endemics

Yellow Honeyeater.

### Other Australian Endemics

Plumed Whistling-Duck, Red-kneed Dotterel, Great Bowerbird, Red-backed Fairywren, Brown Songlark.

### Non-endemic Specialities

Red-backed Buttonquail, Brown-backed Honeyeater.

### Others

Magpie Goose, Wandering Whistling-Duck, Green and Cotton Pygmy-geese, Rufous Night-Heron, Black-necked Stork, Pacific Baza, Brown and Blue-breasted Quails, Brolga, Australian Bustard, Comb-crested Jacana, Bush Thick-knee, Bar-shouldered Dove, Rainbow Lorikeet, Pheasant Coucal, Little Kingfisher, Blue-winged Kookaburra, Rainbow Bee-eater, White-throated Gerygone, White-throated Honeyeater, Torresian Crow, Black-faced Woodswallow, Green Figbird, White-winged and Varied Trillers, Tawny Grassbird, Chestnut-breasted Munia.

### Other Wildlife

Koala.

(Other species recorded here include Plum-headed Finch. Introduced species include Scaly-breasted Munia.)

Townsville Common Environmental Park is situated on the coast off Cape Pallarenda Road 6.5 km north of the town centre. To reach the park, which is best when wet (usually from December to July, but water was in short supply in the mid-1990s), take the Cape Pallarenda Road near the Rowes Bay Country Club. Freshwater Lagoon Road ends at a car park near a hide overlooking the lagoon and there is a good trail through the 'bush' near the ranger's house. Koalas are fairly easy to see alongside the track to the fort on **Magnetic Island**, a resort off Townsville.

## EUNGELLA NATIONAL PARK

Although this isolated area of rainforest, 83 km west of Mackay, supports a relatively poor avifauna, especially when compared with the forests to the north, it does boast an endemic honeyeater, as well as Regent Bowerbird.

### Localised Australian Endemics

Regent Bowerbird, Eungella Honeyeater*, White-eared Monarch.

**EUNGELLA NP**

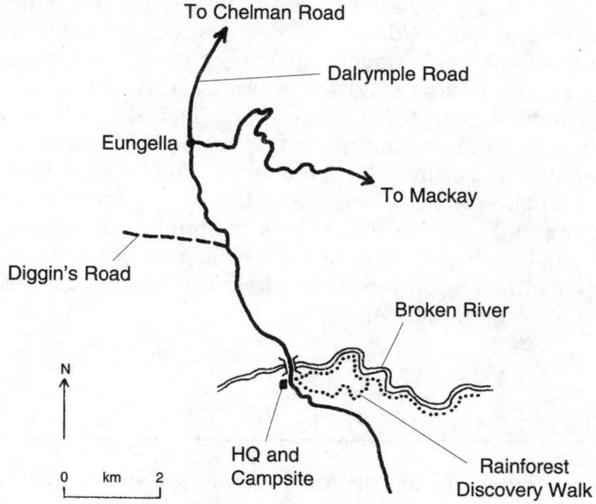


## Other Australian Endemics

Australian Brush-turkey, Brown Cuckoo-Dove, White-headed and Topknot Pigeons, Australian King-Parrot, Crimson Rosella, Laughing Kookaburra, Eastern Whipbird, Red-browed Firetail.

## Non-endemic Specialities

Noisy Pitta.

## Others

Rufous-tailed Bush-hen, Wompoo, Superb and Rose-crowned Fruit-Doves, Channel-billed Cuckoo (Sep–Apr), Azure Kingfisher, Black-faced (Sep–Mar) and Spectacled Monarchs, Yellow-eyed Cuckoo-shrike, Common Cicadabird (Sep–Apr).

## Other Wildlife

Platypus.

At Eungella township turn north on to the narrow track known as Dalrymple Road or south 6 km to the HQ and campsite alongside the Broken River. The honeyeater is an elusive species and the best thing to do on arrival at the HQ is to ask the rangers where the most recent sightings have been. Otherwise try Dalrymple Road, Chelmans Road (on the left 16 km along Dalrymple Road) and Diggin's Road, and the walking tracks which start at the picnic site near Broken River bridge, one of which leads to an observation platform overlooking Broken River, from which platypus is regularly seen. Beware of leeches.

**Bundaberg** lies in a good area for Mangrove Honeyeater and is the gateway to some islands and cays on the Great Barrier Reef, including **Lady Elliot Island**, a coral cay at the south end of the reef and a popular snorkelling and scuba-diving site, mainly thanks to the presence of loggerhead turtles and monstrous manta rays. The island also supports a superb variety of breeding seabirds, including Red-tailed Tropicbird (mostly Dec–Mar), Great and Lesser Frigatebirds, Black-naped Tern, and Brown and Black Noddies. It is accessible by air from Bundaberg (35 minutes) and has relatively cheap bungalows and permanent tents which can be booked in advance through Lady Elliot Island Resort, LMB 6, via Bundaberg 4670 (tel: 071 71 6077). **Raine Island**, an expensive island to get to at the north end of the reef, supports breeding Herald Petrel and Ashy-bellied White-eye. The huge **Fraser Island**, a World Heritage Area which lies off the Queensland coast near Bundaberg, is a good place to look for humpback whales between August and October. Organised whale-watching boat trips depart from a number of places on the shore of Hervey Bay, which lies between Fraser Island and Bundaberg.

## COOLOOLA NATIONAL PARK

This heathy headland east of Tin Can Bay near Gympie on the 'Sunshine Coast' about 150 km north of Brisbane supports the localised Ground Parrot*, as well as Australasian Grass-Owl and Southern Emuwren. There are also pockets of rainforest here which support Noisy Pitta and White-eared Monarch.

### Localised Australian Endemics

Ground Parrot*, White-eared Monarch.

**COOLOOLA NP**

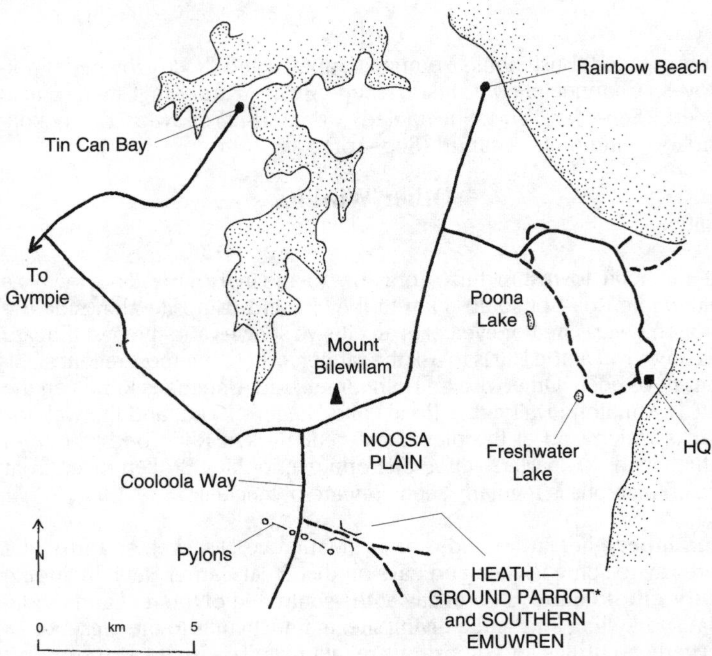

### Other Australian Endemics

Australian Brush-turkey, White-headed and Topknot Pigeons, Australian King-Parrot, Scaly-breasted Lorikeet, Southern Emuwren, Scarlet Myzomela, White-cheeked Honeyeater, Eastern Whipbird, Red-browed Firetail.

### Non-endemic Specialities

Australasian Grass-Owl, Noisy Pitta.

### Others

Blue-breasted Quail, Wompoo and Superb Fruit-Doves, Tawny Grassbird.

Turn east off the road to Tin Can Bay 47 km northeast of Gympie and head for Rainbow Beach. About halfway along this road turn south on to Cooloola Way, then head east along the track which starts before this road reaches some roadside pylons. When this track reaches a log bridge, stop and scan the heath of the Noosa Plain to the north for Ground Parrots*. They may take some finding, but have been known to visit the track puddles to drink. This is an area where access is restricted, so before leaving the track permission should be sought at the HQ, near Rainbow Beach.

## CONONDALE RANGE

The forested steep-sided gorges of the Conondale Range, 100 km or so north of Brisbane, boast a diverse avifauna. Crystal creeks flow through the eucalypt woodlands and subtropical rainforests where localised goodies such as Glossy Black-Cockatoo* and Marbled Frogmouth occur.

### Localised Australian Endemics

Glossy Black-Cockatoo*, Regent Bowerbird, White-eared Monarch, Paradise Riflebird*.

### Other Australian Endemics

Maned Duck, White-headed, Wonga and Topknot Pigeons, Australian King-Parrot, Pale-headed Rosella, Yellow-tailed Black-Cockatoo, Southern Boobook, Laughing Kookaburra, Red-backed and Variegated Fairywrens, Scarlet Myzomela, Lewin's and Yellow-faced Honeyeaters, Eastern Spinebill, Bell Miner, Pale-yellow Robin, Eastern Whipbird, Russet-tailed Thrush, Dusky Woodswallow, Red-browed Firetail.

### Non-endemic Specialities

Marbled Frogmouth, Logrunner.

### Others

Pacific Baza, Grey Goshawk, Brown Quail, Wompoo and Superb Fruit-Doves, Channel-billed Cuckoo (Sep–Apr), Azure Kingfisher, Rainbow Bee-eater.

### Other Wildlife

Koala, platypus, yellow-bellied glider.

## CONONDALE RANGE

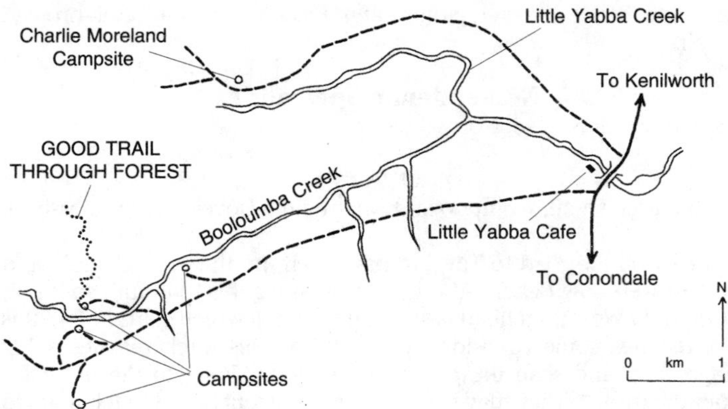


(Other species recorded here include Red Goshawk* and Black-breasted Buttonquail*.)

To reach the best sites in the Conondale Range, turn west off the Bruce Highway at Eumundi (50 km south of Gympie and 129 km north of Brisbane) and head 30 km to Kenilworth. Bird the area around the **Charlie Moreland Campsite**, reached by turning west 5 km south of Kenilworth, and along **Booloumba Creek**, reached by turning west 7 km south of Kenilworth. Glossy Black-Cockatoo* occurs on *casuarina*-covered slopes a few kilometres along the track above the four campsites at Boolumba Creek. In between these two sites, on the west side of the main road south of Kenilworth, look out for the Little Yabba Cafe, which is situated under a large fig tree which attracts Wompoo Fruit-Doves.

One of only a few known and accessible sites for the very rare Black-breasted Buttonquail* is **Neumgna State Forest** near Yarraman, 127 km northwest of Brisbane. Head southwest out of Yarraman on the New England Highway, then turn west after 2 km on to Yarraman Tarong Road until reaching some buildings on the north side of the road after about 800 m. Turn south here, then west after crossing a cattle grid on to a short track. Park at the end of here and explore the surrounding woodland on foot, looking for small 20 cm diameter circular cleared areas, known as platelets, amongst the leaf litter. Birds are usually present near fresh platelets and can be heard amongst the leaf litter. To see them, however, requires careful stalking. Greater Sooty-Owl and many of the species listed for Lamington National Park (see p. 153) occur in **Bunya Mountains National Park**, about 65 km southwest of Kingaroy. To look for the owl, head up the road from Quinalow and turn right to Dandabah where the road ends at a camping area. From here walk along the Scenic Circuit track, which passes through a huge hollow fig tree inside which an owl regularly roosts.

## BRISBANE

The rainforests on the slopes to the west and the coastal mudflats and mangroves to the east of Queensland's sprawling capital combine to support a diverse avifauna which includes an impressive collection of shorebirds and nightbirds, as well as Noisy Pitta, Mangrove Honeyeater and Spotted Quail-thrush.

### Localised Australian Endemics

Green Catbird, Regent Bowerbird, Mangrove Honeyeater, Spotted Quail-thrush, Paradise Riflebird*, Russet-tailed Thrush.

### Other Australian Endemics

Maned Duck, Australian Brush-turkey, Red-capped Plover, White-headed Pigeon, Brown Cuckoo-Dove, Crested, Wonga and Topknot Pigeons, Australian King-Parrot, Crimson and Pale-headed Rosellas, Yellow-tailed Black-Cockatoo, Scaly-breasted and Little Lorikeets, Southern Boobook, Tawny Frogmouth, Laughing Kookaburra, White-throated and Red-browed Treecreepers, Satin Bowerbird, Superb and Variegated Fairywrens, Spotted, Red-browed and Striated Pardalotes, Yellow-throated, White-browed and Large-billed Scrubwrens, Brown Gerygone, Brown and Striated Thornbills, Scarlet Myzomela, Lewin's and Yellow-faced Honeyeaters, Eastern Spinebill, Bell and Noisy Miners, Rose, Pale-yellow and Yellow Robins, Crested Shrike-tit, Eastern Whipbird, Grey and Pied Butcherbirds, Pied Currawong, Australian Reed-Warbler, Red-browed Firetail.

### Non-endemic Specialities

Wandering Tattler, Marbled Frogmouth, White-throated Nightjar (Sep–May), Noisy Pitta, Logrunner.

### Others

Australian Darter, Royal Spoonbill, Pacific Baza, Brahminy Kite, White-bellied Sea-Eagle, Grey Goshawk, Painted Buttonquail, Latham's Snipe* (Oct–Apr), Far Eastern Curlew*, Grey-tailed Tattler, Great Knot, Rufous-necked Stint, Sharp-tailed Sandpiper, Pied Oystercatcher, Pacific Golden-Plover, Mongolian Plover, Greater Sandplover, Double-banded Plover (Feb–Sep), Great Crested-Tern, Wompoo Fruit-Dove, Rainbow Lorikeet, Brush Cuckoo (Sep–Apr), Australian Koel (Sep–Apr), Channel-billed Cuckoo (Sep–Apr), Pheasant Coucal, Greater Sooty-Owl, Forest, Collared and Sacred Kingfishers, Dollarbird (Oct–Apr), White-throated and Mangrove Gerygones, Brown and White-throated Honeyeaters, Golden and Rufous Whistlers, Rufous and Grey Shrike-Thrushes, Willie-wagtail, Grey and Rufous (Sep-Apr) Fantails, Black-faced (Sep–Mar) and Spectacled Monarchs, Leaden Flycatcher (Sep–Apr), Torresian Crow, Australasian Magpie, Magpie-lark, Olive-backed Oriole, Green Figbird, Black-faced and Yellow-eyed (Sep–Mar) Cuckoo-shrikes, Common Cicadabird (Sep–Apr), Varied Triller, Olive-tailed Thrush, Welcome Swallow, Tree Martin, Mistletoebird.

### Other Wildife

Brown antechinus, common dunnart, greater and yellow-bellied gliders, red-legged pademelon.

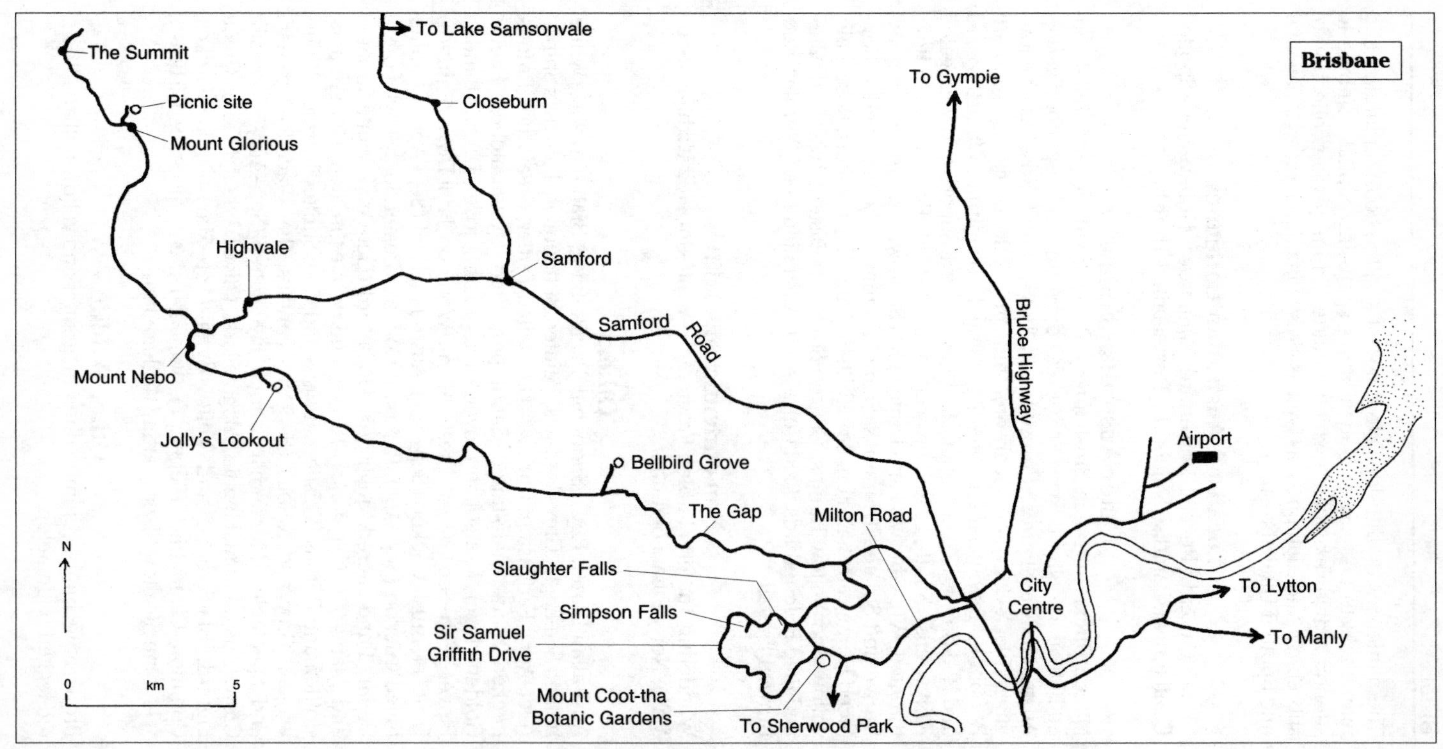
Brisbane
To Lake Samsonvale
The Summit
Picnic site
Mount Glorious
Closeburn
To Gympie
Highvale
Samford
Samford Road
Bruce Highway
Mount Nebo
Jolly's Lookout
Bellbird Grove
Airport
The Gap
Milton Road
Slaughter Falls
Simpson Falls
Sir Samuel Griffith Drive
Mount Coot-tha Botanic Gardens
To Sherwood Park
City Centre
To Lytton
To Manly
N
0
km
5

(Other species recorded here include Black-backed Bittern, Blue-breasted Quail, Red-backed and Black-breasted* Buttonquails, Asian Dowitcher* and Powerful Owl*.)

Birding around Brisbane starts at the airport where the car park is as good a site as any for Mangrove Honeyeater. The **Mount Coot-tha** area, at the southern end of Brisbane Forest Park 6 km west of the city centre via Milton Road, is an excellent place for nightbirds, including Powerful Owl*, Southern Boobook, Tawny Frogmouth and White-throated Nightjar. Bird around Slaughter Falls picnic site and the steep walking track from there to Constitution Hill, as well as the walking track from Simpson Falls picnic site to The Summit, both of which are accessible via the circular Sir Samuel Griffith Drive. The large areas of tall, open eucalypt woodland and subtropical rainforest at the northern end of Brisbane Forest Park in the D'Aguilar Range are full of birds and accessible via the Musgrave, Waterworks and Mount Nebo Roads. Spotted Quail-Thrush, as well as Painted Buttonquail, Red-browed Pardalote and Scarlet Myzomela, occur above **Bellbird Grove** 17 km northwest of the city centre, off Mount Nebo Road. From the car park walk up the track to the left to the top of the ridge (about 2 km) and scour the sparsely vegetated rocky slopes below to the left. About 13 km further up Mount Nebo Road it is worth stopping at **Jolly's Lookout**, where Red-browed Treecreeper is possible. Beyond the village of **Mount Glorious** (in Maiala National Park) park at the picnic site on the right and take the first right to Brown's Road. Walk down here for 500 m and at the 'pedestrians crossing' sign take the walking track left, which descends steeply to some wooden bridges. The forest here and along the track supports Greater Sooty-Owl and Marbled Frogmouth, as well as Noisy Pitta, Green Catbird, Regent Bowerbird, Logrunner, Paradise Riflebird* and Olive-tailed and Russet-tailed Thrushes, plus nocturnal mammals. There are a number of other walking tracks in the area which may be worth trying if time permits.

It is usually necessary to obtain permission from the Brisbane Waterboard before visiting **Lake Samsonvale**, which is about 30 km northwest of the city. Latham's Snipe* winters here, and in suitable conditions Blue-breasted Quail and Red-backed Buttonquail frequent the surrounding grasslands. The lake is best approached along Postman's Track, which is 9 km south of Dayboro. At the end of here park by the gate and walk along the track beyond to reach the lakeshore. Black-backed Bittern and a variety of crakes have occurred on the lake in **Sherwood Park** when the water level has been very low.

About 18,000 shorebirds winter (Nov–Mar) in the Moreton Bay area east of the city, with smaller numbers remaining throughout the summer. North of the Brisbane River Wandering Tattler and Double-banded Plover occur at **Redcliffe** (35 km) and **Scarborough Marina**, whilst nearby mangroves support Mangrove Honeyeater. South of the Brisbane River difficulties with access are compounded by land reclamation and development projects, but try the **Lytton**, **Wynnum**, **Thorneside** and **Manly** areas for Asian Dowitcher*, as well as Far Eastern Curlew*, Grey-tailed Tattler, Great Knot and Red-capped Plover, whilst remnant mangroves and seafront gardens support Mangrove Gerygone and Mangrove Honeyeater.

One of the best places to seawatch from in Australia is Point Lookout at the northeastern tip of **North Stradbroke Island** ('Straddy' to the locals), accessible via ferries from Cleveland, south of Manly. Strong southeasterlies during the austral winter (Apr–Sep) and summer cyclones usually bring the best birds, which have included albatrosses, Black-winged, White-necked*, Cook's*, Kermadec and Providence* Petrels, Streaked, Buller's*, Flesh-footed, Fluttering and Hutton's* Shearwaters, Red-tailed and White-tailed Tropicbirds, Great and Lesser Frigatebirds, Masked Booby, White-fronted, Black-naped, Bridled and Sooty Terns, Blue-grey, Brown and Black Noddies, and Common White-Tern. From May to October there is a also a chance of seeing humpback whales. There is a Wedge-tailed Shearwater colony on Camel Rock and the rocky beaches to the west of the point support Wandering Tattler.

## BRISBANE PELAGIC

Remote sensing satellite images have shown that there are streams of water carrying high concentrations of marine organisms, often hundreds of kilometres long, flowing through the still waters off the east Australian coast, probably originating in the Great Barrier Reef to the north. These 'sea streams' attract numerous seabirds, including Tahiti Petrel, which is rare elsewhere off the Australian coast, and during October up to 37 migrant Mottled Petrels have been seen in one day.

To book a place on the organised boat trips out of Southport, 75 km south of Brisbane, contact the Brisbane Seabird Study Group, c/o Paul Walbridge, 135 Lytton Road, East Brisbane, Queensland 4169, Australia (tel/fax: 07 3391 8839).

### Non-endemic Specialities

Tahiti (Oct–Apr) and Providence* (Apr–Sep) Petrels, White-tailed Tropicbird.

### Others

Cape (Apr–Nov), White-necked* (Nov–Mar), Gould's (Oct–Mar) and Great-winged (Apr–Sep) Petrels, Fairy Prion (Apr–Oct), Streaked (Jan–Apr), Wedge-tailed, Flesh-footed (Nov–Mar), Short-tailed (Oct–May), Fluttering and Hutton's* Shearwaters, Wilson's Storm-Petrel, Australian Gannet, Brown Booby (Nov–Mar), Great Crested-Tern, Bridled and Sooty Terns, Brown Noddy.

(Other species recorded at sea off the Brisbane region include Wandering Albatross* (Apr–Nov), Antarctic Giant-Petrel, Kerguelen, Black-winged, Mottled (Oct), Kermadec (Oct–Nov, Mar/Apr), White-headed, Soft-plumaged (Oct), Blue and White-chinned (Apr–Sep) Petrels, Buller's Shearwater* (Oct–Apr), Black-bellied (Apr–Sep) and White-bellied (Apr–Sep) Storm-Petrels, Red-tailed Tropicbird, Masked Booby, White-fronted Tern (Apr–Sep), Blue-grey and Black Noddies, and Common White-Tern.)

The Gold Coast Seaworld research vessel usually departs the Gold Coast Seaworld every four to six weeks, leaving at 0700 and returning between 1400 and 1500. If the trip is cancelled it may be worth seawatching from Southport, or heading 14 km down the coast to Burleigh Heads National Park, where Sooty Oystercatcher and short-beaked echidna occur.

*One of the best birds of the Brisbane area is the stunning black and yellow Regent Bowerbird. It is particularly common and easy to see at Lamington National Park*

## LAMINGTON NATIONAL PARK

This 205 sq km park, which straddles a 1100 m (3609 ft) escarpment 110 km south of Brisbane, is one of the finest birding sites in Australia. The eucalypt woodland, subtropical rainforest and temperate rainforest support a wealth of rare, spectacular and exciting birds, including Noisy Pitta, the amazing Albert's Lyrebird*, the very rare Rufous Scrub-bird*, the stunning Regent Bowerbird, Eastern Bristlebird*, Logrunner and, last but by no means least, Paradise Riflebird*.

It is warm and wet here from November to March, when leeches can be a serious problem, and dry but cool to cold from April to October.

### Localised Australian Endemics

Black-breasted Buttonquail*, Glossy Black-Cockatoo*, Albert's Lyrebird*, Rufous Scrub-bird*, Green Catbird, Regent Bowerbird, Eastern Bristlebird*, Olive Whistler, White-eared Monarch (Sep–Apr), Paradise Riflebird*, Russet-tailed Thrush.

### Other Australian Endemics

Australian Brush-turkey, White-headed Pigeon, Brown Cuckoo-Dove, Crested, Wonga and Topknot Pigeons, Australian King-Parrot, Crimson and Pale-headed Rosellas, Scaly-breasted Lorikeet, Southern Boobook, Tawny Frogmouth, Laughing Kookaburra, White-throated and Red-browed Treecreepers, Satin Bowerbird, Red-backed, Superb and Variegated Fairywrens, Spotted and Striated Pardalotes, Yellow-throated, White-browed and Large-billed Scrubwrens, Buff-rumped, Brown and Striated Thornbills, Brown Gerygone, Scarlet Myzomela, Lewin's, Yellow-faced and White-naped Honeyeaters, Eastern Spinebill, Bell and Noisy Miners, Rose, Pale-yellow and Yellow Robins, Eastern Whipbird, Grey Butcherbird, Pied Currawong, Red-browed Firetail.

### Non-endemic Specialities

Marbled Frogmouth, Noisy Pitta, Logrunner.

### Others

Pacific Baza, Grey Goshawk, Wedge-tailed Eagle, Bar-shouldered Dove, Wompoo Fruit-Dove, Brush (Sep–Apr) and Fan-tailed (Sep–Apr) Cuckoos, Shining Bronze-Cuckoo (Aug–Apr), Australian Koel (Sep–Apr),

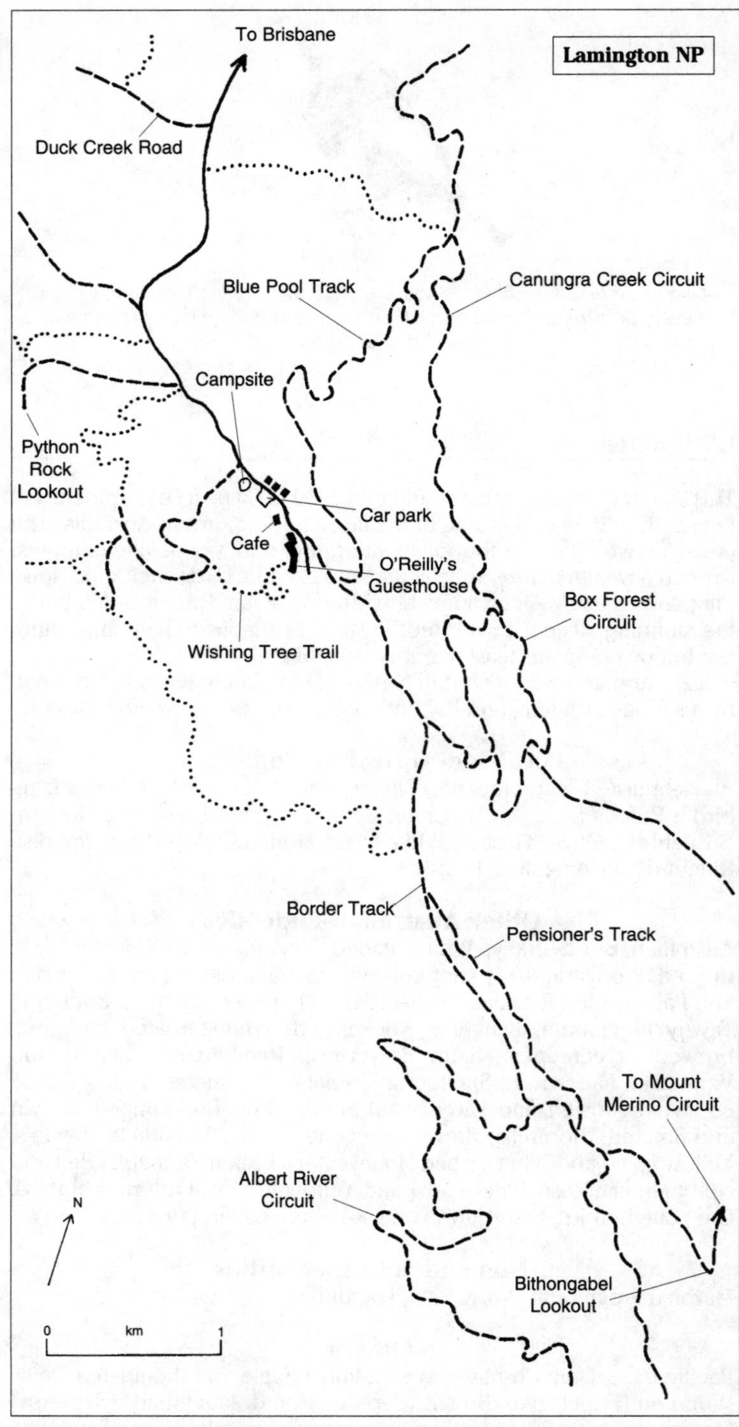
Lamington NP
To Brisbane
Duck Creek Road
Blue Pool Track
Canungra Creek Circuit
Campsite
Python
Rock
Lookout
Car park
Cafe
O'Reilly's
Guesthouse
Box Forest
Circuit
Wishing Tree Trail
Border Track
Pensioner's Track
To Mount
Merino Circuit
Albert River
Circuit
N
Bithongabel
Lookout
0
km
1

Channel-billed Cuckoo (Sep–Apr), White-throated Needletail (Oct–Apr), Australian Owlet-Nightjar, Dollarbird (Sep–Apr), White-throated and Blue-faced Honeyeaters, Varied Sittella, Golden and Rufous Whistlers, Willie-wagtail, Grey and Rufous (Sep–Apr) Fantails, Thrush, Black-faced (Sep–Mar) and Spectacled (Sep–Mar) Monarchs, Leaden Flycatcher (Sep–Apr), Torresian Crow, Magpie-lark, Olive-backed Oriole, Green Figbird, Black-faced Cuckoo-shrike, Common Cicadabird (Sep–Apr), Varied Triller, Olive-tailed Thrush, Welcome Swallow, Mistletoebird.

## Other Wildlife

Brush-tailed phascogale, carpet python, common ringtail possum, common wallaroo, dingo, greater and sugar gliders, green tree-snake, long-nosed bandicoot, mountain brushtail possum (bobuck), pretty-faced and whiptail wallabies, red-necked pademelon, spotted-tailed quoll.

(Other species recorded here include Greater Sooty-Owl, Powerful Owl*, Superb Lyrebird and Spotted Quail-thrush.)

The park HQ is 110 km south of Brisbane via Canungra and 70 km south-west of the Gold Coast via Nerang and Canungra. Scaly-breasted Lorikeet and Pale-headed Rosella occur in Canungra, from where the 30 km long steep and winding road ascends to 700 m (2297 ft) at 'Green Mountains', the park hub. On the way up check clumps of *casuarinas* for Glossy Black-Cockatoo* and the wooded hills for whiptail wallaby, and 500 m below the turning to Duck Creek Road it is worth spending some time in the patch of forest looking for Marbled Frogmouth. Birding begins in earnest around the campsite and O'Reilly's Guesthouse at Green Mountains, for normally skulking birds have become rather tame and conspicuous here, and they include such delights as Wonga Pigeon, Noisy Pitta, and Regent and Satin Bowerbirds. Ask politely at O'Reilly's if you can walk the **Wishing Tree Trail** which lies within their grounds, for there is a Satin Bowerbird's bower along here and it is also a good place to see Regent Bowerbird and canopy dwellers at Mick's Tower. Guests at O'Reilly's can see a number of normally shy forest birds at close quarters as they come to feeding trays throughout the grounds, including Regent Bowerbird, and a floodlit feeding station next to the restaurant attracts mountain brush-tail possums, red-necked pademelons and sugar gliders at night.

Beyond O'Reilly's bird the forest trails. Albert's Lyrebird* and Rufous Scrub-bird* occur along the 21 km long **Border and Pensioner's Tracks**. The lyrebird is most likely to be seen at dawn, along the edge of the tracks, before the many non-birding visitors to the park rise from their slumbers for a stroll. The scrub-bird is a super-skulker in damp, mossy areas of high-altitude temperate forest dominated by Antarctic beech (*Nothofagus*). It favours forest patches with short, but dense, undergrowth and is most likely to be seen between October and December when the birds are at their most vocal. The best places to try are between the Wanungara and Nyamulli Lookouts, 5.5 to 6 km from Green Mountains, and the **Mount Merino Circuit** at the end of the Pensioner's Track. From Green Mountains also bird the **Python Rock Lookout Trail**, which is also good for Albert's Lyrebird*, particularly at dawn, and along **Duck Creek Road**, which is actually a track which passes through dry, open eucalypt woodland which supports Black-breasted Buttonquail*, Pale-headed Rosella (around the farm at the bottom of the track), Glossy Black-Cockatoo*, Marbled Frogmouth (in forest 1 km from the top of the track), Eastern Bristlebird*, Rose Robin and Spotted Quail-thrush (scarce). To look for the rare Black-breasted Buttonquail* park 7.7 km down the track, between the 'Watson's Wood' and 'Fleming Family Crest' signs, walk about 70 m down the track on the right, then look for the buttonquails along the obscure trail which descends off this track on the right into an area of *lantana*, a South American shrub with small pink flowers which forms dense thickets on the woodland floor. To look for the bristlebird, head further down Duck Creek Road, park at the right-hand hairpin and walk down the track for 1 km to 'Bristlebird Creek' (which is signposted) where, aptly enough, this species skulks.

*Accommodation:* O'Reilly's Rainforest Guesthouse (A+), bookable in advance via 'Green Mountains', Lamington National Park, Via Canungra, QLD 4275 (tel: 075 44 0644, fax: 075 44 0638). Camping (C), best booked in advance via the Ranger at the same address as above (tel: 075 44 0634).

Albert's Lyrebird* also occurs on **Mount Tambourine** along the walking tracks in Palm Grove National Park about 3 km east of Doughty Park.

Two national parks near Warwick, 164 km southwest of Brisbane, support Painted Buttonquail, Turquoise Parrot*, Spotted Quail-thrush, Diamond Firetail and Plum-headed Finch. To reach **Girraween National Park** HQ, take the minor road signposted 'Storm King Dam' southeast from Stanthorpe. In this park bird roadsides, the trails leading from the HQ, especially Junction Track (Painted Buttonquail, Turquoise Parrot* and Spotted Quail-thrush) and the Old Wallangarra Road (Turquoise Parrot* and Plum-headed Finch) which is on the left beyond the HQ. To reach **Sundown National Park** head for Tenterfield from Wallangarra, then turn west towards Goondiwindi. The turning to the park is along the road north from here towards Stanthorpe. Turquoise Parrot* and Plum-headed Finch occur alongside the entrance road. Other species recorded here include White-browed Woodswallow and White-backed Swallow.

## *OUTBACK*

### BRISBANE TO BIRDSVILLE

On the 1882 km journey by road and track from Brisbane west to Birdsville via Cunnamulla, Quilpie and Windorah it is possible to see some outstanding outback specialities in some splendid country, including Letter-winged Kite, Inland Dotterel, Crimson and Orange Chats, Hall's Babbler and two quail-thrushes.

Some parts of this route, especially west of Windorah, are very rough, so a 4WD is recommended, especially for people intending to tackle the Birdsville Track from the north. It would also be wise not to take on this journey during the intense heat of summer (Oct–Apr).

### Localised Australian Endemics

Letter-winged Kite, Inland Dotterel, Flock Bronzewing*, Bourke's Parrot, White-browed Treecreeper, Spotted Bowerbird, Rufous-crowned Emuwren, Striated Grasswren, Crimson, Orange and Desert Chats, Hall's and Chestnut-crowned Babblers, Chestnut-breasted (*castaneothorax* race) and Cinnamon Quail-thrushes, Plum-headed Finch.

### Other Australian Endemics

Black Falcon, Spinifex Pigeon, White-winged and Variegated Fairy-wrens, Crested Bellbird, Apostlebird, Little Crow, Masked Woodswallow, Ground Cuckoo-shrike, Brown Songlark.

### Others

Spotted Harrier, Brolga, Australian Bustard, Australian Pratincole, Australian Owlet-Nightjar, Grey-crowned Babbler.

(Other species recorded on this journey include Freckled Duck*, Baillon's, Australian and Spotless Crakes, Red-necked Avocet and Grey-headed Honeyeater.)

From Cunnamulla head west towards **Eulo** and after 40 km or so start looking out for Bourke's Parrots (which visit Eulo Bore, about 50 km west of Cunnamulla, to drink), White-browed Treecreeper, Spotted Bowerbird (which also occurs in Eulo Public School Grounds), Grey-headed Honeyeater, Crested Bellbird, Hall's and Chestnut-crowned Babblers, the eastern *castaneothorax* race of Chestnut-breasted Quail-thrush (on ridges south of the road) and Plum-headed Finch. Freckled Duck* has been recorded on **Lake Bindegolly** between Eulo and Thargomindah, as well as crakes, Brolga, Red-necked Avocet, Spotted Bowerbird and Orange Chat (along west shore). From Thargomindah it is possible to travel south, with 4WD and full survival gear, to the Bulloo Overflow where Grey Grasswren* occurs (see p. 90), and the Strzelecki Track where Chestnut-breasted Whiteface* occurs (see p. 160). To reach Birdsville and the Birdsville Track, however, it is best to travel north from Thargomindah to **Quilpie**. Crimson Chat and Hall's Babbler have been recorded around the usually dry creek 161 km northwest of Quilpie. From here it is 85 km northwest to Windorah where there is a tempting diversion to deal with, because Rufous-crowned Emuwren and Striated Grasswren occur around the mine workings at Opalton, a 700 km round trip to the north.

*One of Australia's most amazing outback birds is the White-winged Fairywren—a long-tailed blue jewel with 'snow on its back'*

About 109 km west of **Windorah**, turn south on to the Birdsville Development Road to reach Birdsville the short way, or, better still, continue northwest to **Bedourie** on the Diamantina Development Road which traverses the sparsely vegetated gravelly plains and *spinifex*-covered red dunes at the edge of the Simpson Desert where Black Falcon, Australian Bustard, Inland Dotterel, Flock Bronzewing*, Spinifex Pigeon, and Orange and Desert Chats occur. A small colony of Letter-winged Kites bred alongside the creek at Bedourie in 1992.

## BIRDSVILLE TRACK

The remote 517 km long rough track between Birdsville and Marree in central Australia traverses sparsely vegetated semi-desert, sandy ridges and stony gibber. This is true outback, at the border between the Simpson Desert to the west and the Sturt Stony Desert to the east, and the stark landscape is relieved only by a few, usually dry, bushy creeks and some, rarely wet, marshes. The Birdsville Track is probably the best in the outback for raptors, especially Letter-winged Kite, and it also enables access to sites which support such great rarities as Grey* and Eyrean* Grasswrens, and Yellow Chat*.

This track passes through dangerously hot desert country where as recently as the early 1990s a British birder died of hyperthermia, despite taking along an adequate supply of water. It is best to not to tackle it during the intense heat of summer (Oct–Apr), but those who do should drink plenty of water even if they don't feel thirsty and take along full survival equipment, including vehicle spares and emergency supplies of fuel and water. A 4WD is recommended if approaching the track from the north, but it is possible to bird the south end, in suitable weather conditions, with a 2WD.

### Localised Australian Endemics

Letter-winged Kite, Inland Dotterel, Banded Lapwing, Flock Bronzewing*, Grey* and Eyrean* Grasswrens, Banded Whiteface, Crimson, Orange, Yellow* (Nov–Mar) and Desert Chats, Hall's Babbler, Chirruping Wedgebill, Cinnamon Quail-thrush.

### Other Australian Endemics

Black-breasted Kite, Black Falcon, Stubble Quail, White-winged Fairywren, Red-browed Pardalote, Little Crow, White-backed Swallow, Brown Songlark.

### Others

Wedge-tailed and Little Eagles, Brolga, Australian Bustard, Australian Pratincole, Spotted Nightjar, Black-faced Woodswallow.

(Other species recorded here include Grey Falcon* and Red-necked Avocet.)

From Birdsville the track descends in to the Diamantina River floodplain and on to **Goyder's Lagoon**, a seasonal swamp 80 km downstream from Birdsville. 100 km from Birdsville the track enters the Sturt Stony Desert, a vast flat expanse of shiny stones which characterise the

## BIRDSVILLE TRACK

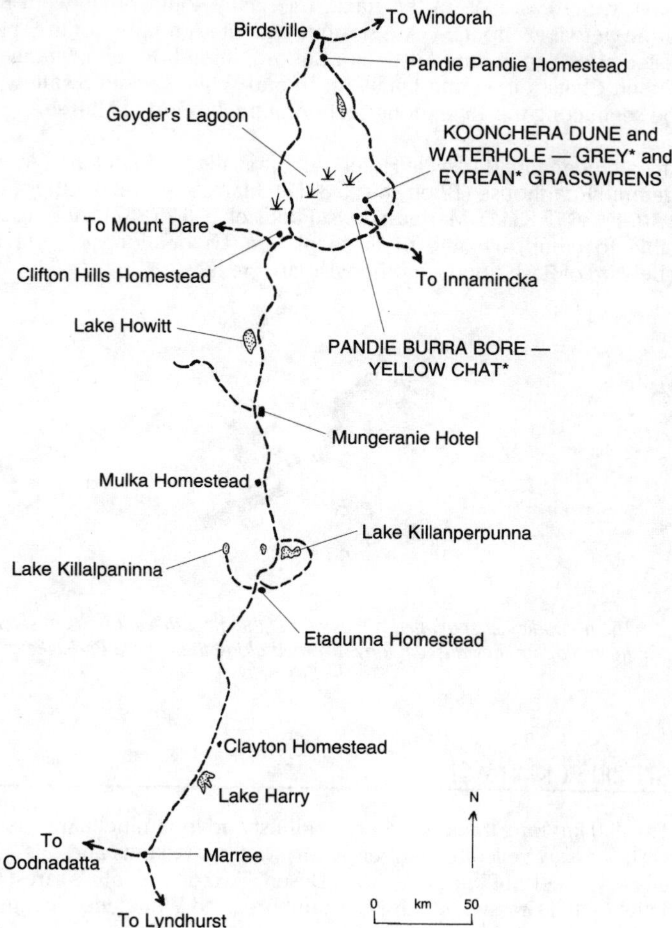


gibber. About 118 km south of Birdsville (400 km north of Marree), turn west to **Koonchera Dune** and the waterhole, 20 km away. Both Grey* and Eyrean* Grasswrens occur here, with Eyrean* present in *spinifex* and canegrass on the top of the dune 1 km east of the waterhole and Grey* present in the *lignum* flats 1–2 km east of the waterhole, on the south side of the dune. Other species present in the Koonchera area include Flock Bronzewing*, Orange and Desert Chats, Cinnamon Quail-thrush and White-backed Swallow. About halfway along the track to the waterhole turn south to **Pandie Burra Bore**, one of the few relatively reliable sites for Flock Bronzewing* and Yellow Chat*, although the latter is usually only present during the height of summer. Back on the main track Eyrean Grasswren* also occurs on Lake Surprise Dune, 20 km south of the turning to Koonchera. South of here the main track crosses more dunes and a couple of coolabah creeks before reaching Clifton Hills homestead, from where it is about 80 km on a very rough section of the track to Mungeranie Hotel where Eyrean Grasswren* occurs in *spinifex* on the larger, more stable sand dunes which run parallel to the east side of the track, especially south of Derwent River. From here it is about 235 km south to Marree. A number of the species listed above, including Australian Bustard, Inland Dotterel, Orange and Desert Chats, Cinnamon Quail-thrush and White-backed Swallow, can be seen along the 15 km long section of track north of Marree.

*Accommodation:* Birdsville Hotel (A). Birdsville Caravan Park (A). Mungeranie Roadhouse (B/tel: 086 75 8317). Marree—Great Northern Hotel (A/tel: 086 75 8344). Marree Tourist Park (tel: 086 75 8371). It is also possible to camp at some of these places (C) or alongside the track (beware of flash floods in otherwise dry creeks).

*The nomadic Letter-winged Kite is one of the most difficult birds to see in Australia, but they are regularly recorded along the remote Birdsville and Strzelecki Tracks.*

## STRZELECKI TRACK

The 499 km long track between Lyndhust and Innamincka traverses the vast, sparsely vegetated gibber plains, wispy grasslands and bushy, usually dry, creeks of the Great Stony Desert. Two of Australia's rarest birds, Thick-billed Grasswren* and Chestnut-breasted Whiteface*, occur here and both can be seen within 30 km of Lyndhurst with a 2WD. Birders brave enough to cover the whole track may also be rewarded with such delights as Letter-winged Kite and Grey Falcon*.

This is fine, if somewhat dangerous, birding country and birders preparing to complete the whole track, rather than concentrate on the southern end, should take along full survival gear, including vehicle spares and emergency supplies of fuel and water. The best time to go is between May and September.

### Localised Australian Endemics

Letter-winged Kite, Grey Falcon*, Inland Dotterel, Thick-billed* and Eyrean* Grasswrens, Chestnut-breasted* and Banded Whitefaces, Desert Chat, Chestnut-crowned Babbler, Chirruping Wedgebill, Cinnamon Quail-thrush.

### Other Australian Endemics

Emu, Bluebonnet, Mulga Parrot, Budgerigar, Pink Cockatoo*, Galah, Brown Treecreeper, White-winged Fairywren, Striated Pardalote, Red-

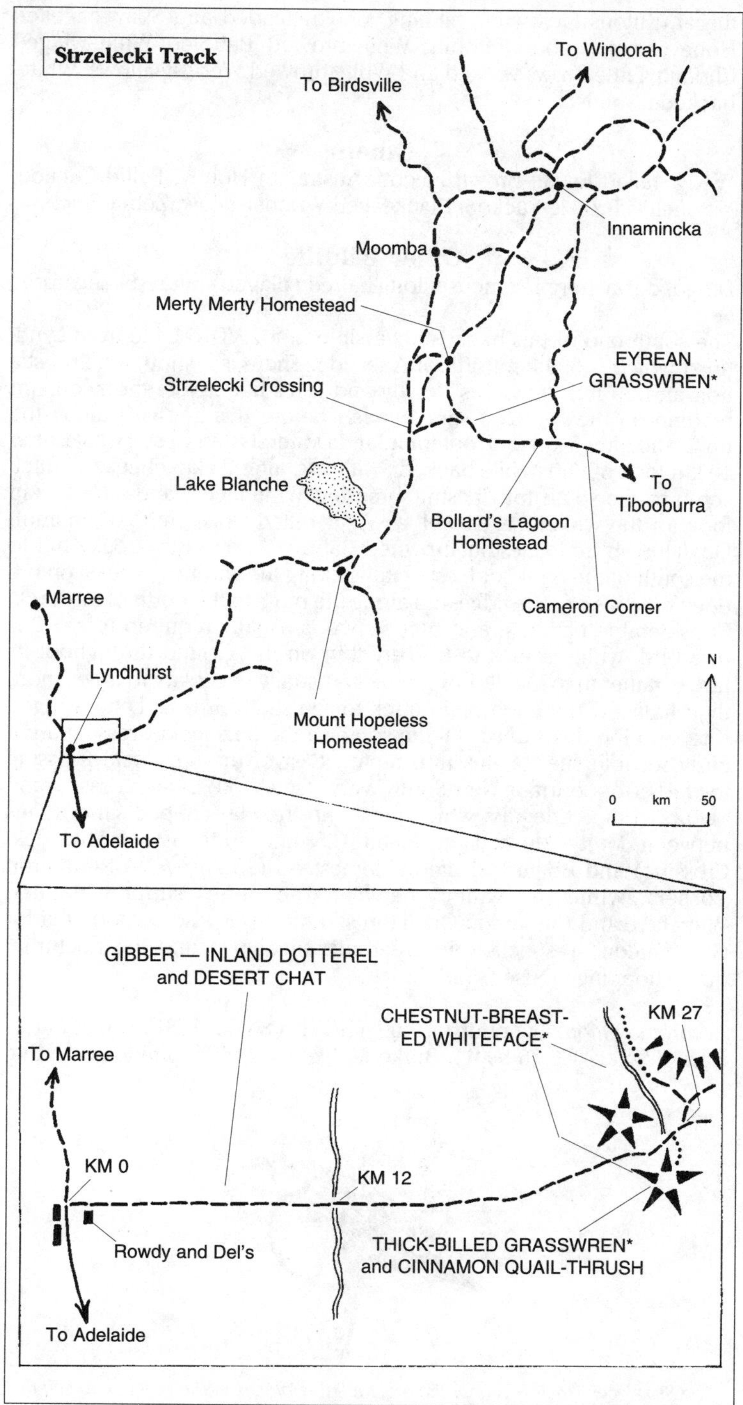
Strzelecki Track
To Windorah
To Birdsville
Innamincka
Moomba
Merty Merty Homestead
EYREAN
GRASSWREN*
Strzelecki Crossing
Lake Blanche
To
Tibooburra
Bollard's Lagoon
Homestead
Marree
Cameron Corner
N
Lyndhurst
Mount Hopeless
Homestead
0 km 50
To Adelaide
GIBBER — INLAND DOTTEREL
and DESERT CHAT
CHESTNUT-BREAST-
ED WHITEFACE*
KM 27
To Marree
KM 0
KM 12
Rowdy and Del's
THICK-BILLED GRASSWREN*
and CINNAMON QUAIL-THRUSH
To Adelaide

throat, Rufous Fieldwren, Singing, Brown-headed and Spiny-cheeked Honeyeaters, Hooded Robin, White-browed Babbler, White-winged Chough, Little Crow, Masked and White-browed Woodswallows, White-backed Swallow.

### Others

Wedge-tailed Eagle, Brown Falcon, Australian Hobby, Pallid Cuckoo, Horsfield's Bronze-Cuckoo, Black-faced Woodswallow, Zebra Finch.

### Other Wildlife

Dingo, dusky hopping-mouse, long-haired (plague) rat, red kangaroo.

The south end of this track is accessible in a 2WD vehicle from Lyndhurst which is 590 km north of Adelaide. There is a shop, a petrol station and an inn known as Rowdy and Del's here. Note the kilometre reading on the vehicle's speedometer before heading east along the track and after 5 km look out for Inland Dotterels and Desert Chats, after 10 km look out for White-backed Swallows, after 24 km check the thick scrub to the south for Chestnut-breasted Whiteface*, and after 27 km look for the whiteface, as well as Thick-billed Grasswren*, Cinnamon Quail-thrush and Chestnut-crowned Babbler, around the rocky hill to the south of the track and, especially, along the shrubby creeks, on the open area west of the ridge and along the ridge to the north of the track. Considerable patience and persistence is usually required to see this rare bird, which seems to be very thin on the ground throughout its range, rather than locally common. It is usually necessary to travel more than halfway along the main track to see such birds as Letter-winged Kite, and the dead trees 5–6 km south of the Strzelecki Crossing are a fairly reliable site for this rare raptor. East of the Strzelecki Crossing towards Tibooburra in New South Wales (see p. 90) Eyrean Grasswren* occurs in the canegrass which grows on the clay-capped sand dunes between Merty Merty Homestead (25 km northeast of Strzelecki Crossing) and Bollard's Lagoon Homestead (15 km west of Cameron Corner), while the valleys between the dunes support Banded Whiteface and Cinnamon Quail-thrush and this is also a good area for Grey Falcon* (especially in creekside eucalypts) and the nocturnal dusky hopping-mouse (sand dunes).

*Accommodation:* Lyndhurst Hotel (B/Tel: 086 75 7781). Innamincka Hotel (A/Tel: 086 75 9901). Burke Lodge, care of Innamincka Trading

*The Strzelecki Track is one of the most reliable places in the outback to see the delightful Inland Dotterel*

Post (B/Tel: 086 75 9900). It is also possible to camp alongside the track (beware of flash floods in otherwise dry creeks).

The 429 km long **Oodnadatta Track** which passes alongside Lake Eyre (South), between Marree and Oodnadatta, traverses flat and undulating desert, gibber and saltbush country where some outback specialities occur, including Bourke's Parrot and Desert Chat, and where a number of nomadic species have been recorded, including Black and Pied Honeyeaters, and Orange Chat. It is possible to tackle this track in a 2WD during the height of the dry season, which is usually in July and August. Lake Eyre has only been anywhere near full on three occasions during the last 150 years and the most recent saturation occurred in 1974, so expect to see a blinding white pan rather than a shallow, saline wetland full of birds.

*The massive Wedge-tailed Eagle is widespread throughout Australia, and, especially in the outback, is often seen standing on roads where they have landed in search of carrion*

## ALICE SPRINGS

The sprawling, dusty tin-roofed ramshackle town of 'Alice' lies in the middle of the most sparsely populated part of the planet, apart from the polar ice-caps and oceans. Apart from the surprisingly well vegetated, but usually dry, deep gorges in the 300 km long red rock ridge known as the MacDonnell Ranges, the town is surrounded by superb desert country with areas of sand, spiky *spinifex* and mulga. There are plenty of birds around Alice despite the harsh terrain and they include Bourke's Parrot, Western Bowerbird, Rufous-crowned Emuwren, Dusky Grasswren, Grey Honeyeater and Crimson Chat.

### Localised Australian Endemics

Bourke's Parrot, White-browed Treecreeper, Western Bowerbird, Rufous-crowned Emuwren, Dusky Grasswren (*purnelli* race), Slaty-backed Thornbill, Banded Whiteface, Black, Pied and Grey Honeyeaters, Crimson Chat, Spinifex-bird, Painted Firetail.

### Other Australian Endemics

Plumed Whistling-Duck, Black Swan, Maned and Pink-eared Ducks, Pacific Heron, Yellow-billed Spoonbill, Black-breasted Kite, Little Buttonquail, Australian Crake, Black-tailed Native-hen, Red-necked Avocet, Red-kneed Dotterel, Common Bronzewing, Crested and Spinifex

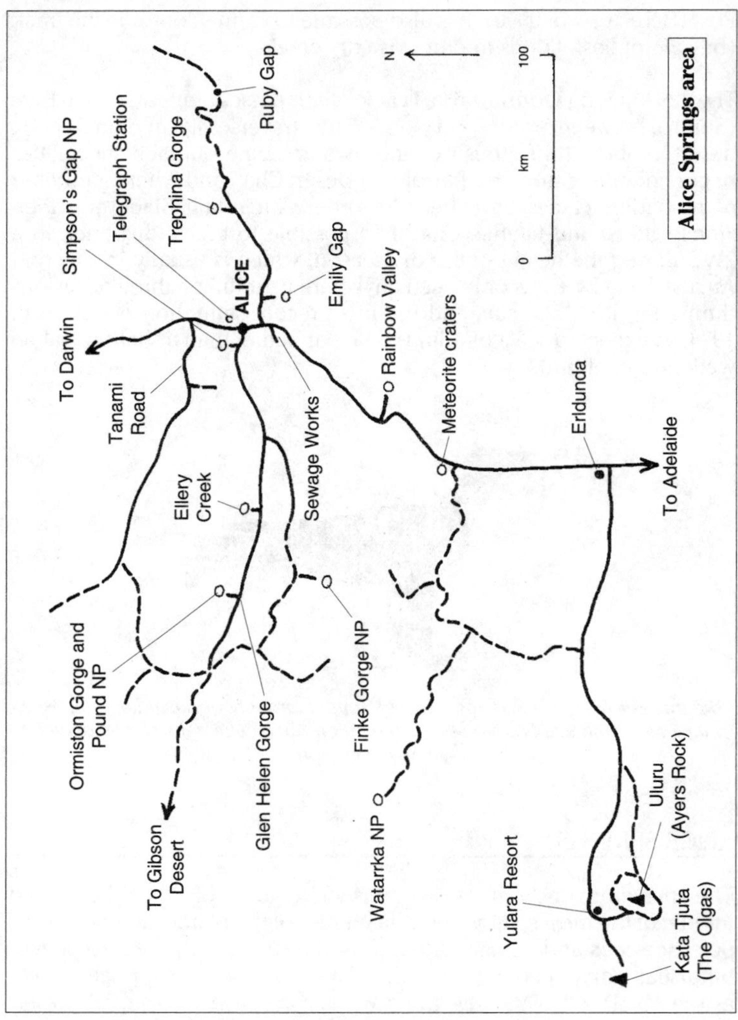


**Alice Springs area**

Pigeons, Diamond Dove, Mallee Ringneck, Mulga Parrot, Budgerigar, Pink Cockatoo*, Galah, Red-backed Kingfisher, White-winged, Splendid and Variegated Fairywrens, Red-browed Pardalote, Redthroat, Inland, Yellow-rumped and Chestnut-rumped Thornbills, Weebill, Western Gerygone, Southern Whiteface, Singing, Grey-headed, White-plumed, Golden-backed and White-fronted Honeyeaters, Yellow-throated Miner, Spiny-cheeked Honeyeater, Red-capped and Hooded Robins, Crested Bellbird, White-browed Babbler, Little Crow, Little Woodswallow, Pied Butcherbird, Ground Cuckoo-shrike, Australian Reed-Warbler, Brown and Rufous Songlarks.

## Others

Hoary-headed Grebe, White-eyed Duck, Intermediate Egret, Royal Spoonbill, Collared Sparrowhawk, Wedge-tailed and Little Eagles, Australian Hobby, Black-fronted Dotterel, Horsfield's Bronze-Cuckoo, Australian

Owlet-Nightjar, Spotted Nightjar, Rainbow Bee-eater, Grey-crowned Babbler, Black-faced Woodswallow, White-winged Triller, Tree and Fairy Martins, Little Grassbird.

## Other Wildlife

Black-footed rock wallaby, red kangaroo, wallaroo.

(Other species recorded here include Freckled Duck*, Grey Falcon*, Inland Dotterel, Banded Lapwing, Cockatiel, Orange Chat, Masked and White-browed Woodswallows, White-backed Swallow, Zebra Finch.)

Alice Springs is accessible by air, or 450 km by road from Uluru National Park (Ayers Rock), 1511 km by road from Darwin and 1542 km by road from Adelaide.

Most of the waterbirds listed above occur only at the **Alice Springs Sewage Works**, 3 km south of the town centre. To reach here, head south on the Stuart Highway towards the airport, then turn west on to Commonage Road, from which it is possible to view the pools from the outside. To look for Grey Honeyeater, head north along the Stuart Highway and after 21 km turn west on to **Tanami Road**. About 30 km along here, 500 m west of the 'Kunoth Well' signpost and a windmill next to a dam, turn south on to the track which leads to Hamilton Downs Youth Camp. Bird the mulga on the west side of this track between 2 and 5 km south of its junction with Tanami Road. Mulga and Bourke's Parrots, White-browed Treecreeper, Inland and Slaty-backed Thornbills, and Crimson Chat also occur here, especially after rain, while Inland Dotterel and Banded Lapwing have been recorded to the east of the track. **Heavitree Gap**, just south of the town centre along the Todd River, supports Dusky Grasswren (at the top of the steep *spinifex*-covered slopes on the west side), but the best place around Alice to see this bird is arguably **Simpson's Gap**, a National Park 22 km west of town. They occur on the *spinifex*-covered slopes above the car park here, to the left before the gorge. Other species present in Simpson's Gap include Spinifex Pigeon, Diamond Dove, Inland Thornbill, Grey-headed Honeyeater, Little Woodswallow, Painted Firetail and black-footed rock wallaby. The secretive Rufous-crowned Emuwren, as well as White-fronted Honeyeater and Spinifex-bird, occur at **Ellery Creek**, a nature park off Namatjira Drive about 90 km west of Alice, but this bird is arguably easier to see at the beautiful **Ormiston Gorge and Pound National Park**, 132 km west of Alice. Take plenty of water and

*One of the best birds in the Alice Springs area is the widespread but scarce Red-kneed Dotterel, another cracking member of the shorebird family which is endemic to Australia*

walk the Pound Walk, which takes about three hours. Along here it is possible to see the emuwrens, as well as Spinifex Pigeon (which feed out of the hand in the car park and campsite), Diamond Dove, Budgerigar, Pink Cockatoo*, Western Bowerbird (around car park and campsite), Dusky Grasswren, Red-browed Pardalote, Spinifex-bird, Australian Reed-Warbler and Painted Firetail, as well as nomads such as Black and Pied Honeyeaters, plus black-footed rock wallaby. The sealed road west of Alice ends at **Glen Helen**, where Australian Reed-Warbler occurs in the reedbeds at the southern end of the large waterhole, along with Little Woodswallow, and the surrounding mulga bushland has attracted Black and Pied Honeyeaters. About 85 km east of Alice, Rufous-crowned Emuwren and Spinifex-bird occur in **Trephina Gorge**, another nature park.

The 900 km round road trip between Alice and Uluru National Park (Ayers Rock) would be one hell of a haul but for the possibility of seeing some good birds in the roadside mulga, gibber and vegetated watercourses. Previously productive spots have included the area between KM posts 48 and 52 from Alice, where Inland Dotterel, White-winged Fairywren, Banded Whiteface and Orange Chat have all been recorded, the lucerne farm (ask permission to enter) near Stuart's Well where Australian Bustard and Banded Lapwing occur, and the open area to the west of the Stuart Highway just north of the KM 180 post from Alice (about 20 km north of Erldunda), where Banded Whiteface is more reliable in the bushy hollows, and other goodies have included Southern Whiteface, Crimson and Orange Chats, Chiming Wedgebill and Cinnamon Quail-thrush. The Lasseter Highway between Erldunda and Uluru passes through one of the best areas in the country for White-backed Swallow, and these beautiful birds can be seen at most of the major creek crossings.

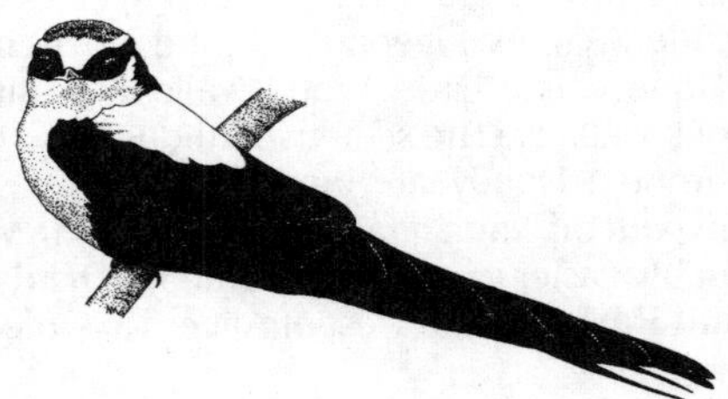

*The beautiful White-backed Swallow is often seen where roads and tracks cross creeks in the outback*

## ULURU NATIONAL PARK

The world's biggest monolith and Australia's top tourist attraction, known as Uluru or Ayers Rock, and the nearby red rock domes known as Kata Tjuta or The Olgas, both lie within this park, 450 km southwest of Alice Springs. Although the 6 km-long hump of rock which rises to 349 m (1145 ft) dominates the scene, the surrounding mulga and *spinifex* do occasionally attract such eye-catching birds as Pied Honeyeater, and are worth scouring for birds such as Western Bowerbird, Striated Grasswren and Chiming Wedgebill.

### Localised Australian Endemics

White-browed Treecreeper, Western Bowerbird, Rufous-crowned Emuwren, Striated Grasswren, Slaty-backed Thornbill, Banded Whiteface, Black and Pied Honeyeaters, Crimson and Orange Chats, Chiming Wedgebill, Cinnamon Quail-thrush, Painted Firetail.

### Other Australian Endemics

Little Buttonquail, Bluebonnet, Mulga Parrot, Budgerigar, Pink Cockatoo*, Red-backed Kingfisher, Red-browed Pardalote, Redthroat, Singing and White-fronted Honeyeaters, Yellow-throated Miner, Crested Bellbird, Little Crow, Little Woodswallow, Grey and Pied Butcherbirds, White-backed Swallow, Brown Songlark.

### Others

Grey-crowned Babbler, Black-faced Woodswallow, Zebra Finch.

### Other Wildlife

Common wallaroo, thorny devil.

(Other species recorded here include Grey Falcon*, Grey Honeyeater, and Masked and White-browed Woodswallows.)

Black and Pied Honeyeaters have been seen visiting the flowering shrubs surrounding Sunset Viewing car park and Striated Grasswren occurs in the *spinifex* on the opposite side of road to the car park. Banded Whiteface is most likely to be found in areas which are being recolonised by plants after controlled burns, especially between Yulara Resort and Uluru.

*Accommodation:* Yulara Resort: hotels (A), camping (B).

## *TASMANIA*

Around 230 species, including 13 endemics, have been recorded on Tasmania, a land of cultivated lowlands and cool, wet mountains which rise to 1617 m (5305 ft) at Mount Ossa. There are large stretches of cool, temperate rainforests on this island, as well as wet and dry sclerophyll forests, heaths and alpine grasslands, and most of the remote southwest coast and adjacent mountainous areas have been designated as a World Heritage Area, contributing significantly to the 25% of land in Tasmania which is 'protected'.

## HOBART

This pleasant modern city is situated on a wide bay surrounded by mountains which rise to 1270 m (4167 ft) at forested Mount Wellington. It is possible to see 12 of the 13 Tasmanian endemics near the city,

including Tasmanian Masked-Owl, as well as some species which are difficult to catch up with on mainland Australia, including breeding summer visitors such as Blue-winged and Swift* Parrots.

## Tasmanian Endemics

Green Rosella, Tasmanian Masked-Owl, Brown Scrubwren, Scrubtit, Tasmanian Thornbill, Yellow-throated, Black-headed and Strong-billed Honeyeaters, Yellow Wattlebird, Dusky Robin, Black Currawong.

## Localised Australian Endemics

Banded Lapwing, Blue-winged (Sep–Mar) and Swift* (Sep–Feb) Parrots, Olive Whistler, Forest Raven.

## Other Australian Endemics

Musk Duck, Black Swan, Chestnut Teal, Yellow-tailed Black-Cockatoo, Musk Lorikeet, Superb Fairywren, White-browed Scrubwren, Striated Pardalote, Brown Thornbill, Crescent and New Holland Honeyeaters, Eastern Spinebill, White-fronted Chat, Flame and Pink Robins, Dusky Woodswallow.

## Others

Australian Shoveler, White-eyed Duck, Pallid (Sep–Apr) and Fan-tailed

(Sep–Apr) Cuckoos, Satin Flycatcher (Sep–Mar), Black-faced Cuckoo-shrike (Sep–Mar), Olive-tailed Thrush, Welcome Swallow, Tree Martin (Sep–Mar).

## Other Wildlife

Spot-tailed quoll.

(Other species recorded here include Tasmanian Native-hen.)

Hobart is accessible by air and sea. Unfortunately, the expensive ferry operates only overnight and is therefore no good for seawatching. If arriving by air look out for Banded Lapwings on the airfield. The best site for Tasmanian Masked-Owl is near the airport. Head towards Sorell from the airport and turn right after about 3 km in response to the 'Seven Mile Beach' signpost on to **Pittwater Road**. About 400 m along here park in the lay-by and point your optics straight ahead from the gate to the hole in the broken branch in the tall tree about 150 m away. The owl occasionally roosts in this hole, but if it is not present try birding this road at night. In Hobart, Swift Parrot*, Yellow-throated Honeyeater and Yellow Wattlebird occur in Lambert Park, opposite the casino. However, the area to concentrate on near Hobart is **Mount Wellington National Park** which is just 8 km southwest of the city and supports several endemics including Scrubtit, Tasmanian Thornbill, Yellow-throated Honeyeater and Black Currawong. There are several walking tracks, the best of which is the Fern Glade Track which starts at Fern Tree, 8 km southwest of Hobart, opposite the cafe, pub and bus-stop. It begins by the side of the church next to the picnic site and follows Longhill Creek through wet sclerophyll forest which supports Scrubtit (in wet gullies) and Tasmanian Thornbill, along with Pink Robin and Olive-tailed Thrush. The 12 km long Pilinger Drive, just north of Fern Tree, climbs steeply to the summit of Mount Wellington where boulder- and bush-strewn slopes support Flame Robin during the summer (try the Collins

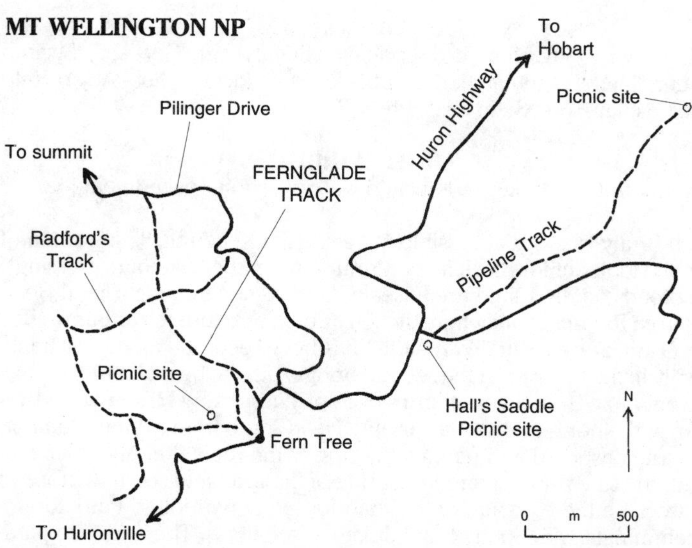

Bonnet Track, 2 km below the summit car park, for this species) and where snow lies during the austral winter. About 500 m up Pilinger Drive from 'The Springs', try the Lenah Valley track if Black Currawong is still proving elusive. A kilometre or so back from Fern Tree towards Hobart, turn east on to Chimney Pot Hill Road at Hall's Saddle and from the picnic site walk the Pipeline Track which passes through dry sclerophyll forest where Green Rosella, Swift Parrot*, Strong-billed Honeyeater, Dusky Robin, Forest Raven and Black Currawong occur.

## BRUNY ISLAND

This sparsely populated scenic 70 km long island, 35 km south of Hobart, supports 12 of the 13 Tasmanian endemics, including Tasmanian Native-hen, which can be elusive near Hobart, and Forty-spotted Pardalote*, which does not occur near Hobart. It is also a good place to look for localised mainland species such as Black-faced Cormorant and Hooded Plover*.

### Tasmanian Endemics

Tasmanian Native-hen, Green Rosella, Forty-spotted Pardalote*, Brown Scrubwren, Scrubtit, Tasmanian Thornbill, Yellow-throated, Black-headed and Strong-billed Honeyeaters, Yellow Wattlebird, Dusky Robin, Black Currawong.

### Localised Australian Endemics

Black-faced Cormorant, Hooded Plover*, Swift Parrot* (Sep–Feb), Olive Whistler, Forest Raven, Beautiful Firetail.

### Other Australian Endemics

Sooty Oystercatcher, Pacific Gull*, Spotted and Striated Pardalotes, Crescent Honeyeater, White-fronted Chat, Flame Robin.

### Others

Little Penguin, Shy Albatross, Short-tailed Shearwater (Oct–Apr), Swamp Harrier, Pied Oystercatcher, Double-banded Plover (Feb–Aug), Kelp Gull, Caspian Tern, Satin Flycatcher (Sep–Mar).

### Other Wildlife

Eastern quoll, platypus, red-necked wallaby, short-beaked echidna.

North Bruny Island is accessible by ferry from Kettering, 35 km south of Hobart (look out for Black-faced Cormorant on the 20 minute crossing). Most roads on the island are unsealed and some are quite rough. Head east from Roberts Point where the ferry docks and turn left to Barnes Bay after 9 km. Forty-spotted Pardalote* has been recorded along this track, usually in the tall trees at the second bridge, but the best place to see this rare endemic is on the northern slopes of **Waterview Hill** near Dennes Point at the northern tip of the island. Head south from Dennes Point on the east coast road and park by the side of the road after about 3.5 km. Climb the steep slope on the west side of the road and scour the tops of the trees on the east side of the road for the Forty-spotted Pardalotes*, which mingle with Spotted and Striated Pardalotes. The endemic pard-

## BRUNY ISLAND

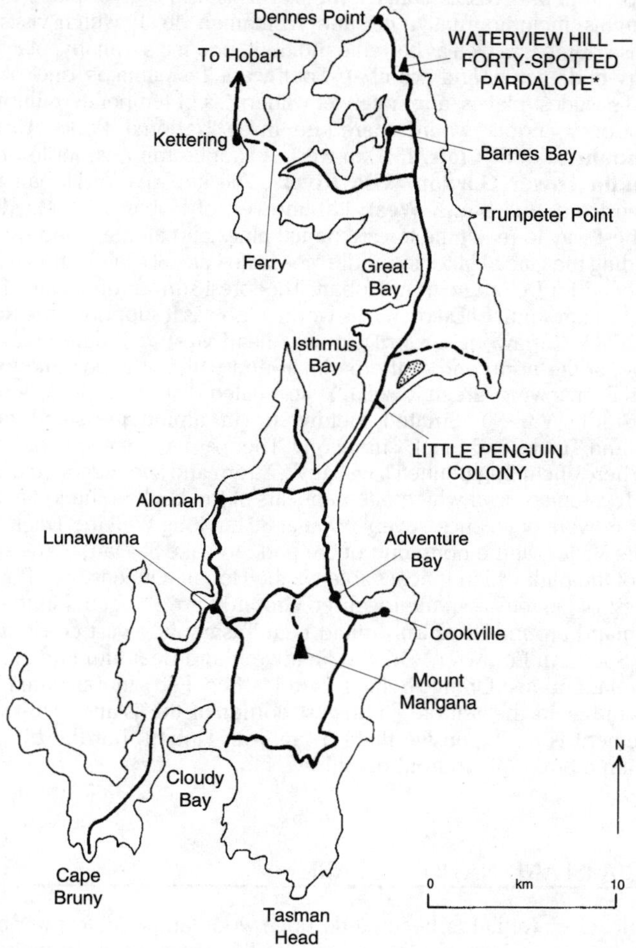


alote also occurs at McCracken's Gully about 2.5 km south of Dennes Point along the west coast road. At the northeast end of the ishtmus between North Bruny Island and South Bruny Island there is a viewing platform for watching Little Penguins coming ashore to their burrows at dusk, along with Short-tailed Shearwaters, while the beach at the southeast end of the isthmus supports Hooded Plover*, as well as Sooty Oystercatcher and Pacific Gull*. At Adventure Bay on South Bruny Island Green Rosella, Swift Parrot* and Yellow Wattlebird occur around the campsite. The road from Adventure Bay west to Lunawanna passes through rainforest which supports Green Rosella, Scrubtit, Tasmanian Thornbill, Strong-billed Honeyeater and Black Currawong, as well as Crescent Honeyeater and Olive Whistler. Seawatching can be good from Cape Bruny at the southwestern tip of South Bruny Island with species such as Shy Albatross flying past. Tasmanian Native-hen is widespread and occurs around most farm dams on both islands.

The forests in **Mount Field National Park**, 72 km west of Hobart, support Scrubtit and Tasmanian Thornbill. This is also a good place to see mammals, including native cat and Tasmanian devil (which visits the rubbish dump), as well as barred bandicoot, Bennett's wallaby, platypus, rufous pademelon and wombat. Southwest Tasmania is one of the world's wildest places, a remote wet wilderness of temperate rainforests and boggy moors where there are three National Parks: **Cradle Mountain-Lake St Clair**, 155 km west of Launceston near Mole Creek, **Franklin Lower Gordon Wild Rivers**, 200 km west of Hobart near Queenstown, and **South West**, 110 km west of Hobart near Maydena. The best way to reach the forests, pencil pines and alpine meadows surrounding the glacial lakes in Cradle Mountain-Lake St Clair National Park is to head for Deloraine from Hobart. The forest surrounding Liffey Falls, about 25 km south of Deloraine, is worth a look as it supports Pink Robin and Black Currawong. From Deloraine head west to Cradle Mountain Lodge, at the north end of the park, around which it is possible to see Brush Bronzewing, Green Rosella, Yellow-tailed Black-Cockatoo, Scrubtit (in Cradle Valley), Striated Fieldwren (in alpine grassland along Overland Track) and Black Currawong. There are also some good mammals here, including Bennett's wallaby, eastern and spotted-tailed quolls, and Tasmanian devil which often appears at the back of the lodge near dusk. Beware of leeches. A very popular 80 km long Walking Track links Cradle Valley, at the north end of the park, to Lake St Clair, at the south end of the park which is accessible via the Hobart–Queenstown Road.

West of Queenstown the localised Ground Parrot* occurs in the low heathland around **Strahan** airfield near Tasmania's west coast, along with Southern Emuwren, Striated Fieldwren and Beautiful Firetail. The best place to see Orange-bellied Parrot* (Sep–Feb) in Tasmania is at **Melaleuca** in the remote southwest corner of the island. This small settlement is an expensive flight away from Hobart, but the birds do feed on a bird table in front of a hide.

## MARIA ISLAND NATIONAL PARK

The beaches, wetlands, heathlands, open woodlands and forests on this 97 sq km island National Park support a fine range of birds, including Hooded Plover* and the largest known colony of Forty-spotted Pardalotes*.

### Tasmanian Endemics

Forty-spotted Pardalote*, Yellow Wattlebird, Dusky Robin, Black Currawong.

### Localised Australian Endemics

Hooded Plover*, Swift Parrot* (Sep–Feb), Beautiful Firetail.

### Other Australian Endemics

Brush Bronzewing, Pink Robin, Grey Currawong.

### Others

Little Penguin, Painted Buttonquail, Satin Flycatcher (Sep–Mar), Olive-tailed Thrush.

### Other Wildlife

Bennett's and rufous wallabies, brushtail possum, forester kangaroo.

(Introduced species include Emu, Cape Barren Goose and Tasmanian Native-hen.)

This island can be visited on a day-trip using the ferry from Triabunna near Louisville, which is 70 km northeast of Hobart on the east coast (look out for Little Penguin on the crossing). The best site for the pardalotes, as well as Swift Parrot*, is around the dam on Reservoir Circuit Walk, a two-hour loop which begins at Darlington (where Hooded Plover* occurs on the beach).

In northern Tasmania the red granite peaks, dry sclerophyll forest, coastal heathland, lagoons and sheltered sandy beaches in **Freycinet National Park** (110 sq km), support Brown Quail (Hazards Lagoon), Green Rosella, Tasmanian Thornbill (Cape Tourville), Yellow-throated, Black-headed and Strong-billed Honeyeaters, Yellow Wattlebird, Dusky Robin (Cape Tourville), Spotted Quail-thrush and Black Currawong, as well as Red-capped Plover, Common Bronzewing, Laughing Kookaburra (introduced), Superb Fairywren, Crescent Honeyeater, Eastern Spinebill, Scarlet Robin, Forest Raven and Beautiful Firetail. Mammals present include Bennett's and rufous wallabies, bottle-nosed dolphin, eastern quoll, long-nosed potoroo and southern right whale (Apr–Sep). To the north of here Little Penguin, Hooded Plover* and Pacific Gull* occur at **Bicheno**. One of the best places to see Swift Parrot* (Sep–Feb) in Tasmania is at the **Forest Glen Tea Gardens**, which are signposted from the Spreyton–Sheffield road about 3 km south of Spreyton, which is 6 km south of Devonport on Tasmania's north coast. The coastal waters, wetlands, savanna and heathland in **Asbestos Range National Park**, 30 km east of Devonport, support Little Penguin, Musk and Pink-eared Ducks, White-bellied Sea-Eagle and Beautiful Firetail.

Birders with time to spare or a passion for seabirds should try to arrange a **Tasmanian Pelagic**, but it is not always easy to charter a boat which is willing to go far enough out, especially off the southeast coast which has been the most rewarding in the past. However, it is worth trying in Hobart, Eaglehawk Neck, Port Arthur and Louisville. Previous pelagics have turned up a variety of moulting vagrant penguins (which also come ashore) including King, Gentoo, Adelie, Chinstrap, Rockhopper, Fiordland Crested* (regular, usually in March), Snares Crested*, Erect-crested*, Royal and even Magellanic, as well as Wandering*, Shy, Yellow-nosed and Buller's* Albatrosses, Mottled, Gould's and Cook's* Petrels, Grey-backed and White-faced Storm-Petrels, and Common Diving-Petrel.

## *OTHER OFFSHORE ISLANDS*

### LORD HOWE ISLAND

This small volcanic island, which is only 11 km long and up to 2.5 km wide, rises spectacularly out of the Tasman Sea about 700 km northeast

## LORD HOWE ISLAND

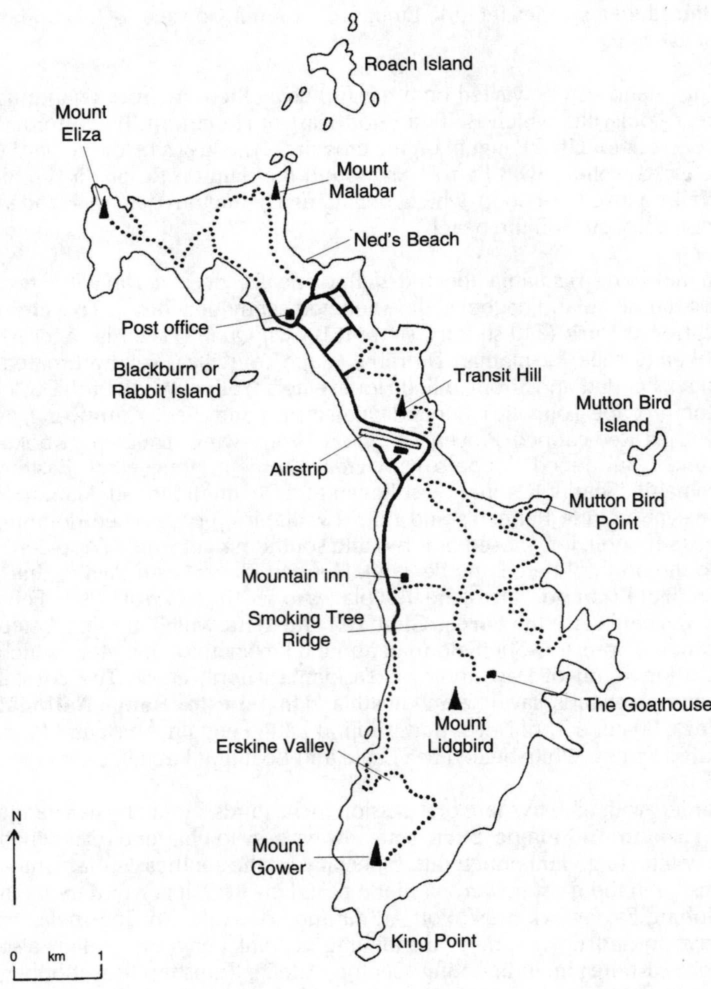


of Sydney to reach a height of 875 m (2871 ft) at Mount Gower. It is an expensive but exceptional place to visit, thanks to the wonderful selection of seabirds and its two very own endemics.

The best time of year to visit this island is from December to March when the seas are relatively calm and the weather at its warmest.

### Lord Howe Island Endemics

Lord Howe Rail*, Lord Howe White-eye.

### Non-endemic Specialities

Providence Petrel* (Apr–Sep), Red-tailed Tropicbird, Blue-grey (Oct–Mar) and Black Noddies, Common White-tern (Nov–Jun), Red-fronted Parakeet, Norfolk Starling.

### Australian Endemics

Pied Currawong.

### Others

Black-winged (Nov–Apr) and Kermadec Petrels, Wedge-tailed (Sep–Apr), Flesh-footed (Sep–May) and Little (Apr–Sep) Shearwaters, White-bellied Storm-Petrel, Masked Booby (*tasmani* race), Purple Swamphen, Grey-tailed Tattler, Double-banded Plover (Feb–Aug), Sooty Tern (Sep–Feb), Brown Noddy (Sep–Mar), Emerald Dove, Sacred Kingfisher, Golden Whistler, Magpie-lark.

(Other species recorded here include Wandering Albatross*, Cape, White-necked* and Great-winged Petrels, Fairy Prion, Sooty Shearwater and Latham's Snipe*. Introduced species include Australian Masked-Owl.)

Lord Howe Island is accessible by air from Sydney, but only passengers who have booked accommodation on the island in advance are allowed to board the flight. Both the flight and the accommodation are expensive, so the cheapest way to visit the island is to take a package trip from Sydney. For more information, contact the Pacific Island Tourist Centre, 7th Floor, 39–41 York Street, Sydney (tel: 02 262 6011). About 300 people live on the island, mainly in the low, central part. There are few roads, but plenty of walking tracks and the best way to get around is on foot or by bicycle. Bicycles are available for hire at a number of places. In calm weather there are also organised hikes and plenty of boat trips to choose from. The boat trip which encircles the island, organised by Wilson's Bike Hire, is the best for close-up views of seabirds, although a number of species breed on Roach Island, which is accessible by boat in calm weather. It is also possible to fly to and around the 551 m (1808 ft) Ball's Pyramid, a sea rock 23 km to the south-west of Lord Howe Island, where Kermadec Petrel breeds. The endemic Lord Howe Rail* occurs throughout the island, but is most common in the remnant forests on the summits of Mounts Lidgbird and Gower at the southern end. There are only 170–200 birds left and these are under threat from Australian Masked-Owls which have been introduced to the island. The other endemic, Lord Howe White-eye*, is also widespread.

*Accommodation:* Pine Trees (A+), guesthouses (A), self-catering (A). There is no camping area.

## NORFOLK ISLAND

This small island (35 sq km) of rolling green pastures, 1700 km north-east of Sydney, supports four endemics, and two rare petrels breed on nearby Philip Island.

The best time to visit this island is between October and May.

### Norfolk Island Endemics

Norfolk Island Parakeet*, Norfolk Gerygone*, Slender-billed* and White-chested* White-eyes.

### Non-endemic Specialities

White-necked* and Providence* Petrels, Long-tailed Triller, Norfolk Starling.

### Others

Masked Booby (*tasmani* race).

Norfolk Island is accessible by air. There is an information centre (tel: 0011 672 32695) and a wide range of accommodation (but no campsite) on the island, and a number of trails worth walking. White-chested White-eye* is restricted to the remote forests of Norfolk Island National Park where the core population of Slender-billed White-eye* also survives.

## ADDITIONAL INFORMATION

### Addresses

The Royal Australasian Ornithologists Union (RAOU) publishes the *Emu* journal. Head Office, 407–415 Riversdale Road, Hawthorn East, Victoria 3123 (tel: 03 882 2622, fax: 03 882 2677, web site: http://www.vicnet.net.au/~raou/raou.html). RAOU New South Wales Office, Locked Bag 600, St James Post Office, Sydney, New South Wales 2000 (Level 10, 8–12 Bridge Street, Sydney) (tel: 02 252 1403, fax: 02 252 1460). Perth Office, PO Box 199, Jolimont, Western Australia 6014 (Perry House, 71 Oceanic Drive, Floreat) (tel: 09 383 7749).

To subscribe to the excellent *Australian Birding* magazine (Aus$20 or £12 per annum), contact David Andrew (Editor), Australian Birding, Suite 4/3 Robe Street, St Kilda, Victoria 3182 (tel: 03 9534 9909, fax: 03 9535 8454).

The Bird Observers Club of Australia (BOCA), 183 Springvale Road, Nunawading, Victoria 3131 (tel: 03 9877 5342. fax: 03 9894 4048), publishes *The Bird Observer* and *The Australian Bird Watcher*.

The New South Wales Field Ornithologists Club Incorporated, PO Box C436, Clarence Street, Sydney, NSW 2000, publishes a newsletter and holds regular indoor and outdoor meetings.

The Cumberland Bird Observers Club Incorporated (Sydney), PO Box 550, Baulkham Hills, New South Wales 2153, publishes a newsletter.

The South Australian Ornithologists Association, c/o South Australian Museum, North Terrace, Adelaide, SA 5000.

The Queensland Ornithological Society, PO Box 97, St Lucia, Queensland 4067.

The Brisbane Seabird Study Group publishes *The Petrel*, an annual field report edited by Paul Walbridge, 135 Lytton Road, East Brisbane, Queensland 4169.

The Bird Observers Association of Tasmania, GPO Box 68A, Hobart, Tasmania 7001.

The Australian Nature Conservation Agency (formerly the Australian National Parks and Wildlife Service), PO Box 1967, 43 Bridge Street, Hurstville, NSW 2220.

The Australian Conservation Foundation, 340 Gore Street, Fitzroy, Victoria 3065 (tel: 03 416 1455).

## Books and Papers

*The Complete Guide to Finding the Birds of Australia*. Thomas R, Thomas S, 1996. Privately published.
*Where to Find Birds in Australia*. Bransbury J, 1987. Century Hutchinson.
*Where to Find Birds in North-East Queensland* (2nd edn). Wieneke J, 1995. C of P: Australia.
*The Slater Field Guide to Australian Birds*. Slater P *et al.*, 1990. Lansdowne.
*Field Guide to the Birds of Australia* (5th edn). Simpson K, Day N, 1998. Helm. Also available, with additional information including songs, on CD.
*Pizzey Field Guide to Australian Birds*. Pizzey G, 1996. Angus and Robertson.
*Birds of Australia* (photographic field guide). Flegg J, Madge S, The Australian Museum, 1995. New Holland.
*Australia: Land of Birds* (photographic guide). Trounson D, Trounson M, 1987. William Collins.
*RAOU Complete Australian Bird List*. RAOU, 1995. RAOU.
*The Atlas of Australian Birds*. Blakers M *et al.*, 1984. Melbourne University Press.
*Birds of Norfolk Island*. Hermes N, 1985. Wonderland Publications.
*Birds of Lord Howe Island*. Hutton I, 1991.
*National Photographic Index of Australian Wildlife* (a series of volumes on birds and other wildlife). Angus and Robertson.
*The Taxonomy and Species of Birds of Australia and its Territories*. Christidis L, Boles W, 1994. RAOU Monograph No. 2. RAOU.
*A Photographic Guide to Mammals of Australia*. Strahan R, 1995.
*Key Guide to Australian Mammals*. Cronin L, 1991. Reed Books.
*The Complete Book of Australian Mammals*. Strahan R, 1983. Angus and Robertson.
*The Complete Guide to Australian Snakes* (photographic guide). Gow G, 1989. Angus and Robertson.
*Tropical Fishes of the Great Barrier Reef*. Marshall T, 1982. Angus and Robertson.

## AUSTRALIAN ENDEMICS (332)

### Widespread (37)

These species occur more or less throughout the country, but are not necessarily common.

| | |
|---|---|
| Black Swan | Occurs on most waterbodies, mainly in the south and on Tasmania |
| Pink-eared Duck | Occurs on most waterbodies, to Tasmania |
| Pacific Heron | Occurs in small numbers around waterbodies, mainly inland |
| Yellow-billed Spoonbill | Occurs in small numbers around waterbodies, mainly inland |
| Australian Kite | Occurs in small numbers, mainly in the south |
| Square-tailed Kite* | Occurs in very small numbers throughout, but rare in the southeast and most likely to be seen in the west |
| Stubble Quail | Scarce in grasslands in all but the north and northwest and most likely to be seen at Deniliquin |

| | |
|---|---|
| Little Buttonquail | Scarce in grasslands in all but the north and most likely to be seen at Deniliquin |
| Black-tailed Native-hen | Mainly an inland nomad, occurring locally on ephemeral wetlands |
| Sooty Oystercatcher | Occurs sparingly around the coast, mainly along rocky shores in the south and on Tasmania |
| Red-capped Plover | Occurs around the whole coast and to a lesser extent inland, including Tasmania |
| Red-kneed Dotterel | Local, mainly on inland wetlands |
| Banded Lapwing | A nomadic grassland species possible anywhere across the country except for the north, although probably most likely around Deniliquin. Also occurs on Tasmania |
| Common Bronzewing | Throughout the mainland and Tasmania |
| Crested Pigeon | Throughout, but mainly in arid areas |
| Red-tailed Black-Cockatoo | Throughout open areas except the extreme southeast and southwest. |
| Galah | Numerous throughout except in rainforests |
| Southern Boobook | Throughout, including Tasmania |
| Tawny Frogmouth | Throughout, including Tasmania |
| Variegated Fairywren | Occurs mainly in arid areas throughout the country except the extreme south |
| Striated Pardalote | Occurs in most woodlands to Tasmania |
| Yellow-rumped Thornbill | Throughout the country in open woodlands but not the extreme north |
| Weebill | Occurs in most dry forests and woodlands |
| Singing Honeyeater | Throughout, although mainly confined to arid areas of the interior and absent from the extreme east |
| White-plumed Honeyeater | Throughout, except for extreme north and southwest |
| Yellow-throated Miner | Woodlands throughout, except extreme east |
| Hooded Robin | Scarce in drier areas except northeast |
| Crested Shrike-tit | Scarce in drier woodlands, mainly in the southeast |
| White-browed Babbler | Throughout the southern interior |
| Australian Raven | Common throughout, except Darwin area |
| Dusky Woodswallow | Common near water in the south, including Tasmania, during the summer. Most move north in the winter |
| Grey Butcherbird | Throughout open areas to Tasmania |
| Pied Butcherbird | Throughout open areas, except extreme southwest and southeast |
| Australian Reed-Warbler | Throughout, although only a summer visitor to the south |
| Brown Songlark | Scarce in grasslands throughout except extreme north and usually only present in the south from July to March |
| Rufous Songlark | Fairly common in grassy woodlands throughout. |

| | |
|---|---|
| Double-barred Finch | Throughout the north and east from The Kimberley to southern New South Wales |

## East (43)

These species are mainly confined to the eastern coastal area, inland to the Great Dividing Range, from Cairns in northeast Queensland south to Sydney, and in some cases west to the Melbourne area in west Victoria.

| | |
|---|---|
| Australian Brush-turkey | Occurs at most forested sites from north New South Wales to Cape York |
| Black-breasted Buttonquail* | Rare in woodlands around Brisbane, but reported quite regularly at Neumgna SF and Lamington NP |
| White-headed Pigeon | Scarce in forests, mainly around Brisbane and Cairns. Most likely at Lamington NP |
| Brown Cuckoo-Dove | Scarce in forests, mainly around Brisbane and Cairns. Most likely at Lamington NP |
| Topknot Pigeon | Occurs in small numbers in most rain-forests. |
| Australian King-Parrot | Occurs in most forests west to Victoria |
| Crimson Rosella | Throughout |
| Pale-headed Rosella | Occurs in most woodlands |
| Glossy Black-Cockatoo* | More or less restricted to localised areas of *casuarinas* and most likely to be seen at Dharug NP near Sydney and Lamington NP near Brisbane |
| Scaly-breasted Lorikeet | Occurs in most woodlands |
| Little Lorikeet | Scarce in woodlands from Cairns to Victoria |
| Laughing Kookaburra | Common throughout. Introduced to south-west and Tasmania |
| White-throated Treecreeper | Occurs in most rainforests west to Victoria |
| Brown Treecreeper | Occurs in most dry forests, inland to the Alice Springs area |
| Albert's Lyrebird* | Restricted to the area in and around Lamington NP near Brisbane |
| Rufous Scrub-bird* | Rare in Antarctic beech forests of south-east Queensland (Lamington NP) and northeast New South Wales (near Gloucester) |
| Green Catbird | Occurs in most rain forests around Brisbane and some other sites south to the Sydney area |
| Regent Bowerbird | Restricted to southeast Queensland and northeast New South Wales where fairly common, especially at Lamington NP |
| Satin Bowerbird | Occurs in most wet forests |
| Eastern Bristlebird* | A rare and localised bird, only likely to be seen near Brisbane in Lamington NP and near Sydney at Barren Grounds and Jervis Bay NRs |
| Yellow-throated Scrubwren | Occurs in most wet forests near Sydney, Brisbane and Cairns |

| | |
|---|---|
| Large-billed Scrubwren | Occurs in most wet forests near Sydney, Brisbane and Cairns |
| Buff-rumped Thornbill | Occurs in most open forests |
| Brown Gerygone | Occurs in most rain forests |
| Scarlet Myzomela | Occurs in most woodlands and forests from the Sydney area north to the Cairns area |
| Lewin's Honeyeater | Occurs in most rain forests |
| Yellow-faced Honeyeater | Occurs in most woodlands |
| Mangrove Honeyeater | Occurs in mangroves along southeast Queensland coast where most likely to be seen in the Brisbane area |
| Fuscous Honeyeater | Occurs in dry open woodlands, especially in the southeast |
| Striped Honeyeater | Throughout drier areas inland |
| Eastern Spinebill | Throughout to Tasmania |
| Noisy Miner | Open woodlands throughout to Tasmania |
| Rose Robin | Scarce in wet forests |
| Pale-yellow Robin | Fairly common in wet forests, especially near Brisbane and on the Atherton Tablelands |
| Yellow Robin | Common in woodlands and forests |
| Eastern Whipbird | Common in wet forests around Sydney, Brisbane and on the Atherton Tablelands |
| Apostlebird | Fairly common inland |
| White-eared Monarch | Scarce in rain forests and most likely to be seen near Brisbane and Cairns |
| Paradise Riflebird* | Localised in rain forests near Brisbane and north New South Wales |
| Pied Currawong | Throughout |
| Russet-tailed Thrush | Restricted to rain forests near Brisbane |
| Red-browed Firetail | Woodland edges throughout |
| Plum-headed Finch | Scarce nomad in grasslands and reedbeds inland, but regularly seen at Glen Davis near Sydney |

## Southeast (47)

These species are mainly confined to the Sydney, Melbourne and Adelaide areas, inland to the mallee reserves in west New South Wales and northwest Victoria such as Wyperfeld and Hattah-Kulkyne National Parks.

| | |
|---|---|
| Wonga Pigeon | Occurs in most temperate forests north to the Brisbane area |
| Superb Parrot* | Occurs mainly in inland west New South Wales and is most likely to be seen at Deniliquin |
| Mallee Ringneck | Occurs in mallee and mulga areas inland north to Mount Isa |
| Eastern Rosella | Occurs in most woodland areas to Tasmania |
| Bluebonnet | Occurs in mallee and mulga areas inland west to the Nullarbor Plain |
| Red-rumped Parrot | Occurs in most open woodland and grass- |

| | |
|---|---|
| | land areas, usually near water |
| Blue-winged Parrot | Scarce, mostly in coastal heathlands to Tasmania, and most likely to be seen in the Melbourne area (Apr–Sep) or on Tasmania (Sep–Mar) |
| Orange-bellied Parrot* | Only around 150 individuals of this species exist along the coast near Melbourne and in remote southwest Tasmania. However, a few can usually be found at Werribee SW or Swan Island between March and July, or in southwest Tasmania between September and February |
| Turquoise Parrot* | Scarce inland, but regular at a few sites, including Glen Davis near Sydney |
| Swift Parrot* | Scarce from May to September inland, at a few sites including Chiltern SF and You Yangs FP, but more localised and concentrated on Tasmania from September to February |
| Ground Parrot* | Restricted to coastal heathlands, mainly near Sydney, Melbourne and Brisbane, and in southwest Tasmania |
| Yellow-tailed Black-Cockatoo | Occurs in most forested areas north to south Queensland and south to Tasmania |
| Gang-gang Cockatoo | Localised, but likely to be seen near Sydney and especially in Canberra |
| Long-billed Corella | Restricted to west New South Wales and Victoria, but common in that region, especially around Deniliquin and near Hall's Gap |
| Musk Lorikeet | Occurs in most woodlands of coastal New South Wales to Tasmania, Victoria and Adelaide |
| Powerful Owl* | Scarce in forested areas around Sydney, Brisbane and Melbourne |
| Red-browed Treecreeper | Scarce in wet forests north to southeast Queensland |
| Superb Lyrebird | Occurs in most wet forests, especially near Sydney and Melbourne. Introduced to Tasmania |
| Superb Fairywren | Occurs in most woodlands to Tasmania |
| Mallee Emuwren* | Restricted to *spinifex* in mallee of South Australia (eg. Ngarkat Conservation Park) and Victoria (e.g. Wyperfeld, Hattah-Kulkyne (most likely site) and Murray-Sunset NPs, and Big Desert Wilderness) |
| Rufous Bristlebird* | A rare bird in coastal heathlands near Melbourne and only likely to be seen along the Great Ocean Road or further west in Coorong NP |
| Pilotbird | Occurs in some areas of wet forest, notably Barren Grounds NR and the Blue Mountains |

| | |
|---|---|
| Rock Warbler* | Restricted to sandstone outcrops near Sydney and most likely to be seen at Dharug NP and the Blue Mountains |
| Speckled Warbler | Local and scarce in open woodlands |
| Striated Fieldwren | Restricted to coastal heathlands on the mainland, but also occurs in alpine scrub on Tasmania |
| Chestnut-rumped Hylacola | Scarce and local in coastal heathlands and open woodlands |
| Brown Thornbill | Throughout |
| Yellow Thornbill | Fairly common in woodlands north to southeast Queensland |
| Striated Thornbill | Occurs in woodlands and rainforests north to southeast Queensland |
| Yellow-tufted Honeyeater | Mainly restricted to areas of ironbark trees, but occurs at a number of sites, especially near Sydney and Melbourne |
| Black-chinned Honeyeater | Mainly restricted to areas of ironbark trees, but occurs at a number of sites, especially between Sydney and Melbourne |
| Crescent Honeyeater | Mainly restricted to wet woodlands and coastal shrublands, to Tasmania |
| Regent Honeyeater* | Rare inland nomad, most regular in recent years at Glen Davis near Sydney |
| Bell Miner | Localised large colonies north to south-east Queensland |
| Black-eared Miner* | A very rare bird restricted to seven mallee areas in northwest Victoria and the adjacent state of South Australia, including Wyperfeld NP where it hybridises with Yellow-throated Miner, the super-species which appears to be eliminating pure-bred individuals of this debatable species |
| Brush Wattlebird | Fairly common near the coast, north to south Queensland and southeast to Tasmania |
| Flame Robin | Fairly common in open woodlands to Tasmania |
| Pink Robin | Scarce, mainly in wet forests of Victoria and Tasmania |
| Olive Whistler | Localised throughout, to Tasmania |
| Red-lored Whistler* | A very rare mallee species which is only likely to be seen at Round Hill NR in September and October. Also recorded from Big Desert Wilderness and Sunset Country |
| Spotted Quail-thrush | Localised in dry woodlands north to the Brisbane area |
| White-winged Chough | Fairly common in drier areas north to southeast Queensland |
| Little Raven | Common throughout southern New South Wales, Victoria and southern South Australia |

| | |
|---|---|
| Relict Raven | Restricted to northeast New South Wales where it occurs on the New England Tablelands and around Coffs Harbour |
| Forest Raven | Restricted to localised coastal areas near Melbourne, such as Wilson's Promontory NP and Portland, but occurs throughout Tasmania |
| Beautiful Firetail | Scarce in heathlands and woodlands near the coast, to Tasmania, and most likely to be seen on the mainland at Barren Grounds NR |
| Diamond Firetail | Localised in open woodlands, but present at a number of sites |

## Southeast and Southwest (38)

These species are mainly confined to the Sydney, Melbourne, Adelaide, Albany and Perth areas, with some penetrating inland to the mallee reserves in northwest Victoria, west New South Wales and Western Australia.

| | |
|---|---|
| Black-faced Cormorant | Coast only. Occurs at a number of sites on the south coast near Melbourne, Adelaide and Esperance, as well as around Tasmania |
| Blue-billed Duck | Occurs on most large freshwater bodies, including those on Tasmania |
| Musk Duck | Occurs on most large freshwater bodies, including those on Tasmania |
| Freckled Duck* | Nomadic, but usually present all year round on Lake George near Canberra |
| Cape Barren Goose | Occurs on short grassy areas, mainly at sites around Melbourne and Adelaide, and on Tasmania |
| Australian Shelduck | Occurs on most waterbodies |
| Maned Duck | Occurs, often far from water, throughout the southeast and southwest, to Tasmania |
| Chestnut Teal | Occurs on most waterbodies near the coast, as well as on Tasmania |
| Black-backed Bittern | Scarce at a few sites and only seen regularly at Deniliquin and Bool Lagoon |
| Malleefowl* | Occurs in pristine mallee, mainly in northwest Victoria where Wyperfeld NP is the best site |
| Australian Crake | Occurs on most waterbodies, to Tasmania. |
| Banded Stilt | Localised on saltwater bodies and estuaries, mainly around Melbourne, Adelaide and Perth |
| Red-necked Avocet | Localised on brackish waterbodies, mainly around Melbourne, Adelaide and Perth |
| Hooded Plover* | Scarce on undisturbed sandy beaches and coastal lagoons, mainly between Melbourne and Adelaide, near Esperance in the southwest, and on Tasmania |
| Pacific Gull* | Scarce along the south coast and on Tasmania, most likely to be seen around |

| | |
|---|---|
| | Melbourne and Adelaide, and on Tasmania |
| Brush Bronzewing | Quite scarce at a number of sites, mostly near the south coast and on Tasmania |
| Regent Parrot | Occurs mainly in northwest Victoria, at Wyperfeld and Hattah-Kulkyne NPs, and near Perth |
| Elegant Parrot | Occurs mainly in the Adelaide and Perth areas |
| Purple-crowned Lorikeet | Occurs in woodlands and mallee, mainly from Melbourne, where Tullamarine Airport is a regular haunt, to the Perth area |
| Southern Emuwren | Occurs in most coastal heathlands and swamps, including those on Tasmania |
| Spotted Pardalote | Occurs in most woodlands and mallee areas, especially in the southeast and Tasmania |
| White-browed Scrubwren | Occurs in most forests north to Queensland and southeast to Tasmania |
| Shy Hylacola | Occurs in most areas of pristine mallee, including Wyperfeld and Hattah-Kulkyne NPs |
| White-eared Honeyeater | Fairly common throughout. |
| Purple-gaped Honeyeater | Scarce in pristine mallee areas |
| Yellow-plumed Honeyeater | Common in pristine mallee areas |
| White-naped Honeyeater | Fairly common in woodlands |
| Brown-headed Honeyeater | Scarce in woodlands throughout |
| New Holland Honeyeater | Throughout to Tasmania |
| White-cheeked Honeyeater | Throughout to an isolated population on the Atherton Tablelands in northeast Queensland |
| Tawny-crowned Honeyeater | Occurs mainly in coastal heathlands, including Tasmania |
| Painted Honeyeater | Scarce in dry woodlands and most likely to be seen near Melbourne in October and November, or at Deniliquin from November to March |
| Red Wattlebird | Common in forests |
| White-fronted Chat | Common near water, including Tasmania |
| Southern Scrub-Robin | Fairly common in mallee areas |
| Gilbert's Whistler | Fairly common in dry inland areas, particularly mallee areas |
| Chestnut Quail-thrush | Occurs sparsely in pristine mallee areas |
| Grey Currawong | Localised, but widespread to Tasmania |

## Southwest (20)

These species are mainly restricted to the southwest corner of the country, around Albany and Perth, with some penetrating inland to south-central Australia and sites near Adelaide.

| | |
|---|---|
| Red-capped Parrot | Occurs in most woodlands |
| Port Lincoln Parrot | Occurs in mallee and mulga areas inland to west-central Australia, and is seen most regularly at Dryandra SF near Perth |

| | |
|---|---|
| Western Rosella | Occurs in most open woodlands |
| Rock Parrot | A coastal species most likely to be seen in the southwest although occurs east to Adelaide |
| White-tailed Black Cockatoo* | Occurs in some woodlands near Perth |
| Slender-billed Black Cockatoo* | Occurs in most mallee areas and dry woodlands, in and around Perth |
| Western Corella* | Scarce in and around Perth |
| Rufous Treecreeper | Occurs in most woodlands of the southwest, east to mallee areas of south-central Australia |
| Noisy Scrub-bird* | This semi-flightless bird was formerly restricted to the Mount Gardner area of the Two People's Bay NR (the best place to look for it), but thanks to translocation and successful habitat management its range has spread over 30 km to Mount Manypeaks and so on. 400 singing males were located in 1993 |
| Red-winged Fairywren | Occurs throughout though most likely to be seen at Two People's Bay NR |
| Blue-breasted Fairywren | Occurs in most woodlands of the southwest, as well as in isolated populations in south-central Australia |
| Western Bristlebird* | A rare bird which occurs only in the coastal heathlands of Fitzgerald River NP and Two People's Bay NR |
| Rufous Fieldwren | A scarce species most likely to be seen in the southwest but also occurs east to south-central Australia and the Strzelecki Track |
| Western Thornbill | Occurs in some forests and open woodlands |
| Western Spinebill | Throughout the southwest corner |
| Little Wattlebird | Fairly common near the coast |
| Grey-breasted Robin | Fairly common in open woodlands of the southwest, as well as in isolated populations in south-central Australia |
| White-breasted Robin | Fairly common at Two People's Bay NR and in the Porongurup Ranges nearby |
| Western Whipbird* | Rare in coastal heathlands of the southwest, as well as in isolated populations in south-central Australia |
| Red-eared Firetail* | Scarce in coastal heathlands and woodlands, and most likely to be seen at Two People's Bay NR or in the Porongurup Ranges |

## Northwest (5)

These species are confined to The Kimberley and other nearby sites.

| | |
|---|---|
| White-quilled Rock-Pigeon | Scarce in The Kimberley and nearby area such as Victoria River and Keep River NP |

| | |
|---|---|
| Black Grasswren* | Restricted to The Kimberley where most likely to be seen at the remote Mertens Creek/Mitchell Falls area |
| Dusky Gerygone | Occurs in mangroves in northwest only, mainly between Carnarvon and Derby |
| Star Finch* | Restricted mainly to areas near water, but occurs at a number of sites, east to Darwin |
| Yellow-rumped Munia* | Rare in grasslands and reedbeds and only likely to be seen around Kununurra |

## North-central (6)

These species are confined to the Darwin area.

| | |
|---|---|
| Chestnut-quilled Rock-Pigeon | Occurs only in Arnhem Land, but fairly easy to see in Kakadu NP |
| Black-banded Fruit-Dove* | Occurs only in Arnhem Land, but fairly easy to see in Kakadu NP |
| Hooded Parrot* | Rare, but possible to see at a number of dry season waterholes, especially around Katherine |
| Rainbow Pitta | Occurs at several lowland forest sites around Darwin and in Kakadu NP. Also occurs in The Kimberley, but scarce there |
| White-throated Grasswren* | Occurs only in Arnhem Land, but fairly easy to see above Waterfall Creek next to Kakadu NP |
| Brown Whistler | Occurs at a number of woodland, forest and mangrove areas around Darwin |

## North (28)

These species are mainly restricted to The Kimberley, Darwin and, in some cases, Alice Springs, Mount Isa and Cairns areas.

| | |
|---|---|
| Plumed Whistling-Duck | Mainly in the north, in the Darwin and Cairns areas, but also regular at Bool Lagoon between Melbourne and Adelaide in south |
| Black-breasted Kite | Occurs more widely but most likely to be seen in the forested areas of the north |
| Red Goshawk* | Very rarely seen and only likely in The Kimberley and Kakadu NP, although it also occurs in east Queensland |
| Chestnut-backed Buttonquail* | Rare in woodlands of The Kimberley and Kakadu NP |
| Partridge Pigeon* | Scarce in The Kimberley and Darwin areas |
| Northern Rosella | Scarce in dry woodlands and most likely to be seen in The Kimberley and Darwin areas |
| Varied Lorikeet | Throughout The Kimberley and Darwin areas |
| Black-tailed Treecreeper | Occurs in dry woodlands, mainly near Darwin |
| Great Bowerbird | Common in the dry areas near Darwin, decreasing in numbers east to the Cairns area |

| | |
|---|---|
| Red-backed Fairywren | Common in dry grasslands and woodlands, south to northern New South Wales in east |
| Purple-crowned Fairywren* | Local and scarce in The Kimberley area and east Northern Territory/west Queensland, and most likely to be seen at Victoria River in the west and Lawn Hill NP in the east |
| Carpentarian Grasswren* | Known only from several areas of mature tussock grassland inland from the south coast of the Gulf of Carpentaria, and most likely to be seen near Caranbirini Springs and Mount Isa |
| Banded Honeyeater | Fairly common in woodlands from The Kimberley area east to inland north Queensland |
| White-lined Honeyeater | Fairly common in The Kimberley and Kakadu NP |
| White-gaped Honeyeater | Fairly common, inland to Victoria River and Caranbirini Springs |
| Golden-backed Honeyeater | Scarce in open woodlands |
| Silver-crowned Friarbird | Fairly common in open woodlands from The Kimberley east to the Cairns area |
| Bar-breasted Honeyeater | Fairly common, mainly in the Darwin area |
| Rufous-throated Honeyeater | Fairly common near water |
| White-browed Robin | Scarce along creeks |
| White-breasted Whistler | Locally common in mangrove areas |
| Sandstone Shrike-Thrush | Scarce on sandstone outcrops east to Caranbirini Springs |
| Little Woodswallow | Scarce south to Alice Springs |
| Australian Yellow White-eye | Common in mangroves from the west coast to Karumba in west Queensland |
| Masked Finch | Fairly common east to Cape York Peninsula |
| Long-tailed Finch | Fairly common east to Caranbirini Springs |
| Gouldian Finch* | Scarce and localised but possible at a number of waterholes from The Kimberley area in the west to Georgetown in the east |
| Pictorella Munia* | Scarce at a few sites from The Kimberley in the west to Georgetown in the east |

## Northeast (21)

These species are mainly confined to the Atherton Tablelands area near Cairns in northeast Queensland, with some species' ranges extending south to Mount Spec National Park and north to the Cape York Peninsula.

| | |
|---|---|
| Buff-breasted Buttonquail* | Rare in the Mount Molloy area near Cairns and at Iron Range NP on the Cape York Peninsula |
| Squatter Pigeon | Localised at a few open sites near Cairns |
| Lesser Sooty-Owl* | Scarce in forests of Atherton Tablelands south to Mount Spec NP |

| | |
|---|---|
| Australian Swiftlet | Common in the Cairns area |
| Tooth-billed Catbird* | Fairly common in forests of Atherton Tablelands south to Mount Spec NP |
| Golden Bowerbird* | Fairly common in forests of Atherton Tablelands south to Mount Spec NP but only likely to be seen if an active bower can be located |
| Lovely Fairywren | Occurs in most rainforests around Cairns and on Cape York Peninsula |
| Fernwren* | Fairly common in forests of Atherton Tablelands south to Mount Spec NP |
| Atherton Scrubwren* | Fairly common in forests of Atherton Tablelands |
| Mountain Thornbill* | Fairly common in forests of Atherton Tablelands south to Mount Spec NP |
| Yellow-spotted Honeyeater | Fairly common in the lowland woodlands and rainforests of the Cairns area north to the Cape York Peninsula |
| Bridled Honeyeater* | Fairly common in the montane rainforests of the Atherton Tablelands south to Mount Spec NP |
| Eungella Honeyeater* | Scarce in and around Eungella NP |
| Yellow Honeyeater | Fairly common in woodlands around Cairns and Townsville |
| Macleay Honeyeater | Fairly common in forests of Atherton Tablelands south to Mount Spec NP |
| Grey-headed Robin | Common in forests of Atherton Tablelands south to Mount Spec NP |
| Bower's Shrike-Thrush | Fairly common in montane forests of Atherton Tablelands south to Mount Spec NP |
| Chowchilla | Fairly common in forests of Atherton Tablelands south to Mount Spec NP |
| Pied Monarch | Fairly common in forests of Atherton Tablelands south to Mount Spec NP |
| Victoria's Riflebird | Fairly common in forests of Atherton Tablelands south to Mount Spec NP |
| Black-throated Finch | Scarce and local and most likely to be seen in the Cairns area west to Georgetown |

## Cape York Peninsula (2)

These species are confined to the Cape York Peninsula in extreme north-east Australia.

| | |
|---|---|
| Golden-shouldered Parrot* | Rare, but regularly recorded around Musgrave |
| White-streaked Honeyeater | Fairly common in Iron Range NP to the northern tip of the peninsula |

## Outback (66)

These species are mainly restricted to the arid interior, around Deniliquin, Broken Hill and Alice Springs, along the Birdsville and Strzelecki Tracks, and in some cases west to the west coast and east and south to the mallee reserves in west New South Wales and northwest Victoria, including Wyperfeld and Hattah-Kulkyne National Parks.

| | |
|---|---|
| Emu | Nomadic in the arid interior, but occurs regularly at a number of sites |
| Letter-winged Kite | Nomadic in the remote arid interior, but occurs regularly on the Birdsville and Strzelecki Tracks, and on the Barkly Tablelands. Occasional irruptions occur when birds can appear almost anywhere |
| Grey Falcon* | Scarce in the remote outback |
| Black Falcon | Quite scarce in the outback and most likely around Deniliquin |
| Red-chested Buttonquail | A scarce nomad in grasslands of north and east, most likely at Deniliquin or on the Barkly Tablelands |
| Plains-wanderer* | Rarely reported from anywhere except the grasslands at Deniliquin where it is possible to see this bird with hired local assistance |
| Inland Dotterel | Grasslands of the mostly remote arid interior, most likely along the Birdsville and Strzelecki Tracks, but also possible at Deniliquin |
| Flock Bronzewing* | A nomad in the remote outback, most likely along the Birdsville Track or on the Barkly Tablelands |
| Spinifex Pigeon | Occurs at a number of sites in the west, centre and north including Cape Range NP, The Kimberley area and near Alice Springs |
| Diamond Dove | Throughout the arid interior, but mainly in the centre and north |
| Alexandra's Parrot* | This rare parrot may be irruptive rather than nomadic and the core population appears to be more or less resident in the Lake Tobin area of the Great Sandy Desert, accessible only in July along the Canning Stock Route |
| Mulga Parrot | Occurs in most mallee and mulga areas |
| Bourke's Parrot | Localised in the remoter mulga areas |
| Scarlet-chested Parrot* | Rare in the Great Victoria Desert of south-central Australia |
| Budgerigar | Nomadic, but numerous in the arid interior |
| Night Parrot* | This very rare nocturnal parrot was only reported on 15 occasions between 1984 and 1994 and several of these records came from near Cloncurry |
| Pink Cockatoo* | Occurs in small numbers at a number of sites throughout the arid interior, including Wyperfeld and Hattah-Kulkyne NPs |
| Cockatiel | Nomadic, but fairly numerous in the arid interior |
| Red-backed Kingfisher | Throughout the arid interior to west and north coasts |

| | |
|---|---|
| White-browed Treecreeper | Scarce in the arid interior of the south, and most likely to be seen in the northern section of Wyperfeld NP, inland from Brisbane or near Alice Springs |
| Western Bowerbird | Localised in the arid interior from the Alice Springs area west to Cape Range NP |
| Spotted Bowerbird | Localised in the east-central arid interior, mainly west of Brisbane |
| White-winged Fairywren | Occurs throughout the arid interior, reaching the coast in some places, including Adelaide and the west coast |
| Splendid Fairywren | Occurs throughout the arid interior, mainly in the mallee and mulga areas of the southeast, and in coastal and inland areas of the southwest |
| Rufous-crowned Emuwren | Localised in the arid interior, mainly around Alice Springs and west to Cape Range NP on the west-central coast |
| Thick-billed Grasswren* | Localised in the arid interior where most likely to be seen along the Strzelecki Track and on the west coast where most likely to be seen on the Peron Peninsula in Shark Bay |
| Dusky Grasswren | Localised in the arid interior and most likely to be seen around Alice Springs or Mount Isa |
| Striated Grasswren | Localised in the arid interior and only likely to be seen at Hattah-Kulkyne and Uluru (Ayers Rock) NPs |
| Grey Grasswren* | Restricted to *lignum* clumps in remote east-central Australia and only likely to be seen near Tibooburra or along the Birdsville Track |
| Eyrean Grasswren* | Restricted to cane grass-covered sand dunes in remote east-central Australia and only likely to be seen along the Birdsville and Strzelecki Tracks |
| Red-browed Pardalote | Throughout the arid interior in the northern half of the country |
| Redthroat | A localised scarce species in the southern arid interior from the Adelaide area to the central west coast |
| Slender-billed Thornbill* | A scarce bird of saltbush and coastal samphire flats from south-central Australia to the central west coast and most likely to be seen near Adelaide and Carnarvon |
| Inland Thornbill | Throughout the southern arid interior |
| Chestnut-rumped Thornbill | Throughout, in mallee and mulga |
| Slaty-backed Thornbill | Local and scarce in mulga areas from Alice Springs to the central west coast where it occurs alongside Route 123 near Mount Magnet |
| Western Gerygone | Throughout open woodlands of the arid interior east to Glen Davis and west to Perth |

| | |
|---|---|
| Southern Whiteface | Throughout the southern arid interior west to the west coast |
| Chestnut-breasted Whiteface* | A great rarity which is only likely to be seen along the southern end of the Strzelecki Track near Lyndhurst in south-central Australia |
| Banded Whiteface | Scarce in the arid interior and most likely to be seen along the Birdsville and Strzelecki Tracks, and in Uluru NP (Ayers Rock) |
| Black Honeyeater | A nomad in the arid interior possible at a number of sites as far south as Deniliquin, but most likely around Alice Springs |
| Pied Honeyeater | A nomad in the arid interior occuring west to the central west coast where most likely to be seen, on the Peron Peninsula in Shark Bay and at Cape Range NP |
| Grey-headed Honeyeater | Occurs along creeks in the arid interior, mainly around Alice Springs and west to Cape Range NP on the west-central coast |
| Grey-fronted Honeyeater | Scarce in the arid interior |
| White-fronted Honeyeater | A nomad in the arid interior, but fairly regular at some sites, including Hattah-Kulkyne NP, Shark Bay and Alice Springs |
| Spiny-cheeked Honeyeater | Fairly common throughout |
| Grey Honeyeater | Rare nomad in mulga areas in central and west, most likely to be seen near Alice Springs or along Route 123 near Mount Magnet near the west-central coast |
| Crimson Chat | Fairly common nomad throughout the arid interior to the central-west coast and possible at a number of remoter sites |
| Orange Chat | Scarce nomad throughout the arid interior with no regular sites, although a distinct possibility along the Birdsville Track and at Deniliquin |
| Yellow Chat* | Rare nomad throughout the arid interior, preferring rushy wetlands, mainly in the north. The only regular sites are near Kununurra in The Kimberley and along the Birdsville Track (but birds are only present here during the oppressive and dangerous heat of summer) |
| Desert Chat | Scarce on stony plains in the arid interior and only likely to be seen along the Birdsville and Strzelecki Tracks |
| Red-capped Robin | Fairly common in mallee and mulga areas |
| Crested Bellbird | Throughout, especially in mallee and mulga |
| Hall's Babbler | Local and scarce in mulga areas of east-central interior, mainly between Brisbane and Birdsville |
| Chestnut-crowned Babbler | Local, but fairly common in mallee and mulga areas of the interior, of which Hattah-Kulkyne NP is the most easily accessible |

| | |
|---|---|
| Chiming Wedgebill | Local, but fairly common in the remoter areas of the centre and west. Most likely to be seen around Alice Springs and west to a few areas along the west-central coast |
| Chirruping Wedgebill | Local, but fairly common in the remoter areas of the eastern interior (e.g. along the Birdsville and Strzelecki Tracks) |
| Chestnut-breasted Quail-thrush | Scarce in mulga areas of the west where most likely along Route 123 near Mount Magnet, and east-central interior where most likely between Brisbane and Birdsville |
| Cinnamon Quail-thrush | Fairly common in the east-central interior, along the Birdsville and Strzelecki Tracks, and on the Nullarbor Plain |
| Little Crow | Fairly common in the arid interior |
| Masked Woodswallow | Nomadic in the arid interior, but regular at some sites including Round Hill NR, Wyperfeld and Hattah-Kulkyne NPs, and Alice Springs |
| White-browed Woodswallow | Nomadic in the arid interior, but regular at some sites including Round Hill NR, and Wyperfeld and Hattah-Kulkyne NPs |
| Ground Cuckoo-shrike | Scarce in the open arid interior and most likely at a number of remoter sites |
| White-backed Swallow | Scarce in arid interior reaching the coast in some places |
| Spinifex-bird | Fairly common in the west-central arid interior and most likely to be seen in the Alice Springs and Mount Isa areas west to Cape Range NP on the west-central coast |
| Painted Firetail | Fairly common on *spinifex*-covered ridges from the Mount Isa and Alice Springs areas to the west-central coast |

The *alisteri* race of Cinnamon Quail-Thrush, which is endemic to the Nullarbor Plain in south-central Australia, is considered to be a full species by some taxonomists.

## Extinct Mainland Endemics

Paradise Parrot (became extinct around 1927, formerly occurred in southeast Queensland and northeast New South Wales).

## Tasmania (13)

| | |
|---|---|
| Tasmanian Native-hen | Wetlands throughout, but most likely on Bruny Island |
| Green Rosella | Woodlands throughout |
| Tasmanian Masked-Owl | Rarely reported away from Hobart area |
| Forty-spotted Pardalote* | A rare localised species, most likely to be seen on Bruny or Maria Islands |
| Brown Scrubwren | Occurs in most dense forests |
| Scrubtit | Occurs in most dense forests |
| Tasmanian Thornbill | Woodlands and forests throughout |

| | |
|---|---|
| Yellow-throated Honeyeater | Woodlands throughout |
| Black-headed Honeyeater | Woodlands and forests throughout |
| Strong-billed Honeyeater | Woodlands throughout |
| Yellow Wattlebird | Woodlands of south and east |
| Dusky Robin | Common in open areas |
| Black Currawong | Common inland but scarce near Hobart |

### Norfolk Island (4)

Norfolk Island Parakeet*, Norfolk Gerygone*, Slender-billed* and White-chested* White-eyes.

### Extinct Norfolk Island Endemics

Norfolk Kaka (became extinct around 1851).

### Lord Howe Island (2)

Lord Howe Rail*, Lord Howe White-eye*.

### Extinct Lord Howe Island Endemics

Lord Howe Swamphen (became extinct around 1834), Lord Howe Gerygone (became extinct around 1879), Robust White-eye (became extinct around 1928).

## NEAR-ENDEMICS

### Cape York Peninsula (19)

Red-cheeked and Eclectus Parrots, Palm Cockatoo*, Chestnut-breasted Cuckoo, Yellow-billed Kingfisher, Red-bellied Pitta, Fawn-breasted Bowerbird, Beccari's Scrubwren, Green-backed and Tawny-breasted Honeyeaters, Yellow-legged Flycatcher, White-faced Robin, Northern Scrub-Robin, Black-winged and Frilled Monarchs, Trumpet Manucode, Magnificent Riflebird, Black-backed Butcherbird, Ashy-bellied White-eye (islands off peninsula).

### Northeast Queensland (Cairns area to Cape York Peninsula) (15)

Southern Cassowary*, Red-necked Crake, Double-eyed Fig-Parrot (south to Brisbane area where rare), Gould's Bronze-Cuckoo, Papuan Frogmouth, Buff-breasted Paradise-Kingfisher, Spotted Catbird, Fairy Gerygone, Graceful and Varied Honeyeaters, New Guinea Friarbird, Brown-backed Honeyeater, Yellow-breasted Boatbill, Yellow-eyed Cuckoo-shrike (south to Brisbane area), Metallic Starling.

### North (mainly Darwin area) (6)

Chestnut Rail, Green-backed Gerygone, Yellow-tinted Honeyeater, Helmeted Friarbird, Grey Whistler, Mangrove Fantail (mainly northwest).

### North and Northeast (mainly Darwin and Cairns areas) (33)

Magpie Goose, Radjah Shelduck, Pied Heron, Rufous-tailed Bush-hen (to Brisbane area), Rose-crowned Fruit-Dove (to Brisbane area), Torresian Imperial-Pigeon, Red-winged Parrot (to Brisbane area), Australian Koel (to Brisbane area), Pheasant Coucal (to Brisbane area), Rufous Owl, Little Kingfisher, Blue-winged Kookaburra (to The

Kimberley), Forest Kingfisher (to Brisbane area), Large-billed and Mangrove (to Brisbane area) Gerygones, Dusky and Red-headed (mainly Darwin area) Myzomelas, White-throated Honeyeater (to Brisbane area), Little Friarbird (to Brisbane area and Victoria), Rufous-banded and Blue-faced (to Brisbane area and Victoria) Honeyeaters, Lemon-bellied Flycatcher, Mangrove Robin, Black-tailed Whistler (mainly Darwin area), Rufous Shrike-Thrush (to Brisbane area), Leaden (to Brisbane area and Victoria) and Shining Flycatchers, Black Butcherbird, Green Oriole, Green Figbird (to Brisbane area), Varied Triller (to Brisbane area), Crimson Finch, Chestnut-breasted Munia (to Brisbane area).

### East (mainly Cairns, Brisbane and Sydney areas) (9)

Wompoo Fruit-Dove, Marbled Frogmouth (only Brisbane area and Cape York Peninsula), White-throated Nightjar (to Victoria), Noisy Pitta, Noisy Friarbird (to Victoria), Logrunner (mainly Brisbane area), Black-faced Monarch (to Victoria), Satin Flycatcher (to Victoria and Tasmania), Olive-tailed Thrush (to Victoria and Tasmania).

### Southeast (mainly Sydney and Melbourne areas) (4)

Lewin's Rail (to Tasmania), Double-banded Plover (to Brisbane and Tasmania), White-fronted Tern (to Tasmania), Greater Sooty-Owl (to Brisbane).

### Widespread (58)

Hoary-headed Grebe, Little Penguin (south coast), Australian Gannet (south coast), Pied Cormorant, Australian Shoveler (to Tasmania), Australasian Bittern* (to Tasmania), Australian (to Tasmania) and Straw-necked Ibises, Royal Spoonbill, Whistling Kite (to Tasmania), Collared Sparrowhawk, Wedge-tailed and Little Eagles, Brown Falcon (to Tasmania), Australian Hobby (to Tasmania), Painted Buttonquail, Brolga, Australian Bustard, Bush Thick-knee, Pied Oystercatcher (coasts including Tasmania), Black-fronted Dotterel (to Tasmania), Masked Lapwing (not southwest, to Tasmania), Silver Gull, Fairy Tern* (not east, to Tasmania), Peaceful (not southwest) and Bar-shouldered Doves, Sulphur-crested Cockatoo (to Tasmania), Little Corella, Pallid (to Tasmania) and Black-eared Cuckoos, Australian Masked-Owl, Barking Owl, Australian Owlet-Nightjar (to Tasmania), Spotted Nightjar, Azure Kingfisher (not southwest), White-throated Gerygone (not southwest), Brown Honeyeater (not southeast), Jacky-winter, Scarlet Robin (not north, to Tasmania), Varied Sittella, Rufous Whistler, Grey Shrike-Thrush (to Tasmania), Grey-crowned Babbler (not southwest), Restless Flycatcher, Torresian Crow (not south), Black-faced Woodswallow, Australasian Magpie, Magpie-lark, Olive-backed Oriole (not southwest), Black-faced Cuckoo-shrike (to Tasmania), White-winged Triller, Welcome Swallow (to Tasmania), Tree (to Tasmania) and Fairy Martins, Little Grassbird (not north), Zebra Finch, Australasian Pipit (to Tasmania), Mistletoebird.

### Norfolk Island

Long-tailed Triller, Norfolk Starling.

### Lord Howe Island

Red-fronted Parakeet, Norfolk Starling.

# FIJI, SAMOA AND TONGA

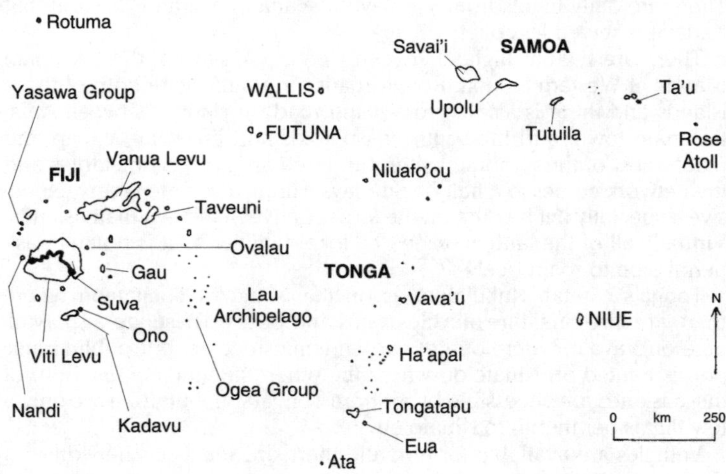


## INTRODUCTION

### Summary

This group of islands supports 41 endemics, 25 of which may be seen on a trip to the main islands of Fiji. Nine endemics are restricted to Samoa, all of which may be seen in Western Samoa, and two species are endemic to Tonga, both of which occur only on different outer islands. There are regular flights between most islands, vehicles available for hire and good public transport networks on the main islands, and a wide range of accommodation near the majority of sites. Some fabulous endemics, an efficient infrastructure and the presence of so many easygoing, friendly local people, all combine to make birding in this part of the Pacific a very enjoyable experience. This is especially true of Taveuni, a small Fijian island which is arguably as close to most people's idea of paradise as it is possible to get. Brilliant Orange Doves and Silktails* light up the island's verdant rainforest, and a coral reef teeming with fantastic fish lies offshore from the beautiful beaches.

### Size

At 18,330 sq km the Fijian islands make up a land area seven times smaller than England and 37 times smaller than Texas. The Samoan islands make up a much smaller land area (3037 sq km) and Tonga is a tiny archipelago (699 sq km).

### Getting Around

On Fiji international flights arrive at Nandi, which is on the west side of the island of Viti Levu. Suva, the capital and hub of the internal air and sea networks, is situated on the opposite coast, 212 km east of Nandi. They are connected by a fairly good road and it is possible to travel between the two by bus (six hours), express bus (three hours), shared taxis (three hours) and hire-car (three hours). Vehicles can be hired on Viti Levu and Vanau Levu, but they are much more expensive than taxis and buses. The cheapest way to island hop is by boat, but reasonably priced airpasses are usually available to visitors with tight schedules. There are daily flights from Viti Levu to Vanau Levu and Taveuni, but Kadavu is served less often.

There are regular flights between Upolu and Savai'i, the two main islands of Western Samoa. Rough roads circumnavigate both of these islands and there is also a cross-island road on Upolu, between Apia, the main town, and the south coast. Taxis and buses are cheap and reach most of the important sites, but there are no bus timetables and the network comes to a halt on Sundays. Hiring a vehicle is very expensive, especially if it is taken on the ferries between the two main islands. Virtually all of the land is owned by local families so it is polite to ask permission to roam freely.

Tonga's capital, Nuku'alofa, is on the island of Tongatapu where there are hire-cars, hire-bicycles, taxis and buses. These are also available on Vava'u, where one of two endemics occurs, but public transport is limited on Niuafo'ou where the other endemic occurs. Both of these islands are accessible by air from Tongatapu, but there are only a few flights per month to Niuafo'ou.

Vehicles are available for hire and there are small bus networks on Wallis and Futuna.

## Accommodation and Food

There is a wide range of accommodation in Fiji, from the numerous luxurious hotels and beach resorts to cheap hotels and guesthouses. Some of the cheaper places have dormitories for budget travellers, but a few double up as brothels. There are campsites at Momi Bay, south of Nandi and on Nukulau, off Suva, as well as on Taveuni, Kadavu, Ovalau and Ono.

In Western Samoa there is a wide range of accommodation in Apia and along the southeast coast of Upolu, as well as along the east coast of Savai'i. One of the best forms of accommodation is thatched beach huts, particularly in Aleipata and Lepa on Upolu and at Satuiatua on Savai'i. It is also possible to stay with local people in their own thatched huts, which they call *fales*. Virtually all of the land is owned by local families so it is necessary to ask for permission to pitch a tent, even on the beaches. In American Samoa there is a good infrastructure on Tutuila, the most westernised island in the Pacific apart from those in Hawaii, but accommodation is expensive unless visitors track down local families willing to accept paying guests.

In Tonga there are hotels and guesthouses on Tongatapu, Eua, Vava'u and Ha'apai, but it will be necessary to enquire about the possibility of staying with local families or camping on Niuafo'ou before venturing there.

Expensive hotels are the only form of accommodation available on Wallis and Futuna, a self-governing Overseas Territory of France, but it may be possible to camp or stay with local families.

Throughout these islands the local people are still uncomfortable with the concept of camping, especially where it is possible to stay with them as paying guests. If you wish to camp, ask for permission very politely and explain carefully why you prefer to sleep under the stars rather than in one of their thatched huts, because they may feel that their generous offer of a roof over your head has been spurned. They also believe that campers are too individualistic, a strange phenomenon in a country where sharing absolutely everything and being part of an extended family is still the norm. Whether you prefer a roof over your head or a tent, repay their generous hospitality with gifts rather than money. Favoured items include kava roots, T-shirts and food. Alcohol is taboo.

There is a wide range of food on offer in the major towns and resorts, and breadfruit, bananas, seafood and raw fish, most of which is marinated in lime juice and served with some concoction of coconut sauce, are available almost everywhere. Favourite local dishes include palusami, a mixture of corned beef, taro, onions and coconut cream, and baked fish in coconut sauce with cassava, taro, breadfruit and sweet potato.

## Health and Safety

Immunisation against hepatitis, polio, typhoid and yellow fever (if arriving from an infected country) is recommended. Malaria has been eradicated, but the local mosquitoes do carry dengue fever.

## Climate and Timing

The peak time to visit this group of islands is July and August, in the middle of the cool and dry season which lasts from May or June to August, September or October.

The best time to visit Fiji is between June and October, the driest and coolest period of the year. The long rainy season lasts from November to May, but most of the rain arrives with the prevailing southeast tradewinds and falls on the southeast coasts and mountain slopes of the high islands. The rains peak in February and March when it is usually extremely wet in these areas. Hence the major tourist complexes are concentrated on the leeward northwestern coasts of each island where the weather is normally dry and sunny for most of the year. Cyclones are most likely from January to March.

The best time to visit Samoa is between May and October, the driest and coolest period of the year, although it is usually hot and humid throughout the year. The long, very wet rainy season lasts from November to April. Severe tropical cyclones occur from December to March and in the early 1990s these caused extensive damage to the forests.

The best time to visit Tonga is between June and August, the driest and coolest time of the year. The hot, wet cyclone season usually lasts from December to April.

The best time to visit Wallis and Futuna is between May and September. The wet season usually lasts from November to March.

## Habitats

Most of the 300 or so Fijian islands are small coral atolls and limestone islets, but the main islands of Viti Levu, Vanua Levu, Taveuni and Kadavu rise to 1323 m (4341 ft) at Mount Tomanivi on Viti Levu. The long rainy season provides enough water to sustain luxuriant, but cool and damp, tropical rainforests, characterised by tall tree ferns. These grow on the southeastern slopes of the rugged highlands of these islands and support most of the endemic birds. Although most of the forest has been cleared on Viti Levu, about 60% remains on Taveuni. The lower slopes support drier woodlands, while coarse grasslands dominate the leeward northwestern slopes and the fertile coastal plains have mostly been turned over to subsistence farming and coconut and sugarcane plantations.

The three main islands of Samoa, which rise to 1858 m (6096 ft) at Mount Silisili on Savai'i, also support luxuriant tropical rainforests, where most of the endemic birds occur, although most of the larger tracts remain only on the steepest slopes.

Rolling forested hills characterise the remaining forested islands of Tonga, but most of the forest has been cleared on islands which support large human populations to make way for subsistence farming, wet taro fields, and numerous coconut and vanilla plantations.

The tiny islands of Wallis and Futuna, which are situated about midway between Fiji and Samoa and rise to 524 m (1719 ft) on Futuna, are also noted for their forested rolling hills. Most of the forest is present on the higher island of Futuna, where there are also patches of 'toafa' fernland.

Throughout this part of the Pacific there are also numerous islets, atolls and coral reefs, all of which help to support a high diversity of seabirds.

## Conservation

Large areas of lowland forest have been cleared on most islands to make way for subsistence farming and sugarcane, vanilla and coconut plantations, and although some relatively extensive tracts of montane forest remain, these are mainly confined to the steepest slopes. Fortunately, the annual natural increase in human population is comparatively low, with a maximum rate of 1.8% on Fiji and rates less than 0.5% in Western Samoa and Tonga, and some areas have been protected, hence some of the montane forest appears to be fairly secure. This will help the 23 threatened and near-threatened species which occur on these islands, but their future is still fraught with problems. In Fiji, for example, natural forests still cover 40% of the land, but a quarter of this has already been deemed suitable for logging. Where reafforestation is taking place, such as in Fiji and Western Samoa, native species which once thrived on the land are being replaced with totally inappropriate non-native exotics such as caribbean pine, teak and mahogany, hence these so-called 'conservation projects' are a pointless exercise as far as the native birds are concerned.

Another problem associated with protecting the rich endemic avifauna is the vicious cyclones which batter these islands every few years and leave considerable damage in their wake. Direct hits to Samoa in 1990 and 1991 reduced the forest canopy cover from 100% to 27%. However, cyclones are hardly a new phenomenon and many species have survived many storms up until now because there has been enough forest to absorb such devastation. Some areas have always managed to escape unscathed from the worst cyclones, leaving the individual birds present in these areas to produce enough offspring to repopulate the damaged areas as they recover. If much more forest is cleared on these islands, one serious cyclone could cause some species to become extinct.

## Bird Species

Over 130 species have been recorded in these islands, including about

100 breeding species and around 70 native landbirds. Fiji's list of about 120 includes 58 native landbirds. Non-endemic specialities and spectacular species in Fiji include Collared Petrel, Polynesian Storm-Petrel, White-tailed Tropicbird, Red-footed Booby, Metallic Pigeon, Scarlet Robin, Black-throated Shrikebill*, Polynesian Triller and Island Thrush. In Samoa such species may include Red-tailed and White-tailed Tropicbirds, Common White-Tern, Crimson-crowned Fruit-Dove, Pacific Imperial-Pigeon, Cardinal Myzomela and Red-headed Parrotfinch.

### Endemics

A total of 41 species only occur on these islands with 25 confined to Fiji, nine to Samoa and two to Tonga. The Fijian endemics include Orange, Golden and Velvet* Doves, two shining-parrots, four honeyeaters, Blue-crested Flycatcher, Silktail* and two parrotfinches. The Samoan endemics include Tooth-billed Pigeon*, Flat-billed Kingfisher, a whistler, a triller and a starling. Tonga supports an endemic scrubfowl and whistler.

### Expectations

It is possible to see around 50 species during a week-long visit to the main Fijian islands of Viti Levu, Taveuni and Kadavu, of which half should be endemics. A few days in Western Samoa should be enough to see all nine Samoan endemics, although Tooth-billed Pigeon* is very rare. More time will be needed to reach the two remote islands in Tonga where the two endemics occur.

## *FIJI*

Twenty-two of the 25 Fijian endemics and four of the five species shared only with the other islands in this group occur on Viti Levu, Taveuni and Kadavu. The three Fijian endemics which do not occur on these main islands are MacGillivray's Petrel*, which is restricted to the small island of Gau off east Viti Levu; Rotuma Myzomela*, which is confined to Rotuma; and Versicoloured Monarch*, which along with the fifth species shared only with the other islands in this group, Blue-crowned Lorikeet, occurs only in the southern Lau Archipelago.

## NAUSORI HIGHLANDS

Most of the original forest cover on Viti Levu, the largest and mostly densely populated of the Fijian islands, has gone. The majority of that which remains lies in the Nausori Highlands near Nandi on the central-west coast where it supports 13 Fijian endemics, including Golden Dove, Masked Shining-Parrot* and Fiji Woodswallow.

### Fijian Endemics

Fiji Goshawk, Golden Dove, Peale's Imperial-Pigeon, Masked Shining-Parrot*, Collared Lory, Orange-breasted Myzomela, Giant Honeyeater, Slaty Monarch, Blue-crested Flycatcher, Fiji Woodswallow, Layard's White-eye, Fiji Bush-Warbler, Fiji Parrotfinch.

## NAUSORI HIGHLANDS

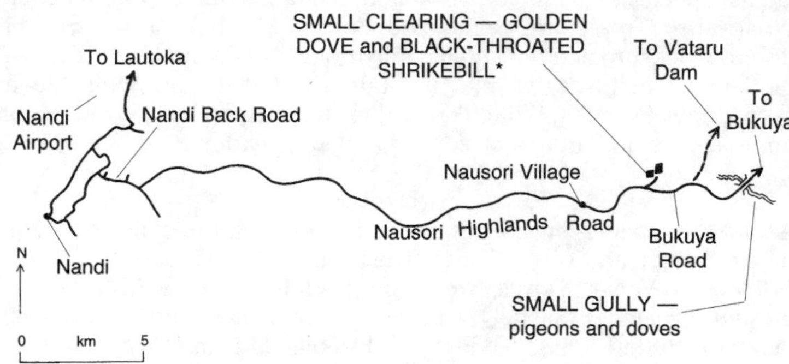


### Fijian, Samoan and Tongan Endemics

Many-coloured Fruit-Dove, Wattled Honeyeater, Fiji Shrikebill.

### Non-endemic Specialities

Streaked Fantail, Black-throated Shrikebill*, Vanikoro Flycatcher, Polynesian Triller, Polynesian Starling.

### Others

Swamp Harrier, Metallic Pigeon, White-rumped Swiftlet, Sacred Kingfisher, Scarlet Robin, Island Thrush, Silver-eye.

(Other species recorded here include Red-throated Lorikeet*. Introduced species include Spotted Dove, Common and Jungle Mynas, Red-vented Bulbul and Red Avadavat.)

From Nandi Airport turn south towards the town of Nandi. After 4 km turn east on to Nandi Back Road, then turn north on to Nausori Highlands Road after 3 km. From here it is 22 km on a rough, winding track to the first remnant forest patches. Bird the roadside from here for the next 10 km or so, especially where there are clearings and gullies.

*Accommodation:* Nandi: Nandi Travelodge. The main resort area on Viti Levu is concentrated along a 100 km stretch of the southwest coast.

*Blue-crested Flycatcher is one of Fiji's best-looking endemics*

Collared Petrel and Polynesian Storm-Petrel have been recorded on boat trips to **Mana Island**, 20 km offshore from Nandi. Some hotels in and around Nandi (e.g. the Hyatt Regency) run regular day-trips to this superb snorkelling and scuba-diving site. Lautoka, 32 km north of Nandi, is the departure point for ferries to a number of small island resorts and the **Yasawa Group**, where seabirds seen on cruises include Wedge-tailed Shearwater, Red-tailed Tropicbird, Great Crested-Tern, Black-naped, Grey-backed and Sooty Terns, and Brown and Black Noddies.

Between Nandi, on the west coast, and Suva, on the east coast, it is worth considering a bit of birding off the beaten track. There is some good forest near **Monasuva Dam**, which lies close to the Nandi-Suva road in the centre of the island and the very rare Long-legged Warbler* was last recorded near here in 1991 when two birds were seen west of Laselevu. Further east along the Nandi-Suva road the presumed extinct Bar-winged Rail was reported near Vunindawa, north of Waisa, in 1973.

In and around **Suva** it is worth birding the Thurston Botanical Gardens where the possibilities include Fiji Goshawk, Many-coloured Fruit-Dove, Collared Lory, White-rumped Swiftlet, Orange-breasted Myzomela, Wattled Honeyeater and Fiji Parrotfinch, as well as the near-by peninsula where Lesser Frigatebird, Pacific Reef-Egret, Wandering Tattler, Pacific Golden-Plover, Great Crested-Tern, Collared Lory, Wattled Honeyeater and Pacific Swallow occur. Any wetlands in the area are worth checking for Spotless Crake.

## THOLO-I-SUVA FOREST PARK

The tropical rainforest in Viti Levu's most important reserve supports 11 Fijian endemics, including Golden Dove and Masked Shining-Parrot*, as well as the near-endemic Shy Ground-Dove*.

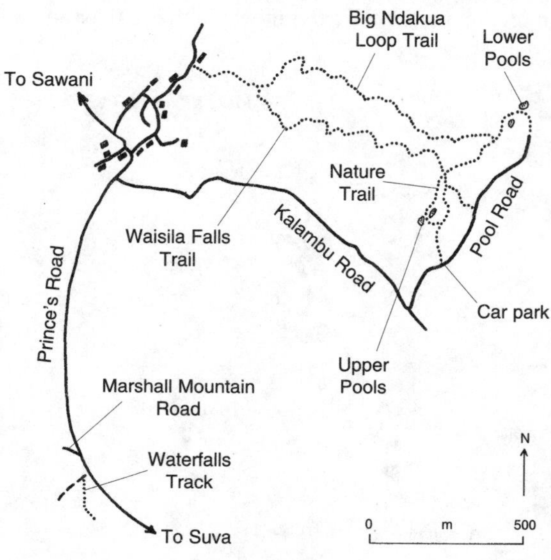

## Fijian Endemics

Golden Dove, Peale's Imperial-Pigeon, Masked Shining-Parrot*, Collared Lory, Orange-breasted Myzomela, Giant Honeyeater, Slaty Monarch, Blue-crested Flycatcher, Layard's White-eye, Fiji Bush-Warbler, Fiji Parrotfinch.

## Fijian, Samoan and Tongan Endemics

Shy Ground-Dove*, Wattled Honeyeater, Fiji Shrikebill.

## Non-endemic Specialities

Streaked Fantail, Black-throated Shrikebill*, Vanikoro Flycatcher, Polynesian Triller, Polynesian Starling.

## Others

Fan-tailed Cuckoo, White-rumped Swiftlet, Scarlet Robin, Golden Whistler, Island Thrush.

(Other species recorded here include Pink-billed Parrotfinch*. Introduced species include Java Sparrow.)

This park is 11 km north of Suva and accessible on the Sawani or Serea buses which depart from the bus station in Suva. Bird the Waterfalls Track which lies to the west of Prince's Road about 500m before the park entrance, and the 3–4 km of excellent trails within the park.

*Accommodation:* camping.

The best site for the very rare Pink-billed Parrotfinch*, which is endemic to Viti Levu, is the remnant forest at Nailagosakelo Creek on the flanks of **Joske's Thumb**, a volcanic plug about 20 km west of Suva. Take the Suva–Nandi road west out of Suva and turn north on to a track called Laikerokoko Road after about 17 km. About 1 km along here bird the track to the right which leads to a dairy farm, and/or continue for a further 2 km on the main track to where it reaches a river and a village.

**JOSKE'S THUMB**

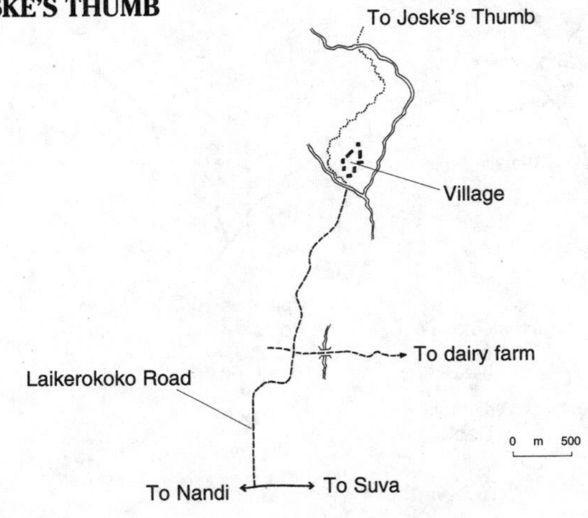

At the village it is possible to hire a guide to explore further. Other species recorded here include Golden Dove, Peale's Imperial-Pigeon, Masked Shining-Parrot*, Vanikoro and Blue-crested Flycatchers, and Fiji Parrotfinch.

## TAVEUNI

In stark contrast with Viti Levu, the small island of Taveuni (just 42 km × 15 km) is less heavily populated and far less popular with conventional tourists, hence it supports 60% of its original forest cover and is still wild enough to be under consideration for World Heritage Site status. The island has a 16 km long mountainous spine which rises to 1241 m (4072 ft) at Mount Uluinggalau, and is surrounded by beautiful beaches and one of the richest coral reefs on earth. However, birders will no doubt be spending most of their time in the cool, misty montane rainforest on Des Voeux Peak. Abundant tall tree ferns fill this forest, which supports the greatest diversity of birds in Fiji. No less than 15 of the endemics have been recorded here, including Orange Dove and Silktail*, both of which are only likely to be seen on this island.

### Fijian Endemics

Fiji Goshawk, Orange Dove, Peale's Imperial-Pigeon, Red Shining-Parrot*, Collared Lory, Orange-breasted Myzomela, Giant Honeyeater, Slaty Monarch, Blue-crested Flycatcher, Silktail*, Fiji Woodswallow, Layard's White-eye, Fiji Bush-Warbler, Fiji Parrotfinch.

### Fijian, Samoan and Tongan Endemics

Shy Ground-Dove*, Many-coloured Fruit-Dove, Wattled Honeyeater, Fiji Shrikebill.

**TAVEUNI**

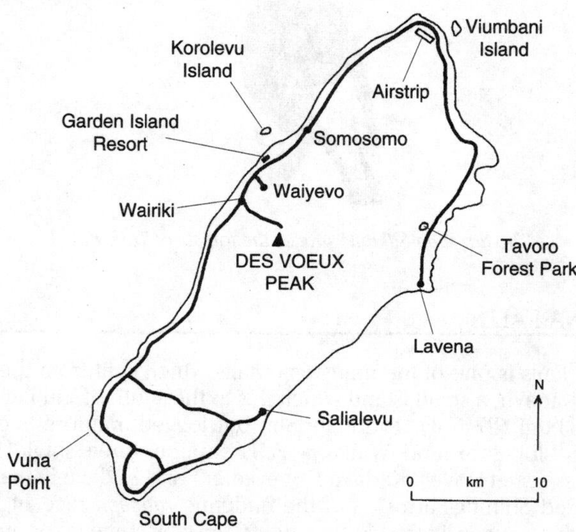

### Non-endemic Specialities

Streaked Fantail, Black-throated Shrikebill*, Vanikoro Flycatcher, Polynesian Triller, Polynesian Starling.

### Others

Lesser Frigatebird, Red-footed and Brown Boobies, Great Crested-Tern, White-rumped Swiftlet, Collared and Sacred Kingfishers, Scarlet Robin, Golden Whistler, White-breasted Woodswallow, Island Thrush, Pacific Swallow, Silver-eye.

(Other species recorded here include Red-throated Lorikeet*. Introduced species include Red Junglefowl, Spotted Dove, Australasian Magpie and Common Myna.)

Taveuni is accessible by air from Viti Levu. From the airstrip at the northern end of the island, head south to the town of Somosomo, just 4 km from the international dateline. About 5.5 km south of here, at Wairiki, head east along the 8 km long winding track (4WD only) to **Des Voeux Peak**, at 1195 m (3921 ft) the highest point accessible by vehicle on Fiji. The best birding strategy is to arrange a lift to the peak at Kaba's Guesthouse in Somosomo, or at a number of other places, and walk slowly down to Wairiki. Birders staying in Somosomo could then hitch a lift back there or, better still, walk alongside the coastal scrub and scan for seabirds such as Lesser Frigatebird and Red-footed Booby, both of which breed on a small islet just offshore. Snorkelling is also highly recommended.

*Accommodation:* Maravu Plantation Resort (good birding), Garden Isle Resort, International Hotel (A+), Kaba's Guesthouse (self-catering chalets).

*The dazzling Silktail* graces the forests of Taveuni*

## WAIKANA FALLS

Waikana Falls is one of the many waterfalls which spill from the highlands of Kadavu, a small island which lies to the south of Viti Levu and rises to 838 m (2749 ft). The luxuriant, but logged, rainforests on the mountain slopes around Waikana Falls support three single island endemics: Velvet Dove*, Kadavu Honeyeater* and Kadavu Fantail*, as well as Red Shining-Parrot* and the endemic *ruficeps* race of Island Thrush which is considered to be a full species by some taxonomists.

## KADAVU

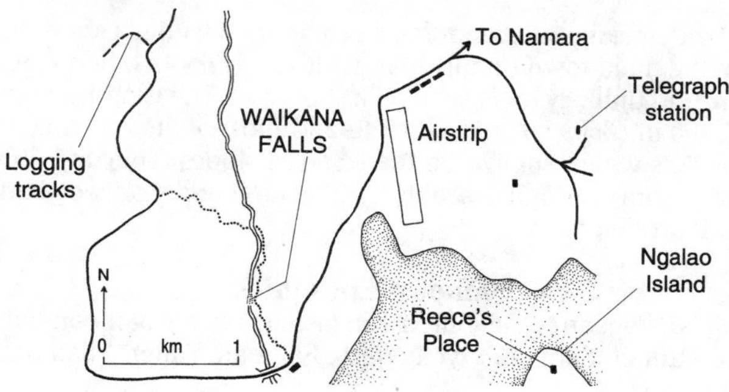


### Fijian Endemics

Velvet Dove*, Peale's Imperial-Pigeon, Red Shining-Parrot*, Collared Lory, Orange-breasted Myzomela, Kadavu Honeyeater*, Kadavu Fantail*, Slaty Monarch, Layard's White-eye.

### Non-endemic Specialities

Vanikoro Flycatcher, Polynesian Triller, Polynesian Starling.

### Others

Lesser Frigatebird, Pacific Black Duck, Pacific Reef-Egret, Swamp Harrier, Grey-tailed and Wandering Tattlers, Pacific Golden-Plover, Great Crested-Tern, White-rumped Swiftlet, Collared Kingfisher, Golden Whistler, Island Thrush (*ruficeps* race), Pacific Swallow, Silver-eye.

Kadavu is accessible by air from Suva. Bird the rainforest around the falls and alongside the nearby logging tracks. The Astrolabe Reef, just to the northeast, is one of the world's best scuba-diving sites.

*Accommodation:* Reece's Place, on the adjacent island of Ngalao, a short boat trip away.

Rotuma Myzomela* is endemic to the island of **Rotuma**, accessible by air from Suva. Tourism is discouraged on this 6 km × 14 km damp island, which rises to 256 m (840 ft) at Mount Suelhof, and there is no accommodation. The islet of Hatana, off the west coast, supports breeding seabirds. Versicoloured Monarch* is endemic to the Ogea group of islands in the southern **Lau Archipelago** and it may be possible to reach these islands via Vanua Mbalavu and Lakemba where there is accommodation.

## *WESTERN SAMOA*

Samoa is comprised of Western Samoa (two major islands known as Upolu and Savai'i, both of which must be visited to see all nine endemics) and American Samoa (two major islands known as Tutuila and Ta'u, neither of which support any localised endemics).

## UPOLU

Eight of the nine Samoan endemics can be seen within a short distance of Apia, the main town on this island, although Tooth-billed Pigeon* is very rare and unlikely to be seen on a short visit. The island's mountains rise to 1100 m (3609 ft) at Mount Fito and most of the endemics occur in the forests which survive on the steepest slopes. They are ably supported by some stunning seabirds, Blue-crowned Lorikeet and Red-headed Parrotfinch.

### Samoan Endemics

Tooth-billed Pigeon*, Flat-billed Kingfisher, Mao*, Samoan Whistler, Samoan Fantail, Samoan Flycatcher*, Samoan Triller*, Samoan Starling.

### Fijian, Samoan and Tongan Endemics

Shy Ground-Dove*, Blue-crowned Lorikeet, Wattled Honeyeater.

### Non-endemic Specialities

Crimson-crowned Fruit-Dove, Cardinal Myzomela, Polynesian Triller, Polynesian Starling, Red-headed Parrotfinch.

### Others

Red-tailed and White-tailed Tropicbirds, Great Frigatebird, Red-footed Booby, Wandering Tattler, Brown Noddy, Common White-Tern, Pacific Imperial-Pigeon, White-rumped Swiftlet.

Faleolo Airport, Western Samoa's main international airport, is 35 km west of Apia on Upolu's north coast. On arrival in Apia, head for the Division of Conservation and Environment, Department of Lands, Survey and Environment, Government Offices, Beach Road, where it may be possible to find out the latest details on the status of species such as Tooth-billed Pigeon*, and where the best birding sites are. Otherwise head straight for **Mount Vaea**, accessible on the Mulivai or Lotofaga buses, which leave from the bus station next to the market (Maketi Fou), or by taxi (agree price before departure). Either way, ask to be dropped off at the entrance to Vailima, Robert Louis Stevenson's old house, which sits at the foot of Mount Vaea 3.5 km inland from Apia. Bird around the botanic gardens and along the trail up Mount Vaea (Flat-billed Kingfisher, Samoan Triller*) which leads to Stevenson's tomb just below the 475 m (1558 ft) summit, then walk back downhill to Apia. After Stevenson's death the local chiefs tabooed the use of guns on the hillside surrounding his tomb so that the birds would continue to sing—and they do.

The other good birding site near Apia is the **Vaisigano Watershed**, accessible by taxi via Magigai Road. On reaching the gravel section of this road look out for a disused concrete water-tank on the right-hand side. About 300 m beyond the tank walk down the track to the right, which leads to a river. Bird upstream from here, searching remnant forest patches for the rare Mao* and Red-headed Parrotfinch. The 28 sq km **O Le Pupu-Pu'e National Park** (tel: 24 294), which stretches from Mount Fito to the south coast and is accessible by bus from Apia, supports Tooth-billed Pigeon*, Flat-billed Kingfisher and Samoan Fantail,

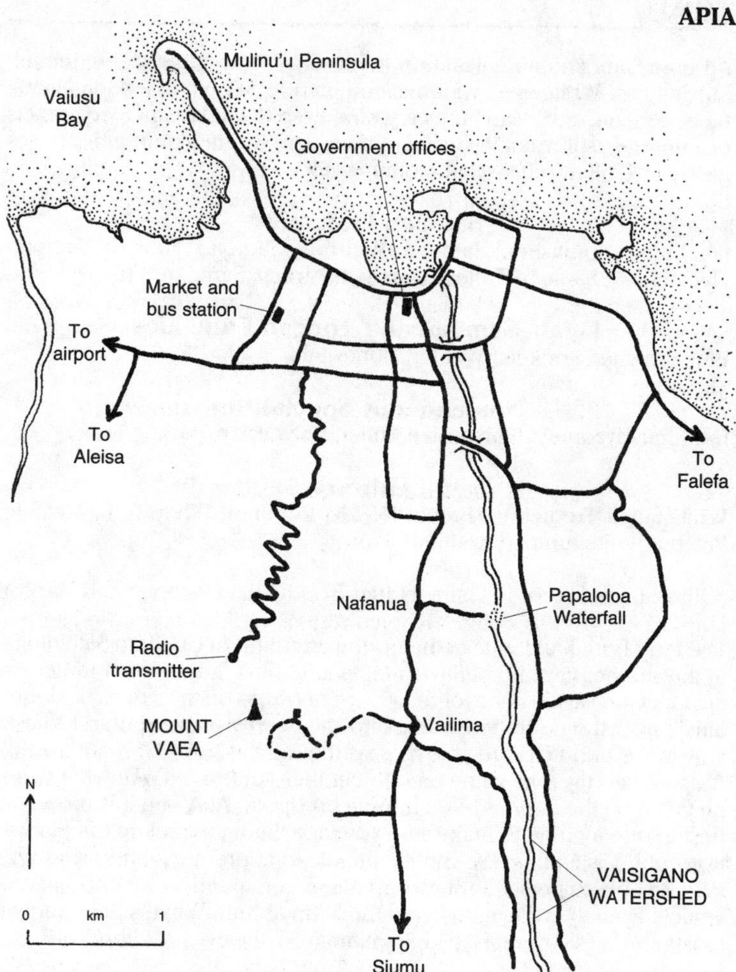


as well as Red-tailed Tropicbird and Blue-crowned Lorikeet. Near the village of **Lalomanu** at the southeast corner of the island, accessible by bus from Apia, Tooth-billed Pigeon* has been recorded at the Lua O Moa Crater, along with Crimson-crowned Fruit-Dove. The islets of Nu'utele and Nu'ulua off Lalomanu support breeding seabirds such as Red-footed Booby, and Shy Ground-Dove* occurs on Nu'utele. Other species recorded around Lalomanu include Great Frigatebird, Wandering Tattler and Flat-billed Kingfisher.

*Accommodation:* Apia—hotels and hostels. Lalomanu—*fales*.

Upolu and Savai'i are connected by air and vehicle ferries which run between Apia and Mulifanua (Upolu) and Salelologa (Savai'i). Birds recorded from the ferry include Great Frigatebird and Red-footed Booby.

## SAVAI'I

All nine Samoan endemics have been recorded on this island, including Samoan White-eye* which is confined to Savai'i. However, Tooth-billed Pigeon* and Mao* are very rare, despite the fact that large tracts of rainforest still remain on this otherwise barren island, which rises gently to 1858 m (6096 ft) at Mount Silisili.

### Samoan Endemics

Flat-billed Kingfisher, Samoan Whistler, Samoan Fantail, Samoan Flycatcher*, Samoan Triller*, Samoan Starling, Samoan White-eye*.

### Fijian, Samoan and Tongan Endemics

Blue-crowned Lorikeet, Wattled Honeyeater.

### Non-endemic Specialities

Cardinal Myzomela, Polynesian Triller, Polynesian Starling.

### Others

White-tailed Tropicbird, Brown Noddy, Common White-Tern, Metallic Pigeon, White-rumped Swiftlet.

(Other species recorded here include Tooth-billed Pigeon* and Mao*.)

The ferry from Mulifanua at the northwestern tip of Upolu to Salelologa at the southeastern tip of Savai'i takes 1.5 hours. It is seven minutes by air. Once on Savai'i head for the village of **A'opo** on the slopes of Mount Silisili near the north coast, and bird the nearby plantation and forest. Few buses and taxis are able to pass the rough stretch of road around A'opo so it may take some time to get there unless a 4WD, which can be taken on the ferry, is hired in Apia on Upolu. At A'opo it is probably best to hire a guide to make sure you take the right track to the plantation, which is 5 km away. Birders unable to afford the luxury of a 4WD may be able to persuade such a guide to commandeer an appropriate vehicle from the village, to avoid the 5 km ascent. What is important is to get above 900 m (2953 ft) into Samoan White-eye* territory.

*Accommodation:* there are several places to stay on Savai'i, including a few hotels which also cater for campers.

The three large atolls of Nukunonu, Atafu and Fakaofo which comprise **Tokelau**, a Dependent Territory of New Zealand, are only accessible via the more or less monthly freightship (complete with passenger cabins) from Apia in Western Samoa. Before embarking on the trip to Tokelau, where there must be some good seabirds, it is necessary to obtain a visitor permit from the Office for Tokelau Affairs, Box 865, Apia (tel: 685 20822, fax: 685 21761). There is no official accommodation on the atolls, but it may be possible to stay with local people as a paying guest and this may also be arranged through the aforementioned address.

## *AMERICAN SAMOA*

Over 60 species have been recorded in American Samoa, including White-tailed Tropicbird, Red-footed Booby, Buff-banded Rail, Many-coloured and Crimson-crowned Fruit-Doves, Pacific Imperial-Pigeon, Wattled Honeyeater and Fiji Shrikebill. This archipelago is also a good place to see humpback whales between August and October. The international airport is at Pago Pago on the small, modern island of **Tutuila** (32 km × 10 km wide). Rugged forested mountains, which rise to 653 m (2142 ft) at Mount Matafao, dominate the eastern half of this island, whereas the western half is composed of a high plateau with forest-filled craters of extinct volcanoes. The two sides are separated by the huge harbour of Pago Pago and there is a wide coastal plain along the south coast of both. Part of Tutuila falls within a 32 sq km national park which was established to protect some of the best remaining rainforest and reefs in American Samoa. It is possible to get near this park at Vatia, a short bus ride from Pago Pago, which lies opposite Pola Island where seabirds breed, but for details on access to the park, contact the Administrative Office, Suite 214, Pago Pago Shopping Plaza (tel: 633 7082, fax: 633 7085). The *powelli* race of Fiji Shrikebill, considered to be a full species by some taxonomists, occurs on the island of **Tau**, which is situated in the Manua Group to the east of Tutuila. Further east lies **Rose Atoll**, a NWR.

## *TONGA*

Neither of the two endemics occur on Tongatapu, the main island, and to see both it is necessary to visit at least two of the outer islands.

### Tongan Endemics

Polynesian Scrubfowl*, Tongan Whistler*.

### Fijian, Samoan and Tongan Endemics

Shy Ground-Dove*, Blue-crowned Lorikeet.

### Others

Collared Kingfisher.

(Introduced species include Red Shining-Parrot*.)

The capital of the Kingdom of Tonga, Nuku'alofa, is situated on the most heavily populated island of Tongatapu, a rather flat island which is dominated by coconut plantations. In contrast, the island of **Eua**, 40 km to the southeast, is comprised of rolling, forested hills surrounded by high cliffs, and it supports Blue-crowned Lorikeet and Collared Kingfisher. Between 188 and 235 pairs of Polynesian Scrubfowl* survive on the 50 sq km island of **Niuafo'ou**, the northernmost island in Tonga. It is also one of the most remote islands in the Pacific, but accessible by air at least twice a month from Tongatapu and Vava'u, crosswinds permitting, The scrubfowl breed at nine communal nesting grounds at least, including those on the islands in the 5 km wide sulphurous crater lake known as Vai Lahi, but they have declined steadily in recent years

**NIUAFO'OU**

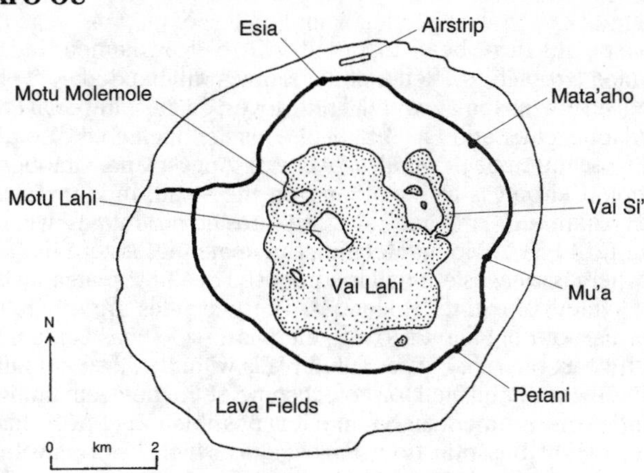


due to over-harvesting of the large, protein-rich eggs, predation by feral cats, and the loss of rainforest due to the spread of plantations and lava, which occasionally pours out of the active volcano and has already spilled over large areas of the south and west. Only 10 sq km of rainforest survives and this is restricted to the crater. There is no accommodation on this island, but it may be possible to stay as paying guests with the locals. In an effort to ensure Polynesian Scrubfowl* has a future, some birds have been introduced to the islands of **Late** and **Fonualei**, both of which support large seabird colonies and Shy Ground-Dove*. Late is also the stronghold of Tongan Whistler*, but this endemic also occurs on **Vava'u** where there are whalewatching trips out of Neiafu between July and October in search of humpback whales. There is a wide range of accommodation on this island and it is possible to get around by hire-car, minibuses, trucks and bicycles.

## *WALLIS AND FUTUNA*

At least 35 species have been recorded in this small archipelago, which is an Overseas Territory of France, including Bristle-thighed Curlew* and some superb seabirds.

### Fijian, Samoan and Tongan Endemics

Blue-crowned Lorikeet, Wattled Honeyeater.

### Non-endemic Specialities

Bristle-thighed Curlew*, Common White-Tern, Crimson-crowned Fruit-Dove, Pacific Imperial-Pigeon, Polynesian Triller, Polynesian Starling.

### Others

White-tailed Tropicbird, Red-footed Booby, Great and Lesser Frigatebirds, Pacific Black Duck, Buff-banded Rail, Purple Swamphen, Wandering Tattler, Pacific Golden-Plover, Black-naped Tern, Brown Noddy, White-rumped Swiftlet.

(Other species recorded here include Red-tailed Tropicbird (Wallis), Shy Ground-Dove* ('Alofi) and Fiji Shrikebill (Futuna).)

These islands are accessible via Hihifo Airport, which is served by flights from Fiji, New Caledonia and Tahiti on Air Caledonie International. There is also a fairly regular freightship service from New Caledonia. The main town, Mata-Utu, is on the east coast of **Wallis** (also known as 'Uvea), a low 96 sq km island of forested rolling hills which rise to 144 m (472 ft) at Mount Lulu Fakahega, and which is surrounded by about 20 islets and a coral lagoon. On this island White-tailed Tropicbirds are most likely to be seen around Lakes Lalolalo and Lanutavake, Red-footed Boobies and Brown Noddies breed on the islets of Nukufutu and Nukuloa, Bristle-thighed Curlews* occur around Nukuloa, Common White-Tern breeds in the pandanus scrub and plantations near the airport, at Matala'a Point and on Nukuloa, and Pacific Imperial-Pigeon occurs in the forest near Utuleve and on Mount Lulufakaenga. **Futuna**, one hour by air to the southwest of Wallis, is a high 80 sq km island which rises to 524 m (1719 ft) at Mount Puke and therefore supports more forest, although much of this was damaged by a cyclone in 1987, and some has been replaced with plantations. 'Toafa' fernland is another major habitat here. Futuna and 'Alofi, its 35 sq km neighbour, have no coral lagoons surrounding them. Blue-crowned Lorikeet, Wattled Honeyeater and Polynesian Triller only occur on Futuna, where the best place for Red-footed Booby, Brown Noddy and Common White-Tern is the coast around Leava. The hills inland from here are the best place for landbirds. For more information on these islands, contact the Bureau des Wallis et Futuna, BP C5, Noumea Cedex, New Caledonia (fax: 687 284283).

*Accommodation:* Wallis and Futuna—hotels (A+). It may be possible to camp inland or stay as a paying guest with local people.

The independent nation of **Niue** is accessible by air from New Zealand. Most of the 2,500 inhabitants live in and around Alofi, the main town on the west coast of this 260 sq km elevated atoll. The central plateau rises to 60 m (197 ft) and supports some forest which may well be worth exploring, but this island is not famous for its birds. It is, however, very popular with scuba-divers. They arrive here from all over the world to swim through the Matapa Chasm, one of a number of underwater limestone chasms which supports 'friendly' sea-snakes. There are a few small hotels, taxis run along the few roads and cars are available for hire. For more information, contact the Tourism Office, Box 42, Alofi (tel: 683 4224, fax: 683 4225).

## ADDITIONAL INFORMATION

### Addresses

The Ornithological Society of New Zealand, PO Box 316, Drury, South Auckland, New Zealand, publishes the *Notornis* journal, which covers Fiji, Samoa and Tonga.
Fiji Visitors Bureau, PO Box 92, Suva, Fiji (fax: 679 300 970).
Western Samoa Visitors Bureau, PO Box 2272, Apia, Western Samoa

(fax: 685 20886).
Office of Tourism, PO Box 1147, Pago Pago, American Samoa (fax: 684 633 1094).
Tonga Visitors Bureau, PO Box 37, Nuku'alofa, Kingdom of Tonga (fax: 676 22129).

## Books and Papers

*The Birds of Hawaii and the Tropical Pacific.* Pratt H D *et al.*, 1987. Princeton University Press.
*The Birds of Fiji, Tonga and Samoa.* Watling D, 1982. Millwood Press.
*The Rainforest and the Flying Foxes: an Introduction to the Rainforest Preserves on Savai'i, Western Samoa.* Elmqvist T, 1993. Salelologa, Western Samoa: Fa'asao Savai'i Society.
Forest bird communities in Western Samoa. Bellingham M, Davis A, 1988. *Notornis* 35: 117–128.
Birds of 'Ata and Late, and additional notes on the avifauna of Niuafo'ou, Kingdom of Tonga. Rinke D, 1991. *Notornis* 38: 131–151.
The status of wildlife in Tonga. Rinke D, 1986. *Oryx* 20: 146–151.
Notes on the birds of Wallis and Futuna, South-West Pacific. Gill B, 1995. *Notornis* 42: 17–22.

## FIJIAN, SAMOAN and TONGAN ENDEMICS (41)

### Fiji, Samoa and Tonga (5)

| | |
|---|---|
| Shy Ground-Dove* | Tholo-i-Suva FP and Des Voeux Peak (Fiji), Upolu (Samoa) and Late and Fonualei (Tonga). Also known from 'Alofi in Wallis and Futuna |
| Blue-crowned Lorikeet | Restricted to the southern Lau Archipelago in Fiji, widespread on Upolu and Savai'i (Samoa), Eua (Tonga) and Futuna |
| Many-coloured Fruit-Dove | Nausori Highlands, Suva and Des Voeux Peak (Fiji), and American Samoa |
| Wattled Honeyeater | Widespread |
| Fiji Shrikebill | Nausori Highlands, Tholo-i-Suva FP and Des Voeux Peak (Fiji), and American Samoa where the *powelli* race may be a separate species. Also known from Futuna |

### Fiji (25)

| | |
|---|---|
| MacGillivray's Petrel* | Breeds on Gau Island, apparently in very small numbers |
| Fiji Goshawk | Viti Levu and Taveuni |
| Orange Dove | Taveuni and Vanau Levu |
| Golden Dove | Viti Levu |
| Velvet Dove* | Kadavu and Ono |
| Peale's Imperial-Pigeon | Viti Levu, Taveuni and Kadavu |
| Red Shining-Parrot* | Taveuni and Kadavu |
| Masked Shining-Parrot* | Viti Levu |
| Collared Lory | Viti Levu, Taveuni and Kadavu |
| Red-throated Lorikeet* | Viti Levu and Taveuni. Very rare and usually only seen in flocks of 2–6 birds. Also known from Vanua Levu and Ovalau |

| | |
|---|---|
| Rotuma Myzomela* | Rotuma |
| Orange-breasted Myzomela | Viti Levu, Taveuni and Kadavu |
| Kadavu Honeyeater* | Kadavu |
| Giant Honeyeater | Viti Levu and Taveuni |
| Kadavu Fantail* | Kadavu |
| Versicoloured Monarch* | Ogealevu, Ogeadriki and Dakuiyanuya in the Ogea Group in the southern Lau Archipelago |
| Slaty Monarch | Viti Levu, Taveuni and Kadavu |
| Blue-crested Flycatcher | Viti Levu and Taveuni |
| Silktail* | Taveuni. Also known from the Natewa Peninsula at the eastern end of Vanua Levu |
| Fiji Woodswallow | Viti Levu and Taveuni |
| Layard's White-eye | Viti Levu, Taveuni and Kadavu |
| Fiji Bush-Warbler | Viti Levu and Taveuni |
| Long-legged Warbler* | Viti Levu. Very rare with recent records only from 1967, 1973 and 1991 when two birds were seen west of Laselevu (which is near Monasavu Dam in the centre of the island, along the Nandi–Suva road). Also known from Vanua Levu where one specimen was taken in 1974 |
| Fiji Parrotfinch | Viti Levu and Taveuni |
| Pink-billed Parrotfinch* | Viti Levu. Very rare and only likely to be seen at Joske's Thumb |

The *ruficeps* race of Island Thrush, which is endemic to Kadavu, is considered to be a full species by some taxonomists.

## Extinct Fijian Endemics

| | |
|---|---|
| Bar-winged Rail | Known only from 12 specimens collected on Viti Levu and Ovalau during the 1800s, and an unconfirmed record of one north of Waisa, near Vunindawa (near the Nandi–Suva road, northwest of Suva) on Viti Levu in 1973 |

## Samoa (9)

| | |
|---|---|
| Tooth-billed Pigeon* | Western Samoa: Upolu. Also known from Savai'i. Very rare with probably less than 50 pairs left |
| Flat-billed Kingfisher | Western Samoa: Upolu and Savai'i |
| Mao* | Western Samoa: Upolu. Also known from Savai'i and from Tutuila in American Samoa |
| Samoan Whistler | Western Samoa: Upolu and Savai'i |
| Samoan Fantail | Western Samoa: Upolu and Savai'i |
| Samoan Flycatcher* | Western Samoa: Upolu and Savai'i |
| Samoan Triller* | Western Samoa: Upolu and Savai'i |
| Samoan Starling | Western Samoa: Upolu and Savai'i |
| Samoan White-eye* | Western Samoa: Savai'i |

The *powelli* race of Fiji Shrikebill, which is endemic to American Samoa, is considered to be a full species by some taxonomists.

### Extinct Samoan Endemics

| | |
|---|---|
| Samoan Moorhen | Last recorded (on Savai'i) in 1873, but there were two possible sightings in montane forest west of Mount Elietoga at the west end of the island in 1987 |

### Tonga (2)

| | |
|---|---|
| Polynesian Scrubfowl* | Niuafo'ou (188–235 pairs). Introduced to Late and Fonualei |
| Tongan Whistler* | Late (stronghold) and Vava'u |

### Breeding Endemics

| | |
|---|---|
| Collared Petrel | Breeds in Fiji and Samoa, and ranges to central Polynesia |

### NEAR-ENDEMICS

Grey-backed Tern, Blue-grey Noddy, Crimson-crowned Fruit-Dove, Cardinal Myzomela (Samoa), Streaked Fantail (Fiji), Black-throated Shrikebill* (Fiji), Vanikoro Flycatcher (Fiji), Polynesian Triller (Fiji and Samoa), Polynesian Starling (Fiji and Samoa), Red-headed Parrotfinch (Western Samoa: Upolu and Savaii).

# HAWAII

## INTRODUCTION

### Summary

The world's most isolated archipelago, which is situated in the north Pacific over 3000 km from the nearest landmass, supports a highly distinctive, but severely depleted, avifauna which includes 35 endemics, many of which maintain a precarious existence in remnant montane forests, and only 20 of which are likely to be seen on a short trip to Kauai, Maui and Big Island. Getting to and around these islands is easy, but virtually all forms of accommodation are very expensive. Although birding in Hawaii is tainted by the large numbers of introduced species in the lowlands, tracking down the endemics is enlivened by the presence of a superb selection of seabirds, as well as large numbers of humpback whales which spend the winter around the islands.

### Size

At 16,640 sq km Hawaii is eight times smaller than England and one-fortieth the size of Texas. However, the 130 or so atolls and islands span 2600 km of the Pacific.

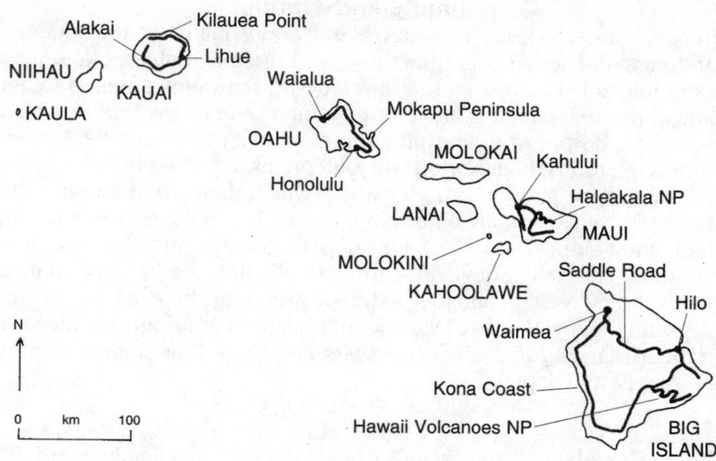


## Getting Around

There is a good inter-island air network, but few ferries. The most effective way to bird each island thoroughly is to hire a vehicle, preferably a 4WD, although all but the remotest high-altitude sites, most of which are not normally accessible to independent birders, are usually accessible in 2WD. On Big Island it is best not to tell hire companies that you intend to take your vehicle on the Saddle Road (they will insist it is too rough even for 4WD, but this is not true) and to make sure you are insured through some other means because if you break down or have an accident on this road the hire companies' insurance will not provide the appropriate cover. Buses cover most of Oahu (where Honolulu is situated), the lowlands of Kauai and Maui, and the coastal plain between Kona and Hilo on Big Island.

It is necessary to obtain permits well in advance to visit a number of important sites. Do not enter wilderness areas without ridding all clothing and footwear of the seeds of non-native plant species. Take a telescope to obtain the best views of seabirds.

Learning a little Hawaiian may help in locating some of the birds and it is useful to know how to pronounce their names—for example, Iiwi is pronounced 'e-EE-vee', Poouli is pronounced 'PO-oh-ou-lee', Akohekohe is pronounced 'AH-KO-ay-KO-ay', Akekee is pronounced 'AH-Key-KAY-e' and Akiapolaau is pronounced 'ah-KEY-ah-PO-LAH-OW'.

## Accommodation and Food

Birders in need of a roof over their heads at the end of a long day in the field will find only very expensive hotels and B&Bs. Camping is free at the widely scattered campsites, but few are situated near the best birding sites and permits are required for camping in state parks on Kauai. Western food, Asian dishes and superb seafood are available throughout the main islands.

## Health and Safety

Beyond the heavily populated Honolulu–Waikiki conurbation on the island of Oahu, the Hawaiian islands are generally safe and free from crime.

## Climate and Timing

The peak times to visit Hawaii are March and April, when the endemic landbirds and seabirds are breeding, and there is a chance of seeing some migrant seabirds, and late October to early November, another time of the year which is good for migrant seabirds. Any time between October and April would be almost as good, but mid-December to mid-April is the tourist high season when all prices are hiked up.

There is little point in worrying about which period of the year is the wettest because virtually all of the endemic landbirds only survive on the highest slopes, which are almost permanently bathed in wet, low clouds. Higher still, above 1524 m (5000 ft), the weather can change rapidly from cold rain and mist to warm, strong sunshine. It is warm and pleasantly sunny, thanks to the cool northeasterlies, for most of the year in the lowlands, especially on leeward coasts, and the hottest months are August and September.

## Habitats

The spectacular volcanic islands of Hawaii rise dramatically out of the Pacific and rise to 4205 m (13,796 ft) at Mauna Kea on Big Island, the highest peak on earth when the 5486 m (18,000 ft) which lie below sea-level are taken into account.

The natural lowland forests and wetlands have long been replaced by built developments, introduced trees (the lush, natural looking forest behind Honolulu is not natural), alien algoroba thickets, huge areas of non-native pasture land and massive sugarcane and pineapple plantations, all of which combine to form a desert as far as endemic landbirds are concerned. Another common crop appears to be marijuana, which has been planted so extensively that Big Island has been known to produce the largest crop of marijuana in the USA. Endemic waterbirds have fared better because they have been able to adapt to artificial wetlands in the form of shrimp ponds, taro fields, small reservoirs and sewage lagoons, but the lowlands are, on the whole, infested with introduced landbirds. Horrified birders can hide from the aliens by taking solace in the seabirds, which thrive on the rich waters surrounding the islands and breed on the rocky headlands and offshore islets. There are also plenty of palm-fringed beaches and, offshore, some outstanding coral reefs.

Fragments of natural forests, known as *kipukas* where they are separated by lava flows, survive only above 1219 m (4000 ft) and this is where virtually all the endemic landbirds occur. The forests are dominated by *ohia-lehua* (usually shortened to *ohia*), a member of the eucalyptus family, and *koa*, a member of the acacia clan. The red flowers of the *ohia* trees are a very important source of nectar for the endemic honeycreepers. Climbing vines, epiphytes, mosses and tree-ferns adorn wet *ohia* forests, which, in the wettest montane areas such as the Alakai Plateau on Kauai, could be described as cloud forests, as they are almost constantly shrouded in low, wet clouds. These forests are particularly important to the endemic thrushes. In drier montane areas such as those on Big Island there are mixed *koa–ohia* forests which support the greatest diversity of the archipelago's rarest endemic birds. Open, park-like and grassy *mamane–naio* forests (where the trees have yellow flowers) also occur in high and dry areas, mainly on the leeward side of the highest mountains such as the western slopes of Mauna Kea on Big Island. Puu Waa Waa on Big Island is one the few sites which support tiny remnants of natural lowland forest. This dry forest is composed of such species as *naio*, *halapepe* and *wiliwili*.

There are alpine zones above 2134 m (7000 ft) on the four highest peaks (Mauna Kea, Mauna Loa, Haleakala and Hualalai), and on Big Island the volcanoes are still active, producing regular flows of molten lava which, when cool, form large barren areas at all altitudes.

## Conservation

A very high total of 33 threatened and near-threatened species occur in Hawaii. At least six of these are on the verge of extinction and seem set to join the 16 species which have become extinct since 1800. It is widely believed that the rapid and formerly mysterious decline of many forest birds after 1820 was probably due to the arrival of disease-carrying mosquitoes, which may well have been introduced deliberately by a crazy seafaring captain. Although there were few endemic species left in the lowlands (most lowland forest on the main islands had been destroyed by 1800), those that were present were soon wiped out and virtually all of the endemics which survive today only do so above 1219 m (4000 ft), the upper altitudinal limit of mosquitoes. If these bloodsuckers adapt to higher, cooler altitudes, or are able to expand their range due to a slight climatic change, then many more birds, most of which are only represented by tiny populations, may also become extinct. Another more pressing problem for the conservationists to solve is the severe disruption of natural regeneration by numerous feral pigs. The only way to provide a potentially secure future for the unique endemic landbirds of Hawaii, apart from rendering the mosquitoes harmless, is to ensure that as much natural forest as possible is protected, restored and created, although even this laudable aim will be difficult to achieve in the face of occasional catastrophic hurricanes. The two most recent severe hurricanes, Iwa in 1982 and Iniki in 1992, are thought to have led to the extinction of at least one species and enhanced the decline of a few others, hence it is crucial to establish and protect as much forest as possible. Naturally, this was realised a long time ago, hence many reserves have been established and the state is trying very hard to conserve its natural resources, but they may have missed the boat, because many species continue to slide down the slippery slope of extinction.

## Bird Families

The Hawaiian Honeycreepers are endemic to Hawaii. The family originally contained 30 species, but at least ten have become extinct since 1800.

## Bird Species

Over 200 species have been recorded in Hawaii. Non-endemic specialities and spectacular species include Black-footed and Laysan Albatrosses, Black-winged, Mottled, Bonin, Dark-rumped (the endemic *sandwichensis* race), Juan Fernandez and Bulwer's Petrels, Buller's* and Christmas Island Shearwaters, Band-rumped and Tristram's* Storm-Petrels, Red-tailed and White-tailed Tropicbirds, Great Frigatebird, Masked and Red-footed Boobies, the endemic *sandvicensis* race of Common Moorhen, Bristle-thighed Curlew*, the endemic *knudseni* race of Black-necked Stilt, Grey-backed and Sooty Terns, Black Noddy and Common White-Tern. There are probably more introduced species in

Hawaii than anywhere else in the world, thanks to the misguided aims of the Hui Manu Society which decided to repopulate the birdless lowlands with anything they could think of between the 1920s and 1950s. Their energy would have been better spent restoring those habitats which used to be present and used to support native birds, but alas they have left a laughable legacy which ranges from the ridiculous (White-rumped Shama) to the extreme (Guam Swiftlet). It was the state, however, which was responsible for destroying most of the natural lowland habitats in an effort to 'improve' the land for gamebirds such as Grey Francolin and, believe it or not, Chestnut-bellied Sandgrouse, which were introduced so they could be shot.

### Endemics

A total of 35 species are endemic to Hawaii, although only 31 are known to be surviving and only about 20 are likely to be seen on a well organised trip that includes a few days each on Kauai (six known surviving single island endemics), Maui (four known surviving single island endemics) and Big Island (seven known surviving single island endemics). The 20 or so endemics likely to be seen include a shearwater, a goose, a duck, a hawk, a coot, a 'monarch' flycatcher known as Elepaio, a 'thrush' known as Omao and 14 honeycreepers. In addition, it is possible to see endemic races of Dark-rumped Petrel*, Common Moorhen and Black-necked Stilt.

### Expectations

It is possible to see 100 to 120 species, including about 20 endemics, on a two week trip to Oahu, Kauai, Maui and Big Island in October and November, but 100 species is a tricky target to hit in April.

## OAHU

Honolulu, the main gateway to the Hawaiian Islands, is on this island where about 80% of the people live. Oahu supports one single island endemic which is extremely rare, single island races of two widespread endemics which may be full species, and the biggest seabird colony on the main islands. Indeed, seabirds are arguably the island's major avian attraction and Oahu is the only island where Masked Booby, Grey-backed Tern and Common White-Tern are likely to be seen.

### Oahu Endemics

Oahu Alauahio*.

### Hawaiian Endemics

Hawaiian Duck* (reintroduced), Hawaiian Coot*, Elepaio (*ibidis* race), Common Amakihi (*chloris* race), Apapane.

### Non-endemic Specialities

Black-footed (Dec–Jun) and Laysan (Jan–Aug) Albatrosses, Bulwer's Petrel, Christmas Island Shearwater, Masked Booby, Grey-backed Tern (Feb–Jul), Common White-Tern.

## Others

Wedge-tailed (Mar–Nov) and Sooty (Apr–Nov) Shearwaters, Red-tailed Tropicbird (most Mar–Sep), Great Frigatebird, Red-footed and Brown Boobies, Black-crowned Night-Heron, Common Moorhen (*sandvicensis* race), Wandering Tattler (Sep–Apr), Black-necked Stilt (*knudseni* race), Pacific Golden-Plover, Sooty Tern (Feb–Sep), Brown and Black Noddies, Pomarine Jaeger (Oct–Apr).

## Other Wildlife

Green sea-turtle, hawaiian monk seal, humpback whale (Jan–Apr).

(Other species recorded on Oahu include Eurasian Wigeon, Garganey, Tufted Duck, Bristle-thighed Curlew* and Sharp-tailed Sandpiper. Introduced species include Cattle Egret, Spotted and Zebra Doves, Rose-ringed Parakeet, Guam Swiftlet, Common Myna, Red-vented Bulbul, Japanese White-eye, Orange-cheeked Waxbill, Scaly-breasted Munia, Java Sparrow, Yellow-fronted Canary, House Finch, and Red-crested and Northern Cardinals.)

The best place to see Common White-Tern in Hawaii is **Waikiki**, the eastern enclave of Honolulu where most of the tourist hotels are situated. These delightful birds breed in large trees in several places amongst the hotels, particularly in the casuarinas near Big Fountain at the Diamond Head end of Kapiolani Park. It is best to visit this park at dawn before the tourists arise from their slumbers and swarm all over it. Great Frigatebirds can also be seen drifting over Waikiki, and off Diamond Head it is possible to see seabirds such as Grey-backed Tern. A little way inland from Honolulu, the *chloris* race of Common Amakihi, potentially a full species, and Apapane occur around **Punchbowl Crater Lookout** on Tantalus Drive. The only site where there is a chance, albeit slim, of seeing the very rare Oahu Alauahio*, is along the **Aiea Ridge Trail**, accessible via Aiea northwest of Honolulu. The *ibidis* race of Elepaio, another candidate for full species status, also occurs along this trail, along with the *chloris* race of Common Amakihi and Apapane.

Birders more interested in seabirds may prefer to forget about spending hours searching for the rare passerines, and avoid bumping into the numerous introduced species, by heading east out of the Honolulu–Waikiki area as soon as they have seen Common White-Tern. To the east of the turn-off to the Kuliouou Trail (a good site for the *ibidis* race of Elepaio, accessible via Kuliouou Road), beyond Koko Head, Red-tailed Tropicbirds regularly fly over the car park at **Halona Blowhole Overlook** and seawatching with a 'scope from here may reveal Christmas Island Shearwater and Grey-backed Tern, as well as green sea-turtle and humpback whale. A little further on the island of Manana, visible from **Makapuu Beach Park**, supports breeding Red-tailed Tropicbird (best seen from Upper Lookout), masses of Sooty Terns and Black Noddy (on the island's beaches), as well as Bulwer's Petrel, but this species is rarely seen from the mainland. Seawatching from opposite the Sealife Centre, or the viewpoint where the coast road passes close to the lighthouse, is also worthwhile, as offshore seabirds may include Masked Booby and Grey-backed Tern. To the northwest of Makapuu Beach Park the Kalanianaole Highway meets Kailua Road, west of Kailua. **Kawainui Marsh**, visible from behind the Castle Medical Centre at this junction, supports Hawaiian Duck*, Common Moorhen,

## SOUTHEAST OAHU

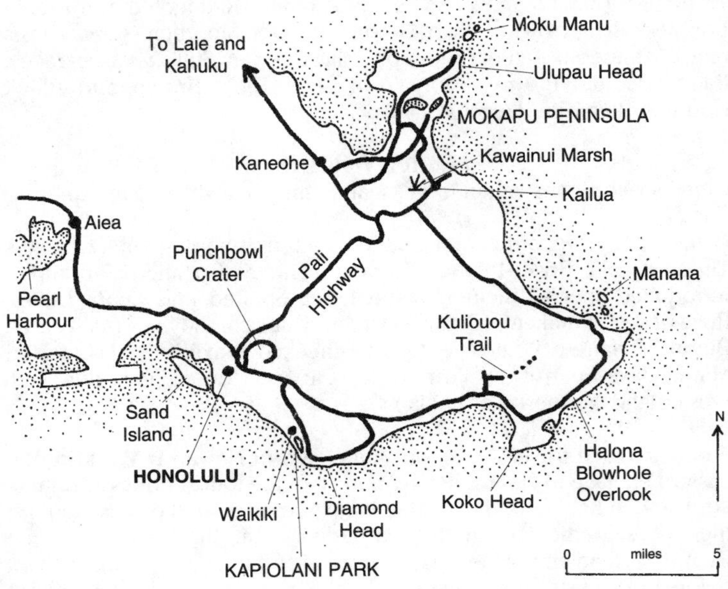


Hawaiian Coot* and Black-necked Stilt. Turn west at the junction, continue along the Kalanianaole Highway, then turn east on to Highway 3 to reach the **Mokapu Peninsula** which, together with the offshore islet of **Moku Manu**, supports the biggest seabird colony on the main Hawaiian islands. The colony lies within a Marine Corps Military Base, but it is possible to obtain an entrance permit by contacting, at least a month in advance, the Joint Public Affairs Officer, Marine Corps Base Hawaii, Kaneohe Bay, Hawaii 96863-5001 (tel: (808) 257 3319).

The road out to the head of the Mokapu Peninsula passes Nuupia Pond, which usually supports at least a few Black Noddies and is a good site for migrant shorebirds. It is best to visit the large booby colony at Ulupau Crater on the peninsula during the late afternoon and Red-footed Boobies are most numerous from April to November. Moku Manu, visible with a 'scope from Ulupau Head at the tip of the peninsula, is the only breeding site on the main islands for Masked Booby (a few pairs) and Grey-backed Tern, and these two species are more likely to be seen here than anywhere else in the archipelago. This islet also supports masses of Sooty Terns, as well as breeding Bulwer's Petrel and Christmas Island Shearwater (both of which are unlikely to be seen from the mainland), and Hawaiian monk seal. Brown and Black Noddies both breed on the cliffs of Ulupau Head and seawatching may reveal Laysan Albatross.

**Laie Point**, on the northeast coast of Oahu, is a good seawatching site where possible seabirds include Christmas Island Shearwater and Masked Booby. To the north of here Bristle-thighed Curlew* has been recorded, in August and September, in the pasture between the James Campbell National Wildlife Refuge and the beach, visible from the small cemetery at the the north end of the golf course outside the village of **Kahuku**. The NWR, accessible via the Pali Highway, supports Hawaiian Duck* and Hawaiian Coot*, as well as the endemic Hawaiian races of Common Moorhen and Black-necked Stilt, and it also attracts passage ducks and shorebirds which have included Eurasian Wigeon, Garganey, Tufted Duck and Sharp-tailed Sandpiper. For more details of this reserve, which is usually closed from-mid February to mid-August, contact the Refuge Manager, PO Box 340, Haleiwa, Hawaii 96712 (tel: (808) 637 6330). West of Kahuku the Kamehameha Highway runs along the north shore, one of the world's top surfing areas and a good stretch of coast for Laysan Albatrosses which have been known to appear on *terra firme* at Dillingham Airfield west of Waialua. Top surfers usually head for Waimea Bay, where non-surfers prefer to look at the 11 m (35 ft) rollers, the biggest in Hawaii, instead of riding them. The best wave tunnels in Hawaii occur at nearby Ekuhai Beach, known amongst surfers as the Banzai Pipeline.

*Accommodation:* New Otani Kaimana Beach Hotel (next to Kapiolani Park).

## OAHU PELAGIC

To see some superb seabirds there is no need to go further than ten miles out from the main islands of Hawaii because they have no continental shelf, and the depth of the surrounding ocean drops suddenly to somewhere in the region of 1829 m (6000 ft). Although the Kauai Pelagics (p. 225) seem to be better for rarities, Oahu Pelagics present the best opportunity of seeing Masked Booby, Grey-backed Tern and Common White-Tern. However, these three species can be seen from mainland Oahu and the real pelagic prizes are *pterodromas.* Up to six species of these superb seabirds may be seen, particularly in April, September and October.

### Non-endemic Specialities

Mottled (Apr–May/Aug–Oct), Bonin (Oct–Nov), Juan Fernandez (Apr–Nov) and Bulwer's Petrels, Buller's* (Apr–Nov) and Christmas Island Shearwaters, Band-rumped (Apr–Oct) and Tristram's* Storm-Petrels, Masked Booby, Grey-backed Tern (Feb–Jul), Common White-Tern.

### Others

Black-winged Petrel (Jun–Oct), Wedge-tailed (Mar–Nov), Flesh-footed (Apr–Nov), Sooty (Apr–Nov) and Short-tailed (Apr–Nov) Shearwaters, Leach's Storm-Petrel (Nov–Mar), Great Frigatebird, Red-footed and Brown Boobies, Red Phalarope (Sep–Apr), Sooty Tern, Brown and Black Noddies, Pomarine Jaeger (Oct–Apr).

(Other possibilities include Black-footed (Dec–Jun) and Laysan (Jan–Aug) Albatrosses, Cook's Petrel* (Apr–Aug), the endemic *sanwichensis* race of Dark-rumped Petrel* and the endemic Newell's Shearwater*.)

Pelagic birding off Oahu is best on expensive deep-sea sport-fishing boats. These boats use feeding parties of birds to locate tuna which are feeding on the same schools of fish as the birds. One example is the *Kono,* PO Box 22012, Honolulu, Hawaii 96822 (tel: 531 4966), which is usually berthed alongside *Golden Eagle* (another possibility) at Kewalo Basin along Ala Moana Boulevard in Honolulu. The Hawaiian Audubon Society also arrange pelagic birding trips. The channels between Oahu and Kauai to the west and Oahu and Molokai to the east are particularly good because they act as bottlenecks. Whale-watching cruises, which run from November to May, are not so good because they rarely venture far enough from land.

## KAUAI

This island, the oldest in the archipelago, rises to 1576 m (5170 ft) at Mount Waialeale—the rainiest place on earth—where it rains on average 360 days a year. Some of this water helps to sustain the fragments of misty montane *ohia-lehua* forests which support seven single island endemics. Although only five of these are likely to be seen on a short trip, it is possible to see more Hawaiian endemics on Kauai than on any other island. In addition to the rich endemic avifauna, this island also supports what is arguably the most diverse, but not the biggest, seabird colony in the main Hawaiian islands, on one of the rocky headlands along the 90 mile long coastline. All this, and the second largest canyon on earth—only the Grand Canyon is bigger than the 10 mile long, 2 mile wide, 1097 m (3600 ft) deep Waimea Canyon.

No birds became extinct in recent times on Kauai until 1969, when Akialoa was last seen, but two hurricanes have caused severe damage to the remaining forests since then and may have played a major part in the presumed extinction of at least one species. In 1982 Hurricane Iwa laid waste to some of the remaining forest fragments, and in the process may have accounted for the few Kauai Oos* left alive at that time, probably helped to reduce the Kamao* and the Puaiohi* populations to a few dozen birds, and presumably left behind only a few pairs of the Ou*. In September 1992 the island received the full force of Hurricane Iniki, which devastated the remaining forest. Most of the island's infrastructure was back in place by 1995, but what little remains of the natural habitat will take a very long time to recover, and since then only the Puaiohi*, out of the four species aforementioned, has been seen.

### Kauai Endemics

Puaiohi*, Kauai Amakihi*, Anianiau*, Akikiki*, Akekee*.

### Other Hawaiian Endemics

Hawaiian Goose* (reintroduced), Hawaiian Duck*, Hawaiian Coot*, Elepaio (*sclateri* race), Iiwi, Apapane.

### Non-endemic Specialities

Laysan Albatross (Jan–Aug).

### Others

Wedge-tailed Shearwater (Apr–Oct), Red-tailed (most Mar–Sep) and White-tailed (most Mar–Sep) Tropicbirds, Great Frigatebird, Red-footed and Brown Boobies, Black-crowned Night-Heron, Common Moorhen (*sandvicensis* race), Wandering Tattler (Sep–Apr), Black-necked Stilt (*knudseni* race), Pacific Golden-Plover, Brown and Black Noddies, Short-eared Owl.

## Other Wildlife

Humpback whale (Jan–Apr).

(Other species recorded on Kauai include the two remaining single island endemics—Kauai Oo* (last recorded in 1985) and Kamao* (very rare)—and two other Hawaiian endemics—Ou* (last recorded in 1989) and Nukupuu* (very rare)—as well as Black-footed Albatross (Dec–Jun), the endemic *sandwichensis* race of Dark-rumped Petrel*, Bulwer's Petrel, the endemic Newell's Shearwater*, and Bristle-thighed Curlew*. Introduced species include Cattle Egret, Erckell's Francolin, Japanese Quail, Red Junglefowl, Spotted and Zebra Doves, Barn Owl, Northern Mockingbird, Common Myna, White-rumped Shama, Japanese White-eye, Japanese Bush-Warbler, Greater Necklaced Laughing-thrush, Hwamei, Scaly-breasted and Black-headed Munias, House Finch, Northern Cardinal and Western Meadowlark.)

Kauai is accessible by air from Honolulu and the major arrival point is Lihue on the east coast. To see the endemic landbirds, head west from Lihue on the Kaumualii Highway (Route 50) to Waimea, 23 miles away, and then north in to the Kokee Region. *En route* it is worth taking a diversion to **Makahuena Point**, which overlooks the Kauai Channel and in April and May at least, offers the opportunity to look for Black-footed Albatross, Dark-rumped* and Bulwer's Petrels and Newell's Shearwater*. Before reaching Waimea it is also worth stopping at **Hanapepe Valley Overlook** where White-tailed Tropicbirds may be seen at eye-level and the **Hanapepe Saltpans and Airstrip** area, southwest of Hanapepe, where migrant shorebirds have included Bristle-thighed Curlew*.

Back on the Kaumualii Highway turn north at Waimea, before the sports ground, on to the rough Waimea Canyon Drive (Route 550), not signposted but recognisable by a '0 Miles' marker by the roadside, or continue west to Kekaha and turn north on to the better Kokee Road (Route 55). These two roads merge several kilometres north of Waimea at **Waimea Canyon**. The lookouts further north are on the canyon's western rim, hence the afternoon is the best time to admire it. The endemic Kauai race of Elepaio, Kauai Amakihi* and Apapane occur near Waimea Canyon and Puu Hianhina Lookouts. Beyond these lookouts the Kokee Road (Route 550) climbs up to the **Kokee Region**, where the best birding strategy is to spend a day walking a circuit that takes in the Alakai Swamp, Pihea Ridge and Kawaikoi Stream Trails. On this circuit it is possible to see the Kauai race of Elepaio, Kauai Amakihi*, Anianiau*, Akikiki* (where the Alakai Swamp Trail crosses the upper reaches of Kawaikoi Stream, east of the Pihea Ridge Trail, and at the upper end of the Kawaikoi Stream Trail), Akekee*, Iiwi and Apapane. There is also the remote chance of coming across such great rarities as Kamao* (where the Alakai Swamp Trail crosses the Pihea Ridge Trail), Ou* (on the Alakai Swamp Trail beyond Kawaikoi Stream) and even a Nukupuu*. The Kauai endemic, Puaiohi* has only been recorded recently along the remote Koaie Stream Trail which starts at the end of Camp 10 Road and penetrates the **Alakai Wilderness**

## KAUAI-ALAKAI REGION

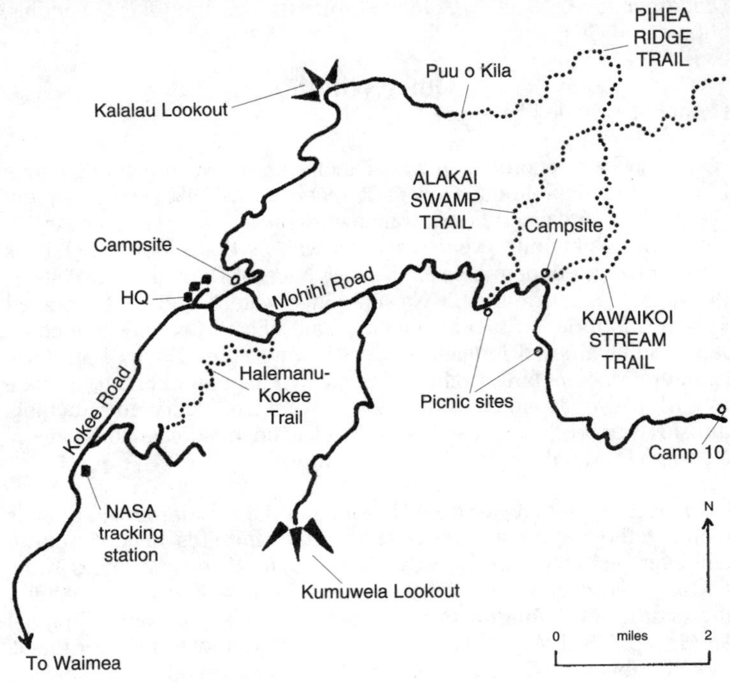


**Preserve** where the Kauai race of Elepaio, Kauai Amakihi*, Anianiau*, Akikiki*, Akekee*, Iiwi and Apapane still survive in good numbers and where Kauai Oo*, Kamao*, Ou* and Nukupuu* may still exist. To arrange a birding trip to this remote region, including camping permits, contact the Division of State Parks, PO Box 1671, Lihue, Kauai, Hawaii 96766. Unfortunately, both White-rumped Shama and Hwamei are present in the Kokee Region and spoil what would otherwise be an almost wholesome experience of natural Hawaii.

There are a number of other excellent birding sites north of Lihue. Six miles north of Lihue, turn west off the Kuhio Highway (Route 56) on to Kuamoo Road (Route 580) to reach **Opaekaa Falls**, an excellent site for White-tailed Tropicbird. These falls are situated in the Wailua River Valley where any wetlands are worth checking for Hawaiian Duck* and Hawaiian Coot*, as well as Common Moorhen and Black-necked Stilt. One of the sites that should be inked into any itinerary for a birding trip to Hawaii is about one hour by road north of Lihue. Turn north off Route 56 at Kilauea to reach **Kilauea Point National Wildlife Refuge**, which is open from 1000 to 1600 on weekdays. This rocky promontory supports over 40 pairs of Laysan Albatross, a large Wedge-tailed Shearwater colony, Red-tailed and White-tailed Tropicbirds, Great Frigatebird, and one of the two main Red-footed Booby colonies in Hawaii. Occasionally in spring Black-footed Albatrosses are attracted to the Laysan Albatross colony. Some Hawaiian Geese* have also been reintroduced and Short-eared Owl occurs in the area. For more details, contact the Refuge Manager, PO Box 87, Kilauea, Kauai, Hawaii 96754. The wet taro and rice fields in **Hanalei National Wildlife Refuge** to the west of Kilauea support Hawaiian Duck* and Hawaiian Coot*, as well as Common Moorhen and Black-necked Stilt, and attract migrant shorebirds. **Haena State Park** at the west end of Route 56 is a good place to seawatch from, with possible pelagic seabirds including Newell's Shearwater*, albatrosses and noddies. The 11 mile long **Kalalau Trail** also starts here, leading to the lofty Na Pali cliffs where Black Noddies breed. Another place worth visiting on Kauai if time allows is Queen's Bath, a large natural seawater pool where it is possible to swim with sea turtles.

During October and November a few young Dark-rumped Petrels* and Newell's Shearwaters* are occasionally found stranded on lawns near bright lights, and once such terrific birds have been admired they should be taken to the nearest fire station. When handling them make sure both the bill and tail are pointing away from you, because they are apt to excrete from either end.

*Accommodation:* Kokee Lodge, PO Box 819, Waimea, Kauai, Hawaii 96796 (tel: (808) 335 6061) needs to be booked well in advance.

Lehua, the offshore islet off the northern tip of **Niihau**, west of Kauai, supports breeding Bulwer's Petrel and Christmas Island Shearwater.

## KAUAI PELAGIC

Pelagic birding trips off Kauai are usually better than those off Oahu (p. 221), as they offer the best chance of seeing Black-footed (which breeds on islets off nearby Niihua) and Laysan Albatrosses, the endemic Hawaiian race of Dark-rumped Petrel, the endemic Newell's* Shearwater and no less than six *pterodromas*, including the marvellous Mottled Petrel. The best times to go are in April, September and October.

### Endemics

Newell's Shearwater* (most Apr–Oct).

### Non-endemic Specialities

Black-footed (Dec–Jun) and Laysan (Jan–Aug) Albatrosses, Mottled (Apr–May/Aug–Oct), Bonin (Oct–Nov), Dark-rumped* (*sandwichensis* race), Juan Fernandez (Apr–Nov) and Bulwer's Petrels, Buller's* (Apr–Nov) and Christmas Island Shearwaters, Band-rumped (Apr–Oct) and Tristram's* Storm-Petrels.

### Others

Black-winged Petrel (Jun–Oct), Wedge-tailed (Mar–Nov), Flesh-footed (Apr–Nov), Sooty (Apr–Nov) and Short-tailed (Apr–Nov) Shearwaters, Leach's Storm-Petrel (Nov–Mar), Great Frigatebird, Red-footed and Brown Boobies, Red Phalarope (Sep–Apr), Sooty Tern, Brown and Black Noddies, Pomarine Jaeger (Oct–Apr).

(Other possibilities include Cook's Petrel* (Apr–Aug), Masked Booby, Grey-backed Tern and Common White-Tern.)

Pelagic birding off Kauai is best on expensive deep-sea sport-fishing boats based in Lihue and Port Allen. The best area of sea to explore is the channel between Kauai and Oahu.

*The endemic Hawaiian race of Dark-rumped Petrel* is a perfectly pied pterodroma which is most likely to be seen on a pelagic birding trip off Kauai*

**Molokai** is a small island which rises to 1512 m (4961 ft) at Mount Kamakou in the east and is famous for its seacliffs, which are reputed to be the highest on earth. They rise to 914 m (3000 ft) on the north coast and can be seen on helicopter trips from Maui, along with humpback whales (Jan–Apr). The dense natural forest, where the brilliant Black Mamo became extinct in 1908 and the Kakawahie managed to survive until 1964, is now confined to the highest altitudes, where much of it is protected within the 11 sq km **Kamakou Preserve**. This is the only known site for Olomao*, another species which seems destined to become extinct, if that is not already the case as it has not been seen since the late 1980s. There is no public transport on Molokai and only a few basic places to stay, but visits to Kamakou Preserve can be arranged through the Preserve Manager, PO Box 40, Kualapuu, Hawaii 96757 (tel: (808) 567 6680). Common Amakihi, Iiwi and Apapane also occur here.

## MAUI

This island consists of two mountain massifs joined by a low isthmus. Three of the five single island endemics occur in the remnant forests on the slopes of the dormant Haleakala Volcano, which rises to 3055 m (10,023 ft) on the eastern side of island and lies within a 111 sq km National Park. The remaining two single island endemics are unlikely to be seen because they are either extinct or very rare.

Most of the humpback whales which spend the summer in the north Pacific and off Alaska migrate south to calve in Hawaii's inshore waters during the winter. Between 600 and 800 are believed to be present in the waters around Maui at this time, hence this island is the best one from which to see these magnificent creatures. Maui is also the best island for snorkelling.

## Maui Endemics

Maui Parrotbill*, Maui Alauahio*, Akohekohe*.

## Other Hawaiian Endemics

Hawaiian Goose* (reintroduced), Hawaiian Coot*, Common Amakihi, Iiwi, Apapane.

## Non-endemic Specialities

Dark-rumped Petrel* (*sandwichensis* race).

## Others

Wedge-tailed Shearwater (Mar–Nov), White-tailed Tropicbird, Great Frigatebird, Black-crowned Night-Heron, Wandering Tattler (Sep–Apr), Black-necked Stilt (*knudseni* race), Pacific Golden-Plover, Black Noddy, Short-eared Owl.

## Other Wildlife

Flying-fish, green sea-turtle, humpback whale (Jan–Apr), moray eel, octopus, spinner dolphin, and many fabulous fish.

(Other species recorded on Maui include the two remaining single island endemics—Bishop's Oo* (last recorded in 1981) and Poo-uli* (very rare) and the Hawaiian endemic—Nukupuu* (very rare)—as well as Bulwer's Petrel, Lesser Scaup, Semipalmated and Sharp-tailed Sandpipers, Semipalmated Plover and Laughing Gull. Introduced species include Cattle Egret, Chukar, Grey Francolin, Common Pheasant, Spotted and Zebra Doves, Northern Mockingbird, Common Myna, Japanese White-eye, Hwamei, Eurasian Skylark, Scaly-breasted Munia, Java Sparrow, House Finch and Northern Cardinal.)

Kahului on the north coast of Maui is accessible by air from Honolulu. Three single island endemic landbirds occur in and around **Haleakala National Park**, accessible via the Haleakala Highway on a road which rises dramatically from sea level to 3055 m (10,023 ft) in 38 miles. Early risers in the park may well be rewarded with the unearthly, but spectacular, sight of the sun rising up over the volcanic moon-like landscape. Worth looking at even if there are birds to find. Just inside the park turn left to Hosmer Grove where Common Amakihi (which feed from the hand), Maui Alauahio*, Iiwi and Apapane occur. Bird around the picnic and campsites, especially if the yellow *mamane* flowers are in bloom, and along the Loop Trail. About 3–4 miles further up the road turn left to the Leleiwi Overlook car park, which is situated at about 2682 m (8800 ft) and is a good place to see reintroduced Hawaiian Geese*. Higher still, the endemic *sandwichensis* race of Dark-rumped Petrel* breeds in tunnels in the lava alongside the one mile stretch of road below the car park at the visitor centre at Lower Crater Overlook, between the service road (which leads left at a sharp right-hand bend) and the visitor centre. Listen for their calls, which usually begin an hour after sunset and look for the birds flying low over the road (spotlights are illegal). Birds may also be seen in the early hours. Otherwise, it may be possible to see these birds behind the building which overlooks a rocky slope at the far side of the Crater Overlook car park just before dawn. The best place to look for soaring White-tailed Tropicbirds is Kalahaku Overlook. For details of organised walks and other good birding sites, contact The

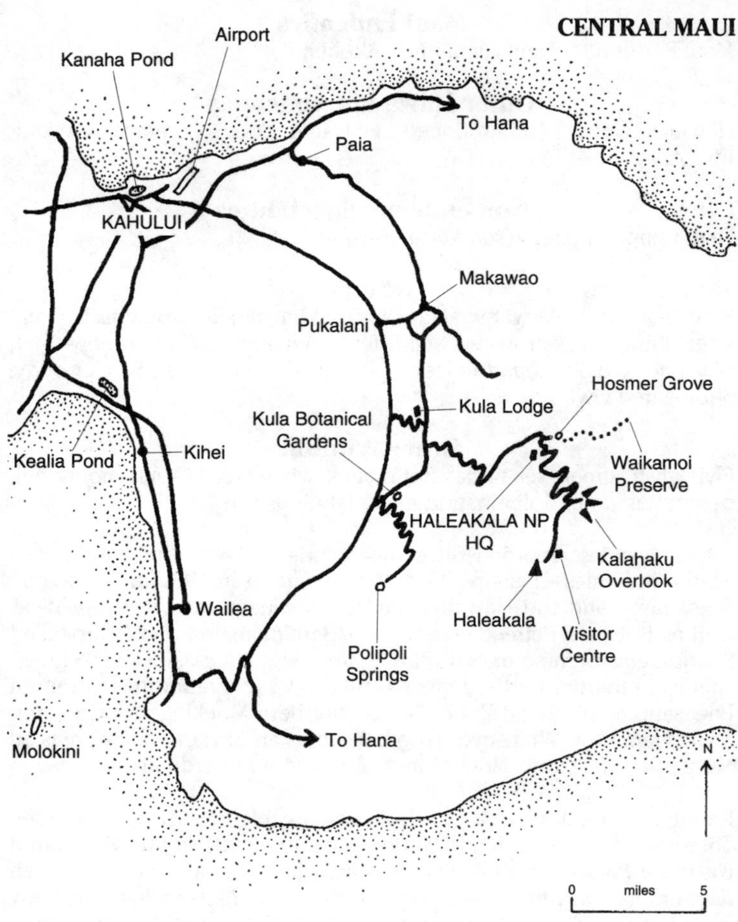


Superintendent, Haleakala NP, Box 369, Makawao, Hawaii 96768. Maui Alauahio* also occurs at Polipoli Springs on the west slope of Haleakala above Kula, and in the **Waikamoi Preserve**, along with Maui Parrotbill* and Akohekohe*, as well as Common Amakihi, Iiwi and Apapane. This important preserve is situated on the north slope of Haleakala adjacent to the National Park and is about two hours walk from Hosmer Grove. Access is restricted, but there is a chance of connecting with the escorted walks organised by the Preserve Manager, Waikamoi Preserve, PO Box 1716, Makawao, Hawaii 96768-1716 (tel: (808) 572 7849). The parrotbill is seen regularly on these walks, but they don't usually penetrate far enough into the preserve to see the cracking 'crested honeycreeper', alias Akohekohe*. To reach the favoured *ohia* areas of this very special endemic it is usually necessary to be accompanied by experienced guides, but it may be possible to arrange access by contacting, at least a month in advance, the Nature Conservation of Hawaii (TNCH), 1116 Smith Street, Suite 201, Honolulu, Hawaii 96817.

A Nukupuu* and three Poo-ulis*, two extremely rare birds, were seen in the remote **East Maui Wilderness** in late 1994. This reserve, which

*The Akohekohe*, one of Hawaii's most amazing honeycreepers, is endemic to the island of Maui*

is situated on the northeast slope of Haleakala, is also the stronghold of Maui Parrotbill* and supports Akohekohe*. To investigate the possibility of birding in this restricted area, contact the Superintendent at Haleakala National Park (address above), or offer to volunteer on the National Biological Survey, PO Box 44, Hawaii NP, Hawaii 96718.

There are a few lowland sites worth birding on Maui. **Kealia Pond National Wildlife Refuge**, which lies north of Kihei near the junction with the road from Kahului, is one of the best sites for shorebirds in Hawaii when the water levels are low. **Keanae Peninsula**, on the north side of the island off Highway 36, is good for seawatching with the possibilities including White-tailed Tropicbird and Black Noddy. Seabirds can also be seen on snorkelling and whale-watching trips out of Kihei and Maaleea Harbour. The boats usually head for the waters around the offshore islet of **Molokini**, where Bulwer's Petrel breeds (Apr–Sep). The reefs here support a stunning variety of underwater life, including flying-fish, green sea-turtle, moray eel, octopus and several species of butterfly-fish and reef-fish. Bulwer's Petrels may be seen offshore anywhere south of Kihea and Wailea, especially opposite Molokini, and whilst looking for them it is worth remembering that there are humpback whales out there in winter. Dive boats, operating out of Lahaina on Maui, visit the waters at the east side of the island of **Lanai** where Red-tailed Tropicbird is regularly seen.

*Accommodation:* Kula Lodge, RR1, Box 475, Kula, Maui, Hawaii 96790 (tel: (808) 878 1535/2517).

## BIG ISLAND

This island, also known as Hawaii, is the youngest, largest and highest in the archipelago. It is dominated by the twin shield volcanoes of active Mauna Loa and dormant Mauna Kea, which rise to 4169 m (13,677 ft) and 4205 m (13,796 ft), respectively, and are high enough to be snow-capped in winter. Their slopes support some of the largest remaining tracts of native forest in the archipelago, and these support five single island endemics, all of which are fairly easy to see. The remaining two single island endemics are the widespread but scarce Hawaiian Hawk* and the virtually extinct Hawaiian Crow*, which can be seen only on organised tours to a private ranch in the lowlands.

## BIG ISLAND

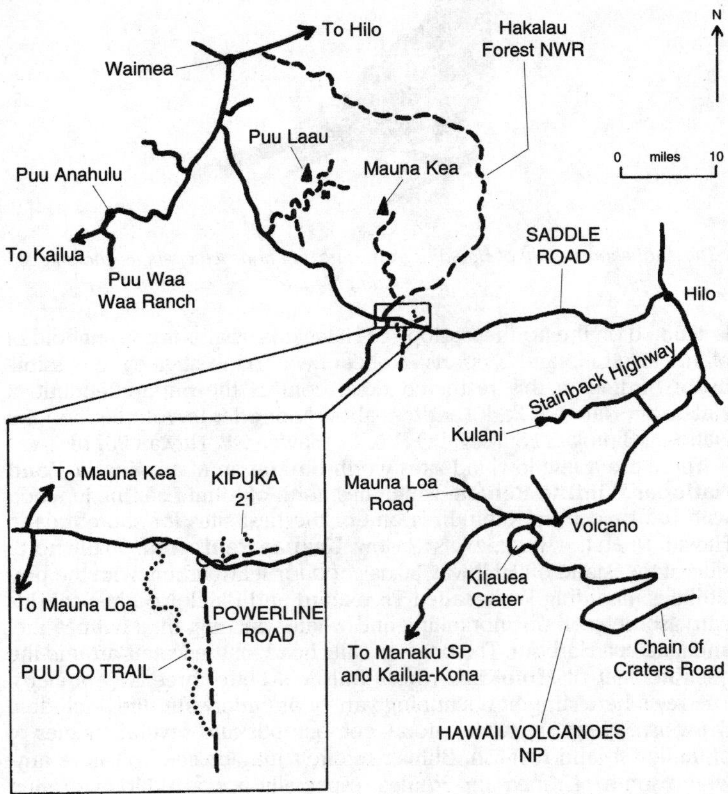


Thanks to the flow of smooth pahoehoe lava and sharp aa lava from the very active Mauna Loa, the landscape in the southeastern part of the island is always changing.

### Big Island Endemics

Hawaiian Hawk*, Hawaiian Crow*, Omao, Palila*, Akiapolaau*, Hawaii Creeper*, Akepa*.

### Other Hawaiian Endemics

Hawaiian Goose*, Hawaiian Duck* (reintroduced), Hawaiian Coot*, Elepaio, Common Amakihi, Iiwi, Apapane.

### Others

Pied-billed Grebe, Wedge-tailed Shearwater (Mar–Nov), White-tailed Tropicbird, Wandering Tattler (Sep–Apr), Black-necked Stilt (*knudseni* race), Pacific Golden-Plover, Black Noddy.

### Other Wildlife

Hoary bat.

(Other species recorded on and around Big Island include Ou* (last recorded in 1983), as well as Black-winged (Jun–Oct) and Mottled (Apr–May/Aug–Oct) Petrels, Eurasian and American Wigeons, Gadwall, Garganey, Blue-winged Teal, Tufted Duck, Bristle-thighed Curlew*, Grey-tailed Tattler and Rufous-necked Stint. Introduced species include Chukar, Black and Erckell's Francolins, Kalij and Common Pheasants, Indian Peafowl, Wild Turkey, California Quail, Chestnut-bellied Sand-grouse, Spotted and Zebra Doves, Common Myna, Japanese White-eye, Hwamei, Red-billed Leiothrix, Eurasian Skylark, Red-cheeked Cordon-bleu, Lavender Waxbill, White-throated and Scaly-breasted Munias, Yellow-fronted Canary, House Finch, Yellow-billed Cardinal, Saffron Finch and Northern Cardinal.)

Big Island is accessible by air from Honolulu and the best arrival point is Hilo on the east coast. Wandering Tattler occurs along the shoreline in front of the Hilo Hawaiian Hotel or on the small beach west of the Hilo Seaside Hotel. Migrant waterbirds and shorebirds are attracted to the large pond (known as Hilo Waiakea) inland from Hilo Bay and the ponds (known as Keokaha and Loko Waka) accessible via Kalanean-eole Avenue beyond Hilo Harbour. The best area for most of the single island endemics is alongside the 50 mile long **Saddle Road** (Route 200), which traverses the northern half of the island. Hawaiian Hawk*, Omao, Palila*, Akiapolaau*, Hawaii Creeper* and Akepa*, as well as Hawaiian Goose*, the pale and dark forms of Elepaio, Common Ama-kihi, Iiwi and Apapane all occur along here. About 21 miles west of Hilo bird **Kipuka 21**, a small fragment of forest amongst the lava flows, to the north of the road. About 400 m beyond the 21 mile marker, park by the side of the road and walk across the 30 m wide lava flow to scan the kipuka from its upper edge, checking the *ohia* trees for the rare, leaf-gleaning Akepa*, and the red *lehua* blossoms for nectar-feeders such as Common Amakihi, Iiwi and Apapane. It is also possible to look for the dark form of Elepaio, Omao and the scarce Hawaii Creeper*, all of which are more likely inside the kipuka, by walking down the very rough track from the main road for about 50 m until reaching a small *koa* tree at the base of a steep part of the track, then taking the obscure trail to the left which leads a few metres in to the forest. Stand at the edge of the drop along here and scan the mid-canopy for the these three species. About 100 m west of Kipuka 21 there is a 4WD track, known as **Powerline Road**, which leads south across barren lava fields with occasional forested kipukas which support Akiapolaau*, Hawaii Creeper* and Akepa*. All of these birds also occur in the kipukas alongside the nearby 4 mile long **Puu Oo Trail**, which leads south about 800 m west of the Powerline Road turning, but throughout the area these birds are very thin on the ground, to say the least. Look out for Hawaiian Goose* and Hawaiian Hawk* passing overhead. Much further west along the Saddle Road, 43 miles west of Hilo, turn north by the Hunter Check Station to reach **Puu Laau**, the best site on the island for Palila*. This bird inhabits the dry, open *mamane-naio* forest above 2134 m (7000 ft), which can be reached by taking the right fork at the cabin, either on foot or in a 4WD, to the gate at the boundary of the Mauna Kea FR. Bird the upper part of this track where the pale form of Elepaio, Common Amakihi, Akiapolaau* and Apapane also occur.

The **Hakalau Forest National Wildlife Refuge** (67 sq km), which supports Hawaiian Hawk*, Akiapolaau*, Hawaii Creeper* and Akepa*, is usually only accessible with experienced guides (try Hawaii Forest and Trail tour operators). For the latest visiting arrangements, contact the Refuge Manager, Hakalau Forest NWR, 154 Waianuenue Avenue, Room 219, Hilo, Hawaii 96720 (tel: (808) 969 9909).

*The dark form of the dinky Elepaio occurs along the Saddle Road and in Hawaii Volcanoes National Park on Big Island*

At the western end of the Saddle Road, turn south on to the Mamalahoa Highway (Route 190) towards Kailua-Kona to reach the **McCandless Ranch**, near **Puu Anahulu**, where the last wild flock (about 15 birds) of Hawaiian Crow* can usually be seen on escorted tours (contact McCandless Ranch Ecotours, PO Box 500, Honaunau, Hawaii 96726 (tel: 808 328 8246, fax: 808 328 8671)). The Puu Anahulu area supports mostly introduced species, especially *estrilid* finches (at Puu Waa Waa Ranch), but the Puu Lani Ranch is a reliable Hawaiian Hawk* site.

**Aimakapa Pond**, a few miles northwest of Kailua, was colonised by Pied-billed Grebe in the early 1980s. It also supports Hawaiian Coot* and Black-necked Stilt, and attracts migrant waterfowl and shorebirds including Blue-winged Teal, which has bred. To reach it head for Honokohau Harbour and turn north before reaching the boat-yard. Walk north from the end of the road through the scrub and along the nudist beach to view the pond from the dunes. South of Kailua Route 11 runs along the Kona coast, where Wandering Tattler occurs and sea-watching has produced Black-winged and Mottled Petrels. The small **Manuka State Park** in the southwest corner of the island supports the intermediate form of Elepaio, as well as Common Amakihi and Apapane. **South Point** (Ka Lae), at the extreme southwesterly point of the island, is also worth a visit, as Bristle-thighed Curlew* is possible on the grassy area to the east.

Mauna Loa, Kilauea Crater and part of the south coast lie within the 840 sq km **Hawaii Volcanoes National Park**, north of South Point and southwest of Hilo. The HQ is situated at about 1219 m (4000 ft) a mile or so west of the town of Volcano and opposite Volcano House, the balcony of which overlooks the massive sunken Kilauea Crater and some forest which is one of the best places on the island to see Omao. The Crater Rim Drive encircles the crater, enabling views of soaring White-tailed Tropicbirds, which breed in the crater walls. The car park area at Thurston Lava Tube is good for the dark form of Elepaio and Omao. The Chain of Craters Road leads south from the crater to the coast. Look out for Hawaiian Hawk* on the descent to the coast where Black Noddies breed on the cliffs, especially near the Holei Sea Arch. Since the late 1980s molten lava has been spilling into the sea across the Chain of Craters Road and there are organised night-time excursions to view this spectacular natural firework display. The northern section of the park is also worth birding. Hawaiian Hawk* occurs along the 10 mile long **Mauna Loa Road** (Strip Road), which reaches a height of nearly 2134 m (7000 ft). The dark form of Elepaio and Omao have been recorded in the 'Bird Park' (Kipuka Puaulu), which is situated on the right-hand side of the road. Sulphurous fumes may fill the air at Hawaii Volcanoes National Park and these can be hazardous to your health and binoculars. People with respiratory problems should take special care and binoculars should be cleaned regularly to avoid the effects of damaging acid.

Between Hilo and Hawaii Volcanoes National Park the **Stainback Highway** (Hawaiian Hawk*) leads to the Kulani Correctional Facility, a minimum security prison which lies next to some good forest. This supports Hawaii Creeper* and Akepa*, and is arguably the best site on the island for Akiapolaau*. Access is usually possible only with tour groups, but the Hawaiian Audubon Society may be worth contacting.

*Accommodation:* Hilo—Hilo Hawaiian Hotel. Hawaii Volcanoes NP—Volcano House, Box 53, Hawaii Volcanoes NP, Hawaii 96718 (tel: 967 7321); Kilauea Lodge (just outside the NP), PO Box 116, Volcano, Hawaii 96785 (tel: 967 7366); and, most reasonable of all, but still expensive, My Island B&B in Volcano Village. Kona Coast—Keauhou Beach Hotel, Sundowner B&B.

The **Northwestern Islands** of Hawaii are largely uninhabited and accessible only with special permits. They support four endemic landbirds, breeding seabirds such as Black-footed Albatross, Bonin Petrel, Tristram's Storm-Petrel* (all of which only occur at sea around the main islands) and Blue-grey Noddy, as well as large numbers of wintering Bristle-thighed Curlews* and Grey-backed Tern. Two of the endemics occur on the island of Nihoa—a reed-warbler known as Millerbird* and a honeycreeper known as Nihoa Finch*—and two occur on the island of Laysan—Laysan Duck* and a honeycreeper known as Laysan Finch*. This island is also a wintering stronghold of Bristle-thighed Curlew*, with 300–350 birds present at that time. At the extreme northwest end of this chain of islands one or two Short-tailed Albatrosses* are usually present on Midway Atoll.

## ADDITIONAL INFORMATION

### Addresses

The Hawaiian Audubon Society, 850 Richards Street, Suite 505, Honolulu, Hawaii 96813 (tel: 808 528 1432, fax: 808 537 5294), publishes the monthly *Elepaio* journal, which covers Hawaii and most of the other Pacific islands, and arranges regular birding walks, boat trips and excursions.

Nature Conservancy of Hawaii, 1116 Smith Street, Honolulu, Hawaii 96817 (tel: 808 537 4508).

Voyagers International, PO Box 915, Ithaca, New York 14851, USA (tel: 800 633 0299), usually organise at least one expertly led birding trip to Hawaii each year.

Please send pelagic seabird records to *American Birds* Regional Editor for Hawaii, B P Bishop Museum, PO Box 19000-A, Honolulu, Hawaii 96819.

Federal Parks are administered by the National Parks Service, 300 Ala Moana Boulevard, Suite 6305, Box 50165, Honolulu, Hawaii 96850 (tel: 808 541 2693).
State Parks are administered by the District Office of the Hawaii Department of Land and Natural Resources, Division of State Parks, 1151 Punchbowl Street, Room 310, Honolulu, Hawaii 96813, or Box 621, Honolulu, Hawaii 96809 (tel: 808 587 0300).
The Hawaii Visitors Bureau, Waikiki Business Plaza, 2270 Kalakaua Avenue, Suite 801, Honolulu, Hawaii 96815 (tel: 808 923 1811), or 56–60 Great Cumberland Place, London W1H 8DD, UK (tel: 0171 723 7011), and various addresses in the USA.
Hawaii Forest and Trail, PO Box 2975, Kailua-Kona, Hawaii 96745 (tel: 1 800 464 1993 or 808 322 8881, fax: 808 322 8883, e-mail: hitrail@aloha.net), can help with travel arrangements on Big Island.

## Books and Papers

*Enjoying Birds in Hawaii: a Birdfinding Guide to the Fiftieth State*. Pratt H D, 1993. Mutual Publishing.
*The Birdwatcher's Guide to Hawaii*. Soehren R, 1996. Hawaii University Press.
*A Field Guide to The Birds of Hawaii and the Tropical Pacific.* Pratt H D *et al.*, 1987. Princeton University Press.
Avifaunal change in the Hawaiian Islands, 1893–1993. Pratt H D, 1994. *Stud. Avian Biol.* 15: 103–118.
*Seabirds of Hawaii: Natural History and Conservation*. Harrison C, 1990. Cornell University Press.
*The Hawaiian Honeycreepers.* Pratt H D, in press. Oxford University Press.
*Oceanwatcher: an Above-water Guide to Hawaiian Marine Animals* (including seabirds). Scott S, 1988. Honolulu: Green Turtle Press.

## HAWAIIAN ENDEMICS (35)

### Widespread (10)

| | |
|---|---|
| Newell's Shearwater* | Breeds in mountains of several islands, mostly Oahu and Kauai, and most likely to be seen on Kauai Pelagics between April and October. Also possible on Oahu Pelagics, or whilst seawatching from Makahuena Point and Haena on Kauai |
| Hawaiian Goose* | Occurs as a wild bird on Big Island (Saddle Road and Hawaii Volcanoes NP), and has been reintroduced to Kauai (Kilauea Point NWR) and Maui (Haleakala NP) |
| Hawaiian Duck* | Occurs as a wild bird on Kauai (widespread), and has been reintroduced to Oahu (widespread) and Big Island (scarce) |
| Hawaiian Coot* | Widespread on Oahu, Kauai, Molokai, Maui and Big Island |
| Elepaio | Widespread, on Oahu (*ibidis* race), Kauai (*sclateri* race) and Big Island where three forms occur: dark (widespread), intermediate (Manuka State Park) and pale (Puu Laau on Saddle Road), all of which may be separate species |

| | |
|---|---|
| Ou* | Unlikely to be seen. Very rare on Kauai (last recorded at Alakai WP in 1989) and Big Island where there were about 400 birds between 1976 and 1983, but some of its habitat was destroyed by molten lava in 1984 and only a few have been seen since |
| Common Amakihi | Widespread and relatively common on Oahu (*chloris* race), Molokai, Maui and especially Big Island |
| Nukupuu* | Unlikely to be seen. Very rare on Kauai (Kokee Region/Alakai WP) and Maui (East Maui Wilderness) |
| Iiwi | Relatively common on Kauai (Kokee Region), Maui (Haleakala NP and Waikamoi Preserve) and Big Island (Saddle and Mauna Loa Roads) |
| Apapane | The commonest endemic, occurring in most *ohia* forests |

The endemic *sandwichensis* race of Dark-rumped Petrel* is considered to be a full species by some taxonomists. It may be seen on the Oahu Pelagic, off Kauai, on the Kauai Pelagic or on Maui in Haleakala NP where it breeds.

The endemic *sandvicensis* race of Common Moorhen is considered to be a full species by some taxonomists. It occurs in most wetlands on Oahu, Kauai and Molokai.

The endemic *knudseni* race of Black-necked Stilt is considered to be a full species by some taxonomists. It occurs in most wetlands on Oahu, Kauai, Maui and Big Island.

## Oahu (1)

| | |
|---|---|
| Oahu Alauahio* | Very rare and only likely to be seen on the Aiea Ridge Trail where there were a few sightings in the 1980s and early 1990s, mostly around the North Halawa Valley where a new freeway was under construction in the mid-1990s |

The endemic *ibidis* race of Elepaio and the endemic *chloris* race of Common Amakihi are considered to be full species by some taxonomists.

## Kauai (7)

| | |
|---|---|
| Kauai Oo* | Unlikely to be seen. Last recorded in 1985 in Alakai WP |
| Kamao* | Unlikely to be seen. Very rare in the Kokee Region/Alakai WP near the junction of the Alakai Swamp and Pihea Ridge Trails, and on the highest reaches of the Alakai Plateau just below the peak of Waialeale |
| Puaiohi* | Rare in the high altitude *ohia* forests of Alakai WP where there were 18 sightings in early 1994 |
| Kauai Amakihi* | Relatively common in the Kokee Region/Alakai WP |

| | |
|---|---|
| Anianiau* | Relatively common in the Kokee Region/Alakai WP |
| Akikiki* | Very rare around the upper reaches of the Kawaikoi Stream in the Kokee Region/Alakai WP |
| Akekee* | Relatively common in the Kokee Region/Alakai WP |

**Molokai (1)**

| | |
|---|---|
| Olomao* | Unlikely to be seen. Last recorded in the late 1980s in Kamakou Preserve |

**Maui (5)**

| | |
|---|---|
| Bishop's Oo* | Unlikely to be seen. Last recorded in 1981 in *ohia* forest on the northeast slopes of Haleakala |
| Maui Parrotbill* | Rare in Waikamoi Preserve and East Maui Wilderness |
| Maui Alauahio* | Relatively common in Haleakala NP, Waikamoi Preserve and at Polipoli Springs |
| Akohekohe* | Rare in Waikamoi Preserve and East Maui Wilderness |
| Poo-uli* | Unlikely to be seen. Very rare in East Maui Wilderness where recorded in late 1994 |

**Big Island (7)**

| | |
|---|---|
| Hawaiian Hawk* | Widespread but scarce |
| Hawaiian Crow* | The last wild flock (15 or so birds) survives on the McCandless Ranch |
| Omao | Relatively common and widespread. |
| Palila* | Saddle Road. Rare in *mamane-naio* forests above 2134 m (7000 ft) on Mauna Kea, but regularly recorded above the cabin at Puu Laau |
| Akiapolaau* | Saddle Road, Hakalau Forest NWR and Kulani Correctional Facility. Rare in montane *koa-ohia* forests, but still regularly recorded |
| Hawaii Creeper* | Saddle Road, Hakalau Forest NWR and Kulani Correctional Facility. Rare in montane *koa-ohia* forests, but still regularly recorded |
| Akepa* | Saddle Road, Hakalau Forest NWR and Kulani Correctional Facility. Rare in montane *koa-ohia* forests, but still regularly recorded |

**Nihoa (2)**

| | |
|---|---|
| Millerbird* | Fairly common. 400–1,000 birds present in 1993. Became extinct on Laysan between 1912 and 1923 |
| Nihoa Finch* | 'Common' |

### Laysan (2)

| | |
|---|---|
| Laysan Duck* | About 500 birds survive on the central lagoon |
| Laysan Finch* | 'Common' |

### Species which have become extinct since 1800

| | |
|---|---|
| Laysan Crake | Became extinct on Laysan around 1944 |
| Hawaiian Crake | Became extinct on Big Island around 1844 |
| Oahu Oo | Became extinct on Oahu around 1837 |
| Hawaii Oo | Became extinct on Big Island around 1898 |
| Kioea | Became extinct on Big Island around 1860 |
| Amaui | Became extinct on Oahu around 1820 |
| Lanai Finch | Known only from a 1913 specimen taken on Lanai |
| Lesser Koa-Finch | Became extinct on Big Island around 1891 |
| Greater Koa-Finch | Became extinct on Big Island around 1896 |
| Kona Grosbeak | Became extinct on Big Island around 1896 |
| Greater Amakihi | Became extinct on Big Island around 1910 |
| Akialoa | Last recorded on Kauai (in Alakai WP) in 1969 |
| Kakawahie | Last recorded on Molokai (in Kamakou Preserve) in 1964 |
| Ula-ai-hawane | Became extinct on Big Island around 1890 |
| Hawaii Mamo | Became extinct on Big Island around 1898 |
| Black Mamo | Became extinct on Molokai around 1908 |

### NEAR-ENDEMICS

Bonin and Dark-rumped* Petrels, Tristram's Storm-Petrel*, Grey-backed Tern, Blue-grey Noddy.

# IRIAN JAYA

## INTRODUCTION

### Summary

Birding is hard work in Irian Jaya. Seeing the best birds in what is one of the wildest places left on earth involves overcoming time-consuming logistical problems such as organising guides, porters, supplies and boats for what amount to expensive mini-expeditions, and tackling some very tough trails, many of which are steep and muddy. Such problems are surmountable, however, and the rewards, which include MacGregor's* and Wilson's* Birds-of-paradise, are out of this world.

Irian Jaya's star birds are harder to get to than Papua New Guinea's, but Irian Jaya is a cheaper and far friendlier place to visit, so where does

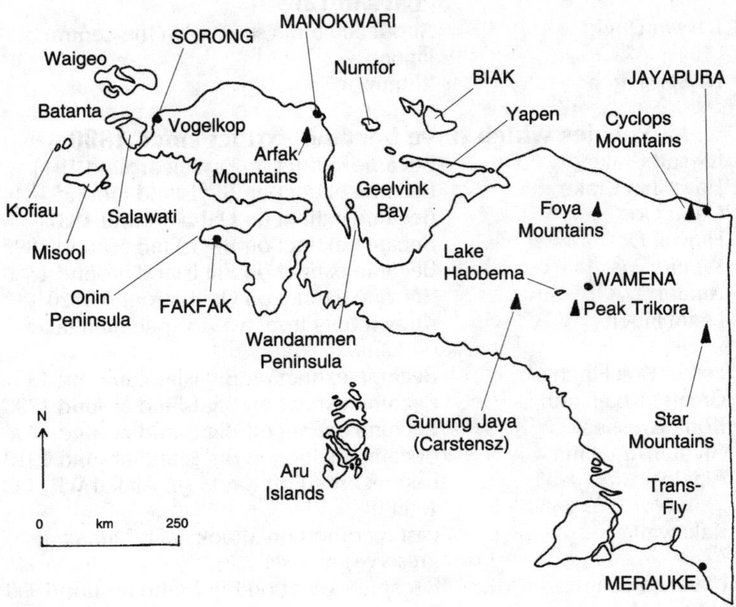


the first time visitor to the island of New Guinea go? Well, as far as birds are concerned, choosing between the two halves of this tropical island is a very difficult decision. On a trip to Irian Jaya one could reasonably expect to see up to 24 birds-of-paradise, including Wilson's* and Red*, the two most spectacular endemics, as well as MacGregor's* which is far easier to see here than in Papua New Guinea. On a trip to mainland Papua New Guinea one could reasonably expect to see up to 23 birds-of-paradise (26 if the Huon Peninsula is included), including Ribbon-tailed Astrapia*, and Raggiana and Blue* Birds-of-paradise, the three most spectacular endemics. Hence, a draw would seem to be a fair result as far as birds-of-paradise are concerned. What may sway the first time visitor to New Guinea, for whom expense is not a problem, to visit one or the other half may therefore come down to personal taste in birds-of-paradise or the chance of seeing other spectacular species. Hence, birders primarily interested in birds-of-paradise will have to decide which is the more fantastic—Wilson's* or Blue* (males of the former are far more likely to be seen, especially displaying), or the more bizarre—MacGregor's* Bird-of-paradise (with its big yellow eye-wattles) or Ribbon-tailed Astrapia* (with its long silky white tail), since Red* and Raggiana are very similar. As far as other goodies go, Shovel-billed Kookaburra* and Blue-black Kingfisher* are more likely to be seen in Irian Jaya, and Southern Crowned-Pigeon* and Painted Quail-thrush are more likely to be seen in Papua New Guinea. Either way, a birding trip to New Guinea which concentrates on such birds is likely to be a tantalising, but ultimately richly rewarding, experience.

## Size

At 421,981 sq km Irian Jaya is about three times larger than England and about half the size of Texas.

## Getting Around

It is necessary to obtain a travel permit (*surat jalan*) to travel beyond the towns in Irian Jaya and one that covers all of the birding areas can be obtained in Jayapura, the major entry point, or in Jakarta, Java. This permit must then be presented at the local police stations at each major destination. To obtain the permit you will need at least six passport photographs, six sets of photocopies of the relevant pages in your passport and six photocopies of the tourist card which is handed out on arrival in the country. Make sure all potential destinations are listed on the permit, especially Genyem (which covers Jayapura, Sentani and Jalan Korea), Wamena (which covers the Snow Mountains), Biak (which covers Biak, Numfor and Warafe), Manokwari (Arfak Mountains) and Sorong (which covers the Batanta and Salawati Islands, and Batu Rumah).

There are few roads away from the major centres of population and birders on an extensive trip will have make use of the expansive, but expensive, internal air network, most of which is run by Merpati but bookable through Garuda. Try to book all flights well in advance and to reconfirm flights as often as possible, because many routes are often overbooked. Also make allowances for the erratic timetables, which are little more than guidelines as many flights are subject to weather conditions. As well as the scheduled internal services run by Merpati, small *Cessnas*, which carry three to five passengers, serve the all-too-many missions. These flights are run by the Missionary Aviation Fellowship (MAF) and Associated Missions Aviation (AMA), both of which have offices at Jayapura Airport in Sentani and at Wamena in the Snow Mountains. They are not too keen on accepting paying passengers, but the planes can be chartered subject to availability and weather.

Some sites are only accessible via long, arduous treks and getting to them will require the help of guides, porters and cooks. Such mini-expeditions can be organised at the nearest towns, often with the help of local ground agents, but be prepared to spend a day or two getting the trek started. Few people speak English in Irian Jaya so it is wise to learn a little Bahasa Indonesian before attempting to organise treks and boat trips. Even a little knowledge of the language will help in greeting people, asking for directions, buying food and, most importantly, checking just how expensive mini-expeditions are. Birding sites around most towns can be reached via the numerous cheap bemos (public taxis), some of which can also be chartered.

## Accommodation and Food

There is a variety of hotels, where a light breakfast is usually included in the price, in most towns, but birders in search of the best sites and birds will not be spending much time in these. Most of the time on extensive birding trips is likely to be spent in village houses and ramshackle huts known as *pondoks*, unless you prefer to camp in what may well be very wet conditions. It is necessary to take camping gear which includes cooking utensils, water containers, karrimat and sleeping bag, as well as a tent and tarpaulin (these can be purchased locally) if you prefer to stay out of the often smoky, flea-filled *pondoks*. Sleeping bags and karrimats should be good enough to ensure a decent night's sleep in the highlands, where temperatures can drop to as low as freezing overnight. Cheap Chinese and Indonesian food is available in towns, while the food eaten on the treks and boat trips depends on what you buy at the small town stores and how good the cook is. Beer is generally available in the lowlands, but all alcohol is banned in the highlands.

## Health and Safety

Immunisation against hepatitis, polio, typhoid and yellow fever (if arriving from an infected country) is recommended. Malaria is particularly prevalent in Irian Jaya, including the *Plasmodium falciparum* species of parasite which can kill its host within a week, so it is wise to take all possible precautions against all forms of this disease, including sleeping under the necessary nets. A number of other diseases, including tuberculosis, are also rife, so treat all water and do not share cutlery or crockery with guides, porters and cooks. Only reasonably fit birders who enjoy trekking should consider making an extensive birding trip to Irian Jaya because it may be necessary to cover as many as 15 km, and ascend 1000 m (3281 ft) in a single day, on steep, narrow, and often wet and muddy trails, to reach the very best sites.

The vast majority of people in Irian Jaya are exceptionally friendly and helpful, and crime is very rare. However, there are pockets of resistance to the Indonesian government and in January 1996 separatists belonging to the Free Papua Movement kidnapped 26 people, mostly Westerners involved in ecological survey work, at Mapunduma in the Snow Mountains. Whilst such a fate is possible here, it is only likely to happen to birders who venture well off the beaten track without asking the local people whether it is safe to do so or not.

## Climate and Timing

Irian Jaya has a humid, warm and wet equatorial climate, and rain falls throughout the year in the highlands, usually in the form of torrential downpours during the afternoon and overnight. However, in the coastal lowlands the normally distinct dry season lasts from May to September. The months of July and August are the driest, and most birds-of-paradise are much more active and more likely to be seen displaying from July onwards, hence this is the peak time to visit Irian Jaya, although southeast tradewinds in August may delay the departure of boats to the Batanta and Salawati Islands, which support the endemic Wilson's Bird-of-paradise*.

Hot weather, cold weather and wet weather birding gear will all be needed for an extensive birding trip, as hot, humid damp days give way to chilly nights in the mountains.

## Habitats

New Guinea is the tallest tropical island on earth, rising to 5029 m (16,499 ft) at Gunung Jaya (Carstensz) in Irian Jaya, the highest peak between the Himalayas and the Andes. Many more high mountains form the island's 2000 km long snow-capped spine and their rugged slopes, together with the lowlands, support 700,000 sq km of forest, the largest tract of forested land away from Amazonia and the Congo Basin. There are no forests above 3000 m (9843 ft), only rolling subalpine meadows with stunted tree-ferns, lakes, bogs and tussock grass. These high-altitiude grasslands give way to stunted moss forests at the treeline, then montane and lowland rainforests, which together still cover 70% of the island. There are no monkeys or large ground-dwelling predators in these forests, only seven species of tree-kangaroo, some mainly nocturnal marsupials such as cuscuses, more species of fruit-bat than anywhere else on earth, some of the world's largest butterflies (birdwings) and moths, and a number of large ground-dwelling birds such as cassowaries and crowned-pigeons. These forests, particularly the moist, mossy montane variety, also support the majority of the world's birds-of-paradise. In parts of the highlands, such as around Wamena in the Snow Mountains, there are broad, intensively cultivated, fertile valleys which have been farmed for centuries. The interior of the island is so wonderfully wild that these valleys were not seen by people from outside New Guinea until the 1930s.

The remote, rugged, forested interior is drained by numerous streams, many of which plunge vertically off the precipitous slopes. Once they reach the coastal lowlands, however, they become wide, muddy, meandering rivers flowing slowly through wide floodplains and lowland peat-swamp forests. In the north the coastal plain is relatively narrow, but in the south it is very wide, especially the Trans-Fly region of the southeast. Here there are rivers, seasonally flooded savanna grasslands and permanent steamy swamps which support masses of waterbirds, many of which also occur in northern Australia, which is only a few hundred kilometres to the south. Areas of mangrove and beaches line the coast, and some of the world's richest coral reefs lie offshore.

## Conservation

A very high proportion of the island of New Guinea (about 70%) is still forested, mainly because the extremely rugged terrain of the interior has prevented local people from spilling out of the densely populated fertile highland valleys, or from spreading inland from the coastal settlements, and deterred most mining and logging companies from moving in. However, the vast expanses of little known and barely touched forest in Irian Jaya are under increasing threat from a burgeoning human population, as well as logging and mining companies, hence the Directorate General of Forest Protection and Nature Conservation will find it increasingly difficult to protect the 64 threatened and near-threatened species which occur in Irian Jaya, and the forests most of them inhabit. The government has established some very large reserves, but these are little more than lines on a map.

## Bird Families

The two families which are endemic to New Guinea (Berrypeckers and Tit/Crested Berrypeckers) are both represented in Irian Jaya, as are the eight families shared with Australia (Cassowaries, Australian Creepers, Bowerbirds, Fairywrens, Logrunners, Pseudo-babblers, Butcherbirds and Magpie-lark/Torrent-lark). Hence ten of the 20 families endemic to Australasia and Oceania occur here.

## Bird Species

Over 650 species have been recorded in Irian Jaya (out of over 700 for the whole of New Guinea). Non-endemic specialities and spectacular species which occur beyond New Guinea include Gurney's Eagle*, Comb-crested Jacana, Dusky Woodcock, Wompoo and Superb Fruit-Doves, Palm Cockatoo*, Channel-billed Cuckoo, Papuan Frogmouth, Moustached Treeswift, Azure, Variable, Beach and Yellow-billed Kingfishers, Common Paradise-Kingfisher, Blue-tailed and Rainbow Bee-eaters, Blyth's Hornbill, Hooded and Red-bellied Pittas, Varied Sittella, Yellow-breasted Boatbill, Magnificent Riflebird, Island Thrush and Blue-faced Parrotfinch. Species restricted to the Trans-Fly region of southeast Irian Jaya, but which also occur and are fairly easy to see in Australia, include Southern Cassowary*, Pied Heron, Brolga, Australian Bustard, Bush Thick-knee, Blue-winged Kookaburra and Magpie-lark.

## Endemics

A total of 44 species are endemic to Irian Jaya, 30 of which occur on the mainland (compared with 25 on the Papua New Guinea mainland and 61 on the islands to the east of Papua New Guinea). In total, 399 species are endemic to New Guinea, of which 269 occur in Irian Jaya and Papua New Guinea. Irian Jaya's 44 endemics, most of which are concentrated on the island of Biak and in the Snow and Arfak Mountains on the mainland, include Western Crowned-Pigeon*, three paradise-kingfishers, three bowerbirds, seven honeyeaters and five birds-of-paradise; Long-tailed Paradigalla*, Western Parotia, Arfak Astrapia* (all three of which occur in the Arfak Mountains), and Wilson's* and Red* Birds-of-paradise (both of which occur on the offshore island of Batanta). New Guinea endemics which are regularly recorded in Irian Jaya include Pheasant Pigeon, Victoria Crowned-Pigeon*, Spangled, Rufous-bellied and Shovel-billed* Kookaburras, Blue-black*, Hook-billed and Mountain Kingfishers, Flame Bowerbird, Black Sittella, two jewel-babblers, 24 birds-of-paradise (including MacGregor's*, King, King-of-Saxony and Twelve-wired) and Crested Berrypecker.

## Expectations

It is possible to see over 250 species on a four-week trip, including about 35 of the 44 endemics (80%), if Jalan Korea, Biak, the Snow and Arfak Mountains, and Batanta are included in the itinerary. Such a total could include as many as 24 birds-of-paradise, including all five endemic species, as well as 27 pigeons, 28 parrots and 33 honeyeaters. The list is likely to be longer if a visit to the Trans-Fly is included or if the whole trip is extended to at least two months, in which case expect to see in the region of 300 species, although this total is only likely to include a few more endemics.

Many external flights arrive at Jayapura Airport, which is 36 km west of Jayapura just outside the lakeside town of **Sentani** in northeast Irian Jaya. It makes sense to stay in Sentani where there is plenty of accommodation to choose from, because the next two major sites are easily accessible from here. Before birding it is crucial to visit Jayapura, 45 minutes away, in order to obtain a travel permit (*surat jalan*). These can be obtained from the local police (POLRES) at Jalan Achmad Yani, next to the Hotel Matos, or the regional police (POLDA) at Jalan Sam Ratulangi, opposite the church (see Getting Around, page 239). The police issue permits only on weekdays. In time it may be possible to obtain a surat jalan in Sentani so it would be wise to ask if this is possible on arrival, in the hope of saving a trip to Jayapura. While sorting this out you are bound to be approached by local people offering to help you find accommodation and to organise a trip to Wamena in the Snow Mountains (p. 245). Any assistance in finding somewhere to stay may be appreciated, but it is better to wait until reaching Wamena before organising the trek into the Snow Mountains. The Hotel Sentani Inn (B), 5 km from airport, the Hotel Ratna (C), and Losmen Minang Jaya are arguably the best places to stay in Sentani. To get to Wamena by air, try to book an early morning flight because cloud cover often means later flights are cancelled. Even if you cannot book an early flight it is a good idea to go to the airport anyway because passengers who have booked often fail to turn up. If there is time to spare in Sentani, take a stroll west out of town along the northern shore of **Lake Sentani** where the possibilities include Oriental Hobby, Brown Quail, Red-backed Buttonquail, White-browed Crake, Dusky Moorhen, Comb-crested Jacana, Orange-fronted Fruit-Dove, Channel-billed Cuckoo (Apr–Sep), Blue-tailed and Rainbow (Apr–Sep) Bee-eaters, Fawn-breasted Bowerbird, Scrub Honeyeater and New Guinea Friarbird. The Cyclops Mountains lie opposite the airport, between Sentani and the coast. The steep forested slopes of these mountains support the endemic Mayr's Honeyeater, but they are difficult to reach without local help and enough time to mount a mini-expedition.

## JALAN KOREA

Jalan Korea is a road which was constructed by a Korean logging company through lowland alluvial swamp forest near the base of the Cyclops Mountains. The road is over 100 km long and beyond the logging zone, more than 100 m from the roadside, there are some superb birds to look for, notably Northern Cassowary*, Victoria Crowned-Pigeon*, Salvadori's Fig-Parrot*, Blue-black Kingfisher*, Brown-headed Crow* and Pale-billed Sicklebill*, as well as the more widespread, but nevertheless exciting, Pesquet's Parrot*, Blue Jewel-babbler and Twelve-wired Bird-of-paradise.

More birds are likely to be seen here with the assistance of local guides, so take enough food for yourself and at least two local people if you intend to employ such help. The best local guide, Jamil, 160/C Nimbokrang, Genyem, Jayapura, Irian Jaya, Indonesia, may still deal in birds-of-paradise, so don't expect to see too many males, if any at all, because he may have shot them. It is therefore wise to offer him a bonus if you see male birds-of-paradise, as well as for certain other species. Expect to pay somewhere in the region of a basic Rp15,000 per day for the guide's services, which will probably include arranging accommodation.

### Irian Jaya Endemics

Salvadori's Fig-Parrot*, Brown-headed Crow*.

### Localised New Guinea Endemics

Northern Cassowary*, Brown-collared Brush-turkey, Orange-fronted Fruit-Dove, Victoria Crowned-Pigeon*, Buff-faced Pygmy-Parrot, Brown Lory, Papuan Nightjar, Blue-black Kingfisher*, Streak-headed Honeyeater, Jobi Manucode, Pale-billed Sicklebill*.

### Other New Guinea Endemics

Long-tailed Honey-buzzard, Grey-headed Goshawk, Pink-spotted, Coroneted, Beautiful and Orange-bellied Fruit-Doves, Purple-tailed, Pinon, Collared and Zoe Imperial-Pigeons, Pesquet's Parrot*, Dusky and Black-capped Lories, Greater Black and Lesser Black Coucals, Papuan Needletail, Rufous-bellied Kookaburra, Hook-billed Kingfisher, White-

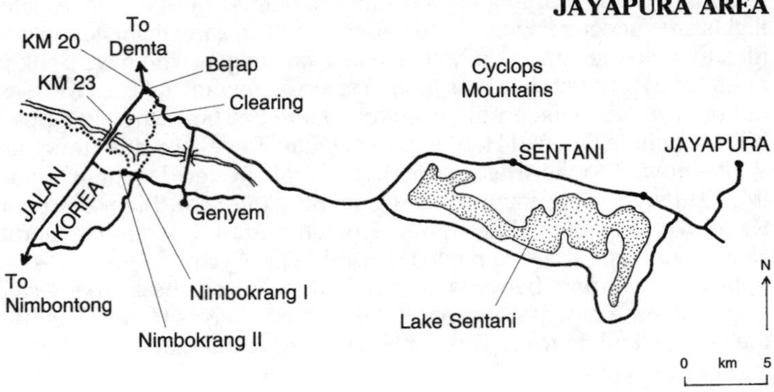


eared Catbird, White-shouldered and Emperor Fairywrens, Pale-billed Scrubwren, Yellow-bellied Gerygone, Long-billed and Yellow-gaped Honeyeaters, Meyer's Friarbird, Torrent Flycatcher, Black-sided Robin, Variable, Hooded and Rusty Pitohuis, New Guinea Babbler, Blue Jewel-babbler, Sooty, Black and White-bellied Thicket-Fantails, Spot-winged, Hooded, Golden and Rufous-collared Monarchs, Grey Crow, Glossy-mantled Manucode, Magnificent, King, Twelve-wired and Lesser Birds-of-paradise, Lowland Peltops, Hooded Butcherbird, Brown Oriole, Boyer's, Papuan, Grey-headed, New Guinea and Golden Cuckoo-shrikes, Black-browed Triller, Golden Myna, Streak-headed Munia, Red-capped Flowerpecker.

## Non-endemic Specialities

Spotted Whistling-Duck, Red-necked Crake, Palm Cockatoo*, Yellow-billed Kingfisher, Magnificent Riflebird.

## Others

Little Pied Cormorant, Rufous Night-Heron, Black Bittern, Pacific Baza, Whistling and Brahminy Kites, White-bellied Sea-Eagle, Grey Goshawk, Collared Sparrowhawk, Gurney's Eagle*, Brown Falcon, Oriental Hobby, Rufous-tailed Bush-hen, Oriental Pratincole (Oct–Apr), Slender-billed and Great Cuckoo-Doves, Stephan's Dove, Wompoo and Superb Fruit-Doves, Papuan Mountain-Pigeon, Double-eyed Fig-Parrot, Red-cheeked and Eclectus Parrots, Sulphur-crested Cockatoo, Rainbow and Red-flanked Lorikeets, Oriental (Oct–Apr) and Channel-billed (Apr–Sep) Cuckoos, Moustached Treeswift, Glossy and Uniform Swiftlets, Variable Kingfisher, Common Paradise-Kingfisher, Rainbow Bee-eater (Apr–Sep), Dollarbird, Blyth's Hornbill, Fairy Gerygone, New Guinea Friarbird, Rufous Shrike-Thrush, Willie-wagtail, Northern Fantail, Shining Flycatcher, Black Butcherbird, White-bellied Cuckoo-shrike, Singing and Metallic Starlings, Yellow-faced Myna, Pacific Swallow, Tree Martin (Apr–Sep), Golden-headed Cisticola, Black and Olive-backed Sunbirds.

(Other species recorded here include Papuan Frogmouth, Little Kingfisher and Plain Honeyeater.)

To reach this site, charter a bemo from Sentani and head to the transmigration camp known as Nimbokrang 1, which is about 75 km away, via Genyem where the guide Jamil lives. From Nimbokrang 1 it is an

8–10 km walk through farmland to the forest alongside Jalan Korea. Previously productive areas alongside the road have included the clearing where there used to be a sawmill (Lesser Bird-of-paradise), KM 29 to KM 32.5, the trail to a Twelve-wired Bird-of-paradise display tree which starts at KM 32.5, and KM 45, which is a good area for Pesquet's Parrot* and Magnificent Bird-of-paradise. A good birding strategy for the area is to prepare for battle with millions of mosquitoes, be in position in the depths of the best forest just after dawn, then leave the forest well before dusk to scan the forest edge, especially dead trees, for birds such as pigeons and parrots preparing to go to roost. To achieve this it will probably be necessary to camp in the vicinity of the road if Jamil cannot come up with an alternative.

*The huge Victoria Crowned-Pigeon* is one of three fantastic crowned-pigeons which are endemic to New Guinea*

## SNOW MOUNTAINS

The Dani and Yali tribes, which inhabit the 60 km long and 15 km wide Grand Baliem Valley at the northern edge of the Snow Mountains in central New Guinea, did not see a Westerner or a wheel until 1938. Unknown to the outside world until then, these friendly people had been cultivating this highly fertile valley with only stone tools. Today, the town of Wamena, which is situated at 1600 m (5249 ft) in the valley, is the centrepoint of tourism in Irian Jaya, despite the fact that in January 1996 separatists from the Free Papua Movement kidnapped 26 people, mainly westerners, at Mapunduma in the Snow Mountains region.

Most people visit Wamena to look at the local people and 'experience' their culture, and only a few, mainly birders, venture further afield into the forested mountains beyond, where they usually experience far more excitement and wonder. The superb montane forests and grasslands above Wamena support some fantastic birds, not least MacGregor's Bird-of-paradise*, Splendid Astrapia, King-of-Saxony Bird-of-paradise and Crested Berrypecker, as well as six endemics.

There are two ways of birding the area. Most birders, up until the mid-1990s, organised their own treks, which usually took about seven days, from Wamena up through the montane forests to the stunted moss forests, where MacGregor's Bird-of-paradise* occurs, and grasslands surrounding Lake Habbema. Some still do this, but others charter a jeep

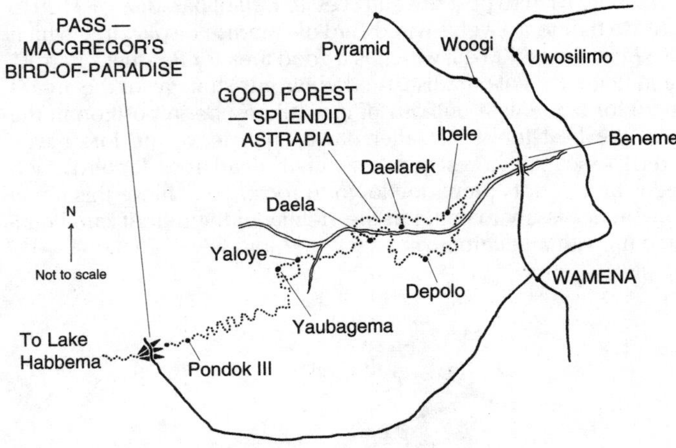


to the lake then walk back to Wamena, downhill. It is now also possible to bird alongside two new roads out of Wamena, one of which reaches MacGregor's Bird-of-paradise* land.

## Irian Jaya Endemics

Snow Mountain Quail* (scarce), Archbold's Bowerbird*, Orange-cheeked and Rufous-sided Honeyeaters, Short-bearded Melidectes, Black-breasted and Snow Mountain Munias.

## Localised New Guinea Endemics

Salvadori's Teal*, Painted and Madarasz's Tiger-Parrots, Goldie's and Orange-billed Lorikeets, Archbold's Nightjar, Mountain Kingfisher, Buff-faced and Papuan Scrubwrens, Papuan Thornbill, Black-throated, Olive-streaked and Black-backed Honeyeaters, Sooty, Belford's and Ornate Melidectes, Smoky Honeyeater, Alpine, White-winged and White-eyed Robins, Black Sittella, Rufous-naped and Lorentz's Whistlers, Wattled Ploughbill, Papuan Whipbird*, Blue-capped Ifrita, Lesser Melampitta, Crested, Loria's and MacGregor's* Birds-of-paradise, Short-tailed Paradigalla, Brown Sicklebill, Splendid Astrapia, King-of-Saxony Bird-of-paradise, Hooded Cuckoo-shrike, Mountain Firetail, Papuan Parrotfinch, Alpine Pipit, Slaty-chinned Longbill, Crested Berrypecker.

## Other New Guinea Endemics

Long-tailed Honey-buzzard, Black-mantled Goshawk, Black-billed Cuckoo-Dove, Rufescent Imperial-Pigeon, Brehm's and Modest Tiger-Parrots, Pygmy, Fairy, Papuan, Plum-faced and Yellow-billed Lorikeets, Rufous-throated Bronze-Cuckoo, Mountain Swiftlet, Papuan Tree-creeper, Orange-crowned and White-shouldered Fairywrens, Mountain Mouse-Warbler, Perplexing and Large Scrubwrens, Mountain and Brown-breasted Gerygones, Olive Straightbill, Red-collared Myzomela, Mimic and Marbled Honeyeaters, Lesser Ground-Robin, Canary Fly-catcher, Garnet, Black-throated and Blue-grey Robins, Rusty, Sclater's and Regent Whistlers, Friendly, Black and Dimorphic Fantails, Black Monarch, Black-breasted Boatbill, Superb Bird-of-paradise, Great

Woodswallow, Mountain Peltops, Torrent-lark, Stout-billed, Papuan and Black-bellied Cuckoo-shrikes, Capped White-eye, Red-capped Flowerpecker, Lemon-breasted and Fan-tailed Berrypeckers, Dwarf Honeyeater, Tit Berrypecker.

## Non-endemic Specialities

Dusky Woodcock, Chestnut-breasted Cuckoo, Australasian Grass-Owl, Tawny-breasted Honeyeater.

## Others

Pacific Black Duck, Eastern Marsh-Harrier, Blue-breasted Quail, Buff-banded Rail, Spotless Crake, Slender-billed and Great Cuckoo-Doves, White-breasted Fruit-Dove, Papuan Mountain-Pigeon, Varied Sittella, Golden Whistler, Island Thrush, Pied Bushchat, Island Leaf-Warbler, Tawny Grassbird, Blue-faced Parrotfinch.

## Other Wildlife

Pygmy ringtail, speckled dasyure.

(Other species recorded here include Meyer's Goshawk, Chestnut Forest-Rail, Swinhoe's Snipe (Oct–Apr), Greater Ground-Robin and Streaked Berrypecker.)

At **Wamena**, one hour by air from Jayapura Airport, Sentani, it is possible to get your *surat jalan* stamped at the airport, thus saving a trip to the local police station. Once out of the airport talk to the numerous potential guides who will be there to greet you, or, better still, head for Chandra Nusantara Tours and Travel, Jalan Trikora No. 17, PO Box 225 Wamena, Irian Jaya, Indonesia (tel: 31293, fax: 31299, telex: 76102 CNTWMX IA), or the Hotel Syahrial Jaya on Jalan Gatot Subroto, five minutes walk along the road alongside the airstrip. The local entrepeneurs, the travel agent or the hotel will be able to make the necessary arrangements for birding the new roads (which will involve hiring a 4WD and, to get the best out of the area, camping at various altitudes) or for a trek to or from Lake Habbema (which will involve hiring guides, porters and cooks, and paying for their food, accommodation and cigarettes). In 1991, a nine-day trek for two cost Rp250,000, but by 1994 the going rate had risen to Rp650,000 and by the late 1990s will probably cost something in the region of a million rupees, which is the equivalent to US$500. Agree on how much each person will be paid per day and which roles they will carry out before departure, and remember that the accommodation amounts to a couple of smoky and flea-filled *pondoks*, so taking a tent and tarpaulin may be a much more comfortable option.

The trek to Lake Habbema begins at Beneme, from where the rest of the first day is usually spent walking through the cultivated, but scenic, Ibele Valley where there are patches of secondary forest and conifer plantations which, surprisingly, support Loria's and Superb Birds-of-paradise. By the end of day one it is possible to reach the village of **Daelarek** (Tailarek), which at 2200 m (7218 ft) is 600 m (1969 ft) above Wamena, or the village of **Daela** (Dyela). From Daelarek it is a 45 minute walk to a finger of forest which supports Short-tailed Paradigalla and Brown Sicklebill. After a short, steep climb above Daela the main trail passes through more forest before descending steeply to a river. From here it is primary, almost pristine, forest all the way up to the pass near Lake Habbema. Now is the time to start looking for King-of-Saxony Bird-of-paradise, and Crested Bird-of-paradise occurs between Yaloye and the small hut known as **Yaubagema** (Jabogema), where the second night is usually spent. The clearing here, in lower montane forest at 2650 m (8694 ft), is well worth birding in late afternoon and early morning, with possibilities including Chestnut Forest-Rail, Archbold's Nightjar, Garnet Robin, Blue-capped Ifrita, Brown Sicklebill, Splendid Astrapia and King-of-Saxony Bird-of-paradise. After searching for these birds early on day three, press onwards along the trail as it ascends to 3200 m (10,499 ft) via a narrow river valley where the excellent moss forest supports Archbold's Bowerbird*, Lesser Melampitta and Crested Berry-pecker. The third night is usually spent at **Pondok III**, three hours or so above Yaubagema. On day four it is best to start out 30 minutes before dawn to reach the pass near Lake Habbema at dawn. This is a good area for MacGregor's Bird-of-paradise* in the early morning and late afternoon, along with Goldie's Lorikeet and Short-bearded Melidectes. Unfortunately, since the new road was built up to Lake Habbema MacGregor's Bird-of-paradise* has become scarcer due to hunting, and it may be necessary to trek some distance from the road along the tree-line to see this exceptional species, if it cannot be found near the pass. The same is true of Snow Mountain Quail*, which is rarely seen near the road. The rest of day four is worth spending in the grasslands, bogs and stunted forest alongside **Lake Habbema**, 1.5 km beyond the pass, in search of Snow Mountain Quail*, Dusky Woodcock, Orange-cheeked Honeyeater, Lorentz's Whistler, Island Thrush, Snow Mountain Munia and Alpine Pipit, while Salvadori's Teal* occurs on the lake itself. The fourth night can be spent back at Pondok III or at Pondok IV by the lake-side (a better base from which to search for the woodcock at dusk). From Pondok III it is a steady three hours down to Yaubagema, a steady five hours from there to Daela, and a five hour walk from there to Beneme, so it is best to allow two days for the return trek to Wamena, as well as an extra day for the whole trip, in case some birds take a long time to find or the weather makes walking difficult.

*Accommodation:* Wamena—Hotel Syahrial Jaya (C), Hotel Nayak (A–B).

*The brilliant black-and-yellow MacGregor's Bird-of-paradise* is the Snow Mountains' star bird*

## WASUR NATIONAL PARK

This park lies near Merauke in the Trans-Fly region of south-central New Guinea and was established to protect a maze of mangroves, seasonally flooded savanna grasslands, paperbark swamps and lowland rainforest where waterbirds otherwise confined to Australia occur, as well as Southern Cassowary*, Southern Crowned-Pigeon*, Spangled Kookaburra, Greater Bird-of-paradise and three species of munia, all of which have very restricted ranges.

The wetlands are particularly impressive from August onwards, at the end of the dry season, when the numerous waterbirds concentrate around the remaining pools to feast on stranded fish and frogs.

### Localised New Guinea Endemics

New Guinea Flightless Rail* (rare), Southern Crowned-Pigeon*, Spangled Kookaburra, Plain Honeyeater, Greater Bird-of-paradise, Fly River Grassbird*, White-spotted, Grey-crowned* and Black* Munias.

### Other New Guinea Endemics

Long-tailed Honey-buzzard, Beautiful Fruit-Dove, Orange-breasted Fig-Parrot, Lesser Black Coucal, Rufous-bellied Kookaburra, White-shouldered Fairywren, Puff-backed Honeyeater, Meyer's Friarbird, Black and White-bellied Thicket-Fantails, Olive Flyrobin, King Bird-of-paradise.

### Non-endemic Specialities

Southern Cassowary*, Palm Cockatoo*, Noisy Pitta, Fawn-breasted Bowerbird, Trumpet Manucode, Black-backed Butcherbird.

### Others

Little Pied and Little Black Cormorants, Australian Darter, Australian Pelican, Magpie Goose, Radjah Shelduck, Green Pygmy-goose, White-faced Heron, Intermediate Egret, Great-billed Heron*, Pied Heron, Rufous Night-Heron, Black Bittern, Glossy, Australian and Straw-necked Ibises, Royal Spoonbill, Black-necked Stork, Pacific Baza, Whistling and Brahminy Kites, White-bellied Sea-Eagle, Swamp Harrier, Grey Goshawk, Collared Sparrowhawk, Wedge-tailed and Little Eagles, Brown Falcon, Orange-footed Scrubfowl, Brown Quail, Brolga, Australian Bustard, Comb-crested Jacana, Far Eastern Curlew*, Great Knot, Rufous-necked Stint, Sharp-tailed Sandpiper, Bush Thick-knee, Australian Pratincole (Apr–Sep), Great Crested-Tern, Peaceful and Bar-shouldered Doves, Wompoo Fruit-Dove, Torresian Imperial-Pigeon, Red-cheeked and Eclectus Parrots, Red-winged Parrot, Sulphur-crested Cockatoo, Little Corella, Rainbow and Red-flanked Lorikeets, Shining (Apr–Sep) and Horsfield's (Apr–Sep) Bronze-Cuckoos, Pheasant Coucal, Barking Owl, Papuan Frogmouth, White-throated (Apr–Sep) and Large-tailed Nightjars, Azure Kingfisher, Blue-winged Kookaburra, Forest Kingfisher, Blue-tailed and Rainbow (Apr–Sep) Bee-eaters, Dollarbird, Blyth's Hornbill, Fairy, Large-billed and Mangrove Gerygones, Brown Honeyeater, Dusky and Red-headed Myzomelas, Graceful, Varied and White-throated Honeyeaters, Little, New Guinea and Noisy Friarbirds, Brown-backed, Rufous-banded and Blue-faced Honeyeaters, Lemon-bellied Flycatcher, Mangrove Robin, Black-tailed Whistler, Rufous and Grey Shrike-Thrushes, Grey-crowned Babbler, Willie-wagtail, Mangrove Fantail, Leaden, Restless and Shining Flycatchers, Torresian Crow, Black

## WASUR NP

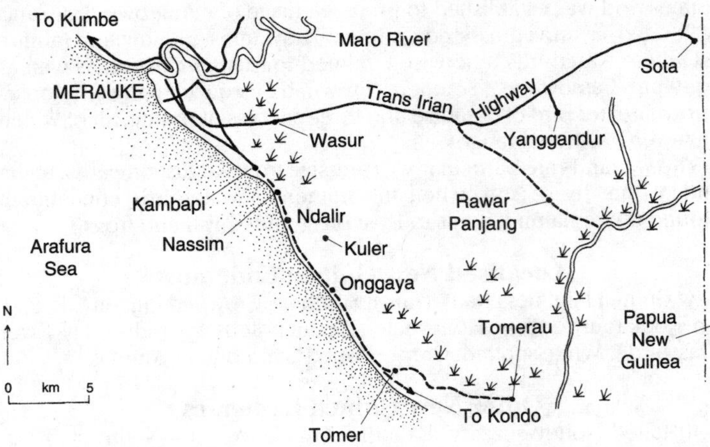


Butcherbird, Australasian Magpie, Magpie-lark, Olive-backed and Green Orioles, Black-faced and White-bellied Cuckoo-shrikes, Common Cicadabird, Yellow-faced Myna, Tree Martin (Apr–Sep), Golden-headed Cisticola, Australasian Bushlark, Crimson Finch, Black and Olive-backed Sunbirds.

### Other Wildlife

Agile wallaby, death adder, greater flying-fox, striped possum, sugar glider, taipan, water monitor.

At Merauke, accessible by air, head for the WWF office which is at Jalan Brawrjayaat Sepaden (tel: 62971 22407) for details on how to get around the area. This will probably involve hiring a 4WD vehicle to traverse the Trans Irian Highway which runs through the park east of Merauke. The sago swamps near the village of Wasur along here support Southern Crowned-Pigeon*. The guesthouse at Yanggandur lies near a Greater Bird-of-paradise display tree. Before reaching the village of Sota at the Papua New Guinea border the road turns north into an area where Greater Bird-of-paradise occurs. Around Merauke the degraded mangroves west of the port support mangrove specialists such as Mangrove Gerygone, Red-headed Myzomela, Mangrove Robin and Black-tailed Whistler, and the beach 2 km southwest of the town centre is good for shorebirds. It is also worth hiring a boat to explore the lowland swamp forest alongside the Maro River. King Bird-of-paradise occurs here. The road along the coast southeast of Merauke passes a large marsh just out of town (Brolga) before becoming a track (impassable from November to May) which passes through open forest beyond Nassim. About 20 km further on, turn inland at Tomer to reach Tomerau 10 km away, or continue down the coast to Kondo, a good area for Southern Cassowary* (although good habitat may be a 5 km walk away if the river is impassable). Gallery forest near the Tomer–Tomerau Road supports Trumpet Manucode and mangrove-lined tidal creeks may support New Guinea Flightless Rail*. At Tomerau it is possible to stay in a local house with permission from the head of the village, who may also be willing to act as a guide. The marshes, savanna and forests around here, especially the reedbeds at Ukra, support Fly River Grassbird*, and White-spotted, Grey-crowned* and Black* Munias. In November–December Southern Cassowaries* drink at remaining areas of water at dawn. Beware of snakes, such as the taipan—one of the most venomous on earth—throughout the park. For more information on visiting arrangements, contact YAPSEL (Foundation for Social, Economic and Environmental Development), PO Box 283, Jalan Missi, Merauke 99602 (tel: 62 971 21489/22088, fax: 62 971 21610), a non-governmental organisation which is endeavouring to encourage small-scale ecotourism in the area.

*Accommodation:* Merauke—Hotel Asmat. Wasur National Park—basic guesthouses, camping.

## BIAK

The forests on this palm-fringed limestone island have been logged, but they still support eight of the nine species endemic to the Geelvink Bay islands, including the beautiful Biak Paradise-Kingfisher*.

### Biak Endemics

Biak Coucal*, Biak Paradise-Kingfisher*, Biak Monarch*, Biak White-eye*.

### Geelvink Bay Islands Endemics

Geelvink Pygmy-Parrot*, Black-winged Lory*, Biak Flycatcher*, Long-tailed Starling.

### Irian Jaya Endemics

Spice Imperial-Pigeon.

### Other New Guinea Endemics

Long-tailed Honey-buzzard, Black-capped Lory, Red-fronted Lorikeet, Emperor Fairywren, Golden Monarch (*kordensis* race), Hooded Butcherbird, Black-browed Triller, Red-capped Flowerpecker.

### Non-endemic Specialities

Dusky Scrubfowl, Meyer's Goshawk, Yellow-bibbed Fruit-Dove, Moluccan Scops-Owl (*beccarii* race).

### Others

Lesser Frigatebird, Collared Sparrowhawk, Gurney's Eagle*, Slender-billed and Great Cuckoo-Doves, Emerald Dove, Superb and Claret-breasted Fruit-Doves, Torresian Imperial-Pigeon, Oriental Cuckoo (Oct–Apr), Papuan Frogmouth, Moustached Treeswift, Beach Kingfisher, Rainbow Bee-eater (Apr–Sep), Dollarbird, Hooded Pitta, Fairy and Large-billed (*hypoxantha* race) Gerygones, Dusky Myzomela, Singing and Metallic Starlings, Black Sunbird.

## BIAK

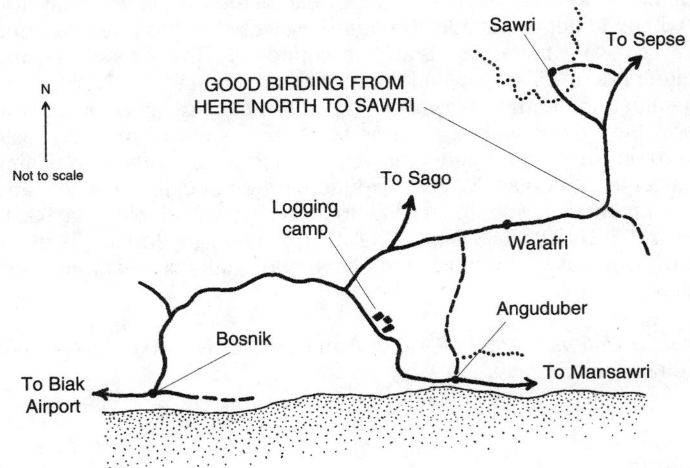


### Other Wildlife

Common cuscus, common echymipera, spinner dolphin.

If time is short, bird the scrub behind the airport (walk across the runway as the locals do or get a taxi around the long way) on both sides of the Biak Town–Bosnik Road, especially the valley to the left on the far side of the road from the airport. Yellow-bibbed Fruit-Dove, Long-tailed Starling and Biak White-eye* occur here. However, the degraded forest beyond the village of **Warafri**, about an hour east of the town of Biak, supports all the endemics (although the white-eye is scarce here) and is accessible by bus or bemo via Bosnik. Bird alongside the road between Warafri and the village of Sawri. Watch out for Dusky Scrubfowl crossing the roads and Papuan Frogmouths perched on roadside wires. Higher quality forest is present in the Pulau Biak Utara Reserve, which is north of Warsa at the northern end of the island, and on the adjacent island of Supiori (see below). Beach Kingfisher occurs along the south coast west of Biak town.

*Accommodation:* Taman Angrek (B, including good food) is a small losmen on the hill behind the airport (ask for directions and help in getting there, to save what could be a long walk, at the Merpati Office in the airport). Hotel Irian (B).

Dusky Scrubfowl, Spice Imperial-Pigeon, Victoria Crowned-Pigeon*, Geelvink Pygmy-Parrot*, Black-winged Lory*, Red-fronted Lorikeet, Biak Coucal*, Biak Paradise-Kingfisher*, Golden Monarch, Biak Flycatcher* and Long-tailed Starling, as well as Papuan Frogmouth, Hooded Pitta and Emperor Fairywren occur on Biak's sister island, **Supiori**. To look for these birds, charter a boat from Biak to Korido on the south coast of Supiori and bird beyond the village. It is usually possible to arrange accommodation at the police station. The island of **Ayawi**, 5–6 hours by boat from Biak, is reported to support a large colony of Nicobar Pigeons* (Aug–Dec) and the nearby island of **Meos**

**Befondi** may support Island Whistler and Island Monarch. The island of **Numfor**, accessible by air, supports the beautiful endemic Numfor Paradise-Kingfisher, which is quite easy to find close to the airport and main town, as well as Dwarf Fruit-Dove and Hooded Pitta.

The forests at Warkapi and in the Arfak Mountains on the Vogelkop Peninsula of mainland Irian Jaya, where a number of endemics occur, are accessible from **Manokwari**. On arrival at this town, which is accessible by air, show your *surat jalan* to the local police then head for the WWF Office, which is situated in a house on the coast five minutes along the road from the airstrip to town (bemo drivers know where to go). The address is WWF, Jaian Pertanian Wosi Dalam, PO Box 174, Manokwani 98312 (tel: 22493). Ask WWF if they will (i) help to get the permit (*surat ijin*) needed to visit the Warkapi area and the Arfak Mountains from the Departemen Kehutanan (Forest Office) nearby, (ii) supply you with a letter of introduction to take to the village of Warkapi and (iii) help to organise guides, porters, cooks and accommodation for the trek from Warkapi and/or the trek up to the Arfak Mountains. If WWF are unable to help, ask Yoris Wonggai, who can be contacted via the Hotel Mutiara. Guides cost Rp10,000 per day for the Arfak Mountains trek in 1994.

The **Maruni Trail** south of Manokwari is second best to the Warkapi area, but species recorded along here include King and Lesser Birds-of-paradise, as well as Gurney's Eagle*, Dwarf Fruit-Dove, Large Fig-Parrot, Common Paradise-Kingfisher and Yellow-faced Myna. Just after the road south from Manokwari to Warkapi leaves the coast there are two bridges. After the second bridge there is a trail to the right to the village of Maruni, 3 km up hill. Bird this trail, especially the last kilometre before the village.

## WARKAPI

The lowland and foothill forests at the base of the Arfak Mountains inland from the coastal village of Warkapi are degraded, but they still support a surprisingly good selection of spectacular birds, including Flame Bowerbird, Blue Jewel-babbler and King Bird-of-paradise, as well as the three birds-of-paradise endemic to mainland Irian Jaya.

### Irian Jaya Endemics

Vogelkop Bowerbird, Vogelkop Scrubwren, Rufous-sided Honeyeater, Vogelkop Melidectes*, Arfak Honeyeater, Smoky and Green-backed Robins, Vogelkop Whistler*, Long-tailed Paradigalla*, Western Parotia, Arfak Astrapia*, Olive-crowned Flowerpecker.

### Localised New Guinea Endemics

Ornate Fruit-Dove, Mountain Owlet-Nightjar, Flame Bowerbird, Wallace's Fairywren, Tawny Straightbill, Black Pitohui, Black Sicklebill*.

### Other New Guinea Endemics

Long-tailed Honey-buzzard, Black-mantled Goshawk, Black-billed Cuckoo-Dove, Pink-spotted, Beautiful and Orange-bellied Fruit-Doves,

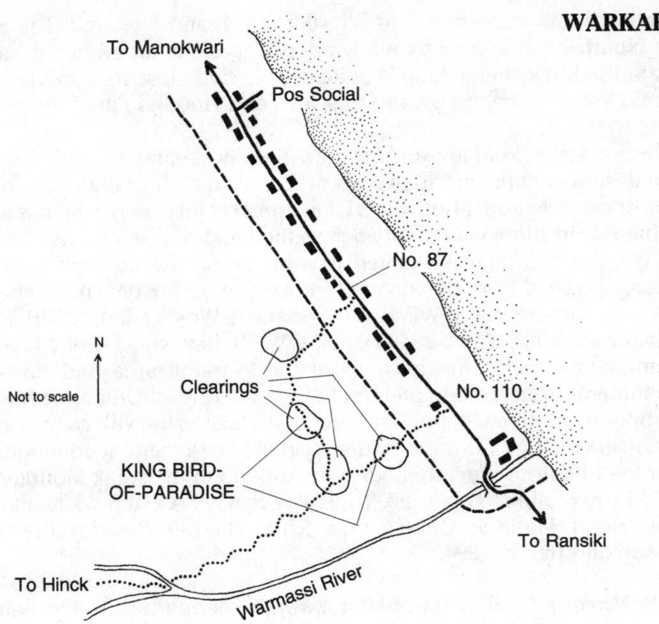


Purple-tailed, Rufescent and Pinon Imperial-Pigeons, Large Fig-Parrot, Brehm's and Modest Tiger-Parrots, Black-capped Lory, Papuan and Yellow-billed Lorikeets, Rufous-throated Bronze-Cuckoo, Lesser Black Coucal, Mountain Swiftlet, Rufous-bellied Kookaburra, Hook-billed Kingfisher, Papuan Treecreeper, Orange-crowned Fairywren, Rusty Mouse-Warbler, Perplexing Scrubwren, Mountain Gerygone, Red-collared Myzomela, Scrub and Puff-backed Honeyeaters, Olive Flyrobin, Canary Flycatcher, Garnet, Black-sided and Black-throated Robins, Dwarf, Sclater's and Regent Whistlers, Variable and Rusty Pitohuis, New Guinea Babbler, Blue Jewel-babbler, Friendly and Black Fantails, Spot-winged, Hooded and Rufous-collared Monarchs, Black-breasted Boatbill, Papuan Drongo, Grey Crow, Glossy-mantled Manucode, King and Lesser Birds-of-paradise, Great Woodswallow, Lowland Peltops, Hooded Butcherbird, Brown Oriole, Boyer's, New Guinea and Black-bellied Cuckoo-shrikes, Black-fronted White-eye, Black, Lemon-breasted and Fan-tailed Berrypeckers, Yellow-bellied Longbill, Tit Berrypecker.

## Non-endemic Specialities

Metallic Pigeon, Yellow-capped Pygmy-Parrot, Palm Cockatoo*, Yellow-billed Kingfisher, Tawny-breasted Honeyeater, White-faced Robin, Magnificent Riflebird.

## Others

Grey Goshawk, Gurney's* and Little Eagles, Slender-billed Cuckoo-Dove, Stephan's Dove, White-breasted Fruit-Dove, Double-eyed Fig-Parrot, Red-cheeked and Eclectus Parrots, Moluccan King-Parrot*, Oriental Cuckoo (Oct–Apr), Rufous Owl, Moustached Treeswift, Glossy and Uniform Swiftlets, Common Paradise-Kingfisher, Rainbow Bee-eater (Apr–Sep), Dollarbird, Blyth's Hornbill, Hooded and Red-bellied Pittas,

Fairy Gerygone, New Guinea Friarbird, Varied Sittella, Grey Whistler, Yellow-breasted Boatbill, Black Butcherbird, Metallic Starling, Yellow-faced Myna.

## Other Wildlife

Black tree-kangaroo, long-nosed echymipera.

(Other species recorded here include Trumpet Manucode, Magnificent Bird-of-paradise and Gray's Warbler (Oct–Apr).)

Warkapi is about 45 km south of Manokwari and can be reached from there by bemo, a journey which usually lasts just over an hour. However, most bemos do not go all the way to Warkapi, so it may be better to charter one if time is short. On arrival, show your WWF letter of introduction and *surat ijin* to the head of the village (*kepala desa*) and you will then almost certainly be shown to some accommodation where food will also be provided at nightfall. In 1994 paying guests of the village said thanks for their generous hospitality with Rp15,000, a sum which was well received. Bird around the village and along the trail towards the mountain village of Hinck (Hing), the lower part of which supports such star birds as King Bird-of-paradise. To reach the upper part of the trail in time for good early morning birding it is necessary to start very early or camp out. Rufous Owl and Flame Bowerbird have been recorded near a *pondok* at 1300 m (4265 ft) and Long-tailed Paradigalla* at 1725 m (5660 ft), below a fairly good spot to camp at 1850 m (6070 ft), next to the bog on the left as you ascend. Look for Mountain Owlet-Nightjar around here and at 1900 m (6234 ft) scan from the viewpoint for Black-mantled Goshawk.

*Accommodation:* Manokwari—Hotel Beringin (C), Losmen Binhar/Era Ria Restaurant. Warkapi—local houses. Trail—camping and pondoks.

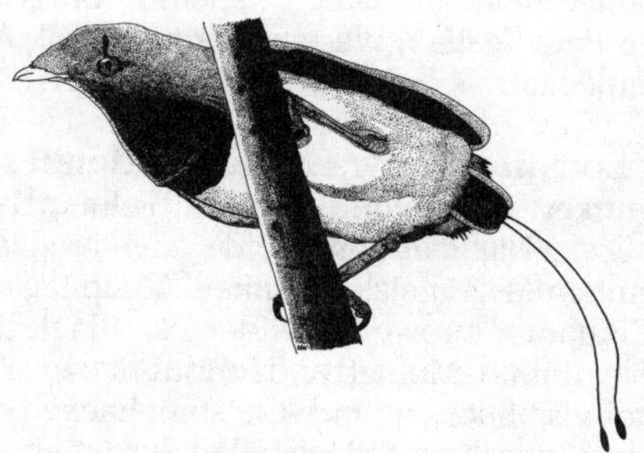

*The fabulous scarlet-and-white King Bird-of-paradise is widespread, but scarce, throughout the lowlands of New Guinea*

It is possible to trek further in to the mountains behind Warkapi or other coastal villages on trails which link up to those in the Arfak Mountains. Thick-billed Ground-Pigeon*, Western Crowned-Pigeon*, Red-throated Myzomela, Crested Pitohui and Chestnut-backed Jewel-babbler have been recorded on the slopes behind **Oransburi** for example.

## ARFAK MOUNTAINS

The montane forests of the rugged Arfak Mountains support many of the species which are endemic or near-endemic to the Vogelkop Peninsula, including three birds-of-paradise, as well as more widespread, but rare and spectacular, species such as White-striped Forest-Rail*, Flame Bowerbird, Spotted and Chestnut-backed Jewel-babblers, and eight other birds-of-paradise. However, seeing these birds is far from easy. Male birds-of-paradise are very thin on the ground, and like most of the other great birds present in the area, they are some of the world's top forest skulkers, most of which would be difficult to find even in flat terrain, let alone the precipitous ridges and deep valleys of the Arfak Mountains. These are only accessible via some of the worst trails in Irian Jaya, trails so bad that after heavy rain they turn into rivers of mud, making birding whilst walking virtually impossible, hence it is hardly surprising that those birders who have been here in bad weather have described their experience as a nightmare. At the very least, birding here is a great challenge, but the rewards could be phenomenal.

It takes at least ten hours walking to reach Bini Bei, where it is best to spend at least a day birding the clearing and surrounding ridges, at least ten hours to reach Mokwam, where it is best to spend at least two days birding the surrounding area, and at least a day to get back to Manokwari, so, taking into account the time needed beforehand to organise guides, porters, cooks, fuel and food, it would be wise to allocate at least a week to enjoy some success at this site. If time is short it is possible to fly from Manokwari, on planes chartered from MAF (Kantor Team, Manokwari 98311 (tel: 21155)), up to Mokwam or Minyambou nearby, and walk one way. A road to Minyambou is also under construction.

### Irian Jaya Endemics

Red-billed Brush-turkey, White-striped Forest-Rail*, Vogelkop Bowerbird, Vogelkop Scrubwren, Rufous-sided Honeyeater, Vogelkop Melidectes*, Arfak Honeyeater, Smoky and Green-backed Robins, Vogelkop Whistler*, Long-tailed Paradigalla*, Western Parotia, Arfak Astrapia*, Olive-crowned Flowerpecker.

### Localised New Guinea Endemics

Wattled Brush-turkey, Josephine's Lorikeet, Feline, Barred, Wallace's and Mountain Owlet-Nightjars, Archbold's Nightjar, Flame Bowerbird, Black and Mountain Myzomelas, Mountain Meliphaga, Black-throated Honeyeater, Cinnamon-browed Melidectes, Black-chinned, White-rumped and Ashy Robins, Mottled and Rufous-naped Whistlers, Crested and Black Pitohuis, Spotted and Chestnut-backed Jewel-babblers, Lesser Melampitta, Black* and Black-billed Sicklebills.

### Other New Guinea Endemics

Long-tailed Honey-buzzard, Black-mantled Goshawk, New Guinea Eagle*, Black-billed Cuckoo-Dove, New Guinea Bronzewing*, Pink-spotted and Beautiful Fruit-Doves, Purple-tailed, Rufescent, Pinon and Zoe Imperial-Pigeons, Brehm's and Modest Tiger-Parrots, Pesquet's Parrot*, Pygmy, Fairy, Papuan, Plum-faced and Yellow-billed Lorikeets, Rufous-throated and White-eared Bronze-Cuckoos, Jungle Hawk-Owl, Mountain Swiftlet, Rufous-bellied Kookaburra, Hook-billed Kingfisher,

Papuan Treecreeper, Orange-crowned and White-shouldered Fairy-wrens, Rusty and Mountain Mouse-Warblers, Perplexing, Large, Grey-green and Pale-billed Scrubwrens, Mountain, Yellow-bellied and Brown-breasted Gerygones, Olive Straightbill, Long-billed Honeyeater, Red-collared Myzomela, Mimic and Marbled Honeyeaters, Lesser Ground-Robin, Torrent and Canary Flycatchers, Garnet, Black-throated and Blue-grey Robins, Dwarf, Rusty, Sclater's and Regent Whistlers, Variable and Hooded Pitohuis, New Guinea Babbler, Friendly and Chestnut-bellied Fantails, Black and White-bellied Thicket-Fantails, Black, Dimorphic and Rufous-backed Fantails, Black Monarch, Black-breasted Boatbill, Papuan Drongo, Grey Crow, Crinkle-collared Manucode, Superb, Magnificent and Lesser Birds-of-paradise, Great Woodswallow, Mountain Peltops, Hooded Butcherbird, Torrent-lark, Stout-billed, Boyer's, Papuan, Grey-headed, New Guinea, Black-bellied and Golden Cuckoo-shrikes, Black-browed Triller, Black-fronted and Capped White-eyes, Streak-headed Munia, Lemon-breasted and Fan-tailed Berrypeckers, Dwarf Honeyeater, Tit Berrypecker.

## Non-endemic Specialities

Dusky Woodcock, Metallic Pigeon, Palm Cockatoo*, Chestnut-breasted Cuckoo, Marbled Frogmouth, Tawny-breasted Honeyeater, Yellow-legged Flycatcher, White-faced Robin, Northern Scrub-Robin, Logrunner, Trumpet Manucode, Magnificent Riflebird.

## Others

Grey Goshawk, Gurney's* and Little Eagles, Blue-breasted Quail, Slender-billed and Great Cuckoo-Doves, Stephan's Dove, Superb, White-breasted and Claret-breasted Fruit-Doves, Papuan Mountain-Pigeon, Red-breasted Pygmy-Parrot, Moluccan King-Parrot*, Greater Sooty-Owl, Papuan Frogmouth, Large-tailed Nightjar, Moustached Treeswift, Glossy and Uniform Swiftlets, Variable Kingfisher, Common Paradise-Kingfisher, Blyth's Hornbill, Red-bellied Pitta, Spotted Catbird, Fairy Gerygone, New Guinea Friarbird, Varied Sittella, Grey Whistler, Black-winged Monarch, Gray's Warbler (Nov–Mar), Island Leaf-Warbler, Tawny Grassbird, Black Sunbird.

## Other Wildlife

Common cuscus, long-nosed antechinus, narrow-striped dasyure.

(Other species recorded here include Swinhoe's Snipe (Oct–Apr), Ornate Fruit-Dove, Pheasant Pigeon, Blue-collared Parrot, Red Myzomela, Ornate Melidectes and Blue-faced Parrotfinch.)

If walking in, it is possible to start at Tanah Merah or Warmare, 40 minutes by bemo from Manokwari. The trail from Tanah Merah ascends Gunung Umsini and after two to three hours reaches a small clearing (a good area to camp in with water close by) at 780 m (2559 ft) where Flame Bowerbird occurs, as well as Lesser Bird-of-paradise. From here the trail ascends to 1800 m (5906 ft) where there is another good area for camping. The clearing at **Bini Bei**, ten hours on foot from Tanah Merah, is situated at 1850 m (6070 ft) and a first class birding area, especially early in the morning. The trees at the top of the clearing are good for birds-of-paradise, including the rare Long-tailed Paradigalla*, and Black* and Black-billed Sicklebills. The first 100 m of the steep trail leading from these trees is also worth a long look. The lower end of the clearing is good for Western Parotia. Other species possible at and around the clearing include Black-mantled Goshawk, Arfak Honey-eater, Black-breasted Boatbill and Great Woodswallow. The trail up to **Gunung Ngribou** from Bini Bei reaches 1900 m (6234 ft) and is good for Vogelkop Bowerbird, Vogelkop Melidectes*, Black Sicklebill* and Arfak Astrapia*. The ten hour trek between Bini Bei and the village of **Mokwam** begins with an ascent to a ridge. The trail follows this ridge for a while (Vogelkop Bowerbird) before turning off to a side ridge (Vogelkop Whistler*, Arfak Astrapia*) and then descending steeply to the River Prafti (Torrent-lark). It is then necessary to wade across the river twice before ascending to Mokwam. Wallace's Owlet-Nightjar is occasionally seen at roost near Ciraubrei between Bini Bei and Mokwam. The forest is poor once across the river, but Magnificent Bird-of-paradise occurs near the village of Gwao. At Mokwam, hire Zeth Wonggor as a guide to look for New Guinea Eagle* (Gunung Indon), White-striped Forest-Rail* (Soiti), Dusky Woodcock (Gunung Indon), New Guinea Bronzewing* (Gunung Indon–Sioubri Trail), Feline (Soiti) and Mountain (Gunung Indon and Soiti) Owlet-Nightjars, Archbold's Nightjar (Gunung Indon), Vogelkop Bowerbird (Soiti), Mottled Whistler (Soiti), Logrunner (Soiti), Black* (Gunung Indon) and Black-billed (Sioubri) Sicklebills, Western Parotia and Arfak Astrapia* (Gunung Indon and Sioubri).

**ARFAK MOUNTAINS**

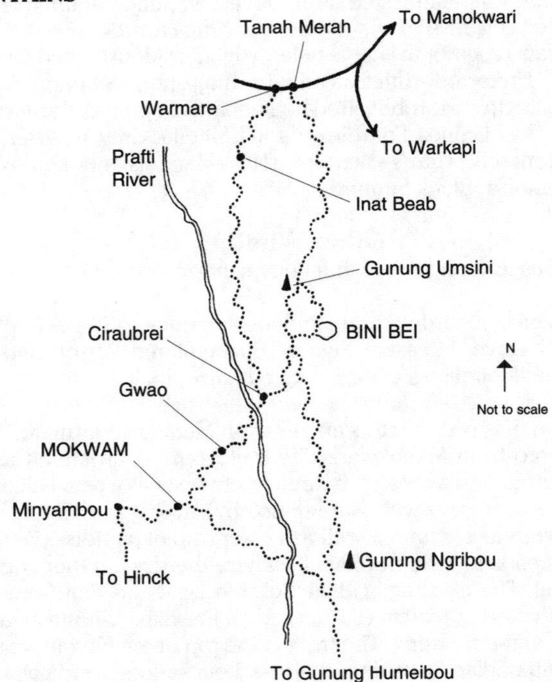

*Accommodation:* Tanah Merah and Warmare—local houses. Trek—basic *pondoks* and/or camping (take a karrimat and sleeping bag, both of which should be able to withstand chilly overnight temperatures, as well as a tent if you wish to avoid spending the night in the flea-filled *pondoks*). Mokwam—WWF hut.

*The very rare Long-tailed Paradigalla* is the star attraction of the Arfak Mountains for most birders*

It is also possible to trek into the Arfak Mountains from Myubi, near Ransiki, up to **Anggi** where Shovel-billed Kookaburra* and Grey-banded Munia*, as well as Black-mantled Goshawk, Wattled Brush-turkey, Lewin's Rail, Vogelkop and Flame Bowerbirds, Spotted and Chestnut-backed Jewel-babblers, Black* and Black-billed Sicklebills, Western Parotia and Torrent-lark occur. The munia is common in wet grasslands around Danau Gigi on the way up to Anggi and the kookaburra is present in swampy pandanus forest near Hunku, a one hour walk from Anggi. Introduce yourself to the village head (*kepala desa*) in Myubi and he will probably find somewhere for you to stay and help to arrange guides, porters and cooks for the two-day trek up to Anggi, where it is possible to stay at the police post. From here head to Hunku and ask for Joseph Seiber, an excellent guide who will probably also let you camp near his house. It is also possible to fly to Anggi, but the flights are often cancelled due to bad weather.

## BATU RUMAH

The primary rainforest at this remote site on the north coast of the Vogelkop Peninsula supports two rare kingfishers: the unique Shovel-billed Kookaburra* and Blue-black Kingfisher*. It is possible to see over 85 species in a week here and the two major attractions are ably supported by Dwarf Cassowary*, Pheasant Pigeon, Western Crowned-Pigeon*, Beach Kingfisher and King Bird-of-paradise.

Batu Rumah is also a turtle conservation project site, run jointly by the local forest office and WWF. Visitors are welcome in small numbers and arrangements must be made in advance via Jopi Bakarbessy at the Kantor Kehutanan (Forest Office), Jalan Sudirman 40 (near the market), PO Box 353, Sorong (tel: 21986). Visiting the site involves hiring a boat, as well as guides and cooks, and paying for fuel, accommodation and food for all members of what amounts to a mini-expedition. Make

**BATU RUMAH**

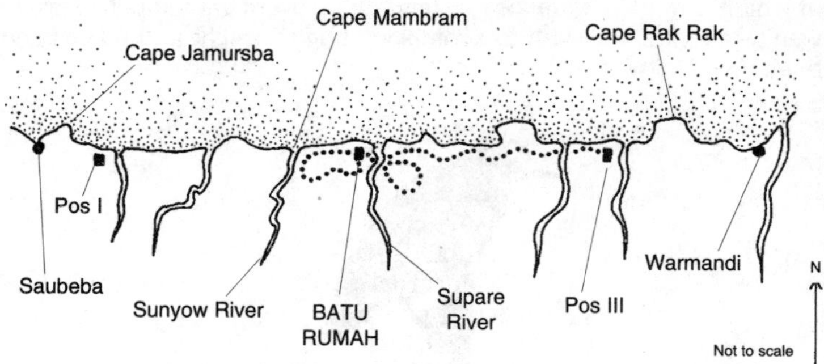


sure the boat has two engines because the sea can be very rough along the northern Vogelkop coast. In 1994 a three-day trip for two cost Rp584,000, and in 1995 a week long trip for two cost Rp1,500,000, but it may be possible to organise a cheaper trip via Bob Furima at the harbour office in Sorong.

## Irian Jaya Endemics

Red-billed Brush-turkey, Western Crowned-Pigeon*.

## Localised New Guinea Endemics

Dwarf Cassowary*, New Guinea Scrubfowl, Thick-billed Ground-Pigeon*, Pheasant Pigeon, Shovel-billed Kookaburra*, Blue-black Kingfisher*, Tawny Straightbill.

## Other New Guinea Endemics

Long-tailed Honey-buzzard, New Guinea Eagle*, Cinnamon Ground-Dove, Pink-spotted, Coroneted and Orange-bellied Fruit-Doves, Rufescent, Pinon and Zoe Imperial-Pigeons, Large Fig-Parrot, Dusky and Black-capped Lories, Greater Black Coucal, Rufous-bellied Kookaburra, White-eared Catbird, Emperor Fairywren, Yellow-bellied Gerygone, Mimic Honeyeater, Variable and Rusty Pitohuis, New Guinea Babbler, Sooty Thicket-Fantail, Grey Crow, Glossy-mantled Manucode, Superb, King and Lesser Birds-of-paradise, Lowland Peltops, Hooded Butcherbird, Brown Oriole, Black-browed Triller, Black Berrypecker, Yellow-bellied Longbill.

## Non-endemic Specialities

Spotted Whistling-Duck, Yellow-capped Pygmy-Parrot, Palm Cockatoo*, Magnificent Riflebird.

## Others

Lesser Frigatebird, Black Bittern, White-browed Crake, Slender-billed and Great Cuckoo-Doves, Stephan's Dove, Wompoo, Superb and Claret-breasted Fruit-Doves, Eclectus Parrot, Papuan Frogmouth, Large-tailed Nightjar, Azure, Variable and Beach Kingfishers, Common Paradise-Kingfisher, Rainbow Bee-eater (Apr–Sep), Blyth's Hornbill, Red-bellied Pitta, Fairy Gerygone, Shining Flycatcher, Yellow-breasted Boatbill, Singing Starling, Yellow-faced Myna, Black Sunbird.

### Other Wildlife

Dorcopsis kangaroo, green (Sep–Nov), hawksbill (Mar–May), leatherback (May–Sep) and Pacific Ridley (Mar–May) sea-turtles, grizzled tree-kangaroo.

The longboat from Sorong takes four to seven hours to reach the small town of Sausapor, where it is necessary to report to the local police with your *surat jalan*. It is worth stopping at Oum Island *en route* to Sausapor, as New Guinea Scrubfowl is common here. From Sausapor it is another two to four hours by boat to Batu Rumah via the village of Saubeba. The whole journey from Sorong may be completed in a day, but it sometimes takes two. There are no trails and it is easy to get lost without a compass if birding without the excellent park guides (Rp3000 per trip). Shovel-billed Kookaburra* and Blue-black Kingfisher*, as well as Black Bittern and Lowland Peltops occur in the flooded forest at Lake Rak Rak, 3 km inland from Cape Rak Rak. This is also a particularly good area for pigeons and parrots and it is usually accessible on foot via a broad, dry river bed. Soaking clothes in a 5% solution of benzyl bezoate will help keep most of the chiggers at bay, but prepare for an itchy time here.

*Accommodation:* share the small wooden house with the park staff, or camp.

## SORONG

The town of Sorong, at the western tip of the Vogelkop Peninsula, is the gateway to the island of Batanta and its star attraction: Wilson's Bird-of-paradise*. It will take some time to organise the trip to Batanta, and while waiting to depart it is worth birding in the degraded lowland forest nearby. Irian Jaya endemics such as Black Lory, and localised New Guinea endemics such as Forest Bittern* and Red-breasted Paradise-Kingfisher, have all been recorded here.

### Irian Jaya Endemics

Black Lory, Olive-crowned Flowerpecker.

### Localised New Guinea Endemics

Forest Bittern*.

### Other New Guinea Endemics

Long-tailed Honey-buzzard, Grey-headed Goshawk, Orange-bellied Fruit-Dove, Purple-tailed and Pinon Imperial-Pigeons, Pesquet's Parrot*, Black-capped Lory, Lesser Black Coucal, Papuan Needletail, Rufous-bellied Kookaburra, Emperor Fairywren, Long-billed Honeyeater, Red-throated Myzomela, Scrub and Mimic Honeyeaters, Rusty Pitohui, White-bellied Thicket-Fantail, Golden Monarch, Glossy-mantled Manucode, Hooded Butcherbird, Brown Oriole, Black-browed Triller, Golden Myna, Streak-headed Munia, Yellow-bellied Longbill.

### Non-endemic Specialities

Spotted Whistling-Duck, Yellow-billed Kingfisher, Tawny-breasted Honeyeater.

### Others

Rufous Night-Heron, Black Bittern, Pacific Baza, Oriental Hobby, Great Cuckoo-Dove, Red-cheeked and Eclectus Parrots, Rainbow Lorikeet, Channel-billed Cuckoo (Apr–Sep), Moustached Treeswift, Glossy and Uniform Swiftlets, Blyth's Hornbill, New Guinea Friarbird, Shining Flycatcher, Black Butcherbird, White-bellied Cuckoo-shrike, Singing Starling, Yellow-faced Myna, Black Sunbird.

(Other species recorded here include Western Crowned-Pigeon* and Red-breasted Paradise-Kingfisher.)

Sorong is accessible by air. The airport for large aircraft is on an offshore island, 30 minutes by water taxi from the town on the mainland, although a new mainland airport is under construction. Once in town set about organising the mini-expedition to the islands of Batanta and Salawati (see below) and, once this has been completed, if there is time to spare, head for the **Klamalu–Kalamomo Road**, 24 km southeast of town. The best way to bird this road is to charter a taxi to get to the roadside forest, which begins at KM 25, at dawn, and return by public transport, or make arrangements through Kris Tindige, care of the Cendrawasih Hotel (see Additional Information, p. 266, for address). The other major birding site near Sorong is the **Intimpura Logging Area**, 18 km out of town. Bird along the track which leads north to a logging camp (signposted PT Intimpura Timber Co.). Forest Bittern* has been recorded in the trackside pools and this is also a good area for Pesquet's Parrot*. To continue beyond the logging camp it is necessary to obtain permission from PT Intimpura Timber Company, Jalan Melati No. 9, Sorong, and this may well be worth the effort because Western Crowned-Pigeon* has been recorded here. Red-breasted Paradise-Kingfisher has been recorded in the secondary woodland on the left-hand side of the road 14–15 km out of Sorong, in what is a 'wooded picnic area' known as **Tamam Wisata**.

*Accommodation:* Hotel Indah (seabirds possible from third floor rooms), Cendrawasih Hotel (good food), Hotel Batanta, Hotel Irian Beach, Losmen Parco-Pole.

## BATANTA AND SALAWATI

One of the most fantastic creatures to grace planet earth, Wilson's Bird-of-paradise*, is endemic to the island of Batanta off the west coast of Irian Jaya, along with Red Bird-of-paradise*, and its neighbouring island, Salawati, supports Red-necked Crake, Western Crowned-Pigeon* and King Bird-of-paradise, which help complete a sensational selection of birds.

To get to these two islands it is necessary to visit Sorong, where a longboat, guides and cooks must be hired, and fuel, oil, water and food for everyone bought and paid for. In 1991 a three-day trip for two cost Rp250,000, but the going rate had risen to Rp830,000 for a six-day trip for four in 1994, and by the end of the 1990s the rate is likely to reach around a million rupees, which is equivalent to about US$500. It is possible to organise this mini-expedition on your own by asking around in

Sorong, but Kris Tindige, care of the Cendrawasih Hotel (see Additional Information, p. 266, for address), will sort things out more quickly and probably save you a lot of time and hassle. Either way, it is important to make sure that Anton Dei, the best local guide, who lives on Batanta, is available.

## Irian Jaya Endemics

Red-billed Brush-turkey, Spice Imperial-Pigeon, Western Crowned-Pigeon*, Wilson's* and Red* Birds-of-paradise.

## Localised New Guinea Endemics

Northern Cassowary*, Pheasant Pigeon.

## Other New Guinea Endemics

Long-tailed Honey-buzzard, Cinnamon Ground-Dove, Beautiful Fruit-Dove, Purple-tailed and Pinon Imperial-Pigeons, Black-capped Lory, Rufous-bellied Kookaburra, Hook-billed Kingfisher, White-eared Catbird, Rusty Mouse-Warbler, Pale-billed Scrubwren, Yellow-bellied Gerygone, Long-billed, Puff-backed, Mimic and Yellow-gaped Honeyeaters, Black-sided Robin, Variable and Rusty Pitohuis, Black Thicket-Fantail, Spot-winged and Golden Monarchs, Grey Crow, Glossy-mantled Manucode, King and Lesser Birds-of-paradise, Brown Oriole, New Guinea Cuckoo-shrike, Black Berrypecker, Yellow-bellied Longbill.

## Non-endemic Specialities

Dusky Scrubfowl, Red-necked Crake, Yellow-capped Pygmy-Parrot, Palm Cockatoo*, Chestnut-breasted Cuckoo, Tawny-breasted Honeyeater.

## Others

Lesser Frigatebird, Radjah Shelduck, Great-billed Heron*, Brahminy Kite, White-bellied Sea-Eagle, Red-necked Phalarope (Oct–Apr), Great Crested-Tern, Black-naped Tern, Stephan's Dove, Wompoo and Superb Fruit-Doves, Moluccan King-Parrot*, Papuan Frogmouth, Moustached Treeswift, Azure, Variable and Beach Kingfishers, Common Paradise-Kingfisher, Dollarbird, Blyth's Hornbill, Hooded and Red-bellied Pittas, New Guinea Friarbird, Grey Whistler, Willie-wagtail, Shining Flycatcher, White-bellied Cuckoo-shrike, Singing Starling, Yellow-faced Myna, Black Sunbird.

## Other Wildlife

Bottle-nosed and spinner dolphins, common cuscus, common echymipera, sugar glider.

(Other species recorded here include Doria's Goshawk*, Bare-eyed Rail and Olive-yellow Robin*.)

The longboat from Sorong usually takes about two hours to reach Yennenes (Beach Kingfisher) and a further one to two hours to reach the tiny beach village of Wai Lebed on the south coast of **Batanta**. Here there is a basic, but cosy, reedmat-and-bamboo hut at the top of the palm-fringed beach which serves as the accommodation (take sleeping bag). The flat, lowland forest just 500 m from the hut supports Red Bird-of-paradise* (which is most likely to be seen near dusk), as well as Hooded and Red-bellied Pittas, and from here a steep trail ascends

Gunung Batanta. One to two hours up this trail there is a display ground, complete with viewing screen, of Wilson's Bird-of-paradise*. The best time to visit it is between 0730 and 1000, and however long it takes for a male to appear, be sure every agonising second is worth it. Once the two endemic birds-of-paradise have been seen and absorbed, it is time to head across the Sagewin Strait to **Salawati**, although it is also worth snorkelling just off the beach at Wai Lebed, if only to relieve the itching caused by the numerous chiggers in the area. From Wai Lebed it is 50 minutes by longboat to Salawati, where the flat lowland forest, usually accessible via a partly dry river bed at Wai Bon or at Kalisisi, supports Western Crowned-Pigeon* (Wai Bon), as well as Red-necked Crake (Wai Bon) and King Bird-of-paradise (Kalisisi). It is possible to visit these sites on a day-trip from Batanta or, if you start out before dawn, on the way back to Sorong. Birders with more time on their hands may wish to stay at the village of Kaliam on Salawati and then bird the surrounding forest via taking a small boat along the beach to the west, or the old quarry road inland. Northern Cassowary*, Cinnamon Ground-Dove, Western Crowned-Pigeon* and King Bird-of-paradise all occur here.

*The blue-headed, yellow-and-red-backed Wilson's Bird-of-paradise*, which only occurs on the small island of Batanta off the west coast of Irian Jaya, is one of the most fabulous birds on earth*

## FAKFAK MOUNTAINS

Before 1991 these mountains on the Onin Peninsula, south of the Vogelkop Peninsula, were so steep and rugged that they were uninhabited and the local people rarely ventured more than a few kilometres from the coast to hunt. However, oil exploration has led to the construction of helipads and numerous trails have been cut between these from coast to coast. Hence it is now possible to bird these mountains, with the assistance of local guides and porters, and via camping at the edge of the helipad clearings. Few birders have ventured to the forested slopes so far, but already they have discovered four potentially new species: a bowerbird, two honeyeaters and a paradigalla. Other little-known birds present here include Red-breasted Paradise-Kingfisher.

### Irian Jaya Endemics

Western Crowned-Pigeon*, Vogelkop Bowerbird, Rufous-sided Honeyeater, Vogelkop Melidectes*, Long-tailed Paradigalla*.

## Localised New Guinea Endemics

Red-breasted Paradise-Kingfisher, Smoky Honeyeater, Olive-yellow Robin*, Black-billed Sicklebill.

## Other New Guinea Endemics

Long-tailed Honey-buzzard, Grey-headed Goshawk, Black-billed Cuckoo-Dove, Ornate Fruit-Dove, Purple-tailed, Pinon and Zoe Imperial-Pigeons, Dusky and Black-capped Lories, Fairy Lorikeet, White-eared Bronze-Cuckoo, Greater Black Coucal, Jungle Hawk-Owl, Rufous-bellied Kookaburra, Hook-billed Kingfisher, Rusty and Mountain Mouse-Warblers, Perplexing, Grey-green and Pale-billed Scrubwrens, Mountain, Yellow-bellied and Brown-breasted Gerygones, Olive Straightbill, Long-billed Honeyeater, Red and Red-collared Myzomelas, Sclater's Whistler (unnamed race), Hooded and Crested Pitohuis, Friendly, Black and Rufous-backed Fantails, Black, Spot-winged and Golden Monarchs, Black-breasted Boatbill, Papuan Drongo, Grey Crow, Crinkle-collared Manucode, Superb, Magnificent and King Birds-of-paradise, Great Woodswallow, Mountain Peltops, Papuan and Black-bellied Cuckoo-shrikes, Black and Lemon-breasted (unnamed race) Berrypeckers, Yellow-bellied Longbill, Dwarf Honeyeater.

## Non-endemic Specialities

Southern Cassowary*, Palm Cockatoo*, Chestnut-breasted Cuckoo, Marbled Frogmouth, Yellow-billed Kingfisher, Yellow-legged Flycatcher, Trumpet Manucode, Magnificent Riflebird.

## Others

Great Cuckoo-Dove, Stephan's Dove, Wompoo, Superb and White-breasted Fruit-Doves, Papuan Mountain-Pigeon, Greater Sooty-Owl, Spotted Catbird, Fairy Gerygone, Black-winged Monarch.

(Greater Melampitta was recorded near Wanggasten, 20 km east of the main trail at this site, in 1981.)

At Kota Fakfak head for Losmen Haranya and ask if Eddy, a local guide, is around. He will probably recommend taking a dugout canoe to the tiny village of Worsaret two hours east along the coast, picking up a couple of porters and heading off along the trail inland. This trail, which soon enters undisturbed forest, reaches 'Helipad 2' at about 600 m (1967 ft), 'Helipad 4' at about 1200 m (3937 ft) ten hours further on, and 'Helipad 5' at about 1500 m (4921 ft) seven hours further on. The potential new species of bowerbird, allied to Vogelkop Bowerbird, which builds a distinctly different type of bower to those in the Arfak Mountains, the two potential new species of honeyeater, allied to Rufous-sided and Smoky, and the potential new paradigalla, allied to Long-tailed*, which has a shorter tail and differently coloured facial wattles to those in the Arfak Mountains, all occur above 'Helipad 4'. The best area for the paradigalla is at the highest point between there and 'Helipad 5'.

About 160 species are resident on the **Aru Islands**, many of which are endemic subspecies. The large areas of mangrove and forest support Chestnut Rail (Pulau Karang and Pulau Enu), Wallace's Fruit-Dove, Elegant Imperial-Pigeon, Spangled and Rufous-bellied Kookaburras, and Brown-headed Crow*.

# ADDITIONAL INFORMATION

## Addresses

Please submit records to the Indonesian Ornithological Society (IOS), c/o BirdLife Indonesia Programme, PO Box 310/B00, Bogor 16003, Java, Indonesia. The IOS publishes the regular *Kukila* bulletin.

Permits (*surat jalans*) to visit some areas may be obtained from the Directorate General of Forest Protection and Nature Conservation (PHPA—Perlindungan Hutan dan Pelestarian Alam), Ministry of Forestry, Gedung Manggala Wanabakti, Jalan Gatot Subroto, Jakarta (tel: 5730311/2, fax: 5734818).

Kris Tindige, Nature Irian, Jalan Sam Ratulangi No. 6, Sorong 98413, Irian Jaya, Indonesia (fax: 951 23665/23500), is a good local travel agent who can help to arrange trips throughout Irian Jaya, and especially around Sorong and the Batanta and Salawati Islands.

Sentosa Tosiga Tours and Travel Limited, Jalan Ahmad Yani No. 36, Biak 98111, Irian Jaya, Indonesia (tel: 961 21398/21956, fax: 961 21988, telex: 76281 SENTOSA IA) is a good local travel agent who can help to arrange trips in the Biak, Manokwari and Sorong areas.

## Books and Papers

*Birding Indonesia*. Jepson P *et al.*, 1997. Periplus Editions.

*Irian Jaya: A Site Guide for Birdwatchers*. Gibbs D, 1997. Privately published and available from the Natural History Book Service.

*Birding in Irian Jaya 1991*. Smith S, 1991. Privately published and available from the Natural History Book Service.

*Birds of New Guinea*. Beehler B *et al.*, 1986. Princeton University Press.

*The Birds of Papua New Guinea*, volumes 1 (*Non-Passerines*) and 2 (*Passerines*). Coates B, 1985 and 1990. Dove Publications.

*Mammals of New Guinea*. Flannery T, 1990. The Australian Museum and Robert Brown & Associates.

Undescribed taxa and new records from the Fakfak Mountains, Irian Jaya. Gibbs D, 1994. *Bull. Brit. Ornithol. Club* 114: 4–12.

## IRIAN JAYA ENDEMICS (44)
## Mainland and Offshore Islands (30)

| | |
|---|---|
| Red-billed Brush-turkey | Arfak Mountains, Batu Rumah, and Batanta and Salawati. Also known from Misool |
| Snow Mountain Quail* | Snow Mountains |
| White-striped Forest-Rail* | Arfak Mountains. Also rarely reported from montane forests of Tamrau and Wandammen Mountains on the Vogelkop Peninsula |
| Spice Imperial-Pigeon | Biak and Supiori, and Batanta and Salawati |
| Western Crowned-Pigeon* | Batu Rumah, Salawati and Fakfak Mountains |
| Salvadori's Fig-Parrot* | Jalan Korea. Also known from lowlands west from here to Geelvink Bay |
| Black Lory | Sorong. Also known from eastern Vogelkop, Onin and Bomberai Peninsulas, and west Papuan Islands |
| Archbold's Bowerbird* | Snow Mountains. Also known from Weyland Mountains. May be conspecific |

| | |
|---|---|
| | with Sanford's Bowerbird* which occurs in the Tari Valley in Papua New Guinea |
| Vogelkop Bowerbird | Warkapi/Arfak Mountains and Fakfak Mountains (where the local race may be a separate species). Also known from Tamrau, Wandammen and Kumawa Mountains |
| Golden-fronted Bowerbird* | Known only from Foya Mountains |
| Vogelkop Scrubwren | Warkapi/Arfak Mountains. Also known from Tamrau and Kumawa Mountains |
| Orange-cheeked Honeyeater | Snow Mountains |
| Brass' Friarbird* | Known only from a small area of flooded canegrass and dense secondary forest around a lagoon on the Idenburg River and from the lower Mamberamo River |
| Rufous-sided Honeyeater | Snow Mountains, Warkapi/Arfak Mountains and Fakfak Mountains (where the local race may be a separate species). Also known from Kumawa Mountains |
| Mayr's Honeyeater | Known from Bewani, Cyclops and Foya Mountains |
| Short-bearded Melidectes | Snow Mountains |
| Vogelkop Melidectes* | Warkapi/Arfak Mountains and Fakfak Mountains. Also known from Kumawa Mountains |
| Arfak Honeyeater | Warkapi/Arfak Mountains. Also known from Tamrau and Wandammen Mountains |
| Snow Mountain Robin* | Known only from Mounts Wilhelmina (Peak Trikora) and Gunung Jaya (Carstensz), the highest peaks of the Snow Mountains. Neither of these mountains is easy to visit, although it may be possible to reach Gunung Jaya on a trek from Ilaga |
| Smoky Robin | Warkapi/Arfak Mountains. Also known from Kumawa, Weyland and Foya Mountains |
| Green-backed Robin | Warkapi/Arfak Mountains. Also known from Wandammen, Foya and western Snow Mountains, as well as Yapen |
| Vogelkop Whistler* | Warkapi/Arfak Mountains |
| Brown-headed Crow* | Jalan Korea. Also known from the lower Mamberamo River, the west Papuan Islands of Waigeo and Gemien, and the Aru Islands |
| Long-tailed Paradigalla* | Warkapi/Arfak Mountains and Fakfak Mountains (where local race may be a separate species). Also known from western Snow Mountains |
| Western Parotia | Warkapi/Arfak Mountains. Also known from Tamrau and Wandammen Mountains |

| | |
|---|---|
| Arfak Astrapia* | Warkapi/Arfak Mountains |
| Grey-banded Munia* | Anggi. Mid-montane areas of Arfak and Tamrau Mountains on the Vogelkop Peninsula |
| Black-breasted Munia | Snow Mountains |
| Snow Mountain Munia | Snow Mountains |
| Olive-crowned Flowerpecker | Warkapi/Arfak Mountains and Sorong. Also known from west Papuan Islands |

## Geelvink Bay Islands (9)

| | |
|---|---|
| Geelvink Pygmy-Parrot* | Biak and Supiori. Also known from Numfor |
| Black-winged Lory* | Biak and Supiori. Also known from Numfor |
| Biak Coucal* | Biak and Supiori |
| Biak Paradise-Kingfisher* | Biak and Supiori |
| Numfor Paradise-Kingfisher | Numfor |
| Biak Monarch* | Biak and Supiori |
| Biak Flycatcher* | Biak and Supiori. Also known from Numfor |
| Long-tailed Starling | Biak and Supiori. Also known from Numfor |
| Biak White-eye* | Biak |

The *beccarii* race of Moluccan Scops-Owl, the *hypoxantha* race of Large-billed Gerygone and the *kordensis* race of Golden Monarch, are considered to be full species by some taxonomists.

## West Papuan Islands (5)

| | |
|---|---|
| Bruijn's Brush-turkey* | Waigeo. Also probably seen on Batanta in 1986 |
| Kofiau Paradise-Kingfisher | Kofiau |
| Black-backed Monarch | Kofiau. Known only from a 1959 specimen |
| Wilson's Bird-of-paradise* | Batanta. Also known from Waigeo |
| Red Bird-of-paradise* | Batanta. Also known from Waigeo and Gemien |

For a full list of the New Guinea Endemics which occur in Irian Jaya, see p. 368.

## Near-endemics

Dusky Scrubfowl (west Papuan Islands and islands in Geelvink Bay), Moluccan Scrubfowl (Misool Island), Wallace's Fruit-Dove, Moluccan King-Parrot*, Violet-necked Lory (west Papuan islands), Olive Honeyeater (west Papuan islands), Little Grassbird, Mistletoebird (Aru Islands).

For a full list of the New Guinea Near-endemics which occur in Irian Jaya see p. 380.

# MICRONESIA

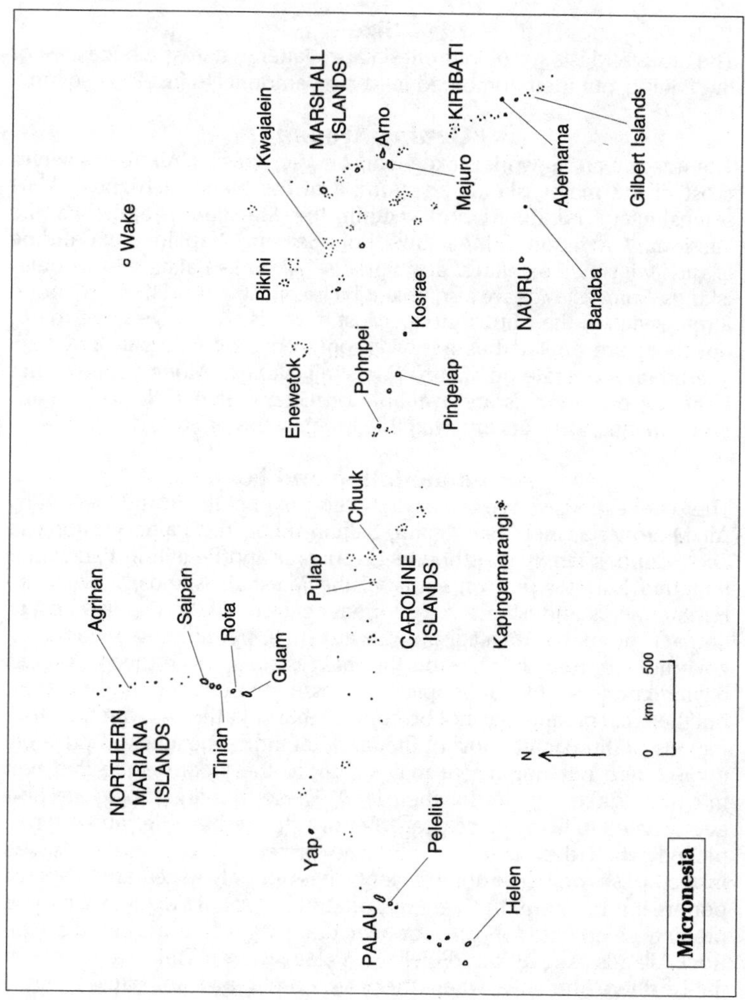


## INTRODUCTION

### Summary

This large group of atolls and islands supports 40 endemics, the majority of which are confined to the Caroline Islands (15), Palau (ten), and the Northern Mariana Islands (eight). While it will be necessary to visit at least seven atolls and islands scattered across a huge part of the northwest Pacific to stand a chance of seeing these endemics, there is an excellent internal air network, all of the atolls and islands are small and fairly easy to get around, and virtually all of the birds can be found without too much trouble. Together with the friendly folk, fantastic coral reefs and often picturesque surroundings, Micronesia has the potential to conjure up a very fine, if expensive, birding trip.

## Size

The atolls and islands of Micronesia are scattered across a huge area of the Pacific, but their combined land area amounts to just 2937 sq km.

## Getting Around

The internal air network is excellent. Air Micronesia ('Air Mike') serves most of the major islands; the Airline of the Marshall Islands (AMI) serves every inhabited atoll within the Marshall Islands; Pacific Missionary Aviation (PMA) links Pohnpei and Yap in the Caroline Islands with their satellites; and Paradise Air links Palau with its outer islands. Some islands are also linked by freight ships and there is a good ferry service in the Chuuk group. Most major islands have good roads, but there are limited bus networks only on Guam, Saipan and Yap. Shared taxis operate on Majuro (Marshall Islands), Moen (Chuuk) and Pohnpei; private taxis are available on Guam, Saipan, Koror (Palau) and Yap; and hire-cars are available on most major islands.

## Accommodation and Food

There are expensive Western-style hotels on all of the islands served by Air Micronesia, including Guam, Saipan, Rota, the Palau group, Yap and Pohnpei; family guesthouses on Angaur and Peleliu in Palau; and thatched huts for rent on some of the Marshall Islands. Few of the remoter atolls and islands have formal accommodation so it is best to contact the mayor or magistrate in advance, by radioing ahead from governor's or tourist offices on the main islands, to arrange to stay as paying guests with local people. It is possible to camp in these places, but the local people may not be comfortable with this. As with the other regions of the Pacific most of the land, including beaches, is privately owned, and pitching a tent may signify to the local people that you intend to stake a claim for their land. These friendly people are also accustomed to living closely together in extended families and are perplexed when they meet people who prefer to sleep under canvas instead of sharing their homes. Hence it is not only necessary to ask for permission to camp, but very important to carefully explain why you prefer to sleep outdoors on your own. Camping is now accepted on the Rock Islands, Angaur and Peleliu in Palau, and on Tinian and Rota in the Northern Marianas, where there are even a few campsites.

A wide range of food is available on major islands, but survival on the outer atolls and islands will probably depend on bananas, breadfruit, coconuts, fresh tuna, rice, tapioca and taro. Beer, usually in the form of Budweiser, is available everywhere except on Chuuk and the Marshall Islands. Local concoctions include tuba, made from coconut sap and yeast, which will probably only appeal to hardened drinkers.

## Health and Safety

Immunisation against hepatitis, polio, typhoid and yellow fever (if arriving on Nauru from an infected country) is recommended. Once there, stick to bottled water and beware of eating poisonous fish, especially in the Marshall Islands.

## Climate and Timing

The peak time to visit Micronesia is between January and March, the coolest, least humid and driest time of year throughout the region, although rain is possible even during this period, especially on the island of Pohnpei, where up to 10 m (33 ft) of rain may fall in 12 months. The main rainy seasons of the island groups within Micronesia fall between June and November. During this time the heat and humidity build up enough to produce stifling conditions from August to December, which is also the typhoon season.

## Habitats

The 2,000 or so atolls and islands of Micronesia are sprinkled liberally across the northwest Pacific in an area the size of the USA. There are many small, low, slender, sparsely vegetated palm-fringed coral cays, which usually occur in circular or horseshoe-shaped chains, known as atolls, as well as some high, forested volcanic islands which rise to 965 m (3166 ft) on Agrihan in the Northern Mariana Islands. The remnant rainforests on such islands are dominated by *Ficus* species and characterised by numerous climbing vines and tree-ferns. Some of these high islands also support large areas of mangrove. Many atolls and some high islands lie next to numerous coral reefs, some of which are amongst the richest on earth. The Mariana Trench, which spans nearly 3000 km and runs parallel to Guam and the Northern Mariana Islands, reaches a depth of 11,022 m (36,161 ft), making it the second deepest ocean trench on earth.

## Conservation

Owing to the small size of the islands, which means many birds survive only in tiny populations, habitat loss and degradation, and some short-sighted introductions, 23 of the species which are endemic or occur regularly in Micronesia are threatened and near-threatened with extinction. Island ecosystems are very fragile. Their avifaunas are particularly susceptible to sudden ecological changes, and events on the island of Guam provide a poignant reminder of what not to do to protect these birds and their habitats in the future. Despite the presence on this island of disease-carrying mosquitoes, introduced birds, mammals and reptiles, widespread habitat degradation, and habitat loss through forest clearance and the effects of the Second World War, most of the birds on Guam were still numerous throughout the island in the late 1960s. However, over the ensuing 20 years they suffered a rapid decline, almost certainly because of the introduction of the brown tree snake, a voracious bird predator. By 1990 the endemic avifauna of the island had been wiped out and most of the near-endemics pushed to the brink of local extinction.

Such mistakes will hopefully not be repeated in the future, but there are still plenty of other problems facing the birds in Micronesia, not least an annual natural increase in the human population of 2.4%. There is barely enough room for the birds now, so how they will survive if the human population continues to grow at such a high rate is a major concern for conservationists.

Despite the vulnerability of many of Micronesia's endemic and near-endemic birds, there are very few managed reserves and only the odd atoll is protected on paper. Even such designations will not protect these low-lying island chains, which rarely reach more than 10 m (33 ft), from rising sea levels. There is little the local governments and ruling bodies can do about this potentially catastrophic problem except lobby those countries from outside the region which may end up being responsible. The same applies to those countries who have carried out numerous nuclear explosions on the atolls of Bikini and Enewetok in the northwestern Marshall Islands. The effects of nuclear tests are difficult to detect, but they may have played their part in the decline of some species up to now, and who knows what their long-term effects will be?

### Bird Species

Over 225 species have been recorded in Micronesia including around 85 breeding species. Non-endemic specialities and spectacular species include Red-tailed and White-tailed Tropicbirds, Masked and Red-footed Boobies, Bristle-thighed Curlew*, Grey-backed and Sooty Terns, Blue-grey and Black Noddies, Crimson-crowned Fruit-Dove and Long-tailed Koel.

### Endemics

A total of 40 species are endemic to Micronesia (compared with 42 in Polynesia), including 15 which occur only on the Caroline Islands, ten which occur only on Palau and eight which are confined to the Northern Mariana Islands and Guam. The Caroline Islands endemics include two monarchs and five white-eyes, the Palau endemics include a fruit-dove, a scops-owl, two white-eyes and a bush-warbler, and the Northern Mariana Islands and Guam endemics include a fruit-dove, a monarch and two white-eyes. Other Micronesian endemics include a scrubfowl, three swiftlets, a kingfisher (which is most likely to be seen on Palau) and two reed-warblers.

### Expectations

It is possible to see virtually all of the endemics and Micronesian Kingfisher on a quick whizz around the Caroline Islands, all of the Palau endemics and Micronesian Kingfisher during a short trip to Peleliu, and all of the Northern Mariana Islands and Guam endemics plus Micronesian Scrubfowl* on a short trip to the three islands of Saipan, Tinian and Rota.

## NORTHERN MARIANA ISLANDS

These high volcanic islands with remnant forests lie in a 650 km long north to south chain. They support five endemics, three species which are shared only with Guam and four other more widespread Micronesian endemics.

### Northern Mariana Islands Endemics

Guam Rail*, Mariana Fruit-Dove*, Tinian Monarch*, Golden White-eye*, Nightingale Reed-Warbler*.

### Northern Mariana Islands and Guam Endemics

Guam Swiftlet, Mariana Crow*, Bridled White-eye.

## Other Micronesian Endemics

Micronesian Scrubfowl*, White-throated Ground-Dove*, Micronesian Myzomela, Micronesian Starling.

## Others

Rufous Fantail.

The island of **Saipan** (122 sq km) is the largest and most populated of the Northern Mariana Islands, and part of the island is full of high-rise resorts which are particularly popular with the Japanese. Micronesian Scrubfowl* (reintroduced), Guam Swiftlet, Micronesian Myzomela and Nightingale Reed-Warbler* occur in the Marpi Commonwealth Forest, which surrounds the radar station at the 287 m (942 ft) summit of Mount Petosukara at the north end of the island. This forest is accessible via the Laderan Tangke Trail, a 3 km long loop. To reach it, turn off Marpi Road on to Matuis Road just past the Hotel Nikko and the trail head is on the left after 2.4 km. Golden White-eye*, which is restricted to Saipan

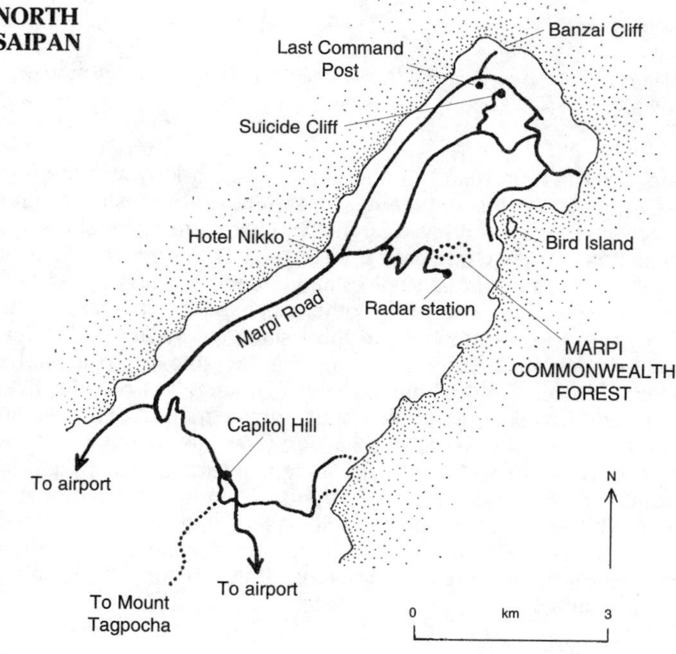


and Aguijan, as well as Rufous Fantail, occur along the Banadero Trail at the top of the 250 m (820 ft) Suicide Cliff nearby. White-throated Ground-Dove*, Mariana Fruit-Dove* and Bridled White-eye also occur on Saipan. Tinian Monarch* is a 'common' single island endemic on the island of **Tinian** (101 sq km), accessible by air from Saipan. Mariana Fruit-Dove*, Guam Swiftlet and Bridled White-eye also occur here. The uninhabited island of **Aguijan** (Agiguan) is accessible by boat (20 minutes) from Tinian with a permit obtainable from the mayor of Tinian. Micronesian Scrubfowl*, White-throated Ground-Dove*, Marian Fruit-

Dove*, Guam Swiftlet, Bridled and Golden* White-eyes, and Nightingale Reed-Warbler* have all been recorded here. Guam Rail*, extinct in the wild on Guam, is being introduced to the island of **Rota** (83 sq km), where Mariana Crow* still survives in large numbers and the *rotensis* race of Bridled White-eye, probably a separate species, occurs on the Sabana Plateau. White-throated Ground-Dove* and Mariana Fruit-Dove* have also been recorded here.

*The rare Micronesian Scrubfowl* is most likely to be seen on the island of Saipan*

**Guam** is the largest island in Micronesia (549 sq km) and the most heavily populated. It is a modern island with high-rise resorts catering for package tourists and has a large US military presence. The stupid introduction of brown tree snake is believed to have been the main factor in the extinction of one single-island endemic (Guam Flycatcher), the extinction in the wild of the other single-island endemic (Guam Rail*), and the extinction on this island of more widespread Micronesian endemics such as Micronesian Scrubfowl*, White-throated Ground-Dove* and Nightingale Reed-Warbler*. It also seems likely that unless the snake is controlled or exterminated most of the remaining birds will also be wiped out, leaving Guam to claim fame as the world's only ornithological desert. Although Micronesian Kingfisher, Micronesian Myzomela, Mariana Crow*, Micronesian Starling and Bridled White-eye are all probably still present, they are no doubt very thin on the ground, hence any birders unfortunate enough to be marooned on this serpent-ridden outpost of the Pacific are unlikely to enjoy themselves.

## PALAU

The independent nation of Palau supports the richest flora and fauna in Micronesia, including ten single-island endemics and Micronesian Kingfisher, all of which can be seen fairly easily on the island of Peleliu. This group of islands lies at the covergence of three major ocean currents and its reefs support a dazzling variety of marine life which survives in 80° F, crystal-clear waters with spectacular drop-offs which are very popular with scuba-divers.

## Palau Endemics
Palau Ground-Dove*, Palau Fruit-Dove, Palau Scops-Owl, Palau Swiftlet, Morningbird, Palau Fantail, Palau Flycatcher, Dusky and Giant* White-eyes, Palau Bush-Warbler.

## Other Micronesian Endemics
Micronesian Scrubfowl*, Micronesian Imperial-Pigeon, Micronesian Kingfisher, Micronesian Myzomela, Micronesian Starling, Caroline Islands White-eye.

## Non-endemic Specialities
Slaty-legged Crake, Nicobar Pigeon*.

## Others
Little Pied Cormorant, Pacific Reef-Egret, Rufous Night-Heron, Yellow Bittern, Buff-banded Rail, Bridled Tern, Oriental Cuckoo (most Oct–Apr), Jungle Nightjar, Common Cicadabird.

## Other Wildlife
Dugong, Pacific island boa, Palau tree snake, saltwater crocodile.

(Other species recorded here include Japanese Night-Heron*.)

All of the Palau endemics, as well as most of the other Micronesian endemics, can be seen with some ease around the small town of Klouklubed on the island of **Peleliu** (62 sq km), despite the fact that most of the forest on this island was burnt to the ground during the Second World War. Take care not to wander off the well-trodden paths here because the countryside is still littered with live ammunition left over from one of the worst battles of the war. Birders who don a snorkel and take a leisurely swim off White and Bloody Beaches on Peleliu may return home with tales of bigeyes, blackfin barracudas and massive

**PELELIU**

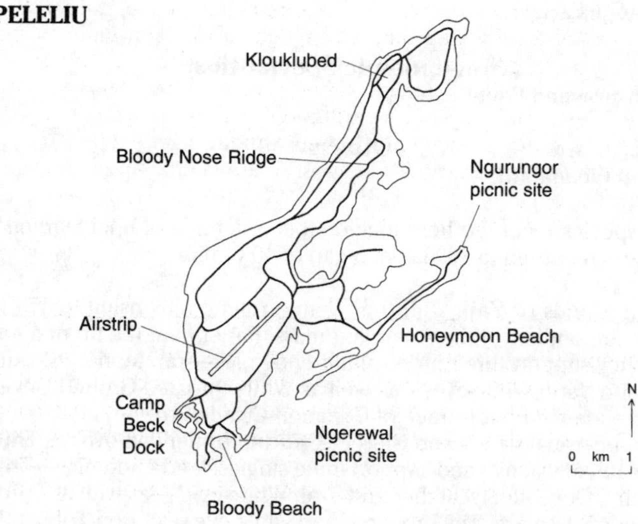

Napoleon wrasses rather than swiftlets and white-eyes, because the reefs which lie off the western shores of the islands in Palau support over 1,400 species of fish and are regarded as one of the world's top scuba-diving destinations. The fantastic coral gardens which adorn the reef have to be seen to be believed, and further afield it is possible to scuba-dive through gigantic chimneys (known as blue holes) in the underwater rocks and across the tops of high underwater cliffs (known as drop-offs). There are also many Second World War wrecks within the inner lagoon around Palau which are equally popular with scuba-divers.

*Accommodation:* Wenty Inn, Peleliu State, Republic of Palau, 96940, is a family guesthouse and allows camping in the grounds.

## CAROLINE ISLANDS

The 600 or so Caroline Islands span nearly 3000 km of the Pacific. They support 15 endemics, and to see all of these it is necessary to visit the islands of Yap, Chuuk and Pohnpei, all of which support three single island endemics each. More widespread Micronesian endemics are also present, but White-throated Ground-Dove* is confined to Yap and Micronesian Kingfisher to Pohnpei.

### Caroline Islands Endemics

Caroline Ground-Dove*, Pohnpei Lorikeet, Caroline Islands Swiftlet, Pohnpei Fantail, Truk* and Yap* Monarchs, Pohnpei and Oceanic Flycatchers, Plain*, Grey, Yap*, Truk* and Long-billed* White-eyes, Caroline Reed-Warbler.

### Other Micronesian Endemics

White-throated Ground-Dove*, Micronesian Imperial-Pigeon, Micronesian Kingfisher, Micronesian Myzomela, Micronesian Starling, Caroline Islands White-eye.

### Non-endemic Specialities

Crimson-crowned Fruit-Dove.

### Others

Common Cicadabird.

(Other species recorded here include the endemic Pohnpei Starling*, which was recorded in 1996 after a gap of 40 years.)

The four islands of **Yap**, with their gentle rolling hills rising to 174 m (571 ft), are outliers of the Asian landmass, rather than the tip of a volcano. They support three single-island endemics—Yap Monarch*, and Plain* and Yap* White-eyes—as well as White-throated Ground-Dove* and the endemic *nesiotis* race of Common Cicadabird.

The numerous islands and islets of **Chuuk**, formerly known as Truk, are volcanically active and support three single-island endemics—Truk Monarch*, Oceanic Flycatcher and Truk White-eye*—as well as Caroline Islands White-eye. The monarch and white-eye occur on Tol South,

**CHUUK**

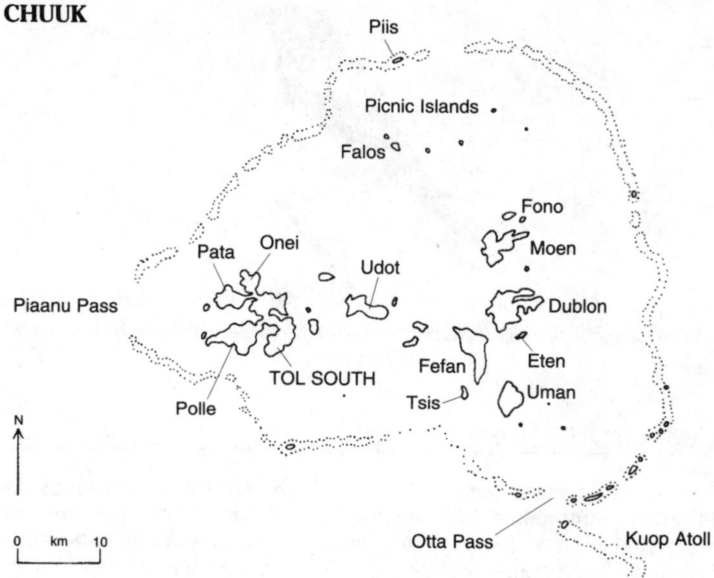


the largest and most populated of the Faichuk Group in the western part of Chuuk Lagoon. Both are most likely to be seen in the forest on Mount Winipot. The island is accessible by boat (one hour) from Moen (Weno), the capital and gateway to Chuuk. There are no cars or accommodation here, but it is possible to trek into the forested interior mountains and to camp with permission of the magistrate. The Chuuk Lagoon is a popular tourist attraction due to the sunken Japanese wartime fleet which lies on its bed and is now an underwater museum.

Five species as well as the endemic *insperatum* race of Common Cicadabird and the endemic *cinereus* race of Grey White-eye are restricted to the island of **Pohnpei** (334 sq km). The endemic Pohnpei Starling* was recorded in 1996, the first record since 1956. Three of the remaining endemics—Pohnpei Fantail, Pohnpei Flycatcher and Long-billed White-eye*—as well as the scarce Micronesian Kingfisher and Caroline Islands White-eye are most likely to be seen in the wet, mossy forests on the slopes of the active volcanic mountains which rise to 791 m (2595 ft) at Ngihneni. These forests are sustained by up to 10 m (33 ft) of rain each year, making this island one of the wettest places in the world. Most of the coastline is surrounded by mangroves and tidal flats, hence there are very few beaches. However, the island, which is accessible by air and sea from Kosrae, is still a popular tourist attraction due to its ruined city.

The endemic *cinerea* race of Grey White-eye occurs on the island of **Kosrae** (109 sq km), one of the least spoiled of the Micronesian islands. It is a high, active volcanic island, rising to 629 m (2064 ft) at Mount Finkol and a popular tourist attraction due to its ruined city. There are a number of trails in to the interior and large areas of mangrove around the coast.

*Accommodation:* hotels (A).

*The black-and-white Yap Monarch* is one of three monarchs which only occur in Micronesia*

## MARSHALL ISLANDS

The group of sparsely vegetated atolls known as the Marshall Islands are still largely untouched by mass tourism. Unfortunately, they are not untouched as far as nuclear testing in the Pacific is concerned, because there have been many nuclear explosions on the outer atolls of Bikini and Enewetok, and missiles are still being tested on Kwajalein. Presumably, most birders will therefore be pleased to hear that there are no endemics. However, there are plenty of seabirds, including Blue-grey Noddy, and shorebirds such as Bristle-thighed Curlew*, even though all seabirds have been heavily predated by the islanders for centuries.

### Non-endemic Specialities

Bristle-thighed Curlew*, Blue-grey Noddy, Long-tailed Koel (Apr–Sep).

### Others

Wedge-tailed Shearwater, Red-tailed and White-tailed Tropicbirds, Masked, Red-footed and Brown Boobies, Great Frigatebird, Pacific Reef-Egret, Grey-tailed and Wandering Tattlers, Sharp-tailed Sandpiper, Pacific Golden-Plover, Mongolian Plover, Great Crested-Tern, Black-naped and Sooty Terns, Brown and Black Noddies, Common White-Tern.

(Other species recorded here include Common (Green-winged) Teal, Northern Pintail, Northern Shoveler, Tufted Duck, Greater Scaup and Micronesian Imperial-Pigeon.)

The gateway to the Marshall Islands is Majuro, which is accessible by air. This 100 km long atoll is the base for a modern settlement where it is possible to hire a car or make use of cheap taxis to bird alongside the atoll's 56 km long road. The 20 or so other inhabited atolls are accessible by air and those that are not may be accessible by boat (ask for details at the hotels). Previously productive atolls beyond Majuro include Likiep (20 hours by boat), Taka (Bristle-thighed Curlews* in the Eluk area, Sooty Terns on Bwokwen and a Black Noddy colony), Bikar (White-tailed Tropicbird and Bristle-thighed Curlew*) and Waatwerik (large Sooty Tern colony).

*Accommodation:* hotels (A).

# ADDITIONAL INFORMATION

## Addresses

The Hawaiian Audubon Society, 850 Richards Street, Suite 505, Honolulu, Hawaii 96813 (tel: 808 528 1432, fax: 808 537 5294) publishes the monthly *Elepaio* journal which covers Micronesia.

The University of Guam, Mangilao, Guam 96913, External Territory of the USA, publishes the *Micronesica* journal.

Micronesian Islands Conservation, Box 159, Kolonia, Pohnpei 96941, Federal States of Micronesia, sells maps with localities of bird colonies for US$12, including postage.

Zegrahm Expeditions Inc., 1414 Dexter Avenue North, #327 Seattle, WA 98109, USA (tel: 206 285 4000 or 1 800 628 8747, fax: 206 285 5037, e-mail: zoe@zeco.com, Website: www.zeco.com).

## Books and Papers

*A Field Guide to The Birds of Hawaii and the Tropical Pacific.* Pratt H D *et al.*, 1987. Princeton University Press.

*Field Guide to the Birds of Palau.* Engbring J, 1988. Koror, Palau: Conservation Office and Bureau of Education.

*A 1991 Survey of the Forest Birds of the Republic of Palau.* Engbring J, 1992. Honolulu: US Fish and Wildlife Service.

*Micronesian Forest Bird Surveys, the Federated States: Pohnpei, Kosrae, Chuuk (Truk) and Yap.* Engbring J *et al.*, 1990. Honolulu: US Fish and Wildlife Service.

*Checklist of the Birds of Micronesia.* Pyle P, Engbring J. Available for US$2 from Hawaiian Audubon Society.

*Micronesian Reef Fishes.* Myers R, 1989. Guam: Coral Graphics.

## MICRONESIAN ENDEMICS (40)

### Northern Mariana Islands (5)

| | |
|---|---|
| Guam Rail* | Rota. This species is being introduced to Rota because it is now extinct in the wild on Guam. As recently as 1981 there were about 2000 wild birds on Guam, but they were wiped out by the brown tree snake which was foolishly introduced |
| Mariana Fruit-Dove* | Saipan, Tinian, Aguijan and Rota |
| Tinian Monarch* | Tinian. 'Common' |
| Golden White-eye* | Saipan and Aguijan. 'Common' on both islands |
| Nightingale Reed-Warbler* | Saipan, Aguijan and Alamagan. 'Common' on Saipan and Alamagan, rare on Aguijan, probably extinct on Pagan and extinct on Guam |

'Rota White-eye*' (*Zosterops rotensis*) is probably a separate species, based on unpublished differences in plumage, vocalisations and behaviour, from Bridled White-eye and is endemic to the Sabana plateau region of Rota.

### Northern Mariana Islands and Guam (3)

| | |
|---|---|
| Guam Swiftlet | Saipan, Tinian, Aguijan and Guam. Scarce |
| Mariana Crow* | Rota and Guam. About 500 birds were |

| | |
|---|---|
| | estimated to be present on Rota in 1993, but less than 50 birds remained on Guam at that time |
| Bridled White-eye | Saipan, Tinian, Aguijan, Rota (scarce on central plateau) and Guam (rare) |

### Northern Mariana Islands and Palau (1)

| | |
|---|---|
| Micronesian Scrubfowl* | Saipan (reintroduced), Aguijan (rare), Sarigan and Guguan (two remote volcanic islands north of Saipan) in the Northern Mariana Islands, and Babelthuap (rare) and Kayangel in Palau. Extinct on Guam |

### Northern Mariana Islands, Guam, Palau and Caroline Islands (2)

| | |
|---|---|
| Micronesian Myzomela | Larger Northern Mariana Islands, Guam (rare), Palau, Yap, Chuuk, Pohnpei and Kosrae |
| Micronesian Starling | Widespread to Kosrae, but rare on Guam |

### Northern Mariana Islands and Yap (Caroline Islands) (1)

| | |
|---|---|
| White-throated Ground-Dove* | Saipan south to Rota, and Yap. Extinct on Guam |

### Guam, Palau and Pohnpei (Caroline Islands) (1)

| | |
|---|---|
| Micronesian Kingfisher | Guam (rare), Palau ('common' on larger islands) and Pohnpei (scarce) |

### Palau (10)

| | |
|---|---|
| Palau Ground-Dove* | Babelthuap (rare) and 'Rock Islands' south of Koror, including Peleliu |
| Palau Fruit-Dove | 'Common' on larger islands including Peleliu |
| Palau Scops-Owl | 'Common' on larger islands including Peleliu |
| Palau Swiftlet | 'Common' throughout |
| Morningbird | 'Common' from Babelthuap south to Peleliu |
| Palau Fantail | 'Common' from Babelthuap south to Peleliu |
| Palau Flycatcher | 'Common' on larger islands including Peleliu |
| Dusky White-eye | 'Common' on larger islands including Peleliu |
| Giant White-eye* | 'Common' on Peleliu and Urukthapel |
| Palau Bush-Warbler | 'Common' from Babelthuap south to Peleliu |

### Palau and Caroline Islands (1)

| | |
|---|---|
| Caroline Islands White-eye | Widespread on Palau, Chuuk and Pohnpei |

### Palau, and Caroline and Marshall Islands (1)

| | |
|---|---|
| Micronesian Imperial-Pigeon | Palau, Yap, Chuuk (rare), Pohnpei, Kosrae and Marshall Islands (rare) |

## Caroline Islands (15)

| | |
|---|---|
| Caroline Ground-Dove* | Chuuk (rare) and Pohnpei (mostly in mangroves) |
| Pohnpei Lorikeet | Pohnpei: lowlands |
| Caroline Islands Swiftlet | Chuuk, Pohnpei and Kosrae |
| Pohnpei Fantail | Pohnpei |
| Truk Monarch* | Chuuk. Known from most islands and some islets, but rare and most likely to be seen on Tol South (three to four birds in 1993) |
| Yap Monarch* | Yap |
| Pohnpei Flycatcher | Pohnpei |
| Oceanic Flycatcher | Chuuk |
| Pohnpei Starling* | Pohnpei. A specimen was obtained in 1996, the first confirmed record since 1956 |
| Plain White-eye* | Yap |
| Grey White-eye | Pohnpei and Kosrae |
| Yap White-eye* | Yap. 'common' |
| Truk White-eye* | Chuuk. Occurs on four islands in the Faichuk Group, especially on Tol South in the forest on Mount Winipot |
| Long-billed White-eye* | Pohnpei. Scarce |
| Caroline Reed-Warbler | Widespread, including Chuuk and Pohnpei |

The *nesiotis* race of Common Cicadabird, which is endemic to Yap, the *insperatum* race of Common Cicadabird, which is endemic to Pohnpei, the *cinereus* race of Grey White-eye, which is endemic to Pohnpei and the *cinerea* race of Grey White-eye, which is endemic to Kosrae, are all considered to be a full species by some taxonomists.

## Extinct Endemics

| | |
|---|---|
| Wake Island Rail | Became extinct on Wake around 1944 |
| Kosrae Crake | Became extinct on Kosrae around 1828 |
| Guam Flycatcher | Became extinct on Guam in the 1980s or 1990s |
| Kosrae Starling | Became extinct on Kosrae around 1828 |

## Near-endemics

Grey-backed Tern, Blue-grey Noddy, Crimson-crowned Fruit-Dove (Caroline Islands).

# NEW CALEDONIA

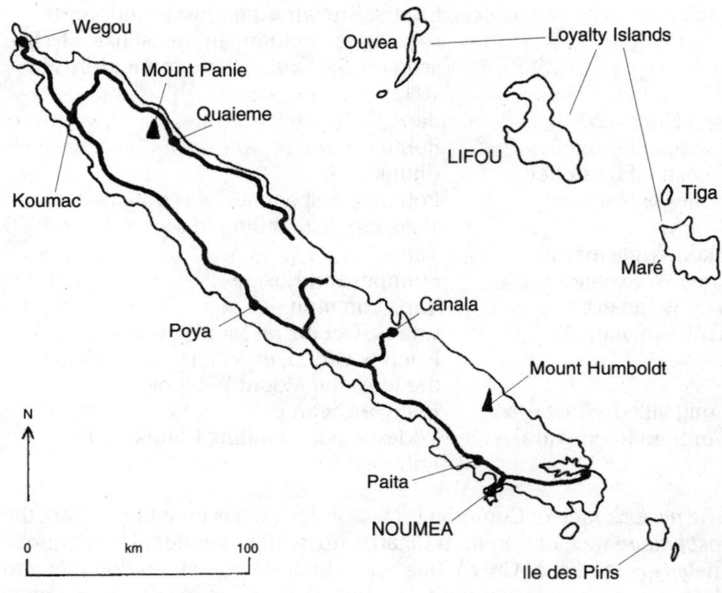


## INTRODUCTION

### Summary

This archipelago, which is an Overseas Territory of France, supports 19 known surviving endemics, all of which are fairly easy to see within 70 km of the modern capital, Noumea. These endemics include the island's major avian attraction, the unique Kagu*, which is most likely to be seen with assistance from the friendly local Ornithological Society.

### Size

At 19,105 sq km New Caledonia is seven times smaller than England and 36 times smaller than Texas. The main island is about 400 km long and 50 km wide.

### Getting Around

A package tour from Australia or New Zealand is the cheapest way to visit New Caledonia, especially in November, which is in the low season. A vehicle is almost essential on the main island, Grand Terre, especially if time is short, as there is only an irregular, unscheduled bus network away from the capital, Noumea. Most roads and tracks are passable in 2WD during the dry season (May–November) but even a 4WD may not be good enough to get to the best sites in the wet season (Dec–Apr). There are regular flights to Lifou, Ile des Pins, Ouvea and Tiga, as well as the east and west coasts of the main island. To book in advance, contact Air Caledonie, BP 212, Noumea (tel: 25 2177, fax: 25 0326). Lifou can also be reached by ferry.

## Accommodation and Food

New Caledonia is an Overseas Territory of France and has a modern infrastructure. Most hotels are very expensive, especially in and around the capital, Noumea, and particularly during the high seasons of May, mid-August to mid-September and mid-December to the end of January. However, there is a wide range of other accommodation to choose from, including small country hotels (*relais*), thatched beach bungalow resorts (*gites*) which also cater for campers, youth hostels (*auberge de jeunesse*) and campsites. A wide range of food is available in Noumea, from couscous, French bread and pizza to the delights on offer in expensive French restaurants, but away from the capital and other large towns local dishes include bougna, a mixture of vegetables and coconut with chicken, pork or seafood wrapped in banana leaves.

## Health and Safety

Immunisation against hepatitis, polio, typhoid and yellow fever (if arriving from an infected country) is recommended.

## Climate and Timing

The peak time to visit New Caledonia is during November and December. This may be the beginning of the wet season, but most birds are breeding at this time of the year and therefore easier to locate. When the wet season reaches its peak in February and March it may be very difficult to get around, even with a 4WD. The cyclone season usually lasts from December to March. It is generally drier and cooler from May to November.

## Habitats

New Caledonia is a land of rugged mountains, rising to 1639 m (5377 ft) at Mount Panie. The northeast side of the main island, Grand Terre, is particularly high, wild and wet, whereas the southwest lies in a drier rainshadow where there are lowland swamps and savanna. Only a little primary rainforest, watered with the help of the southeast tradewinds, remains, but there are still extensive areas of mangrove along the west coast. Many coastal hills are pine-clad and form a strange backdrop to a tropical coast liberally sprinkled with palm-fringed beaches, and a 1600 km long coral reef which surrounds the main island.

## Conservation

Much of the original tropical rainforest has been cleared, leaving an eroded, degraded landscape, full of mountain slopes left scarred by many mineral mines, and littered with patches of secondary growth. Fortunately, several parks and reserves have been established to help protect the best remaining natural habitats, and, in turn, the ten threatened species which occur on New Caledonia. However, three of these species may already be extinct and a lot more needs to be done to protect the remaining species, even those which have yet to meet the criteria for threatened status.

### Bird Families

One bird family is endemic to New Caledonia and is represented by its sole member, the Kagu*.

### Bird Species

Over 90 species have been recorded on New Caledonia. Non-endemic specialities and spectacular species include Metallic Pigeon, Red-fronted Parakeet, Fan-tailed Gerygone, Dark-brown Honeyeater, Cardinal Myzomela, Streaked Fantail, Southern Shrikebill, New Caledonian Flycatcher, Melanesian Cuckoo-shrike, Long-tailed Triller and Blue-faced Parrotfinch, while possible seabirds on a pelagic trip include Tahiti and Gould's Petrels, Red-tailed Tropicbird, Fairy Tern* and Common White-Tern.

### Endemics

A total of 22 species (50% of the landbirds) are endemic to New Caledonia, two of which are confined to the Loyalty Islands and three of which may be extinct. The endemics likely to be seen on a short trip include Kagu*, two pigeons, four honeyeaters, three white-eyes and a parrotfinch.

### Expectations

It is possible to see about 60 species during a trip lasting four to seven days, including all of the known surviving endemics, and more if a pelagic trip is included.

## NOUMEA

The cosmopolitan capital of New Caledonia, at the south end of the main island, lies next to some excellent birding sites where most of the endemics occur, including Cloven-feathered Dove*, which is more likely to be seen here than in Parc Provincial de la Riviere Bleue, and New Caledonian Grassbird, which is only likely to be seen here.

### Localised New Caledonian Endemics

Cloven-feathered Dove*, New Caledonian Grassbird.

### Other New Caledonian Endemics

White-bellied Goshawk, New Caledonia Imperial-Pigeon*, Horned Parakeet*, New Caledonian Myzomela, Barred Honeyeater, Yellow-bellied Robin, New Caledonian Whistler, New Caledonian Crow, New Caledonian Cuckoo-shrike, Striated Starling, Green-backed White-eye, Red-throated Parrotfinch.

### Non-endemic Specialities

Fan-tailed Gerygone, Dark-brown Honeyeater, Streaked Fantail, Southern Shrikebill, New Caledonian Flycatcher, Melanesian Cuckoo-shrike, Long-tailed Triller.

### Others

Australasian Grebe, Little Pied Cormorant, White-faced Heron, Rufous Night-heron, Whistling Kite, Swamp Harrier, Brown Goshawk, Grey-

## NOUMEA

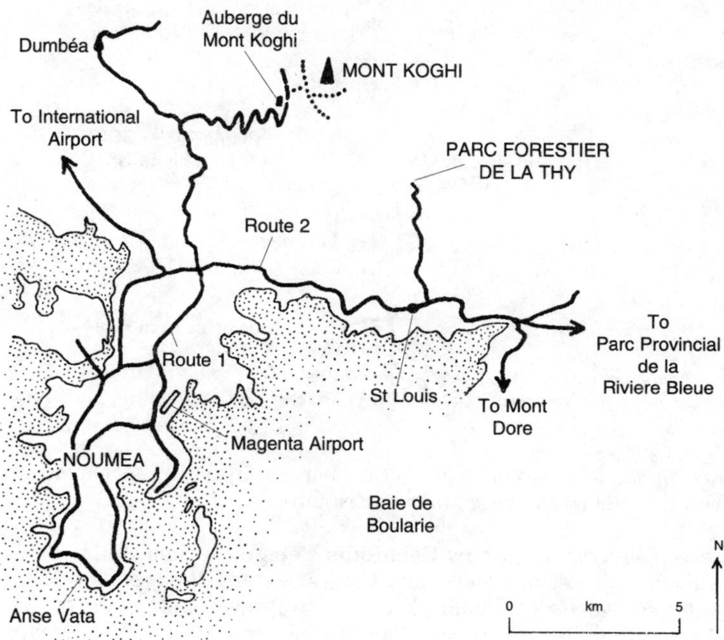


tailed and Wandering Tattlers, Black-naped Tern, Metallic Pigeon, Fan-tailed Cuckoo, Shining Bronze-Cuckoo, White-rumped Swiftlet, Rufous Whistler, Grey Fantail, Silver-eye.

(Other species recorded here include Bristle-thighed Curlew*. Introduced species include Spotted Dove, Common Myna and Common Waxbill.)

Noumea is accessible by air via La Tontouta Airport, which is 45 km northwest of town. Several endemics are easier to see on **Mont Koghi**, a forest-clad hill 18 km north of town, than in Parc Provincial de la Riviere Bleue (p. 286), including White-bellied Goshawk, Cloven-feathered Dove* and New Caledonian Grassbird. To reach this site, turn east at the bottom of the hill at the north end of Col de Tonghoue, 13 km north of Noumea off the road to Dumbea. From this turning it is 5 km up a steep, winding road to a car park, restaurant and viewpoint. Bird around the Auberge du Mont Koghi at dawn, checking fruiting trees for Cloven-feathered Dove*, and then walk the Point de Vue Trail above the cafe which passes through forest and, after a few kilometres, an area of ferns and long grass where the localised New Caledonian Grassbird occurs. The roadside up to the car park at Mont Koghi is also worth birding. Other sites worth birding in and around Noumea if time is available include the bay near Magenta Airport and at Anse Vata, where Bristle-thighed Curlew* and both tattlers have been seen, and the open savanna woodland and pools to the north of town, which are good for waterbirds.

**MONT KOGHI**

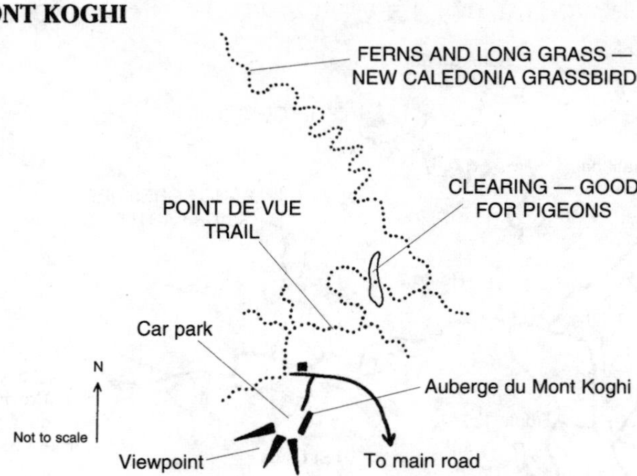


*Accommodation:* Hotel Tontouta (at the main airport). Hotel Laperouse. Youth hostel (Auberge Jeunesse de Noumea).

Seabirds recorded on **New Caledonia Pelagics** include Tahiti, Black-winged (Nov–Mar), Gould's and Cook's* Petrels, Wedge-tailed Shearwater, Red-tailed Tropicbird, Masked and Brown Boobies, Silver Gull, Great Crested-Tern, Roseate, Black-naped, Bridled and Fairy* Terns, Brown and Black Noddies, and Common White-Tern. It is possible to charter boats in Noumea. Seawatching from land is unlikely to provide even a flavour of such birds because the island is encircled by a reef which deters birds from entering the offshore coastal lagoon.

Cloven-feathered Dove* occurs in **Parc Forestier de la Thy**, which is situated off the main road between Noumea and Parc Provincial de la Riviere Bleue. To visit this reserve it is necessary to obtain a permit in advance from Service des Forets et du Patrimoine Naturel. The rough entrance track leads north just east of the St Louis Mission, which is 15 km east of Noumea. Bird the trails beyond the park sign, 7 km from the main road. Other species recorded here include Buff-banded Rail, Metallic Pigeon, Fan-tailed Gerygone, New Caledonian Myzomela, Barred Honeyeater, Yellow-bellied Robin, New Caledonian Whistler, Streaked Fantail, New Caledonian Crow, Melanesian and New Caledonian Cuckoo-shrikes, Striated Starling, Green-backed White-eye and Red-throated Parrotfinch. (Red Junglefowl has been introduced). There is no accommodation, but camping is allowed.

## PARC PROVINCIAL DE LA RIVIERE BLEUE

The kauri forest within this 90 sq km reserve resounds with the very loud pre-dawn barks and yelps of the unique night-heron-sized Kagu*, the sole member of its family. This great rarity is doing so well here now that it is possible to see as many as ten different birds in a day! The site's star bird is ably supported by all of the remaining known surviving endem-

## PARC PROVINCIAL DE LA RIVIERE BLEUE

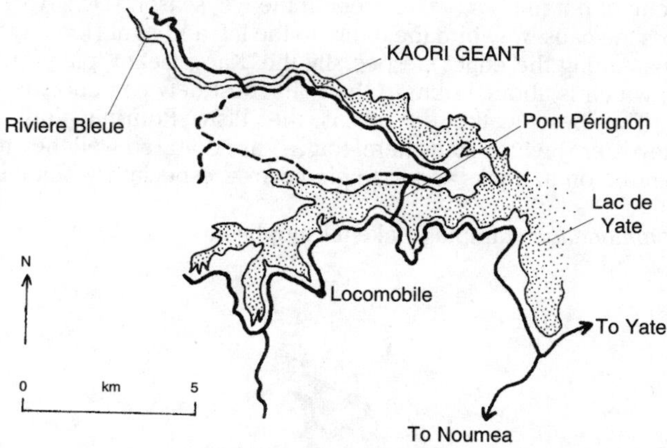


ics except New Caledonian Grassbird, and these include the rare Crow Honeyeater*.

To visit this park it is necessary to obtain a permit in advance from Service des Forets et du Patrimoine Naturel, and seeing a Kagu* and the other endemics is most likely with the assistance of Monsieur Serge Sirgouant, Societe Caledonienne d'Ornithologie, 21 rue G. Clemenceau, BP 4338-98847 Noumea Cedex, Nouvelle-Caledonie. Write well in advance to make the necessary arrangements. Weekends are best avoided and prepare for chilly nights if camping in the reserve.

### Localised New Caledonian Endemics

Kagu*, New Caledonian Friarbird, Crow Honeyeater*.

### Other New Caledonian Endemics

White-bellied Goshawk, Cloven-feathered Dove*, New Caledonian Imperial-Pigeon*, Horned Parakeet*, New Caledonian Myzomela, Barred Honeyeater, Yellow-bellied Robin, New Caledonian Whistler, New Caledonian Crow, New Caledonian Cuckoo-shrike, Striated Starling, Green-backed White-eye, Red-throated Parrotfinch.

### Non-endemic Specialities

Red-fronted Parakeet, Fan-tailed Gerygone, Dark-brown Honeyeater, Streaked Fantail, Southern Shrikebill, New Caledonian Flycatcher, Melanesian Cuckoo-shrike, Long-tailed Triller.

### Others

Little Pied Cormorant, Whistling Kite, Metallic Pigeon, Emerald Dove, Rainbow Lorikeet, Fan-tailed Cuckoo, Shining Bronze-Cuckoo, Glossy and White-rumped Swiftlets, Sacred Kingfisher, Rufous Whistler, Grey Fantail.

Turn north off the main road to Yate at Col de Ouenarou in response to the signpost 35 km east of Noumea. From the main road it is 2.5 km to the HQ. Ask here for details of recent sightings of Kagus*, but brush up your French first because few people here speak English. From the HQ it is 9.5 km to Pont Perignon, a causeway across Lac de Yate which is difficult, if not impossible, to cross in the wet season (Dec–Apr). Once across the causeway bird the tracks to the left and right (looking out for Kagus* along the edges), especially the 'Kaori Geant' picnic site section, which is about 18 km to the right (best between culverts 12 and 14). The best walking track is the Piste Pourina Trail (Crow Honeyeater*) which starts here. Kagus* are doing so well they regularly venture on to tracks and in to picnic area, especially when it is wet.

*Accommodation:* camping (take all supplies).

*The unique Kagu* is New Caledonia's major avian attraction*

## LIFOU

This small forested island is in the Loyalty Group to the east of the main island. It supports two endemic white-eyes, which are easy to see, as well as Red-bellied Fruit-Dove, which is rare on the main island, Cardinal Myzomela, which does not occur on the main island, and distinct races of Sacred Kingfisher, New Caledonian Flycatcher, Long-tailed Triller, Striated Starling and Silver-eye.

### Lifou Endemics

Large Lifou (scarce) and Small Lifou White-eyes.

### Other New Caledonian Endemics

Striated Starling (*Lifou* race).

### Non-endemic Specialities

Red-bellied Fruit-Dove, Cardinal Myzomela, New Caledonian Flycatcher (*Lifou* race), Melanesian Cuckoo-shrike, Long-tailed Triller (*Lifou* race).

### Others

Brown Goshawk, Emerald Dove, Shining Bronze-Cuckoo, Sacred Kingfisher (*Lifou* race), Pacific Swallow, Blue-faced Parrotfinch, Silver-eye (*Lifou* race).

Lifou is accessible by air and sea from Noumea. By flying to the island and back it is possible to 'clean-up Lifou' on a day-trip from Noumea. The flight schedules normally allow for eight hours on the island, but this is likely to be seven hours too long, because all of the species listed above can be found within a kilometre of the airstrip. Take some food and water for yourself, and some cigarettes and/or alcohol for the Melanesian people who live there. On receipt of such a gift they will almost certainly allow you to roam freely through their gardens and coconout groves. Otherwise stick to the road.

*Accommodation:* gites in We, the main town accessible by bus from the airstrip.

## ADDITIONAL INFORMATION

### Addresses

Le Chef, Service des Forets et du Patrimoine Naturel, BP 256, Noumea. It is best to write in advance for permits which can then be collected from the office at the northern end of Rue du General Gallieni on arrival. The street number on the gatepost is 2BIS.

The Royal Australasian Ornithologists Union (see p. 176 for address) publishes the *Emu* journal which covers New Caledonia.

Office du tourisme de Noumea, BP 2828, Noumea (fax: 687 287585).

### Books and Papers

*Oiseaux de Nouvelle Caledonie et des Loyautes* (two volumes). Hannecart F, Letocart Y.

### NEW CALEDONIAN ENDEMICS (22)
### Main Island (20)

| | |
|---|---|
| White-bellied Goshawk | Mt Koghi and Parc Provincial de la Riviere Bleue |
| New Caledonian Rail* | Possibly extinct. Last collected in 1890, but local reports suggest it may not be extinct |
| Kagu* | Parc Provincial de la Riviere Bleue. About 200 birds were present here in 1992. Also occurs on Mts Do and Nakada, and Pic Ningua. In the early 1990s 403 birds were counted in Southern Province and 88 in Northern Province |
| Cloven-feathered Dove* | Widespread, but most likely on Mt Koghi, since only about 30 birds are present in Parc Provincial de la Riviere Bleue. This species is more 'common' in the north and it also occurs on Ile des Pins |
| New Caledonian Imperial-Pigeon* | Mt Koghi and Parc Provincial de la Riviere Bleue. Also occurs on Ile des Pins |
| Horned Parakeet* | Mt Koghi and Parc Provincial de la Riviere Bleue. Also occurs on Ouvea (northwest Loyalty Islands) |
| New Caledonian Lorikeet* | Possibly extinct. A possible sighting in for- |

| | |
|---|---|
| | est west of Mount Panie in 1980 suggests this species may still survive, but the last sighting before that was in 1913. Otherwise only known from two females collected in 1859 |
| New Caledonian Owlet-Nightjar* | Possibly extinct. Known only from a specimen collected near Noumea in 1880 and a single bird killed by a hunter in the Paita region in 1960 |
| New Caledonian Myzomela | Widespread |
| New Caledonian Friarbird | Parc Provincial de la Riviere Bleue. Also known from Mare and Lifou (Loyalty Islands) |
| Crow Honeyeater* | Parc Provincial de la Riviere Bleue. Also occurs in the Mt Humboldt region |
| Barred Honeyeater | Widespread in montane forests |
| Yellow-bellied Robin | Widespread |
| New Caledonian Whistler | Widespread |
| New Caledonian Crow | Widespread |
| New Caledonian Cuckoo-shrike | Widespread in montane forests |
| Striated Starling | Widespread |
| Green-backed White-eye | Widespread |
| New Caledonian Grassbird | Mt Koghi |
| Red-throated Parrotfinch | Widespread |

## Loyalty Islands (2)

| | |
|---|---|
| Large Lifou White-eye | Lifou |
| Small Lifou White-eye | Lifou |

## Near-endemics

Australasian Bittern*, Whistling Kite, Painted Buttonquail, Silver Gull, Fairy Tern*, Red-bellied Fruit-Dove (including Loyalty Islands), Red-fronted Parakeet, Fan-tailed Gerygone, Dark-brown Honeyeater, Rufous Whistler, Streaked Fantail, Southern Shrikebill, New Caledonian Flycatcher (including Loyalty Islands), Melanesian Cuckoo-shrike (including Loyalty Islands), Long-tailed Triller.

# NEW ZEALAND

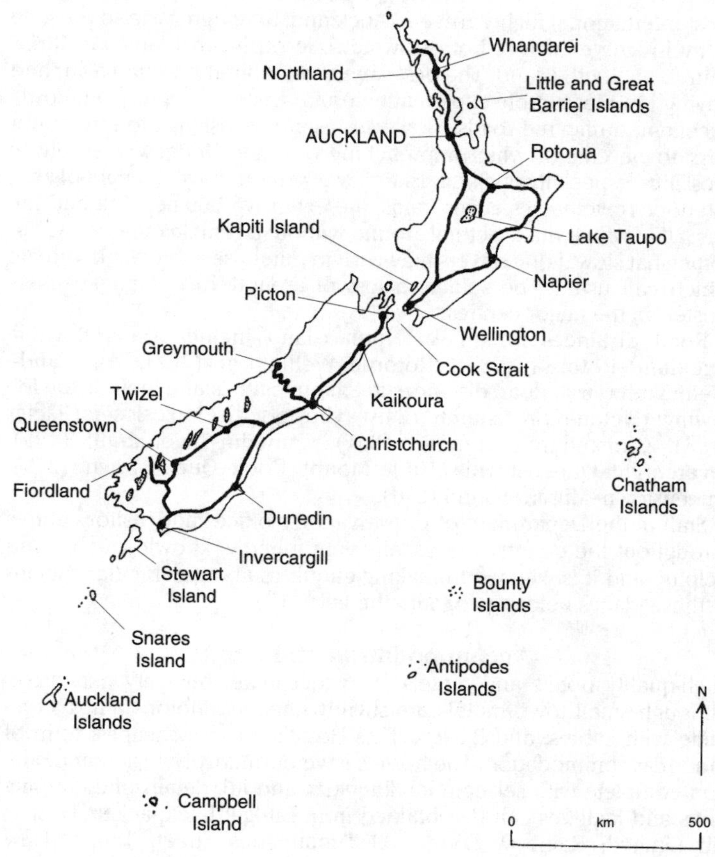


## INTRODUCTION

### Summary

Scenically spectacular New Zealand is a wonderful country to go birding in. There are few native landbirds, some of which now only exist in translocated populations on predator-free offshore islands, and too many introduced species, but the high total of 43 endemics which occur on the main islands includes three kiwis, Kea* and Kokako*, as well as two penguins and five shorebirds, including the unique Wrybill*. Most sites and the important offshore islands are easily accessible, hence it is possible to see as many as 42 of these 43 endemics on a short trip, and a rich diversity of seabirds in the process. Some of the seabirds are visitors from their breeding colonies on the remote Chatham and Subantarctic Islands, which also support a further 18 endemics, including Shore Plover*, but these islands are much more difficult to get to.

## Size

At 265,150 sq km New Zealand is twice the size of England and 2.6 times smaller than Texas.

## Getting Around

Most international flights arrive in Auckland, although it is also possible to fly in to Wellington, both of which are on North Island, or Christchurch on South Island. The best way to get around is to hire a car and driving is a pleasurable experience in such a scenic country on mostly excellent, traffic-free roads. However, useful roadsigns are rare and it pays to be careful when approaching one-lane bridges and railway crossings, especially on South Island, where trains have the right-of-way! InterCity Travelpasses cover trains, the extensive bus network and ferries, all of which make getting around without a vehicle rather easy, but somewhat slow. Long stayers may wish to purchase a 'buyback' vehicle which can usually be sold at a loss of around 10% at Backpackers Hostels in the major centres.

Road distances in km on North Island include the following: Auckland–Rotorua (233), Rotorua–Wellington (462), Auckland–Wellington (660). Road distances in km on South Island include the following; Picton–Christchurch (349), Greymouth–Franz Josef Glacier (188), Christchurch–Dunedin (361), Dunedin–Invercargill (195), Invercargill–Queenstown (104), Mount Cook–Queenstown (270), Queenstown–Milford Sound (270).

Staff at the Department of Conservation's offices and visitor centres throughout the country are usually very friendly, knowledgeable and helpful, and it is well worth making enquiries about particular species at these places before going into the field.

## Accommodation and Food

High-quality hotels and motels are widespread, but very expensive, although small town motels are slightly cheaper. Motor Camps, complete with cabins, and Backpackers Hostels are the cheapest form of indoor accommodation. The hostels have dormitory-style accommodation complete with self-catering kitchens, and full details of their locations and facilities can be obtained from Budget Backpackers Hostels NZ Limited, Rainbow Lodge, 99 Titiraupenga Street, Taupo, New Zealand. There are also plenty of campsites, some of which are state-of-the-art, complete with cooking facilities, showers and laundrettes. It is difficult to rough it in New Zealand.

The food is generally excellent and many restaurants operate a 'bring your own' policy, so take beer and wine if you wish to wash down your food with alcohol.

## Health and Safety

Squeamish travellers can delight in the fact that there is no need to visit their local health centre for numerous jabs before setting off to New Zealand. This is virtually a disease-free country, although it is wise to treat stream water because it may harbour the giardia parasite in some areas. Arguably, the biggest health danger in New Zealand, at least between November and March, is the strong sunlight, hence it would be wise to take plenty of the appropriate sun block. There are also a few little critters to cope with, especially sandflies, which are ubiquitous on South and Stewart Islands where it is advisable to wear long trousers, especially in Fiordland National Park. Fortunately, the poisonous katipo spider is rarely encountered.

## Climate and Timing

The peak time to visit New Zealand is during the austral spring in November and December, although the warm sunny weather at this time usually lasts until March. Birders keen to see Royal Albatrosses* at their only mainland breeding colony in the world should avoid September and early November because the reserve near Dunedin on South Island is closed at this time. While spring may be warm and sunny, and it is fairly mild all year round, it can still be very wet, especially in mountainous areas where heavy downpours, snow and gales sweep in unexpectedly all year round. This is especially true of the west coast of South Island, which is one of the wettest places in the world and may receive up to 7.6 m (25 ft) of rain in one year. Two days without rain in this part of the country and the locals start talking about a possible drought.

## Habitats

New Zealand, especially South Island, is a wild, scenically spectacular country with volcanoes, snow-capped peaks, glaciers, fiords, huge high-altitude lakes, tussocklands, primeval *podocarpus* forests, wide valleys with braided rivers, coastal cliffs, beaches and mudflats. The volcanic mountains of North Island rise to 2752 m (9029 ft) at Mount Ruapehu in Tongariro National Park south of Lake Taupo. South Island is dominated by the Southern Alps, which run parallel to the west coast and rise much higher to 3754 m (12,136 ft) at Mount Cook, the highest peak between New Guinea and the Andes. These magnificent mountains divide the rugged west coast from the rolling sheep-grazed hills to the east.

This lofty landmass which rises out of the Pacific Ocean has a wide continental shelf, but because it lies within a subtropical ocean convergence zone the coastal waters are extremely rich, and therefore attract a diverse array of seabirds.

## Conservation

Some of the world's most famous extinct birds include the Moas, flightless giants which roamed New Zealand without fear of predation before the Polynesian settlers arrived and killed every last one of them. These settlers also burnt large areas of forest, but they were nowhere near as destructive as the Europeans, mainly British, who arrived in the nineteenth century, seemingly determined to fell as much forest as possible, drain all the wetlands they could, and shoot everything with feathers that came near enough. Shooting for the pot led to serious declines in many species and was probably the sole reason for the extinction of the Auckland Islands Merganser. The Europeans also brought predators such as rats, cats, dogs, stoats and ferrets with them, the first mammalian predators to be let loose on the mainland, and they decimated the populations of ground-dwelling flightless native landbirds, as well as seabirds and others. The last remaining Stephen Island Wren, for example, was killed by a lighthouse keeper's cat in 1894. Such wanton vandalism and totally thoughtless introductions resulted in the extinction of at least eight (possibly ten) species and several subspecies, and led to the virtual extinction of many more endemics, including Shore Plover*, Stitchbird* and Saddleback*, many of which now only survive in mainly translocated populations on predator-free offshore island sanctuaries.

A lot of effort has been put in since those bad old days to protect those species which survived the onslaught, but it is only possible to get a taste of what birding must have been like before the Europeans arrived on a couple of offshore islands. Nevertheless, the authorities responsible for conserving the natural habitats and the birds that inhabit them in New Zealand deserve a lot of credit for trying to redress the balance. Few countries in the world can boast about designating 10% of their land as National Parks. Now the government, developers and conservationists must work together to tackle equally serious modern-day problems such as proposed hydroelectric power schemes which threaten specialist species such as Blue Duck* and Black Stilt*, and knuckle down to the task of improving a far less impressive statistic—58 of the birds which regularly occur in New Zealand are threatened or near-threatened with extinction, one of the highest totals in the world.

## Bird Families

Three families are unique to New Zealand: Kiwis (three species), New Zealand Wrens (two species) and Wattlebirds (two species).

## Bird Species

Over 320 species have been recorded in New Zealand, not including over 30 species which have been introduced. The vast majority of the birds which occur regularly are non-passerines and there are only about 40 breeding landbird species.

Non-endemic specialities and spectacular species include a superb assortment of seabirds such as Little Penguin, Wandering*, Royal*, Shy, Grey-headed* and Buller's* Albatrosses, Antarctic and Hall's* Giant-Petrels, Cape, Mottled, Cook's*, Pycroft's*, Parkinson's* and Westland* Petrels, Buller's*, Fluttering and Hutton's* Shearwaters, White-faced Storm-Petrel and Common Diving-Petrel, as well as other more widespread species such as Australasian Bittern*, Buff-banded Rail, Spotless Crake, Double-banded Plover, Black-fronted Dotterel, White-fronted and Fairy* Terns, Red-fronted Parakeet, Long-tailed Koel, Morepork and Sacred Kingfisher. In addition, such species present in the Subantarctic Islands include King Penguin and Light-mantled Albatross.

The birding experience in New Zealand is tainted by the presence of too many introduced species, and these include Mute and Black Swans, Brown and California Quails, Spotted Dove, Eastern Rosella, Sulphur-crested Cockatoo, Rook, Australasian Magpie, Eurasian Blackbird, Song Thrush, Common Starling, Common Myna, Eurasian Skylark, Dunnock, Chaffinch, European Greenfinch, European Goldfinch, Common Redpoll and Yellowhammer, many of which are, unfortunately, much more common than the native species.

## Endemics

A total of 61 species are endemic to New Zealand. An amazing 43 of the 88 species breeding on the main islands are endemic (49%), and the remaining 18 endemics are confined to the Chatham (seven) and Subantarctic Islands. Endemics which are relatively easy to see on a trip covering North, South, Tiritiri Matangi and Stewart Islands include Brown* and Little Spotted* Kiwis, Fiordland Crested* and Yellow-eyed* Penguins, Rough-faced*, Bronze* and Spotted Shags, Blue Duck*,

Weka*, Takahe*, South Island and Variable Oystercatchers, Black Stilt*, Red-breasted Dotterel*, Wrybill*, Black-fronted Tern*, Kea*, Common Kaka*, Rifleman, Stitchbird*, Tui, Kokako*, Saddleback*, Whitehead, Yellowhead* and Pipipi.

On the Chatham Islands the endemics include Chatham* and Pitt* Shags, Chatham Snipe* and Shore Plover*. Species restricted to the Subantarctic Islands include Royal Penguin, Flightless Teal* and Subantarctic Snipe*.

### Expectations

It is possible to see between 90 and 100 native species (and over 20 introduced species) during a well-prepared and thorough three-week trip to the main islands, including as many as 42 of the 43 endemics!

## *NORTH ISLAND*

## AUCKLAND

A good selection of species can be seen in and around this city on the shores of the Hauraki Gulf, including four of the five shorebirds which are endemic to the main islands.

### New Zealand Endemics

Spotted Shag, Paradise Shelduck, South Island (most Jan–Jul) and Variable Oystercatchers, Red-breasted Dotterel*, Wrybill* (most Feb–Jul), Red-billed Gull, Grey Gerygone, Tui, Tomtit.

### Non-endemic Specialities

White-fronted Tern.

### Others

Australian Gannet, Little Pied Cormorant, Grey Teal, Pacific Black Duck, Australian Shoveler, Royal Spoonbill (Feb–Jul), Swamp Harrier, Buff-banded Rail, Spotless Crake, Purple Swamphen, Rufous-necked Stint, Sharp-tailed Sandpiper, White-headed Stilt, Pacific Golden-Plover, Double-banded Plover, Kelp Gull, Caspian Tern, Morepork, Welcome Swallow, Silver-eye.

(Other species recorded here include Australasian Bittern* and Marsh Sandpiper. Introduced species include Spotted Dove and Common Myna.)

The best birding site near the city is **Mangere Sewage Works**. From the airport take the George Bolt Memorial Drive, then turn left at its junction with McKenzie Road, then left again on to Ascot Road, right on to Greenwood Road and left on to Island Road, which leads to the visitors' car park. Collect the free entry permit at the adjacent office, then proceed by vehicle through the complex to the track which leads northwest alongside the sewage ponds. Shorebirds, including Wrybills*, roost quite regularly on the shingle banks of these ponds. Further along this track, at the end of Puketutu Island, look west for roosting Royal Spoonbills. Further out of Auckland, about 30 km northwest of the city via State Highway 16, there is a 2,000-strong Australian Gannet colony at **Muriwai Beach**. This is also a good site for Red-breasted Dotterel*.

*The unique Wrybill* is one of New Zealand's eight endemic shorebirds, five of which occur on the main islands*

From Auckland it is also possible to take organised boat trips out to the **Hauraki Gulf**, where the possibilities include Little Penguin, Wandering*, Royal* and Yellow-nosed (Feb–Jul) Albatrosses, Cook's* (Oct–Mar), Pycroft's* (Oct–Mar) and Great-winged (May–Dec) Petrels, Broad-billed and Fairy Prions, Parkinson's Petrel* (Dec–May), Buller's* (Sep–May) and Little Shearwaters, White-faced Storm-Petrel (Aug–Apr) and Common Diving-Petrel. Most boats depart from the wharves near the Ferry Building on the waterfront, and the best day-trips are run by the Fullers Cruise Centre (tel: 09 377 1771). They operate the *Supercat* which departs on Tuesdays, Thursdays and weekends, and usually visits Great Barrier Island, which supports Brown Teal*, breeding colonies of Cook's* and Parkinson's* Petrels, and Whitehead.

## TIRITIRI MATANGI ISLAND

All five localised New Zealand endemics which occur on this island have been introduced, as they have been on a number of other predator-free offshore islands. Birders on short trips to New Zealand who wish to see as many endemics as possible must visit one of these islands to see such great rarities as Stitchbird* and Saddleback*, which have long been extinct on the mainland, and most choose Little Barrier Island in the Hauraki Gulf (see p. 298). There are plenty of good birds there, but as with Kapiti Island (p. 307) it is necessary to write months in advance for a permit; there are no birds there which cannot be seen on Tiritiri Matangi or elsewhere in New Zealand (Kakapos* are out of bounds), and neither Little Spotted Kiwi* or Takahe* are present. Hence Tiritiri Matangi, which can be visited without obtaining a permit in advance, is *the* offshore island to visit in New Zealand.

### Localised New Zealand Endemics

Little Spotted Kiwi*, Brown Teal*, Takahe*, Stitchbird*, Saddleback*.

### Other New Zealand Endemics

New Zealand Pigeon, New Zealand Bellbird, Tui, New Zealand Robin, Whitehead.

### Non-endemic Specialities

Cook's* (Oct–Mar) and Parkinson's* (Dec–May) Petrels, Red-fronted Parakeet.

### Others

Little Penguin, Great-winged Petrel (May–Dec), Fluttering Shearwater, Common Diving-Petrel, Australian Gannet, Spotless Crake, Purple Swamphen, Shining Bronze-Cuckoo (Oct–Feb), Grey Fantail, Australasian Pipit.

(Introduced species include Brown Quail and other species which may be introduced in the future include Tomtit and Fernbird.)

There are several regular boats to the island, including those operated by Hibiscus Coast Charters (tel: 09 424 5561, fax: 09 424 5510) which leave from Gulf Harbour Marina, north of Auckland, every Thursday and Sunday. Boats can also be chartered. The Department of Conservation boat to Little Barrier Island may also stop here. For further details of boat times and accommodation, contact The Wardens, Tiritiri Matangi Island, Private Bag, DOC, Auckland (tel: 09 479 4490). There are only about 20–25 Little Spotted Kiwis* on the island, but they can be seen by day and night (torch filters are provided), and are most likely to be seen along the Kawerau Track, along with Stitchbird*. Like the other two species of kiwi they are attracted to sniffing and snorting noises, but extremely wary.

*Accommodation:* (B), bookable in advance through the wardens.

*The Saddleback* is one of two surviving members of the wattlebird family, which is endemic to New Zealand*

## LITTLE BARRIER ISLAND

This forested predator-free 30 sq km offshore island in the Hauraki Gulf rises to 700 m (2297 ft) and supports an excellent selection of endemics, including Stitchbird* and Saddleback*, but, unfortunately, the introduced population of Kakapos* inhabit remote heavily forested areas which are not usually accessible to the visiting public. Boat trips to and from the island, which is about 20 km offshore, also offer the opportunity to see some rare seabirds, including Pycroft's Petrel*.

To visit this island it is necessary to book at least eight months in advance via the Department of Conservation.

### Localised New Zealand Endemics

Brown Teal*, Common Kaka*, Stitchbird*, Saddleback*.

### Other New Zealand Endemics

New Zealand Pigeon, Rifleman, Grey Gerygone, New Zealand Bellbird, Tui, Tomtit, New Zealand Robin, Whitehead.

### Non-endemic Specialities

Cook's* (Oct–Mar), Pycroft's* (Oct–Mar) and Parkinson's* (Dec–May) Petrels, Buller's Shearwater* (Sep–May), Red-fronted Parakeet, Long-tailed Koel (Oct–Mar).

### Others

Little Penguin, Hall's Giant-Petrel*, Fairy Prion, Cape (Feb–Jul) and Great-winged (May–Dec) Petrels, Flesh-footed (Nov–Apr), Fluttering and Little Shearwaters, White-faced Storm-Petrel (Aug–Apr), Common Diving-Petrel, Australian Gannet, Little Black Cormorant, Shining Bronze-Cuckoo (Oct–Feb), Morepork, Grey Fantail, Silver-eye.

### Other Wildlife

Bottle-nosed dolphin, hammerhead shark, minke whale, tuatara (the closest living relative to the dinosaurs).

(Other species present on this island include Yellow-fronted Parakeet*, Kakapo* and Kokako*.)

Details of boat trips to the island can be obtained from the Department of Conservation when arranging visits. Access is restricted to a small part of the island, but most of the landbirds are common and occur in and around the warden's garden. However, the Summit Track and Tirikawa Stream are the best sites for Stitchbird* and Saddleback*. It is possible to volunteer for a fortnight's work on the Kakapo Supplementary Feeding Programme (transport, accommodation and food provided) by contacting the Department of Conservation in Auckland.

*Accommodation:* bunkhouse.

A few Shore Plovers*, one of the world's rarest shorebirds which is otherwise confined to the virtually inaccessible island of Rangatira in the Chatham Islands, were translocated to **Motuora Island** in the Hauraki Gulf in the mid-1990s, and a few birds have moved to the mainland.

## NORTHLAND

There are a number of excellent birding sites on the peninsula north of Auckland where it is possible to see Brown Teal* and Kokako*, as well as a Black-fronted* and Fairy* Terns.

### Localised New Zealand Endemics

Brown Teal*, Kokako*.

## NORTHLAND

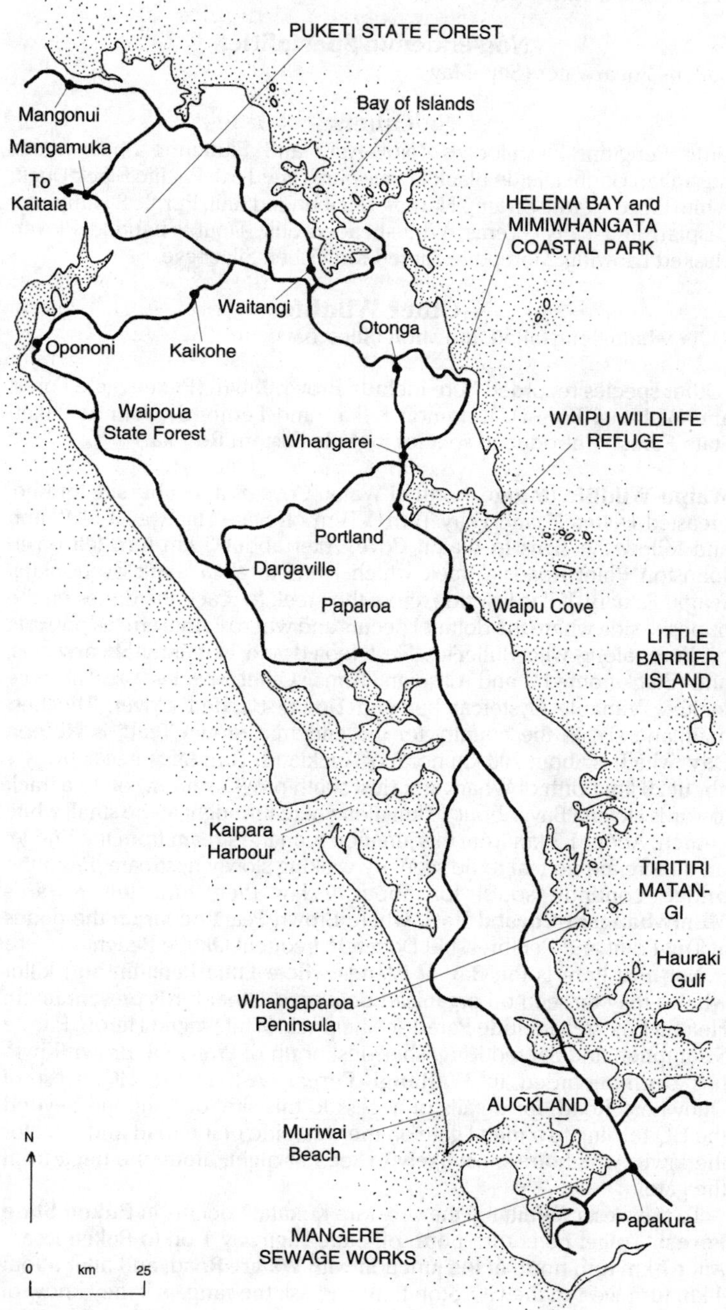
PUKETI STATE FOREST
Bay of Islands
Mangonui
Mangamuka
To Kaitaia
HELENA BAY and MIMIWHANGATA COASTAL PARK
Waitangi
Otonga
Opononi
Kaikohe
Waipoua State Forest
WAIPU WILDLIFE REFUGE
Whangarei
Portland
Dargaville
Paparoa
Waipu Cove
LITTLE BARRIER ISLAND
Kaipara Harbour
TIRITIRI MATAN-GI
Hauraki Gulf
Whangaparoa Peninsula
AUCKLAND
Muriwai Beach
N
Papakura
MANGERE SEWAGE WORKS
0 km 25

## Other New Zealand Endemics
Paradise Shelduck, Variable Oystercatcher, Red-breasted Dotterel*, Black-fronted Tern* (Apr–Aug), Grey Gerygone, Tui.

## Non-endemic Specialities
Buller's Shearwater (Sep–May).

## Others
Little Penguin, Flesh-footed (Nov–Apr) and Fluttering Shearwaters, Australian Gannet, Little Black Cormorant, Grey Teal, Pacific Black Duck, White-faced Heron, Swamp Harrier, Buff-banded Rail, Purple Swamphen, Caspian and Fairy* Terns, White-headed Stilt, Double-banded Plover, Masked Lapwing, Morepork, Sacred Kingfisher, Silver-eye.

## Other Wildlife
Killer whale, long-tailed and short-tailed bats.

(Other species recorded here include Brown Kiwi* (Puketi State Forest and Waitangi Forest), Common Kaka* and Fernbird (both at Puketi State Forest). Introduced species include Eastern Rosella.)

**Waipu Wildlife Refuge**, north of Waipu Cove, is a reliable site for Red-breasted Dotterel* and Fairy Tern*. Turn off State Highway 1 at Waipu and follow the signs to Waipu Cove. After about 3 km turn left on to Johnston Point Road, a track which leads to a car park overlooking Waipu Estuary. If it is low tide, cross the creek to reach the dunes on the opposite side where the dotterel occurs and where Fairy Tern* is possible offshore, along with Buller's*, Flesh-footed and Fluttering Shearwaters, and Black-fronted* and Caspian Terns. Other species present here include Variable Oystercatcher and Double-banded Plover. The best mainland site in the country for the endemic Brown Teal* is **Helena Bay**, which is about 200 km north of Auckland. Turn off State Highway 1 about 20 km north of Whangarei (just south of Whakapara) on to a track towards Helena Bay. About 19 km along here turn right at the small white church. About 1.7 km from this junction scan the stream from the bridge, or, if there are no teal to be seen, try walking slowly upstream. From the bridge continue south for about 6 km then turn left towards **Mimiwhangata Coastal Park** where Brown Teal* occur on the ponds at Trig Point and Red-breasted Dotterel* frequent Okupe Beach.

North of here is the Bay of Islands where Little Penguin and killer whales may be seen on organised boat trips. Other birds present in the Helena Bay area include Paradise Shelduck, White-faced Heron, Purple Swamphen and Sacred Kingfisher. Just north of Waitangi, Brown Kiwi* has been recorded in **Waitangi Forest**. Ask at the HQ, west of Ouewhero Road, for details of access to this site, or continue beyond the HQ turning to a metal gate on the west side of the road and look for the kiwis, which are most likely to seen at night, along the track from the gate.

To the west of Waitangi the very rare Kokako* occurs in **Puketi State Forest**. To get here, turn north off State Highway 1 on to Puketi Road. After 7 km turn north at the junction with Waiare Road, and after about 4 km turn west to the HQ. Stop here and ask the rangers if they know of any Kokako territories. In the mid-1990s there was a reliable spot on the Takapau Kauri Track which leads north halfway along Puketi Road and

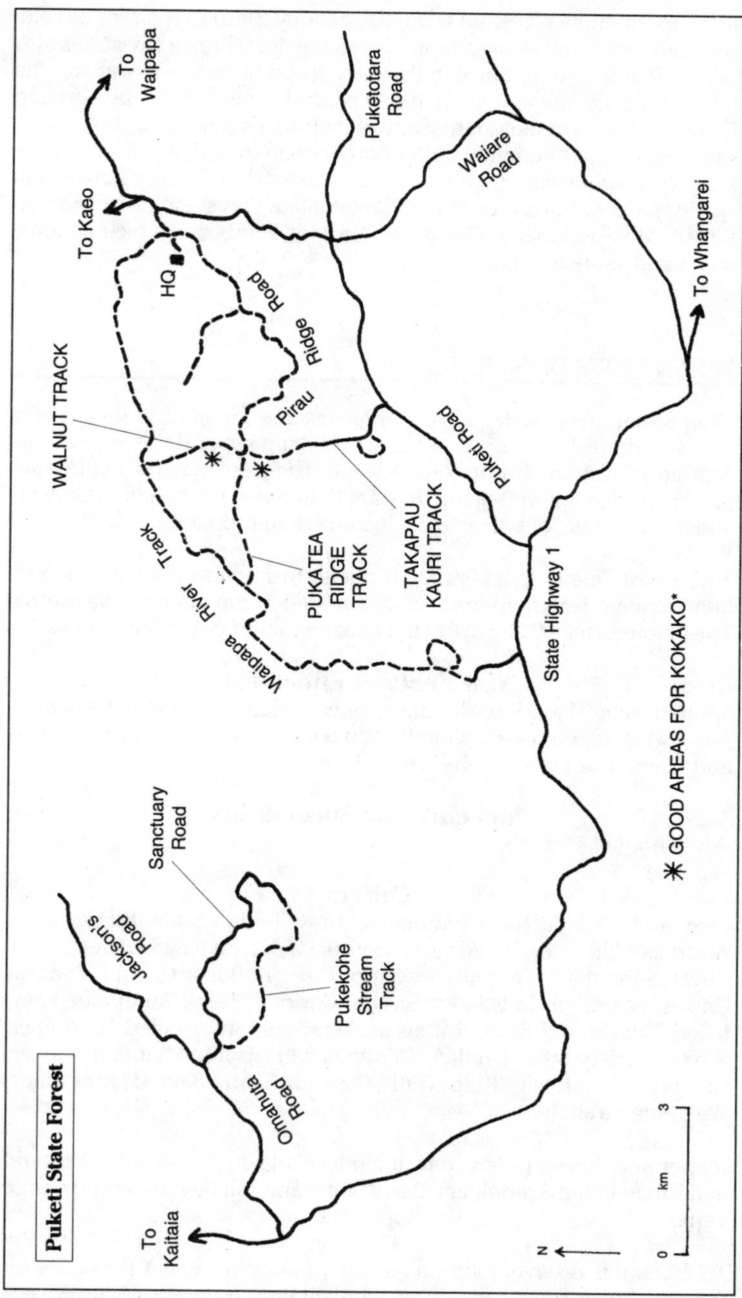


is also accessible via the Pirau Ridge Road, a track which leads west from the HQ. The spot was 40 m or so along the Takapau Kauri Track from its junction with Pirau Ridge Road. Another spot worth trying lies along the Walnut Track to the north of the Pirau Ridge–Takapau Kauri Track. Aim to be at either of these sites as soon after dawn as possible, listen for the fluty song and scour the canopy for the Jay-sized, but elusive, bird which rarely flies more than a few feet. Brown Kiwi* has also been recorded here, but is only likely to be seen while walking the tracks in the Omahuta Road part of the forest at night. Both the kiwi and Kokako* are extremely rare and difficult to find here, so birders on short trips would be much better off concentrating their efforts for the kiwi on Stewart Island (p. 320) and the Kokako* at Pureora Forest Park (p. 304). Other birds recorded at Puketi State Forest include Common Kaka*, Morepork, Grey Gerygone, Tui and Fernbird, as well as long-tailed and short-tailed bats.

## MIRANDA WILDLIFE RESERVE

The coastal marshes, lagoons, mangroves and mudflats in this reserve on the Firth of Thames southeast of Auckland support the largest concentration of shorebirds in New Zealand. The great majority of birds are present during the winter and they are dominated by Bar-tailed Godwits and Red Knots, but they also include Red-breasted Dotterel* and Wrybill*.

The best time to visit Miranda is one to two hours either side of high tide, hence it is wise to contact the warden at the Miranda Naturalists Trust Centre (tel: 09 232 2781) in advance to find out the tide times.

### New Zealand Endemics

Spotted Shag, Paradise Shelduck, South Island Oystercatcher (most Jan–Jul), Red-breasted Dotterel*, Wrybill* (most Feb–Jul), Red-billed and Black-billed (most Feb–Jul) Gulls.

### Non-endemic Specialities

White-fronted Tern.

### Others

Pied and Little Black Cormorants, Grey Teal, Pacific Black Duck, Australian Shoveler, White-faced Heron, Pacific Reef-Egret, Great Egret, Royal Spoonbill (Feb–Jul), Swamp Harrier, Baillon's and Spotless Crakes, Bar-tailed Godwit, Far Eastern Curlew*, Terek Sandpiper, Grey-tailed Tattler, Red Knot, Rufous-necked Stint, Sharp-tailed Sandpiper, White-headed Stilt, Pacific Golden-Plover, Double-banded Plover, Greater Sandplover, Kelp Gull, Caspian Tern, Sacred Kingfisher, Welcome Swallow.

(Other species recorded here include Hudsonian Godwit*, Pectoral and Broad-billed Sandpipers, Black Stilt*, and White-winged and Fairy* Terns.)

To reach this reserve, follow signs for Thames from near Papakura on State Highway 1 and look out for the Miranda Naturalists Trust Visitor Centre on the west side of the road about 4 km south of Kaiaua. Miranda is a large reserve where the shorebirds can be hard to pin down, especially at low tide, hence it is best to call in at the Visitor Centre to ask for the latest information on their feeding and roosting habits before getting stuck in to the birding. If the Visitor Centre is

## MIRANDA WILDLIFE RESERVE

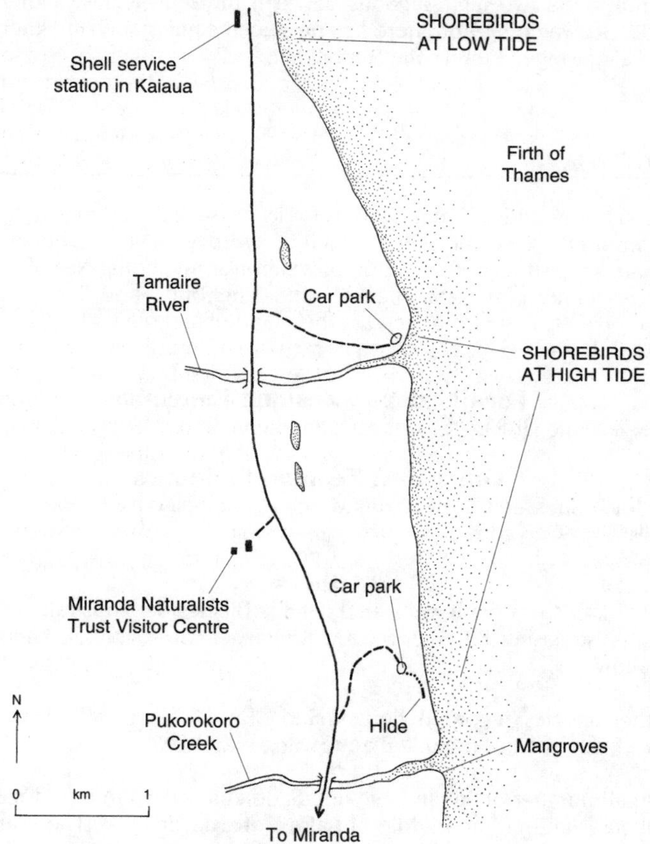


closed, check the usual high tide roost sites a couple of kilometres north and south of here. Red-breasted Dotterel* occurs most regularly at the roost site to the north, near the mouth of the Tamaire River, but the majority of other birds tend to favour the one to the south, where there is a hide 200 m beyond the car park. The mangroves at the mouth of Pukorokoro Creek are also worth a look. If it is low tide try the shore opposite the Shell service station in Kaiaua.

*Accommodation:* Visitor Centre (B).

Across the Coromandel Peninsula from Miranda near the coastal town of **Tairua** there is a reserve at Opoutere Beach which was established to protect breeding Variable Oystercatchers and Red-breasted Dotterels*.

The localised Fernbird, as well as New Zealand Grebe*, Australasian Bittern*, Australian Shoveler, New Zealand Scaup, Buff-banded Rail, Baillon's and Spotless Crakes, Black-fronted Dotterel and Black-fronted Tern* (Apr–Aug) occur on and around the **Matata Lagoons** which lie near the village of Matata alongside the Bay of Plenty, about 70 km east of Tauranga on State Highway 2. Check the marshy vegetation surrounding the two large lagoons between the road and sea for Fernbird*. Seawatching from here has produced some good birds, including Great-winged Petrel (May–Dec).

## ROTORUA

The lakes around Rotorua, famous for its geysers, hot springs and boiling mud pools, as well as the stench of hydrogen sulphide hanging in the air, support a good selection of waterbirds, including New Zealand Grebe* and Australasian Bittern*, and Stitchbird* and Saddleback* have recently been introduced to the island of Mokoia in the middle of Lake Rotorua.

### Localised New Zealand Endemics

New Zealand Grebe*, Stitchbird*, Saddleback*.

### Other New Zealand Endemics

Paradise Shelduck, New Zealand Scaup, Red-billed and Black-billed Gulls, Grey Gerygone.

### Others

Little Black Cormorant, Grey Teal, Pacific Black Duck, Australian Shoveler, Australasian Bittern*, Sacred Kingfisher, Grey Fantail, Welcome Swallow.

(Other species recorded here include Brown Kiwi* and Kokako*. Introduced species include Black Swan.)

A small number of Stitchbirds* and Saddlebacks* were introduced to Mokoia Island, in the middle of **Lake Rotorua**, in 1994. The island is accessible on organised boat trips from the waterfront. One of the best areas for waterbirds such as New Zealand Grebe* is at the south end of Lake Rotorua, which can be reached by driving through the Government Gardens near the town centre. Once there, scan the shore and small islands behind the Bath House-Polynesian Pools complex. New Zealand Grebe* also occurs, along with Australasian Bittern*, on **Lakes Rotoiti** (viewable from State Highway 33 just south of Okere Falls) and **Rotoma**. Rotoehu Forest, between Lakes Rotoiti and Rotoehu (turn off State Highway 30 towards Rotoma Hot Springs) may be worth a look if time permits, as Brown Kiwi* and Kokako* may still occur here.

## PUREORA FOREST PARK

The ancient podocarpus forest in and around this park is the best area in New Zealand to see the endemic Kokako*, a very rare Jay-sized semi-flightless bird which runs along high canopy branches and glides between trees rather like turacos. There are plenty of other more wide-

**PUREORA FP**

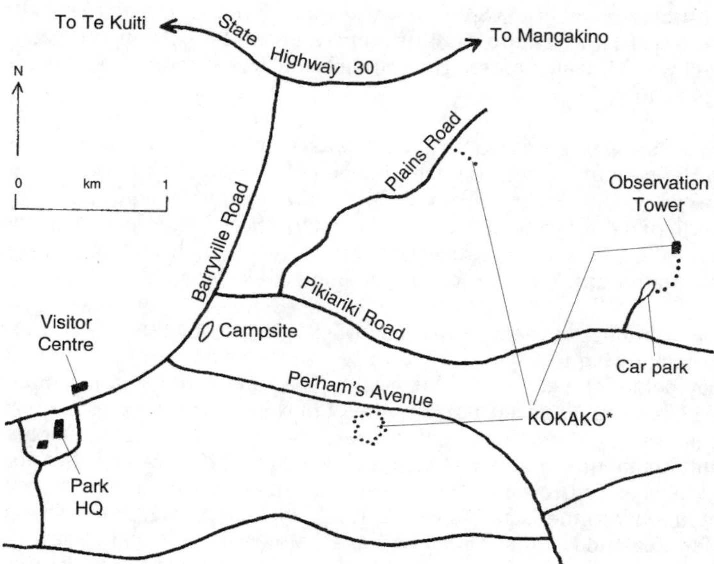


spread endemics here, including Common Kaka* which can be tricky to find elsewhere.

## Localised New Zealand Endemics

Common Kaka*, Kokako*.

## Other New Zealand Endemics

New Zealand Falcon*, New Zealand Pigeon, Yellow-fronted Parakeet*, Rifleman, Grey Gerygone, New Zealand Bellbird, Tui, Tomtit, New Zealand Robin, Whitehead.

## Non-endemic Specialities

Long-tailed Koel (Oct–Mar).

## Others

Shining Bronze-Cuckoo (Oct–Feb), Morepork, Sacred Kingfisher, Grey Fantail, Silver-eye, Australasian Pipit.

(Other species recorded here include Brown Kiwi*, but this species is only present in restricted areas.)

Between Te Kuiti and Mangakino on State Highway 30, turn south on to Barryville Road to reach the HQ and Visitor Centre (tel: 08 134 8773) where the friendly rangers are usually happy to divulge the latest Kokako* localities. Be prepared to return at dawn the following day, for these elusive birds are almost impossible to see at any other time. Otherwise, bird the Ngaherenga Campsite, Plains Road (a bird was seen regularly at dawn 1.3 km along here in late 1996), Perham's Avenue and Pikiariki Road, where there is an excellent observation tower.

*Accommodation:* Tokoroa, Waitangi.

Australasian Bittern*, Spotless Crake and Fernbird occur along the shores of **Lake Taupo**, east of Pureora Forest Park. Scan from State Highway 41, which passes close to the south shore between Waihi and Tokaanu.

State Highway 4 south to Wellington passes close to one of the best sites in the country for the very rare, endemic Blue Duck*, the antipodean answer to the 'Andean' Torrent Duck. Drive towards Raetihi and 5 km north of there turn west to Orautoha on the Ohura Road. About 11.5 km along here the road crosses a white bridge, after which it runs alongside the **Manganui A Te Ao River** which the ducks inhabit.

For a number of years a stray Blue Duck* (this specialist usually sticks to fast-flowing rocky rivers) has appeared somewhat irregularly in the bay behind the kitchen building of the Waikaremoana Motor Camp in **Te Urewara National Park** northeast of Napier. This species has also been recorded on Hopuruahine Stream between Lake Waikaremoana and Ruatahuna, in this vast national park (tel: 06 837 3803). Other possiblities at Te Urewara, most of which have been seen along the one-hour walk to the Lake Waikareiti Track, include New Zealand Scaup, New Zealand Falcon*, Common Kaka*, Morepork, Rifleman, New Zealand Robin and Whitehead. South of the park the small **Lake Tutira**, alongside State Highway 2, about midway between Wairoa and Napier, supports New Zealand Grebe* and other waterbirds.

## NAPIER

This small town lies next to the Ahuriri Estuary which supports a fine selection of waterbirds, and close to Cape Kidnappers which supports the largest mainland colony of Australian Gannets.

### New Zealand Endemics

New Zealand Scaup.

### Non-endemic Specialities

White-fronted Tern.

### Others

Australian Gannet (most Oct–Mar), Little Pied Cormorant, Australian Shoveler, Royal Spoonbill (Feb–Jul), Rufous-necked Stint, Sharp-tailed Sandpiper, White-headed Stilt, Pacific Golden-Plover, Double-banded Plover, Black-fronted Dotterel, Masked Lapwing, Kelp Gull, Caspian Tern.

Bird the Westshore Wildlife Reserve and the Ahuriri Estuary Wildlife Refuge, both of which are on the **Ahuriri Estuary** at the northern edge of Napier next to State Highway 2. There is a hide near the car park at Westshore, where birding can also be good alongside Watchman Road which crosses the reserve, and from the causeway across the estuary (Embankment Road). About 7,500 pairs of Australian Gannets and a small colony of White-fronted Terns are present at **Cape Kidnappers** between October and March. The cape is accessible via an 8 km long walk along the beach from Clifton, 24 km south of Napier (begin walk at least three hours after high tide and return no later than 1.5 hours after low tide); via tractor-trailers run by Gannet Beach Adventures (tel: 06 875 0898) which depart from Charlton Road, Te Awanga, 21 km south of Napier; via 4WD buses run by Gannet Safaris (tel: 06 875 0511) which departs from Summerlee Station, just past Te Awanga; and via boats run by Kidnappers Sea Escape (tel: 06 875 0556) which depart from Te Awanga.

Between Napier and Wellington, Black-fronted Dotterel occurs on the shingle banks of the **Manawatu River** near Palmerston. From Woodville, head east on State Highway 3 through Manawatu Gorge and turn left 3 km after the Ashhurst Junction on to Ruakawa Road which leads down to the river. The **Manawatu Estuary**, southwest of Palmerston, supports other shorebirds including Grey-tailed Tattler. Turn off State Highway 1 at Foxton, about 19 km north of Levin, towards Foxton Beach and walk down to the estuary from the Motor Camp. The **Taranaki Peninsula** on the west shore of North Island is a good place to seawatch from and it is possible to hitch rides on trawlers operating out of nearby New Plymouth to look for such pelagic species as White-bellied Storm-Petrel, as well as cetaceans which may include the endemic Hector's dolphin.

## KAPITI ISLAND

Almost all of the 1,000 or so surviving Little Spotted Kiwis* are on this island, together with a number of other introduced rarities, including Weka*, Takahe* and Kokako*, which, at the very least, puts it on a par with the island of Tiritiri Matangi (p. 297). However, unlike Tiritiri Matangi, permission to visit this island is very difficult to obtain.

### Localised New Zealand Endemics

Little Spotted Kiwi*, Weka* (*greyi* race), Takahe*, Common Kaka*, Stitchbird*, Kokako*, Saddleback*.

### Other New Zealand Endemics

Tui, New Zealand Robin, Whitehead.

### Non-endemic Specialities

Red-fronted Parakeet, Long-tailed Koel (Oct–Mar).

Kapiti Island is 10 km off Paraparaumu Beach northwest of Wellington. To attempt to arrange a visit, write at least eight months in advance to the New Zealand Department of Conservation, stressing the need to stay at least one night on the island, as the kiwi is most likely to be seen during the hours of darkness.

## *COOK STRAIT*

The 17 km wide Cook Strait which separates North Island from South Island is an excellent place for seabirds. Up to six species of albatross, along with Buller's Shearwater*, may be seen from the Wellington–Picton vehicle-ferry, but such a selection and better views are more likely from trawlers based in Wellington.

### New Zealand Endemics

Spotted Shag, Red-billed and Black-billed Gulls.

### Non-endemic Specialities

Grey-headed* and Buller's* Albatrosses, Buller's Shearwater* (Sep–May).

### Others

Little Penguin, Wandering*, Royal*, Black-browed (most May–Sep) and Shy Albatrosses, Antarctic and Hall's* Giant-Petrels, Cape Petrel, Fairy Prion, Flesh-footed (Nov–Apr), Sooty, Fluttering and Hutton's* Shearwaters, White-faced Storm-Petrel (Aug–Apr), Common Diving-Petrel, Australian Gannet, Kelp Gull, Brown Skua (Aug–Apr).

### Other Wildlife

Common, dusky and Hector's dolphins, killer whale.

It is fairly easy to arrange a trip on a trawler, but the waters of the Cook Strait are rarely smooth, hence birders who suffer from seasickness may prefer to stick to the vehicle-ferry and hope for better views of the seabirds elsewhere. The ferry, which sails five times each day and takes between 1.5 and 3 hours, leaves Wellington at 0130, 0930, 1430, 1730 and 2030, and Picton at 0530, 1030, 1330, 1830 and 2130. Morning sailings are usually the best for seabirds, hence it would be wise to head south from Wellington on the 0930 and north from Picton on the 1030. To book in advance, telephone (0800) 802 802.

## *SOUTH ISLAND*

The 500 or so remaining Rough-faced Shags* are confined to the rock stacks and their surrounding seas at the entrance to Pelorus Sound in **Marlborough Sound Maritime Park** and it is possible to see some of them by sailing on the Pelorus Mail Boat or by chartering a water-taxi, both of which are based in Havelock. The mail boat sails from Havelock at 0930 on Tuesdays, Wednesdays and Thursdays and can be booked in advance at Havelock Visitor Centre. However, only the Wednesday boat ventures far enough into the sound to guarantee seeing the shag, and such a trip will take up much of the day, hence the best way to see this species is to charter a water-taxi which takes just three hours to visit Duffers Reef, a reliable site for the shags, and a small colony of Australian Gannets, and works out cheaper for a crew of birders. There are several water-taxi operators, including Meteor (tel: 03 579 8292). While looking for the shags it is also possible to see some of the seabirds listed for the Cook Strait (above), as well as killer whale. It may also be worth contacting the Department of Conservation in Nelson to see if it is possible to visit nearby islands which support Little Spotted Kiwi*, Takahe* (Maud), Kakapo* (Maud) and Saddleback* (Moutuara).

South of Picton State Highway 1 crosses the wetlands alongside the **Wairau River**, which support Australasian Bittern*, Buff-banded Rail, and Baillon's and Spotless Crakes. **Lake Elterwater**, a small roadside lake next to State Highway 1 about 36 km south of Blenheim, supports a good selection of waterfowl, including Hoary-headed Grebe and Australian Shoveler, and the **Awatere River** nearby is worth checking for Black-fronted Dotterel.

## KAIKOURA

The deep sea trench a few hundred metres offshore from the small town of Kaikoura causes an upwelling of nutrients, which in turn provides food for a fine selection of seabirds, including Buller's Albatross* and Buller's Shearwater*. However, these waters are much more famous for whales, and people from all over the world come to Kaikoura in the hope of seeing such wonders as humpback, killer and sperm whales at close quarters.

### New Zealand Endemics

Spotted Shag, Red-billed and Black-billed (most Feb–Jul) Gulls, Black-fronted Tern* (Apr–Aug), Rifleman, New Zealand Bellbird, Tui.

### Non-endemic Specialities

Buller's Albatross*, Buller's Shearwater* (Sep–May), White-fronted Tern.

### Others

Little Penguin, Wandering*, Royal*, Black-browed (most May–Sep) and Shy Albatrosses, Antarctic and Hall's* Giant-Petrels, Cape Petrel, Fairy Prion, Great-winged (May–Dec) and White-chinned (Jun–Nov) Petrels, Flesh-footed (Nov–Apr), Sooty and Hutton's* Shearwaters, White-faced Storm-Petrel (Aug–Apr), Australian Gannet, Pied Cormorant, White-faced Heron, Pacific Reef-Egret, Grey-tailed Tattler, Parasitic Jaeger (Nov–Mar), Australasian Pipit.

### Other Wildlife

Blue shark, common (scarce), dusky and Hector's dolphins, humpback, killer, minke, short-finned pilot and sperm (Oct–Dec) whales, New Zealand fur seal.

(Other species recorded here include Parkinson's* (Dec–May) and Westland* Petrels, and Black-bellied Storm-Petrel.)

Kaikoura is about 130 km south of Blenheim and 190 km north of Christchurch via State Highway 1. The easiest way to see seabirds, dolphins and whales is to join one of the many expensive organised boat trips, but more species, especially seabirds, are likely to be seen from trawlers which venture much further from land. Ask the local fishing folk, who can usually be found in the Pier Hotel bar, if you can join them on a fishing trip or two. They usually go to sea from 0500 to 1400 and sometimes travel as far south as the Banks Peninsula near

Christchurch, presenting the chance to see such species as Parkinson's Petrel* and Black-bellied Storm-Petrel. Landlubbers may prefer to stick to seawatching from the cliff above the car park near the New Zealand fur seal colony at the eastern end of the peninsula. Little Penguins usually appear in the bay towards dusk. Rifleman, New Zealand Bellbird and Tui occur around Mount Fyfe. For more information on organised boat trips, contact Whale Watch Kaikoura Limited, The Whaleway Station, PO Box 89, Kaikoura, New Zealand (freephone: 0800 65 5121).

## CHRISTCHURCH

The Christchurch area is excellent for waterbirds and lies close to the Banks Peninsula, the only place on earth where the white-flippered form of Little Penguin, thought by some taxonomists to be a separate species, occurs.

### New Zealand Endemics

Paradise Shelduck, New Zealand Scaup, South Island (most Jan–Jul) and Variable Oystercatchers, Red-billed Gull, Black-fronted Tern* (Apr–Aug).

### Non-endemic Specialities

White-fronted Tern.

### Others

Little Penguin (white-flippered *albosignata* race), Little Pied, Pied and Little Black Cormorants, Grey Teal, Pacific Black Duck, Australian Shoveler, White-faced Heron, Pacific Reef-Egret, Great Egret, Royal Spoonbill (Feb–Jul), Purple Swamphen, White-headed Stilt, Masked Lapwing, Kelp Gull, Welcome Swallow.

### Other Wildlife

Hector's dolphin.

(Other species recorded here include Black-browed Albatross (most May–Sep), White-chinned Petrel (Jun–Nov), Brown Skua (Aug–Apr) and Pomarine Jaeger (Nov–Mar). Introduced species include Black Swan.)

The best place to see the white-flippered *albosignata* race of Little Penguin is **Akaroa Harbour**, which is situated at the southeast end of the Banks Peninsula 82 km from Christchurch via State Highway 75. The penguins are usually fairly easy to see here on 90 minute boat trips run by Akaroa Harbour Cruises (tel: 03 304 7641). Their boat, the *Canterbury Cat,* sails three times a day at 1100, 1330 and 1540. Seawatching from Akaroa Head can be excellent in southeasterlies when possible species include Black-browed Albatross, White-chinned Petrel and Brown Skua. Large numbers of waterbirds, including Black-fronted Tern* occur on **Lake Ellesmere**, just south of Christchurch. The best places to view the lake from are Kaituna Lagoon, which lies at the north end adjacent to State Highway 75 between Christchurch and Banks Peninsula, and Harts Creek Wildfowl Refuge, which lies at the south end and can be reached by turning off State Highway 1 about 40 km south of Christchurch. Head towards Leeston and follow the signs from there.

State Highway 73 between Christchurch and Greymouth on the west coast of South Island passes through the Otira Gorge before crossing the Southern Alps at **Arthur's Pass**, one of the few sites in the country where there is a reasonable chance of seeing Blue Duck*. To look for this river-dwelling rarity follow the track on the south side of the road from the car park at the Dobson Memorial for about 3 km to a foot-bridge over the Otira River and scan from there, or try Bealey and Mingha Rivers just south of Arthur's Pass Township. Otherwise, it may be worth asking for up-to-date information at the visitor centre in the township (tel: 03 318 9211). Other species recorded in the Arthur's Pass region include Great Spotted Kiwi*.

## STATE HIGHWAY SIX

The bays, beaches, forests and scree slopes alongside State Highway Six, which runs along the wild west coast of South Island, support six localised endemics, including Great Spotted Kiwi*, which is only likely to be seen here, South Island Wren* and Yellowhead*.

### Localised New Zealand Endemics

Great Spotted Kiwi*, Weka*, Kea*, South Island Wren*, Yellowhead*, Pipipi.

### Other New Zealand Endemics

Fiordland Crested Penguin* (Aug–Nov).

### Non-endemic Specialities

Westland Petrel* (Feb–Dec).

### Others

Great Egret (Nov–Feb), Royal Spoonbill (Nov–Feb), South Polar Skua (Mar–Oct).

### Other Wildlife

Hector's dolphin, New Zealand fur seal.

The highly localised Westland Petrel* breeds in the hills around **Greymouth**, mainly between April and August, but occasionally as late as December. At Scotchman's Creek, between the Ilmenite Mining Plant and the Nikau Scenic Reserve about 4 km south of Punakaiki, it is possible to see petrels flying inland across State Highway 6 to their breeding colonies at dusk. It is also possible to see the birds at one of their breeding colonies, on escorted tours run by Paparoa Nature Tours, PO Box 36, Punakaiki (tel: 03 731 1826), or at sea, on trawlers which sail from Greymouth.

The mossy forest in **Paparoa National Park**, near Punakaiki, is the only area in New Zealand where Great Spotted Kiwi* is likely to be seen. Head north out of Punakaiki and turn right towards Bullock Creek Farm after crossing Bullock Creek. Park by a gate 6.3 km along this track and walk beyond the gate for 300 m to where there are three signposted tracks; one to the left, one to the right, and a more obscure one which leads straight on. The best way to see this very rare and elusive bird is to wander along these tracks at night, listening out for their sniffing and snorting noises. They are also attracted to such sounds, but still very wary and seeing one may well take several hours. However, birds have been known to investigate snoring birders who have fallen asleep after hours of fruitless stalking. Crashing into the forest is not recommended because the birds will hear you before you see them, and the area is riddled with dangerous pot holes. This species of kiwi may be crepuscular rather than nocturnal, so dawn and dusk may be the best times to try. For more information on Paparoa National Park, contact the visitor centre (tel: 03 731 1895). **Cape Foulwind**, near Westport, much further north of Greymouth, supports Weka* and a New Zealand fur seal colony, and seawatching from here has produced Westland Petrel*. Another site for Great Spotted Kiwi* is the **Heaphy Track** near Karamea, a small village 100 km north of Westport via State Highway 67.

South of Greymouth the road enters Westland National Park where there are over 60 glaciers. At **Whataroa** it is possible to join the organised boat trips (Nov–Feb) run by White Heron Sanctuary Tours, PO Box 19, Whataroa (tel: 03 753 4120) which follow the Waitangi–Taona River to a heronry where Great Egrets (Nov–Feb) and Royal Spoonbills (Nov–Feb) breed. These birds feed on nearby Okarito Lagoon, which is signposted off State Highway 6 south of Whataroa. The rare South Island Wren* has been recorded on guided walks to **Franz Josef and Fox Glaciers** (which are 24 km apart), especially the latter where it is also wise to keep an eye on the Keas* which have a penchant for windscreen wipers and rubber window rims. The rare Yellowhead* occurs in the Antarctic beech forest around roadside **Lake Paringa** about 70 km south of the glaciers towards Haast. About 15 km further south from here walk down the 2 km long track by the stream from Lake Moeraki Wilderness Lodge to **Monroe's Beach**, a good site for Fiordland Crested Penguin* (Aug–Nov), as well as Hector's dolphin and New Zealand fur seal. One of the largest Fiordland Crested Penguin* colonies is at **Jackson Head**, reached via a 40 km long track which leads off State Highway 6 south of Haast. From Haast the road crosses the Southern Alps at Haast Pass to Lake Te Anau in Fiordland National Park (p. 317).

## WAITAKI VALLEY

The entire world population of about 60 Black Stilts* breeds in the upper Waitaki Valley, on the braided rivers which spill down from Mount Cook, the highest mountain in New Zealand at 3754 m (12,316 ft). This great rarity is rarely seen elsewhere in the country, hence this valley should be on every birder's New Zealand itinerary. The wild rivers graced by the stilts also support breeding Double-banded Plover, Wrybill* and Black-fronted Tern*.

### Localised New Zealand Endemics

Black Stilt*, Kea*.

## WAITAKI VALLEY

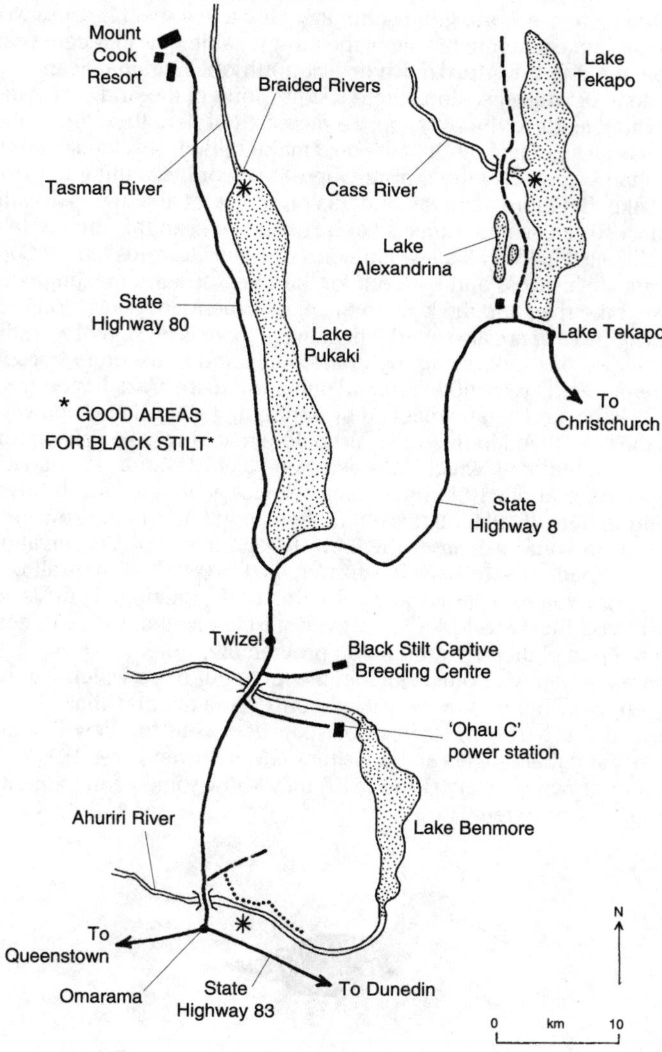


### Other New Zealand Endemics

Paradise Shelduck, New Zealand Scaup, New Zealand Falcon*, South Island Oystercatcher (Aug–Dec), Wrybill* (Aug–Jan), Black-billed Gull (Nov–Feb), Black-fronted Tern* (Sep–Jan).

### Others

Little Pied Cormorant, Grey Teal, Pacific Black Duck, White-faced Heron, White-headed Stilt (Aug–Dec), Double-banded Plover (Aug–Feb), Australasian Pipit.

(Other species recorded here include South Island Wren*.)

Black Stilts* occur sparingly throughout the area, usually in ones or twos on pools and, especially, braided rivers. All such habitats in the area are therefore worth grilling, but there are a few specific areas worthy of prolonged attention. One of the most reliable sites in recent years has been along the **Ahuriri River** just north of Omarama. Scan from the bridge or walk east along the track just north of the bridge to join a trail which leads to the riverside. To the north of here there is another track leading east just south of the next major bridge. This track leads to the 'Ohau C' power station, from where it is worth scanning the river and Lake Benmore. The second major site is at the mouth of the **Tasman River**, where it meets Lake Pukaki. To scan this inland delta turn off State Highway 8 a few km north of Twizel towards Mount Cook on State Highway 80 and look out for the often obscure meeting point between the river and the lake, to the east of the road. Pools alongside State Highway 80 are also worth checking. If there is no sign of any stilts in these two particular areas, try not to panic and move on to hot spot number three. This is another inland delta, where the **Cass River** meets Lake Tekapo, and can be reached by continuing along State Highway 8 from the turn-off to Mount Cook. Just before reaching Lake Tekapo turn north on to the track which runs between Lake Alexandrina and Lake Tekapo. After about 10 km this track reaches a bridge over the river. Scan from here. If, after all this effort, there is still no stilt to show for it, try to glean some gen from the Twizel Department of Conservation, Wairepo Road, Private Bag, Twizel (tel: 03 435 0802), or start all over again. Once you have tasted success, if the birds were ringed purists will want to visit the Twizel DOC anyway, just to check that the birds seen were not part of their reintroduction programme.

There are plenty of other birds in the area, but none which can not be seen elsewhere. However, it is worth remembering that Hooker Valley, at the base of Mount Cook, is a good site for New Zealand Falcon*, and that rangers at the Visitor Centre, Bowen Drive, PO Box 5, Mount Cook Village (tel: 03 435 1819) may know some good local sites for South Island Wren*.

*The Black Stilt* is one of the rarest shorebirds on earth*

At the lower end of the Waitaki Valley, near **Oamaru** on the east coast of South Island, the world's rarest penguin can be seen at Waitaki Beach near the picnic area alongside State Highway 1 just south of the Waitaki River. Walk north from the picnic area towards the large rocks and watch out for Yellow-eyed Penguins* popping out of the Pacific towards dusk. They can also be seen at Bushy Beach Scenic Reserve to the south of here, along with Little Penguins. Ask at the visitor centre just south of the Oamaru town centre for details of escorted tours (C) which start at 1830 on weekdays, or about access to the hide at other times. The penguins breed here in burrows which they normally return to as the sun goes down. While some birds may be present at any time of the year, the period of peak activity is October and November.

## DUNEDIN

This town on the southeast coast of South Island lies at the base of the Otago Peninsula which supports the only mainland breeding colony of Royal Albatrosses* in the world. Nearby, there is a breeding colony of Yellow-eyed Penguins*, the world's rarest penguin, and the seas surrounding the peninsula support some superb seabirds, including the *salvini* race of Shy Albatross, which is considered to be a full species by some taxonomists.

### New Zealand Endemics

Yellow-eyed Penguin* (most Oct–May), Bronze* and Spotted (*punctatus* race) Shags, South Island Oystercatcher (most Jan–Jul), Red-billed Gull, Rifleman, New Zealand Bellbird, Pipipi.

### Non-endemic Specialities

Grey-headed* and Buller's* Albatrosses, White-fronted Tern.

### Others

Little Penguin, Wandering*, Royal* (*sanfordi* and *epomophera* races), Black-browed (most May–Sep) and Shy (*salvini* race) Albatrosses, Hall's Giant-Petrel*, Cape and White-chinned (Jun–Nov) Petrels, Sooty and Hutton's* Shearwaters, Common Diving-Petrel, Australian Gannet, Little Pied and Little Black Cormorants, Grey Teal, Australian Shoveler, White-faced Heron, Double-banded Plover (Mar–Aug), Black-fronted Dotterel, Masked Lapwing, Kelp Gull, Brown Skua (Aug–Apr), Australasian Pipit.

### Other Wildlife

Hooker's sea-lion, New Zealand fur seal.

(Other species recorded here include Erect-crested Penguin* which has attempted to breed on the Otago Peninsula in the past. Introduced species include Australasian Magpie, Eurasian Skylark and Dunnock.)

The small Royal Albatross* colony is on **Taiaroa Head**, about 30 km from Dunedin at the northeast tip of the Otago Peninsula. There are usually around 15 pairs and they can be seen at very close quarters on guided tours run by the Trust Bank Royal Albatross Centre between mid-November and August. These escorted walks start every half hour from 0930 to 1900 seven days a week, but it is still best to book a place in advance by contacting the Trust Bank Royal Albatross Centre, Otago Peninsula Trust, PO Box 492, Dunedin (tel: 03 478 0498/0499). It may also be possible to see the birds through the fence near the lighthouse

**OTAGO PENINSULA**

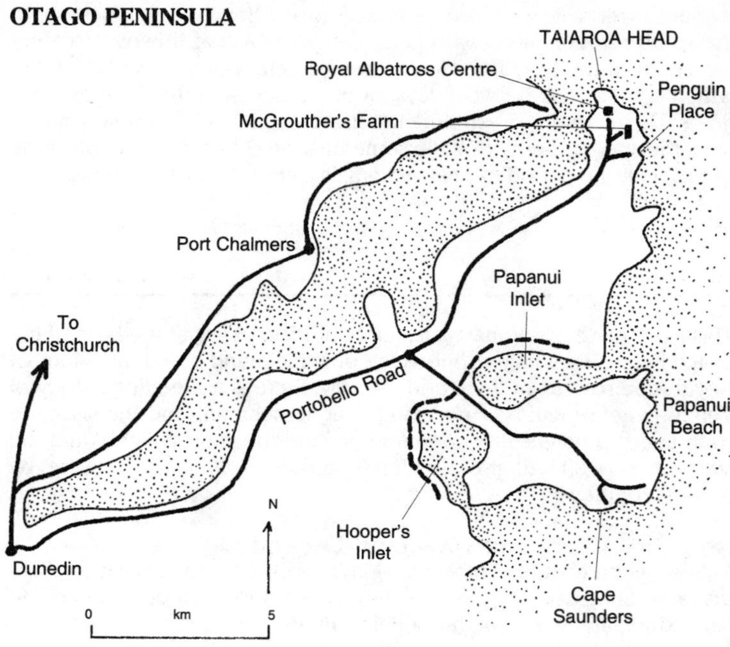


or from the cliff-top near the car park, and it is possible to visit Taiaroa Head by boat. Late afternoon is usually the busiest time at the albatross colony. There is also a large colony of Bronze Shags* here and a few Spotted Shags. The adjacent McGrouther's Farm (tel: 03 478 0286) supports a colony of Yellow-eyed* and Little Penguins, which can be visited by arrangement. **Cape Saunders** at the southeast tip of the Otago Peninsula is a great seawatching site in southeasterlies, while waterbirds occur in the nearby Papanui and Hoopers Inlets and the rare Hooker's sea-lion has been recorded on Papanui Beach. It may be possible to organise a pelagic birding trip aboard the *RV Munida,* which is moored at Port Chalmers.

## DUNEDIN TO INVERCARGILL

There are a number of sites worth visiting between Dunedin and Invercargill, at the the southern tip of South Island, where the possibilities include the localised Yellowhead* and Fernbird, as well as Australasian Bittern*.

### Localised New Zealand Endemics

Yellowhead*.

### Other New Zealand Endemics

Yellow-eyed Penguin*, Bronze Shag*, Paradise Shelduck, New Zealand Falcon*, South Island Oystercatcher (most Jan–Jul), Red-breasted Dotterel* (Mar–Aug), Tomtit, New Zealand Robin, Fernbird.

### Others

Australasian Bittern*, Royal Spoonbill (Mar–Aug), Spotless Crake, Double-banded Plover (Mar–Aug), Australasian Pipit.

### Other Wildlife

Hooker's sealion, New Zealand fur seal, southern elephant seal.

Australasian Bittern* and Fernbird occur at **Sinclair Wetlands**, a private reserve adjacent to Lake Waihola, just south of Berwick, about 35 km south of Dunedin (tel: 03 486 2654). Further south, turn off State Highway 1 at Balclutha on to State Highway 92 to reach the **Catlins** area, where Yellow-eyed Penguin* can be seen at close quarters from the Department of Conservation hide at Roaring Bay, on the south side of Nugget Point, about 20 km south of Balclutha, along with southern elephant seal, and Yellowhead* occurs around Chaslands in Catlins State Forest, south of Owaka. Marshy areas around **Waituna Lagoon**, 20 km east of Invercargill, support Fernbird. To reach this site turn off State Highway 92 at Kapuka, midway between Fortrose and Invercargill, on to a road which skirts the east end of the brackish lagoon. Fernbird also occurs at **Awarua Bay**, 20 km south of Invercargill, along with Bronze Shag*, Australasian Bittern* and Red-breasted Dotterel*. To reach here turn off State Highway 1 about 10 km south of Invercargill towards the aluminium smelter on Tiwai Point, turn left before the bridge over the bay, and park by Muddy Creek to search for Fernbird and roosting shorebirds. Beyond the bridge turn left, along the south shore of the bay, park opposite Cow Island and scan the shoreline for Red-breasted Dotterel*.

The road south of Invercargill leads to **Bluff**, where the ferry to Stewart Island leaves from. It is possible to hitch rides on the trawlers in Bluff Harbour but they don't usually venture very far out in to the Foveaux Strait because it is so rough. However, even on a short trip it is possible to see lots of seabirds including Mottled Petrel (Nov–Apr), as well as Broad-billed Prion and Common Diving-Petrel. While waiting for the ferry to Stewart Island it may be worth taking a stroll because Pipipi and Fernbird occur in the area.

## FIORDLAND NATIONAL PARK

This 12,000 sq km wild expanse of wet *podocarpus* forests, lakes, braided rivers, alpine meadows, boulder fields, glaciers, snow-capped peaks and fiords, supports one of the best selections of endemics in the whole of the country, and is the site where South Island Wren* is most likely to be seen. Don't be put off by this bird's boring name—it can take some tracking down, but it is a perky little mini-pitta of a bird and, once seen well, often ends up being voted bird-of-the-trip by visiting birders.

### Localised New Zealand Endemics

Kea*, Common Kaka*, South Island Wren*, Yellowhead*.

### Other New Zealand Endemics

Fiordland Crested* (Jul–Dec) and Yellow-eyed* Penguins, Paradise

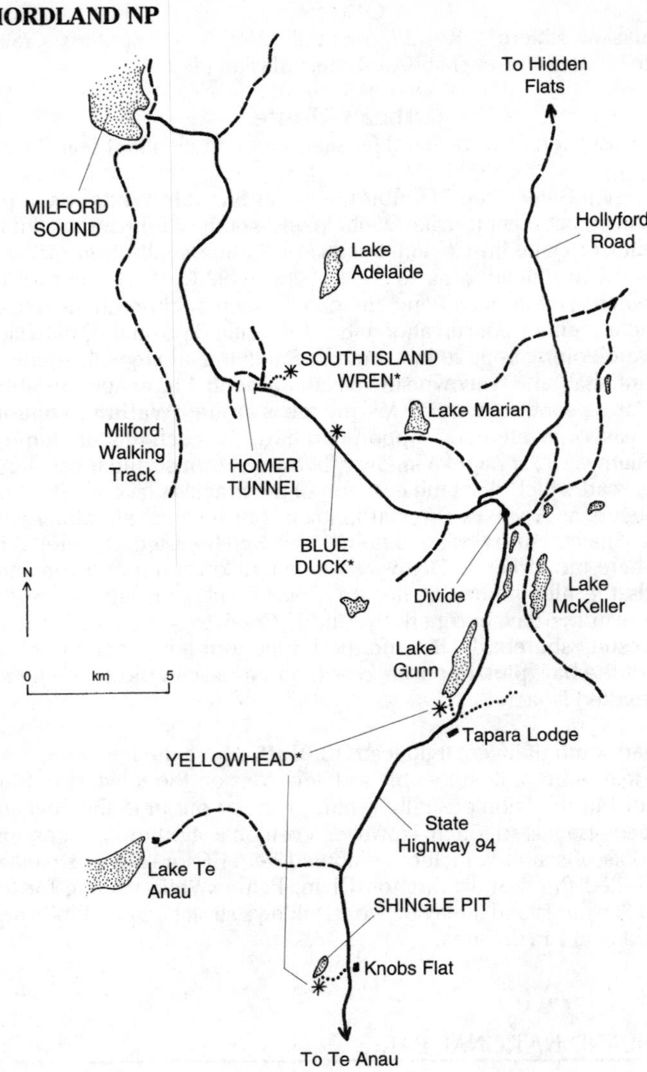


Shelduck, New Zealand Scaup, New Zealand Falcon*, Wrybill* (Aug–Dec), Black-billed Gull (Nov–Feb), Black-fronted Tern* (Sep–Jan), New Zealand Pigeon, Yellow-fronted Parakeet*, Rifleman, Grey Gerygone, New Zealand Bellbird, Tui, Tomtit, New Zealand Robin, Pipipi.

## Non-endemic Specialities

Long-tailed Koel (Oct–Mar).

## Others

Little Penguin, Little Pied Cormorant, Pacific Black Duck, Swamp Harrier, Purple Swamphen, White-headed Stilt (Aug–Dec), Double-banded

Plover (Aug–Feb), Shining Bronze-Cuckoo (Oct–Feb), Morepork, Grey Fantail, Australasian Pipit.

## Other Wildlife

Dusky dolphin, New Zealand fur seal.

(Other species recorded here include Brown Kiwi* and Blue Duck*.)

The visitor centre is on Lake Front Drive, PO Box 29, Te Anau (tel: 03 249 7921). From here a 120 km long road runs north and west to Milford Sound, alongside red beech forests, lakes, braided rocky rivers and boulder slopes, and below scenically spectacular snow-capped mountains. The best areas of forest for Yellowhead* are around the shingle pit at **Knobs Flat**, at **Kiosk Creek**, 12 km south of Tapara Lodge, and alongside the **Lake Gunn Nature Walk** opposite Tapara Lodge. Forested white water stretches of rivers and streams between Divide and the Homer Tunnel support the rare Blue Duck*, but they are much harder to find here than elsewhere in the country. *The* place to look for South Island Wren* is on the boulder-strewn slopes just before the **Homer Tunnel**. From the car park at the southeast end of the tunnel, cross the road and walk along the track for 200 m to an area of large boulders. Search these boulders and the surrounding area diligently for the dinky little numbers, or try around the weather station 500 m below the tunnel. The Homer Tunnel area is also good for Keas*, which are partial to windscreen wipers and gloves. West of the tunnel the road ends up at the enchanting **Milford Sound**, one of nature's finest works of art. The sheer rock walls of this 21 km long fiord rise to 1219 m (4000 ft) opposite the 159 m (520 ft) Bowen Falls and the surrounding snow-capped mountains, with hanging glaciers, reach 1695 m (5560 ft) at Mitre Peak. What a place to look for birds! There aren't many, but they include Fiordland Crested* and Yellow-eyed* Penguins, which are most likely to be seen on the early morning Red Boat Cruise from the wharf, bookable in advance through Fiordland Travel, Steamer Wharf, Queenstown (tel: 03 442 7500). New Zealand Falcon*, Kea*, Common Kaka*, Yellow-fronted Parakeet*, Yellowhead* and Pipipi can all be seen on the wait-listed three day long trek along the **Milford Walking Track**. This is reputed to be one of the finest (and wettest) walks in the world, but there are a number of other, less heavily-pounded trails in this and other parts of New Zealand where the scenery is just as spectacular. Remember Fiordland National Park is one of the wettest places on earth and that sandflies abound, so it is best to wear long trousers at all times.

*Accommodation:* Milford Lodge (B), near Milford Sound.

Yellowhead* is one of hardest endemics to see in New Zealand, even at Fiordland National Park, but one of the most reliable sites is **Lake Sylvan**. To reach this site take the minor road out of Queenstown alongside the lake and drive through the small village of Glenorchy, then turn right at the crossroads and follow the signs to Routeburn. After 22 km turn off to Lake Sylvan, just before the 'Mount Aspiring National Park' sign. Less than 1 km along here the track reaches a campsite from where a trail leads to the lake. Look for the birds in the high canopy along this trail, where Rifleman and New Zealand Robin are also present.

## *STEWART ISLAND*

This large forested island (1751 sq km) with granite headlands and sandy bays lies off the southern end of South Island and is the best place in New Zealand to see a kiwi. The island is sparsely inhabited and there are only 15 km of roads, hence many native forest birds are common and confiding, none more so than Brown Kiwi*, which may be seen down to just a few feet. The surrounding waters support some superb seabirds, including five species of albatross and Mottled Petrel, but most of these are difficult to see without organising boat trips.

**STEWART ISLAND**

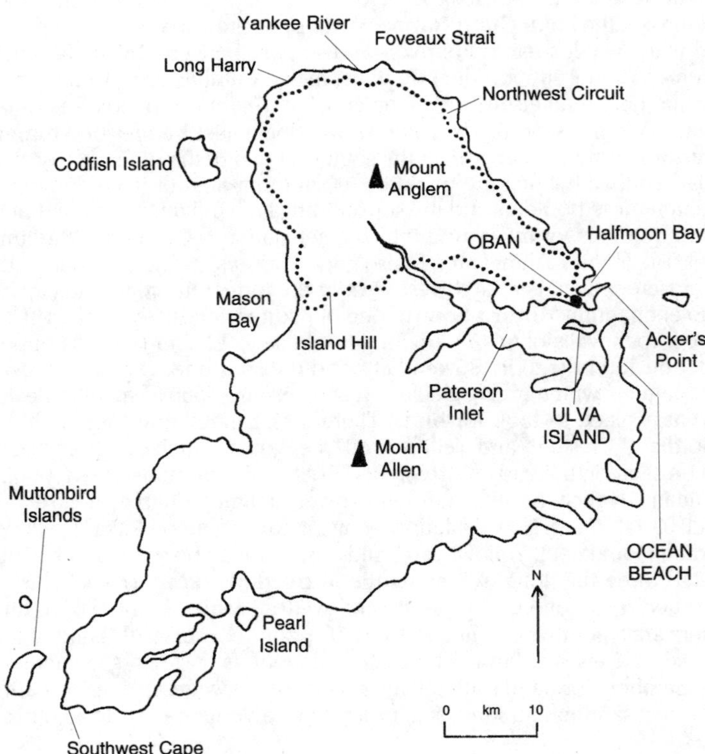


### Localised New Zealand Endemics

Brown Kiwi* (*lawryi* race), Weka* (*scotti* race), Common Kaka*.

### Other New Zealand Endemics

Fiordland Crested* (Jul–Nov) and Yellow-eyed* Penguins, Bronze* and Spotted (*steadi* race) Shags, Paradise Shelduck, Variable Oystercatcher, Red-billed and Black-billed (Apr–Sep) Gulls, Black-fronted Tern* (Mar–Jul), New Zealand Pigeon, Yellow-fronted Parakeet*, Grey Gerygone, New Zealand Bellbird, Tui, Tomtit, Pipipi.

## Non-endemic Specialities

Grey-headed* and Buller's* Albatrosses, Mottled Petrel (Nov–Apr), Broad-billed Prion, White-fronted and Antarctic Terns, Red-fronted Parakeet, Long-tailed Koel (Oct–Mar).

## Others

Little Penguin, Wandering*, Royal*, Black-browed (most May–Sep) and Shy Albatrosses, Antarctic and Hall's* Giant-Petrels, Cape Petrel, Fairy Prion, Sooty Shearwater, White-faced Storm-Petrel (Aug–Apr), Common Diving-Petrel, Australian Gannet, Pied Cormorant, White-faced Heron, Pacific Reef-Egret, Swamp Harrier, Spotless Crake, Kelp Gull, Brown Skua (Aug–Apr), Shining Bronze-Cuckoo (Oct–Feb), Morepork, Sacred Kingfisher, Grey Fantail, Silver-eye, Australasian Pipit.

(Other species recorded here include Cook's* (Nov–Mar), White-chinned (Jun–Nov) and Grey (Nov–Mar) Petrels, Black-bellied Storm-Petrel, South Georgia Diving-Petrel (breeds on South West Cape) and Fernbird. Introduced species include California Quail. There are introduced populations of Kakapo* and Saddleback* on Codfish Island, which is usually inaccessible to the public, and there are plans to introduce Saddleback* and New Zealand Robin to Ulva Island.)

The small town of Oban on Stewart Island is accessible by air from Invercargill (20 minutes) and sea from Bluff (one hour). The catamaran ferry trip from Bluff across the 24 km wide Foveaux Strait offers the opportunity to see some seabirds such as Fiordland Crested* and Yellow-eyed* Penguins, Wandering* and Royal* Albatrosses, and Mottled Petrel, but views are likely to be distant and brief. The ferry, which is operated by Stewart Island Marine (tel: 03 212 7660), runs twice daily between December and April (leaving Bluff at 0930 and 1700, and Oban at 0800 and 1530), but less frequently at other times of the year.

The highlight for most visitors to Stewart Island is the 'kiwi excursion', a nightime boat trip to **Ocean Beach**, beyond the neck of Paterson Inlet, where Brown Kiwis* often feed on sandhoppers along the tideline just a few metres away from observers. These confiding birds have been known to investigate smelly shoes and may also be seen along the trail to the beach. The boat can only take 15 people at a time and only runs every other night, so to avoid serious disappointment it is crucial to book the trip at least one week in advance by contacting Bravo Adventure Cruises (tel/fax: 03 219 1144). The birds have only failed to appear three times over many years.

Once in Oban head for the Department of Conservation Visitor Centre 100 m from the South Sea Hotel for the latest information on other boat trips, as these are usually the only way to see most of the seabirds, including Fiordland Crested Penguin*, which is only likely in the Foveaux Strait. However, negotiating trips on local trawlers to the west side of the island, especially around Codfish Island, is the best way to see the rarest seabirds. Even birds such as South Georgia Diving-Petrel are possible there.

Regular boat trips (B) include those to **Ulva Island**, where landbirds such as tame Wekas*, Red-fronted Parakeet and Pipipi are usually easy to see. While waiting for these trips it is worth exploring the vicinity of Oban. Try the Scenic Reserve Track for landbirds including Red-fronted Parakeet and walk out across Halfmoon Bay to Acker's Point, 3 km away, in the late afternoon to seawatch. Bronze* and Spotted Shags occur here and in summer Little Penguins and Sooty Shearwaters return to their burrows at dusk. Few birders have undertaken the 10 day long hike around the northern coast of the island on the muddy, undulating Northwest Circuit, but those with the time and inclination to do so have been rewarded with such birds as Brown Kiwi* (some birds around Island Hill homestead, about 1 km upstream from Mason Bay hut, are diurnal), Yellow-eyed Penguin* (in bays viewable from the huts at Yankee River and Long Harry), Red-breasted Dotterel* (along river near Mason Bay hut) and Fernbird (along river near Mason Bay hut). Permits to walk this trail and to stay in the Department of Conservation huts must be obtained at the visitor centre in Oban.

*Accommodation:* South Sea Hotel, Rakiura Motel (A+), Stewart Island Lodge (A++). It is wise to book accommodation in advance via the Visitor Centre, Main Road, PO Box 3, Oban (tel: 03 219 1130/1218), or Stewart Island Travel, PO Box 26, Oban (tel: 03 219 1269).

*Although most birders visit Stewart Island to see Brown Kiwi*, there are plenty of seabirds around, including the superb Mottled Petrel*

## *THE CHATHAM ISLANDS*

This remote archipelago, which lies approximately 800 km east of New Zealand's main islands, supports seven endemic birds, most of which are on the brink of extinction. They include a *pterodroma* petrel, two shags and two shorebirds, one of which is the superb Shore Plover*. In addition, the endemic races of Shy Albatross and Variable Oystercatcher are candidates for full species status according to some taxonomists.

Getting to the main island, Chatham, where it is possible to see the two endemic shags and the endemic gerygone, is not a problem, but permits are needed to visit the island of Rangatira, where the remaining endemics occur, and these are far from easy to obtain.

### Chatham Islands Endemics

Chatham Petrel*, Chatham* and Pitt* Shags, Chatham Snipe*, Shore Plover*, Chatham Gerygone*, Chatham Robin*.

### Chatham and Subantarctic Islands Endemics

Fulmar Prion.

## Other New Zealand Endemics

Weka*, Variable Oystercatcher (*chathamensis* race), Red-billed Gull, New Zealand Pigeon, Yellow-fronted Parakeet* (*forbesi* race), Tui.

## Non-endemic Specialities

Magenta Petrel*, Broad-billed Prion, White-fronted Tern (Sep–Mar), Red-fronted Parakeet.

## Others

Royal* and Shy (*eremita* race) Albatrosses, White-faced Heron, Double-banded Plover (Aug–Feb), Masked Lapwing, Kelp Gull, Brown Skua (Aug–Apr).

## Other Wildlife

New Zealand fur seal.

The main island is accessible by air. Most of the 700 or so residents live in four fishing settlements on the main island known as Chatham, where there is a motel and a pub in Waitangi, and on farms on the island of Pitt. Cars are available for hire on **Chatham**, where the rare endemic *chathamensis* race of Variable Oystercatcher occurs along the north coast either side of Cape Pattison, along with Double-banded Plover and Masked Lapwing. Also on Chatham there is a breeding colony of Chatham* and Pitt* Shags, as well as Kelp and Red-billed Gulls at Matarakau Point. The two shags also breed at Okawa Point, at the northwest corner of the island, along with White-faced Herons, Red-billed Gulls and White-fronted Terns. The thick *terehinau* scrub at the Rangaikia Reserve on the southeast coast of Chatham supports New Zealand Pigeon, Chatham Gerygone* and Tui. The Tuku Valley Nature Reserve also supports the pigeon and gerygone, as well as Red-fronted Parakeet. The major avian attraction of the Chatham Islands, however, is the very rare and highly localised Shore Plover*. It is confined, along with Chatham Snipe*, to the southeasternmost island, known as **Rangatira**, where there are about 130 birds left. This small island (2 sq km) is only accessible with prior permission from the Department of Conservation. Write to the Chatham Islands office, *not* the 'mainland' office, with a very good reason for wanting to see the birds and, if permission is granted, fly to the main island, then to Pitt Island and ask the local fishermen there if one is willing to take you to Rangatira. 'Casual', unprofessional, independent birders have virtually no chance of getting permission, although a letter of introduction from the New Zealand Ornithological Society might help and they may even point you to the right fisherman on Pitt Island to approach. The confiding Shore Plovers* occur on the flat, rocky platforms around the coast. In the 1970s an attempt was made to transfer some birds to the nearby island of **Mangere**, but the birds simply disappeared or returned to Rangatira. One bird flew back immediately, passed the boat carrying the scientists who had taken it to Mangere, and was back on Rangatira before them! Chatham Snipe* has been successfully reintroduced to Mangere. Chatham Petrel* is also endemic to Rangatira, at least as a breeding species, and Chatham Robin* survives only on Rangatira and Mangere.

*Accommodation:* Chatham—motel in Waitangi.

## *THE SUBANTARCTIC ISLANDS*

The nutrient-rich waters surrounding these islands which lie south and east of New Zealand support the greatest diversity and concentration of seabirds on earth, including nine species of penguin and 30 species of albatrosses, petrels and shearwaters. Six seabirds (three penguins and three shags) are endemic along with four other species; a teal, a rail, a snipe and a parakeet. Non-endemic avian superstars include King Penguin, Light-mantled Albatross and Mottled Petrel.

### Subantarctic Islands Endemics

Snares Crested*, Erect-crested* and Royal Penguins, Campbell*, Auckland* and Bounty* Shags, Flightless Teal*, Auckland Rail*, Subantarctic Snipe*, Antipodes Parakeet*.

### Chatham and Subantarctic Islands Endemics

Fulmar Prion.

### Other New Zealand Endemics

Yellow-eyed Penguin*, New Zealand Falcon*, Yellow-fronted Parakeet*, New Zealand Bellbird, Tui, Tomtit, Fernbird.

### Non-endemic Specialities

Grey-headed* and Light-mantled Albatrosses, Mottled (Nov–Apr) and White-headed Petrels, Broad-billed Prion, Grey Petrel, Red-fronted Parakeet.

### Others

King, Gentoo and Rockhopper Penguins, Wandering*, Royal*, Black-browed and Shy Albatrosses, Imperial Shag (*purpurascens* race), Brown Skua.

### Other Wildlife

Hooker's sealion, killer, southern right and sperm whales, leopard, New Zealand fur and southern elephant seals.

All of the islands are reserves. A number of tour companies offer occasional cruises to these islands, but more regular trips are organised by Southern Heritage Expeditions, who can be contacted via New Zealand Travel, 7 Macquarie Place, Sydney, NSW 2000, Australia (tel: 02 241 5188, fax: 02 252 2775). One recent trip to these islands took place in January 1994 (the height of the breeding season) when the *MY Pacific Ruby* (chartered by Naturetrek) with room for 20 passengers left South Island and visited the Chatham, Bounty, Antipodes, Campbell, Macquarie, Auckland and Snares Islands before returning to Stewart Island. Another cruise, to Australian Antarctic Territory, is being planned for 1997/98 by Inland Bird Tours, Australian Ornithological Services Pty Ltd, PO Box 382 (127 Whitehorse Road), Balwyn 3103, Victoria, Australia (tel/fax: 03 9817 6555).

Birders with enough time and money to visit these islands should book themselves on the next cruise as soon as possible, for the seabird statistics speak for themselves. The 11 granite stacks that make up the **Bounty Islands** (135 ha) are crammed with breeding seabirds, including over 100,000 pairs of Erect-crested Penguins*, at least 75,000 pairs of

Shy Albatrosses (*salvini* race), similar numbers of Fulmar Prions, and up to 1,200 Bounty Shags*, the rarest member of its family. The **Antipodes Islands** support large colonies of Rockhopper Penguins and are one of the world strongholds of Wandering Albatross*. They also support the endemic Antipodes Parakeet*, as well as Erect-crested Penguin*, Mottled, White-headed and Grey Petrels, and Red-fronted Parakeet. The hillsides of **Campbell Island** support tussock grass instead of trees, ideal breeding habitat for about 7,500 pairs of Royal Albatrosses*. There is a huge colony of these birds on Colonel Lyall Saddle near the meteorological station in Perseverance Harbour, as well as massive colonies of Black-browed and Grey-headed* Albatrosses on the north coast. Other species present include the endemic Campbell Shag*, as well as Rockhopper, Erect-crested* and Yellow-eyed* Penguins, and Light-mantled Albatross plus Hooker's sea-lion and southern elephant seal. Three to four million penguins breed on **Macquarie Island** (administered by Australia), including about 850,000 pairs of the endemic Royal Penguin, mostly at Lusitania Bay, and over 200,000 King Penguins at Sandy Bay, as well as Gentoo and Rockhopper Penguins. Other species present on this wonderful island include Wandering Albatross* and the endemic *purpurascens* race of Imperial Shag, which is considered by some taxonomists to be a full species. The surrounding seas support killer whale, leopard seal, southern right and sperm whales, and about 150,000 southern elephant seals. The **Auckland Islands** are just as exciting. Enderby Island at the northern end of this group, where endemic races of Subantarctic Snipe*, Red-fronted Parakeet, New Zealand Bellbird and Tomtit all occur in the *bulbinella* meadows, boasts the greatest diversity and Port Ross hosts the world's largest breeding colony of Wandering Albatrosses*. The archipelago as a whole supports the endemic Auckland Shag*, Flightless Teal* (Derrycastle Reef) and Auckland Rail*, as well as Yellow-eyed Penguin*, Royal*, Shy and Light-mantled Albatrosses, and an endemic race of Yellow-fronted Parakeet*. Hooker's sea-lions are usually present on Sandy Bay beach. Landing on the **Snares Islands** is prohibited, but from zodiacs it is possible to see the endemic Snares Crested Penguin*. Other breeding species here include Buller's Albatross*, Cape Petrel and an estimated six million Sooty Shearwaters. The dense *olearia* forests provide additional room for the endemic races of Subantarctic Snipe*, Tomtit and Fernbird.

*A trip to the Subantarctic Islands offers the chance to see Light-mantled Albatross, arguably the world's most elegant bird*

# ADDITIONAL INFORMATION

## Addresses

New Zealand Department of Conservation (DOC) Head Office, 59 Boulcott Street, PO Box 10420, Wellington, New Zealand (tel: 04 471 0726).

Auckland DOC, corner of Karangahape Road and Liverpool Street, Private Bag 68908, Newton, Auckland, New Zealand (tel: 09 307 9279).

Wellington DOC, 2nd Floor, Bowen State Building, 58 Bowen Street, PO Box 5086, Wellington, New Zealand (tel: 04 472 5821).

The Ornithological Society of New Zealand, PO Box 316, Drury, South Auckland, New Zealand, publishes *Notornis*, a quarterly journal, as well as a newsletter.

The Royal Forest and Bird Protection Society of New Zealand, 172 Taranaki Street, PO Box 631, Wellington, New Zealand (tel: 04 385 7374), publishes *Forest and Bird*, a bimonthly journal.

Manu Tours, 106 Ocean Beach Road, Tairua 2853 (tel/fax: 07 864 7475), organise birding tours and personal trips throughout the mainland.

## Books and Papers

*Birdwatching in New Zealand.* Burfield I, 1995. Privately published.

*A Guide to Birding in New Zealand.* Harrop H, 1992. Privately published.

*Field Guide to the Birds of New Zealand.* Heather B and Robertson H, due May 1997. Oxford University Press.

*Collins Field Guide to the Birds of New Zealand.* Falla R *et al.*, 1979. HarperCollins.

*Complete Book of New Zealand Birds.* Robertson C, 1985. Readers Digest.

*Checklist of the Birds of New Zealand* (3rd edn). Turbott E, 1990. Ornithological Society of New Zealand.

*Rare and Endangered New Zealand Birds—Conservation and Management.* Gaze P, 1994. Canterbury University Press.

*The Conservation of Critically Endangered Flightless Birds in New Zealand.* Clout M, Craig J, in press. Ibis.

*The Handbook of Australian, New Zealand and Antarctic Birds* (HANZAB), volumes 1 (1991) to 3 (1996) and continuing. Marchant S, Higgins P (RAOU), continuing. Oxford University Press.

## NEW ZEALAND ENDEMICS (61)

### North and South Islands and Smaller Offshore Islands (43)

| | |
|---|---|
| Brown Kiwi* | Possible in Northland but most likely to be seen on Stewart Island. Known from four localities on North Island, including Rotorua and Pureora FP, the west coast and Fiordland of South Island, and Stewart Island |
| Little Spotted Kiwi* | Introduced to a number of offshore islands including Tiritiri Matangi (where it is most likely to be seen) and Kapiti where 95% of the 1,000 or so surviving birds are present. Has also been introduced to Red Mercury (off Coromandel Peninsula), Hen (north of Little Barrier Island) and Long Islands, all of which are around North Island, although there is one record from Franz Josef on the west coast of South Island |

| | |
|---|---|
| Great Spotted Kiwi* | Only likely to be seen in Paparoa NP, along State Highway Six, South Island, although also known from the Southern Alps at northwest Nelson and near Arthur's Pass |
| New Zealand Grebe* | Matata Lagoons, Rotorua and Lake Tutira on North Island where only 600–700 pairs survive |
| Fiordland Crested Penguin* | State Highway Six along the southwest coast of South Island, Fiordland NP and Stewart Island |
| Yellow-eyed Penguin* | The world's rarest penguin, with a mainland population of about 385 pairs, occurs along the southeast coast of South Island between Christchurch and Invercargill, in Fiordland NP, on Stewart Island, and in the Subantarctic Islands |
| Rough-faced Shag* | The surviving population of about 500 birds is confined to rock stacks and their surrounding seas in Marlborough Sound Maritime Park, and can be seen on boat trips from Havelock on South Island |
| Bronze Shag* | Along the southeast coast of South Island between Dunedin and Invercargill, and on Stewart Island |
| Spotted Shag | Widespread |
| Paradise Shelduck | Widespread |
| Blue Duck* | Rare on mountain streams and rivers, and difficult to find. Most likely to be seen on the Manganui A Te O River on North Island, and at Arthur's Pass on South Island, but also occurs in Fiordland NP |
| Brown Teal* | Tiritiri Matangi, Little Barrier and Great Barrier (the stronghold) Islands, and Northland |
| New Zealand Scaup | Widespread |
| New Zealand Falcon* | Widespread but scarce, to the Auckland Islands in the Subantarctic Islands |
| Weka* | Kapiti Island, State Highway Six and Stewart Island, where most likely to be seen, to Chatham Islands |
| Takahe* | Introduced to a number of offshore islands including Tiritiri Matangi and Kapiti. Over 150 birds were also still present in the virtually inaccessible Murchison and Stuart Mountains of South Island in 1994 |
| South Island Oystercatcher | Breeds in highlands of South Island (e.g. Waitaki Valley) between August and December, and disperses to coasts of North and South Islands between January and July (although some birds remain at the coast all year round) |
| Variable Oystercatcher | Widespread around coasts, to Stewart and Chatham Islands |

| | |
|---|---|
| Black Stilt* | Resident in Waitaki Valley, South Island where about 60 birds maintain a fragile existence, alongside White-headed Stilts with which it sometimes hybridises and migrates to the coast between January and July |
| Red-breasted Dotterel* | Widespread along northern coast of North Island where it is resident. Also winters (Mar–Aug) along the southeast coast of South Island and breeds on Stewart Island |
| Wrybill* | Breeds on riverbeds in highlands of South Island (e.g. Waitaki Valley and Fiordland NP) between August and December, and disperses to northern coast of North Island between February and July (although some birds remain at the coast all year round) |
| Red-billed Gull | Widespread, to Chatham Islands |
| Black-billed Gull | Widespread |
| Black-fronted Tern* | Breeds in highlands of South Island (e.g. Waitaki Valley and Fiordland NP) between September and January, and disperses to coasts and Stewart Island between March and August |
| New Zealand Pigeon | Widespread |
| Kea* | State Highway Six, Waitaki Valley and Fiordland NP on South Island |
| Common Kaka* | Widespread but scarce and most likely to be seen on Little Barrier Island and at Pureora FP on North Island, or on Stewart Island |
| Yellow-fronted Parakeet* | Widespread but scarce, to Chatham and Subantarctic Islands. |
| Kakapo* | Unlikely to be seen by visiting birders because this flightless, nocturnal parrot—the world's largest—is extinct in its natural range and only present in restricted areas on Little Barrier, Codfish and Maud Islands where it has been introduced |
| Rifleman | Widespread |
| South Island Wren* | Rare in highlands of South Island where most likely to be seen at Fiordland NP, but also occurs along State Highway Six and in the Waitaki Valley |
| Grey Gerygone | Widespread |
| Stitchbird* | Introduced to Tiritiri Matangi, Little Barrier, Mokoia (in Lake Rotorua), Kapiti, Hen and Cuvier (off Coromandel Peninsula) Islands |
| New Zealand Bellbird | Widespread, to Subantarctic Islands |
| Tui | Widespread, to Chatham Islands and Auckland Islands in the Subantarctic Islands |
| Kokako* | Possible on Little Barrier and Kapiti |

| | |
|---|---|
| | Islands, and in Northland, but most likely at Pureora FP, North Island. Has also been recorded around Rotorua and may also occur on Stewart Island |
| Saddleback* | Introduced to Tiritiri Matangi, Little Barrier, Mokoia (in Lake Rotorua) and Kapiti Islands. Also present on Hen Island (north of Little Barrier Island), Moutuara Island (in Marlborough Sound) and Codfish Island (off Stewart Island) |
| Tomtit | Widespread, to Subantarctic Islands |
| New Zealand Robin | Widespread |
| Whitehead | Widespread, on North Island and its off-shore islands |
| Yellowhead* | Rare and localised on South Island. Most likely to be seen at Fiordland NP or Lake Sylvan near Mount Aspiring NP, but also occurs along State Highway Six and between Dunedin and Invercargill |
| Pipipi | Dunedin, Bluff and Fiordland NP on South Island, and Stewart Island |
| Fernbird | Widespread but localised and most likely at Matata Lagoons and Lake Taupo on North Island, and along southeast coast of South Island between Dunedin and Bluff, especially at Waituna Lagoon. Also present in Northland, and on Stewart and Subantarctic Islands |

The *malherbi* race of Yellow-fronted Parakeet*, known as Orange-fronted Parakeet, is considered to be a full species by some taxonomists. It is known from the Nelson area on South Island.

## Extinct 'Mainland' Endemics

| | |
|---|---|
| New Zealand Quail | Last recorded around 1870 |
| Laughing Owl | Last recorded around 1914 |
| Bush Wren | Last recorded on South Island in 1972 |
| Stephen Island Wren | Last recorded around 1894 on Stephen Island in the Cook Strait |
| Huia | Last recorded around 1907 on North Island |
| New Zealand Thrush | Last recorded in 1908 on North Island |

## Chatham Islands (7)

| | |
|---|---|
| Chatham Petrel* | Less than 150 birds breed on Rangatira |
| Chatham Shag* | Less than 1,000 birds remain, some of which still breed on the main island |
| Pitt Shag* | Less than 1,000 pairs remain, some of which still breed on the main island |
| Chatham Snipe* | About 1,000 pairs survive on Rangatira and Mangere (where reintroduced) |
| Shore Plover* | About 130 birds survive on Rangatira. This species was once common throughout New Zealand but it became extinct on the |

| | |
|---|---|
| | 'mainland' by the 1880s. A captive breeding programme at Mount Bruce National Wildlife Centre near Wellington was started in 1991 and has proved successful, hence the authorities are now considering releasing viable populations on predator-free offshore islands. Some have already been introduced to Motuora in the Hauraki Gulf (from where a few have moved to the mainland) and others may be introduced to Mana which is also in the Hauraki Gulf |
| Chatham Gerygone* | Widespread but localised |
| Chatham Robin | About 155 birds survive on Rangatira and Mangere, a remarkable total considering only seven birds were still alive in the late 1970s |

The endemic *eremita* race of Shy Albatross, the endemic *chathamensis* race of Variable Oystercatcher (approximately 100 birds survive on Chatham, Pitt, Rangatira and Mangere), and the endemic *forbesi* race of Yellow-fronted Parakeet*, are considered to be full species by some taxonomists.

## Extinct Chatham Islands Endemics

| | |
|---|---|
| Dieffenbach's Rail | Last recorded around 1900 |
| Chatham Rail | Last recorded around 1900 |
| Chatham Islands Fernbird | Last recorded around 1900 |

## Chatham and Subantarctic Islands (1)

| | |
|---|---|
| Fulmar Prion | Apparently resident around Chatham and Subantarctic Islands |

## Subantarctic Islands (10)

| | |
|---|---|
| Snares Crested Penguin* | Over 20,000 pairs were present on the Snares Islands in the mid 1980s |
| Erect-crested Penguin* | About 200,000 pairs, mainly on Antipodes and Bounty Islands. Has also attempted to breed on the Otago Peninsula near Dunedin on South Island, 'mainland' New Zealand |
| Royal Penguin | Endemic to Macquarie Island (under Australian administration) where there are about 850,000 pairs |
| Campbell Shag* | About 8,000 birds were present on Campbell Island in the mid-1970s |
| Auckland Shag* | About 4,000 birds survive on the Auckland Islands |
| Bounty Shag* | Less than 1,200 birds survive on the Bounty Islands |
| Flightless Teal* | About 1,500 birds survive on the Auckland Islands and between 60 and 100 on Dent Island, an islet off Campbell Island. Some taxonomists believe this is a subspecies of |

| | |
|---|---|
| | Brown Teal* |
| Auckland Rail* | Over 1,000 birds survive on Adams and Disappointment Islands in the Auckland Islands |
| Subantarctic Snipe* | Survives in small numbers on Auckland, Snares and Antipodes Islands |
| Antipodes Parakeet* | Between 2,000 and 3,000 birds are believed to survive on the Antipodes Islands |

The endemic *purpurascens* race of Imperial Shag, present on Macquarie Island, is considered to be a full species by some taxonomists.

## Extinct Subantarctic Islands Endemics

| | |
|---|---|
| Auckland Islands Merganser | Last recorded around 1905 |

## Breeding Endemic Seabirds

Mottled Petrel (on and around Stewart and Snares Islands), Cook's Petrel* (Little Barrier, Great Barrier and Codfish Islands), Pycroft's Petrel* (islands off northeast New Zealand), Magenta Petrel* (only four pairs of this mysterious species are known to be breeding on the Chatham Islands, but the population may actually lie between 45 and 150 birds—the type-specimen was collected south of the Pitcairn Islands in 1867 and that remains the only record away from the breeding colony), Parkinson's Petrel* (Little Barrier and Great Barrier Islands), Westland Petrel* (coastal hills around Punakaiki on South Island), Buller's Shearwater* (islands off New Zealand), Fluttering Shearwater (islands off New Zealand), Hutton's Shearwater* (Kaikoura Range in northeast South Island).

## Near-endemic Breeding Seabirds

White-necked Petrel* (Macauley Island in the Kermadec Islands).

## Near-endemics

Hoary-headed Grebe, Little Penguin, Australian Gannet, Pied Cormorant, Australian Shoveler, Australasian Bittern*, Australian Ibis, Pied Oystercatcher, Double-banded Plover, Black-fronted Dotterel, Masked Lapwing, White-fronted and Fairy* Terns, Red-fronted Parakeet, Long-tailed Koel, Australasian Pipit.

# PAPUA NEW GUINEA

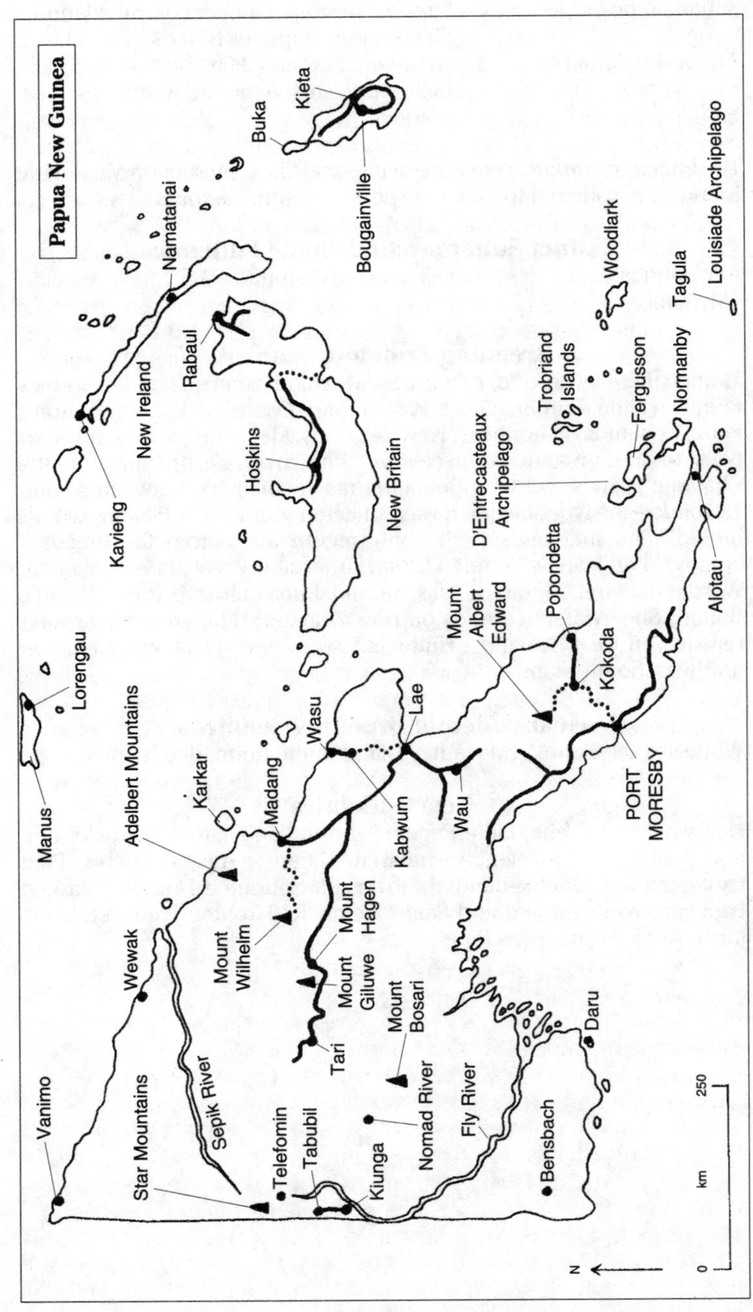

# INTRODUCTION

## Summary

This country's modern infrastructure makes birding here much easier than in Irian Jaya, but Papua New Guinea is nowhere near as friendly and safe as its western neighbour. Most of the best sites are accessible by air and road and lie close to good, but expensive, accommodation, hence there is no need to organise mini trekking expeditions to see such high quality birds as Ribbon-tailed Astrapia* and Blue Bird-of-paradise*.

First-time visitors to New Guinea face a difficult decision when it comes to choosing between Papua New Guinea and Irian Jaya, at least as far as the birds are concerned. On a trip to mainland Papua New Guinea one could reasonably expect to see up to 23 birds-of-paradise (26 if the Huon Peninsula is included), including Ribbon-tailed Astrapia*, and Raggiana and Blue* Birds-of-paradise, the three most spectacular endemics, whereas in Irian Jaya one could reasonably expect to see up to 24 birds-of-paradise, including Wilson's* and Red* Birds-of-paradise, the two most spectacular endemics, as well as MacGregor's Bird-of-paradise*, which is much easier to see in Irian Jaya. So, a draw would seem a fair result as far as birds-of-paradise are concerned. What may sway the first time visitor to New Guinea, for whom expense is not a problem, to visit one or the other half may therefore come down to personal taste in birds-of-paradise or the chance of seeing other spectacular species. Hence, birders primarily interested in birds-of-paradise will have to work out which is the more fantastic—Wilson's* or Blue* (males of the former are much more likely to be seen, especially displaying)—or the more bizarre—MacGregor's Bird-of-paradise* (with its big yellow eye-wattles) or Ribbon-tailed Astrapia* (with its long silky white tail), since Red* and Raggiana are very similar. As far as other species go, Southern Crowned-Pigeon* and Painted Quail-thrush are most likely to be seen in Papua New Guinea, and Shovel-billed Kookaburra* and Blue-black Kingfisher* are more likely to be seen in Irian Jaya. Either way, a birding trip to New Guinea which concentrates on such birds is likely to be a tantalising, but ultimately richly rewarding experience.

## Size

At 462,840 sq km Papua New Guinea is 3.6 times larger than England and 1.5 times smaller than Texas.

## Getting Around

There are still only a few major roads in Papua New Guinea and because the interior terrain is so rugged one has yet to be built which crosses the mountainous central spine of the country. Hence the best way to get from site to site is by air and Public Motor Vehicle (PMV), although the majority of birding visitors tend to be on organised tours which provide transport between airstrips and lodges, because travelling by PMV is only totally safe in some areas of the country. The far-reaching internal air network makes use of numerous airstrips, but most flights are expensive. The major carriers are Air Niugini, Talair and the Missionary Aviation Fellowship, which can be contacted at PO Box 273, Mount Hagen, Western Highlands (tel: 55 1506). Where there are roads there are usually plenty of PMVs, in the form of minibuses and trucks. It is also possible to hire 4WD vehicles in most towns, but this is an expensive and dangerous form of transport (see under 'Health and Safety'). Passenger boats ply the coastal waters along the north coast and between the islands to the north and east of the mainland. Lutheran Shipping, PO Box 1459, Lae, Morobe Province (tel: 42 2066, fax: 42 5806) is one of the major operators and they run a regular service to New Britain. The few sites which are off the beaten track can be reached on foot, via steep, often wet and muddy trails, and with the assistance of local guides and porters. When hiring such help a grasp of 'pidgin', a local form of English, would be helpful. Many local people speak 'pidgin', despite the fact that Papua New Guinea is home to thousands of tribes, many of which have been isolated for a long time by the rugged terrain, and there are well over 700 languages.

## Accommodation and Food

All types of formal accommodation, from the luxurious Western-style hotels and lodges to mission-run guesthouses and hostels, are very expensive. These types of accommodation can be found almost everywhere on the mainland, and in most towns on the offshore islands. In remote regions it is possible to stay as paying guests with local people, but don't expect to sleep on anything other than one hell of a dirty floor. Hence birders intending to bird away from the beaten track may prefer to take a tent, since permission to camp in villages is usually granted. It is much safer to camp with the locals than to pitch a tent in the forest, but whether you camp or move in with the locals, you are still a paying guest, and should therefore repay their hospitality. Gifts are usually appreciated much more than money, especially matches, tobacco, fishing gear, pens and pencils, salt and clothes. Remember that all land in the country is under private ownership and failure to seek permission to 'use' it may lead to unacceptable demands for compensation.

In towns Western and Chinese foods are widely available but expensive. The staple food of the local people in the highlands is sago and sweet potato, supplemented with bananas and the occasional pig, a diet which certainly suits budget birders. Locally brewed SP beer is widely available.

## Health and Safety

Immunisation against hepatitis, polio, typhoid and yellow fever (if arriving from an infected country) is recommended, as are all possible precautions against malaria. Take care to treat river and stream water for it may harbour many diseases, including amoebic dysentery.

Apart from the expense the major reason why Papua New Guinea has been out of favour with independent budget birders for many years is because it is a very dangerous country to travel in. Parts of Port Moresby, where violent crime is commonplace, look like war zones with heavily barricaded buildings, and it would be foolish to walk around this town, or Wau, Lae or Mount Hagen alone after dark, especially on the fortnightly friday pay-days when drunks often get out of hand. However, as is the case in many parts of the world where the Western influence is still in its fledgling stages, the further one gets away from so-called civilization, the friendlier the people are, especially if one makes an effort to be friendly towards them, and Papua New Guinea is no exception. Furthermore, the country is mercifully free of corrupt and violent officials, and blessed with careful PMV drivers who live in fear of 'payback', a traditional form of compensation where if something is destroyed it must be returned promptly. PMVs are the targets for armed hold-ups. These are rarely violent once out of the main towns, but in 1995 one birder, who was working for Conservation International, had to travel between Wau and Bulolo in the company of an armed police escort. It would be much more expensive, dangerous and potentially life-threatening to hire a vehicle. Especially in and around Port Moresby, where such vehicles are a prime target for highway robbers, and if someone is killed in a road accident payback may be sought. Birders who use PMVs carefully during the day might just complete a budget birding trip to Papua New Guinea without too many harrowing tales to tell.

## Climate and Timing

Papua New Guinea has a warm, wet equatorial climate and rain falls throughout the year in the highlands, usually in the form of torrential downpours during the afternoon and overnight. However, in the coastal lowlands there is a normally distinct dry season which lasts from May to September. The months of July and August are the wettest of the year on the islands to the east though, hence the driest time to visit the mainland and islands such as New Britain during the same trip is May and June. However, male birds-of-paradise are much more active and are more likely to be seen displaying from July onwards.

Hot weather, cold weather and wet weather birding gear will all be needed for an extensive birding trip, as hot, humid damp days give way to chilly nights in the highlands, when the temperature can drop to freezing.

## Habitats

New Guinea is the tallest tropical island on earth, rising to 4508 m (14,790 ft) at Mount Wilhelm in Papua New Guinea, but even higher, to 5209 m (16,499 ft) at Gunung Jaya (Carstensz) in neighbouring Irian Jaya, the highest peak between the Himalayas and the Andes. Many more high mountains form the island's 2000 km long snow-capped spine and their rugged slopes, together with the lowlands, support 700,000 sq km of forest, the largest tract of forested land away from Amazonia and the Congo Basin. There are no forests above 3000 m (9843 ft), only rolling subalpine meadows, with stunted tree-ferns, lakes, bogs and tussock grass. These high-altitude grasslands give way to stunted moss forests at the tree-line, then montane and lowland rainforests which together still cover 70% of the island. There are no monkeys or large ground-dwelling predators in these forests, only seven species of tree-kangaroo, some mainly nocturnal marsupials such as cuscuses, more species of fruit-bat than anywhere else on earth, the world's largest butterfly (Queen Alexandra's Birdwing) and moth (Hercules Moth), and a number of large ground-dwelling birds such as cassowaries and crowned-pigeons. These forests, particularly the moist, mossy montane variety, also support the vast majority of the world's birds-of-paradise. In parts of the highlands there are broad fertile valleys, such as the Tari Basin, which have been farmed for centuries. The interior of the island is so wonderfully wild that these valleys were not seen by people from outside New Guinea until the 1930s.

The remote, rugged forested interior is drained by numerous streams, many of which plunge vertically off the precipitous slopes. Once they reach the coastal lowlands, however, they become wide, muddy, meandering rivers flowing slowly through floodplains and tall lowland peat-swamp forests. In the north the coastal plain is relatively narrow, but in the south it is very wide, especially in the Trans-Fly region of the south-west. Here there are rivers, seasonally flooded savanna grasslands and permanent steamy swamps which support masses of waterbirds, many of which also occur in northern Australia, which is only 100 km or so to the south. Areas of mangrove and beaches line the coast, and some of the world's richest coral reefs lie offshore. The offshore volcanic islands, including New Britain, New Ireland and Bougainville, are also heavily forested and rise above 2000 m (6562 ft).

## Conservation

Extensive tracts of natural habitat still remain in Papua New Guinea. The forested areas, especially montane forests on the rugged, inhospitable slopes of the interior mountains, have escaped the axe until now. However, with an annual natural increase in the human population of 2.3%, many of whom still practice the slash-and-burn style of cultivation, and the imminent arrival of Malaysian logging companies who practise clear-felling, some of the world's richest forests and wildest places look doomed. The 83 threatened and near-threatened species which occur in Papua New Guinea have proved difficult to protect anyway, as every square metre of land is under long-established local ownership, and whilst it has been possible for the government to purchase some small blocks of land, such as that within the four National Parks, landowners are much more likely to sell their land for the large sums of money offered by logging and mining companies than the paltry amounts on offer from the government. The government and some landowners are at least attempting to overcome this crisis by establishing Wildlife Management Areas where over-exploitation is discouraged, but with many birds declining and so few male birds-of-paradise around, far more needs to be done to conserve this country's amazing avifauna.

## Bird Families

The two families which are endemic to New Guinea (Berrypeckers and Tit/Crested Berrypeckers) are represented, as are the eight families shared with Australia (Cassowaries, Australian Creepers, Bowerbirds, Fairywrens, Logrunners, Pseudo-babblers, Butcherbirds and Magpie-lark/Torrent-lark). Hence ten of the 20 families endemic to Australasia and Oceania are present.

## Bird Species

Over 646 species have been recorded in Papua New Guinea (out of over 700 species which have been recorded in New Guinea). Non-endemic specialities and spectacular species which occur outside New Guinea include Southern Cassowary*, Green Pygmy-goose, Great-billed* and Pied Herons, Black-necked Stork, Wedge-tailed Eagle, White-browed Crake, Brolga, Australian Bustard, Comb-crested Jacana, Dusky Woodcock, Bush Thick-knee, Black Noddy, Wompoo and Superb Fruit-Doves, Palm Cockatoo*, Channel-billed Cuckoo, Papuan and Marbled Frogmouths, Moustached Treeswift, Azure, Little and Variable Kingfishers, Blue-winged Kookaburra, Forest, Beach and Yellow-billed Kingfishers, Common and Buff-breasted Paradise-Kingfishers, Blue-tailed and Rainbow Bee-eaters, Blyth's Hornbill, Hooded and Red-bellied Pittas, Varied Sittella, Logrunner, Yellow-breasted Boatbill, Magnificent Riflebird, Island Thrush and Blue-faced Parrotfinch.

## Endemics

A total of 86 species are endemic to Papua New Guinea, 25 of which occur on the mainland, and 61 of which are restricted to offshore islands, mainly in the Bismarck Archipelago (compared with 44 species which are endemic to Irian Jaya). In total 399 species are endemic to New Guinea, of which 269 species occur in Papua New Guinea and Irian Jaya. Papua New Guinea's mainland endemics include Brown-headed Paradise-Kingfisher and ten birds-of-paradise, notably Ribbon-tailed Astrapia*, and Raggiana and Blue* Birds-of-paradise. The off-shore island endemics include Bismarck and New Britain Kingfishers, Black-headed Pitta* and two birds-of-paradise; Curl-crested Manucode and Goldie's Bird-of-paradise*, both of which occur in the remote D'Entrecasteaux Archipelago. New Guinea endemics which are regularly recorded in Papua New Guinea include Pheasant Pigeon, Victoria* and Southern* Crowned-Pigeons, Spangled and Rufous-bellied Kookaburras, Hook-billed and Mountain Kingfishers, Flame Bowerbird, Black Sittella, Painted Quail-thrush, three jewel-babblers, 26 birds-of-paradise (including King, King-of-Saxony and Twelve-wired) and last, but by no means least, the beautiful Crested Berrypecker.

There are many near-endemics, most of which are shared only with Australia, but 25 species which are otherwise confined to the Solomon Islands occur on the islands of Buka and Bougainville, which are politically part of Papua New Guinea but ecologically akin to the Solomon Islands. These include Solomon Sea-Eagle*, Ultramarine and Moustached* Kingfishers, and Black-faced Pitta*.

## Expectations

It is possible to see around 300 species on a three- or four-week trip to the mainland, including 15 of the 25 mainland endemics (20 if the Huon Peninsula is included in the itinerary), 14 species of kingfisher and up to 23 birds-of-paradise (26 if the Huon Peninsula is included in the itinerary), of which six of the ten endemic to the mainland are likely (nine if the Huon Peninsula is included in the itinerary). On a longer trip that lasts at least six weeks and includes the offshore islands of Manus, New Ireland and New Britain it would be possible to add most of the 50 Bismarck Archipelago endemics and end up with a trip list in the region of 370.

# *MAINLAND*

## PORT MORESBY

Papua New Guinea's capital, which straddles Paga Point, a hilly promontory on the southeast coast, lies in the richest region for birds in the country. The nearby palm-fringed beaches, mangroves, lagoons, sago swamps, *pandanus*-dotted 'kunai' grasslands, eucalypt savanna and lowland rainforests support a superb assortment of birds, including Blue-winged and Rufous-bellied Kookaburras, Common Paradise-Kingfisher,

Blue and Chestnut-backed Jewel-babblers, and King, Twelve-wired and Raggiana Birds-of-paradise.

Unfortunately, independent birders will find it very difficult to see such wonderful birds because the Port Moresby area is one of the most dangerous in the world. The latest in a long line of curfews (2200 to 0400) was declared in November 1996 due to a series of vehicle hijacks, as well as violent murders, muggings and sexual assaults. Hence before contemplating birding around Port Moresby it is wise to contact the Papua New Guinea Bird Society in advance. The committee members are usually extremely helpful and welcome visitors to join their society outings. If it proves impossible to link up with the society's activities and you are desperate to get into the field, it is possible to reach most of the sites near Port Moresby via PMVs or a 4WD hire-vehicle, but remember to keep windows up, doors locked and only leave the vehicle if it is absolutely necessary.

### Papua New Guinea Endemics

White-bellied Whistler, Eastern Riflebird, Raggiana Bird-of-paradise, Grey-headed Munia.

### Localised New Guinea Endemics

Orange-fronted Fruit-Dove, Yellow-streaked Lory, Silver-eared Honeyeater, Black Myzomela, Spot-breasted Meliphaga, Olive-yellow* and White-rumped Robins.

### Other New Guinea Endemics

Long-tailed Honey-buzzard, Grey-headed Goshawk, Black-billed Brush-turkey, Black-billed Cuckoo-Dove, Pink-spotted, Ornate, Coroneted, Orange-bellied and Dwarf Fruit-Doves, Purple-tailed, Pinon and Zoe Imperial-Pigeons, Buff-faced Pygmy-Parrot, Orange-breasted Fig-Parrot, Papuan King-Parrot, Black-capped Lory, White-crowned Koel, Greater Black Coucal, Jungle Hawk-Owl, Papuan Needletail, Rufous-bellied Kookaburra, Hook-billed Kingfisher, White-shouldered and Emperor Fairywrens, Rusty Mouse-Warbler, Pale-billed Scrubwren, Yellow-bellied Gerygone, Red-throated and Red Myzomelas, Puff-backed, Mimic, Yellow-gaped and Spotted Honeyeaters, Olive Flyrobin, Black-sided Robin, Dwarf and Rusty Whistlers, Rusty and Crested Pitohuis, Blue and Chestnut-backed Jewel-babblers, Chestnut-bellied Fantail, Sooty and White-bellied Thicket-Fantails, Rufous-backed Fantail, Spot-winged and Golden Monarchs, Grey Crow, Glossy-mantled and Crinkle-collared Manucodes, King and Twelve-wired Birds-of-paradise, Lowland Peltops, Hooded Butcherbird, Brown Oriole, Stout-billed, Boyer's, Grey-headed, New Guinea and Golden Cuckoo-shrikes, Golden Myna, Red-capped Flowerpecker, Black Berrypecker, Dwarf and Pygmy Honeyeaters.

### Non-endemic Specialities

Spotted Whistling-Duck, Chestnut-breasted Cuckoo, Yellow-billed Kingfisher, Fawn-breasted Bowerbird, Green-backed and Tawny-breasted Honeyeaters, Yellow-legged Flycatcher, White-faced Robin, Northern Scrub-Robin, Frilled Monarch, Yellow-breasted Boatbill, Trumpet Manucode, Black-backed Butcherbird.

### Others

Australasian Grebe, Lesser Frigatebird, Little Pied and Little Black

Cormorants, Australian Darter, Wandering Whistling-Duck, Radjah Shelduck, Green Pygmy-goose, Pacific Black Duck, Pacific Reef-Egret, Intermediate Egret, Great-billed* and Pied Herons, Rufous Night-Heron, Pacific Baza, Whistling and Brahminy Kites, White-bellied Sea-Eagle, Eastern Marsh-Harrier, Swamp Harrier, Grey and Brown Goshawks, Collared Sparrowhawk, Little Eagle, Orange-footed Scrubfowl, Brown Quail, Buff-banded Rail, White-browed Crake, Purple Swamphen, Dusky Moorhen, Comb-crested Jacana, Little (Oct–Apr) and Far Eastern* Curlews, Grey-tailed Tattler, Sharp-tailed Sandpiper, Pacific Golden-Plover, Great Crested-Tern, Roseate and Black-naped Terns, Great Cuckoo-Dove, Emerald, Stephan's, Peaceful and Bar-shouldered Doves, Wompoo and Superb Fruit-Doves, Torresian Imperial-Pigeon, Papuan Mountain-Pigeon, Red-cheeked and Eclectus Parrots, Sulphur-crested Cockatoo, Rainbow and Red-flanked Lorikeets, Oriental (Oct–Apr) and Brush Cuckoos, Australian Koel, Pheasant Coucal, Moustached Tree-swift, Glossy and Uniform Swiftlets, Azure, Little and Variable Kingfishers, Blue-winged Kookaburra, Forest and Collared Kingfishers, Common Paradise-Kingfisher, Rainbow Bee-eater, Dollarbird, Blyth's Hornbill, Hooded and Red-bellied Pittas, Green-backed, Fairy, White-throated, Large-billed and Mangrove Gerygones, Brown Honeyeater, Dusky and Red-headed Myzomelas, Graceful, Yellow-tinted and White-throated Honeyeaters, New Guinea Friarbird, Brown-backed and Rufous-banded Honeyeaters, Lemon-bellied Flycatcher, Mangrove Robin, Grey and Black-tailed Whistlers, Rufous and Grey Shrike-Thrushes, Willie-wagtail, Northern, Mangrove and Rufous Fantails, Black-faced Monarch (Apr–Aug), Leaden, Broad-billed, Restless and Shining Flycatchers, Torresian Crow, Black Butcherbird, Green Figbird, Black-faced, Yellow-eyed and White-bellied Cuckoo-shrikes, Common Cicadabird, White-winged and Varied Trillers, Singing and Metallic Starlings, Yellow-faced Myna, Pied Bushchat, Pacific Swallow, Tree Martin (Apr–Aug), Golden-headed Cisticola, Clamorous Reed-Warbler, Chestnut-breasted Munia, Black and Olive-backed Sunbirds.

(Other species recorded here include Doria's Goshawk*, New Guinea Bronzewing* (Veimauri), Thick-billed Ground-Pigeon* (Veimauri), Collared Imperial-Pigeon, Long-billed Cuckoo, Black Noddy, Rufous Owl, Barred Owlet-Nightjar, Spotted Catbird, Wallace's Fairywren and Black Thicket-Fantail.)

The **Moitaka Sewage Works**, 12 km from the town centre, is a good site for waterbirds including Spotted Whistling-Duck, as well as other species such as Orange-fronted Fruit-Dove. To reach here, turn left a few kilometres beyond the end of the Jackson Airport runway, off the road to Sogeri and Varirata National Park. Other sites near town worth checking out if time allows are the safe grounds of the **South Pacific Adventists' College**, 20 km from town (White-browed Crake, Comb-crested Jacana and Fawn-breasted Bowerbird), the small botanical gardens on the university campus and Paga Point (terns, possibly including Black Noddy). The lowland forest at **Brown River**, about 30 minutes to the north of town via the Hiritano Highway, was badly affected by fire in late 1992, but may still support Black-billed Brush-turkey, Orange-breasted Fig-Parrot, Rufous-bellied Kookaburra, Common Paradise-kingfisher, Emperor Fairywren, Crested Pitohui, Blue Jewel-babbler, King (display tree) and Raggiana Birds-of-paradise, and Dwarf

Honeyeater. Bird the roadside and logging tracks (4WD recommended). One hour north from town via the Hiritano Highway bird the logging tracks (4WD recommended) at **Veimauri** where New Guinea Bronzewing*, Long-billed Cuckoo, Wallace's Fairywren, Olive-yellow Robin* and Golden Cuckoo-shrike have been recorded. The **Vanapa River** area is also accessible via the Hiritano Highway, about 45 minutes northwest of town. The remnant humid lowland forest here supports Olive-yellow Robin* and Twelve-wired Bird-of-paradise, as well as Common Paradise-Kingfisher, Emperor Fairywren and Blue Jewel-babbler. Further north, the Hiritano Highway passes **Kanosia Lagoon** (Little Curlew, Blue-winged Kookaburra. White-shouldered Fairywren, Grey-headed Munia), **Hisiu Lagoon** (Radjah Shelduck, Pied Heron), **Hisiu Beach** (shorebirds) and **Cape Suckling** (mangrove specialities). Food and fuel are available at Aroa.

*Accommodation:* University of Australia Guesthouse (in Boroko), Port Moresby Travelodge (A+), Airways Hotel (A+), Ela Beach Hotel, Salvation Army (A).

*One of the best birds to look for around Port Moresby is the widespread and whacky Twelve-wired Bird-of-paradise*

## VARIRATA NATIONAL PARK

Over 180 species have been recorded in the eucalypt savanna, gallery forest and low montane rainforest in this small (10 sq km) park, which is situated at about 580 m (1903 ft) in the Astrolabe Range above Port Moresby. It is a particularly good site for ground-dwelling species such as Dwarf Cassowary*, Black-billed Brush-turkey, Pheasant Pigeon, Painted Quail-thrush and Chestnut-backed Jewel-babbler, although all of these birds are very thin on the ground and difficult to find, especially after early morning.

The wettest time of year here lasts from December to April, but most rain falls in the afternoon, so birding is still possible at this time of year. The park is very popular at weekends and best avoided at that time.

### Papua New Guinea Endemics

Brown-headed Paradise-kingfisher, Eastern Riflebird, Raggiana Bird-of-paradise.

## Localised New Guinea Endemics

Dwarf Cassowary*, Pheasant Pigeon, Black Myzomela, Painted Quail-thrush, Black Fantail, Slaty-chinned Longbill.

## Other New Guinea Endemics

Long-tailed Honey-buzzard, Black-billed Brush-turkey, Black-billed Cuckoo-Dove, Cinnamon Ground-Dove, Pink-spotted, Beautiful and Orange-bellied Fruit-Doves, Purple-tailed and Zoe Imperial-Pigeons, Buff-faced Pygmy-Parrot, Papuan King-Parrot, Black-capped Lory, White-crowned Koel, Hook-billed Kingfisher, White-eared Catbird, White-shouldered Fairywren, Rusty Mouse-Warbler, Pale-billed Scrubwren, Yellow-bellied Gerygone, Long-billed Honeyeater, Red and Mountain Myzomelas, Puff-backed, Mimic and Spotted Honeyeaters, Dwarf Whistler, Hooded and Crested Pitohuis, Chestnut-backed Jewel-babbler, Chestnut-bellied Fantail, Black and Spot-winged Monarchs, Papuan Drongo, Grey Crow, Crinkle-collared Manucode, Magnificent Bird-of-paradise, Brown Oriole, Stout-billed, Papuan and New Guinea Cuckoo-shrikes, Black-fronted White-eye, Red-capped Flowerpecker, Black Berrypecker, Dwarf Honeyeater.

## Non-endemic Specialities

Yellow-billed Kingfisher, Fawn-breasted Bowerbird, Tawny-breasted Honeyeater, Yellow-legged Flycatcher, White-faced Robin, Northern Scrub-Robin, Frilled Monarch, Yellow-breasted Boatbill.

## Others

Australasian Grebe, Pacific Baza, Whistling Kite, Little Eagle, Great Cuckoo-Dove, Emerald Dove, Wompoo and Superb Fruit-Doves, Papuan Mountain-Pigeon, Red-flanked Lorikeet, Papuan Frogmouth, Glossy Swiftlet, Azure Kingfisher, Blue-winged Kookaburra, Forest Kingfisher, Rainbow Bee-eater, Dollarbird, Hooded Pitta, Fairy Gerygone, Dusky Myzomela, Graceful and White-throated Honeyeaters, New Guinea Friarbird, Lemon-bellied Flycatcher, Grey Whistler, Black-faced Monarch (Apr–Aug), Leaden Flycatcher, Torresian Crow, Black Butcherbird, Black-faced, Yellow-eyed and White-bellied Cuckoo-shrikes, Varied Triller, Yellow-faced Myna.

The park is 45 minutes by road from Port Moresby, about 45 km to the east via Rouna Falls. The best way to reach the park is by taxi, although PMVs go to the park turn-off near Sogeri, 5 km from the entrance gate. It is open from 0700 to dusk daily and there is a small entrance fee. Bird the steep, obscure trail to the south of the road 300 m before the entrance gate and just before the 'National Park' signpost, and the excellent network of trails within the park itself. The trail before the entrance gate runs through forest to an open scrubby area and is good for Black-billed Brush-turkey, Brown-headed Paradise-kingfisher, White-eared Catbird, Crested Pitohui and Crinkle-collared Manucode. The best trail inside the park is the Varirata Circuit Trail, which winds back from the picnic site near the HQ, 1 km beyond the entrance gate, to the entrance road. Dwarf Cassowary* and Pheasant Pigeon are most likely along here with careful stalking, and there is a Raggiana Bird-of-paradise display tree signposted about halfway along the trail which is usually in use between 0600 and 0700, and around 1600, especially between June and November. The trail to Gare's Lookout is also worth

**VARIRATA NP**

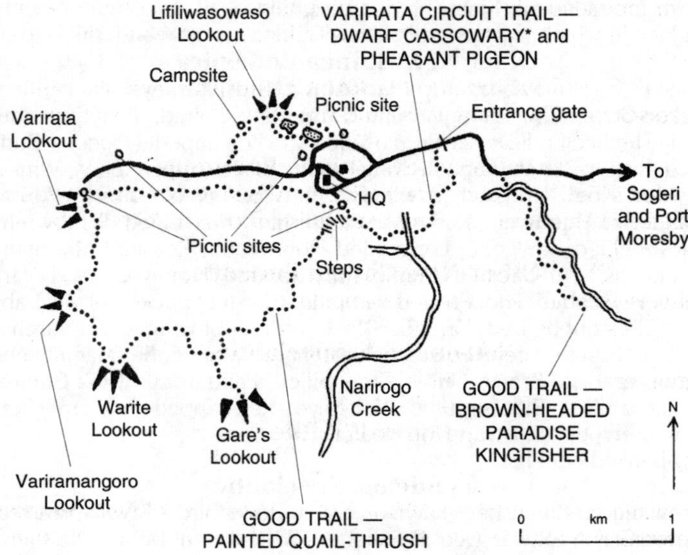


birding, with the possibilities including Painted Quail-thrush. There is another Raggiana Bird-of-paradise display tree on the top of a hill to the south of the road to Varirata Lookout 2 km from the HQ.

*Accommodation:* lodge (A—bookable on arrival/take food and utensils/no electricity) and campsite (not totally safe/take supplies), bookable in advance via National Parks, Department of Environment and Conservation, Waigani, or the Chief Ranger (tel: 25 9340). Weekends are usually booked well in advance.

## OWEN STANLEY RANGES

The scenic forested mountain slopes, small alpine lakes and swampy montane meadows, including the Neon Basin, a level grassy plain situated at 3000 m (9843 ft), around Mount Albert Edward, which rises to 3990 m (13,091 ft), support the full set of species one would expect at this altitude in southeast New Guinea. The avifauna is similar to that found in the Tari Valley (p. 352), with such notable exceptions as Greater Ground-Robin and MacGregor's Bird-of-paradise*, a bird which is only likely to be seen here, in Papua New Guinea, and in the Snow Mountains of Irian Jaya.

Hence independent budget birders may wish to consider birding these rarely visited ranges, particularly the Mount Albert Edward area, instead of the Tari Valley. Both sites are served by daily flights from Port Moresby and both boast conveniently situated tourist lodges. It is possible to see most of the goodies in the Tari Valley on daily excursions from the lodge, whereas it will be necessary to organise a four-day trek, with local guides, to see some of the best birds here, including MacGregor's Bird-of-paradise*. However, this is a far cheaper and safer site for independent birders to visit, and, best of all, a far more beautiful place in which to see some of New Guinea's most wonderful birds.

### Papua New Guinea Endemics

Princess Stephanie's Astrapia, Alpine Munia.

### Localised New Guinea Endemics

Salvadori's Teal*, Greater Ground-Robin, Alpine Robin, Black Sittella, Crested and MacGregor's* Birds-of-paradise, Brown Sicklebill.

### Other New Guinea Endemics

Spotted Jewel-babbler, Lesser Melampitta.

### Non-endemic Specialities

Logrunner.

### Other Wildlife

Long-beaked echidna.

The mixed montane forests above 2100 m (6890 ft) at **Myola** support Greater Ground-Robin (above 3000 m (9843 ft)), as well as Spotted Jewel-babbler, Lesser Melampitta, Crested Bird-of-paradise, Brown Sicklebill and Princess Stephanie's Astrapia. The local guides know where the display trees of the birds-of-paradise are. The Myola area is accessible via charter flights from Port Moresby, or on foot (two hours each way) from between Kagi and Efoge Creek on the Kokoda Trail. The rough 94 km long Kokoda Trail, popular with travelling backpackers, traverses the Owen Stanley Ranges, reaching a height of 2190 m (7185 ft), and takes a week to complete. It begins at Owers' Corner, 50 km east of Port Moresby, and ends at Kokoda after passing through numerous small villages. At Kokoda another trail leads west to Tapini via Woitape, from where it is possible to bird the **Mount Albert Edward** area where MacGregor's Bird-of-paradise* (in upper montane forest on southwest slope of Neon Basin), as well as Greater Ground-Robin, Alpine Robin, Logrunner, Crested Bird-of-paradise and Alpine Munia, occur. TransNiugini Airways and Milne Bay Air operate flights from Port Moresby to Woitape on a daily basis, landing somewhat spectacularly on a small airstrip near the Owen Stanley Lodge where guides and porters can be organised. Many locals will assure you that they know the area well, but few do, so it is best to ask at the lodge for help in organising a trek as they know the best guides. Guests of the lodge may be offered free guides. From Woitape, which lies at 1600 m (5249 ft) it is possible to reach lower montane forest at 3000 m (9843 ft) within a day, but it is a four-day round trip to the summit and back. To tackle this trek it will be necessary to take camping gear, all supplies, including food for all, and full cold weather gear.

*Accommodation:* Myola—Myola Guesthouse (A). Woitape—Owen Stanley Lodge (A), bookable in advance via PO Box 6036, Boroko (tel: 25 7999). Catholic Mission (C).

## LAKEKAMU BASIN

The vast expanse of lowland rainforest in the wild Lakekamu Basin supports almost the complete set of New Guinea's lowland forest birds and the highest diversity of pigeons (24), parrots (17) and kingfishers (11) found at any one site on earth! The avian stars include Southern Cassowary*, Forest Bittern*, Southern Crowned-Pigeon*, Shovel-billed Kookaburra* and Golden-backed Whistler.

Inevitably, one of the few wildernesses left on planet earth is under threat from logging companies, but the indigenous people are being helped in their fight to protect their land by a project aimed at involving them in adventure tourism and ongoing research. This project is managed by Conservation International, 1015 18th Street NW, Washington DC 20036, USA, and this organisation is keen to see more birders visiting the area, so for the latest information on visiting arrangements contact them or the Lakekamu Project, Foundation of Peoples of the South Pacific, PO Box 1119, Boroko, NCD, Papua New Guinea.

### Papua New Guinea Endemics

Eastern Riflebird, Raggiana Bird-of-paradise, Grey-headed Munia.

### Localised New Guinea Endemics

Salvadori's Teal*, Forest Bittern*, Thick-billed Ground-Pigeon*, Pheasant Pigeon, Southern Crowned-Pigeon*, Yellow-streaked Lory, Goldie's and Striated* Lorikeets, Papuan Nightjar, Shovel-billed Kookaburra*, Tawny Straightbill, Plain and Streak-headed Honeyeaters, Golden-backed Whistler, Yellow-eyed Starling*, Yellow-bellied Longbill.

### Other New Guinea Endemics

Long-tailed Honey-buzzard, Grey-headed Goshawk, Black-billed Brush-turkey, Black-billed Cuckoo-Dove, Pink-spotted, Ornate, Coroneted, Beautiful, Orange-bellied and Dwarf Fruit-Doves, Purple-tailed, Pinon and Zoe Imperial-Pigeons, Buff-faced Pygmy-Parrot, Orange-breasted and Large Fig-Parrots, Pesquet's Parrot*, Dusky and Black-capped Lories, Pygmy and Fairy Lorikeets, White-eared Bronze-Cuckoo, White-crowned and Dwarf Koels, Greater Black Coucal, Jungle Hawk-Owl, Papuan Needletail, Rufous-bellied Kookaburra, Hook-billed Kingfisher, White-eared Catbird, Emperor Fairywren, Rusty Mouse-Warbler, Yellow-bellied Gerygone, Long-billed Honeyeater, Red-throated Myzomela, Scrub, Puff-backed, Mimic and Obscure Honeyeaters, Meyer's Friarbird, Torrent Flycatcher, Olive Flyrobin, Black-sided Robin, Variable, Rusty and Crested Pitohuis, New Guinea Babbler, Blue Jewel-babbler, Sooty, Black and White-bellied Thicket-Fantails, Rufous-backed Fantail, Black, Spot-winged, Hooded and Golden Monarchs, Papuan Drongo, Grey Crow, Glossy-mantled and Crinkle-collared Manucodes, King and Twelve-wired Birds-of-paradise, Lowland Peltops, Hooded Butcherbird, Brown Oriole, Boyer's, Grey-headed, New Guinea and Golden Cuckoo-shrikes, Golden Myna, Red-capped Flowerpecker, Black Berrypecker, Dwarf and Pygmy Honeyeaters.

### Non-endemic Specialities

Southern Cassowary*, Palm Cockatoo*, Marbled Frogmouth, Yellow-billed Kingfisher, Green-backed and Tawny-breasted Honeyeaters, Frilled Monarch, Yellow-breasted Boatbill, Trumpet Manucode.

### Others

Great-billed Heron*, Bat Hawk, Great Cuckoo-Dove, Papuan Mountain-Pigeon, Red-cheeked and Eclectus Parrots, Red-flanked Lorikeet, Papuan Frogmouth, Moustached Treeswift, Little and Variable Kingfishers, Common Paradise-kingfisher, Blyth's Hornbill, Rainbow Bee-eater, Hooded and Red-bellied Pittas, Green-backed, Fairy and Large-billed Gerygones, Graceful Honeyeater, New Guinea Friarbird, Black Butcherbird, Varied Triller, Singing and Metallic Starlings, Yellow-faced Myna, Blue-faced Parrotfinch, Black Sunbird.

(Other species recorded here include New Guinea Eagle*, Red-necked Crake, Bare-eyed Rail, New Guinea Bronzewing*, Cinnamon Ground-Dove, Long-billed Cuckoo and Buff-breasted Paradise-kingfisher.)

Kakoro airstrip in the Lakekamu Basin is just 30 minutes by air from Wau and an hour from Port Moresby. Shovel-billed Kookaburra* occurs in the Nagore River Forest, 6.5 km southeast of Kakoro, where Southern Cassowary*, Southern Crowned-Pigeon*, Pesquet's Parrot* and Variable Pitohui also occur. There is a research camp here due to be run to the late 1990s at least. Golden-backed Whistler (in high canegrass alongside the Biaru River) and Twelve-wired Bird-of-paradise (in trees surrounding the small wetland) occur around the village of Mirimas.

*Accommodation:* camping.

## WAU

Over 250 species have been recorded in the forests surrounding Wau in the mountains of central Papua New Guinea, including Red-breasted Paradise-Kingfisher, Garnet Robin and Blue Bird-of-paradise*. The wide altitudinal range of habitats includes mid-montane forests, which are hard to get to elsewhere in the country, but these are being replaced all too hastily by coffee and pine plantations, despite the efforts of the Wau Ecology Institute.

### Papua New Guinea Endemics

Rufous-backed Honeyeater, Brown-backed Whistler, Princess Stephanie's Astrapia, Raggiana and Blue* Birds-of-paradise.

### Localised New Guinea Endemics

Blue-collared Parrot, Red-breasted Paradise-Kingfisher, Black-billed Sicklebill, Streaked and Spotted Berrypeckers.

### Other New Guinea Endemics

Rufescent Imperial-Pigeon, Madarasz's Tiger-Parrot, Papuan King-Parrot, Fairy and Yellow-billed Lorikeets, White-eared Bronze-Cuckoo, Mountain Swiftlet, Papuan Treecreeper, MacGregor's Bowerbird, White-shouldered Fairywren, Mountain Mouse-Warbler, Large, Buff-faced and Papuan Scrubwrens, Papuan Thornbill, Mountain Gerygone, Long-billed Honeyeater, Mountain and Red-collared Myzomelas, Mountain Meliphaga, Scrub, Puff-backed, Mimic, Black-throated, Obscure and Marbled Honeyeaters, Belford's Melidectes, Smoky Honeyeater, Torrent and

Canary Flycatchers, Garnet and Blue-grey Robins, Regent and Black-headed Whistlers, Hooded Pitohui, Spotted Jewel-babbler, Blue-capped Ifrita, Friendly Fantail, Black Monarch, Papuan Drongo, Lesser Melampitta, Great Woodswallow, Mountain Peltops, Hooded Butcherbird, Stout-billed, Hooded, Papuan and Black-bellied Cuckoo-shrikes, Black-fronted and New Guinea White-eyes, Hooded Munia, Red-capped Flowerpecker, Fan-tailed Berrypecker, Slaty-chinned Longbill, Tit Berrypecker.

## Others

Papuan Mountain-Pigeon, Red-breasted Pygmy-Parrot, Double-eyed Fig-Parrot, Green-backed Gerygone, New Guinea Friarbird, Yellow-faced Myna, Blue-faced Parrotfinch.

(Other species recorded here include Olive Straightbill, Olive-streaked Honeyeater, Brown Sicklebill and Lawes' Parotia (all alongside the Wau–Biaru Road), as well as Dwarf Cassowary*, New Guinea Eagle*, Brown-collared and Wattled Brush-turkeys, Forbes' Rail, Cinnamon and Bronze Ground-Doves, Pheasant Pigeon, Mountain Owlet-Nightjar, Bicoloured Mouse-Warbler and Chestnut-backed Jewel-babbler (all on Mount Mission).)

Wau is accessible by air and the best base is the Wau Ecology Institute (WEI), which caters for guests and is a couple of kilometres west of town, off the road to Mount Kaindi. This independent ecological research station is situated at 1000 m (3281 ft) on the lower slopes of **Mount Kaindi**, which rises to 2350 m (7710 ft) and is well worth birding. To find out where the best birding areas are, ask at the institute. Otherwise, continue on the track past the institute to about 2100 m (6890 ft) where there are remnant patches of lower montane forest which support Garnet Robin, Black-headed Whistler, Lesser Melampitta, New Guinea White-eye, Blue-faced Parrotfinch, Streaked and Spotted Berrypeckers, and Slaty-chinned Longbill. When ascending the road up Mount Kaindi, take the track to the left at 1900 m (6234 ft). This follows a watercourse and after about 1 km, near the end of the track, it is possible to scramble up a steep path to look for Spotted Jewel-babbler. The institute used to concentrate their activities on Mount Mission (Missim), but they have recently turned their attention to the **Kuper Range**, which is easily reached with their assistance. Their field station here is situated at the Kolorong Pass, which lies beyond the village of Ilauru on the track to Biaru south of Wau. Madarasz's Tiger-Parrot, MacGregor's Bowerbird, Black-throated Honeyeater, Black-billed Sicklebill, Princess Stephanie's Astrapia (display tree) and Blue Bird-of-paradise* all occur near here. It is also worth asking at the institute about any new field stations which have been set up, and if it is possible to stay at them. Over 200 species, including Red-breasted Paradise-Kingfisher, have been recorded in the 21 sq km **McAdam National Park** which lies alongside the road between Wau and Bulolo and was established to protect a large stand of hoop and klinkii pines, but also supports lowland, submontane and montane forests. The WEI may be able to arrange lifts to this park. For more information on the Wau area, contact the Institute or The Ranger, PO Box 127, Bulolo, Morobe Province.

*Accommodation:* Wau Ecology Institute (A-B), PO Box 77, Wau (tel: 44 6218, fax: 44 6381). Kuper Range—WEI Field Station.

## HUON PENINSULA

The isolated forested mountains of the Huon Peninsula in north Papua New Guinea support a distinct avifauna which includes four peninsula endemics, two of which are birds-of-paradise. The Huon 'paradise' hat-trick is completed by Wahnes' Parotia* which otherwise only occurs in the Adelbert Mountains to the west.

### Huon Peninsula Endemics

Spangled Honeyeater, Huon Astrapia, Emperor Bird-of-paradise*.

### Other Papua New Guinea Endemics

Rufous-backed Honeyeater, Wahnes' Parotia*.

### Localised New Guinea Endemics

Cinnamon-browed Melidectes.

### Other New Guinea Endemics

Black-mantled Goshawk, Ornate Fruit-Dove, Papuan King-Parrot, Dusky Lory, Fairy, Papuan and Orange-billed Lorikeets, Hook-billed and Mountain Kingfishers, MacGregor's Bowerbird, Orange-crowned and White-shouldered Fairywrens, Mountain Mouse-Warbler, Buff-faced and Grey-green Scrubwrens, Red-collared Myzomela, Black-throated Honey-eater, Lesser Ground-Robin, Canary Flycatcher, Blue-grey Robin, Mottled, Sclater's and Regent Whistlers, Spotted Jewel-babbler, Blue-capped Ifrita, Friendly Fantail, White-bellied Thicket-Fantail, Black-breasted Boatbill, Lesser Melampitta, Glossy-mantled Manucode, Superb Bird-of-paradise, Great Woodswallow, Mountain Peltops, Hooded Butcherbird, Hooded and Black-bellied Cuckoo-shrikes, Black-fronted and New Guinea White-eyes, Hooded Munia, Red-capped Flowerpecker, Black, Lemon-breasted, Fan-tailed and Tit Berrypeckers.

### Others

Great and Lesser Frigatebirds, Pacific Reef-Egret, Pacific Baza, Brahminy Kite, Great Crested-Tern, Black Noddy, Great Cuckoo-Dove, White-breasted Fruit-Dove, Torresian Imperial-Pigeon, Papuan Mount-ain-Pigeon, Red-cheeked and Eclectus Parrots, Glossy and Uniform Swiftlets, Variable and Beach Kingfishers, Blue-tailed Bee-eater, Varied Sittella, Shining Flycatcher, Metallic Starling, Pacific Swallow, Golden-headed Cisticola, Tawny Grassbird, Blue-faced Parrotfinch, Olive-backed Sunbird.

(The fourth peninsula endemic, Huon Melidectes, seems to occur only at higher altitudes which are difficult to reach.)

The town of Wasu, on the north coast of the peninsula, is accessible by boat or plane from Madang and Lae. Black Noddy, Beach Kingfisher and White-bellied Thicket-Fantail occur around here. The peninsula endemics occur around and above the village of Satop, a few kilometres inland. Just before the village a trail to the left used to lead to an Emperor Bird-of-paradise* display area (ask at village). From the village bird alongside the road up to the viewpoint on an 1850 m (6070 ft) peak, two to three hours on foot from Satop.

*Accommodation:* Wasu—ask at police station. Satop—negotiate staying in a house or camping in the village with village elders.

From Wasu it is also possible to walk across the Sarawaget Range, which rises to 4212 m (13,819 ft), south to Lae via Kabwum (accessible by air). This may be the best way to see Huon Melidectes. Species recorded near **Lae**, Papua New Guinea's second city, include Edwards' Fig-Parrot, Dwarf Koel, Lesser Black Coucal, Red-breasted Paradise-Kingfisher, Crinkle-collared Manucode, Magnificent Bird-of-paradise, and Streak-headed and Grand Munias. This sprawling city is accessible by air (the airport is a long way from the city centre) and road (four hours by PMV from Wau).

## MADANG

This town on Papua New Guinea's northeast coast next to the Bismarck Sea lies near lowland and foothill rainforests which support Chestnut-shouldered Goshawk*, Brown-collared Brush-turkey and Olive-yellow Robin*, and the island of Karkar where Red-chinned Lorikeet, Beach Kingfisher and Scarlet-bibbed Myzomela occur.

### Papua New Guinea Endemics

Chestnut-shouldered Goshawk*, Red-chinned Lorikeet.

### Localised New Guinea Endemics

Brown-collared Brush-turkey, Scarlet-bibbed Myzomela, Olive-yellow Robin*.

### Other New Guinea Endemics

Coroneted and Dwarf Fruit-Doves, Purple-tailed Imperial-Pigeon, Rufous-bellied Kookaburra, Olive Flyrobin, Variable Pitohui, White-bellied Thicket-Fantail, Hooded and Golden Monarchs, Grey Crow, Magnificent, King and Lesser Birds-of-paradise, Boyer's Cuckoo-shrike.

### Others

Streaked Shearwater (Oct–Apr), Lesser Frigatebird, White-browed Crake, Black Noddy, MacKinlay's Cuckoo-Dove, Moustached Treeswift, Azure, Variable and Beach Kingfishers, Common Paradise-kingfisher, Blyth's Hornbill, Island Monarch.

The relatively pleasant town of Madang has a few parks and ponds worth strolling around, including a lily-covered lake where White-browed Crake occurs. From Madang there is a daily ferry to the volcanic island of **Karkar**, about 50 km offshore, where Mackinlay's Cuckoo-Dove, Red-chinned Lorikeet (which otherwise only occurs on New Ireland and New Britain), Scarlet-bibbed Myzomela (which is restricted to islands off the northeast coast and New Britain) and Island Monarch occur in the remaining forest above the cocoa and coconut plantations. Look out for Streaked Shearwater, Lesser Frigatebird and Black Noddy on the crossing, and Beach Kingfisher around the coast. The island is also a superb scuba-diving and snorkelling site. The **Malolo Plantation Lodge**, 42 km northwest of Madang, lies near forested hills where Magnificent, King and Lesser Birds-of-paradise occur. It is possible to bird these hills along logging tracks. Chestnut-shouldered Goshawk*, Brown-collared Brush-turkey, Variable Pitohui, Hooded Monarch and King and Lesser Birds-of-paradise have been recorded in the lowland rainforest near the village of **Nauru**, about 50 km south of Madang. The village lies next to the Nauru River and is accessible via the Ramu Highway between Madang and Lae. It is best to hire a local guide here, to help find the best tracks and trails, especially those which reach the ridges.

*Accommodation:* Malolo Plantation Lodge (A+), bookable in advance through Trans Niugini Tours.

## MANUS ISLAND

This island, at the western end of the Bismarck Archipelago, supports five endemics, one of which is a pitta, and Manus Fantail* occurs on the nearby island of Tong. Manus is accessible by air and sea, and the boat trip from Madang presents the opportunity to see the rarely reported Heinroth's Shearwater*, as well as Tahiti Petrel.

### Manus Island Endemics

Manus Owl*, Manus Hawk-Owl, Black-headed Pitta*, White-naped Friarbird, Manus Fantail*, Manus Monarch*.

### Bismarck Archipelago Endemics

Pied Cuckoo-Dove, Meek's Pygmy-Parrot, Ebony Myzomela, Black-headed White-eye.

### Non-endemic Specialities

Heinroth's Shearwater*, Melanesian Scrubfowl, Nicobar Pigeon*, Bronze Ground-Dove, Island Imperial-Pigeon, Finsch's Pygmy-Parrot, Chestnut-breasted Cuckoo.

### Others

Tahiti Petrel (Oct–Apr), Streaked Shearwater (Oct–Apr), Lesser Frigatebird, Meyer's Goshawk, Brown and Black Noddies, MacKinlay's Cuckoo-Dove, White-breasted and Claret-breasted Fruit-Doves, Torresian Imperial-Pigeon ('yellow-tinted' race), Moustached Treeswift, Variable and Beach Kingfishers.

### Other Wildlife

Manus cuscus.

The boat trip from Madang to Lorengau, the island's gateway, takes a day. At Lorengau or the village of Rossun, about 6 km up the main road from there, ask around for Adam Jonathon, who will help to arrange accommodation (which may involve camping) and guides at Rossun, as well as a day trip to the island of Tong where Manus Fantail* occurs. All of the other endemics except for Manus Owl* occur around Rossun and Black-headed Pitta* is most likely to be seen on 'Solomon's Hill', just 30 minutes walk away from the village.

*Accommodation:* Lorengau—hotel (A). Rossun—local huts or camping.

It is possible to travel by boat from Manus to Rabaul on the island New Britain and on this trip seabirds such as White-tailed Tropicbird, Masked Booby, Sooty Tern and Brown Noddy have been recorded.

## KARAWARI LODGE

The extensive humid lowland forest around this lodge, which is situated on a tributary of the Sepik River in northwest Papua New Guinea, supports the rare Victoria Crowned-Pigeon*, as well as some other localised species and Twelve-wired Bird-of-paradise.

### Localised New Guinea Endemics

Victoria Crowned-Pigeon*.

### Other New Guinea Endemics

Orange-bellied Fruit-Dove, Pinon, Collared and Zoe Imperial-Pigeons, Edwards' Fig-Parrot, Black-capped Lory, Dwarf Koel, Greater Black Coucal, White-eared Catbird, Mimic Honeyeater, Rusty Pitohui, King and Twelve-wired Birds-of-paradise, Lowland Peltops, Boyer's Cuckoo-shrike, Golden Myna, Pygmy Honeyeater.

### Non-endemic Specialities

Spotted Whistling-Duck, Palm Cockatoo*.

### Others

Red-flanked Lorikeet, Blyth's Hornbill, Hooded and Red-bellied Pittas, Yellow-faced Myna.

It is possible to bird by boat and on foot near the lodge, which is best reached by air.

*Accommodation:* Karawari Lodge (A+), bookable in advance through Trans Niugini Tours.

## VANIMO

This town in extreme northwest Papua New Guinea lies on a small peninsula surrounded by beaches, just 30 km east of the border with Irian Jaya. The remnant forests between the town and the border are the only known locality in Papua New Guinea for Pale-billed Sicklebill*, and they also support a number of other localised rarities, including Forest Bittern*, Victoria Crowned-Pigeon*, Broad-billed Fairywren* and Jobi Manucode.

### Localised New Guinea Endemics

Northern Cassowary*, Forest Bittern*, Victoria Crowned-Pigeon*, Brown Lory, Papuan Hawk-Owl*, Broad-billed Fairywren*, Rufous Monarch, Jobi Manucode, Pale-billed Sicklebill*.

### Other New Guinea Endemics

Edwards' Fig-Parrot, White-eared Catbird, Yellow-gaped Honeyeater, Blue Jewel-babbler, King, Twelve-wired and Lesser Birds-of-paradise.

### Others

Gurney's Eagle*, Wandering Tattler.

(Species recorded on the two-day boat trip from Madang include Tahiti Petrel (Oct–Apr), Streaked Shearwater (Oct–Apr) and Black Noddy.)

Vanimo is accessible by air and sea (from Madang). It is possible to hire a vehicle at the airport. Bird along the road inland to Bewani where Pale-billed Sicklebill* has been recorded after 15 km (heading south), the logging areas east of Vanimo and the Wuting area on the border with Irian Jaya (Forest Bittern*). It may be best to hire local guides here, as some of them will know the best areas of forest and where to look for tricky species such as Victoria Crowned-Pigeon*.

*Accommodation:* Vanimo Resort Hotel (A), PO Box 42, Vanimo (tel: 87 1102, fax: 87 1131. Sandaun Motel (A+), PO Box 35, Vanimo (tel: 87 1000, fax: 87 1119).

## MOUNT HAGEN

The forests around Mount Hagen are rarely explored by birders these days due to problems with safety, but if the area becomes visitor-friendly again it will no doubt be a very popular destination, for a number of localised rarities have been recorded here, including Yellow-breasted Bird-of-paradise*.

### Papua New Guinea Endemics

Blue Bird-of-paradise*.

### Localised New Guinea Endemics

Dwarf Cassowary*, Wattled Brush-turkey, New Guinea Bronzewing*, Yellow-breasted Bowerbird, Leaden Honeyeater, Yellow-breasted Bird-of-paradise*, Carola's Parotia.

### Other New Guinea Endemics

New Guinea Eagle*, Cinnamon Ground-Dove, Jungle Hawk-Owl, Mountain Kingfisher, Pale-billed Scrubwren, Papuan Thornbill, Black-sided Robin, Spotted and Chestnut-backed Jewel-babblers, Crinkle-collared Manucode, Superb, Magnificent and Lesser Birds-of-paradise.

### Non-endemic Specialities

Red-necked Crake, Chestnut-breasted Cuckoo, Marbled Frogmouth.

### Others

Papuan Frogmouth, Spotted Catbird.

(Other species recorded here include Victoria Crowned-Pigeon*.)

An old stomping ground for birders used to be the lowland and mid-montane forests in and around the tiny **Baiyer River Wildlife Sanctuary**, about 55 km north of Mount Hagen. However, in the early 1990s this became a very dangerous area to visit, with even PMVs being held up on the road nearby. The sanctuary used to be run by the National Parks service and there used to be a self-catering hostel, but due to the lack of visitors it has become run down. It is worth asking the National Parks Service, or in Mount Hagen, about the possibilities of visiting the site safely, because species recorded here include such rare and spectacular birds as Dwarf Cassowary*, Red-necked Crake, New Guinea Bronzewing*, Yellow-breasted Bowerbird, Chestnut-backed Jewel-babbler and Lesser Bird-of-paradise. It is also worth asking about the current safety situation at nearby **Jimi Ridge**, one of the few known sites for Yellow-breasted Bird-of-paradise*. Other species recorded in the forest here include New Guinea Eagle*, Wattled Brush-turkey, Papuan Thornbill, Leaden Honeyeater, Spotted Jewel-babbler, Carola's Parotia and Blue Bird-of-paradise*. It used to be possible to bird along the road either side of the lay-by at the highest point of the road, 9 km from Baiyer River Wildlife Sanctuary, and along the Trauna Ridge Track from here, and when the sanctuary was open to visitors lifts to the lay-by could be arranged. Victoria Crowned-Pigeon* has been recorded in the Jimi Valley further on.

Some high-altitude specialities such as Salvadori's Teal*, Sooty and Long-bearded* Melidectes, and Alpine Pipit occur on **Mount Wilhelm**, at 4508 m (14,790 ft) the highest peak in Papua New Guinea. It is possible to ascend this mountain from Kegsugl, 51 km from Kundara. Allow three or four days and take full cold weather gear. **Mount Giluwe**, which at 4367 m (14,327 ft) is the second highest peak in Papua New Guinea, may also be worth birding. It is accessible from the DASF agricultural station on the Mount Hagen–Mendi road 18 km southwest of Tambul, and takes two days to tackle.

## TARI VALLEY

There is little point in visiting Papua New Guinea if the Tari Valley is not on the itinerary, despite the extortionate costs involved, although the Owen Stanley Ranges (p. 342) beckon budget birders and may yet present a serious challenge to this site's claim as the best birding area in Papua New Guinea. No less than 15 birds-of-paradise have been recorded here, including Short-tailed Paradigalla, Black Sicklebill*, Lawes' Parotia, Ribbon-tailed Astrapia*, and King-of-Saxony and Blue* Birds-of-paradise. This heady all-star cast has a support band to match, and it includes Archbold's Bowerbird*, Wattled Ploughbill, Torrent-lark and the gorgeous Crested Berrypecker.

Most of these great birds inhabit the mossy oak and southern beech upper montane forests of Mount Kerewa and the fringes of the intensively cultivated Tari valley, home of the Huli Tribe, the 'Wigmen' who decorate their wigs with birds-of-paradise plumes. These indigenous people had been farming the fertile valley for centuries and did not see their first 'whiteman' until the 1930s when a few Australian gold-diggers managed to scramble over the rugged mountains which surround the valley. The area is far from being remote today and it is possible to look for all of the birds listed below on daily excursions from a luxurious lodge.

## Papua New Guinea Endemics

Sanford's Bowerbird*, Rufous-backed Honeyeater, Brown-backed Whistler, Lawes' Parotia, Ribbon-tailed* and Princess Stephanie's Astrapias, Raggiana and Blue* Birds-of-paradise.

## Localised New Guinea Endemics

Chestnut Forest-Rail, Brehm's, Painted and Modest Tiger-Parrots, Goldie's and Plum-faced Lorikeets, Rufous-throated Bronze-Cuckoo, Archbold's Nightjar, Bicoloured Mouse-Warbler, Brown-breasted Gerygone, Olive Straightbill, Olive-streaked and Black-backed Honeyeaters, Sooty and Yellow-browed Melidectes, Black-throated, White-winged and Ashy Robins, Black Sittella, Rufous-naped Whistler, Black Pitohui, Wattled Ploughbill, Papuan Whipbird*, Dimorphic Fantail, Crested and Loria's Birds-of-paradise, Short-tailed Paradigalla, Black*, Brown and Black-billed Sicklebills, King-of-Saxony Bird-of-paradise, Capped White-eye, Mountain Firetail, Alpine Pipit, Crested Berrypecker.

## Other New Guinea Endemics

Long-tailed Honey-buzzard, Black-mantled Goshawk, New Guinea Eagle*, Black-billed Cuckoo-Dove, Cinnamon Ground-Dove, Rufescent Imperial-Pigeon, Madarasz's Tiger-Parrot, Papuan King-Parrot, Dusky Lory, Papuan, Yellow-billed and Orange-billed Lorikeets, White-eared Bronze-Cuckoo, Jungle Hawk-Owl, Mountain Swiftlet, Mountain Kingfisher, Papuan Treecreeper, MacGregor's Bowerbird, Orange-crowned and White-shouldered Fairywrens, Mountain Mouse-Warbler, Large, Buff-faced, Grey-green and Papuan Scrubwrens, Papuan Thornbill, Mountain Gerygone, Red-collared Myzomela, Mountain Meliphaga, Scrub, Black-throated and Marbled Honeyeaters, Belford's and Ornate Melidectes, Smoky Honeyeater, Lesser Ground-Robin, Canary Flycatcher, Garnet and Blue-grey Robins, Mottled, Rusty, Sclater's, Regent and Black-headed Whistlers, Spotted Jewel-babbler, Blue-capped Ifrita, Friendly and Black Fantails, Black Monarch, Black-breasted Boatbill, Grey Crow, Lesser Melampitta, Superb and Magnificent Birds-of-paradise, Great Woodswallow, Mountain Peltops, Torrent-lark, Stout-billed, Hooded and Black-bellied Cuckoo-shrikes, Hooded Munia, Red-capped Flowerpecker, Lemon-breasted, Fan-tailed and Tit Berrypeckers.

## Non-endemic Specialities

Dusky Woodcock, Metallic Pigeon, Bronze Ground-Dove, Logrunner.

## Others

Pacific Baza, Eastern Marsh-Harrier, Collared Sparrowhawk, Little Eagle, Brown Falcon, Brown Quail, Buff-banded Rail, Great Cuckoo-Dove, White-breasted Fruit-Dove, Papuan Mountain-Pigeon, Papuan Frogmouth, Large-tailed Nightjar, Glossy Swiftlet, Forest Kingfisher (Apr–Sep), Rainbow Bee-eater (Apr–Sep), Dollarbird, Varied Sittella, Willie-wagtail, Black Butcherbird, Long-tailed Shrike, Island Thrush, Pied Bushchat, Pacific Swallow, Island Leaf-Warbler, Tawny Grassbird, Blue-faced Parrotfinch, Australasian Pipit.

## TARI VALLEY

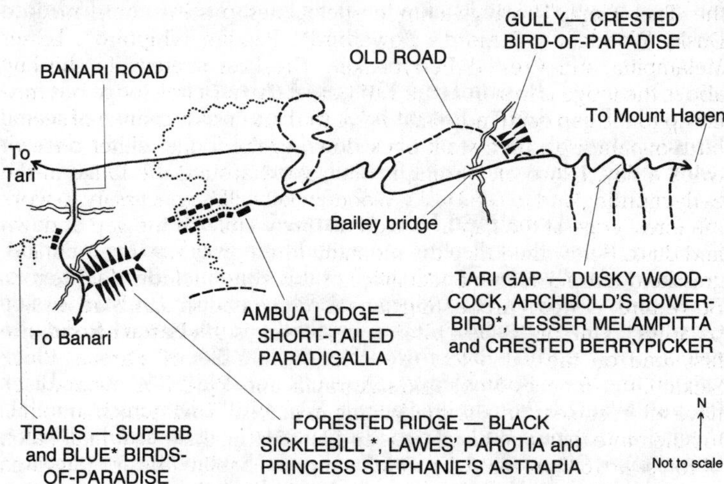


(Other species recorded here include Dwarf Cassowary* (bred in lodge grounds in 1987), Salvadori's Teal*, Meyer's Goshawk, Wattled Brush-turkey, Bare-eyed Rail, Pheasant Pigeon, Josephine's Lorikeet, White-crowned Koel, Feline and Mountain Owlet-Nightjars, and Moustached Treeswift.)

The best base for birding the Tari Valley is **Ambua Lodge**, one hour by road from the airstrip at Tari. Staying in Tari and hitching lifts up to the valley each day would be a much cheaper, but less safe and reliable, way to approach birding in the area. Once there, ask for Joseph, the best local guide. The superb, but extremely expensive, lodge lies at 2092 m (6864 ft) at the lower edge of montane forest, overlooking the Tari Valley. Over 55 species have been recorded in the lodge grounds alone, including eight birds-of-paradise. These include Loria's Bird-of-paradise, Short-tailed Paradigalla (which usually nests (Jul–Sep) behind cabin 5), Superb Bird-of-paradise, and Ribbon-tailed* and Princess Stephanie's Astrapias. The 9 km long stretch of road above the lodge to Tari Gap at about 2804 m (9200 ft) passes through superb montane forest festooned with ferns and epiphytes, and some fantastic birds, not least Crested Bird-of-paradise, three species of sicklebill, Ribbon-tailed Astrapia* and King-of-Saxony Bird-of-paradise. The latter can often be picked up on its call, which sounds like 'static' on the radio, while Brown Sicklebill sounds remarkably like a muffled machine gun.

Other possiblities between the lodge and Tari Gap include New Guinea Eagle*, Chestnut Forest-Rail, Brehm's Tiger-Parrot and Wattled Ploughbill, which is a bamboo specialist. Birding along this road can be brilliant, but it is usually even better along the quieter, though longer, **Old Road**, and to see Chestnut Forest-Rail, Logrunner and Crested Bird-of-paradise it is normally necessary to scramble down into the long gully to the west of an old bend in the old road a kilometre or so above Bailey's Bridge and search the very wet, dense forest thoroughly. Back on the new road the montane forest ends at about 2646 m (8681 ft) and gives way to stunted moss forest, scrub and rolling alpine grasslands in the **Tari Gap**. The high-altitude specialities possible here include Dusky Woodcock, Sanford's Bowerbird*, Papuan Whipbird*, Lesser Melampitta and Crested Berrypecker. The best strategy for birding above the lodge is to start at the Tari Gap at dawn (a free lodge bus travels up to the gap each morning to give tourist guests a chance of seeing birds-of-paradise), then walk back down to the lodge, either once or twice a day. However, birding is often good around the lodge in the early morning and to see Dusky Woodcock it will be necessary to work the forest edge at the gap at dusk. It is pretty chilly at the gap at dawn and dusk. Below the lodge the montane forest gives way to woodland, grassland and farmland. Specialities of this zone include MacGregor's Bowerbird, Lawes' Parotia, Raggiana Bird-of-paradise and Blue Bird-of-paradise*. One of the best birding areas here is the **Banari Road**, the first road on the left below the lodge, where Lawes' Parotia, Black Sicklebill*, Princess Stephanie's Astrapia and Blue Bird-of-paradise* have all been seen in a single fruiting tree. Near **Tari**, which amounts to little more than a few buildings and an airstrip, there is a small patch of forest at 1680 m (5512 ft) which supports display trees of Raggiana and Blue* Birds-of-paradise. Many species, especially birds-of-paradise, feed high in the canopy at Tari Valley, hence using a telescope is recommended.

*Accommodation:* Ambua Lodge (A++)—PO Box 371, Mount Hagen, Papua New Guinea (tel: 675 521438, fax: 675 522470, telex: 52012), bookable in advance through Trans Niugini Tours. In 1995 it cost £170/US$254 per day (all inclusive) to stay here, and even Air Nuigini's 'Weekend Getaways', bookable at Port Moresby airport, are only slightly cheaper. Rumours that cheaper hostel accommodation is under construction have been circulating for years, and it may be possible to camp in the lodge grounds (take all supplies) but permission to do so will probably not be granted due to the possibility of being robbed. Tari—Tari Women's Guesthouse, Koli Guesthouse.

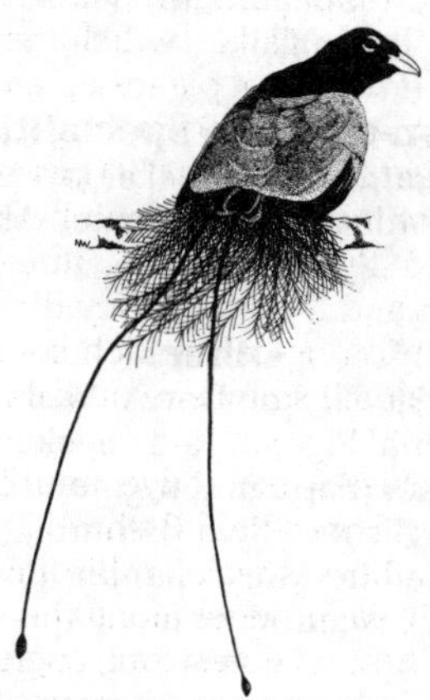

*The bizarre Blue Bird-of-paradise* hangs upside down when displaying, producing a shimmering blue fan of feathers and an almost unbelievable rapid metallic rattle*

## KIUNGA

This shipping port was built to serve the Ok Tedi mine near Tabubil to the north. It is situated on the west bank of the northern Fly River in a remote part of central New Guinea near the border with Irian Jaya and is the gateway to the third largest expanse of lowland tropical forest on earth. Only Amazonia and the Ituri Forest in the Congo Basin cover more ground. This forest supports a top class selection of birds, including Southern Crowned-Pigeon*, Little Paradise-Kingfisher*, Flame Bowerbird, Campbell's Fairywren*, White-bellied Pitohui and Greater Bird-of-paradise, all of which can be seen near Kiunga.

### Papua New Guinea Endemics

Campbell's Fairywren*.

### Localised New Guinea Endemics

Forest Bittern*, New Guinea Bronzewing*, Southern Crowned-Pigeon*, Papuan Hanging-Parrot, Long-billed Cuckoo, Lesser Black Coucal, Little Paradise-Kingfisher*, Flame Bowerbird, Wallace's Fairywren, White-bellied Pitohui, Greater Bird-of-paradise, Yellow-eyed Starling*, White-spotted Munia, Yellow-bellied Longbill.

### Other New Guinea Endemics

Long-tailed Honey-buzzard, Grey-headed Goshawk, Black-billed Brush-turkey, Pink-spotted, Ornate, Beautiful, Orange-bellied and Dwarf Fruit-Doves, Purple-tailed, Pinon, Collared and Zoe Imperial-Pigeons, Orange-breasted and Large Fig-Parrots, Pesquet's Parrot*, Black-capped Lory, White-crowned Koel, Greater Black Coucal, Hook-billed Kingfisher, Emperor Fairywren, Yellow-bellied Gerygone, Yellow-gaped and Obscure Honeyeaters, Meyer's Friarbird, Black-sided Robin, Golden-backed Whistler, Variable Pitohui, New Guinea Babbler, Blue Jewel-babbler, White-bellied Thicket-Fantail, Rufous-backed Fantail, Spot-winged and Golden Monarchs, Grey Crow, Glossy-mantled and Crinkle-collared Manucodes, Magnificent, King and Twelve-wired Birds-of-paradise, Lowland Peltops, Papuan, Grey-headed and Golden Cuckoo-shrikes.

### Non-endemic Specialities

Yellow-capped Pygmy-Parrot, Palm Cockatoo*, Yellow-billed Kingfisher, Buff-breasted Paradise-Kingfisher, Trumpet Manucode, Magnificent Riflebird.

### Others

Slender-billed and Great Cuckoo-Doves, Wompoo and Superb Fruit-Doves, Torresian Imperial-Pigeon, Red-cheeked and Eclectus Parrots, Channel-billed Cuckoo, Papuan Frogmouth, Variable Kingfisher, Common Paradise-Kingfisher, Blyth's Hornbill, Hooded and Red-bellied Pittas, Spotted Catbird, New Guinea Friarbird, Grey Whistler, Northern Fantail, Black-faced Monarch (Apr–Aug), Satin Flycatcher (Apr–Aug).

### Other Wildlife

Spotted cuscus, synchronised fireflies.

(Other species recorded here include Southern Cassowary*, Doria's Goshawk*, New Guinea Flightless Rail* and Black Munia*, while Olive-yellow Robin* also probably occurs here.)

Kiunga is accessible by air, and is connected by road to Tabubil. Once in town ask for Samuel Kepuknai, an excellent local guide who can arrange boat trips in search of local specialities such as Southern Crowned-Pigeon* and Twelve-wired Bird-of-paradise, and also assist with birding at Tabubil (see next site). Southern Crowned-Pigeon* occurs along the tributaries of the Fly River to the north of Kiunga, particularly the Elevara River, where there is a display site for Twelve-wired Bird-of-paradise. Other species which occur along this river include New Guinea Bronzewing*, Collared Imperial-Pigeon, Large Fig-Parrot, Palm Cockatoo*, Blue Jewel-babbler and King Bird-of-paradise, whilst Southern Cassowary* and New Guinea Flightless Rail* must be in there somewhere! Make sure the boat leaves a couple of hours before dawn to reach the Twelve-wired Bird-of-paradise display trees at dawn. Elsewhere, bird the local roads and hunting trails at different elevations. It is almost invariably hot, humid and wet here, and, at times, some areas of forest are inaccessible due to flooding.

*Accommodation:* Kiunga Guest House (A+), PO Box 20, Kiunga (tel: 58 1188, fax: 58 1195). Camping (ask permission at police station).

Kiunga lies at the start of the privately owned 135 km road to Tabubil and the Ok Tedi mine. Aim to be at 'Lorikeet Lookout', the first major rise in elevation north of Kiunga, by dawn to see the numerous pigeons and parrots pouring out from their roosts to feed in the surrounding forests. These birds include Striated Lorikeet*, as well as Papuan Mountain-Pigeon, Pesquet's Parrot*, Dusky Lory, and Pygmy and Red-flanked Lorikeets, while other species present in the area include Grey-headed Goshawk and Golden-backed Whistler.

*It is possible to see the rare Little Paradise-Kingfisher* around Kiunga*

## TABUBIL

The town of Tabubil is situated at about 610 m (2000 ft) in the Ok Tedi River valley and is the gateway to the forested foothills of the Star Mountains, where the avifauna includes those species which are more or less restricted to the mid-montane altitudinal range between 488 m (1600 ft) and 1524 m (5000 ft), a habitat which is barely accessible elsewhere in Papua New Guinea. The star avian attractions of the area include Golden-backed Whistler, Greater Melampitta and Obscure Berrypecker*.

Tabubil was built to serve the monstrous Ok Tedi mine, one of the largest gold and copper mines in the world. The dam which used to contain the waste from the mine collapsed in 1984, since when contaminated slurry has been flowing unchecked into the local rivers. However, BHP, the large Australian mining company which manages and co-owns the mine, was successfully sued by the local people in 1996, resulting in compensation and a clean-up campaign, although many conservationists believe the damage to the local ecosystem is already well beyond repair after 12 years of continuous uncontrolled pollution.

### Localised New Guinea Endemics

Blue-collared Parrot, Striated* and Josephine's Lorikeets, Wallace's Fairywren, Silver-eared Honeyeater, Spot-breasted Meliphaga, White-rumped and White-eyed Robins, Golden-backed Whistler, Sooty Shrike-Thrush, Greater Melampitta, Short-tailed Paradigalla, Carola's Parotia, Greater Bird-of-paradise, Yellow-eyed Starling*, Obscure Berrypecker*.

### Other New Guinea Endemics

Black-mantled Goshawk, New Guinea Eagle*, Ornate Fruit-Dove, Pesquet's Parrot*, Dusky Lory, Pygmy and Fairy Lorikeets, White-eared Bronze-Cuckoo, White-crowned and Dwarf Koels, Mountain Kingfisher, Grey-green Scrubwren, Red and Mountain Myzomelas, Scrub, Obscure and Spotted Honeyeaters, Ornate Melidectes, Torrent Flycatcher, Garnet Robin, Mottled, Dwarf and Rusty Whistlers, Variable Pitohui, Crinkle-collared Manucode, Superb and Magnificent Birds-of-paradise, Great Woodswallow, Torrent-lark.

### Non-endemic Specialities

Palm Cockatoo*, Chestnut-breasted Cuckoo.

### Others

Red-breasted Pygmy-Parrot, Blyth's Hornbill.

(Other species recorded here include Yellow-breasted Bird-of-paradise* which occurs high above Tabubil in areas only accessible via chartered helicopters.)

Bird the roads and trails around the town, from the nearby foothill forest to the lower slopes of the Star Mountains up to 1524 m (5000 ft), preferably with the assistance of Samuel Kepuknai who lives in Kiunga and knows the haunts of Golden-backed Whistler (islands in river near 'heliport'), Greater Melampitta (around sinkholes along Ok Ma Road) and Obscure Berrypecker* (at Dablin Creek, a favourite local picnic spot). Otherwise concentrate on birding alongside the road from Tabubil to the Ok Tedi mine, and the trails which lead off it. Also ask permission at the 'Whitehouse' in town to visit (and stay at) the mine, and to bird the forest above 701 m (2300 ft) which lies beyond it. This is a very wet area, but mornings are usually fine.

*Accommodation:* Cloudlands Hotel (A+), PO Box 266, Tabubil (tel: 58 9277, fax: 58 9301) and Ok Tedi Mining Camp.

The forests surrounding the remote station of **Telefomin**, accessible by air, support Splendid Astrapia, as well as New Guinea Eagle*, Marbled Honeyeater, White-eyed and Ashy Robins, Crested Pitohui, Spotted Jewel-babbler, Carola's Parotia, King-of-Saxony Bird-of-paradise and Papuan Parrotfinch. Accommodation is limited to an expensive mission guesthouse nearby, but it may be possible to hire guides and set up a camping trip, which would probably produce more birds anyway.

## BENSBACH

The seasonally flooded savanna grasslands, steamy swamps, rivers and eucalypt and monsoon woodlands in the Trans-Fly region of extreme southwest Papua New Guinea, near the border with Irian Jaya, support thousands of breeding waterbirds, as well as Spangled Kookaburra and Fly River Grassbird*. These birds also occur at Wasur National Park in Irian Jaya (p. 249) which also supports three localised munias, hence birders planning to visit there may wish to avoid adding Bensbach to their Papua New Guinea itinerary, especially when considering the only place to stay here is in a very expensive lodge.

The best time for waterbirds, many of which are widespread in northern Australia, is from August onwards when they concentrate on remaining pools at the end of the dry season.

### Localised New Guinea Endemics

Spangled Kookaburra, Fly River Grassbird*.

### Other New Guinea Endemics

New Guinea Eagle*, Scrub and Dwarf Honeyeaters, King Bird-of-paradise.

### Non-endemic Specialities

Beccari's Scrubwren, Green-backed Honeyeater.

### Others

Little Pied and Little Black Cormorants, Australian Darter, Australian Pelican, Magpie Goose, Radjah Shelduck, Green Pygmy-goose, White-faced Heron, Intermediate Egret, Pied Heron, Rufous Night-Heron, Australian and Straw-necked Ibises, Royal Spoonbill, Black-necked Stork, Whistling and Brahminy Kites, Swamp Harrier, White-bellied Sea-Eagle, Brown Goshawk, Wedge-tailed Eagle, Australian Kestrel, Orange-footed Scrubfowl, Brown Quail, Dusky Moorhen, Brolga, Australian Bustard, Comb-crested Jacana, Bush Thick-knee, Australian Pratincole (Apr–Sep), Peaceful, Bar-shouldered and Emerald Doves, Torresian Imperial-

Pigeon, Red-winged Parrot, Barking Owl, Morepork, Large-tailed Nightjar, Grey Shrike-Thrush, Grey-crowned Babbler, Varied Triller.

### Other Wildlife

Agile wallaby, frilled dragon, rusa deer (introduced), water monitor.

(Other species recorded here include White-spotted Munia.)

The luxurious, but very expensive, Bensbach Lodge, which caters mainly for deer hunting and fishing, is accessible by air from Port Moresby, via the island of Daru. Guests of the lodge can cruise through the wetlands on motorboats complete with armchairs to look for the rare Fly River Grassbird*.

*Accommodation:* Bensbach Lodge (A++), bookable through Trans Niugini Tours.

The main islands of the **D'Entrecasteaux Archipelago** are accessible by air from Gurney, near Alotau in the extreme southeast corner of the country. To see Goldie's Bird-of-paradise*, which is endemic to the islands of Normanby and Fergusson, fly to Salamo on Fergusson, purchase supplies then charter a boat to reach Nade, 30 km away. It is possible to stay with the local people here and to hire guides who know where the display areas are. Curl-crested Manucode, which occurs throughout the archipelago, also occurs here in lowland forest. It is also possible to stay on Normanby and at Dobu on Goodenough where there are a couple of missions.

The three main islands in the **Louisiade Archipelago** are accessible by air from Port Moresby, via Gurney. These islands support five endemics, three of which are confined to Tagula (Sudest). This island rises to 915 m (3002 ft) and two of the endemics were seen on the trek to Mount Riu in 1992: Tagula Honeyeater* and Tagula Butcherbird*.

## *OFFSHORE ISLANDS*

## NEW IRELAND

Despite the rough terrain and lack of transport on this island in the Bismarck Archipelago, east of the Papua New Guinea mainland, most of the seven endemics, as well as a number of species which are restricted to the archipelago, are fairly easy to see. However, during the wet season especially from November to February overland travel is usually subject to serious disruption.

### New Ireland Endemics

White-naped Lory*, Bismarck Hawk-Owl, New Ireland Myzomela, New Ireland Friarbird, Ribbon-tailed Drongo, Mottled and New Ireland Munias.

### New Ireland and New Britain Endemics

Knob-billed Fruit-Dove, Pied Coucal, Bismarck Fantail, Black-tailed Monarch, Dull Flycatcher, Bismarck Woodswallow, Red-banded Flowerpecker.

### Other Bismarck Archipelago Endemics

Pied Cuckoo-Dove, Black-headed White-eye.

### Other New Guinea Endemics

Purple-bellied Lory, Red-chinned Lorikeet, Red Myzomela, Golden Monarch.

### Non-endemic Specialities

Melanesian Scrubfowl, Red-knobbed Imperial-Pigeon, Finsch's Pygmy-Parrot, Singing Parrot.

### Others

Streaked (Oct–Apr), Wedge-tailed and Flesh-footed Shearwaters, Lesser Frigatebird, Grey-tailed and Wandering Tattlers, Bridled and Sooty Terns, Brown and Black Noddies, Stephan's Dove, Superb Fruit-Dove, Torresian Imperial-Pigeon ('yellow-tinted' race), Beach Kingfisher, Varied Triller.

(Other species recorded here include Yellow-legged Pigeon* (1984) and a possible new species of *Microeca* flycatcher.)

**Kaeving**, at the northwest end of the island, is accessible by air. Mottled Munia occurs around the airport, but to see the rest of the endemics it is necessary to visit **Taron** in the middle of the island. This village is accessible via road, but travelling to it overland, especially during the wet season, is not recommended because it may take as long as two weeks to get there, do some birding, and get back, via foot and motor-canoes. The best way to get to Taron is to fly to Silur via Rabul, from where it is possible to walk to Taron. New Ireland Munia occurs around the airstrip at Silur. Once at Taron hire guides, cooks and porters to walk to Lake Madeh, which is one to two days away in the foothills of the Hans Meyer Ranges. Set up base camp here and walk up to the forest above 1300 m (4265 ft) for the montane specialities.

Elsewhere on the island Finsch's Pygmy-Parrot and Ribbon-tailed Drongo occur around **Namatanai**, from where it is possible to get a boat to Lihir Island where Pied Cuckoo-Dove, Red-knobbed Imperial-Pigeon and Singing Parrot occur. In summer, seawatching from this boat can be excellent.

*Accommodation:* local houses, camping.

## NEW BRITAIN

The rainforests on this island, the largest in the Bismarck Archipelago, support 16 endemics, most of which are fairly easy to see. The black-headed *nigriceps* race of Buff-breasted Paradise-Kingfisher, a separate species according to some taxonomists, is also endemic, and this is also the place where Red-throated Myzomela is most likely to be seen in New Guinea.

### New Britain Endemics

Black Honey-buzzard*, New Britain Goshawk*, New Britain Rail, New

Britain Bronzewing*, Blue-eyed Cockatoo, Russet Hawk-Owl, New Britain Kingfisher, Black-bellied Myzomela, New Britain Friarbird, New Britain Thrush*, Rusty Thicketbird.

## New Britain and New Ireland Endemics

Knob-billed Fruit-Dove, Finsch's* and Bismarck* Imperial-Pigeons, Green-fronted Hanging-Parrot*, Violaceous and Pied Coucals, Bismarck Kingfisher, Bismarck Fantail, Black-tailed Monarch, Dull Flycatcher, Bismarck Woodswallow, Red-banded Flowerpecker.

## Other Bismarck Archipelago Endemics

Pied Cuckoo-Dove, Black-headed White-eye.

## Other New Guinea Endemics

Purple-bellied Lory, Red-throated and Scarlet-bibbed Myzomelas, Bismarck Munia.

## Non-endemic Specialities

Melanesian Scrubfowl, Nicobar Pigeon*, White-bibbed and Bronze Ground-Doves, Red-knobbed and Island Imperial-Pigeons, Singing Parrot, Buff-breasted Paradise-Kingfisher (*nigriceps* race).

## Others

Great and Lesser Frigatebirds, Rufous-tailed Bush-hen, Slender-billed and MacKinlay's Cuckoo-Doves, Stephan's Dove, Superb and White-breasted Fruit-Doves, Torresian Imperial-Pigeon ('yellow-tinted' race), Eclectus Parrot, Red-flanked Lorikeet, Moustached Treeswift, Variable Kingfisher, Blyth's Hornbill, Varied Triller, Metallic Starling, Yellow-faced Myna, Black Sunbird.

(Other species recorded here include Slaty-mantled* and New Britain* Sparrowhawks, Bismarck Owl*, Bismarck Melidectes and Bismarck Thicketbird*.)

**LAVEGE**

The small town of **Hoskins** on the north coast of central New Britain is accessible by air from Port Moresby. Bismarck Munia occurs at the back of the airstrip. From here it is 45 km (4WD or bus) to the village of **Lavege**, just off the Kimbe–Bialla road, where the coastal rainforest supports many of the lowland specialities. Concentrate on the Pokili Wildlife Management Area, a few kilometres from Lavege, and the forest alongside the road back to Hoskins, especially that on the small volcano a little way east of town. New Britain Kingfisher favours forest clearings. To see some montane specialities such as White-bibbed Ground-Dove, Finsch's* and Bismarck* Imperial-Pigeons, and Rusty Thicketbird, head for the village of **Bereme**, 30 minutes along the road south from Ubai (which is on the main road), and bird the logged forest alongside the road near Bereme. However, more montane specialities are likely to be seen in the Nakanai Mountains which can be reached from **Salelubu**, east of Kimbe. Hire guides and porters here to tackle the difficult ascent to Widaguida via Bibise and Wagu Cave, which normally takes more than a day. From base camp at Widaguida bird the montane forest which supports White-bibbed Ground-Dove, Bismarck Fantail, New Britain Thrush* and Rusty Thicketbird. Other species which may be found here in the future include Bismarck Melidectes and Bismarck Thicketbird*. The latter does occur in the Whiteman Mountains, but they are only accessible via a long trek from Lombon, which is served by New Tribes Mission flights from Hoskins.

The logged hill forest around **Sabeltepun** in west New Britain may still support Finsch's Imperial-Pigeon*, Singing Parrot, the endemic *nigriceps* race of Buff-breasted Paradise-kingfisher, Black-bellied Myzomela, Black-tailed Monarch, Bismarck Woodswallow, Black-headed White-eye and Red-banded Flowerpecker. East of Kimbe and Bialla there is a trail, which passes the active Mount Ulawun volcano, between **Ulamona** on the north coast and **Pomio** on the south coast which may well reward a pioneering birder. Pomio is connected by boat to Rabaul or can be reached on foot in a day from the airstrip at Pamalmal. Allow at least four days to walk the whole trail.

*Accommodation:* Hoskins—Hoskins Hotel (A+). Kimbe—Palm Lodge Hotel (A+). Lavege—camping.

*The cracking New Britain Kingfisher could be the highlight of a trip to this island in the Bismarck Archipelago, off east Papua New Guinea*

The boat trip between **Rabaul**, the capital of New Britain, and the island of **Buka** is good for seawatching, with pelagic possibilities including Heinroth's Shearwater*, as well as Tahiti Petrel (Oct–Apr), Streaked Shearwater (Oct–Apr), Red-footed Booby, Black-naped and Sooty Terns, and Brown and Black Noddies. However, Buka, which is only separated by a narrow channel from the neighbouring island of Bougainville, has been out of bounds for most of the 1990s due to the activities of secessionist rebels and a blockade of the island which has been enforced by the government of Papua New Guinea. Bismarck Munia has been recorded in swampy areas around the airstrip, and other species present on the island include Solomon Sea-Eagle*, Pied Goshawk, Cardinal Lory, Ducorps' Cockatoo, Bougainville Crow*, Yellow-throated White-eye and Midget Flowerpecker.

## BOUGAINVILLE

This wild, remote island is politically part of Papua New Guinea, but ecologically akin to the Solomon Islands, hence many of the species present are those which only occur in the Solomon Islands and on Bougainville and Buka. Unfortunately, seeing birds such as Ultramarine Kingfisher is virtually impossible, because the island has been out of bounds to travellers for most of the 1990s due to the activities of secessionist rebels, and a blockade of the island which has been enforced by the government of Papua New Guinea. Fresh attempts to end the crisis began in March 1997 when the government of Papua New Guinea offered to buy a controlling stake in the copper mine at Panguna, which has been at the centrepoint of the crisis since it was closed by the rebels in 1989.

### Bougainville Endemics

Bougainville Honeyeater.

### Bougainville and Solomon Islands Endemics

Pale Mountain-Pigeon, Ducorps' Cockatoo, Meek's and Duchess* Lorikeets, Fearful Owl*, Ultramarine Kingfisher, Scarlet-naped Myzomela, Mountain Whistler*, Brown Fantail, Black-and-white Monarch, Steel-blue Flycatcher, Bougainville Crow*, Solomon Cuckoo-shrike, Brown-winged Starling, Yellow-throated and Grey-throated White-eyes, Midget Flowerpecker.

### Non-endemic Specialities

Metallic Pigeon, Yellow-bibbed Fruit-Dove, Red-knobbed and Island Imperial-Pigeons, Singing Parrot, Cardinal Lory.

### Others

Claret-breasted Fruit-Dove, Beach Kingfisher, Blyth's Hornbill.

(The other Bougainville endemic, Bougainville Thicketbird*, is confined to the virtually inaccessible Crown Prince Range.)

Most of the birds listed have been recorded in the forests surrounding the massive open copper mine at **Panguna** which was closed down by

**PANGUNA**

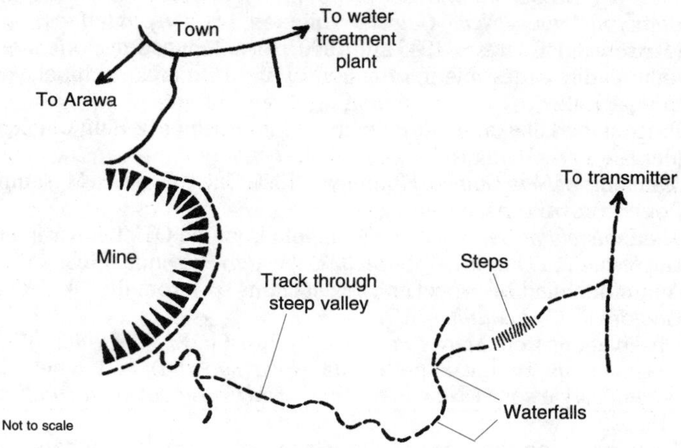


the rebels in 1989. The mine, which is inland from Kieta on the east coast, used to be accessible by road via Arawa, and the best place to go birding once there was along the track above the mine to the radio transmitter, with the high-altitude specialities being confined to the forest above the waterfalls. Elsewhere, Duchess Lorikeet* and Beach Kingfisher have been recorded just north of **Loloho Beach**, 45 minutes by road from Panguna; Ultramarine Kingfisher has been recorded 1.5 km south of the petrol station at **Tunuru** in the direction of Arawa; and Metallic Pigeon, Claret-breasted Fruit-Dove, Island Imperial-Pigeon, Singing Parrot, Steel-blue Flycatcher and Brown-winged Starling have been recorded in remnant lowland forest near the village of **Oria**, about 50 km south of Kieta on the road to Buin.

# ADDITIONAL INFORMATION

## Addresses

The Papua New Guinea Bird Society, PO Box 1598, Boroko, NCD, Papua New Guinea, publishes the *Muruk* journal three times per year.
National Parks Service, PO Box 5749, Boroko, NCD, Papua New Guinea (tel: 25 4247).
Contact the Wildlife Conservation Section, Department of Environment and Conservation, PO Box 6601, Boroko, NCD, Papua New Guinea, for more information on Wildlife Management Areas.
Trans Niugini Tours, PO Box 371, Mount Hagen, Papua New Guinea (tel: 675 521 438, fax: 675 522 470, telex: NE52012). UK contact address: 27 Silverdale Avenue, Oxshott, Leatherhead, Surrey KT22 0JX (tel/fax: 01372 843032). USA contact address: 850 Colorado Blvd., Suite #105, Los Angeles, CA 90041 (tel: 213 256 1991, toll free: 800 521 7242, fax: 213 256 0647).
Air Niugini, PO Box 7186, Boroko, NCD, Papua New Guinea (tel: 259 000, telex: NE22225).

## Books and Papers

*Birds of New Guinea.* Beehler B *et al.*, 1986. Princeton University Press.
*Birds of Papua New Guinea,* volumes 1 (*Non-passerines*) and 2 (*Passerines*). Coates B, 1985 and 1990. Dove Publications. (includes the only readily accessible information on the Bismarck Archipelago and Bougainville).
Birds of the Lakekamu–Kunamaipa Basin. Beehler B, Burg C, Filardi C, Merg K, 1994. *Muruk* 6: 1–8.
*Mammals of New Guinea.* Flannery T, 1990. The Australian Museum and Robert Brown & Associates.
*The Birds of the Ok Tedi Area.* Available from the OTML Environmental Department, PO Box 1, Tabubil 332, Western Province, PNG.
An unidentified berrypecker (*Melanocharis* sp.) from the Ok Tedi area. Gregory P, 1993. *Muruk* 6: 1.
Observations from Manus Province. Tolhurst L, 1993. *Muruk* 6: 15–18.
Observations on the Superb Pitta (*Pitta superba*) and other Manus endemics. Dutson G, Newman J, 1991. *Bird Conservation International* 1: 215–222.
Some notes on the birds of the Bismarcks. Finch B, McKean J, 1987. *Muruk* 2: 3–28.
Some interesting observations from Bougainville and west New Britain. Gardner N, 1987. *Muruk* 2: 38–39.
Some observations from lowland swamp forest in south Bougainville. Kaestner P, 1987. *Muruk* 2: 34–38.
*A Naturalist in New Guinea.* Beehler B, 1991. University of Texas Press.

## PAPUA NEW GUINEA ENDEMICS (86)
## MAINLAND (25)

| | |
|---|---|
| Chestnut-shouldered Goshawk* | Very rare in Central Highlands, Huon Peninsula, North Coastal Range and Port Moresby area. (There is also one record from the Foya Mountains in Irian Jaya.) |
| Purple-bellied Lory | Southeast, islands off southeast and Bismarck Archipelago |
| Brown-headed Paradise Kingfisher | Varirata NP |
| Sanford's Bowerbird* | Tari Valley. Some taxonomists treat this as the eastern race of Archbold's Bowerbird* |
| Streaked Bowerbird | Montane forests |
| Fire-maned Bowerbird* | Adelbert Mountains |
| Campbell's Fairywren* | Kiunga. Also known from Mount Bosari and probably occurs in the Nomad River area |
| Rufous-backed Honeyeater | Wau, Huon Peninsula and Tari Valley |
| Long-bearded Melidectes* | Mount Wilhelm. Also known from Mounts Hagen, Giluwe and Michael, and the Kubor Range near Wau |
| Huon Melidectes | Huon Peninsula |
| Spangled Honeyeater | Huon Peninsula |
| Brown-backed Whistler | Wau and Tari Valley |
| White-bellied Whistler | Port Moresby area |
| Lawes' Parotia | Tari Valley. Also known from the Wau area |
| Eastern Parotia | Mid-montane oak forest |
| Wahnes' Parotia* | Huon Peninsula and Adelbert Mountains |

| | |
|---|---|
| Eastern Riflebird | Port Moresby area, Varirata NP and Lakekamu Basin |
| Ribbon-tailed Astrapia* | Tari Valley |
| Princess Stephanie's Astrapia | Owen Stanley Ranges, Wau area and Tari Valley |
| Huon Astrapia | Huon Peninsula |
| Raggiana Bird-of-paradise | Widespread in low montane forests |
| Emperor Bird-of-paradise* | Huon Peninsula |
| Blue Bird-of-paradise* | Wau, Mount Hagen and Tari Valley, in primary lower montane oak forests |
| Grey-headed Munia | Port Moresby area and Lakekamu Basin |
| Alpine Munia | Owen Stanley Ranges |

## BISMARCK ARCHIPELAGO (50)

This includes the Admiralty Islands (such as Manus), the St Matthias Group, New Hanover, New Ireland and New Britain, all of which lie to the northeast of the Papua New Guinea mainland.

### Widespread (3)

Pied Cuckoo-Dove, Ebony Myzomela, Black-headed White-eye.

(The 'yellow-tinted' race of Torresian Imperial-Pigeon, which is endemic to the archipelago, is regarded as a separate species by some taxonomists.)

### Manus (6)

Manus Owl*, Manus Hawk-Owl, Black-headed Pitta*, White-naped Friarbird, Manus Fantail* (San Miguel, Tong ('common') and nearby islands. Not recorded on Manus since 1934), Manus Monarch (also Rambutyo Islands).

### Manus and St Matthias Group (1)

Meek's Pygmy-Parrot.

### Mussau (St Matthias Group) (2)

Matthias Fantail*, White-breasted Monarch*.

### New Ireland (7)

White-naped Lory*, Bismarck Hawk-Owl, New Ireland Myzomela, New Ireland Friarbird, Ribbon-tailed Drongo, Mottled and New Ireland Munias.

### New Britain (16)

Black Honey-buzzard*, Slaty-mantled Sparrowhawk*, New Britain Goshawk*, New Britain Sparrowhawk*, New Britain Rail, New Britain Bronzewing*, Blue-eyed Cockatoo, Bismarck Owl*, Russet Hawk-Owl, New Britain Kingfisher, Black-bellied Myzomela, New Britain Friarbird, Bismarck Melidectes, New Britain Thrush*, Bismarck* (confined to montane forests of Whiteman Mountains) and Rusty Thicketbirds.

(The black-headed *nigriceps* race of Buff-breasted Paradise-Kingfisher, which is regarded as a separate species by some taxonomists, is endemic to New Britain and nearby Duke of York Island.)

## New Ireland and New Britain (12)

Knob-billed Fruit-Dove, Finsch's* and Bismarck* Imperial-Pigeons, Green-fronted Hanging-Parrot*, Violaceous and Pied Coucals, Bismarck Kingfisher, Bismarck Fantail, Black-tailed Monarch, Dull Flycatcher, Bismarck Woodswallow, Red-banded Flowerpecker.

## New Britain, New Ireland and Karkar (2)

Red-chinned Lorikeet, Scarlet-bibbed Myzomela.

## New Hanover (1)

New Hanover Munia (lowland grasslands).

## BISMARCK ARCHIPELAGO and BUKA (1)

Bismarck Munia.

## BOUGAINVILLE (2)

Bougainville Honeyeater, Bougainville Thicketbird* (confined to Crown Prince Range).

## BISMARCK and LOUISIADE ARCHIPELAGOS (1)

Louisiade White-eye.

## EAST PAPUAN ISLANDS and D'ENTRECASTEAUX ARCHIPELAGO (1)

Curl-crested Manucode.

## D'ENTRECASTEAUX ARCHIPELAGO (1)

Goldie's Bird-of-paradise* (Fergusson and Normanby).

## LOUISIADE ARCHIPELAGO (5)

| | |
|---|---|
| White-chinned Myzomela* | Smaller islands |
| Tagula Honeyeater* | Tagula (Sudest). Seen (in lowland forest) on trek to Mount Riu in 1992 |
| Tagula Butcherbird* | Tagula (Sudest). Seen on trek to Mount Riu in 1992 |
| White-throated White-eye* | Tagula (Sudest). Not seen on trek to Mount Riu in 1992 |
| Louisiade Flowerpecker | Tagula (Sudest), Misima and Rossel |

## NEW GUINEA ENDEMICS (269)

This list deals with the 269 species which are endemic to the island of New Guinea and occur in both Irian Jaya and Papua New Guinea. Together with the 44 species which are endemic to Irian Jaya and the 86 species which are endemic to Papua New Guinea this brings the total number of species endemic to New Guinea to 399.

| | |
|---|---|
| Dwarf Cassowary* | PNG: Varirata NP. Also recorded at Wau, Mount Hagen and Tari Valley, and known from New Britain<br>IRIAN: Batu Rumah. Also known from Yapen |
| Northern Cassowary* | PNG: Vanimo. Present in northern lowlands<br>IRIAN: Jalan Korea. Also known from northern lowlands west to Vogelkop |

| | |
|---|---|
| | Peninsula, Batanta, Salawati and Yapen |
| Salvadori's Teal* | PNG: Owen Stanley Ranges, Lakekamu Basin and Mt Wilhelm. Also recorded at Tari Valley in Central Ranges and known from Huon Peninsula<br>IRIAN: Snow Mountains. Also known from Vogelkop Peninsula |
| Forest Bittern* | PNG: Lakekamu Basin, Vanimo and Kiunga<br>IRIAN: Sorong. Also known from Salawati and Aru Islands |
| Long-tailed Honey-buzzard | Widespread, to Aru Islands |
| Black-mantled Goshawk | Widespread |
| Grey-headed Goshawk | Widespread |
| Doria's Goshawk* | PNG: recorded around Port Moresby and Kiunga<br>IRIAN: recorded on Batanta |
| New Guinea Eagle* | Widespread but rare |
| New Guinea Scrubfowl | PNG: known from north<br>IRIAN: recently reported from Batu Rumah |
| Black-billed Brush-turkey | PNG: widespread<br>IRIAN: known from southern lowlands, to Aru Islands |
| Brown-collared Brush-turkey | PNG: Madang. Also recorded at Wau<br>IRIAN: Jalan Korea. Also known from Yapen |
| Wattled Brush-turkey | PNG: Mount Hagen. Also recorded at Wau and Tari Valley<br>IRIAN: Arfak Mountains. Also known from Yapen and Misool |
| Chestnut Forest-Rail | PNG: Tari Valley<br>IRIAN: Snow Mountains |
| Forbes' Rail | PNG: recorded at Wau<br>IRIAN: known from montane forests |
| Mayr's Rail* | Isolated mountain ranges of Cyclops, Bewani and Torricelli near central north coast |
| New Guinea Flightless Rail* | PNG: Kiunga. Known from Fly, Setekwa, Noord and Digul Rivers in the south, and Idenburg River, Humboldt Bay and Sepik River in the north<br>IRIAN: Wasur NP |
| Black-billed Cuckoo-Dove | Widespread, to Bismarck Archipelago |
| New Guinea Bronzewing* | PNG: widespread<br>IRIAN: Arfak Mountains. Known throughout, to west Papuan Islands, Yapen and Aru Islands |
| Cinnamon Ground-Dove | PNG: widespread<br>IRIAN: Batu Rumah, and Batanta and Salawati. Also known from Yapen and Aru Islands |
| Thick-billed Ground-Pigeon* | PNG: Lakekamu Basin. Also recorded around Port Moresby<br>IRIAN: Batu Rumah. Also known from Salawati |

| | |
|---|---|
| Pheasant Pigeon | PNG: Varirata NP and Lakekamu Basin. Also recorded at Wau and Tari Valley<br>IRIAN: Batu Rumah, and Batanta and Salawati. Also known from Aru Islands |
| Pink-spotted Fruit-Dove | Widespread, to west Papuan Islands, Yapen and Aru Islands |
| Ornate Fruit-Dove | PNG: widespread<br>IRIAN: Warkapi/Arfak Mountains and Fakfak Mountains |
| Orange-fronted Fruit-Dove | PNG: Port Moresby area<br>IRIAN: Lake Sentani and Jalan Korea. Also known from west Papuan Islands, Yapen and Aru Islands |
| Coroneted Fruit-Dove | PNG: Port Moresby area, Lakekamu Basin and Madang<br>IRIAN: Jalan Korea and Batu Rumah. Also known from Salawati, Yapen and Aru Islands |
| Beautiful Fruit-Dove | Widespread, to west Papuan Islands |
| Orange-bellied Fruit-Dove | Widespread, to west Papuan and Aru Islands |
| Dwarf Fruit-Dove | PNG: widespread<br>IRIAN: Numfor and Manokwari area. Also known from west Papuan Islands |
| Purple-tailed Imperial-Pigeon | Widespread, to west Papuan Islands |
| Rufescent Imperial-Pigeon | Widespread |
| Pinon Imperial-Pigeon | Widespread |
| Collared Imperial-Pigeon | Widespread, to Aru Islands |
| Zoe Imperial-Pigeon | Widespread |
| Victoria Crowned-Pigeon* | PNG: Karawari Lodge area and Vanimo. Also recorded at Mount Hagen<br>IRIAN: Jalan Korea and Supiori. Also known from Biak and Yapen |
| Southern Crowned-Pigeon* | PNG: Lakekamu Basin and Kiunga<br>IRIAN: recorded at Wasur NP |
| Buff-faced Pygmy-Parrot | PNG: Port Moresby area, Varirata NP and Lakekamu Basin<br>IRIAN: Jalan Korea |
| Orange-breasted Fig-Parrot | PNG: Port Moresby area, Lakekamu Basin and Kiunga<br>IRIAN: Wasur NP. Also known from Salawati and Aru Islands |
| Large Fig-Parrot | Widespread, to west Papuan Islands |
| Edwards' Fig-Parrot | PNG: Lae, Karawari Lodge area and Vanimo<br>IRIAN: known from Jayapura east to border |
| Brehm's Tiger-Parrot | PNG: Tari Valley<br>IRIAN: Snow Mountains and Warkapi/Arfak Mountains |
| Painted Tiger-Parrot | PNG: Tari Valley<br>IRIAN: Snow Mountains |
| Modest Tiger-Parrot | PNG: Tari Valley<br>IRIAN: Snow Mountains and Warkapi/ |

| | |
|---|---|
| | Arfak Mountains |
| Madarasz's Tiger-Parrot | PNG: Wau and Tari Valley. Also known from Huon Peninsula<br>IRIAN: Snow Mountains |
| Blue-collared Parrot | PNG: rare, Wau and Tabubil<br>IRIAN: rare, Arfak Mountains |
| Pesquet's Parrot* | Widespread but rare |
| Papuan King-Parrot | PNG: widespread<br>IRIAN: known from mountains west to Geelvink Bay |
| Papuan Hanging-Parrot | PNG: Kiunga. Known from lowlands.<br>IRIAN: known from lowlands, to west Papuan Islands |
| Brown Lory | PNG: Vanimo<br>IRIAN: Jalan Korea |
| Yellow-streaked Lory | PNG: Port Moresby area and Lakekamu Basin<br>IRIAN: known from southern lowland savanna, to Aru Islands |
| Dusky Lory | Widespread, to Salawati and Yapen |
| Goldie's Lorikeet | PNG: Lakekamu Basin and Tari Valley<br>IRIAN: Snow Mountains |
| Black-capped Lory | Widespread, to west Papuan Islands |
| Striated Lorikeet* | PNG: Lakekamu Basin and Kiunga/Tabubil<br>IRIAN: known from southern slopes of Snow Mountains |
| Pygmy Lorikeet | Widespread |
| Red-fronted Lorikeet | PNG: known from Sepik-Ramu region of northwest<br>IRIAN: Biak. Also known from Salawati |
| Fairy Lorikeet | Widespread |
| Josephine's Lorikeet | PNG: Tabubil. Also recorded at Tari Valley<br>IRIAN: Arfak Mountains |
| Papuan Lorikeet | PNG: Huon Peninsula and Tari Valley<br>IRIAN: Snow Mountains and Warkapi |
| Plum-faced Lorikeet | PNG: Tari Valley<br>IRIAN: Snow and Arfak Mountains. |
| Yellow-billed Lorikeet | Widespread |
| Orange-billed Lorikeet | PNG: Huon Peninsula and Tari Valley<br>IRIAN: Snow Mountains |
| Long-billed Cuckoo | PNG: Kiunga. Also recorded around Port Moresby and at Lakekamu Basin<br>IRIAN: known from lowlands, to west Papuan and Aru Islands |
| Rufous-throated Bronze-Cuckoo | PNG: Tari Valley<br>IRIAN: Snow Mountains and Warkapi/Arfak Mountains |
| White-eared Bronze-Cuckoo | Widespread, to Batanta |
| White-crowned Koel | PNG: widespread<br>IRIAN: known throughout, to Salawati |
| Dwarf Koel | PNG: widespread<br>IRIAN: known from lowlands |

| | |
|---|---|
| Greater Black Coucal | Widespread, to west Papuan Islands, Numfor, Yapen and Aru Islands |
| Lesser Black Coucal | Widespread, to Salawati |
| Jungle Hawk-Owl | PNG: widespread<br>IRIAN: Arfak and Fakfak Mountains |
| Papuan Hawk-Owl* | PNG: Vanimo<br>IRIAN: known from lowlands |
| Feline Owlet-Nightjar | PNG: recorded at Tari Valley. Also known from lowlands of upper Fly River<br>IRIAN: Arfak Mountains |
| Barred Owlet-Nightjar | PNG: recorded around Port Moresby<br>IRIAN: Arfak Mountains. Known from lowland and hill forests, to Aru Islands |
| Wallace's Owlet-Nightjar | PNG: Known throughout<br>IRIAN: Arfak Mountains. Known throughout, to Aru Islands |
| Archbold's Owlet-Nightjar | PNG: known from Star Mountains<br>IRIAN: known from Snow and Star Mountains |
| Mountain Owlet-Nightjar | PNG: recorded at Wau and Tari Valley<br>IRIAN: Warkapi/Arfak Mountains |
| Papuan Nightjar | PNG: recorded Lakekamu Basin<br>IRIAN: Jalan Korea |
| Archbold's Nightjar | PNG: Tari Valley<br>IRIAN: Snow and Arfak Mountains |
| Mountain Swiftlet | Widespread |
| Bare-legged Swiftlet | Known from mountains of centre and east |
| Papuan Swiftlet | Known from the north |
| Papuan Needletail | Widespread in lowlands |
| Spangled Kookaburra | PNG: Bensbach, in Trans-Fly region<br>IRIAN: Wasur NP, in Trans-Fly region |
| Rufous-bellied Kookaburra | Widespread in lowlands, to west Papuan Islands, Yapen and Aru Islands |
| Shovel-billed Kookaburra* | PNG: Lakekamu Basin<br>IRIAN: Anggi and Batu Rumah |
| Blue-black Kingfisher* | PNG: known from north and south but scarce<br>IRIAN: Jalan Korea and Batu Rumah. Also known from west Papuan Islands |
| Hook-billed Kingfisher | Widespread, to west Papuan Islands and Yapen |
| Mountain Kingfisher | PNG: widespread in montane forests<br>IRIAN: Snow Mountains |
| Little Paradise-Kingfisher* | PNG: Kiunga<br>IRIAN: known from Trans-Fly region in southeast, to Aru Islands |
| Red-breasted Paradise-Kingfisher | PNG: Wau and Lae<br>IRIAN: Sorong and Fakfak Mountains |
| Papuan Treecreeper | Widespread in montane forests |
| White-eared Catbird | Widespread in lowlands, to west Papuan Islands |
| Flame Bowerbird | PNG: Kiunga<br>IRIAN: Warkapi/Arfak Mountains |
| MacGregor's Bowerbird | PNG: widespread in montane forests |

| | |
|---|---|
| | IRIAN: known from central highlands |
| Yellow-breasted Bowerbird | PNG: Mount Hagen<br>IRIAN: known from Snow Mountains |
| Orange-crowned Fairywren | Widespread in montane forests |
| Wallace's Fairywren | PNG: Kiunga-Tabubil. Also recorded around Port Moresby<br>IRIAN: Warkapi. Also known from west Papuan and Aru Islands |
| Broad-billed Fairywren* | PNG: Vanimo<br>IRIAN: known from northern lowlands |
| White-shouldered Fairywren | Widespread in lowland and mid-montane grasslands |
| Emperor Fairywren | Widespread in lowlands, to west Papuan and Aru Islands |
| Rusty Mouse-Warbler | Widespread, to west Papuan Islands, Yapen and Aru Islands |
| Bicoloured Mouse-Warbler | PNG: Tari Valley. Also recorded at Wau<br>IRIAN: known from montane forests |
| Mountain Mouse-Warbler | Widespread in high montane forests |
| Perplexing Scrubwren | PNG: known from montane forests<br>IRIAN: widespread in montane forests |
| Large Scrubwren | Widespread in montane forests |
| Buff-faced Scrubwren | PNG: widespread in montane forests<br>IRIAN: Snow Mountains |
| Grey-green Scrubwren | Widespread in montane forests |
| Papuan Scrubwren | PNG: Wau and Tari Valley<br>IRIAN: Snow Mountains |
| Pale-billed Scrubwren | Widespread in lowlands, to west Papuan Islands, Yapen and Aru Islands |
| Papuan Thornbill | PNG: widespread in montane forests<br>IRIAN: Snow Mountains |
| Mountain Gerygone | Widespread in montane forests |
| Yellow-bellied Gerygone | Widespread, to west Papuan Islands, Yapen and Aru Islands |
| Brown-breasted Gerygone | PNG: Tari Valley<br>IRIAN: Snow, Arfak and Fakfak Mountains |
| Olive Straightbill | PNG: Tari Valley. Also recorded at Wau<br>IRIAN: Snow, Arfak and Fakfak Mountains |
| Tawny Straightbill | PNG: Lakekamu Basin<br>IRIAN: Warkapi and Batu Rumah |
| Long-billed Honeyeater | Widespread, to west Papuan and Aru Islands |
| Silver-eared Honeyeater | PNG: Port Moresby area and Tabubil<br>IRIAN: known from lowlands of northwest |
| Red-throated Myzomela | PNG: Port Moresby area, Lakekamu Basin and New Britain<br>IRIAN: Sorong. Also known from west Papuan Islands |
| Red Myzomela | PNG: widespread, to New Ireland<br>IRIAN: Fakfak Mountains. Also recorded at Arfak Mountains, and known from Yapen |
| Black Myzomela | PNG: Port Moresby area and Varirata NP<br>IRIAN: Arfak Mountains. Also known from west Papuan Islands, Yapen and Aru |

| | |
|---|---|
| | Islands |
| Mountain Myzomela | PNG: Varirata NP, Wau and Tabubil<br>IRIAN: Arfak Mountains |
| Red-collared Myzomela | Widespread in montane forests |
| Forest Honeyeater | Known from northern hill forests |
| Spot-breasted Meliphaga | PNG: Port Moresby area and Tabubil<br>IRIAN: known from southern hill forests |
| Mountain Meliphaga | PNG: Wau and Tari Valley<br>IRIAN: Arfak Mountains |
| Scrub Honeyeater | Widespread |
| Puff-backed Honeyeater | Widespread |
| Mimic Honeyeater | Widespread, to west Papuan and Aru Islands |
| Yellow-gaped Honeyeater | PNG: Port Moresby area, Vanimo and Kiunga<br>IRIAN: Jalan Korea, and Batanta and Salawati |
| Black-throated Honeyeater | PNG: widespread in montane forests<br>IRIAN: Snow and Arfak Mountains |
| Obscure Honeyeater | PNG: widespread in hill forests<br>IRIAN: known from hill forests |
| Spotted Honeyeater | PNG: Port Moresby area, Varirata NP and Tabubil<br>IRIAN: known from hill forests, to west Papuan Islands |
| Plain Honeyeater | PNG: Lakekamu Basin<br>IRIAN: Wasur NP. Also recorded at Jalan Korea |
| Marbled Honeyeater | Widespread in montane forests |
| Streak-headed Honeyeater | PNG: Lakekamu Basin<br>IRIAN: Jalan Korea. Also known from Salawati and Aru Islands |
| Meyer's Friarbird | PNG: Lakekamu Basin and Kiunga<br>IRIAN: Jalan Korea and Wasur NP |
| Leaden Honeyeater | PNG: Mount Hagen. Rare<br>IRIAN: known from mid-montane forests but rare |
| Olive-streaked Honeyeater | PNG: Tari Valley. Also recorded at Wau<br>IRIAN: Snow Mountains |
| Black-backed Honeyeater | PNG: Tari Valley<br>IRIAN: Snow Mountains |
| Sooty Melidectes | PNG: Mt Wilhelm and Tari Valley<br>IRIAN: Snow Mountains |
| Cinnamon-browed Melidectes | PNG: Huon Peninsula<br>IRIAN: Arfak Mountains |
| Belford's Melidectes | PNG: Wau and Tari Valley<br>IRIAN: Snow Mountains |
| Yellow-browed Melidectes | PNG: Tari Valley<br>IRIAN: known from Star Mountains |
| Ornate Melidectes | PNG: Tari Valley and Tabubil<br>IRIAN: Snow and Arfak Mountains |
| Smoky Honeyeater | PNG: Wau and Tari Valley<br>IRIAN: Snow and Fakfak Mountains |
| Greater Ground-Robin | PNG: Owen Stanley Ranges |

| | |
|---|---|
| | IRIAN: recorded in Snow Mountains |
| Lesser Ground-Robin | Widespread in montane forests |
| Torrent Flycatcher | Widespread |
| Olive Flyrobin | PNG: Port Moresby area, Lakekamu Basin and Madang<br>IRIAN: Wasur NP and Warkapi. Also known from west Papuan Islands, Yapen and Aru Islands |
| Canary Flycatcher | Widespread in montane forests |
| Garnet Robin | Widespread in montane forests |
| Alpine Robin | PNG: Owen Stanley Ranges<br>IRIAN: Snow Mountains |
| Black-chinned Robin | PNG: known from northern lowlands from Sepik River west to border<br>IRIAN: Arfak Mountains |
| Black-sided Robin | Widespread, to west Papuan Islands |
| Olive-yellow Robin* | PNG: Veimauri and Vanapa River area near Port Moresby, and Madang are three of six known localities on mainland New Guinea. Probably also occurs at Kiunga<br>IRIAN: Fakfak Mountains. Also recorded on Batanta |
| Black-throated Robin | PNG: Tari Valley<br>IRIAN: Snow Mountains and Warkapi |
| White-winged Robin | PNG: Tari Valley<br>IRIAN: Snow Mountains |
| Blue-grey Robin | Widespread in montane forests |
| White-rumped Robin | PNG: Port Moresby area and Tabubil<br>IRIAN: Arfak Mountains |
| White-eyed Robin | PNG: Tabubil and Telefomin<br>IRIAN: Snow Mountains |
| Ashy Robin | PNG: Tari Valley and Telefomin<br>IRIAN: Arfak Mountains |
| Black Sittella | PNG: Owen Stanley Ranges and Tari Valley<br>IRIAN: Snow Mountains |
| Mottled Whistler | PNG: widespread in montane forests<br>IRIAN: Arfak Mountains |
| Dwarf Whistler | PNG: Port Moresby area, Varirata NP and Tabubil<br>IRIAN: Warkapi/Arfak Mountains |
| Rufous-naped Whistler | PNG: Tari Valley<br>IRIAN: Snow and Arfak Mountains |
| Rusty Whistler | Widespread in montane forests |
| Sclater's Whistler | Widespread in montane forests |
| Lorentz's Whistler | PNG: known from Star Mountains<br>IRIAN: Snow Mountains |
| Regent Whistler | Widespread in montane forests |
| Golden-backed Whistler | PNG: Lakekamu Basin and Kiunga-Tabubil<br>IRIAN: known from southern slopes of Snow Mountains |
| Black-headed Whistler | PNG: Wau and Tari Valley<br>IRIAN: known from Snow Mountains |
| Sooty Shrike-Thrush | PNG: Tabubil |

| | |
|---|---|
| | IRIAN: known from Snow and Star Mountains |
| Variable Pitohui | Widespread, to west Papuan Islands, Yapen and Aru Islands. This species may be poisonous. As is the case with its close relative, Hooded Pitohui, it may have a powerful natural nerve toxin in its flesh and feathers |
| Hooded Pitohui | Widespread, to Yapen Island. This is a poisonous species! It has a powerful natural nerve toxin in its flesh and feathers |
| White-bellied Pitohui | PNG: Kiunga<br>IRIAN: known from Bivak Island in Noord River |
| Rusty Pitohui | Widespread in lowlands, to west Papuan Islands, Yapen and Aru Islands |
| Crested Pitohui | PNG: Port Moresby area, Varirata NP, Lakekamu Basin and Telefomin<br>IRIAN: Fakfak Mountains |
| Black Pitohui | PNG: Tari Valley<br>IRIAN: Warkapi/Arfak Mountains |
| Wattled Ploughbill | PNG: Tari Valley<br>IRIAN: Snow Mountains |
| New Guinea Babbler | PNG: Lakekamu Basin and Kiunga<br>IRIAN: widespread in lowlands |
| Painted Quail-thrush | PNG: Varirata NP<br>IRIAN: known from Trans-Fly region and lowlands along western side of Geelvink Bay |
| Spotted Jewel-babbler | PNG: widespread in high montane forests<br>IRIAN: Arfak Mountains |
| Blue Jewel-babbler | PNG: widespread in lowland forests<br>IRIAN: Jalan Korea and Warkapi |
| Chestnut-backed Jewel-babbler | PNG: Port Moresby area, Varirata NP and Mount Hagen. Also recorded at Wau<br>IRIAN: Arfak Mountains. Also known from Batanta and Yapen |
| Papuan Whipbird* | PNG: Tari Valley<br>IRIAN: Snow Mountains. Also known from Mt Goliath and Weyland Mountains |
| Blue-capped Ifrita | PNG: widespread in montane forests<br>IRIAN: Snow Mountains |
| Friendly Fantail | Widespread in montane forests |
| Chestnut-bellied Fantail | Widespread in lowlands, to Yapen and Aru Islands |
| Sooty Thicket-Fantail | PNG: Port Moresby area and Lakekamu Basin<br>IRIAN: Jalan Korea and Batu Rumah. Also known from west Papuan Islands, Yapen and Aru Islands |
| Black Thicket-Fantail | Widespread in lowlands, to west Papuan and Aru Islands |
| White-bellied Thicket-Fantail | Widespread in lowlands |

| | |
|---|---|
| Black Fantail | PNG: Varirata NP<br>IRIAN: widespread in montane forests |
| Dimorphic Fantail | PNG: Tari Valley<br>IRIAN: Snow and Arfak Mountains |
| Rufous-backed Fantail | PNG: Port Moresby area, Lakekamu Basin and Kiunga<br>IRIAN: Arfak and Fakfak Mountains |
| Black Monarch | Widespread in montane forests |
| Rufous Monarch | PNG: Vanimo<br>IRIAN: known from lowlands west to Geelvink Bay |
| Spot-winged Monarch | Widespread, to west Papuan Islands |
| Hooded Monarch | PNG: Lakekamu Basin and Madang<br>IRIAN: Jalan Korea and Warkapi |
| Golden Monarch | Widespread in lowlands, to west Papuan and Aru Islands, and Bismarck Archipelago |
| Rufous-collared Monarch | PNG: known from north, east to Madang<br>IRIAN: Jalan Korea and Warkapi |
| Black-breasted Boatbill | Widespread in montane forests |
| Papuan Drongo | Widespread in montane forests |
| Grey Crow | Widespread, to west Papuan Islands |
| Lesser Melampitta | PNG: widespread in montane forests<br>IRIAN: Snow and Arfak Mountains |
| Greater Melampitta | PNG: Tabubil. Also known from Torricelli Mountains (Sepik-Ramu region) and Mt Simpson in the southeast<br>IRIAN: known from Arfak, Fakfak and Kumawa Mountains, and Nassau Range |
| Yellow-breasted Bird-of-paradise* | PNG: Mount Hagen and above Tabubil. Rare<br>IRIAN: known from central ranges |
| Crested Bird-of-paradise | PNG: Owen Stanley Ranges and Tari Valley<br>IRIAN: Snow Mountains |
| Loria's Bird-of-paradise | PNG: Tari Valley<br>IRIAN: Snow Mountains |
| MacGregor's Bird-of-paradise* | PNG: Owen Stanley Ranges<br>IRIAN: Snow Mountains |
| Glossy-mantled Manucode | Widespread in lowlands, to west Papuan and Aru Islands |
| Crinkle-collared Manucode | PNG: widespread<br>IRIAN: Arfak and Fakfak Mountains |
| Jobi Manucode | PNG: Vanimo<br>IRIAN: Jalan Korea. Also known from Yapen |
| Short-tailed Paradigalla | PNG: Tari Valley and Tabubil<br>IRIAN: Snow Mountains |
| Black Sicklebill* | PNG: Tari Valley<br>IRIAN: Warkapi/Arfak Mountains |
| Brown Sicklebill | PNG: Owen Stanley Ranges and Tari Valley. Also recorded at Wau<br>IRIAN: Snow Mountains |
| Black-billed Sicklebill | PNG: Wau and Tari Valley |

| | |
|---|---|
| | IRIAN: Arfak and Fakfak Mountains |
| Pale-billed Sicklebill* | PNG: Vanimo<br>IRIAN: Jalan Korea |
| Superb Bird-of-paradise | Widespread in montane forests |
| Carola's Parotia | PNG: Mount Hagen, Tabubil and Telefomin<br>IRIAN: known from Foya, Snow and Star Mountains |
| Magnificent Bird-of-paradise | Widespread, to Salawati and Yapen |
| King Bird-of-paradise | Widespread in lowlands, to west Papuan Islands, Yapen and Aru Islands |
| Splendid Astrapia | PNG: Telefomin<br>IRIAN: Snow Mountains |
| King-of-Saxony Bird-of-paradise | PNG: Tari Valley and Telefomin<br>IRIAN: Snow Mountains |
| Twelve-wired Bird-of-paradise | Widespread in lowlands, to Salawati |
| Lesser Bird-of-paradise | Widespread in north, to Yapen |
| Greater Bird-of-paradise | PNG: Kiunga-Tabubil<br>IRIAN: Wasur NP. Also known from Aru Islands |
| Great Woodswallow | Widespread in mountains |
| Mountain Peltops | Widespread in mountains |
| Lowland Peltops | Widespread in lowlands, to west Papuan Islands |
| Hooded Butcherbird | Widespread in lowlands, to Aru Islands |
| Torrent-lark | Widespread in mountains |
| Brown Oriole | Widespread, to west Papuan Islands |
| Stout-billed Cuckoo-shrike | Widespread, to Yapen and Aru Islands |
| Boyer's Cuckoo-shrike | Widespread, to Salawati and Yapen |
| Hooded Cuckoo-shrike | PNG: widespread in montane forests<br>IRIAN: Snow Mountains |
| Papuan Cuckoo-shrike | Widespread in montane forests, to west Papuan Islands and Yapen |
| Grey-headed Cuckoo-shrike | Widespread |
| New Guinea Cuckoo-shrike | Widespread, to west Papuan Islands, Yapen and Aru Islands |
| Black-bellied Cuckoo-shrike | Widespread in montane forests |
| Golden Cuckoo-shrike | Widespread |
| Black-browed Triller | PNG: known from northwestern lowlands.<br>IRIAN: widespread in northern lowlands, to west Papuan Islands |
| Yellow-eyed Starling* | PNG: Lakekamu Basin and Kiunga-Tabubil<br>IRIAN: known from lowlands |
| Golden Myna | PNG: Port Moresby area, Lakekamu Basin and Karawari Lodge area<br>IRIAN: Jalan Korea and Sorong. Also known from Salawati and Yapen |
| Black-fronted White-eye | PNG: Varirata NP, Wau and Huon Peninsula<br>IRIAN: Warkapi/Arfak Mountains |
| Capped White-eye | PNG: Tari Valley<br>IRIAN: Snow and Arfak Mountains |

| | |
|---|---|
| New Guinea White-eye | PNG: Wau and Huon Peninsula<br>IRIAN: known from mountains on Vogelkop Peninsula and Trans-Fly region, to Aru Islands |
| Fly River Grassbird* | PNG: Southwest: known only from two localities: Lake Daviumbu on Middle Fly River and Bensbach River. May also occur along upper Bonader Creek and Morehead River<br>IRIAN: Wasur NP |
| Mountain Firetail | PNG: Tari Valley<br>IRIAN: Snow Mountains |
| Papuan Parrotfinch | PNG: Telefomin. Also known from other mountain regions<br>IRIAN: Snow Mountains. Also known from Arfak Mountains |
| Streak-headed Munia | PNG: Lae<br>IRIAN: widespread |
| White-spotted Munia | PNG: Kiunga. Also recorded at Bensbach<br>IRIAN: Wasur NP |
| Grand Munia | PNG: Lae. Also known from north and southeast<br>IRIAN: known from Mamberamo and Idenburg Valleys in north-central Irian Jaya |
| Grey-crowned Munia* | PNG: known from Trans-Fly region<br>IRIAN: Wasur NP |
| Hooded Munia | PNG: widespread in north, to New Britain<br>IRIAN: known from northeast |
| Black Munia* | PNG: recorded at Kiunga. Also known from Trans-Fly region<br>IRIAN: Wasur NP |
| Alpine Pipit | PNG: Mt Wilhelm and Tari Valley<br>IRIAN: Snow Mountains |
| Red-capped Flowerpecker | PNG: widespread<br>IRIAN: Jalan Korea, Snow Mountains and Biak |
| Obscure Berrypecker* | PNG: Tabubil. Also known from one specimen taken in the upper Angabunga River valley in 1933<br>IRIAN: one specimen taken in Arfak Mountains in 1867 |
| Black Berrypecker | Widespread, to west Papuan and Aru Islands |
| Lemon-breasted Berrypecker | Widespread in montane forests |
| Fan-tailed Berrypecker | Widespread in montane forests. |
| Streaked Berrypecker | PNG: Wau. Also known from other mountain ranges<br>IRIAN: recorded in Snow Mountains |
| Spotted Berrypecker | PNG: Wau. Also known from other mountain ranges<br>IRIAN: known from mountain ranges |
| Yellow-bellied Longbill | PNG: Lakekamu Basin and Kiunga |

| | |
|---|---|
| | IRIAN: widespread, to west Papuan and Aru Islands |
| Slaty-chinned Longbill | PNG: Varirata NP and Wau<br>IRIAN: Snow Mountains |
| Dwarf Honeyeater | Widespread, to Yapen |
| Pygmy Honeyeater | PNG: Port Moresby area, Lakekamu Basin and Karawari Lodge area<br>IRIAN: known throughout, to west Papuan Islands |
| Tit Berrypecker | Widespread in montane forests |
| Crested Berrypecker | PNG: Tari Valley<br>IRIAN: Snow Mountains |

## NEAR-ENDEMICS

### Papua New Guinea

Beck's Petrel* (possibly seen off Wuvula in the northeast and in the Admiralty Islands of the Bismarck Archipelago; otherwise known only from a specimen taken in 1928 at sea east of New Ireland and north of Buka; may breed on Bougainville), White-throated Gerygone, Yellow-tinted Honeyeater, Jacky-winter, Green Figbird.

### New Guinea

Radjah Shelduck, Pied Heron, Australian and Straw-necked Ibises, Whistling Kite, Collared Sparrowhawk, Gurney's*, Wedge-tailed and Little Eagles, Brown Falcon, Australian Hobby, Lewin's and Bare-eyed Rails, Rufous-tailed Bush-hen, Brolga, Australian Bustard, Dusky Woodcock, Bush Thick-knee, Pied Oystercatcher (south), Masked Lapwing, Great Cuckoo-Dove, Peaceful and Bar-shouldered Doves, White-bibbed and Bronze Ground-Doves, Wompoo, White-breasted, Yellow-bibbed (Bismarck Archipelago and Geelvink Bay islands) and Claret-breasted Fruit-Doves, Torresian Imperial-Pigeon, Papuan Mountain-Pigeon, Yellow-capped and Red-breasted Pygmy-Parrots, Double-eyed Fig-Parrot, Eclectus and Red-winged Parrots, Palm* and Sulphur-crested Cockatoos, Little Corella, Red-flanked Lorikeet, Pallid, Chestnut-breasted and Black-eared Cuckoos, Australian Koel, Pheasant Coucal, Australian Masked-Owl, Rufous (including Waigeo and Aru Islands) and Barking Owls, Papuan (including west Papuan and Aru Islands) and Marbled Frogmouths, Australian Owlet-Nightjar, Spotted (New Ireland and Aru Islands) and White-throated Nightjars, Uniform Swiftlet, Azure and Little Kingfishers, Blue-winged Kookaburra, Forest (including New Britain and Aru Islands), Beach and Yellow-billed Kingfishers, Common and Buff-breasted Paradise-Kingfishers, Blyth's Hornbill, Noisy Pitta, Spotted Catbird, Fawn-breasted Bowerbird, Beccari's Scrubwren, Green-backed (including west Papuan and Aru Islands), Fairy (including west Papuan and Aru Islands), Large-billed and Mangrove (south) Gerygones, Green-backed (including west Papuan and Aru Islands) and Brown (south, as well as Aru Islands) Honeyeaters, Dusky (south, as well as Biak and Aru Islands) and Red-headed (south, as well as Aru Islands) Myzomelas, Graceful (south, as well as Aru Islands), Varied, Tawny-breasted and White-throated (south, savanna) Honeyeaters, Little, New Guinea and Noisy Friarbirds, Brown-backed (south), Rufous-banded (south, as well as Aru Islands) and Blue-faced Honeyeaters, Lemon-bellied (south) and Yellow-legged Flycatchers, White-faced (including Yapen Island) and Mangrove (including Aru Islands) Robins,

Northern Scrub-Robin (including Aru Islands), Varied Sittella, Grey (including west Papuan and Aru Islands) and Black-tailed (south and Bismarck Archipelago) Whistlers, Rufous and Grey Shrike-Thrushes, Logrunner, Grey-crowned Babbler, Mangrove Fantail, Island, Black-winged, Black-faced and Frilled (including west Papuan and Aru Islands) Monarchs, Leaden (south, savanna), Satin (including New Britain), Restless (south) and Shining Flycatchers, Yellow-breasted Boatbill (including west Papuan and Aru Islands), Trumpet Manucode (including Aru Islands), Magnificent Riflebird (west and central), Black-backed and Black (including west Papuan and Aru Islands) Butcherbirds, Australasian Magpie, Magpie-lark, Olive-backed and Green (including Aru Islands) Orioles, Black-faced and Yellow-eyed Cuckoo-shrikes, White-winged (south) and Varied Trillers, Olive-tailed Thrush (including Bismarck Archipelago), Singing (including Bismarck Archipelago) and Metallic Starlings, Yellow-faced Myna (including west Papuan and Aru Islands), Tree and Fairy Martins, Island Leaf-Warbler (including Bismarck Archipelago), Crimson Finch, Chestnut-breasted Munia, Australasian Pipit.

## Bismarck Archipelago

Heinroth's Shearwater* (recorded in Bismarck Sea. May breed on Bougainville in the Crown Prince Range), Melanesian Scrubfowl (Admiralty Islands), Yellow-legged Pigeon* (very rare), Mackinlay's Cuckoo-Dove, Red-knobbed and Island Imperial-Pigeons, Finsch's Pygmy-Parrot, Singing Parrot, Cardinal Lory, Mayr's Swiftlet (New Ireland and Bougainville Island), Atoll Starling (coral islands).

## Bougainville

The 25 species listed below are otherwise confined to the Solomon Islands.

Solomon Sea-Eagle* (also occurs on Buka), Pied Goshawk (also occurs on Buka), Imitator Sparrowhawk* (south), Woodford's Rail*, Pale Mountain-Pigeon, Ducorps' Cockatoo (also occurs on Buka), Meek's and Duchess* Lorikeets, Fearful Owl*, Ultramarine and Moustached* (possibly heard near Arawe on north coast in 1986) Kingfishers, Black-faced Pitta* (south), Scarlet-naped Myzomela, Mountain Whistler*, Brown Fantail, Bougainville (Buka, Bougainville and Shortland Islands only) and Black-and-white Monarchs, Steel-blue Flycatcher, Bougainville Crow* (Buka, Bougainville and Shortland Islands only), Solomon Cuckoo-shrike, Brown-winged and White-eyed* Starlings, Yellow-throated and Grey-throated White-eyes, Midget Flowerpecker.

# POLYNESIA

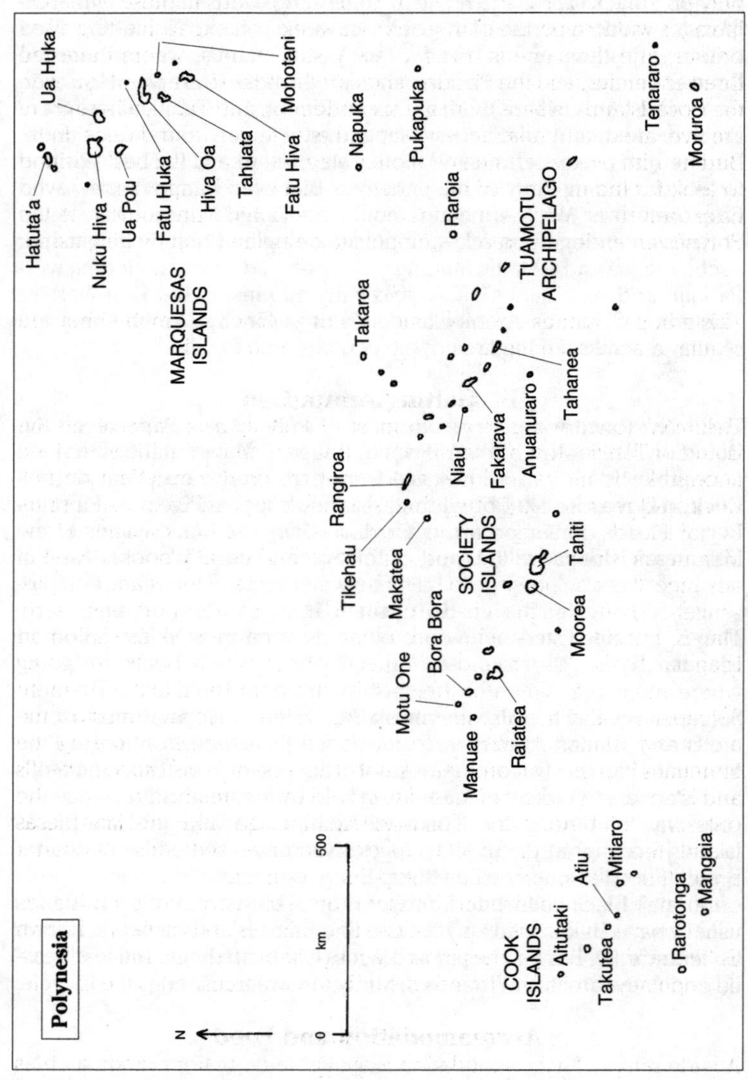


## INTRODUCTION

### Summary

This large group of atolls and islands, which stretches across a massive area of the Pacific, supports 42 endemic species, many of which survive only in very low numbers. It will be necessary to visit at least 20 different atolls and islands to look for all of the endemics, including six in the Marquesas Islands where there are ten endemics and five in the Tuamotu Archipelago where there are six endemics, including what is arguably the region's top bird, the very rare Tuamotu Sandpiper*. It is only possible to get to the relevant atolls and islands in these two archipelagos within a period of three to four weeks, on expensive organised cruises, and the same is true for the Austral Islands, where there are three endemics, and the Pitcairn Islands, where there are five. However, the Cook Islands, where there are six endemics, and Tahiti, where there are five, are much more accessible, and easy to get around once there. Birders with plenty of time and money are therefore in the best position to look for the majority of the endemics, but even budget birders who have only time on their hands could see a high proportion of the Polynesian endemics in a few months if they island-hop by freightship.

## Size

This group of islands covers a land area of just 5503 sq km, but they are scattered across a huge area of the central-south Pacific.

## Getting Around

The main town and gateway to most of Polynesia is Papeete on the island of Tahiti. Most of the islands in this part of the Pacific which are accessible by air can be reached from here on the excellent air network, and reasonably priced air passes make it possible to visit a number of islands on a short trip without breaking the bank. Flights to the Marquesas Islands are the most expensive, and usually booked well in advance. It is also possible to travel between some of the islands on passenger-carrying freightships, a cheaper form of transport than aeroplanes, but a lot more time consuming because most ships sail on an irregular basis. Ask around in Papeete about which boats are going where and when. A monthly freightship runs from Tahiti to the Tuamotu Archipelago and the Marquesas Islands, where it stops at most of the atolls and islands. However, to maximise the chances of seeing the endemics in these two archipelagos it is necessary to visit specific atolls and islands, and not all of these are served by the freightship, hence the only way of birding the Tuamotu Archipelago and the Marquesas Islands thoroughly and quickly is to join an organised cruise or charter a yacht, both of which are very expensive options.

On major islands hire-cars and taxis are expensive, but such islands usually have an unscheduled but cheap public minibus network, known as 'le truck', which reaches most places of habitation. On the less heavily populated atolls and islands the only form of transport is the bicycle.

## Accommodation and Food

A wide range of accommodation is available on major islands such as Rarotonga in the Cook Islands and Tahiti in the Society Islands, and there are hotels and guesthouses in the form of thatched beach bungalows on most of the other islands, although it will be necessary to stay with local people or camp on a few of the remoter atolls and islands.

Ask at the tourist information offices about homestays, the local form of bed and breakfast, which can be found on most inhabited islands. On remote islands local families usually take in paying guests, who should show their gratitude with gifts such as food, rather than money. Travellers who prefer to camp should ask for permission from the local people and explain very carefully why they would rather sleep in a tent than in a local house. Individuals who prefer to sleep outdoors puzzle the local people because they are accustomed to their extended families, and some may think such individuals are staking a claim for their land. There are campsites on Tahiti and Raiatea, and it is possible to camp in hotel grounds on Rangiroa. It is not possible to stay with local people or camp in the Cook Islands.

In the few major towns it is possible to find a wide range of food, from French to Vietnamese, but once off the well beaten tourist track it will be necessary to survive on root crops such as breadfruit, cassava, sweet potato, taro and yam, which may be served up with fish or pork, and raw fish marinated in lime juice and served with a coconut sauce. Various fruits are also generally available when in season. In most places food can be washed down with Hinano, the local beer which is brewed by Heineken.

## Health and Safety

Immunisation against hepatitis, polio, typhoid and yellow fever (if arriving in Kiribati, Niue, Pitcairn Islands, French Polynesia (Tahiti) and Tuvalu from an infected country) is recommended.

Falling coconuts (don't camp under coconut trees) and eating poisonous fish are minor concerns compared with the potential effects of long-term nuclear testing which may or may not be, according to which side of the fence one stands on, a major cause of concern throughout the region. France, the UK and the USA have exploded numerous nuclear weapons on or under Christmas Island, Mururoa and Fangataufa, but who knows for sure how far-reaching the fall-out from these tests has been?

## Climate and Timing

The peak time to visit Polynesia is between May and August, the coolest and driest period of the year, thanks to the southeast tradewinds which blow across most of the region at this time. However, it is also possible to visit areas such as the Tuamotu Archipelago from March to October, although most of Polynesia is usually hot, humid and wet from November to April and cyclones can cause serious problems with travel any time between January and April.

## Habitats

There are two major types of island in Polynesia. Small, slender, low coral islands, which usually occur in circular or horseshoe-shaped chains known as atolls (individual 'island' components in this chain are often referred to as *motus*), and rugged, volcanic high islands which rise to a maximum height of 2241 m (7352 ft) on Tahiti. Atolls support sparse vegetation and few birds, but the damp, windward slopes of the high islands usually support luxuriant rainforests where the diversity of birds is much greater. Such forests are usually dominated by *Ficus* species and are also characterised by climbing vines and tree-ferns. The drier, leeward slopes of these islands normally support grasslands, savanna or subsistence farming and plantations.

## Conservation

Thirty threatened and near-threatened species, a high percentage of the Polynesian avifauna, occur in the region. Many of these survive in very low numbers, primarily because they inhabit very small islands and forested land is being eaten away by subsistence farming. Managed reserves are non-existent, but the odd atoll is protected on paper. Such designation will not protect these low islands, most of which reach heights of less than 10 m (33 ft), from rising sea levels, but there is little the local people can do about this potentially catastrophic problem except lobby those countries which may end up being primarily responsible. The same applies to nuclear testing, where the effects are difficult to detect, but years of nuclear explosions may or may not have played a part in the decline of some species.

### Bird Species

Over 100 species have been recorded in Polynesia. Non-endemic specialities and spectacular species include Tahiti, Black-winged, Cook's*, Collared, Phoenix, Herald and Kermadec Petrels, Polynesian Storm-Petrel, Red-tailed and White-tailed Tropicbirds, Red-footed Booby, Bristle-thighed Curlew*, Grey-backed and Sooty Terns, Blue-grey and Black Noddies, Common White-Tern, Pacific Imperial-Pigeon and Polynesian Starling.

### Endemics

A total of 42 species are endemic to Polynesia (compared with 39 in Micronesia). The ten Marquesas Islands endemics include a kingfisher and three monarchs, the six Cook Islands endemics include a kingfisher and a monarch, the six Tuamotu Archipelago endemics include Tuamotu Sandpiper* and a kingfisher, the five Pitcairn Islands endemics include a crake and the five Tahiti (Society Islands) endemics include a kingfisher and a monarch. More Polynesian endemics include Little White-Tern, two ground-doves, seven fruit-doves, four lorikeets, three swiftlets, another kingfisher, making a total of five, and eight reed-warblers.

### Expectations

On short trips it is possible to see all six Cook Islands endemics and at least three of the five Tahiti (Society Islands) endemics. Longer trips will be necessary to see at least four of the six Tuamotu Archipelago endemics, all five Pitcairn Islands endemics, all three Austral Islands endemics and at least eight of the ten Marquesas Islands endemics.

## COOK ISLANDS

The 15 widely spaced Cook Islands, which rise to 653 m (2142 ft) on Rarotonga, the only high, well-forested island in the archipelago, support six endemics, as well as some excellent seabirds, including Herald Petrel, the rare Bristle-thighed Curlew* and Chattering Kingfisher. To see all six endemics plus these notable species it is necessary to visit three islands, all of which are easy to get to and around.

### Cook Islands Endemics

Rarotongan Fruit-Dove*, Atiu Swiftlet*, Mangaia Kingfisher*, Rarotonga Monarch*, Rarotonga Starling*, Cook Islands Reed-Warbler.

## Non-endemic Specialities

Herald Petrel, Bristle-thighed Curlew* (most Nov–Mar), Pacific Imperial-Pigeon, Long-tailed Koel (Apr–Sep), Chattering Kingfisher.

## Others

Red-tailed and White-tailed Tropicbirds, Lesser and Great Frigatebirds, Masked and Red-footed Boobies, Sooty Tern, Common White-Tern.

(Other species introduced to Aitutaki include Tahitian Lorikeet*.)

Most of the islands are accessible by air via the international airport on Rarotonga, the main island. Three days here and single days on Atiu and Mangaia would be enough to see all six endemics, as well as the near-endemic Chattering Kingfisher, but this is not usually possible due to the domestic flight schedules which will probably necessitate two nights on Atiu and three nights on Mangaia. Book inter-island flights in advance and arrange the appropriate itinerary via a travel agent or Air Rarotonga, Box 79, Rarotonga (tel: 22 888, fax: 23 288). Otherwise it is possible to travel between islands by freightship, but they are very irregular and offer only very basic on-board accommodation.

On **Rarotonga** there are buses and taxis, and cars, scooters and bicycles for hire. Over 130 Rarotonga Monarchs* survive as a single-island endemic here on the only island with luxuriant rainforest growing on the misty mountains. The stronghold for this species is 30 minutes walk up the Totokoitu Stream from the Turoa Research Station at the south end of the island. It is necessary to obtain permission to visit this area from the research station, or, better still, from the Conservation Offices (tel: 21256) which are situated about 2 km east of Avarua on the seaward side of the road, or the National Heritage Office, a further 2 km out of town. The other single-island endemic is Rarotonga Starling*, which also occurs along the Totokoitu Stream and, along with Rarotongan Fruit-Dove*, in forested areas along the cross-island walk (via The Needle). This trail is also one of the best sites for Red-tailed and White-tailed Tropicbirds (common around The Needle), Common White-Tern and Pacific Imperial-Pigeon. Herald Petrel breeds on Te Manga, Rarotonga's highest peak, and can be seen in small numbers in the afternoon (after 1500) flying over Muri Beach at the southeast end of the island towards the mountain. In front of the rugby pitch, north of the sailing club, is a good position from which to scan. Bristle-thighed Curlew* occurs on the small islets off Muri Beach and Avarua Airport and whilst November to March is the best period for this species, a few individuals, probably first-summers, may be present during the summer. The island of **Takutea** is one of this species' wintering strongholds and supports large seabird colonies, including 1,500 pairs of Red-tailed Tropicbirds.

Rarotongan Fruit-Dove* is much more common, and confiding, on **Atiu**, an elevated atoll with a 71 m (233 ft) high central plateau and forested low rolling hills where the single-island endemic, Atiu Swiftlet*, is widespread. It is possible to hire a guide here to visit a breeding colony of swiftlets in caves near the accommodation. Along the coast road it is possible to see Great Frigatebird, Rarotongan Fruit-Dove*, Pacific Imperial-Pigeon, Chattering Kingfisher and Cook Islands Reed-Warbler. The single-island endemic, Mangaia Kingfisher*, occurs in roadside scrub 30 minutes walk from the war memorial, going away from the airstrip, on **Mangaia**, an elevated atoll with low rolling hills, wet taro fields and banana plantations. Along the coast road it is possible to see Red-tailed and White-tailed Tropicbirds, Great Frigatebird and Common White-Tern, while Cook Islands Reed-Warbler is widespread on the island. Tahitian Lorikeet* has been introduced to **Aitutaki**, a middle-aged volcanic island with surrounding reef, where about 1,200 birds were present in 1994. For more information on the Cook Islands, contact Cook Islands Tourist Authority, PO Box 14, Rarotonga (fax: 682 21435).

*Accommodation:* there is a wide range of accommodation, including backpackers' hostels (eg. Vara's at Muri Beach), on Rarotonga and Aitutaki, and smaller establishments on Atiu and Mangaia. Local regulations prohibit the residents from putting up tourists and camping is banned, apparently because the government aims to discourage budget travellers and rake in as much cash as possible via the mega-expensive resort hotels.

## AUSTRAL ISLANDS

The seven Austral (Tubuai) Islands, five of which are inhabited, stretch across 1300 km of the southern Pacific, and include Tubuai and Rurutu, both of which are accessible by air from Tahiti. The three endemics occur on the islands of Rapa and Rimitara, which can only be reached from Tubuai via the irregular freightship service.

### Austral Islands Endemics

Rapa Fruit-Dove*, Kuhl's Lorikeet*, Rimatara Reed-Warbler*.

There are bicycles and canoes for hire on the small island of Tubuai (10 km × 5 km), from where a freightship runs to the other islands on an occasional basis, stopping at Raivavae, Rapa and Rimatara. Rapa Fruit-Dove* is endemic to the misty, ferny forests on the western slopes of the isolated, reefless island of **Rapa** (40 sq km). This is the highest island in the archipelago, rising spectacularly to 650 m (2133 ft). Birders determined to see the pink, grey and green fruit-dove should write to the Subdivision Administrative des Iles Australes, BP 82, Mataura, Tubuai for a permit, and to the mayor of the island for help in arranging some form of accommodation. Some of the 1,000 or so inhabitants of **Rimitara**, the smallest (8 sq km), lowest island in the archipelago, do rent out rooms and houses, but visitors should take food and drink. Kuhl's Lorikeet* is most likely to be found in the mixed horticultural woodlands here.

*Accommodation:* Tubuai and Rurutu—beach bungalows. Rapa and Rimitara—local houses.

## PITCAIRN ISLANDS

These remote islands support five endemics, four of which only occur on uninhabited Henderson Island. While these birds are easy to see once there, this British Dependent Territory is an extremely difficult place to get to, as there is no airstrip or harbour. However, a couple of tour companies do arrange occasional cruises on chartered yachts, and make a special effort to visit Henderson Island.

### Pitcairn Islands Endemics

Henderson Island Crake*, Henderson Island Fruit-Dove*, Stephen's Lorikeet*, Pitcairn* and Henderson Island* Reed-Warblers.

Birders without yachts will probably find their best chance of visiting these islands lies with tour companies such as Ocean Voyages, who arrange two-week cruises. Otherwise write to the magistrate on the island of Pitcairn asking if it would be possible to visit the island and to stay with a local family as a paying guest. Birders who manage to reach these islands and stay with the locals should not repay their hospitality with cigarettes or alcohol because the residents are Seventh Day Adventists and all such vices are banned. The only single-island endemic on **Pitcairn** is the Pitcairn Reed-Warbler*. This high, volcanic island may be tiny (4.5 sq km), but it still manages to rise to 347 m (1139 ft) at Pawala Ridge. The soil is very fertile and manages to provide enough fruit and vegetables to sustain a resident human population of about 60. The four remaining endemics occur only in the 'plateau forest', a more or less dense tangle of prickly vines on a 30 m (98 ft) high interior plateau, on the uninhabited elevated atoll known as **Henderson** (31 sq km), a World Heritage Site. Many seabirds also frequent the Pitcairn Islands and some breed on the remote small atoll known as Ducie.

## TAHITI

Tahiti is the largest and highest island in Polynesia, measuring 1045 sq km and rising to 2241 m (7352 ft) at Orohena, one of the two old volcanoes which dominate the island. The luxuriant rainforest, most of which is now confined to the deep valleys in the sparsely populated interior, supports most of the five endemics, as well as the near-endemic Polynesian Imperial-Pigeon* and Chattering Kingfisher.

### Society Islands Endemics

Grey-green Fruit-Dove, Polynesian Swiftlet*, Tahiti Kingfisher*, Tahiti Monarch*, Tahiti Reed-Warbler*.

### Society Islands and Tuamotu Archipelago Endemics

Polynesian Imperial-Pigeon*.

### Non-endemic Specialities

Pacific Imperial-Pigeon, Chattering Kingfisher.

A 117 km long road runs around the coast of Tahiti Nui, the western part of the figure-of-eight island of **Tahiti**, and provides access to at least the lower part of the forested valleys. The Papeno'o Valley, which is situated near the northeast coast, is the largest valley on the island and it supports Tahiti Reed-Warbler*, as well as Polynesian Imperial-Pigeon*, which also occurs in the Hitia'a Valley. Such valleys also support Tahiti Monarch*, while Grey-green Fruit-Dove, Polynesian Swiftlet* and Tahiti Kingfisher* are more widespread.

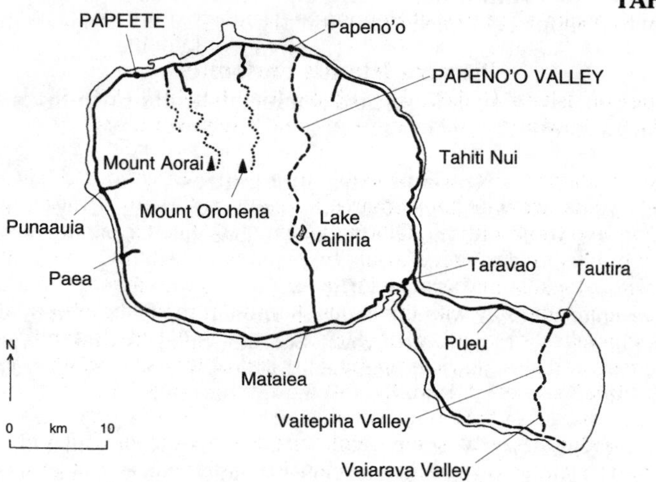


Grey-green Fruit-Dove and Tahiti Kingfisher* also occur on the island of **Moorea**, 16 km northwest of Tahiti and accessible on a regular ferry. Tahitian Lorikeet* occurs on the island of **Manuae** (Scilly), a 15 km wide atoll at the western edge of the Society Islands, and on the 280 ha **Motu One** (Bellingshausen), along with plenty of seabirds. For more information on Tahiti and Polynesia, contact Tahiti Tourisme, BP 65, Papeete (fax: 689 43 6619).

*Accommodation:* plenty to choose from.

The seas between Tahiti and the Tuamotu Archipelago support Tahiti, Black-winged (most Apr–Oct), Collared (most Apr–Oct) and Phoenix Petrels, Christmas Island Shearwater and Polynesian Storm-Petrel.

## TUAMOTU ARCHIPELAGO

This beautiful archipelago of atolls, to the east of Tahiti, is well known to many birders, especially shorebird fanatics, because it is the only place on earth where the rare and unique Tuamotu Sandpiper* occurs. About 45 of the widely spaced 75 or so atolls, the largest group of atolls on earth, are sparsely populated and support a further five endemics, including two fruit-doves and a kingfisher, as well as Bristle-thighed Curlew* and a superb selection of seabirds.

Twelve atolls are served by air, but Tuamotu Sandpiper* has only been recorded in recent decades on one of these: Fakarava. The most accessible site for this bird in the 1990s has been the islets offshore from the uninhabited island of Tahanea, which is accessible only on boats hired from local people (fly to the nearest island and negotiate in French), cargo boats such as the 'Aranui' and chartered yachts, but visited fairly regularly by tour companies. To look for the remaining five endemics it is necessary to visit Rangiroa, Mahatea and Niau, the only island the kingfisher occurs on.

## Tuamotu Archipelago Endemics

Tuamotu Sandpiper*, Polynesian Ground-Dove*, Atoll* and Mahatea* Fruit-Doves, Tuamotu Kingfisher*, Tuamotu Reed-Warbler.

## Tuamotu Archipelago and Society Islands Endemics

Polynesian Imperial-Pigeon*.

## Non-endemic Specialities

Tahiti Petrel, Bristle-thighed Curlew* (most Nov–Mar), Grey-backed Tern, Blue-grey Noddy, Tahitian Lorikeet*, Long-tailed Koel (Apr–Sep).

## Others

Wedge-tailed Shearwater, White-tailed Tropicbird, Great and Lesser Frigatebirds, Red-footed and Brown Boobies, Spotless Crake, Wandering Tattler, Pectoral Sandpiper, Pacific Golden-Plover, Great Crested-Tern, Brown and Black Noddies, Common White-Tern.

Tuamotu Sandpiper* was recorded in March 1995, 1996 and 1997 on two islets (Toreatai and Noiokao) off the uninhabited, predator-free atoll known as **Tahanea**. This strange sandpiper, which is known locally as 'titi' or 'kivi-kivi', may be found in all types of vegetation on predator-free atolls, from coral rubble along the shoreline to bushes and palms inland. Bustle-thighed Curlew* also occurs on Tahanea's islets, along with Common White-Tern, Atoll Fruit-Dove* (on Noiokao) and Tuamotu Reed-Warbler (on Noiokao). Mahatea Fruit-Dove* is endemic to the 8 km long island of **Mahatea** (Makatea). This island, which is scarred by abandoned phosphate mines, rises to over 91 m (300 ft) and also supports Pacific Imperial-Pigeon*, as well as colonies of Red-footed and Brown Boobies, noddies and Common White-Tern. **Rangiroa**, the largest atoll in the archipelago and the third largest on earth (80 km × 25 km), supports Tahiti Petrel, Wedge-tailed Shearwater, White-tailed Tropicbird and Bristle-thighed Curlew*, as well as a colony of Great Frigatebirds and Red-footed Boobies. The nearby atoll of **Tikehau** supports Atoll Fruit-Dove*, Tahitian Lorikeet* and Tuamotu Reed-Warbler, as well as breeding seabirds such as Red-footed and Brown Boobies, Great Crested-Tern, Grey-backed Tern (about 20 pairs), Blue-grey, Brown (about 1,500 pairs) and Black (about 800 pairs) Noddies, and Common White-tern (about 1,500 pairs). Other species recorded here include Great and Lesser Frigatebirds, Spotless Crake, Bristle-thighed Curlew*, Wandering Tattler, Pectoral Sandpiper, Pacific Golden-Plover and Long-tailed Koel. **Raroia** atoll, where Thor Heyerdahl's *Kontiki* expedition came to an end, supports an inland breeding colony of Black Noddies and Common White-Terns. The small atoll of **Takaroa**, famous for its black pearls, is a good site for Wandering Tattler. Widespread terrestrial species in the archipelago include Atoll Fruit-Dove* and Tuamotu Reed-Warbler. Some of the best coral reefs on earth are also here, but they are a navigator's nightmare and littered with wrecks.

It seems almost inevitable that the beauty of the tropical Pacific should be tainted, albeit by an invisible phenomenon. Mururoa, the atoll on the southern fringe of this archipelago, is a French nuclear test site, so it is possible that at least the surrounding atolls may be subject to radioactive fall-out.

*Accommodation:* there are hotels and guesthouses, mostly comprised of thatched beach bungalows, on Rangiroa and Tikehau, a campsite on Rangiroa, and it is possible to stay with local families (ask at the tourist information office in Papeete) or camp, with permission, elsewhere.

The seas between the Tuamotu Archipelago and the Marquesas Islands support Cook's* (Apr–Sep), Herald and Kermadec Petrels, Short-tailed Shearwater (Apr–Sep), White-bellied and Polynesian Storm-Petrels, and Blue-grey, Brown and Black Noddies.

*No doubt about the most exciting bird in the Tuamotu Archipelago, if not the whole of Polynesia—Tuamotu Sandpiper**

## MARQUESAS ISLANDS

The ten major Marquesas Islands, which provided the inspiration for Robert Louis Stevenson's *Treasure Island,* are an administrative division of the Overseas Territory of French Polynesia. The islands of Hiva Oa, Tahuata and Fata Hiva, at the southern end of the 300 km long chain, are high, wild, wet and forested, whereas the islands of Nuku Hiva, Ua Huka and Ua Pou, at the northern end of the chain, are also high, but considerably drier. Together these islands support ten endemics, including a kingfisher and three monarchs, as well as seabirds such as the near-endemic Little White-Tern.

Travelling to the Marquesas Islands is something of an obstacle course, unless it is possible to join the occasional cruises on chartered yachts organised by a couple of tour companies. Tahiti Air does operate very expensive flights to Nuku Hiva, Ua Huka, Ua Pou and Hiva Oa, but has been known to tell prospective travellers that all flights are full, possibly in an effort to keep tourists on Tahiti. It may be possible to obtain a seat by booking at least three weeks in advance, but this cannot be done outside Polynesia. One possible alternative is to wait at the airport in the hope that a passenger fails to turn up for a flight, but such an optimistic technique may involve days of waiting. In 1996 one hotel-owner in the Marquesas Islands was planning to fly tourists in directly from Australia and Los Angeles, but such an arrangement is likely to prove very expensive. The final option available for getting to these remote islands is to travel on the monthly freightship which runs from Papeete. However, the basic accommodation costs cruise-liner prices.

## Marquesas Islands Endemics

Marquesas Ground-Dove*, White-capped Fruit-Dove, Marquesas Imperial-Pigeon*, Ultramarine Lorikeet*, Marquesas Swiftlet, Marquesas Kingfisher*, Iphis*, Marquesas* and Fatuhiva* Monarchs, Marquesan Reed-Warbler.

## Polynesian Endemics

Little White-Tern.

## Others

Sooty Tern.

(Introduced species include Great Horned Owl, Common Myna and Chestnut-breasted Munia.)

White-capped Fruit-Dove, Ultramarine Lorikeet*, Marquesas Swiftlet, the single-island endemic, Iphis Monarch*, and Marquesan Reed-Warbler occur on the forested slopes of **Ua Huka**, which rises to 884 m (2900 ft) at Mount Hitikau, as well as on the offshore islets of Teuaua and Hemeni. These islets also support hundreds of thousands of Sooty Terns. **Nuku Hiva** is the largest and most heavily populated island in the archipelago, rising to 1224 m (4016 ft) at Mount Tekao. It is seven minutes by helicopter or two hours by truck on a very rough track, from the airport in the northwest to Taiohae on the south coast, the administrative capital which is little more than a village with about 2,000 inhabitants. Marquesas Imperial-Pigeon*, which occurs only on this island, and Ultramarine Lorikeet*, appear to be restricted to high valleys at the western end of the island, but this is a difficult area to get to and explore. One area which is relatively easy to bird is the trail to the 350 m (1150 ft) Vaipo Waterfall, which lies 4 km inland from Hakaui. This village, which is about 12 km west of Taiohae, is accessible by boat or in a very expensive hired Land-rover with compulsory driver. The waterfall spills off the fertile volcanic plateau in the centre of the island where

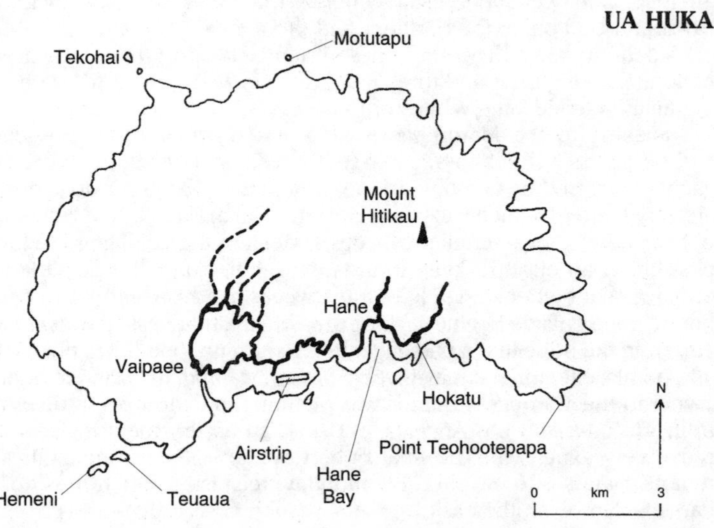

much of the natural vegetation has been destroyed by dairy cows, wild horses and goats.

Marquesas Monarch* is still 'common' on the island **Ua Pou**, where the rocky ridges rise to 1203 m (3947 ft) at misty Mount Oave. Bird off the track which runs around this island. Marquesas Kingfisher* is scarce on **Hiva Oa**, an island which rises to 1276 m (4186 ft) at Mount Temetiu. Paul Gauguin is buried here, above the main town of Atuona where it is possible to hire a Land-rover. The kingfisher is commoner on **Tahuata**, which is only accessible by boat from Hiva Oa. **Fatu Hiva** is also only accessible by boat from Hiva Oa. This island rises to 960 m (3150 ft) at Mount Tauaouoho and the large areas of forest which remain support the single-island endemic, Fatuhiva Monarch*. The best way to see this bird on this, the remotest inhabited island, is to walk the 17 km scenic trail between the two main villages. Marquesas Monarch* still survives on the island of **Mohotani** (Motane), despite the fact that large areas have been turned into treeless desert thanks to felling and the subsequent introduction of sheep. Unfortunately, what is arguably the Marquesas Island's most beautiful endemic, the rare Marquesas Ground-Dove*, is now restricted to the uninhabited islets of **Fatu Huku** and **Hatuta'a**, having been exterminated on all other islands by cats. These islets may prove impossible to get to without joining an organised cruise.

*Accommodation:* there are hotels and guesthouses in the form of thatched bungalows on Nuku Hiva, Hiva Oa, Ua Huka, Ua Pou and Fatu Hiva, but little for budget birders, except for the possibilties of staying with local families or camping (with permission).

*The rare Marquesas Ground-Dove* is confined to two remote islets in the Marquesas Islands, but seeing this black, white and purple beauty would be more than ample reward for any birders who manage to reach them*

The low atolls and islands of **Kiribati**, formerly known as the Gilbert Islands, include the Line and Phoenix Islands. Some of the Pacific's biggest and most easily accessible seabird colonies are situated on the world's largest atoll, known as **Kiritimati** or Christmas Island, at the northern end of the Line Islands. This atoll is accessible by air from Honolulu in Hawaii and there is one hotel. Christmas Island Warbler also occurs here, as well as on Teraina and Tabueran, the two islands which lie between Kiritimati and the atoll known as Palmyra. Teraina and Tabueran also support introduced populations of Kuhl's Lorikeet* and **Palmyra** is a winter stronghold of Bristle-thighed Curlew*. In Kiribati there is also a hotel on Abemama, which is accessible by air from Tarawa. There are buses and taxis on this island and it is also possible to hire cars here.

The small island of **Nauru** (21 sq km), an independent nation where tourism is not encouraged, has been severely damaged by 80 years of phosphate mining, but the endemic reed-warbler was reported by the local people to be surviving in bushy areas in 1983.

Very little is known about the birds of **Tuvalu** (formerly the Ellice Islands), an archipelago which is accessible by air from Fiji and the Marshall Islands (in Micronesia), and, more rarely, by freightship from Fiji. The main town and gateway to other islands is Funafuti. Camping is not allowed here, but there is one expensive hotel and several guesthouses scattered across the nine main islands. Getting around is possible via bus, motorbike and bicycle, and the islands are connected by a fortnightly freightship. For more information on Tuvalu, contact the Tourism Officer, Ministry of Commerce, Trade and Industries, Box 33, Vaiaku, Funafuti (tel: 688 20184, fax: 688 20829).

## ADDITIONAL INFORMATION

### Addresses

The Hawaiian Audubon Society, 850 Richards Street, Suite 505, Honolulu, Hawaii 96813 (tel: 808 528 1432, fax: 808 537 5294) publishes the *Elepaio* journal, which covers Polynesia.

The Ornithological Society of New Zealand, PO Box 316, Drury, South Auckland, New Zealand, publishes the *Notornis* journal, which covers Polynesia.

The Smithsonian Institution, Washington DC 20560, USA, publishes the *Atoll Research Bulletin*, which covers Polynesia.

The Moorings (tour company), Fourth Floor, 19345 US, 19 North, Clearwater, FL 34624, USA (tel: 800 535 7289).

Ocean Voyages Incorporated, 1709 Bridgeway, Sausalito, CA 94965, USA (tel: 415 332 4681, fax: 415 332 7460).

Zegrahm Expeditions Inc., 1414 Dexter Avenue North, #327 Seattle, WA 98109, USA (tel: 206 285 4000 or 1 800 628 8747, fax: 206 285 5037, e-mail: zoe@zeco.com, website: www.zeco.com).

Tourism Council of the South Pacific, 375 Upper Richmond Road West, East Sheen, London SW14 7NX, UK (fax: 0181 878 0998), and 475 Lake Boulevard, Tahoe City, CA 96145, USA (fax: 916 583 0154).

### Books and Papers

*A Field Guide to the Birds of Hawaii and the Tropical Pacific.* Pratt H D *et al.*, 1987. Princeton University Press.

*Guide to Cook Island Birds.* Holyoak D, 1981. Privately published.

*Bird Conservation in the Pacific Islands.* Hay R, 1986. ICBP (BirdLife) Study Report No. 7. BirdLife International.

The modern avifauna of the Pitcairn Islands, South Pacific. Brooke M, in press. *Biol. J. Linn. Soc.*

The endemic land birds of Henderson Island, southeastern Polynesia: notes on natural history and conservation. Graves G, 1992. *Wilson Bulletin* 104: 32–43.

Stability and changes during the twentieth century in the breeding landbirds of Tahiti. Monnet C *et al.*, 1993. *Bird Conservation International* 3: 261–280.
The Tuamotu Sandpiper: little known, little cared for. Hay R, 1984. *Forest and Bird* 15(4): 17.
Distribution, numbers and habitat of Bristle-thighed Curlews (*Numenius tahitiensis*) on Rangiroa Atoll. Gill R, Redmond R, 1992. *Notornis* 39: 17–26.

## POLYNESIAN ENDEMICS (42)

### Widespread (1)

| | |
|---|---|
| Murphy's Petrel | Breeds and ranges throughout south Polynesia, mainly around Tuamotu Archipelago, and the Austral and Pitcairn Islands |

### Cook Islands (6)

| | |
|---|---|
| Rarotongan Fruit-Dove* | Rarotonga and Atiu |
| Atiu Swiftlet* | Atiu. 175 active nests were found in two caves in 1995–96 |
| Mangaia Kingfisher* | Mangaia. Up to 700 birds |
| Rarotonga Monarch* | Rarotonga. Over 130 birds in 1996 |
| Rarotonga Starling* | Rarotonga. Widespread |
| Cook Islands Reed-Warbler | Widespread |

### Cook Islands and Society Islands (1)

| | |
|---|---|
| Chattering Kingfisher | Mainly a montane forest species on Atiu, Mangaia and Mauke in the Cook Islands, and Tahiti, Bora Bora, Raiatea and other islands in the Society Islands |

### Cook Islands, Society Islands and Tuamotu Archipelago (1)

| | |
|---|---|
| Tahitian Lorikeet* | Aitutaki in the Cook Islands, Motu One and Manuae in the Society Islands, and northern atolls of the Tuamotu Archipelago (e.g. Tikehau) |

### Austral Islands (3)

| | |
|---|---|
| Rapa Fruit-Dove* | Rapa. About 274 birds in 1989–90 |
| Kuhl's Lorikeet* | Rimitara. About 900 birds. (Introduced to Teraina and Tabuaeran in Kiribati) |
| Rimatara Reed-Warbler* | Rimitara |

### Pitcairn Islands (5)

| | |
|---|---|
| Henderson Island Crake* | Henderson. This flightless crake is endemic to the plateau forest and surrounding scrub |
| Henderson Island Fruit-Dove* | Henderson. Endemic to the plateau forest |
| Stephen's Lorikeet* | Henderson. Endemic to the plateau forest |
| Pitcairn Reed-Warbler* | Pitcairn |
| Henderson Island Reed-Warbler* | Henderson. Endemic to the plateau forest |

## Society Islands Endemics (5)

| | |
|---|---|
| Grey-green Fruit-Dove | Tahiti and Moorea |
| Polynesian Swiftlet* | Tahiti |
| Tahiti Kingfisher | Tahiti and Moorea |
| Tahiti Monarch* | Tahiti. Found in four valleys only (out of 39 surveyed) between 1986 and 1991 |
| Tahiti Reed-Warbler* | Tahiti. Found in 12 valleys only (out of 39 surveyed), including Papeno'o, between 1986 and 1991 |

## Extinct Society Islands Endemics

| | |
|---|---|
| Tahiti Rail | Became extinct around 1800 |
| White-winged Sandpiper | Became extinct on Tahiti and Moorea around 1790 |
| Black-fronted Parakeet | Became extinct on Tahiti around 1844 |
| Society Parakeet | Became extinct on Raiatea around 1773 |
| Mysterious Starling | Became extinct on Raiatea around 1700 |

## Society Islands and Tuamotu Archipelago Endemics (1)

| | |
|---|---|
| Polynesian Imperial-Pigeon* | Rare in Papeno'o and Hitia'a valleys on Tahiti, and on Mahatea (Makatea) where 100–500 birds survive |

## Tuamotu Archipelago (6)

| | |
|---|---|
| Tuamotu Sandpiper* | This bird was first discovered on Kiritimati (Christmas Island), 2000 km north of the Tuamotus, and was believed to be widespread in this area of the Pacific. However, the introduction of dogs, cats and rats led to its inevitable decline and by the 1920s it was only known from 16 atolls. A major expedition in 1989 found 12–15 birds on a few tiny islets off the south side of Tahanea, the most accessible place in which to see this bird today. In 1990 another expedition found 150–200 birds on the southern Morane and Anuana Runga atolls. Since 1980 it has also been recorded on Tenararo (1986), the Raevski Group (1984) and Fakarava (1980s). |
| Polynesian Ground-Dove* | The most recent records come from Rangiroa Atoll (1990–91) |
| Atoll Fruit-Dove* | Widespread (e.g. Tikehau) |
| Mahatea Fruit-Dove* | Mahatea (Makatea) |
| Tuamotu Kingfisher* | Niau. 400–600 birds in 1974 |
| Tuamotu Reed-Warbler | Widespread |

## Marquesas Islands (10)

| | |
|---|---|
| Marquesas Ground-Dove* | Only present on the uninhabited islets of Fatu Huku and Hatuta'a |
| White-capped Fruit-Dove | Widespread |
| Marquesas Imperial-Pigeon* | Nuku Hiva. 150–300 birds were estimated to be present in 1993, mainly in high valleys at the western end of the island |

| | |
|---|---|
| Ultramarine Lorikeet* | Ua Huka ('common'), Ua Pou and Nuku Hiva (rare in high valleys and on high ridges in the northwest). Has recently been translocated to Fatu Hiva |
| Marquesas Swiftlet | Widespread |
| Marquesas Kingfisher* | Hiva Oa (less than 50 pairs) and Tahuata (300–500 pairs) |
| Iphis Monarch* | Ua Huka. Mainly on vegetated tops of coastal cliffs |
| Marquesas Monarch* | Mohotani ('common') and Ua Pou ('common'). Possibly extinct on Nuku Hiva, Hiva Oa and Tahuata |
| Fatuhiva Monarch* | Fatu Hiva: 'common' in 1990 |
| Marquesan Reed-Warbler | Widespread |

## Extinct Marquesas Islands Endemics

| | |
|---|---|
| Red-moustached Fruit-Dove | Nuku Hiva (became extinct in 1922) and Hiva Oa (not recorded during 1985 survey) |

## Marquesas Islands and Kiribati (1)

| | |
|---|---|
| Little White-Tern | Marquesas Islands and Kiribati (Line and Phoenix Islands) |

## Kiribati Endemics (1)

| | |
|---|---|
| Christmas Island Warbler | 'Common' on Kiritimati, Teraina and Tabueran in the Line Islands |

## Extinct Kiribati Endemics

| | |
|---|---|
| Gilbert Rail | Known only from a 1928 specimen |

## Nauru Endemics (1)

| | |
|---|---|
| Nauru Reed-Warbler* | Still present in 1983 according to local people, despite 80 years of phosphate mining which has caused considerable habitat loss |

## Near-endemics

Grey-backed Tern, Blue-grey Noddy, Polynesian Starling.

# SOLOMON ISLANDS

## INTRODUCTION

### Summary

The Solomon Islands, which lie to the east of New Guinea, support 45 endemics, as well as a further 25 species, including two kingfishers and a pitta, which are shared only with Bougainville and Buka, the two islands which lie at the north end of the archipelago within the political boundaries of Papua New Guinea. As it is possible to see a high percentage of these 70 species, a very high total of endemics for such a small archipelago, during a short trip, the Solomon Islands seem set to become a popular birding destination in the near future. Most of the islands are easily reached by air, but it is still necessary to organise a couple of camping treks with local guides to notch up a high percentage of the endemics. Birders without lists to worry about will find a couple of islands with good accommodation and more easily accessible forests where there are plenty of good birds to complete the scenic surroundings.

### Size

At 29,790 sq km the Solomon Islands cover a land area a quarter the size of England and over 20 times smaller than Texas.

### Getting Around

The excellent cheap internal air network, based on the gateway island of Guadalcanal, serves most islands. The flights are very popular, hence it is wise to book well in advance. There are also weekly boat services to most islands, including a 24-hour ferry between Guadalcanal and Gizo, although the island of Isabel is less well served. Travelling overland is more difficult as there are few long stretches of road away from Guadalcanal and Malaita due to the rugged terrain. On Guadalcanal there are public taxis, in the form of trucks and minibuses, and it is possible to hire vehicles. On Malaita there are also trucks to get around in. However, there are several long, steep and difficult trails on most islands which enable access to montane forests, and it will be necessary to tackle a couple of these with the aid of local guides and camping gear to see the widest possible cross-section of endemics.

It is important to always ask for permission to roam around in search of birds in the Solomon Islands, because all of the land away from the towns is under local ownership, and the indigenous people are very sensitive about strangers walking about freely over their property, especially in the remoter regions of Guadalcanal and Malaita. It is therefore wise to report to the provincial government offices when arriving on each island, to visit the village chief when reaching each village, to ask for assistance in getting around the local area, and to show the appropriate level of appreciation (the daily rate for guides and porters in 1993 was Solomons$10 per day). These time-consuming procedures will severely test the patience of saintly birders, but they will also almost certainly result in the most productive and enjoyable birding.

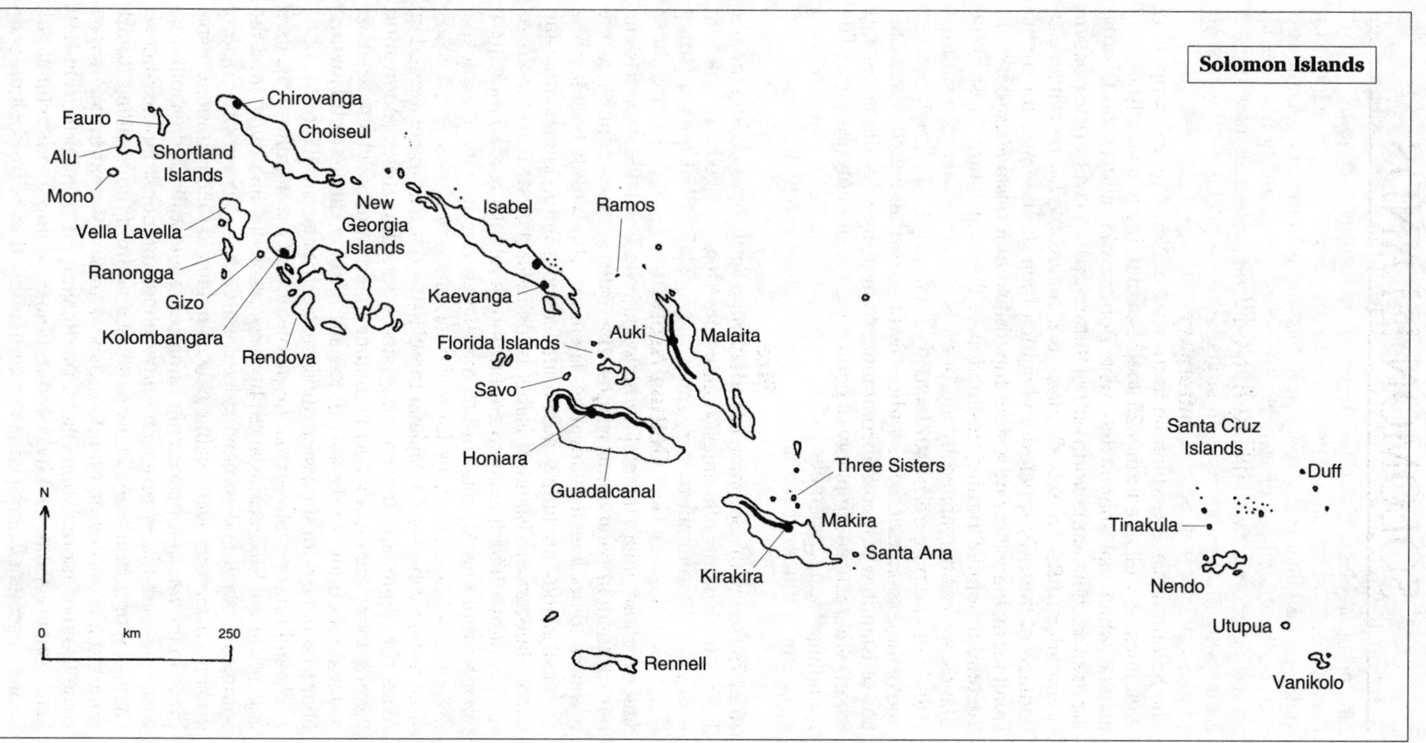
Solomon Islands
Chirovanga
Fauro
Choiseul
Alu
Shortland Islands
Mono
New Georgia Islands
Isabel
Ramos
Vella Lavella
Ranongga
Gizo
Kaevanga
Kolombangara
Rendova
Auki
Malaita
Florida Islands
Savo
Honiara
Guadalcanal
Santa Cruz Islands
Three Sisters
Duff
Tinakula
Makira
Santa Ana
Kirakira
Nendo
Utupua
Rennell
Vanikolo
N
0
km
250

## Accommodation and Food

A thorough exploration of the Solomon Islands will necessitate a certain amount of camping, but there are a couple of good hotels in Honiara on Guadalcanal, a couple of tourist lodges on Gizo, a lodge on Malaita, and cheaper, more basic hotels and government guesthouses with cooking facilities elsewhere. To camp, ask permission, although on asking you may well be invited to stay with a local family instead. Either way, it is best to repay their generous hospitality with gifts such as stick tobacco or food.

## Health and Safety

Immunisation against hepatitis, polio, typhoid and yellow fever (if arriving from an infected country) is recommended, as are all possible precautions against malaria, which is dominated by *Plasmodium falciparum*, the species of parasite which can kill its host within a week. Don't drink the water without treating it first and beware of sharks on the reefs.

## Climate and Timing

The peak time to visit the Solomon Islands is during the coolest, driest and least humid period of the year, which lasts from July to September when the southeast tradewinds blow across the archipelago. The cyclone season, December to March, is also the hottest, wettest and most humid time of the year, and therefore best avoided.

## Habitats

There are six main islands, all of which are high, rugged and volcanic with central mountain ranges which rise to 2447 m (8028 ft) at Mount Makarakomburu on Guadalcanal. The steep slopes of these mountains support mossy montane rainforests, while the lowlands support remnant humid tropical rainforests. These forests support most of the endemic birds, as well as several species of birdwing butterflies. Coconut plantations and sago swamps are widespread throughout the coastal lowlands. There are plenty of palm-fringed sandy beaches, as well as some areas of mangrove around the coast, and some superb coral reefs offshore.

## Conservation

All of the remaining lowland forest and accessible montane forest on the Solomon Islands is threatened by clear fell logging, which points to a bleak future for the 41 threatened and near-threatened birds which occur here. Most of the forest on Gizo and that below 400 m (1312 ft) on neighbouring Kolombangara was felled by the Japanese by 1990 and by the mid-1990s Malaysian timber companies had convinced the Solomon Islands government to let them carry out large-scale logging throughout the archipelago. In 1996 Australian aid to the Timber Control Unit (TCU) was cut, apparently in protest against the increase in logging, especially in Western Province where the corals of the Marovo Lagoon World Heritage Site are under threat from the resulting runoff. With the aid cut the Solomon Islands government then threatened to close the unit down. An allegedly pro-logging prime minister does not help, especially one who has been rumoured to have deployed military police to protect logging camps from being damaged by the local people, who are rightly infuriated about their forests being destroyed. One possible way to pacify the local victims would be to introduce them to portable sawmills and selective logging. This method of logging causes far less damage than clear felling by foreign companies, and should result in most of the profits being returned to the people who own the land the forests grow on.

### Bird Species

Over 190 species have been recorded in the Solomon Islands. Non-endemic specialities and spectacular species include Melanesian Scrubfowl, Beach Thick-knee, Sooty Tern, Nicobar Pigeon*, Finsch's Pygmy-Parrot, Singing Parrot, Moustached Treeswift, Beach Kingfisher, Fan-tailed Gerygone, Cardinal Myzomela, New Caledonian Flycatcher, Melanesian Cuckoo-shrike, Long-tailed Triller, Island Thrush, Yellow-faced Myna and Blue-faced Parrotfinch.

### Endemics

A high total of 45 species are endemic to the Solomon Islands, with a further 25 shared only with Bougainville and Buka, two islands at the north end of the archipelago which are politically part of Papua New Guinea, but ecologically akin to the Solomon Islands. The zoogeographical total of 70 endemics includes Solomon Sea-Eagle*, two fruit-doves, Ultramarine and Moustached* Kingfishers, Black-faced Pitta*, seven honeyeaters, five fantails, a shrikebill, eight monarchs and 12 white-eyes.

### Expectations

It is possible to see a little over 100 species, including most of the common endemics, during a week or two of island-hopping across the archipelago.

## GUADALCANAL

The largest and loftiest of the Solomon Islands supports the best selection of endemics, and those which are widespread but most likely to be seen here include Ultramarine and Moustached* Kingfishers, Mountain Whistler*, Brown Fantail, Black-and-white Monarch, White-billed Crow* and Midget Flowerpecker, as well as the endemic *turipavae* race of San Cristobal Thrush*. Unfortunately, most of these species, as well as the endemic Guadalcanal Honeyeater and the near-endemic Guadalcanal Thicketbird*, are montane specialities which are only likely to be seen on an arduous week-long trek into the mountains.

### Guadalcanal Endemics

Black-headed Myzomela, Guadalcanal Honeyeater.

### Other Solomon Islands Endemics

Yellow-bibbed Lory, Buff-headed Coucal, Solomon Hawk-Owl, White-winged Fantail, Chestnut-bellied Monarch, White-billed Crow*, San Cristobal Thrush* (*turipavae* race).

### Solomon Islands, Bougainville and Buka Endemics

Pied Goshawk, Ducorp's Cockatoo, Duchess Lorikeet*, Ultramarine and Moustached* (*excelsus* race) Kingfishers, Mountain Whistler*, Brown Fantail, Black-and-white Monarch, Steel-blue Flycatcher, Solomon Cuckoo-shrike, Brown-winged and White-eyed* Starlings, Grey-throated White-eye, Midget Flowerpecker.

## Non-endemic Specialities

Melanesian Scrubfowl, Mackinlay's Cuckoo-Dove, Red-knobbed Imperial-Pigeon, Finsch's and Red-breasted Pygmy-Parrots, Singing Parrot, Cardinal Lory, Melanesian Cuckoo-shrike, Yellow-faced Myna, Guadalcanal Thicketbird*.

## Others

Little Pied Cormorant, Rufous Night-Heron, Pacific Baza, Brahminy Kite, Swamp Harrier, Grey Goshawk, Buff-banded Rail, Wandering Tattler, Sharp-tailed Sandpiper, Pacific Golden-Plover, Sooty Tern, Stephan's Dove, Superb and Claret-breasted Fruit-Doves, Eclectus Parrot, Rainbow Lorikeet, Shining Bronze-Cuckoo, Moustached Treeswift, Glossy and Uniform Swiftlets, Variable, Collared, Beach and Sacred Kingfishers, Dollarbird, Blyth's Hornbill, Golden Whistler, Willie-wagtail, Rufous Fantail, Yellow-eyed and White-bellied Cuckoo-shrikes, Common Cicadabird, Singing and Metallic Starlings, Pacific Swallow, Clamorous Reed-Warbler.

(Other species recorded here include Woodford's Rail*.)

**Honiara** is accessible by air. In and around the town Yellow-bibbed Lory, Black-headed Myzomela and Midget Flowerpecker occur in the botanical gardens, and Wandering Tattler, Red-knobbed Imperial-Pigeon, Finsch's Pygmy-Parrot, Ducorp's Cockatoo, Yellow-bibbed Lory and Buff-headed Coucal have been recorded around Selwyn College. The old road over Mount Austen near town enters a lush river valley where the good species selection includes Ultramarine Kingfisher. Head towards the airport and turn right a couple of km east of town, at the junction where there is a bakery. This road accends a hill. Stop at the top and walk along the other side. An unknown species of rail was seen here in mid-1996. About 10 km east of Honiara explore the path leading down to the Lungga River. The scrubland here supports Ultramarine Kingfisher, Chestnut-bellied and Black-and-white Monarchs, White-billed Crow* and White-eyed Starling*. About 10 km further east turn south to Tenaroo Falls, a good area for Ducorp's Cockatoo and Black-and-white Monarch.

In 1994 an individual of the endemic *excelsus* race of Moustached Kingfisher*, previously known only from three specimens, the last two of which were collected in 1953, was seen and others heard above Turipava, along the route used by Gain and Galbraith's hunters in 1953, through the mist forests south of the now abandoned village of Betilonga. To see this very rare and beautiful kingfisher, as well as the other montane specialities listed above, head for **Ando** near Tenaroo Falls and ask for Luke Lendi who will help to organise a trek to Turipava and Mount Mbutohaina. It is also possible to contact Luke in advance by writing to him at PO Box 654, Honiara. This very difficult trek, part of which involves wading along a fast-lowing river, will take about a week to complete. The only porters who know the best way to go are Ansento, Ini, John, Love, Pano and Stanley, at least one of whom should be taken along. The usual route is as follows: Ando–Betilonga (6.5 hours), Betilonga–Talakelako River (9.5 hours), Talakelako River–Turipava (6.5 hours). Bird around Turipava, which is situated on a steep ridge at 1130 m (3707 ft), and on Mount Mbutohaina up to 1565 m (5135 ft).

Most of the montane specialities also occur on the highest reaches of **Mount Popomanseu**, which can be reached via a long and hard two or three day walk from Gold Ridge, which is accessible by 4WD track from Honiara, or via a shorter, but much steeper ascent from Viso, which is west of Avu Avu (accessible by air) on the south coast.

*Accommodation:* Honiara—Hotel Mendana.

White-eyed Starling* occurs on northern **Choiseul**, alongside Metallic Starling, in and around gardens cut out of primary forest. Other species recorded on this island include Solomon Sea-Eagle*, Imitator Sparrowhawk*, Crested Cuckoo-Dove, Fearful Owl* and White-billed Crow*. Rumours surrounding the survival of the endemic Choiseul Pigeon probably relate to sightings of Crested Cuckoo-Doves. The pigeon was discovered and last reliably recorded in 1904, hence it has been presumed extinct for many years. Few travellers, let alone birders, make it to Choiseul, but there are a couple of roads and it is possible to stay at a few small government and mission outposts.

## GIZO

This small island (11 km × 5km) in the New Georgia group supports a single endemic, as well as a good selection of other endemics and near-endemics, hence it is worth spending at least a few hours birding here *en route* to or from neighbouring Kolombangara.

### Gizo Endemics

Splendid White-eye*.

### Other Solomon Islands Endemics

Buff-headed Coucal, Yellow-vented Myzomela, White-capped Monarch.

### Solomon Islands, Bougainville and Buka Endemics

Solomon Sea-Eagle*, Pied Goshawk, Ducorp's Cockatoo, Steel-blue Flycatcher, Solomon Cuckoo-shrike, Brown-winged Starling.

### Non-endemic Specialities

Melanesian Scrubfowl, Red-knobbed and Island Imperial-Pigeons, Singing Parrot, Cardinal Lory, Yellow-faced Myna.

### Others

Lesser Frigatebird, Pacific Baza, Grey-tailed and Wandering Tattlers, Black-naped and Sooty Terns, Claret-breasted Fruit-Dove, Eclectus Parrot, Golden Whistler, Rufous Fantail.

(Other species recorded here include Beach Kingfisher, on Olasana Island.)

Gizo is accessible by air from Honiara and is the gateway to the island of Kolombangara. The airstrip is on Nusatape Island, just offshore, and the town, Gizo, is reached by boat. The main island has been completely logged, but the endangered endemic, Splendid White-eye*, is quite common in secondary scrub alongside the road towards Saeraghi and in well-vegetated gullies elsewhere on the island. It is possible to penetrate the interior by road and track, and to travel by motor-canoe around the coast and to the island of Simbo. On Simbo there is a trail to the rim of an active volcano which passes through forest where Melanesian Scrubfowl occurs.

*Accommodation:* expensive hotels and resthouses.

On the boat trip between Gizo and Kolombangara look out for Heinroth's Shearwater*, as well as Bridled Tern and Brown Noddy.

## KOLOMBANGARA

This island is a classic volcanic cone which is 30 km across and rises to 1770 m (5807 ft). Most of the lowland forest below 400 m (1312 ft) was clear felled by 1990, but the remaining mossy montane forest, the most easily accessible in the Solomon Islands, still supports three single-island endemics, as well as Nicobar Pigeon* and Black-faced Pitta*.

### Kolombangara Endemics

Roviana Rail*, Kulambangra White-eye, Kulambangra Leaf-Warbler*.

### Other Solomon Islands Endemics

Crested Cuckoo-Dove, Buff-headed Coucal, Yellow-vented Myzomela, White-winged Fantail, White-capped and Kulambangra* Monarchs, Solomon Islands White-eye.

### Solomon Islands, Bougainville and Buka Endemics

Solomon Sea-Eagle*, Pied Goshawk, Pale Mountain-Pigeon, Ducorp's Cockatoo, Meek's and Duchess* Lorikeets, Black-faced Pitta*, Steel-blue Flycatcher, Solomon Cuckoo-shrike, Brown-winged Starling, Grey-throated White-eye.

### Non-endemic Specialities

Heinroth's Shearwater*, Meyer's Goshawk, Melanesian Scrubfowl, Beach Thick-knee, Mackinlay's Cuckoo-Dove, Nicobar Pigeon*, Yellow-bibbed Fruit-Dove, Red-knobbed and Island Imperial-Pigeons, Finsch's and Red-breasted Pygmy-Parrots, Singing Parrot, Cardinal Lory, Melanesian Cuckoo-shrike, Yellow-faced Myna.

### Others

Pacific Baza, Grey Goshawk, Grey-tailed Tattler, Metallic Pigeon, Stephan's Dove, Superb and Claret-breasted Fruit-Doves, Eclectus Parrot, Rainbow Lorikeet, Shining Bronze-Cuckoo, Moustached Tree-swift, Variable, Forest, Beach and Sacred Kingfishers, Dollarbird, Blyth's Hornbill, Scarlet Robin, Golden Whistler, Willie-wagtail, Rufous Fantail, Yellow-eyed and White-bellied Cuckoo-shrikes, Common Cicadabird,

Island Thrush, Singing and Metallic Starlings, Pacific Swallow, Island Leaf-Warbler, Blue-faced Parrotfinch.

(A possible new species of cuckoo-shrike was recorded here in 1990.)

The best base for birders on Kolombangara is **Iriri** on the southwest coast. This village is accessible by boat from Gizo (direct or via Ringi) or on foot from Kukundu, which is connected to Gizo by boat. There is a good self-catering guesthouse at Kukundu where Roviana Rails* feed on the lawn! If this bird fails to appear here try the short grass at the south end of the airstrip at dawn. Take all supplies from Gizo and once at Iriri hire a guide and a couple of porters to climb up to 'Camp Professor' at 960 m (3150 ft) on Mount Veve, one day away. Use this as a base camp and take day-trips up to the 1750 m (5742 ft) summit to look for many montane specialities including Crested Cuckoo-Dove, Pale Mountain-Pigeon, Meek's Lorikeet, Kulambangra White-eyes, and Island and Kulambangra* (only near summit) Leaf-Warblers. All arrangements for birding Mount Veve can be made via the Gizo Hotel on Gizo. In Iriri it is also possible to hire a dug-out canoe to search the inshore waters for Heinroth's Shearwater*. The degraded forest surrounding **Kena Hill** on the southwest coast supports Meyer's Goshawk, Singing Parrot, Duchess Lorikeet*, White-winged Fantail, White-capped Monarch, Steel-blue Flycatcher and Grey-throated White-eye, while Solomon Sea-Eagle* may be present around the school and Beach Thick-knees grace the reef just west of the village. The harbour area around **Ringi**, where the Gizo ferry docks at the southeast end of the island, is good for Melanesian Scrubfowl, and Nicobar Pigeons* fly over the bay. Elsewhere there are plenty of logging tracks leading off the coast road and finding one of these which rises to 900 m (2953 ft) will present the best chance of finding the rare Black-faced Pitta*.

*Accommodation:* Kukundu—self-catering guesthouse. Iriri—local huts, camping.

The endemic *nigrotectus* race of Kulambangra Monarch* and the endemic Banded White-eye occur near the village of Maravari on the island of **Vella Lavella**, which is accessible by boat from Gizo. There is a house for visitors at Maravari, but it is necessary to take all supplies. From here it is possible to charter a boat to the village of Koriovuku on the island of **Ranongga**, where the endemic Ganongga White-eye is easy to see in nearby secondary scrub and plantations.

Black-faced Pitta* is easily heard but very difficult to see in secondary growth around the village of Tirotonga on the seldom visited island of **Isabel**. To look for the pitta fly to Buala (the airport is on the nearby island of Fera), from where it is a few hours walk to Tirotonga. Ask the village chief if it is possible to stay there and where to look for 'Toi-toi', the local name for the pitta. Other species recorded on this island include Pied Goshawk, Imitator Sparrowhawk*, Woodford's Rail*, Nicobar Pigeon*, Fearful Owl*, Solomon Hawk-Owl, Scarlet-naped Myzomela and White-billed Crow*.

The montane forests, accessible from Auki, on the island of **Malaita** support three single-island endemics: Red-bellied Myzomela, Malaita

Fantail* and Malaita White-eye. From Auki head south to Lolana (buses available) where it is possible with perseverance to hire guides and porters for the one-day trek up to the small ridge-top village of Aruilange. It is possible to stay with the local people here and to reach 1100 m (3609 ft) on day-trips, a sufficiently high altitude to see Malaita Fantail*. This, the rarest of the three endemics, occurs alongside Rufous Fantail here. Other species recorded on Malaita, the most densely populated in the archipelago, include Solomon Sea-Eagle* and Melanesian Scrubfowl.

*Although the major attraction on the island of Isabel is Black-faced Pitta*, seeing this rare bird could be overshadowed by the even rarer black-and-white Imitator Sparrowhawk**

## MAKIRA (SAN CRISTOBAL)

The forested mountains of Makira support the most single-island endemics in the archipelago, a total of ten known surviving species, as well as the endemic *margaretae* race of San Cristobal Thrush*, a full species according to some taxonomists, and the very rare Yellow-legged Pigeon*. It will be necessary to organise a trek with local guides to see most of these species.

### Makira Endemics

Chestnut-bellied Imperial-Pigeon*, Sooty Myzomela, San Cristobal Melidectes, Dusky Fantail*, White-collared Monarch, Ochre-headed Flycatcher*, San Cristobal Starling, Shade Warbler*, San Cristobal Leaf-Warbler*, Mottled Flowerpecker.

### Other Solomon Islands Endemics

Crested Cuckoo-Dove, White-headed Fruit-Dove*, Yellow-bibbed Lory, Solomon Hawk-Owl, Chestnut-bellied Monarch, San Cristobal Thrush* (*margaretae* race).

### Solomon Islands, Bougainville and Buka Endemics

Solomon Sea-Eagle*, Pied Goshawk, Duchess Lorikeet*, Grey-throated White-eye.

### Non-endemic Specialities

Melanesian Scrubfowl, Mackinlay's Cuckoo-Dove, Bronze Ground-Dove, Yellow-legged Pigeon*, Yellow-bibbed Fruit-Dove, Red-knobbed and Island Imperial-Pigeons, Finsch's Pygmy-Parrot, Singing Parrot, Cardinal Lory, Cardinal Myzomela, Long-tailed Triller.

### Others

Rufous Night-Heron, Buff-banded Rail, Rufous-tailed Bush-hen, Spotless and White-browed Crakes, Grey-tailed Tattler, Rufous-necked Stint, Metallic Pigeon, Stephan's Dove, Eclectus Parrot, Rainbow Lorikeet, Australian Koel, Moustached Treeswift, Variable, Collared, Beach and Sacred Kingfishers, Dollarbird, Scarlet Robin, Golden Whistler, Willie-wagtail, Rufous Fantail, Yellow-eyed Cuckoo-shrike, Common Cicadabird, Singing and Metallic Starlings, Pacific Swallow, Island Leaf-Warbler.

Makira is accessible by air from Honiara. The best birding area is around the village of Hauta at 500 m (1640 ft) which is a long day's walk from Kirakira. The local people here have started an ecotourism project, to provide an alternative source of revenue to logging, and the village chief should be contacted in advance to make the necessary arrangements for guides and accommodation. Write to John Waihuru, Hauta Village, Bauro East, Kirakira, Makira. It is also possible to contact the chief via the Solomon Islands Development Trust in Honiara or by radio through Solomon Telekom.

*Accommodation:* Kirakira—government guesthouse (poor). Hauta—ask village chief for permission to stay in a local hut, or to camp.

The **Three Sisters**, a small island group which can be visited by boat on a day-trip from Makira, support Silver-capped Fruit-Dove, as well as Buff-banded Rail, Beach Thick-knee, Beach Kingfisher and Sooty Myzomela.

## RENNELL

This island is one of the world's best examples of a raised limestone atoll and the eastern half, where the 155 sq km Lake Te Nggano lies, is a World Heritage Site. It is the most southerly and geographically isolated island in the archipelago and, unlike the others, it is largely flat and lacks a central mountain range, although most of the coastal cliffs are about 100 m (328 ft) high. About 80% of the island's 692 sq km is still covered with tropical rainforest which supports most of the birds, including five single-island endemics, as well as Silver-capped Fruit-Dove, Pacific Imperial-Pigeon, Fan-tailed Gerygone, New Caledonian Flycatcher and Island Thrush.

### Rennell Endemics

Rennell Fantail, Rennell Shrikebill*, Rennell Starling*, Rennell* and Bare-eyed White-eyes.

### Other Solomon Islands Endemics

Silver-capped Fruit-Dove, Yellow-bibbed Lory.

### Non-endemic Specialities

Mackinlay's Cuckoo-Dove, Bronze Ground-Dove, Pacific Imperial-Pigeon, Finsch's Pygmy-Parrot, Singing Parrot, Fan-tailed Gerygone, Cardinal Myzomela, New Caledonian Flycatcher.

### Others

Great and Lesser Frigatebirds, Red-footed Booby, Australian Ibis, Brown Goshawk, Sharp-tailed Sandpiper, Black-naped Tern, Shining Bronze-Cuckoo, Moustached Treeswift, Uniform Swiftlet, Collared and Sacred Kingfishers, Golden Whistler (*feminina* race), Yellow-eyed Cuckoo-shrike, Island Thrush.

Rennell is accessible by air and most of the birds listed above can be seen alongside the only road which runs through the centre of the island, especially either side of the village of Lavanggu or by Lake Te Nggano. Both of which are accessible from Tinggoa, where the plane lands, via tractor-trailer, the only mode of motorised transport on the island. The two islets in Lake Te Nggano where Red-footed Boobies nest are 3 hours by boat from Kia Koe Lodge.

*Accommodation:* Lavanggu—local huts. Lake Te Nggano—Kia Koe Lodge, bookable in advance via Lance Tango, Kia Koe Lodge, East Rennell, Rennell Bellora Province.

Santa Cruz and Sanford's* White-eyes, as well as Rusty-winged Starling* occur on the island of Nendo in the **Santa Cruz Islands** at the south-east end of the Solomon Islands chain. From Lata, where there is an adequate government guesthouse, walk south to Pala, then head inland along Head Road and back to Lata. All three species can be seen on this short circuit. The island of Vanikolo is more difficult and expensive to reach. The ferry from Nendo runs every fortnight or so, hence it will probably be necessary to charter a boat with boatman from the government offices to reach the island to look for the endemic Vanikoro Monarch*, the near-endemic Vanikoro Flycatcher and a race of Santa Cruz White-eye which may be a full species. From Lata on Nendo it takes about seven hours to reach the island of Utapua and a further three hours to reach Vanikolo. Guides are available in the village of Lavaka to bird the nearby forest where all three species occur.

## ADDITIONAL INFORMATION

### Addresses

The Royal Australasian Ornithologists Union (see p. 176 for address) publishes the *Emu* journal which covers the Solomon Islands.
Solomon Islands Tourist Authority, PO Box 321, Honiara (fax: 677 23986).

### Books and Papers

Birds of Manus, Kolombangara and Makira (San Cristobal) with Notes on Mammals and Records from Other Solomon Islands. Buckingham D *et al.*, in prep.
Notes on Solomon Island birds. Gibbs D, 1996. *Bull. B.O.C.* 116 (1): 18–25.
*Birds of the North Solomons.* Hadden D, 1981. Wau, Papua New Guinea: Wau Ecology Institute Handbook No. 8.
Field observations of the birds of Santa Isabel, Solomon Islands. Webb H, 1992. *Emu* 92: 52–57.

Checklist and notes on the current status of birds of New Georgia, Western Province, Solomon Islands. Blaber S, 1990. *Emu* 90: 205–214.
Five new subspecies from the mountains of Guadalcanal (British Solomon Islands). Cain A, Galbraith I, 1955. *Bull. B.O.C.* 75: 90–93.

## SOLOMON ISLANDS ENDEMICS (45)

An additional 25 species are shared only with Bougainville and Buka, which are politically part of Papua New Guinea, but ecologically akin to the Solomon Islands, bringing the total of Solomon Islands zoogeographical endemics to 70.

### Widespread (12)

| | |
|---|---|
| Crested Cuckoo-Dove | Choiseul, Kolombangara and Makira |
| Silver-capped Fruit-Dove | Three Sisters (off Makira), Santa Ana (off Makira), Rennell and Ugi |
| White-headed Fruit-Dove* | Makira |
| Yellow-bibbed Lory | Guadalcanal, Makira and Rennell |
| Buff-headed Coucal | Guadalcanal, Gizo and Kolombangara |
| Solomon Hawk-Owl | Guadalcanal, Makira and Isabel |
| Yellow-vented Myzomela | Gizo and Kolombangara |
| White-winged Fantail | Guadalcanal and Kolombangara |
| Chestnut-bellied Monarch | Guadalcanal, Makira and Ugi |
| White-capped Monarch | Gizo and Kolombangara |
| White-billed Crow* | Guadalcanal, Choiseul and Isabel |
| San Cristobal Thrush* | Guadalcanal and Makira |

The *ugiensis* race of Chestnut-bellied Monarch which is endemic to Ugi is considered to be a full species by some taxonomists.

### Guadalcanal (2)

| | |
|---|---|
| Black-headed Myzomela | Also occurs on Florida and Savo |
| Guadalcanal Honeyeater | Montane forests |

The endemic *turipavae* race of San Cristobal Thrush* is considered to be a full species by some taxonomists.

### Ranongga (Ganongga) (1)

| | |
|---|---|
| Ganongga White-eye | Scrub, gardens and secondary growth |

### Vella Lavella (1)

| | |
|---|---|
| Banded White-eye | Scrub and forest edge |

The endemic *nigrotectus* race of Kulambangra Monarch* is considered to be a full species by some taxonomists.

### Vella Lavella and Kolombangara (1)

| | |
|---|---|
| Kulambangra Monarch* | Secondary growth and gardens |

### Gizo (1)

| | |
|---|---|
| Splendid White-eye* | Scrub and secondary growth |

### Kolombangara (Kulambangra) (3)

| | |
|---|---|
| Roviana Rail* | Scrub. Also known from New Georgia where a single specimen was taken near |

| | |
|---|---|
| | Munda in 1977 |
| Kulambangra White-eye | Montane forests |
| Kulambangra Leaf-Warbler* | Montane forests |

## Kolombangara and New Georgia Group (1)

| | |
|---|---|
| Solomon Islands White-eye | Kolombangara, New Georgia Group and Rendova |

## Malaita (3)

| | |
|---|---|
| Red-bellied Myzomela | Montane forests and gardens |
| Malaita Fantail* | Rare near village of Raihora on Mount Ire (Kolovrat), above 900 m (2953 ft) |
| Malaita White-eye | Montane forests. |

## Makira (San Cristobal) (12)

| | |
|---|---|
| San Cristobal Moorhen* | Known only from the type-specimen which was collected in 1929, a sighting in 1953 and reports from local people, but the forests in the Central Ranges where it was originally collected have not been surveyed since the 1950s |
| Thick-billed Ground-Dove* | Not recorded since 1927 but very similar to Bronze Ground-Dove. Also known from Ramos |
| Chestnut-bellied Imperial-Pigeon* | Also known from Guadalcanal and Malaita |
| Sooty Myzomela | Also occurs on adjacent islands of Santa Ana and the Three Sisters |
| San Cristobal Melidectes | Montane forests |
| Dusky Fantail* | Montane forests |
| White-collared Monarch | Montane forests |
| Ochre-headed Flycatcher* | Lowlands |
| San Cristobal Starling | Montane forests |
| Shade Warbler* | Montane forests. |
| San Cristobal Leaf-Warbler* | Montane forests |
| Mottled Flowerpecker | Montane forests |

The endemic *margaretae* race of San Cristobal Thrush is considered to be a full species by some taxonomists.

## Rennell (5)

| | |
|---|---|
| Rennell Fantail | Lowland forests |
| Rennell Shrikebill* | Lowland forests |
| Rennell Starling* | Lowland forests |
| Rennell White-eye* | Lowland forests |
| Bare-eyed White-eye | Lowland forests |

## Santa Cruz Islands (3)

| | |
|---|---|
| Vanikoro Monarch* | Forest and secondary growth on the remote island of Vanikolo (Vanikoro) |
| Santa Cruz White-eye | Forest, scrub and gardens on Nendo |
| Sanford's White-eye* | Forest on Nendo |

(A white-eye species observed on Vanikolo in early 1994 may be a new species or a sub-species of Santa Cruz White-eye.)

## Extinct Endemics

Choiseul Pigeon (not reliably reported from Choiseul since 1904).

## NEAR-ENDEMICS
### Species shared with Bougainville and Buka (25)

| | |
|---|---|
| Solomon Sea-Eagle* | Choiseul, Gizo, Kolombangara, New Georgia Group, Malaita, Makira and Kohinggo |
| Pied Goshawk | Guadalcanal, Gizo, Kolombangara and Makira |
| Imitator Sparrowhawk* | Very rare on Choiseul and Isabel |
| Woodford's Rail* | Very rare on Guadalcanal, Isabel and possibly Choiseul |
| Pale Mountain-Pigeon | Kolombangara |
| Ducorp's Cockatoo | Guadalcanal, Gizo and Kolombangara |
| Meek's Lorikeet | Kolombangara |
| Duchess Lorikeet* | Guadalcanal, Kolombangara and Makira |
| Fearful Owl* | Very rare on Choiseul and Isabel |
| Ultramarine Kingfisher | Guadalcanal |
| Moustached Kingfisher* | Guadalcanal |
| Black-faced Pitta* | Kolombangara, southeast Isabel and possibly Choiseul |
| Scarlet-naped Myzomela | Widespread |
| Mountain Whistler* | Guadalcanal |
| Brown Fantail | Guadalcanal |
| Bougainville Monarch | Shortland Islands |
| Black-and-white Monarch | Guadalcanal |
| Steel-blue Flycatcher | Guadalcanal, Gizo and Kolombangara |
| Bougainville Crow* | Shortland Islands |
| Solomon Cuckoo-shrike | Guadalcanal, Gizo and Kolombangara |
| Brown-winged Starling | Guadalcanal, Gizo and Kolombangara |
| White-eyed Starling* | Guadalcanal and Choiseul. Also known from Rendova |
| Yellow-throated White-eye | Widespread in lowlands and foothills |
| Grey-throated White-eye | Guadalcanal, Kolombangara and Makira |
| Midget Flowerpecker | Guadalcanal |

### Others

Beck's Petrel* (specimen taken northeast of Rendova in 1928), Heinroth's Shearwater* (recorded off Kolombangara where it may breed), Melanesian Scrubfowl (lowlands), Yellow-legged Pigeon* (very rare on Guadalcanal and Makira), Mackinlay's Cuckoo-Dove, White-bibbed, Santa Cruz* (Tinakula and Utupua Islands in the Santa Cruz Islands) and Bronze Ground-Doves, Red-bellied (Santa Cruz Islands), Yellow-bibbed and Claret-breasted Fruit-Doves, Red-knobbed and Island Imperial-Pigeons, Finsch's and Red-breasted Pygmy-Parrots, Singing and Eclectus Parrots, Cardinal Lory, Palm* (Duff and Santa Cruz Islands) and Red-flanked (north) Lorikeets, Papuan and Marbled Frogmouths, White-throated Nightjar, Mayr's* (Guadalcanal) and Uniform Swiftlets, Little Kingfisher, Fan-tailed Gerygone (southeast), Cardinal Myzomela, Black-throated Shrikebill* (Santa Cruz Islands), New Caledonian and

Vanikoro (Vanikoro Island in the Santa Cruz Islands) Flycatchers, Melanesian and Yellow-eyed Cuckoo-shrikes, Polynesian (Santa Cruz Islands) and Long-tailed (Makira) Trillers, Olive-tailed Thrush (north-west), Rusty-winged* (Santa Cruz Islands), Singing, Atoll (coral islands) and Metallic Starlings, Yellow-faced Myna, Tree Martin, Island Leaf-Warbler, Guadalcanal Thicketbird* (Guadalcanal).

# VANUATU

## INTRODUCTION

### Summary

This rugged mountainous archipelago, which lies between the Solomon Islands and New Caledonia, supports nine endemics, including a kingfisher and a parrotfinch, all of which occur on the island of Espiritu Santo. Getting to and around this large island is fairly easy, but it will be necessary to organise a trek into the interior mountains with local guides to stand a chance of seeing the complete set of endemics.

### Size

The 80 or so islands which span about 1300 km cover a land area of just 14,765 sq km, nine times smaller than England and nearly 50 times smaller than Texas.

### Getting Around

Port Vila, on the island of Efate, is a modern cosmopolitan capital and the gateway to the whole archipelago. This town and Luganville on Espiritu Santo are the only two 'urban' centres in Vanuatu and the only places where it is possible to hire cars. On Espiritu Santo and Tanna there are also public taxis, in the form of cars, minibuses and trucks. There are regular, but expensive, flights from Port Vila to Espiritu Santo and Tanna. Inter-island travel is cheaper by boat, but the passenger-carrying freightships run irregularly and offer very basic accommodation. There are well-used trails on most islands, but these should only be tackled with local guides on Espiritu Santo.

### Accommodation and Food

A fairly wide range of accommodation is available in Port Vila and Luganville, and on Tanna. Elsewhere there are some basic local government resthouses. As in most of the Pacific virtually all of the land is owned by local families and camping is not generally tolerated because the local people believe it is one way of staking a claim for their land.

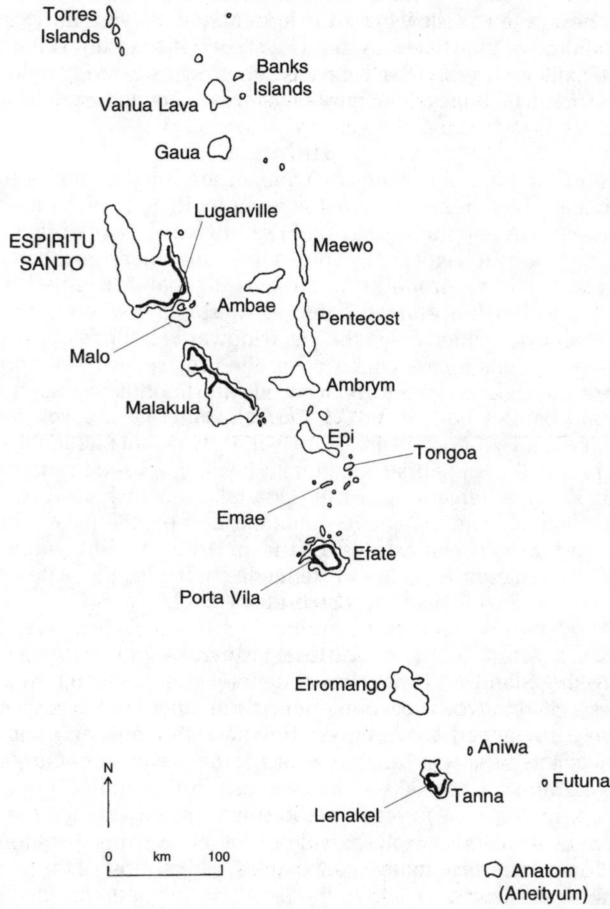


If you insist on camping ask politely for permission and explain very carefully why you wish to sleep outdoors. A French influence means the food is good in the towns. The national dish is *Lap Lap,* a vegetable and banana paste served with coconut cream and, sometimes, pork or seafood. The national drink is *kava,* a mild tranquiliser made from the roots of a local plant. It is narcotic not alcoholic, and most users do not suffer hangovers. However, it looks and tastes foul, and a few coconut shells full can lead to temporary paralysis of the arms and legs.

## Health and Safety

Immunisation against hepatitis, polio and typhoid is recommended, as are all possible precautions against malaria, because the *Plasmodium falciparum* species of parasite is the dominant form and it can kill its host within a week. The local mosquitoes also carry dengue fever. Also beware of tiger sharks if scuba-diving or snorkelling and remember that Vanuatu is renowned for regular cyclones (usually between January and April), volcanic eruptions and earthquakes.

## Climate and Timing

The best time to visit Vanuatu is from May to August, the coolest and driest time of the year. Between November and April it is hot and wet, especially in January and February. The islands are very vulnerable to cyclones, which usually occur between January and April.

## Habitats

Most of the 80 or so islands of Vanuatu are rugged and mountainous with stepped limestone plateaus, rising to 1879 m (6165 ft) at Mount Tabwemasana on the west side of Espiritu Santo. Some islands are volcanic—there are eight active volcanoes—but others are little more than raised coral reefs. Around 70% of the natural habitats remain, mainly in the form of lush evergreen rainforests festooned with climbing lianas and epiphytes which cover the wet windward eastern slopes, and open semi-deciduous forests which cover the drier leeward western slopes. There are also swamp forests on alluvial floodplains, such as those around Big Bay northeast of Mount Tabwemasana, as well as freshwater lakes and some small areas of savanna. Coconut plantations used for the production of copra (coconut flesh which is used in soaps and cosmetics) cover large areas of the coastal plains, where there are also some lagoons, but mangroves, mudflats and palm-fringed beaches are few and far between as most coasts are rocky and fringed with coral reefs. The islands lie on the western edge of the Pacific plate next to the 8000 m (26,247 ft) deep New Hebrides Trench.

## Conservation

Only the island of Tanna has a densely populated interior and the forests covering the rugged interiors of the other islands have remained largely untouched for centuries. However, the most accessible forests seem set to disappear before the end of the twentieth century thanks to logging and an annual natural increase in the human population of 2.4%, which is sure to result in the spread of subsistence farming and coconut plantations, both of which have already been responsible for the loss of forests in many coastal areas, where most of the people live. Hunting and cyclones add to the problems piling up for the ten threatened and near-threatened birds which occur in Vanuatu, but the first terrestrial reserve, the Loru Protected Area on the east coast of Espiritu Santo, was opened in 1995.

## Bird Species

Over 120 species have been recorded in Vanuatu. Non-endemic specialities and spectacular species include Polynesian Storm-Petrel, Red-tailed and White-tailed Tropicbirds, Sooty Tern, Metallic Pigeon, Santa Cruz Ground-Dove*, Palm Lorikeet*, Long-tailed Koel, Cardinal Myzomela, Scarlet Robin, Polynesian Triller, Island Thrush, Guadalcanal Thicketbird*, and Blue-faced and Red-headed Parrotfinches.

## Endemics

A total of nine species are endemic to Vanuatu and all of them occur on Espiritu Santo. They include a scrubfowl, a fruit-dove, an imperial-pigeon, Chestnut-bellied Kingfisher*, a honeyeater, a monarch, a starling, a white-eye and a parrotfinch.

## Expectations

It is possible to see about 50 species on a short one- or two-week trip, including all nine endemics, so long as Espiritu Santo is included in the itinerary.

Birds recorded on **Efate**, on Golf Island opposite the Intercontinental Hotel and in the forest between the hotel and hospital include Pacific Reef-Egret, Swamp Harrier, Buff-banded Rail, Spotless Crake, Wandering Tattler, Pacific Golden-Plover, Emerald Dove, Rainbow Lorikeet, Glossy Swiftlet, Collared Kingfisher, Dark-brown Honeyeater, Streaked Fantail, White-breasted Woodswallow, Polynesian Triller, Island Thrush, Yellow-fronted White-eye and Blue-faced Parrotfinch. A 132 km long road runs around this island, mostly through extensive coconut plantations, but it may well be worth birding some stretches alongside it.

## ESPIRITU SANTO

All of Vanuatu's nine endemics, as well as the near-endemic Guadalcanal Thicketbird*, occur on this island. It is the largest and highest in the archipelago, rising to 1879 m (6165 ft) at Mount Tabwemasana, and some of the species listed here are only likely to be seen in the montane forests on the slopes of the interior mountains, with the assistance of local guides.

**ESPIRITU SANTO**

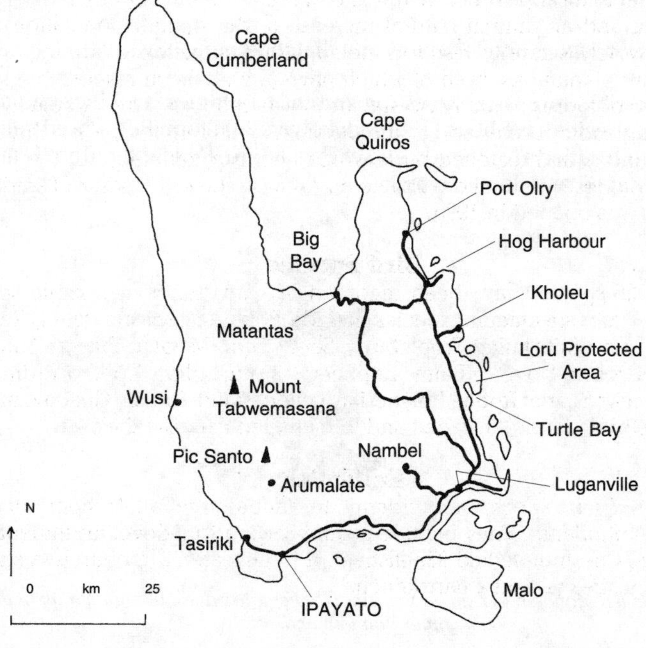

## Vanuatu Endemics

New Hebrides Scrubfowl*, Tanna Fruit-Dove*, Baker's Imperial-Pigeon*, Chestnut-bellied Kingfisher*, New Hebrides Honeyeater, Buff-bellied Monarch, Mountain Starling*, Yellow-fronted White-eye, Royal Parrotfinch*.

## Non-endemic Specialities

Mackinlay's Cuckoo-Dove, Palm Lorikeet*, Cardinal Myzomela, Polynesian Triller, Guadalcanal Thicketbird*.

## Others

Pacific Reef-Egret, Swamp Harrier, Buff-banded Rail, Emerald Dove, Pacific Imperial Pigeon, Uniform Swiftlet, Collared Kingfisher, Scarlet Robin, Golden Whistler, Pacific Swallow.

(Other species recorded here include Santa Cruz Ground-Dove*, Melanesian Cuckoo-shrike and Rusty-winged Starling*. Introduced species include Black-headed Munia.)

Luganville, at the southeast corner of the island, is accessible by air from Port Vila. Most of the endemics and specialities occur in the forested mountains, which can be visited via a trail from Ipayato, a village on the south coast about 60 km west of Luganville. Guides were available in Ipayato in August 1991 to ascend **Pic Santo**, which rises to 1704 m (5591 ft) and supports the rarest endemic, Mountain Starling*, which appears to be restricted to the high cloud forest on this mountain. The **Loru Protected Area** covers 220 ha of reef and lowland rainforest on the east coast of Espiritu Santo and supports 25 species, including New Hebrides Scrubfowl*, Chestnut-bellied Kingfisher*, Cardinal Myzomela and Buff-bellied Monarch.

*Accommodation:* hotels, resorts and thatched bungalows.

It is possible to charter boats for **Vanuatu Pelagics** on which the following species have been recorded: Polynesian Storm-Petrel, Red-tailed and White-tailed Tropicbirds, Lesser Frigatebird, Red-footed Booby, and Black-naped and Sooty Terns.

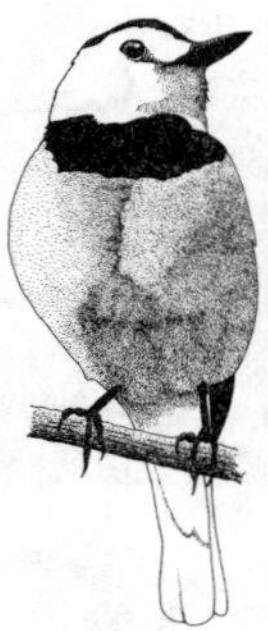

*Buff-bellied Monarch occurs on the island of Espiritu Santo, along with all of the other Vanuatu endemics*

The belt of floating vegetation around the edge of Lake Sini, and nearby swamps on the active volcanic island of **Tanna**, support White-browed Crake. This island, which rises to 361 m (1184 ft) at Yasur Volcano, is the most heavily populated in Vanuatu and the villages are connected by public taxis in the form of cars, minibuses and trucks. There are several guesthouses and tourist bungalows in which to stay.

# ADDITIONAL INFORMATION

## Addresses

Vanuatu National Tourism Office, PO Box 209, Port-Vila (tel: 678 22685, fax: 678 23889).

## Books and Papers

*Birds of Vanuatu.* Bregulla H, 1992. Anthony Nelson.

## VANUATU ENDEMICS (9)

| | |
|---|---|
| New Hebrides Scrubfowl* | Mainly in lowland forests of central and northern islands including Espiritu Santo. It is particularly common on the island of Ambrym, accessible by air from Port Vila |
| Tanna Fruit-Dove* | Widespread, mainly in lowland areas including those on Espiritu Santo, but scarce |
| Baker's Imperial-Pigeon* | Montane forests of central and northern islands including Espiritu Santo |
| Chestnut-bellied Kingfisher* | Mainly in lowland forests of central islands, including Espiritu Santo, as well as Malakula and Malo |
| New Hebrides Honeyeater | Widespread on central and northern islands, including Espiritu Santo |
| Buff-bellied Monarch | Widespread on islands north of Efate, including Espiritu Santo |
| Mountain Starling* | Cloud forests on the highest peaks of Espiritu Santo. Most recently recorded on Pic Santo in August 1991, but also known from Mount Watiamasan and Mount Tabwemasana |
| Yellow-fronted White-eye | Probably the most numerous bird in the archipelago, especially in montane forests. |
| Royal Parrotfinch* | Most 'common' on northern islands, including Espiritu Santo |

## Extinct Endemics

| | |
|---|---|
| Tanna Ground-Dove | Known only from a 1774 specimen which may have been a race of Santa Cruz Ground-Dove*. The specimen was supposedly collected on Tanna but it is now generally assumed that it was collected elsewhere |

### Near-endemics

Mackinlay's Cuckoo-Dove, Santa Cruz Ground-Dove* (Espiritu Santo), Red-bellied Fruit-Dove, Palm Lorikeet* (including Banks Islands), Fan-tailed Gerygone (including Banks Islands), Dark-brown Honeyeater, Cardinal Myzomela, Streaked Fantail, Southern Shrikebill (most likely on northern islands), New Caledonian Flycatcher (including Banks and Torres Islands), Melanesian Cuckoo-shrike (Espiritu Santo, Malakula, Malo and Erromango), Polynesian and Long-tailed Trillers, Rusty-winged Starling* (including Banks Islands), Guadalcanal Thicketbird* (montane forests of Espiritu Santo), Red-headed Parrotfinch (Efate and Aneityum).

# ANTARCTICA

The part of Antarctica which lies to the south of Australia and New Zealand is occasionally accessible during November and December on state-of-the-art Russian icebreakers, which are chartered by tour companies such as Wildlife Worldwide and Zegrahm. Although such cruises are extremely expensive, they do provide the opportunity to see some sensational seabirds, including Light-mantled Albatross, Snow Petrel and what is arguably the hardest bird in the world to get to: the Emperor Penguin. Seeing these four-foot-tall birds standing up would probably make most birders happy, but watching them toboggan by belly across the ice has to rank amongst the most entertaining and enthralling experiences any birder could wish for.

For the purpose of this section those species which usually occur only on Antarctica itself or amongst the surrounding pack-ice and adjacent seas to 63 degrees south are regarded as endemics.

### Antarctica Endemics

Emperor and Adelie Penguins, Antarctic and Snow Petrels.

### Non-endemic Specialities

Wandering*, Grey-headed* and Light-mantled Albatrosses.

### Others

Black-browed Albatross, Southern Fulmar, Cape, Soft-plumaged and White-chinned Petrels.

### Other Wildlife

Killer, minke and southern bottle-nosed whales, leopard and weddell seals.

The **Ross Sea**, south of New Zealand, is a major fishing area for Emperor Penguins, as well as killer, minke and southern bottle-nosed whales. The black volcanic slopes behind Borchgrevinks' Hut at Cape Adare, at the mouth of the Ross Sea, supports hundreds of thousands of breeding Adelie Penguins. South of Cape Evans where Scott's Hut still stands is McMurdo, at 730 nautical miles from the South Pole as close as any ship can sail.

Seabirds recorded between Perth, Western Australia, and the high, icy Bowman Island to the south include Wandering*, Black-browed, Grey-

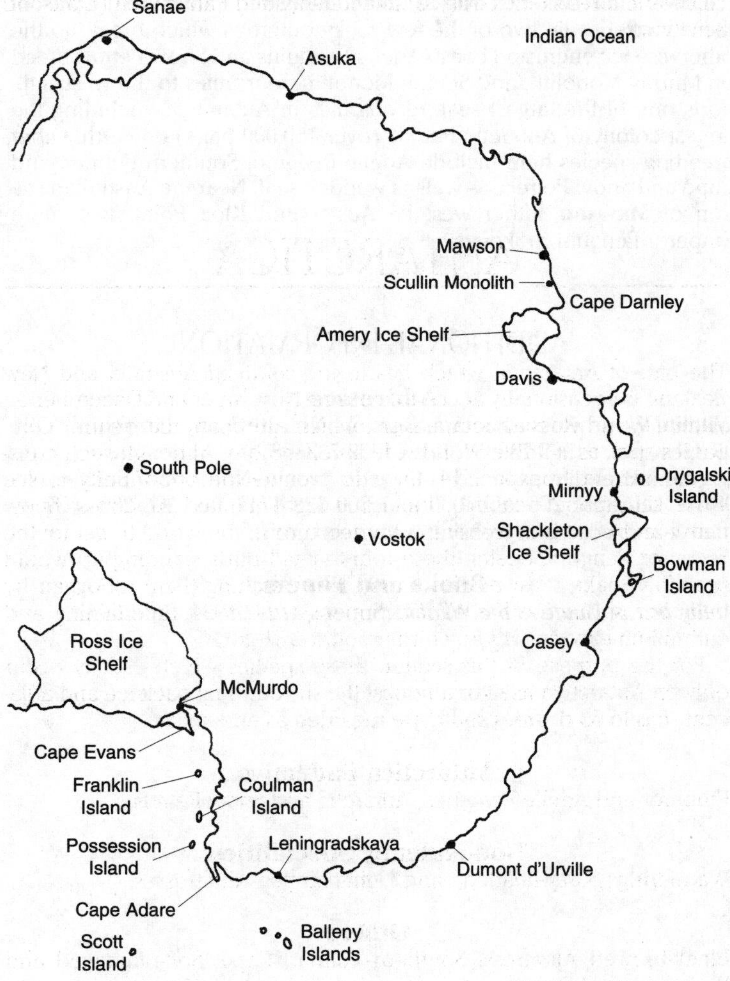

headed* and Light-mantled Albatrosses, and Soft-plumaged and White-chinned Petrels. To the west of Bowman Island, beyond the Shackleton Ice Shelf, Adelie Penguins and weddell seals breed on islands near the Russian station of **Mirnyy**. Adelie Penguins also breed, along with attendant leopard seals, on Lucas and Rookery Islands near the Australian station of **Davis**, which is situated on Prydz Bay southwest of Mirnyy. There are a number of Emperor Penguin rookeries in this part of Antarctica, some of the 42 known breeding colonies which are currently estimated to support approximately 200,000 pairs. West of the Amery Ice Shelf such rookeries exist at Amanda Bay and Flutter. To the west of these rookeries lie two of the few rocky outcrops which break up the otherwise ice-encrusted coast. Adelie Penguins and Snow Petrels breed on Murray Monolith, and Scullin Monolith, four miles to the west, supports one of the largest seabird colonies in Antarctica, including the largest colony of Antarctic Petrels (over 150,000 pairs) on earth. Other breeding species here include Adelie Penguin, Southern Fulmar, and Cape and Snow Petrels, as well as weddell seal. Near the Australian station of **Mawson** futher west lie Auster and Kloa Point, two more Emperor Penguin rookeries.

## ADDITIONAL INFORMATION

### Addresses

Wildlife Worldwide, Chautara, Bighton, Nr. Alresford, Hampshire SO24 9RB, UK (tel: 01962 733051, fax: 01962 733368).
Zegrahm Expeditions Inc., 1414 Dexter Avenue North, #327 Seattle, WA 98109, USA (tel: 206 285 4000 or 1 800 628 8747, fax: 206 285 5037, e-mail: zoe@zeco.com, website: www.zeco.com).

### Books and Papers

*Antarctica: A Guide to the Wildlife.* Soper T *et al.*, 1994. Bradt.

# REQUEST

This book is intended to be a first edition. If you would like to contribute to the second edition, please send details of any errors or changes, and information on any new sites you feel deserve inclusion, to:

Nigel Wheatley, c/o A & C Black (Publishers) Limited, 35 Bedford Row, London WC1R 4JH, UK.

It would be extremely helpful if information could be submitted in the following format:

1 A summary of the site's position (in relation to the nearest city, town or village), altitude, access arrangements, habitats, number of species recorded (if known), best birds, best time to visit, and its richness compared with other sites.
2 A species list, preferably using the names and taxonomic order in Clements' *Check List* and supplements.
3 Details of how to get to the site and where to bird once there, with information on trails, etc.
4 A map complete with scale and compass point.
5 Any addresses to write to for permits etc.
6 Any details of accommodation.

Any information on the following species would also be very useful:

Dwarf* and Northern* Cassowaries, Beck's*, Collared and Murphy's Petrels, Heinroth's Shearwater*, Red Goshawk*, Chestnut and White-striped* Forest-Rails, Forbes', Mayr's*, Bare-eyed and New Guinea Flightless* Rails, Yellow-legged Pigeon*, Blue-collared and Night* Parrots, Australian and Tasmanian Masked-Owls, Australasian Grass-Owl, Feline, Barred, Wallace's, Archbold's and Mountain Owlet-Nightjars, Blue-black Kingfisher*, Red-breasted Paradise-Kingfisher, Streaked and Yellow-breasted Bowerbirds, Plain Honeyeater, Orange and Yellow* Chats, and Greater Melampitta.

I would be extremely grateful if you could also include a statement outlining your permission to use your information in the next edition, and, finally, your name and address, so that you can be acknowledged appropriately.

# CALENDAR

The following is a brief summary of the best countries and regions to visit according to the time of year. This calendar is aimed to help those birders who have set holidays to choose the best destination. Alternatively, if there are birders out there fortunate enough to have a year to go birding in Australasia and Oceania, then following this schedule could produce the best birding and the most birds.

If anyone trys this please let me know how they get on! Better still, if there is a willing sponsor out there, contact me immediately! Were such a dream to come true the following route may prove to be the most rewarding.

Start the year's epic journey amongst the masses of shorebirds in Adelaide, Australia and spend the first couple of months of the year working your way east from there, to the Melbourne and Sydney regions, then north to the Brisbane and Cairns areas. In early March move to the North Mariana Islands in Micronesia. From there, head south to Peleliu in Palau, then travel east through the Caroline Islands, sweeping up the single-island endemics on Yap, Chuuk and Pohnpei. Spend April in Hawaii looking for the surviving endemics and some superb seabirds, before moving south into Polynesia where you will need at least a month to mop up most of the endemics on the Marquesas Islands, Tahiti, the Tuamotu Archipelago and the Cook Islands. Stay in the Pacific in June and head west through Samoa, Tonga, Fiji and Vanuatu to spend the last two weeks of the month on the Solomon Islands. Make time to take the odd break on a beach here and there, if you need to catch up with the first six months' notes, because there will be little time for such pleasures from here onwards. Pop over to Papua New Guinea for the first three weeks of July, then clear up the birds-of-paradise in Irian Jaya before mid-August, because by then it will be time to return to Australia. Start the second leg down under in Darwin, then head west to The Kimberley and south to the Perth area before moving inland in mid-September to track down the outback specialities whilst it is still relatively cool. Spend October, the austral spring, mopping up any missing goodies in Australia, and leave a few days at the end of the month to nip over to New Caledonia to catch up with Kagu and the rest of the endemics. November in New Zealand should be long enough to see all but one of the endemics, as well as numerous seabirds, before boarding an icebreaker bound for the Subantarctic Islands, Antarctica and Emperor Penguins, the ultimate way to end a fantastic birding year.

**JANUARY:** Australia (south and east), Hawaii, Micronesia, New Zealand.
**FEBRUARY:** Australia (south and east), Hawaii, Micronesia.
**MARCH:** Hawaii, Micronesia.
**APRIL:** Hawaii.
**MAY:** Hawaii, Polynesia, Vanuatu.
**JUNE:** Australia (Darwin area), Polynesia, Vanuatu.
**JULY:** Australia (Darwin area), Fiji/Samoa/Tonga, Irian Jaya, Papua New Guinea, Polynesia, Solomon Islands, Vanuatu.

**AUGUST:** Australia (Darwin area, Perth area and Outback), Fiji/Samoa/Tonga, Irian Jaya, Papua New Guinea, Polynesia, Solomon Islands, Vanuatu.
**SEPTEMBER:** Australia (Perth area and Outback), Hawaii, Solomon Islands.
**OCTOBER:** Australia (south and east), Hawaii.
**NOVEMBER:** Australia (south and east), Hawaii, New Caledonia, New Zealand, Antarctica.
**DECEMBER:** Australia (south and east), Hawaii, New Caledonia, New Zealand, Antarctica.

# USEFUL ADDRESSES

### Clubs and Conservation Organisations

**BirdLife International**, Wellbrook Court, Girton Road, Cambridge CB3 0NA, UK. Membership of this vitally important organisation costs from £25 per year and members receive a quarterly magazine and an annual report.

**Southern Oceans Seabird Study Association**, PO Box 142, Unanderra, NSW 2526, Australia.

### Trip Reports

**Dutch Birding Travel Report Service (DBTRS)**, PO Box 737, 9700 AS Groningen, The Netherlands (tel: 050 527 4993; fax: 050 527 2668; email: Ib.Huysman@net.HCC.nl; website: http://www.mebweb.nl/DBTRS.). To obtain a copy of the catalogue, which lists an extensive selection of reports, covering most of the Australasian and Oceania region, send £5 or US$10.

**Foreign Birdwatching Reports and Information Service (FBRIS)**, (organised and owned by Steve Whitehouse), 6 Skipton Crescent, Berkeley Pendesham, Worcester WR4 0LG, UK (tel: 01905 454541). To obtain a copy of the catalogue, which lists over 400 reports from around the world and covers much of the Australasia and Oceania region, send £1.20.

### Tour Companies

**Bird Holidays**, Mantra WGT Ltd, Oxford House, Oxford Road, Guiseley LS20 9AA, UK (tel: 01943 882805/882811; fax: 01943 873349).

**Birding**, Finches House, Hiham Green, Winchelsea, East Sussex TN36 4HB, UK (tel: 01797 223223; fax: 01797 222911).

**Birdquest**, Two Jays, Kemple End, Birdy Brow, Stonyhurst, Lancashire BB7 9QY, UK (tel: 01254 826317; fax: 01254 826780, e-mail: birders@ birdquest.co.uk).

**Cygnus Wildlife Holidays**, 57 Fore Street, Kingsbridge, Devon TQ7 1PG, UK (tel: 01548 856178; fax: 01548 857537).

**Field Guides**, PO Box 160723, Austin, Tx 78716-0723, USA (tel: (800) 728 4953 and (512) 327 4953; fax: (512) 327 9231, e-mail: fgileader@ aol.com; website: http://www.fieldguides.com).

**Inland Bird Tours**, PO Box 382 (172 Whitehorse Road), Balwyn 3103, Victoria, Australia (tel/fax: (03) 9817 6555; mobile: 041 931 0200)

**KingBird Tours Inc.**, PO Box 196, Planetarium Station, New York, NY 10024, USA (tel: (212) 866 7923; fax: (212) 866 4225).

**Limosa Holidays**, Suffield House, Northrepps, Norfolk NR27 0LZ, UK (tel: 01263 578143; fax: 01263 579251).

**Naturetrek**, Chautara, Bighton, Nr. Alresford, Hampshire SO24 9RB, UK (tel: 01962 733051; fax: 01962 733368).

**Ornitholidays**, 1–3 Victoria Drive, Bognor Regis, West Sussex PO21 2PW, UK (tel: 01243 821230; fax: 01243 829574).

**Sunbird/Wings**, PO Box 76, Sandy, Beds. SG19 1DF, UK (tel: 01767 682969; fax: 01767 692481; e-mail: sunbird@sunbird.demon.co.uk), and 1643 North Alvernon Way, Suite 105, Tucson, Az 85712, USA (tel: (520) 320 9868; fax: (520) 320 9373).

**Victor Emanuel Nature Tours**, PO Box 33008, Austin, Tx 78764, USA (tel: 800/328-VENT; fax: 512/328 2919, e-mail: Ventbird@aol.com).

**Wildlife Worldwide**, 170 Selsdon Road, South Croydon, Surrey CR2 6PJ, UK (tel: 0181 667 9158; fax: 0181 667 1960; e-mail: 100775.757@ Compuserve.Com).

**Wildwings**, International House, Bank Road, Bristol BS15 2LX, UK (tel: 0117 984 8040; brochureline: 0117 961 0874; fax: 0117 967 4444; website: http://www.wildwings.co.uk). This is also a travel agency which specialises in arranging birding holidays.

**Zegrahm Expeditions**, 1414 Dexter Avenue North #327, Seattle, WA 98109, USA (tel: (206) 285 4000 or (800) 628 8747; fax: (206) 285 5037; e-mail: zegrahm@accessone.com; website: http://www.zeco.com).

## Books

**Natural History Book Service Limited (NHBS)**, 2–3 Wills Road, Totnes, Devon TQ9 5XN, UK (tel: 01803 865913; fax: 01803 865280; e-mail: nhbs@nhbs.co.uk; website: http://www.nhbs.com).

**Subbuteo Natural History Books Limited**, Pistyll Farm, Nercwys, Nr. Mold, Flintshire CH7 4EW, UK (tel: 01352 756551; fax: 01352 756004, e-mail: sales@subbooks.demon.co.uk).

## Bird Sounds

**Wildsounds**, Cross Street, Salthouse, Norfolk NR25 7XH, UK (tel/fax: 01263 741100).

# USEFUL GENERAL BOOKS


## Regional Field Guides

*Birds of New Guinea.* Beehler B, Pratt T, Zimmerman D, 1986. Princeton University Press.

*The Birds of Hawaii and the Tropical Pacific.* Pratt D, Bruner P, Berrett D, 1987. Princeton University Press.

*Birds of the Southwest Pacific.* Mayr E, 1945. Macmillan (1945) and Charles E Tuttle Company (1978).

## Handbooks and Reference Works

*Handbook of Australian, New Zealand and Antarctic Birds (HANZAB).* Volumes 1 to 3 and continuing. Higgins P, Marchant S (eds), 1991 onwards. Oxford University Press.

*Handbook of the Birds of the World.* Volumes 1 to 3 and continuing to volume 12. del Hoyo *et al.*, 1992 onwards. Lynx Edicions.

## Conservation

*A Fragile Paradise: Man and Nature in the Pacific.* Mitchell A, 1990. Fontana. Published in the USA by University of Texas Press under the title *The Fragile South Pacific: an Ecological Odyssey.*

*Birds to Watch 2: the World List of Threatened Birds.* Collar N *et al.*, 1994. BirdLife International.

*Megapodes: an Action Plan for their Conservation 1995–1999.* Dekker R, McGowan P, 1995. IUCN.

*The Lost Birds of Paradise.* Fuller E, 1995. Swan Hill Press.

*Endemic Bird Areas of the World.* Stattersfield A *et al.*, in press. BirdLife International.

## Bird Families

*Cormorants, Darters and Pelicans of the World.* Johnsgard P, 1993. Smithsonian Institute.

*Crows and Jays.* Madge S, Burn H, 1992. Helm.

*Fairy-Wrens and Grass-Wrens.* Rowley I *et al.*, in press. Oxford University Press.

*Finches and Sparrows.* Clement P *et al.*, 1993. Helm.

*Kingfishers, Bee-eaters and Rollers.* Fry C *et al.*, 1992. Helm.

*Larks, Pipits and Wagtails.* Alstrom P *et al.*, in prep. Helm.

*Munias and Mannikins.* Restall R, 1997. Pica Press.

*Nightjars.* Cleere N and Nurney D, in prep. Pica Press.

*Parrots of the World* (3rd edn). Forshaw J, 1989. Blandford.

*Penguins of the World.* Reilly P, 1994. Oxford University Press.

*Pittas, Broadbills and Asities.* Lambert F, Woodcock M, 1996. Pica Press.

*Photographic Handbook of the Seabirds of the World.* Enticott J, Tipling D, 1997. New Holland.

*Seabirds.* Harrison P, 1985. Helm.

*Seabirds of the World: a Photographic Guide* (2nd edn). Harrison P, 1997. Helm.

*Shorebirds.* Hayman P, Marchant J, Prater T, 1986. Helm.

*Skuas.* Olsen K M and Larsson H, 1997. Pica Press.

*Storks, Ibises and Spoonbills of the World.* Hancock J *et al.*, 1992.

Academic Press.
*Swallows and Martins.* Turner A, Rose C, 1989. Helm.
*Swifts.* Chantler P, Driessens G, 1995. Pica Press.
*The Hamlyn Photographic Guide to the Waders of the World.* Rosair D, Cottridge D, 1995. Hamlyn.
*The Herons Handbook.* Hancock J, Kushlan J, 1984. Helm.
*The Megapodes.* Jones D, Dekker R, Roselaar C, 1995. Oxford University Press.
*The Penguins.* Williams T, 1995. Oxford University Press.
*The Skuas.* Furness R, 1988. Poyser.
*Wildfowl.* Madge S, Burn H, 1988. Helm.

## Lists

*Birds of the world: a check list.* Clements J, 1991. *Ibis.*
*Birds of the world: a check list,* English name index and supplement no. 1. Clements J, 1992. *Ibis.*
*Birds of the world: a check list,* supplement no. 2. Clements J, 1993. *Ibis.*

## Travel

The Lonely Planet, Rough Guides and Moon Publications handbooks to many of the countries, islands and regions within Australasia and Oceania are all, on the whole, excellent, although they do not usually cover the more remote birding areas.

# BIRD NAMES WHICH DIFFER BETWEEN *CLEMENTS* AND VARIOUS OTHER BIRD BOOKS

Only those name differences which are not immediately obvious are given.

| **Name used by *Clements*** | **Name used by other books** | **Latin name** |
|---|---|---|
| Little Penguin | Fairy/Little Blue Penguin | *Eudyptula minor* |
| Antarctic Giant Petrel | Southern Giant Petrel | *Macronectes giganteus* |
| Hall's Giant Petrel* | Northern Giant Petrel | *Macronectes halli* |
| Cape Petrel | Cape Pigeon/Pintado Petrel | *Daption capense* |
| MacGillivray's Petrel* | Fiji Petrel | *Pseudobulweria macgillivrayi* |
| Providence Petrel* | Solander's Petrel | *Pterodroma solandri* |
| Great-winged Petrel | Grey-faced Petrel | *Pterodroma macroptera* |
| Parkinson's Petrel* | Black Petrel | *Procellaria parkinsoni* |
| White-faced Storm-Petrel | Frigate Petrel | *Pelagodroma marina* |
| Polynesian Storm-Petrel | White-throated Storm-Petrel | *Nesofregetta fuliginosa* |
| Band-rumped Storm-Petrel | Madeiran Storm-Petrel | *Oceanodroma castro* |
| Rough-faced Shag* | New Zealand King Cormorant | *Phalacrocorax carunculatus* |
| Bronze Shag* | Stewart Island Cormorant | *Phalacrocorax chalconotus* |
| Hawaiian Goose* | Nene | *Branta sandvicensis* |
| Maned Duck | Wood Duck | *Chenonetta jubata* |
| Pacific Black Duck | Grey Duck | *Anas superciliosa* |
| White-eyed Duck | Hardhead | *Aythya australis* |
| Pacific Heron | White-necked Heron | *Ardea pacifica* |
| Rufous Night-Heron | Nankeen Night-Heron | *Nycticorax caledonicus* |
| Black-backed Bittern | Australian Little Bittern | *Ixobrychus novaezelandiae* |
| Pacific Baza | Crested Hawk | *Aviceda subcristata* |
| Solomon Sea-Eagle* | Sanford's Fish-Eagle | *Haliaeetus sanfordi* |
| Eastern Marsh-Harrier | Papuan Harrier | *Circus spilonotus* |
| Australian Kestrel | Nankeen Kestrel | *Falco cenchroides* |
| Australian Hobby | Little Falcon | *Falco longipennis* |
| Blue-breasted Quail | King Quail | *Coturnix chinensis* |
| Buff-banded Rail | Banded Rail | *Gallirallus philippensis* |
| Australian Crake | Australian Spotted Crake | *Porzana fluminea* |
| Purple Swamphen | Pukeko | *Porphyrio porphyrio* |
| Latham's Snipe* | Japanese Snipe | *Gallinago hardwickii* |
| Mongolian Plover | Lesser Sandplover | *Charadrius mongolus* |
| Masked Lapwing | Spur-winged Plover | *Vanellus miles* |
| Great Crested-Tern | Swift Tern | *Sterna bergii* |
| Grey-backed Tern | Spectacled Tern | *Sterna lunata* |
| Blue-grey Noddy | Grey Ternlet | *Procelsterna cerulea* |
| Brown Noddy | Common Noddy | *Anous stolidus* |
| Black Noddy | White-capped Noddy | *Anous minutus* |
| Common White-Tern | Fairy Tern | *Gygis alba* |
| Brown Skua | Southern Skua | *Catharacta lonnbergi* |
| South Polar Skua | Antarctic Skua | *Catharacta maccormicki* |

| | | |
|---|---|---|
| Parasitic Jaeger | Arctic Skua | *Stercorarius parasiticus* |
| Metallic Pigeon | White-throated Pigeon | *Columba vitiensis* |
| Slender-billed Cuckoo-Dove | Brown Cuckoo-Dove | *Macropygia amboinensis* |
| Great Cuckoo-Dove | Long-tailed Cuckoo-Dove | *Reinwardtoena reinwardtsi* |
| Emerald Dove | Green-winged Pigeon | *Chalcophaps indica* |
| Bronze Ground-Dove | Beccari's Ground-Dove | *Gallicolumba beccarii* |
| Black-banded Fruit-Dove* | Banded Pigeon | *Ptilinopus alligator* |
| Crimson-crowned Fruit-Dove | Purple-capped Fruit-Dove | *Ptilinopus porphyraceus* |
| Velvet Dove* | Whistling Dove | *Ptilinopus layardi* |
| Island Imperial-Pigeon | Grey Imperial-Pigeon | *Ducula pistrinaria* |
| Pesquet's Parrot* | Vulturine Parrot | *Psittrichas fulgidus* |
| Red Shining-Parrot | Red-breasted Musk Parrot | *Prosopeia tabuensis* |
| Masked Shining-Parrot* | Yellow-breasted Musk Parrot | *Prosopeia personata* |
| Alexandra's Parrot* | Princess Parrot | *Polytelis alexandrae* |
| White-tailed Black-Cockatoo* | Long-billed Black-Cockatoo | *Calyptorhynchus baudinii* |
| Slender-billed Black-Cockatoo* | Carnaby's Black-Cockatoo | *Calytporhynchus latirostris* |
| Pink Cockatoo* | Major Mitchell's Cockatoo | *Cacatua leadbeateri* |
| Yellow-streaked Lory | Greater Streaked Lory | *Chalcopsitta sintillata* |
| Black-capped Lory | Western Black-capped Lory | *Lorius lory* |
| Purple-bellied Lory | Eastern Black-capped Lory | *Lorius hypoinochrous* |
| Tahitian Lorikeet* | Blue Lorikeet | *Vini peruviana* |
| Striated Lorikeet* | Streaked Lorikeet | *Charmosyna multistriata* |
| Fairy Lorikeet | Little Red Lorikeet | *Charmosyna pulchella* |
| Jungle Hawk-Owl | Papuan Boobook | *Ninox theomacha* |
| Archbold's Nightjar | Mountain Nightjar | *Eurostopodus archboldi* |
| Jungle Nightjar | Grey Nightjar | *Caprimulgus indicus* |
| Glossy Swiftlet | White-bellied Swiftlet | *Collocalia esculenta* |
| Polynesian Swiftlet* | Tahiti Swiftlet | *Collocalia leucophaeus* |
| Fork-tailed Swift | Pacific Swift | *Apus pacificus* |
| Variable Kingfisher | Dwarf Kingfisher | *Ceyx lepidus* |
| Blue-black Kingfisher* | Black-sided Kingfisher | *Todirhamphus nigrocyaneus* |
| Collared Kingfisher | Mangrove Kingfisher | *Todrihamphus chloris* |
| Mountain Kingfisher | Mountain Yellow-billed Kingfisher | *Syma megarhyncha* |
| Little Paradise-Kingfisher* | Aru Paradise-Kingfisher | *Tanysiptera hydrocharis* |
| South Island Wren* | Rock Wren | *Xenicus gilviventris* |
| Black-headed Pitta* | Superb Pitta | *Pitta superba* |
| Red-bellied Pitta | Blue-breasted Pitta | *Pitta erythrogaster* |
| Rock Warbler* | Origma | *Origma solitaria* |
| Beccari's Scrubwren | Tropical Scrubwren | *Sericornis beccarii* |
| Rufous Fieldwren | Rufous Calamanthus | *Calamanthus campestris* |
| Striated Fieldwren | Striated Calamanthus | *Calamanthus fuliginosus* |
| Chestnut-rumped Hylacola | Chestnut-rumped Heathwren | *Hylacola pyrrhopygius* |
| Shy Hylacola | Shy Heathwren | *Hylacola cautus* |
| Slender-billed Thornbill* | Samphire Thornbill | *Acanthiza iredalei* |
| Scarlet-bibbed Myzomela | Sclater's Myzomela | *Myzomela sclateri* |
| Ebony Myzomela | Bismarck Black Myzomela | *Myzomela pammelaena* |
| Sooty Myzomela | Tristram's Myzomela | *Myzomela tristrami* |
| Forest Honeyeater | Forest White-eared Meliphaga | *Meliphaga montana* |
| Scrub Honeyeater | Scrub White-eared Meliphaga | *Meliphaga albonotata* |
| Puff-backed Honeyeater | Puff-backed Meliphaga | *Meliphaga aruensis* |
| Graceful Honeyeater | Slender-billed Meliphaga | *Meliphaga gracilis* |
| Olive-streaked Honeyeater | Yellowish-streaked Honeyeater | *Ptiloprora meekiana* |
| Black-backed Honeyeater | Grey-streaked Honeyeater | *Ptiloprora perstriata* |
| Arfak Honeyeater | Western Smoky Honeyeater | *Melipotes gymnops* |

| | | |
|---|---|---|
| Desert Chat | Gibberbird/Gibber Chat | *Ashbyia lovensis* |
| Alpine Robin | Mountain Robin | *Petroica bivittata* |
| Yellow Robin | Eastern Yellow Robin | *Eopsaltria australis* |
| Grey-breasted Robin | Western Yellow Robin | *Eopsaltria griseogularis* |
| Olive-yellow Robin* | Banded Yellow Robin | *Poecilodryas placens* |
| Black-tailed Whistler | Mangrove Golden Whistler | *Pachycephala melanura* |
| Regent Whistler | Schlegel's Whistler | *Pachycephala schlegelii* |
| Mountain Whistler* | Hooded Whistler | *Pachycephala implicata* |
| Sooty Shrike-Thrush | Sooty Whistler | *Colluricincla umbrina* |
| Rufous Shrike-Thrush | Little Shrike-Thrush | *Colluricincla megarhyncha* |
| White-winged Fantail | Cockerell's Fantail | *Rhipidura cockerelli* |
| Rufous Fantail | Rufous-fronted Fantail | *Rhipidura rufifrons* |
| Versicoloured Monarch* | Ogea Monarch | *Mayrornis versicolor* |
| Black-throated Shrikebill* | Black-faced Shrikebill | *Clytorhynchus nigrogularis* |
| White-capped Monarch | Richard's Monarch | *Monarcha richardsii* |
| Kulambangra Monarch | Brown's Pied Monarch | *Monarcha browni* |
| Steel-blue Flycatcher | Solomons Flycatcher | *Myiagra ferrocyanea* |
| Ochre-headed Flycatcher* | San Cristobal Flycatcher | *Myiagra cervinicauda* |
| Black-billed Sicklebill | Buff-tailed Sicklebill | *Epimachus albertisi* |
| Green Oriole | Yellow Oriole | *Oriolus flavocinctus* |
| Yellow-eyed Cuckoo-shrike | Barred Cuckoo-shrike | *Coracina lineata* |
| Papuan Cuckoo-shrike | Black-shouldered Cuckoo-shrike | *Coracina incerta* |
| New Guinea Cuckoo-shrike | Black Cuckoo-shrike | *Coracina melas* |
| Solomon Cuckoo-shrike | Black-bellied Cuckoo-shrike | *Coracina holopolia* |
| Long-tailed Shrike | Rufous-backed Shrike | *Lanius schach* |
| Olive-tailed Thrush | Australian/Bassian Ground-Thrush | *Zoothera lunulata* |
| Russet-tailed Thrush | Russet Ground-Thrush | *Zoothera heinei* |
| Island Thrush | Mountain Blackbird | *Turdus poliocephalus* |
| Metallic Starling | Shining Starling | *Aplonis metallica* |
| Capped White-eye | Western Mountain White-eye | *Zosterops fuscicapillus* |
| Christmas Island Warbler | Bokikokiko | *Acrocephalus aequinoctialis* |
| Long-legged Warbler* | Long-legged Thicketbird | *Trichocichla rufa* |
| Australasian Bushlark | Singing Bushlark | *Mirafra javanica* |
| Mountain Firetail | Crimson-sided Mountain Finch | *Oreostruthus fuliginosus* |
| Grand Munia | Great-billed Munia/Mannikin | *Lonchura grandis* |
| Grey-banded Munia* | Arfak Munia/Mannikin | *Lonchura vana* |
| Grey-crowned Munia* | White-crowned Munia/Mannikin | *Lonchura nevermanni* |
| Hooded Munia | New Britain Munia/Mannikin | *Lonchura spectabilis* |
| Mottled Munia | Hunstein's Munia/Mannikin | *Lonchura hunsteini* |
| Black-breasted Munia | Grand Valley Munia/Mannikin | *Lonchura teerinki* |
| Snow Mountain Munia | Western Alpine Munia/Mannikin | *Lonchura montana* |
| Alpine Munia | Eastern Alpine Munia/Mannikin | *Lonchura monticola* |
| Bismarck Munia | Thick-billed Munia/Mannikin | *Lonchura melaena* |
| Midget Flowerpecker | Solomons Flowerpecker | *Dicaeum aeneum* |
| Mottled Flowerpecker | San Cristobal Flowerpecker | *Dicaeum tristrami* |
| Olive-backed Sunbird | Yellow-bellied Sunbird | *Nectarinia jugularis* |
| Lemon-breasted Berrypecker | Mid-mountain Berrypecker | *Melanocharis longicauda* |
| Akikiki* | Kauai Creeper | *Oreomystis bairdi* |
| Maui Alauahio* | Maui Creeper | *Paroreomyza montana* |
| Kakawahie* | Molokai Creeper | *Paroreomyza flammea* |
| Oahu Alauahio* | Oahu Creeper | *Paroreomyza maculata* |
| Akohekohe* | Crested Honeycreeper | *Palmeria dolei* |

# INDEX TO SITES

# INDEX TO SPECIES